ENCYCLOPEDIA LATINA
History, Culture, and Society In the United States

ENCYCLOPEDIA
LATINA

History, Culture, and Society in the United States

Ilan Stavans
Editor in Chief

Harold Augenbraum
Associate Editor

4

Radio

—

Zorro

Grolier Academic Reference, an imprint of
Scholastic Library Publishing, Inc.
Danbury, Connecticut

Published by Grolier Academic Reference, an imprint of Scholastic Library Publishing, Inc.
Danbury, Connecticut

Cover image: by Margaret García: 12 Portraits of Latinos: *Adriana, Alma Cervantes, Jose Luis Lopez, Juan Rodriguez, Marian Elena Gaitan, Bill Martinez, Saint Leo, Glenna Avila, Ernie Sanchez, Kay Reiko Torres, Elias Nahmias,* and *Cindy Ramirez.*

Library of Congress Cataloging-in-Publication Data

Encyclopedia Latina: History, Culture, and Society in the United States/Ilan Stavans, editor in chief;
p. cm.
Includes bibliographical references and indexes.
ISBN 0-7172-5815-7 (set)
1. Hispanic Americans--History--Encyclopedias.
2. Hispanic Americans--Intellectual life----Encyclopedias.
3. Hispanic Americans--Social conditions--Encyclopedias.
4. United States--Ethnic relations--Encyclopedias.
5. United States--Civilization--Hispanic influences--Encyclopedias.
6. Civilization, Hispanic--Encyclopedias.
I. Stavans, Ilan. II. Augenbraum, Harold.
E184.S75E587 2005
973'.0468'003--dc

2004023603

Printed and Manufactured in the United States of America.

1 3 5 4 2

ENCYCLOPEDIA LATINA

History, Culture, and Society In the United States

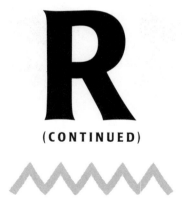

R

(CONTINUED)

RADIO

An invaluable source of communication and entertainment, the relationship between radio and the Latino community dates to the early days of the 20th century. Its reasonable cost, portability, and wide reach have made the radio an ideal companion for migrant workers as well as for urban dwellers. This entry approaches the role of Latinos in radio from two perspectives, dividing the topic between the history and development of Spanish-language radio in the United States and the contribution of Latinos to its English-language counterpart.

SPANISH-LANGUAGE RADIO

With nearly 700 Spanish-language radio stations, Spanish radio can be heard in nearly every part of the United States, from metropolitan areas with large Latino populations to remote rural areas with relatively small numbers of newly arrived immigrants. Wherever they happen to be, these stations are an important source of social capital for U.S. Latinos. They help new arrivals socialize and adapt to American life, promote the maintenance of ethnic and linguistic identity among the acculturated, and create a sense of community among the different subgroups of Latinos within a given location.

The roots of Spanish-language radio in the United States reach back to the late 1920s and early 1930s. At that time Latino deejays and radio managers would buy blocks of time from English-language radio stations during the early morning or weekend hours when listenership was at its lowest. One of

the first pioneers of this brokerage system was Rodolfo Hoyos, who broadcast in Los Angeles from 1932 to 1974. Hoyos's early programs featured live music, poetry, drama, and discussion. Over time, however, Hoyos transitioned to playing recorded music, following a common practice among brokers to keep costs down and maximize profits. In 1939 the International Broadcasting Company of El Paso, Texas, began to produce and distribute Spanish-language programs to stations throughout the country. By 1941 brokers in New York, Arizona, Texas, and California were broadcasting a combined total of over 250 hours per week in Spanish, most of which consisted of recorded music.

Seen as potentially subversive, foreign-language media operated under significant restrictions during World War II. For that reason, despite the popularity of Spanish-language radio, the first full-time Spanish station did not emerge until after the war ended and restrictions were eased. In 1946, the Federal Communications Commission (FCC) issued a license to Raúl Cortéz, a broker from San Antonio, Texas, to operate a full-time radio station. Cortéz launched KCOR amid widespread skepticism about the commercial viability of broadcasting in Spanish on a full-time basis. However, such doubts were quickly allayed when Spanish-language programming emerged as a highly profitable business in the 1950s and 1960s.

Facing growing competition from Spanish-language television, in the 1970s radio oriented itself to reaching local communities of U.S. Latinos. To this end it turned to marketing agencies for help with fine-tuning its programming to local demographics. This strategy has proven highly successful. Since 1980 the number of Spanish-language radio stations in the United States has increased by a factor of ten, from 67 to 664 in 2003, and Spanish radio's market share has nearly doubled. Today, radio is widely recognized as the medium of choice of U.S. Latinos. Spanish-language radio, in particular, reaches over 80 percent of Spanish-dominant and bilingual Latinos, and even 16 percent of English-dominant Latinos.

While commercial gain has always been the main force driving the growth and development of Spanish-language radio, examples of the industry's strong tradition of community service abound. In the 1950s KLVL-AM of Pasadena, California, established a reputation as *la madre de los mexicanos* (the mother of Mexicans) for programs such as *Yo necesito trabajo* (I need a job), which gave unemployed Latinos job referrals, and *Que Dios se lo pague* (May God repay you), where listeners contributed to needy causes in the community. Continuing this tradition, in 2002 Los Angeles radio personality Renan Almendárez Coello ("El Cucuy") raised a record $1.75 million for Padres contra el Cáncer at his annual *Radioton de la Esperanza*. Spanish-language radio has been a launching pad for national campaigns to prevent teenage pregnancy, to disseminate information on health issues affecting the Latino community, to educate Latinos about their legal rights, and to teach parenting techniques.

Spanish radio has also served to galvanize Latinos around political and social causes. One of the earliest examples of this involves Rosa Pesotta, a Russian Jewish garment worker and community activist who used Spanish-language radio in 1933 to organize a strike in Los Angeles against the garment industry. In the 1980s farmworkers relied on public station Radio Cadena of Yakima Valley, California, to learn about boycotts and strikes. Miami's Radio Mambi (WAQI-AM) has been mobilizing the Cuban American community around key political issues for over 25 years. Even mainstream politicians have turned to Spanish-language radio to get out their messages and to court Latino voters.

Past and present successes notwithstanding, industry analysts question whether Spanish-language radio will retain its popularity over the coming decades, as Latinos become increasingly acculturated to American life. In what may be a sign of things to come, broadcaster Entravisión recently switched two of its Spanish-language stations to English (in Los Angeles and Dallas) in an attempt to boost listenership among young Latinos. There is also significant concern regarding the pending merger of Univision Communications, the nation's largest media company, and the Hispanic Broadcasting Corporation, the largest radio corporation. At issue is whether such a move will limit the diversity of programming and reduce the number of outlets that advertisers have to reach U.S. Latinos by giving a single company control over 70 percent of the national advertising dollars spent on Latino media.

Spanish-Language Radio Corporations

Ownership of Spanish-language radio stations in the United States is largely consolidated in four companies: The Hispanic Broadcasting Corporation, The Spanish Broadcasting System, Entravisión, and Radio Unica.

The Hispanic Broadcasting Corporation (HBC) is the nation's largest Spanish-language broadcaster, with over 60 stations in 12 of the 15 radio markets in the United States. These markets account for 80 percent of the U.S. Latino population and reach over 22 million Latinos. This media giant also operates the HBC Ratio Network, a Spanish-language public interest and educational radio service, as well as a network of Web sites that focus on cultural and community issues.

The origins of HBC date back to 1949, when McHenry Tichenor bought station KGBT in Harlinger, Texas, and started broadcasting in Spanish at night. Prompted by the popularity of these broadcasts, in 1962 KGBT switched to Spanish-language programming on a full-time basis. Beginning in the early 1980s, under the leadership of McHenry Tichenor, Jr., Tichenor Media System (TMS) made a strategic decision to focus on Spanish radio. In 1997, TMS merged with Heftel Broadcasting Corporation and became the Hispanic Broadcasting Corporation in 1999. HBC owns and operates the following stations in the nation's five top radio markets (Los Angeles, New York, Chicago, Miami, and Houston).

The Spanish Broadcasting System (SBS) is the largest Latino-owned radio broadcasting company and the second largest Spanish-language broadcaster in the United States, after HBC. Headquartered in

Coconut Grove, Florida, SBS controls 27 stations in seven of the ten largest U.S. Latino markets. The company also runs a Web site that features information on Latin music, entertainment, and news.

SBS was founded by Cuban-born Raúl Alarcón, who emigrated to the United States in 1960 and purchased his first radio station in 1983, WSKQ-AM of New York. Success came quickly to the company. In 1983 SBS-owned KLAX-FM became the first Spanish-language station to rank number one in the Los Angeles area. According to Arbitron, a market research and radio ratings service, in 2002 the top rated stations in New York (WSKQ), Miami (WAMR), and Chicago (WLEY) belonged to SBS. Although publicly owned since 1999, chief executive officer (CEO) and president Raúl Alracón, Jr., owns 41 percent of SBS and controls 83 percent of the voting power. SBS owns ten stations in four of the top five markets (Los Angeles, New York, Miami, and Chicago).

Entravisión is an affiliate of Univisión, the largest Spanish-language network in the world. Entravisión reaches over 7 million U.S. Latinos through its 55 radio stations in 26 markets. The company also publishes New York's daily *El Diario*/LA PRENSA, and it owns and operates 20 television stations and 11,000 billboards in Los Angeles and New York City.

Headquartered in Santa Monica California, Entravisión was established in 1996 by Walter F. Ulloa and Philip C. Wilkinson. In 2000 the company merged with Z-Spanish Radio Network, once the largest Latino-owned satellite radio network in the United States. Entravision owns 11 radio stations in four of the top five Spanish-language markets in the United States (Los Angeles, Miami, Chicago, and Houston).

Radio Unica's 15 AM radio stations and its 30 affiliated stations reach the key markets where over 80 percent of U.S. Latinos reside. The Miami-based company produces 19 hours of Spanish-language programming a day covering primarily news and talk. Its national interactive talk shows are a particularly popular format among U.S. Latinos, along with its exclusive coverage of major sporting events such as the 2000 and 2004 Summer Olympics, and the 2002 World Cup (soccer) qualifying matches.

Radio Unica was formed in 1996 by Chilean-born Joaquín F. Blaya, former president of Univisión Holdings and CEO of Telemundo Group. The company began broadcasting in 1998, becoming the nation's first 24-hour Spanish-language talk and news radio network. Radio Unica owns and operates six stations in the top five U.S. Latino markets. In addition to these national corporations, there are regional owners, notably Liberman Broadcasting and Lotus in Los Angeles, El Dorado in Houston, and Big City Radio in Los Angeles and Chicago.

Radio Information Networks

Radio information networks produce, distribute, and market radio programs for the U.S. Latino population. These include the Latino Broadcasting Corporation, the Latino Radio Network, Radio Bilingüe, and Latino USA.

The Miami-based Latino Broadcasting Corporation (LBC) operates the largest satellite-delivered Spanish-language radio network in the United States, reaching 92 percent of the U.S. Latino market through its 100 affiliated stations. The company was formed in 1996 to produce and distribute Spanish-language radio programs in the United States and Latin America with a focus on sports, news, and talk. In its short time of existence, LBC has carved out a niche as a leader in sports coverage, procuring exclusive U.S. Spanish-language radio rights to Major League Baseball, the National Basketball Association, HBO Boxing, Major League Soccer, and other major sports events in Latin America. Currently, the company owns exclusive rights to over 85 Mexican professional soccer matches. LBC's programs feature prominent television personalities such as Jorge Ramos, Teresa Rodríguez, Jessi Losada, and Chef Pepín.

The Hispanic Radio Network (HRN) produces bilingual radio programs for U.S. Latinos dealing with health, environment, education, social justice, and community resources. These programs are heard on more than 100 popular Spanish-language radio stations in the United States. HRN also operates a public service project with the Self Reliance Foundation, which links listeners to local resources in their own communities, including Spanish-speaking health clinics, after school programs, immigration counseling services, and migrant farm labor services. HRN's radio broadcasts are also available online.

Radio Bilingüe is a network of five public radio stations in California that produces and distributes Latino programming for commercial and National Public Radio. The company's trademark Noticiero Latino is heard on stations across the United States,

Puerto Rico, and Mexico. In partnership with Radio Educación in Mexico and Radio Universidad de Puerto Rico, Radio Bilingüe produces programming that is particularly relevant to American audiences of Mexican and Caribbean origin. The company broadcasts in English, Spanish, and Mixteco, a Native American language spoken in Mexico. Radio Bilingüe is headquartered in Fresno, California, and it has its production studios in San Francisco, California. Programs are available online at www.radiobilingue.org.

Latino USA is the only English-language radio program for Latinos. This weekly half-hour program features news, cultural information, and public service segments. Distributed by National Public Radio and the Longhorn Radio Network, Latino USA is heard in 172 radio stations in 31 states. The program is a collaborative project of KUT Radio of Austin, Texas, and the Center for Mexican American Studies at the University of Texas at Austin. Latino USA programming can also be heard on the Web.

Formats and Listening Patterns

Latinos are avid listeners of Spanish-language radio. On average, they spend 22 hours a week listening to radio in Spanish. Non-Latinos, on the other hand, listen to radio for 16.5 hours a week. When tuned in, 51 percent of Latinos choose a Spanish-language radio program over an English-language one. By contrast, 32 percent of African Americans and 26 percent of Asian Americans prefer their own ethnic radio formats over mainstream (English-language) formats.

Approximately as many Latino men as women listen to Spanish-language radio on a weekly basis. Peak listening times for adults are weekdays from 6:00 A.M. to 6:00 P.M. and weekends between 9 A.M. and 3 P.M. Teens and young adults (18-24) dominate the nighttime market (7:00 P.M. to midnight). Women and older adults (65 and over) are more likely than men to listen to the radio at home. Older adults are the least likely to listen to the radio.

Spanish-language radio owes its phenomenal popularity more to culture than to language. More than half of the Spanish-language radio listeners are either bilingual or English-dominant. Although these listeners are perfectly comfortable speaking English, they turn to Spanish-language radio for culturally meaningful content, which they find in predominantly

musical programming that caters to their ethnic or national preferences. Listed in descending order of market share, the six top Spanish-language radio formats are: Mexican Regional, Contemporary, Tropical, News and Talk, Variety, and Tejano. Format preferences vary along geographical lines. Arbitron defines eight listening regions as Pacific, Mountain, West North Central, East North Central, New England, South Central, South Atlantic, and Middle Atlantic.

With nearly 18 percent of the Spanish-language market share, Mexican Regional is by far the preferred format of U.S. Latinos. Offering a mix of *banda, corridos,* mariachi, and *ranchera* music, this is the format of choice in the Pacific, Mountain, East North Central, and South Central regions, where the majority of Latinos are of Mexican origin. Los Angeles's KSCA-FM is the top-rated Mexican Regional radio station in the nation.

Spanish Contemporary is the second most popular Spanish-language radio format, with a market share of 13.4 percent. The format emphasizes top-40 hits from the Spanish-speaking world, as well as Spanish-language versions of English-language hits by Latin artists looking to cross over into English pop. Although Spanish Contemporary enjoys its highest popularity in the South Atlantic region, the highest rated Spanish Contemporary station in the nation is Los Angeles's KLEV-FM.

Spanish Tropical follows at a distant third, with a 6.1 percent market share. This format offers a selection of salsa and merengue music. It captures its biggest share of the Spanish-language market in New England and the Middle Atlantic regions, where the majority of Latinos are of Caribbean origin. The nation's top Spanish Tropical radio station is WSQK in New York City.

News and Talk, Spanish Variety, and Tejano have respective market shares of 4.2 percent, 3.1 percent, and 1.4 percent. News and Talk emphasizes news, business information, talk, and sports. This is the format of choice of older listeners (65 and over), who make up 25 percent of the format's audience. News and Talk is particularly strong in the Middle Atlantic, South Atlantic, and East North Central regions. Spanish Variety features information and a variety of music styles from all of Latin America. This format is most popular in the West North Central region. Featuring Tex-Mex and Mexican music, Tejano is a preferred format in the South Central region, were the Latino population is predominantly of Mexican origin. Often, Tejano stations have English-speaking disc jockeys and Spanish-language musical programming.

Top Markets

The top five Spanish-language radio markets in the United States are Los Angeles, New York, Miami, Chicago, and Houston. According to Arbitron, the top-rated radio station in 2001 in each of these markets was a Spanish-language station. Except in Miami, these top players doubled the ratings of the closest English-language station within its target. However, recent changes in the way that Arbitron measures language preferences among Latinos have knocked most of these stations off the number-one spot and have resulted in overall lower rankings for Spanish-language radio stations around the nation. Some analysts speculate that a growing preference among young, acculturated Latinos for English-language radio may account for the drop in ratings as well. Despite this, Spanish-language radio remains an undisputed major player in the nation's largest radio markets.

Los Angeles is the top-ranked Spanish-language radio market in the country, with over 4 million Latinos who make up 46 percent of the city's total population. Nearly 80 percent of Los Angeles's Latinos are of Mexican origin, a fact that is reflected in the strong preference for the Mexican Regional format in this market. Spanish Contemporary is the second most popular format, followed by News and Talk and Spanish Variety.

Los Angeles lays claim to important milestones in Spanish-language radio. In 1986 the city's KLAX-FM made history when it became the first Spanish-language radio station in the United States to rank number one in a major radio market. Los Angeles has a greater variety of Spanish-language radio formats and more Spanish-language radio stations consistently ranked in the top-ten category than any other city in the United States. KSCA's "El Cucuy" holds the record for the highest rating shares in the history of Los Angeles radio. For six consecutive years the show occupied the number-one spot in the coveted morning-commute time. The show lost this ranking in February 2003 when, citing personal reasons, host Renán Almendárez Coello moved "El Cucuy" to the afternoon.

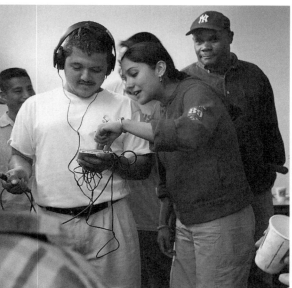

© NURI VALLBONA/MIAMI HERALD/KRT

Luz Aida Ruiz, right, explains the art of the radio interview in a workshop to teach the Coalition of Immokalee workers how to run their new radio station in Miami, Florida.

Los Angeles Latinos have a buying power of $78 billion. Sixty-five percent prefer Spanish to English and 78 percent have Spanish as the language most spoken at home. Besides Mexico, major countries of origin for Latinos in Los Angeles are El Salvador (9.5 percent), Guatemala (4 percent), Argentina (1.7 percent), Cuba (1.5 percent), Costa Rica (1.3 percent), and Puerto Rico (1.1 percent), according to Scarborough, a market research firm. Nearly three-quarters of the city's Latino population is foreign born.

New York is the second largest, as well as the most diverse, Spanish-language radio market in the United States. The city's 3 million Latinos come from Puerto Rico (30 percent), Dominican Republic (19 percent), Mexico (12.2 percent), Colombia (7.6 percent), Cuba (5.8 percent), El Salvador (3.1 percent), Ecuador (2.9 percent), Uruguay (2.8 percent), Peru (2.7 percent), Honduras (2.4 percent), Argentina (2.4 percent), Costa Rica (2.3 percent), and Bolivia (1.8 percent).

Although the popularity of Spanish radio in New York has soared in the recent past, La Mega (WSKQ-FM) is the only Spanish-language station in the city that consistently ranks in the top-ten category. The station's "El Vacilón" is New York's third most popular radio show during the morning commute

(6 to 10 A.M.), behind Howard Stern in WXRK-FM and the all-news 1010 WINS-AM. Lately, El Vacilón has come under fire for its alleged denigrating depictions of homosexuals, its sexually explicit content, and its offensive language. Tropical is the area's favorite Spanish-language radio format, followed by Spanish Contemporary, and News and Talk.

Latinos make up 27 percent of the total population of New York City and have a buying power of $47 billion. Three-quarters speak Spanish at home. In social situations, 55 percent speak Spanish and 14 percent use both English and Spanish. Of the top five radio markets, New York has the lowest percentage of Latinos who are English monolingual (18 percent).

The third largest Spanish radio market is Miami-Ft. Lauderdale-Hollywood, Florida. At 1.7 million, Latinos make up 65 percent of the total population of this area and wield a buying power of $26 billion. In the recent past the area's Latino population has undergone a dramatic population shift, becoming significantly more diverse. Cubans, once 80 percent of the total Latino population, now account for 51 percent of this population, followed by Nicaraguans at 10 percent, Colombians at 10 percent, Dominicans at 4 percent, Puerto Ricans at 3.8 percent, Hondurans at 2.8 percent, Chileans at 2.3 percent, and Venezuelans at 1.7 percent.

This demographic shift has had an impact on Spanish-language radio ratings. In 2003, for the first time ever, Radio Mambí (WAQI-AM) lost its number-one ranking among Spanish-language listeners to WQBA-AM in the hours of the morning commute. Analysts speculate that this situation reflects a growing preference on the part of Miami listeners for WQBA-AM's pan-Hispanic coverage of news and issues to Radio Mambí's Cuban-based coverage.

More than any other Spanish-language radio market, Miami stations make as well as report the news. In 1976 WQBA station director and radio personality Emilio Milián was seriously injured by a car bomb that exploded outside his studio. The radio personality had been an outspoken critic of the violence perpetrated by anti-Castro political extremists in Miami in the mid 1970s. Milián rebuilt his life and his career, returning to WQBA in 1989 with a program that gave air time to dissenting voices. In 2000, Radio Mambí led massive protests against the return of Elián González (a young boy who had been found

drifting at sea, whose mother drowned during their ill-fated attempt to come to the United States) to Cuba, as well as against the recount of the presidential vote. In 2003 WXDJ-FM deejays Enrique Santos and Joe Ferrero made headlines for perpetrating two hoaxes, one on Venezuelan president Hugo Chávez, and the other on Cuba's Fidel Castro. In January, the deejays called Chávez and, using sound bites, fooled him into thinking that it was Castro calling. Then, in June they called Castro and made him believe that he was talking to Chávez.

Among major markets, Miami ranks first in the proportion of Latinos who speak Spanish at home (80 percent), in the workplace (36 percent), and in social situations (62 percent). It is also the country's most affluent and best-educated Spanish-language market. According to Nielsen, 69 percent of Latino households in the area are Spanish-dominant, 15 percent are English-dominant, and 16 percent are bilingual.

Comparatively speaking, the growth of Spanish-language radio in Chicago, the nation's fourth largest Spanish market, has been moderate. The city did not register a top-ten Spanish language radio station until 2003, when WOJO-FM and WLEY-FM were ranked eighth and ninth, respectively. Despite their success, both stations continue to encounter difficulty in procuring advertising dollars. To some extent, demographic and economic factors account for this state of affairs. With 1.6 million Latinos, Chicago follows Miami closely in terms of the size of its Latino population. However, while Miami has the highest density of Latinos among the five major Spanish radio markets (65 percent of the total population), Chicago has the lowest, at 17 percent. Chicago Latinos are also considerably less affluent, with a buying power of $17.3 billion compared to Miami's $26 billion.

Programming missteps have also contributed to the medium's limited success. Although over 80 percent of Chicago's Latinos are of Mexican origin, it is only in the last few years that radio stations have started to cater to this population. WLEY pioneered this trend in 1997, adopting a Mexican Regional format. WOJO followed suit in 2002, recruiting radio personality Rafael Pulido from Fresno, California, and adopting "con orgullo mexicano" as a trademark exclamation of the station's disc jockeys. Preferred radio formats are Regional Mexican, News and Talk, and Tropical.

Eighty percent of Latinos in Chicago are foreign born, 79 percent speak Spanish at home, and 71 percent are Spanish-dominant. Besides Mexicans, Puerto Ricans (3.7 percent), Guatemalans (2.9 percent), Ecuadorians (2.3 percent), and Cubans (1.7 percent) live in the city. Because this composition mirrors closely that of the national Latino population, advertisers often use the city as a Latino test market.

Houston-Galveston (Greater Houston) rounds out the top-five Spanish-language radio markets, with 1.5 million Latinos totaling 30 percent of the area's total population. This thriving Spanish-language radio market has 15 stations, more than New York and Chicago. The area's morning drive time is dominated by Spanish-language radio personality Raúl Brindis's of KLTN-FM. Brindis's program features *norteño* music and discussions of issues such as domestic violence, education, sports, and politics. Most listeners are bilingual, drawn to the program's cultural content as well as Brindis's strong rapport with his audience. Preferred radio formats are Tejano, Mexican Regional, and Spanish Contemporary.

The major countries of origin for greater Houston's Latino community are Mexico (81 percent), El Salvador (7.3 percent), Colombia (2.3 percent), Honduras (2.3 percent), Guatemala (1.9 percent), and Cuba (1 percent). Over half of local Mexicans in the area are U.S.-born, but other Latinos are overwhelmingly foreign-born. Sixty percent of local Latinos prefer to speak Spanish, 26 percent speak this language at work, 71 percent speak it at home, and 50 percent speak it in social situations. Houston's Latino community has a buying power of $16.9 billion.

In terms of overall radio rankings, New York is the country's largest radio market, followed by Los Angeles and then Chicago. Houston and Miami rank 11th and 17th, respectively. Other top-ten Spanish-language radio markets as ranked by Arbitron are San Francisco (6); Dallas–Fort Worth (7); San Antonio (8), and McAllen-Brownsville-Harlingen, Texas (9); and Phoenix (10).

RELATED ARTICLES

Hispanic Radio Network; Journalism; Popular Culture; Radio Martí; Salazar, Rubén.

FURTHER READING

Ferreira, Rui. "Cambios en la audiencia de radios hispanas." *El Nuevo Herald* (August 1, 2003): 5A.

Gutiérrez, Félix, and Jorge Reina Schement. *Spanish-Language Radio in the Southwestern United States.* Monograph 5, Ctr. for Mexican American Studies, Univ. of Tex. at Austin, 1979.

Pugh, Clifford. "Changes in the Airwaves. As Corporations Gobble up Local Stations, Will Listeners Be Winners or Losers?" *Houston Chronicle* (July 14, 2002): 8.

Veciana-Suárez, Ana. *Hispanic Media, USA.* Washington, D.C.: Median Inst., 1988.

SELECTED WEB SITES

Hispanic Radio Network. www.hrn.org
La Musica.com. www.lamusica.com
Latino USA. www.latinousa.org/program/index.html
Univision.com. www.netmio.com

MARÍA M. CARREIRA

RADIO, ENGLISH-LANGUAGE

Since the introduction of broadcast technology in 1902, radio has become an efficient means of spreading the genres of news and entertainment within the multicultural milieu of the United States. The Latino population, which shows a particular affinity for radio in both English and Spanish, is exemplary for its use of the medium as a cultural tool. For recent immigrants radio is both a means of acculturation into a new society and a way to keep in touch with events in the home country, while the growing native Latino population is a driving force of change across many genres and regions of the country. While Spanish-language broadcasts remain wildly popular, English-language radio is growing as an alternative for the Latino population.

The Listeners

For many years after its introduction in the United States radio was exclusively broadcast in the English language. But as station managers sought ways to turn a profit from the hours where listenership was low, they began selling time blocks to outside brokers. Historically, this was the most common way in which radio targeted Latino audiences, with broadcasts in Spanish language and music. As Spanish-language radio began to grow in popularity, even eclipsing English stations in some major markets such as New York City and Los Angeles, the industry viewed the two audiences as being starkly segmented by language. But recently that has all begun to change, as the radio industry has acknowledged the loyalty and buying power of the Latino community. According to a report issued in 2004 by the Pew Hispanic Center, a growing number of Hispanics tune in to English and Spanish broadcasts for news and information. The Pew report shows that even those fluent in English tune in to Spanish broadcasts for news from Latin America and about Latino communities. But as the native Latino population grows, all trends are in flux.

As has been demonstrated in past waves of immigration, the first generation often learns only enough English to survive; the second generation shows a tendency towards bilingualism; and the third may be English-dominant or monolingual. Percentages of bilingual and English- and Spanish-dominant Hispanics are important to English-language radio executives because into these numbers they read trends in buying power. According to *Hispanic Business* higher levels of income and education among Latinos directly correlate with English-language use. Of Latinos who speak English exclusively or enjoy bilingualism, an overwhelming number choose to receive their information via English-language media. A 2003 Pew Hispanic Center study reports that native-born

Hispanics showed a preference (71 percent) for English-language media, while another 20 percent chose English and Spanish equally. The breakdown is very different among the foreign-born: only 15 percent predominantly tune in to English media; 30 percent split equally between Spanish and English media; and 55 percent rely on predominantly Spanish media.

The number of Latinos living in the United States is growing rapidly and, according to media and marketing firm Arbitron, now represents more than 13 percent of the population in the top metropolitan areas. According to Arbitron's spring 2003 Hispanic population rankings, the top five Latino markets are, predictably, as follows: Los Angeles, New York City, Miami-Ft. Lauderdale-Hollywood; Chicago; and Houston-Galveston.

As the Latino population continues to grow, their use of English as a dominant language will certainly grow as will their demand for English-language radio that caters to their specific values and needs. Accord-

© SHAWN BALDWIN/AP/WIDE WORLD PHOTOS

Radio personality Alipio "Cocco" Cabrera speaks to members of his audience from his studio at station WADO in New York City.

ing to the research firm Cultural Access Group, Latinos aged 14 to 24 prefer to use English over Spanish by a margin of 57 percent to 28 percent. This same group prefers English-language radio programming over its Spanish-language counterpart.

The Latino population is extremely biased to radio compared to other segments of the population. Latinos show the same news media preferences as other Americans except in regards to radio, which garners a much higher audience share among Latinos. Of Latino adults, 58 percent say they receive at least some news from radio every weekday. This same audience shows a preference for English (43 percent) compared to those listeners who get all their news in Spanish (34 percent) or in both languages. But it is important to note that within the Latino radio audience the share of the foreign-born who get all their news in Spanish (56 percent) is larger than in any other medium.

Mexican Regional, a radio music format that includes artists of Mexican and Latin American descent and features romántica, mariachi and tropic music, is by far the leading music format among the Latino population. Latinos aged 18 to 44 compose three-quarters of this listening audience. Second overall is the English-language format Contemporary Hit Radio (CHR). CHR, otherwise known as Top 40, appeals equally to Latino men and women in the 18+ demographic with more than 83 percent of Latino listeners under the age of 35. In fact, Latino teens account for almost one-third of the Hispanic CHR audience, whose average age is 25. CHR is particularly popular among Latinos in the New England and Middle Atlantic regions where it garners shares well above the national average.

Of those Latino adults listening to CHR, 67 percent have household incomes under $50,000 per year and are slightly less likely than the average Latino consumer to own their own homes. Of these young adults, 13 percent are college graduates and 36 percent report having attended some college. Latino CHR listeners tune in on an average of nine hours per week.

Of particular interest to advertisers is the purchasing power of the CHR listeners. According to Hispanic Radio Today, more than 50 percent of Latinos who said they plan to buy or lease a new luxury vehicle within the next year listen to CHR. Latino CHR listeners participate in active leisure activities such as in-line skating and bowling and are

34 percent more likely to have gone to see a movie three or more times in the past three months.

These numbers are a reflection of what many radio executives have identified as the fastest-growing segment of the Latino population, the third generation, which is expected to triple by 2040. As Latinos become less an immigrant market and more an ethnic market, listening trends are slowly changing. Los Angeles has the nation's largest Latino immigrant population and Spanish-language radio has consistently topped the charts. But as the growth of Spanish-language stations begins to level off, the lasting impact of Latino listeners becomes more apparent. In 2002, KROQ, an alternative youth-oriented rock station, received the region's best overall ratings. Although the station has not actively sought to bolster its ethnic appeal, it now finds its audience to be 40 percent Latino. Patricia Suárez, president of Suárez/Frommer & Associates, an advertising firm in Pasadena, California, stated in the *New York Times,* "Right when everyone is discovering the importance of using Spanish, we're seeing Latinos become the backbone of the English-language audience." These changes are apparent in CHR, but the same is seen in another format called Adult Contemporary.

The Adult Contemporary (AC) category includes Soft-Light, Hot AC, Mainstream AC, Modern AC, and Adult Rock. In these categories women make up 62 percent of the Latino audience. Of the Latino audience for Adult Contemporary, 56 percent are between the ages of 25 and 44. AC is a popular choice for at-work listening among Latinos and captures above-average shares in many regions across the United States, especially New England, where it garners 93 percent. This Latino audience, who listens an average of 9.5 hours per week, is better off financially and better-educated than its CHR counterpart. Forty-five percent of Latino adults who listen to AC have incomes greater than $50,000 and nearly two-thirds of those Latinos have education beyond the high school level. The average age of Latino AC listeners is 41 and they are slightly more likely than the average Latino consumer to own their own homes.

The purchasing behavior of Latinos who tune in to AC is a little different from that of the CHR format. Latino AC listeners are 28 percent more likely than the average Latino consumer to live in a household planning to buy or lease a new minivan within the next year and 11 percent more likely to obtain a new SUV. Latino AC listeners are also 45 percent more likely to live in a household that invests in stocks or bonds. Members of this Latino demographic also choose slightly more affluent leisure activities.

Another segment of the Latino population that shows a dominant preference for English-language media is likely voters in U.S. elections. Fifty-three percent of Latino voters receive all their news in English, 40 percent listen in both Spanish and English, and only 6 percent choose all Spanish. These results from the Pew Hispanic Center also show that compared to those Latinos who receive all their news in Spanish, those who tune in to English stations have less favorable views of illegal immigrants and tend to trust news organizations far less than do their counterparts. Seventy-seven percent of Latinos who listen to English-language media follow news of U.S. presidential elections closely compared with 51 percent of those who listen in Spanish.

Even those who choose English-language radio exclusively see the Spanish-language fare as an important part of the economic and civic development of the Latino community. Perhaps the reason for this support of Spanish-language radio among those who rarely listen to it is due to the skeptical feelings Latinos have for the English-language media in general. Forty-four percent of all Latinos believe that English-language media purveys a negative stereotype of the Hispanic population among English-speaking Americans.

Perhaps some of this skepticism toward English-language radio is related to the whitewashed nature of the early history of radio in the United States, where there is little if any documentation of minority involvement in early development. The few existing entries that do concern minorities tend to play down the well-known racial binary of black and white. Advertising followed the same general ideas as they attempted to market their goods to what they saw as a general audience. But with the changing appearance of the U.S. population, new definitions of consumers increasingly recognize not only language differences, but also those of taste and culture. There is no homogeneous Latino market, but instead a diverse population from many different regions in Central and South America as well as Cuba and Puerto Rico. Latinos often adapt to the customs and habits of the United States without leaving behind those relevant to their own cultures, and English-language radio advertisers have taken note.

Advertisements from the general market simply translated to Spanish may not be well received. Savvy marketers have left behind the idea of a population sharply segmented along linguistic lines in favor of Spanish-English blends.

The Broadcasters

Historically, radio was virtually impenetrable for non-white performers. The only work available in broadcasting was bit parts as servants or minstrels and then only if they fit a stereotype. The lack of correspondence to reality of the ethnic stereotypes commonly found in early radio programs centered on cultural customs that clashed with white American norms; strange dress, exaggerated speech, odd superstitions, communication gaffes, financial difficulties, or being duped because of cultural ignorance. Commonly these stereotypical caricatures were portrayed by white actors who exaggerated linguistic characteristics to the point of absurdity.

There were some Latino musicians who enjoyed minor success in the early days of radio. Carmen Cavallaro, also known as the poet of the piano, hosted the program *The Schaeffer Parade* in the 1940s. Alfonso D'Artega conducted orchestras for various programs and Colombian singer Sarita Herrera appeared on the variety show circuit. Perhaps one of the more successful Latinos in early radio was Vincent López, who began broadcasting with his band in 1921. He started shows with the signature line, "Hello everybody, López speaking," and through the help of radio became one of the most popular band leaders in the United States through the 1940s.

Historically, a major reason for media underrepresentation is the lack of minority employment in the broadcast industry. But as the diversity of the U.S. population grows, radio trends, thanks in part to the efforts of Latino organizations, mirror that growing diversity. The National Association of Hispanic Journalists (NAHJ) began an initiative to broaden the diversity of all media outlets, including radio. The initiative, known as the Parity Project, has a heavy hitter on board in the radio industry, National Public Radio, or NPR.

NPR garners 22 million listeners spread over 750 member stations throughout the United States. In August 2004 it agreed to partner with NAHJ and the Parity Project. Organization president Juan González expressed pride in an association with one of the most important news organizations in the country and looked forward to increasing the Latino presence in the NPR newsroom and programming. He pointed out that a study by the Radio-Television News Directors Association (RTNDA) showed that Latinos accounted for only 3.9 percent of the total workforce in the newsrooms of English-language radio stations in the United States. Along with his work at NAHJ, Juan González is a columnist at the *New York Daily News* and cohost of the radio program *Democracy Now!,* a national independent daily news program that is broadcast on over 225 stations in North America. Along with host Amy Goodman, González brings to the show guests and perspectives that are often overlooked by mainstream corporate news agencies.

Latino USA, a program in the style of a radio journal concerning news and culture, is the only national English-language radio program produced from a Latino perspective. The increasingly popular show originates from the University of Texas at Austin through a partnership between KUT Radio and the Center for Mexican American Studies. *Latino USA* is distributed by National Public Radio and the Longhorn Radio Network to 172 stations in 31 states, the District of Columbia, and Puerto Rico. *Latino USA* can also be heard worldwide through its distribution by Radio Bilingüe and the Armed Forces Radio service. Alex Avila is the senior producer of the show and oversees its weekly production. *Latino USA* is hosted by María Hinojosa, a veteran of NPR. In 1997 Hinojosa became a correspondent for CNN, but she continued her affiliation with NPR and *Latino USA.* Another Latina gaining tenure in radio is Mandalit del Barco, a correspondent for *Latino USA* and NPR.

Noteworthy is the career of Ray Suárez, who, before becoming a senior correspondent for *The NewsHour with Jim Lehrer* in 1999, worked primarily in radio. For six years in the mid-1990s, he hosted the NPR afternoon call-in program *Talk of the Nation.* Suárez has reported for radio from New York, Rome, and in the service of many U.S. and British stations, over the years narrating, anchoring, and reporting many special stories; he has also worked in television and written for many national publications.

Latino personalities and programming are also growing in local radio. Many stations across the country are beginning to air salsa music programs that are more bilingual in nature and enjoy a cross-cultural appeal. The host, as well as the music, may be speaking a mix of Spanish and English during the course of a show. *Tertulia,* broadcast from the University of Massachusetts, Amherst, discusses Latino music, news, and culture in a bilingual format. In Denver, Colorado, KUVO 89.3 FM broadcasts the shows *Salsa On Sundays,* hosted by Ed Martínez and Rico Rogers, and *The Latin Musicians Show.* Tomás Algarín, who has also had shows in New York City and Houston, now hosts *Latin Aura* at WCLK 91.9 FM in Atlanta, Georgia. KOOP 91.7 FM in Austin, Texas, has Radio Havana and Sancocho Boricua.

Another genre that enjoys a cross-cultural appeal and a strong Latino presence is hip-hop. In Southern California a couple of Latino radio DJs have enjoyed success in the underground hip-hop scene. On station 1580 AM KDAY's *The Mix Master Show* DJs Ralph M., Tony G., and Julio G. gained respect throughout the hip-hop world, and their shows have become classics.

RELATED ARTICLES

Hispanic Radio Network; Journalism; Popular Culture; Radio Martí.

FURTHER READING

"2004 Hispanic Radio Today." *How America Listens to Radio.* Arbitron Inc., 2004.

"The Changing Face of Radio. " *Latin Beat Magazine.* February 1999. www.findarticles.com/p/articles

Clancy, Kevin J., and Peter C. Krieg. *A Counterintuitive Discovery About Media Buying for the U.S. Hispanic Market: The Bipolar Approach Wastes Marketing Dollars.* Copernicus Marketing Consulting, February 4, 2002. www.copernicusmarketing.com/about/docs

Latinos' Choices in News Media Are Shaping Their Views of Their Communities, the Nation and the World. Pew Hispanic Center. www.pewtrusts.com/news/news_subpage

"National Public Radio Signs on to NAHJ Parity Project During UNITY Convention in Washington, D.C." *The National Association of Hispanic Journalists.* August 7, 2004. www.nahj.org/nahjnews/articles/2004/august/parityproject-npr080704.shtml

Rodríguez, Gregory. "Hispanic Demographics Show Shift toward English." *The New York Times,* April 7, 2002. www.asu.edu/educ/epsl/LPRU/newsarchive/art229.txt

Sonderup, Laura. "Hispanic Marketing: A Critical Market Segment." *Advertising & Marketing Review.* www.ad-mkt-review.com/public_html/docs/fs075.html

SELECTED WEB SITE

Latino USA. www.latinousa.org

RANDALL GANN

© HILLERY SMITH SHAY/AP/WIDE WORLD PHOTOS

Before dropping out of the 2004 presidential race, Democratic candidate Senator Joseph Lieberman appealed to Florida's Cuban American voters on Radio Martí with host Margarita Rojo.

RADIO MARTÍ

Radio Martí, named after the 19th-century Cuban writer Jose Martí, is a U.S.-funded Cuban American radio station specifically developed to encourage anticommunist sentiment and provide news to the people of Cuba. Lobbied for by the Cuban American National Foundation (CANF), a nonprofit organization whose principal goal is to help the U.S. administration formulate its foreign policy toward Cuba, Radio Martí has developed into a vital tool for U.S. policy regarding Cuba and is conceived to ostensibly counter propaganda by Castro and his government.

Proposed in 1982, Radio Martí was initially voted down by the U.S. Senate. Although critics condemned the project as an overt act of hostility against a sovereign nation, the Radio Broadcasting to Cuba Act was passed on October 4, 1983. On May 20, 1985, the date of Cuban independence, Radio Martí transmitted its first broadcast to Cuba from Marathon Key, Florida.

Radio Martí transmits 24 hours a day, 7 days a week on shortwave and noncommercial, medium wave (AM) frequencies. However the program has always been vulnerable to jamming by the Cuban government, which retaliated against installation of Radio Martí by suspending the 1984 immigration accords. Calling it an insult and offense to the Cuban people, Castro threatened to interfere with regular broadcasts of several hundred U.S. radio stations and briefly disrupted commercial broadcasts.

Radio Martí's mission is to "fill the vacuum of information generated for more than four decades of censure created by the Cuban government." It claims to offer its listeners an extensive and balanced perspective of current events without censure. Its various programming includes interviews with former political prisoners, immigrants, and human rights activists; readings of suppressed literature; discussions with various religious leaders; musical programs; vintage radio shows; radio *novellas* (soap operas); and messages from Cuban Americans to their relatives on the island. The station also provides analytical news coverage on various topics and events ranging from Communist Party congresses in Havana to AIDS to defection of high-ranking military and government officials to changes in the Soviet Union and Eastern Bloc, and other news stories from around the world.

Radio Martí has been considered so successful in its ideological war against Castro that in March 1990 Congress voted to add TV Martí and created the Office of Cuba Broadcasting to regulate the authority of both programs. Again the Cuban government condemned the operation as a form of military aggression and responded by jamming broadcasts, consequently further limiting reception. Controversy still surrounds Radio Martí. The station has been criticized for being too one-sided and not following standards of objectivity and accuracy. Recent criticism has also cited statistics of plummeting audiences. The effect of Radio Martí on the island continues to remain subject to debate.

Fundamentally a political project, Radio Martí aims to modify the political identity of Cubans and spur the end of communism. Its transmissions evoke the image of a separated Cuban community and work to translate the exiles' sense of loss into political agency. In projecting an imagined community, Radio Martí offers a sentimental attachment to Cuba and Cuban people, inviting those on the island to identify themselves with those abroad. It works to combat isolationist constructions of Cubanness, instead presenting Cuban identity not as insular or fixed but as a diverse and permeable entity that includes those outside the boundaries of the island. Thus Radio Martí plays an influential role in attempting to rearticulate understandings of Cubanness and bridge a geographically divided Latino community.

RELATED ARTICLES

Cuban American National Foundation; Martí, Jose; Radio.

FURTHER READING

García, Maria Cristina. *Havana USA: Cuban Exiles and Cuban Americans in South Florida, 1959–1994.* Berkeley: Univ. of Calif. Press, 1996.

Saco, Diana. *Radio Martí and the (Pen)Insular Construction of Cuban Identity.* Boca Raton: Fla. Atlantic Univ. [masters thesis].

SELECTED WEB SITE

Radio Martí, U.S Office of Cuba Broadcasting.
  http://www.martinoticias.com/radio.asp

ALYSSA GARCIA

RAILWAYS

For the United States, the construction of an extensive railway system during the 19th century represented a transportation revolution on an unprecedented scale. In addition to employing millions of people, the railroads provided ordinary Americans with the means to travel long distances in a short period of time. With more than 200,000 miles (322,000 km) of railroads crisscrossing the country by 1900, the railroad industry dramatically transformed the U.S. economy.

Although the construction of a modern rail network did not take place in the Mexican Republic until the last two decades of the 19th century, the industry had an equally dynamic effect on the economic and social structure of Mexico. In 1877, when President Porfirio Díaz of Mexico initiated the construction of Mexico's railroad system, the country owned only a few hundred miles of trackage. By 1910, however, Mexico's trackage had increased to 15,000 miles (24,000 km).

Originally, President Díaz had envisioned the development and expansion of a major railroad network throughout the country as a means of utilizing Mexico's rich natural resources and expediting the shipping of Mexican goods to U.S. markets. To that end the Mexican National and the Mexican Central railroads were built and soon became major north-south conduits of people and goods that operated for the better part of the 20th century; however, the construction of Mexico's rail network would have unforeseen repercussions that became apparent only with the passage of time.

From 1880 to 1884, an aggressive railroad-building program brought the Mexican Central Railway (Ferrocarril Central Mexicano) up the Central Valley of Mexico, providing a direct link between Mexico City and the northern border. By April 1884, this route consisted of 1,224 miles (1,969 km) of rails that ran from Mexico City through Aguascalientes, Zacatecas, and Chihuahua to the border town of Ciudad Juárez, Chihuahua (across the border from El Paso, Texas). The states located along this railroad became significant contributors of Mexican immigration to the United States during the entire 20th century.

The second major rail route constructed from Mexico City to the northern border was the Mexican National Railway (Ferrocarriles Nacionales de México). When it was completed in the 1880s, this railway ran 737 miles (1,187 km) from Mexico City through Saltillo and Monterrey to Nuevo Laredo, Tamaulipas. Across the border from Nuevo Laredo lay Laredo, one of the most important ports of entry along the Texas border.

Starting in 1883, the Ferrocarril Internacional Mexicano (International Mexican Railroad) brought travelers from the states of Zacatecas, San Luis Potosí, Nuevo León, and Coahuila to Piedras Negras, the Mexican town across the Río Grande from Eagle Pass, Texas. The Piedras Negras–Eagle Pass connection represented a more convenient departure point than El Paso for Mexican nationals going to Houston and other eastern Texas cities.

Nogales, Arizona, lies across the border from its sister city, Nogales, Sonora. In the 1880s, railroad links from both the south and north linked the towns with the interiors of their respective nations. Initially, however, Nogales had no direct access to Mexico City or to Guadalajara (Mexico's second largest city). Up until 1927 most immigrants from Guadalajara and the populous state of Jalisco had to take existing railway lines to El Paso, Texas, even if their destination was California or Arizona.

In April 1927, however, with the completion of the Southern Pacific of Mexico Railroad linking Guadalajara with Nogales, Arizona, the dynamics of the northward migration changed significantly. Statistics show that an immediate influx of immigrants from Jalisco were able to make their way north to work in California and Arizona by way of Nogales.

Although the railroad initiated a temporary period of prosperity for the Mexican Republic, the long-term effect of the railroads was to provide Mexican laborers with an escape route from a nation that was on the brink of social and economic chaos. As the railroads spread out across the landscape of Mexico's Central Plateau, poor Mexican laborers found that they could travel long distances in order to seek employment far from home.

The labor needs of the Mexican railways soon led to a significant wage differential, which drew tens of thousands of laborers north. While an agricultural laborer in the state of Jalisco earned only 15 cents for a day of work, section hands working along the Mexican National Railway received 50 cents per day. Railroad laborers working in the northern state of Chihuahua were able to pull in between 75 cents and $1 a day. Quickly, however, these laborers learned that a railroad job in the United States could pay even more—somewhere between $1.00 and $1.25 for a day's labor. Essentially, a laborer could make more money by working on a seasonal maintenance crew for three months in the United States than he could earn during a whole year of railroad work in central Mexico.

Starting in the first decade of the 20th century, U.S. railroad companies had begun an active campaign to recruit Mexican laborers to work their railroads. The 1882 Chinese Exclusion Act and the 1907 Gentlemen's Agreement with Japan had led to the virtual exclusion of Chinese and Japanese laborers from the railroad, construction, and agricultural industries. As a result, the railroad companies found their most willing and able laborers in the Mexican migrants who were crossing the border in ever-increasing numbers looking for gainful employment.

In order to find Mexican laborers for the construction of new railroads, the large U.S. railroad companies had to recruit and transport construction workers from the border regions to their destination. Some railroads even sponsored employment agencies that met with the Mexican nationals as they crossed the border from Ciudad Juárez into El Paso, Texas. By 1910, 2,000 Mexican citizens were crossing the border each month looking for railroad work.

When the provisions of the Immigration Act of 1917 introduced a literacy test for prospective immigrants crossing the southern border, the railroad industry pressured the U.S. government to create an exclusion for Mexican railroad and agricultural laborers. The United States had just entered World War I and the resulting labor shortages had dramatically increased the need for Mexican labor in the States. In July 1918, Secretary of Labor William Wilson acceded to the railroad industry, permitting the unrestricted entrance of Mexican railroad, mining, and construction workers. The waiver was valid until 1921.

Initially, most Mexican laborers were hired to work on section crews from May to October; it was assumed that many of the laborers would return to Mexico in the off-season. As the labor needs grew in the second decade of the 20th century, however, more immigrants were able to find permanent employment in the railroad industry. For this reason, many Mexican laborers never returned to their native homes. Instead, they joined railroad section gangs and spread out across many parts of the United States. The journalist and historian Carey McWilliams estimated that between 60 and 90 percent of the section and extra gangs on 18 railroads between 1900 and 1940 were Mexican laborers.

At some point, many of the Mexican railroad workers would send for their wives and children and establish new roots in the United States. These enclaves of Mexican laborers and their families were called *colonias* (settlements) and eventually developed throughout the Southwest and the Midwest.

One of the most famous *colonias* was in the area round the railroad yards of Kansas City, Kansas, which were crisscrossed by 12 railroads entering from all directions. Starting about 1904, the Atchison, Topeka, and Santa Fe Railroad and the Chicago, Rock Island, and Pacific Railroad became principal conduits for the migration of Mexican labor to Kansas City. With the influx of Mexican railroad workers into Kansas City, a small barrio cropped up in the flood-prone Argentine district, where laborers made their homes in abandoned boxcars, provided by the Santa Fe Railroad. The railroad industry brought a steady stream of Mexican immigrants into Argentine for the next two decades. By 1927 it is believed that 91 percent of all track laborers in the Kansas City area were Mexican.

The completion of the San Pedro, Los Angeles, and Salt Lake Railroad, linking Salt Lake City with Los Angeles in 1905, gave birth to the city of Las Vegas and brought in a significant number of Mexican laborers. In the same year, the Southern Pacific Railroad started bringing Mexican laborers to Los Angeles, California, where they settled in a *colonia* called Tijuata, better known today as the Watts district.

Other immigrant laborers made their way to the Northwest to work with the Oregon Railroad and Navigation Company, the Union Pacific Railroad, and the Oregon Short Line. Large numbers of Mexican railroad workers also arrived in Chicago, Detroit, Milwaukee, Wisconsin, and other Midwestern cities during and after World War I. In Chicago, the population of Mexican natives increased from 3,854 in 1920 to 19,362 in 1930.

The Great Depression of the 1930s had an adverse affect on the railroad industry. With the severe decline in both freight service and passenger usage, the railroads were forced to dismiss employees and reduce wages. It was during this decade that some Mexican immigrants returned to Mexico, either by choice or through government-sponsored forced repatriation, although many of the inhabitants of the *colonias* looked for and found employment in other industries, thus reinforcing their connection to their adopted land.

With the beginning of World War II, the United States once again looked to its southern neighbor for help in alleviating severe labor shortages. Starting in 1943 more than 100,000 contracts were signed to recruit and transport Mexican workers to the United States for employment in the railroad industry. The railroad *bracero* program of World War II has been explored in depth by the author Barbara A. Driscoll, in her publication *The Tracks North: The Railroad Bracero Program of World War II*. The recruitment program was officially discontinued in August 1945.

More than any other American industry, the railroads were instrumental in bringing Mexican laborers across the southern border and dispatching them to many disparate parts of the United States. It was the railroad industry that gave Latino immigrants an opportunity to settle down and establish permanent roots in new communities far from their native lands, and many Mexican Americans living in the United States today are descended from those Mexican railroad laborers of the early 20th century.

RELATED ARTICLES

Immigration, Latino; Labor; Mexican Americans; Mexico.

FURTHER READING

Driscoll, Barbara A. *The Tracks North: The Railroad Bracero Program of World War II.* Austin: The Center for Mexican American Studies, Univ. of Tex. at Austin, 1998.

García, Juan R. *Mexicans in the Midwest, 1900–1932.* Tucson: Univ. of Ariz. Press, 1996.

Laird, Judith. *Argentine, Kansas: The Evolution of a Mexican-American Community, 1905–1940.* Ph.D. dissertation, Univ. of Kan., 1975.

McNeely, John H. "The Railways of Mexico: A Study in Nationalization." Southwestern Studies 5. El Paso: Tex. Western Press, 1964.

McWilliams, Carey. *North from Mexico: The Spanish-Speaking People of the United States.* 1948. Reprint. New York: Greenwood Press, 1968.

Mexican Central Railway Company Limited. *Facts and Figures about Mexico and Her Great Railroad, The Mexican Central.* 3d ed. Mexico City: Mexican Central Railway Company Limited, 1900.

"New S.P. de M.R.R. Open to Traffic." *Nogales International,* April 17, 1927.

Parlee, Lorena M. *Porfirio Díaz, Railroads, and Development in Northern Mexico: A Study of Government Policy toward the Central and Nacional Railroads, 1876–1910.* Ann Arbor, Mich.: University Microfilms International, 1981.

Reisler, Mark. *By the Sweat of Their Brow: Mexican Immigrant Labor in the United States, 1900–1940.* Westport, Conn.: Greenwood Press, 1976.

Smith, Michael M. "Beyond the Borderlands: Mexican Labor in the Central Plains, 1900–1930." *Great Plains Quarterly* 1 (Fall 1981): 239–251.

SELECTED WEB SITE

Mexlist: The Mexican List for Railway Information. http://mexican.railspot.com/minsk1.htm

JOHN P. SCHMAL

RAMÍREZ, MARTÍN

Born: 1895; Los Altos, Jalisco, Mexico
Died: February 17, 1963; Auburn, California

Martín Ramírez, a diagnosed paranoid schizophrenic who spent the last 30 years of his life in California mental institutions, was also the creator of colored drawings that won him posthumous acclaim. It is believed that Ramírez immigrated to the United States during the Mexican Revolution, that he stopped speaking in 1915, and that he did itinerant work for railroads. Ramírez was institutionalized after being picked up by the police in Los Angeles about 1930.

In 1949 Ramírez was transferred to the DeWitt Hospital in Auburn, where he was able to pass a roll of drawings to Dr. Tarmo Pasto, a visiting psychiatrist, in 1954. Ramírez worked obsessively under a table, in fear of violent patients and of hospital wardens who destroyed patient art. Pasto provided art supplies and persuaded the hospital staff to regard these drawings as therapy, thus ensuring their survival. Ramírez typically drew with pencil. He made pigments from colored pencils and crayons, which he applied with matchsticks but sometimes also utilized tempera and collaged pictures.

Ramírez fashioned his drawings into scrolls several feet long by attaching sections of brown paper bags with adhesive made of mashed potatoes or bread and saliva. The works depict complex (and often disorienting) linear arches that can be read as concave or convex. These arches form tunnels and bridges, some of which are traversed by trains made of similarly abbreviated forms. Mounted Mexican soldiers and Catholic saints appear frequently in his draw-

Martín Ramírez's *Soldado with American Flag,* circa 1950–1953; crayon, watercolor, and pencil on various papers.

ings, but not enough is known about Ramírez (such as his view of the Mexican Revolution) to properly contextualize his work.

In 1968 the artist Jim Nutt saw the drawings Pasto had collected, resulting in the first public exhibition of Ramírez's work. Nutt and art dealer Phyllis Kind purchased the 300 drawings Pasto had collected in 1971. Since that time Ramírez's art has been widely exhibited, often under the "outsider art" rubric that has come under fire for being applied to many singular artists who have little in common save their exclusion from mainstream art institutions. Ramírez was first shown in a Latino context in the much criticized Hispanic Art in the United States exhibition in which Octavio Paz deemed the mute artist a "symbol." Ilan Stavans discussed him in the first chapter of *The Hispanic Condition,* meditating on his muteness as a collective emblem of the Latino minority as a whole. But in a review entitled "Homogenizing Hispanic Art," Shifra Goldman termed Ramírez's inclusion in this show a "linchpin" of the curators' "primitivistic" view of ethnicity: "folkloric, naive, popular, exotic, religious, and traditional."

RELATED ARTICLES

Art, Galleries and Collections; Art, Mexican American and Chicano; Art Criticism; Goldman, Shifra.

FURTHER READING

Cardinal, Roger. *Outsiders: An Art without Precedent or Tradition.* London: Arts Council of Great Britain, 1979.

Goldman, Shifra. "Homogenizing Hispanic Art." In *Dimensions of the Americas: Art and Social Change in Latin America and the United States.* Chicago: Univ. of Chicago Press, 1994.

Hall, Michael D., and Eugene W. Metcalf, Jr., eds. *Artist Outsider: Creativity and the Boundaries of Culture.* Washington, D.C.: Smithsonian Inst. Press, 1994.

Heart of Creation: The Art of Martín Ramírez. Philadelphia: Moore College of Art, 1985.

Morris, Randall. "Martín Ramírez Revisited." *Folk Art* 27 no. 4: 52–59.

Paz, Octavio, et al. *Hispanic Art in the United States: Thirty Contemporary Painters & Sculptors.* Houston: Mus. of Fine Arts, 1987.

Smith, Roberta, et al. *Heart of Creation: The Art of Martín Ramírez.* Philadelphia: Moore College of Art, 1985.

Stavans, Ilan. *The Hispanic Condition: The Power of a People.* 2d ed. New York: Rayo, 2001.

RUBÉN CORDOVA

RAP

Rap music grew out of a late-1970s hip-hop subculture formed by young African Americans and Puerto Ricans living in New York City's South Bronx. During this nascent period, rap was largely characterized by the scratching and mixing of different sounds and lyrics to produce beats and rhythms to which young men could "break-dance." Since its South Bronx hip-hop origins, rap music has experienced many acoustic splinterings and transformations. It has also become a musical phenomenon heard throughout the world.

Rap began its migration from the New York City boroughs to other urban centers in the United States such as Miami, Chicago, Philadelphia, and Los Angeles in the early 1980s. This was partly the result of the early appeal and modest success of African American artists such as Africa Bambata, DJ Kool Herc, and Grandmaster Flash. Rap moved from a street-grown musical form to a musical form that began to win airtime across the nation. This expansion was helped greatly by the popularizing of the music video form and the appearance of docudramas such as *Wild Style* (1982) and films such as *Electric Boogaloo* (1984) and *Break Dancing* (1984). Spike Lee's *Do the Right Thing* popularized Public Enemy's politically engaged rap lyrics and inspired disc jockeys across the country. By the mid-1980s, rap had grown into a nationwide cultural phenomenon and a big business enterprise that was no longer tied to a specific location or disenfranchised urban community.

Although rap has traditionally been identified as an African American musical form, the Latino presence in its formation and evolution has been significant. Nuyoricans such as the Fearless Four, Fat Boys, and Latin Empire gave it a doo-wop beat and Latin meringue spin in its earlier days. After the Bronx-based Latino rap group Mean Machine aired and produced the first bilingual rap song in 1981, the

Rap artist Fat Joe at the 2003 Hip-Hop Music Awards in Miami, Florida.

patterns and rhythms of Spanglish were added to the rap recipe. By the late 1980s and early 1990s, Puerto Rican rappers such as Vico-C and Chicanos such as Kid Frost (whose song *La Raza* topped the Billboard charts) continued to weave Spanish lyrics into their bass lines and riffs. Other Latino rap artists who appeared during this period, such as the Cuban-born Mellow Man Ace, whose track *Mentirosa* went gold, paved the way for others to get radio airplay; musicians such as the Funky Aztecs, JV, Funkdoobiest, Tony Touch, and the Beatnuts were all starting to gather respect in their regions. The massive crossover success (selling over 15 million albums worldwide) of Los Angeles–based Cypress Hill (members include the Mexican Cuban B Real, Cuban Sen Dog, and Italian American DJ Muggs), which combined Spanglish and funk samples with a West Coast gangsta-rap style, conclusively moved bilingual Latino rap from the sidelines to the mainstream.

Although rap has wide appeal and became a big moneymaking enterprise, its success has not been without controversy. The media—and the Christian Right—often have identified it as perverse (in the 1980s, 2Live Crew made headlines defending their 1st Amendment rights in lawsuits in Florida). Rap has been associated with gang activity (Public Enemy's *Fight the Power* came out when gang warfare between the Crips and Bloods in Los Angeles had gained national attention). While rap music has largely been produced by male artists, over the years women rappers have appeared, including Queen Latifah, California-based Conscious Daughters, and Nuyorican Hurricane G. In spite of its detractors, rap has become a global musical phenomenon. Rappers south of the border, such as Molotov and Control Machete from Mexico, DJ Kun from Argentina, and 7 Notas 7 Colores from Spain, all add their own homegrown musical variations to the rap musical form, and young people in places as far afield as Canada, France, Scotland, Poland, Japan, and South Africa are listening and innovatively reforming the Spanglish-driven American-styled rap.

RELATED ARTICLES

African Americans, Influence and Relations; Afro-Latino Influences; Gangs; Music, Popular.

FURTHER READING

Bogdanov, Vladimir, ed. *All Music Guide to Hip-Hop: The Definitive Guide to Rap & Hip-Hop.* San Francisco: Backbeat Bks., 2003.

Rivera, Raquel Z. *New York Ricans from the Hip-Hop Zone.* New York: Palgrave, 2003.
Rodríguez, Richard T. "The Verse of the Godfather: Signifying Family and Nationalism in Chicano Rap and Hip-Hop Culture." In *Velvet Barrios: Popular Culture & Chicana/o Sexualities.* Ed. by Alicia Gaspar de Alba. New York: Palgrave, 2003.

FREDERICK LUIS ALDAMA

RAZA UNIDA PARTY, LA

La Raza Unida Party (RUP) was organized to establish Chicano community control over Crystal City, located in Zavala County in southwestern Texas, just 45 miles (72 km) from the U.S.-Mexican border (part of Mexico until the mid-19th century when northwestern Mexico became the southwestern United States). In the 1960s the area, known as Cristal, was home to 9,100 people, 80 percent of whom shared Mexican heritage, yet the Anglo American elite controlled elected political offices and government employment, and the Poll Tax burdened low-income residents. This control skewed the benefits of public spending toward the Anglo minority and away from the Mexican American majority. Segregation reigned in this semirural area, and many scholars used the concept of "internal colonialism" to describe the exploited predicament of Mexican Americans.

The two-party system in U.S. politics can result in tyranny against the minority, and Mexican Americans in Texas had little representation in their state, then a virtual one-party system ruled by conservative Democrats. Occasionally, "third parties," such as RUP, emerge in U.S. politics when interests are not represented in the two mainstream parties.

La Raza Unida Party exerted control over elected offices in Crystal City, Zavala county, and the local school board. Once elected, RUP officials changed public policies and recruitment practices in the educational and economic realms. The party valued cultural and linguistic (Spanish) identity, but after brief terms in office, factionalism and personal fissures undermined temporary electoral unities. The white elite also divided people through threats and intimidation.

The Cristal context is best analyzed in the autobiographical narrative of José Angel Gutiérrez, the controversial RUP organizer and leader. His narrative provides compelling testimony to Chicano struggles, most visible from the mid-1960s to the mid-1970s. Gutiérrez's account tells the story of anger over injustice that gave rise to a movement and an experiment in community control that extended well beyond the minute population of Cristal. His leadership began in secondary school and continued in higher education through the Mexican American Youth Organization (MAYO) and other organizations whose genius lay in tactics that ranged from voter registration drives and bloc voting mobilizations to school walkouts and protests.

Scholars refer to the Cristal experiment as a Chicano revolt and a militant but peaceful revolution. The revolt came in two stages: in 1963, when "los cinco" took control of the city council, and in 1970, when the newly organized RUP elected its slates to city, council, and school board slots.

Armando Navarro analyzes Ciudadanos Unidos (CU), RUP's organizing arm, as a political machine, with Gutiérrez as its political boss. Like political machines elsewhere in the United States, CU used the patronage of government benefits and jobs as incentives to bind people to the organization. Moreover, the Cristal Experiment attracted major external funding from private foundations along with state and federal government agencies.

La Raza Unida Party spread to other states in the southwestern United States, also known as Aztlán, the mythical Chicano homeland. At the 1972 conference in the heart of this legendary homeland, El Paso, Texas, several thousand Latinos attempted to set a national agenda, memorialized in the four-part Public Broadcasting Service (PBS) series *Chicano!* (1996). Personal conflicts broke out between two men vying for national leadership: Gutiérrez and Rodolfo "Corky" Gonzáles, a Colorado-based leader. Although Gutierrez won national leadership, the conflicts divided the convention and its aftermath. True to its third-party status, RUP remained independent, refusing to endorse the presidential nominees from either the Republican or Democratic parties. With the Gutiérrista-Corkyite split, RUP went into serious decline after 1975, with, according to Armando Navarro, a "politics of self-destruction" paralleled both nationwide and in Cristal.

RELATED ARTICLES

Gonzáles, Rodolfo; Inter-Latino Relations; Politics, Mexican American; Yzaguirre, Raúl.

FURTHER READING

Gutiérrez, José Angel. *The Making of a Chicano Militant: Lessons from Cristal.* Madison: Univ. of Wis. Press, 1998.

Navarro, Armando. *Mexican American Youth Organization: Avant-Garde of the Chicano Movement in Texas.* Austin: Univ. of Tex. Press, 1995.

Navarro, Armando. *The Cristal Experiment: A Chicano Struggle for Community Control.* Madison: Univ. of Wis. Press, 1998.

Shockley, John Staples. *Chicano Revolt in a Texas Town.* Notre Dame, Ind.: Univ. of Notre Dame Press, 1974.

KATHLEEN STAUDT

RECONQUISTA, LA

La Reconquista (Reconquest) is the name given to the Christian conquest of Moorish peoples of the Iberian Peninsula between the 8th and the 15th century. The term is accompanied by overtones of messianism, which were later incorporated into Spain's image of the development of its American empire and its conquest and conversion of the indigenous peoples of the Western Hemisphere, which took place from the late 15th to the 18th century.

For five years beginning in 711, Moorish kings in Africa migrated northward across the Straits of Gibraltar and conquered the Visigoths and most of the Iberian Peninsula as far north as the Pyrenees. The "reconquest" began in 718 with the Moorish defeat at the Battle of Alcama and lasted over 700 years, although later in the period reigning Catholic kings often exacted tribute from Moors rather than wage war. In the late Middle Ages, the concept of restoration of an earlier Christian kingdom coalesced into a Crusade-like calling; by the time of the 1467 marriage of Ferdinand of Aragon and Isabella of Castile, through which most of the peninsular kingdoms were united, the homogenization of Spain had become central to Spain's geopolitical competition with Portugal and other expansionist powers.

By January 1492 Ferdinand and Isabella had driven the last Moorish king from Spain, expelled the Jews from the peninsula, strengthened the power and reach of the Inquisition, accepted the first comprehensive Spanish grammar, and financed Columbus's first voyage to the Indies. This consolidation of Spanish identity helped create a millenarist sensibility, by which Spanish conquistadors translated the concept of reconquering Spain from the infidels (*los infieles,* or "those without faith") to conquering the newly encountered infidels of the Americas—the indigenous peoples. Examples of this transference are the naming of the town Matamoros, located along the Rio Grande, after the protector of Spain, Saint James the Moor-killer; a 16th-century statue of the Virgin Mary still extant in New Mexico called *La Conquistadora* (The Conqueror); and the 1598 performance of the play *Los moros y cristianos* (The Moors and the Christians) in New Mexico, which chronicles aspects of the Reconquest in Spain and which was used to celebrate the defeat of the indigenous peoples at the hands of the Spanish *conquistadores*—and to send a message to the defeated. Literary texts of the time have substituted the word *indio* (Indian) for Moor, but the rhetoric is remarkably similar to that of late-medieval conquest texts in Iberia. Expansion of Spanish missionary activity in the Americas was also a derivation of both military and inquisitional forms.

In more recent years the term *reconquest* has also been used to describe the demographic movement of peoples northward from Mexico as a "re-taking" of Mexico's northern provinces appropriated by the United States in the Mexican-American War (1846–1848). Several Mexican and Mexican American radicals—as well as conservative U.S. political commentators—have taken note of these demographic shifts and interpreted them as a popular movement to establish political control of the American Southwest by Spanish-speaking peoples, thus reconquering the formerly Mexican region by means of the ballot box, with the possible re-adhesion of the territory to Mexico.

RELATED ARTICLES

Politics, Latino; Politics, Mexican American; Southwestern United States, Anglo Immigration to; Spain.

FURTHER READING

Elliott, John Huxtable. *Imperial Spain, 1469–1716.* New York: Penguin Bks., 1963.

Harris, Max. *Aztecs, Moors, and Christians: Festivals of Reconquest in Mexico and Spain.* Austin: Univ. of Tex. Press, 2000.

Lomax, Derek W. *The Reconquest of Spain.* New York: Longman, 1978.

O'Callaghan, Joseph F. *Reconquest and Crusade in Medieval Spain.* Philadelphia: Univ. of Pa. Press, 2003.

HAROLD AUGENBRAUM

REFORMA

Known as REFORMA, the National Association to Promote Library and Information Services to Latinos and the Spanish Speaking was founded in 1971 by Arnulfo Trejo (1922–2002). REFORMA was the first organization in the nation to focus on library and information services for Latino populations. The goal of REFORMA is first and foremost the recruitment and training of bilingual, bicultural librarians who can provide culturally appropriate library and information services and collections to U.S. Latinos. To this end, REFORMA provides numerous annual scholarships to students who pursue a degree in library or information science, sponsors conferences, conducts research studies, maintains a mentoring program, and disseminates information through a quarterly newsletter and a Web site. Many of REFORMA's key positions, such as the development of Spanish-language collections and bilingual-bicultural programming in public libraries, were viewed as controversial and experimental within the American library profession until the mid-1990s. However, these services have now become fairly mainstream owing in part to the educational and organizational efforts of REFORMA.

The organization is composed of 21 autonomous local chapters, at-large members, and a national board. As an affiliate of the American Library Association (ALA), REFORMA conducts national board meetings and programs at ALA's national summer and midwinter conferences. Chapters are involved in local, regional, and state issues affecting Latino populations. While the membership is primarily professionally trained librarians, anyone interested in library services for Latinos—including library staff, community members, library board members, or institutions—can join by filling out an application form on the organization's Web site. The national REFORMA office is based in Scottsdale, Arizona.

The impact of individual REFORMA members on American public library services over the last 30 years has been profound. REFORMISTAS (REFORMA members) have served in public, academic, and special libraries across the nation promoting a culturally specific vision of reading, research, and learning that promotes the best aspects of Latino heritage. The inclusion of Spanish-language materials, the development of English-language collections that reflect the experiences of Latino cultural groups, and relevant programming for children and adults are core issues for REFORMA members employed in public libraries. In academic libraries REFORMISTAS have worked jointly with Chicano, Latino, and Puerto Rican Studies departments to create scholarly collections and research tools and to direct special libraries and archives.

A few of REFORMA's major accomplishments include the initiation of Día de los Niños (Day of the Children) celebrations on April 30th as a national observance in libraries across the country, and the Pura Bulpré Award, a children's book award that recognizes an author or illustrator whose work best portrays, affirms, and celebrates the Latino cultural experience in an outstanding work of literature for children and youth. Additionally, REFORMA has held periodic national conferences. A key national policy accomplishment in which REFORMA played an influential role was the American Library Association's *Guidelines for Library Services to Hispanics* (1998). This policy statement outlines essential features of quality library services for Latinos, including the need for language pluralism in staffing and collection building.

RELATED ARTICLES
Education; Education, Higher; Libraries and Archives.

FURTHER READING
Alire, Camila, and Orlando Archibeque. *Serving Latino Communities: A How-to-Do-It Manual for Librarians.* New York: Neal-Schuman, 1998.

Güereña, Salvador, ed. *Library Services to Latinos: An Anthology.* Jefferson, N.C.: McFarland & Co., 2000.

Güereña, Salvador, and Edward Erazo. "Latinos and Librarianship." *Library Trends* 49, no. 1 (Summer 2000): 138–181.

Luévano-Molina, Susan, ed. *Immigrant Politics and the Public Library.* Westport, Conn.: Greenwood Press, 2001.

McCook, Kathleen de la Peña. "Poverty, Democracy and Public Libraries." In *Libraries and Democracy: The Cornerstones of Liberty.* Ed. by Nancy Kranich. Chicago: Am. Lib. Assn., 2001.

SUSAN LUÉVANO-MOLINA

RELIGION

In general, religion among U.S. Latinos is best understood as the continuing result of the encounter between Christian and non-Christian traditions that was initiated in what is now Latin America. This encounter began in 1492 with the arrival of Christopher Columbus. European Catholic Christianity was characterized by an imperialistic approach that sought to convert indigenous peoples and expand the Christian empire. This attitude is apparent in Columbus's *Libro de las profecías* (1501–1502), which outlines reasons for destroying indigenous religious traditions. The imposition of Catholicism, however, was not uniform throughout the Americas, which helps explain the large variety of indigenous practices that still exist as well as the rise of Protestant Christianity.

Christianity is graphocentric, privileging writing as the primary record of divine communication. As in most "enscripturated" traditions, an elite group preserves and interprets scriptures, especially if literacy is a skill not possessed by the majority. Written traditions may become relatively more fixed than oral traditions, and interpretations may become relatively more rigid. At the same time, putting divine communications in textual form may undermine authority, especially if populations become literate and begin to see themselves as competent interpreters of these sacred texts.

The response of indigenous peoples to Christianity assumed a variety of forms, ranging from conversion to resistance. Indigenous traditions were recontextualized in light of Christianity when they did not disappear altogether. The elite who safeguarded orthodoxy were usually in tension with the interpretation of Christianity that predominated among the nonelite. This situation was complicated by the introduction of African slaves and their traditions into the Americas by the early 16th century. Yoruba religious traditions, mainly from Nigeria, flourished in Cuba, while other African traditions flourished in Puerto Rico and the Dominican Republic.

By the time that substantial populations from Cuba, Puerto Rico, and Mexico became part of the United States, the basic profile of U.S. Latino religion had been established. For much of the last 500 years, a blend of Catholicism and native American traditions has predominated among Mexican Americans, and a blend of Catholicism and African traditions has been practiced by Puerto Ricans, Cuban Americans, and Dominicans. Protestantization has complicated this history even further, especially since the middle part of the 20th century.

Religious Demographics of U.S. Latinos
Although the specifically American story of U.S. Latino religion begins in 1848 with the signing of the Treaty of Guadalupe Hidalgo, the study of U.S.

Latino religious behavior is in its infancy, with detailed sociological studies having begun in the late 20th century. One primary impulse for such study stems from Catholic sociologists' wish to assess the health of their denomination in the face of Protestantization. Examples include Andrew Greeley's two brief but often cited surveys (1988, 1997) and the more detailed survey of Roberto O. González and Michael LaVelle (1985). Another impulse comes from secular sociologists (including Rodolfo de la Garza) who are interested in the role of religion in various aspects of Latino behavior, and particularly in politics.

Academic scholars of religion combine both impulses into studies that seek basic information about the history and evolution of religion among U.S. Latinos. At present, the most ambitious survey of U.S. Latino religious behavior is that of the Hispanic Churches in American Public Life Project (HCAPL), headed by Gastón Espinosa. Collaborators include Virgilio Elizondo, a noted Mexican American Catholic priest, and Jesse Miranda, an Evangelical Protestant leader.

The HCAPL reports that 74 percent of U.S. Latinos identify as Catholic, about 22 percent identify as Protestant, with smaller proportions identifying as Jewish and Muslim (there are some 15,000 Latino Muslims according to some estimates). The Catholic figure has remained relatively constant, but it is being sustained by influxes of Latino Catholics from Latin America. Latino subgroups also show some important distinctions. For example, de la Garza reports an over 70 percent Catholic affiliation for Mexican Americans and Cubans. This compares with 65 percent of Puerto Ricans who identify as Catholic.

Certain criteria (such as church attendance) that are used to measure "religiosity" can provide contradictory results, however. For example, while 70 percent of Mexican Americans identify as Catholic in some surveys, the proportion of Mexican Americans who report "never" attending religious services is placed at 46.8 percent. This sort of paradoxical result reminds us that laypersons and the elite sometimes continue to define "Catholic" (or almost any other major designation) in very different manners.

There also seem to be some differences among generations. González and LaVelle reported that 8.3 percent of Hispanics age 50–59 attended church daily, while only 1.9 percent of those under 30 attended Catholic Mass daily. The importance of the Blessed Virgin Mary was placed at over 80 percent by those age 40 and older, while it was about 70 percent for those under 30. On social issues, the older generation seems more conservative. For example, more than 80 percent of Hispanic Catholics over 80 believe abortion is wrong, according to González and LaVelle, while only 58.9 percent of those under 30 believe so. Sixty-six percent of Hispanic Catholics over age 70 think that contraception is wrong, while only 31 percent of those under 30 believe it is wrong. The importance of the sacraments is similar among men and women of all generations.

The proportion of Catholics declines in the second and third generations to about 72 and 62 percent, respectively, according to the HCAPL. Indeed, younger generations are more inclined to switch to Protestantism and to experiment with non-Christian religions, such as Buddhism and Islam. Some 10 percent of Latinos, mostly of younger generations, describe themselves as having no religious preference, which raises questions about secularization, a process still not widely studied among Latinos. In part, generational differences reflect educational and other socioeconomic differences between immigrant and U.S.-born generations. In general, the younger generations exemplify an eclectic and highly individualized approach to religion typical among Anglo-Americans.

Art and Religion

Art can represent the visual mode of religious experience. Pre-Columbian peoples in the Americas had a variety of religious artistic expressions, ranging from personal ornaments to large monumental architecture. Deities and religious myths were visualized and depicted in all types of media, ranging from stone to painted vessels. Likewise, African traditions (for instance, Santería) portray deities and powers through visual media manufactured from plant, mineral, and metallic substances. Color symbolism is particularly important in distinguishing the *orishas* (Santería divine manifestations). For example, red and white are associated with Shangó, the god of thunder and fire; blue is associated with Yemayá, the goddess of the sea.

The Catholicism that arrived in the Americas saw the depiction of any non-Christian divine entities as idolatry, and three distinct strategies followed. The first was outright destruction of indigenous sacred images. The second involved Christianizing indigenous images, as exemplified by the Afro-Cuban tradition known as Santería. Third, Christian images were indigenized, for example the ubiquitous icon of Mexican Catholicism, the Virgin of Guadalupe.

The home continues to be a repository of religious art, especially in Catholic and Afro-Caribbean traditions. Catholic home altars may have candles and pictures of loved ones or even beloved Catholic political figures such as John F. Kennedy. Adherents of Santería may decorate the interior and exterior of their houses with Catholic and African sacred art. *Retablos,* painted wooden panels, sometimes provide personalized stories (for example, healings) within a religious context.

Protestantization is changing the very definition of artistic expression among U.S. Latinos. Historically, Protestantism has been opposed to images of the Virgin Mary and saints. Simple unadorned crosses appear in Protestant churches while depictions of the bloodied crucified Christ are typically found in Catholic churches. Evangelicals, in particular, usually avoid personal religious art such as crucifixes. In general, Protestantism has shifted from the visual to the aural and oral in its aesthetics with sermons serving as "works of art."

The rise of film and television as the main myth-making force in the United States has also had important effects on religion. American commercial audiovisual media have often suppressed religious expression in order to enhance mass-market appeal. Nonetheless, religious themes can be found, as in *Mi Familia* (1995), which shows the diversity of traditions (indigenous, Protestant, and Catholic) among Mexican Americans. Televangelism, with its flamboyant personalities and dramatic moments, reflects how religion can also use television as a new mode of proselytization. In the future, visual religious expression may become more variegated or recontextualized as U.S. Latinos enter mainstream commercial media in greater numbers.

Health Care and Religion

Health care can shape, and be shaped by, religion. It is useful to think of health care as a system of interacting resources, institutions, and strategies that are intended to maintain or restore health in a particular community. In practice, people often utilize overlapping systems, even if each of them could theoretically stand alone. The history of religion and health care among Latinos can be seen as a triangular tension involving Christian traditions, non-Christian religious traditions, and modern medical views of the causes of illness and the proper modes of therapy.

In most indigenous traditions, health care is an integral part of the religious system. Supernatural forces or beings or both are believed to be responsible for illness and healing. Personal responsibility also has a role, especially if patients believe illness is a punishment for misdeeds.

Christianity held its own God responsible for illness and healing, and usually responded by labeling non-Christian healing concepts as superstition and magic. By the turn of the 20th century, however, a stark disjunction developed between religion and health care in modern Western countries. The discovery of microbes and the success of antibiotics, among other developments, led modern medicine to emphasize the idea that illness was not caused by supernatural forces. Such scientific secular ideas became particularly predominant in urban areas. Although one consultant could routinely combine religious and healing functions in premodern societies, in modern Western societies, the religious consultant was charged with healing the soul; the physician with healing the body.

This disjunction between body and soul is one of the main issues in the role of religion in the health-care practices of Latinos. Mexican folk healers, often called *curanderos,* seek to heal both body and soul through Christian and indigenous methods. Santería is also largely a health-care system that does not restrict itself to the body. Likewise, Puerto Rican *espiritistas,* who focus on communications with departed spirits, see religion as integral to healing the whole person.

As Latinos have become more urbanized and affluent, they have increasingly utilized modern physicians. Rather than dying out completely, however, alternative medicine has assumed new forms. For example, the growing shift to Pentecostalism can be understood, in part, as a shift to an alternative health-care system. Some studies show that Pentecostalism, which has historically emphasized healing, can be attractive in areas where conventional health care is not available or has not yielded satisfactory results.

There is also a growing interaction among the health-care systems of Latino and Latina subgroups in the United States. For example, in New York City, Puerto Ricans are increasingly turning to forms of healing associated primarily with Cuban American Santería, and many Latinas and Latinos appeal to religious healing systems derived from other parts of the globe (such as Ayurvedic medicine). In any case, the complex configurations of etiologies and therapeutic strategies that are still evolving among Latinas and Latinos form a new and dynamic episode in the long history of the interaction of religion and health care.

Literature and Religion

Since its development, literature has been a medium of religious expression, especially for the elite educated classes, and authors do not always mirror the religious attitudes of their broader communities. Likewise, U.S. Latino and Latina authors often exhibit the religious attitudes of the elite educated strata rather than the religious behavior of the broader Hispanic communities. In general, U.S. Latino literature is characterized by a movement away from the European Christianity that it inherited under Spanish colonialism, and such a trend can be detected by studying the attitudes toward religion and specific religious traditions.

Indigenous and African religions, which were often represented as superstitious and evil by early Spanish writers, are now often represented quite positively. For example, Gloria Anzaldúa's *Borderlands/ La Frontera* (1987) sees Náhuatl traditions centering on goddesses as part of her salvation from an institutional and repressive Catholicism. Tato Laviera, the best-selling U.S. Latino poet, uses Afro-Caribbean religions as an antidote to Catholicism in *La Carreta Made a U-Turn* (1979).

Catholicism is often criticized or rejected by modern Latino authors—a reversal of its depiction in U.S. Latino literature from about 1848 to the late 1950s. For example, Fray Angélico Chávez (1910–1996) of New Mexico wrote poetry and short stories that celebrate the advent of Catholicism in the Americas and the Southwest. Starting in the late 1950s, the Catholic Church became increasingly challenged by authors such as José Antonio Villarreal (*Pocho*, 1959), Rudolfo Anaya (*Bless Me, Ultima*, 1972), and Oscar "Zeta" Acosta (*The Revolt of the Cockroach People*, 1973). *Mr. Ives' Christmas* (1995), by the Pulitzer Prize–winning Oscar Hijuelos, is one of the few contemporary works to see the Church as having a generally positive effect.

Protestantism has never fared well in U.S. Latino and Latina literature. It is seen as comical, foreign, and disingenuous in Rolando Hinojosa's *Klail City* (1987), and it is only a temporary fix in Piri Thomas's *Savior, Savior, Hold My Hand* (1972). But perhaps the most salient example of Protestantism's continuing low status among Hispanic literati is the virtual exclusion from most "canons" of a work such as *Run, Baby, Run* (1968), the autobiography of Nicky Cruz, a zealous Pentecostal Protestant. This exclusion comes despite many similarities with the autobiographical work of Piri Thomas, who is accepted into many anthologies.

Judaism is portrayed in a mixed fashion. Oscar Z. Acosta's *The Autobiography of a Brown Buffalo* (1972) spouts forth many anti-Jewish stereotypes that seemingly derive from Acosta's Christian background. Other authors depict characters who manifest anti-Jewish sentiments (for example, Lourdes in Cristina García's *Dreaming in Cuban*, 1992). Nicholasa Mohr's *El Bronx Remembered* (1986), on the other hand, encourages compromise and friendship between Judaism and Christianity. Ilan Stavans has explored his own Latino Jewish identity within the larger history of Judaism in "Xerox Man" (2000), among other works.

Islam and Eastern religions, although still not much of a factor in Latino literature, are usually seen either neutrally or positively. Piri Thomas experiments with Islam in *Down These Mean Streets* (1967). Elements of Eastern religions are portrayed positively in Rudolfo Anaya's *Jalamanta* (1996) and in Hijuelos's *Mr. Ives' Christmas*. In general, pluralistic, eclectic, and individualistic approaches to religion continue to permeate contemporary U.S. Latino literature.

Music and Religion

Music represents a primary mode of the aural and oral religious experience. The history of music in the U.S. Latino and Latina religious experience has been one of tension between orthodox European musical forms and those of indigenous traditions or more popular Anglo-American traditions. Catholicism brought to the Americas musical forms that originated in Medieval Latin ecclesiastical traditions. At the time of the Renaissance, stringed instruments were seen as more "sacred," and wind instruments more "profane." Later, the organ became a standard sacred instrument among major Christian denominations. In contrast, indigenous and African traditions often emphasize percussion and wind instrumentation. Dancing, which was central to many indigenous and African religious traditions, was not highly valued as a form of worship in Catholicism or Protestantism.

Within the United States, these differences resulted in conflict. For example, rhythm and blues were not seen as proper in many white southern churches. This antipathy toward African American forms was transferred into a number of Latino Pentecostal traditions. Thus, the Church of God (headquartered in Cleveland, Tennessee) favored Appalachian musical styles in its Spanish-speaking churches and disdained anything deemed to be rock and roll for much of the 1960s and 1970s. Overall, mainstream Protestantism retains some traditions found in Catholicism, including choirs and organs, but also favors participation by the congregation in singing.

Vatican II (1962–1965), a policy-making general council of the Catholic Church, instituted a number of reforms in its liturgy, which helped to broaden the scope of musical expression among Latino Catholics. Protestant denominations have increasingly insisted that Latino musical forms (*cumbias,* salsa) be deemed sacred. The numerous works of the Mexican-born musician Carlos Santana, a self-described devotee of the angel Metatron, exemplifies how U.S. Latina and Latino artists continue to change the very meaning of sacred music.

Politics, Civil Rights, and Religion

Politics refers here to the set of practices and institutions that allocate power in a society. The degree of separation between church and state that is practiced in the United States has not characterized much of European and Latin American history. The U.S. Latino religio-political experience has sought to re-evaluate the meaning of political participation in light of the turbulent history of church-state establishments in Latin America.

For most of the last 500 years, Catholicism was the established denomination in Latin America. At the same time, this union of church and state began to be seen as a problem when Latin Americans sought independence from their European colonizers. Nonetheless, this did not necessarily mean the rejection of religion in politics, but rather its recontextualization. For example, the Mexican revolutionist Miguel Hidalgo's banner, which prominently displayed the Virgin of Guadalupe, reflects how an indigenized European icon could serve to rally Mexicans against European colonialists. More recently,

liberation theology sees politics as a vehicle by which Christians can liberate the poor and oppressed.

It is not yet clear, however, how religion is influencing politics among U.S. Latinos. The presidential race between Richard Nixon and John F. Kennedy in 1960 was the first to generate visible Latino activism for a presidential candidate. Some Mexican Americans thought that Kennedy's Catholicism was an important factor in voting for him. At the same time, the Viva Kennedy Clubs, which originally came to prominence among Mexican Americans in Texas, emphasized Kennedy's concern for the poor and his sympathy toward Latin America as the main reason for Latino support.

The civil rights movement of the 1950s and 1960s also had a strong religious base. Martin Luther King, Jr., was a Baptist minister and Malcolm X was a Nation of Islam member; however, large churches did not always support racial and economic equality. César Chávez, for example, complained that he often received more help from Protestants than from the Catholic Church. Religious institutions also played a role in sheltering political refugees from Latin America, especially during the 1980s. Yet disputes, publicized in summer 2003, between workers of the Brownsville, Texas, diocese and its bishop, Raymundo

© JUDY WALGREN / DALLAS MORNING NEWS/KRT

A father in Texas spreads holy water from the shrine of the Virgen de San Juan del Valle on his son's head to protect him from evil.

25 ☀

Peña, show that laypersons and officials sometimes continue to disagree on civil rights.

The HCAPL reports that Hispanic Protestants and Catholics do not differ radically in their voting patterns. For example, the HCAPL notes that 73 percent of Latinos voted for Clinton in 1996, while only 37 percent of whites in mainline denominations and 51 percent of white Catholics did so. In the 2000 election, an estimated 35 percent of Latino Pentecostals voted for Bush and about 35 percent for Gore. In 2004, 54 percent of Latinos voted for Kerry. In general, the effect of religion, and especially Protestantization, on Latino and Latina politics remains an open question.

Urbanization and Religion

The Catholicism that first arrived in the Americas highly valued urban civilization. Rome, the Eternal City, was the seat of Catholicism. The Catholic hierarchy had its roots in the complex organization developed to manage cities and empires. In contrast, most indigenous traditions were rural and had relatively small groups as adherents, a notable exception being the large Aztec Empire.

Many anthropologists note that urbanization has at least two important religious consequences. One is the diminution of kinship as a primary mode of social organization; in cities people primarily organize themselves by common interests. Some scholars argue that urbanization increases individualistic orientations, especially since it is possible to live more anonymously in cities than in small rural communities. Second, modern urban centers tend to offer a larger variety of religious choices.

The year 1848 marks the first incorporation into the United States of a Spanish-speaking territory— what was then the northern half of Mexico—and most of the early Spanish-speaking settlers were of rural origins. Large influxes of Mexican immigrants came after the revolution of 1910 and during World War II. Many came as farmworkers, and thus continued living in a rural sector of society in the United States.

In America, the Catholic Church directed a disproportionate number of its resources to the cities. Priests were concentrated in large cities, not rural environments. Consequently, migrant farmworkers were often left to develop their own understanding of Catholicism, which did not always conform to orthodox beliefs. At the same time, Latinos in large cities were frequently attracted to religious choices that were not available in rural environments. Thus, the rise of Protestantism, Islam, and Eastern religions among Latinos and Latinas in the United States is partially the result of the urbanization of U.S. Latinos.

Women and Religion

One of the most significant recent revolutions in Christianity is the ascendance of women's voices. Christianity, whether Catholic or Protestant, historically has been androcentric. Thus in Catholicism, women cannot be priests, despite the fact that women attend Mass daily at a rate almost equaling that of men (3.2 percent to 3.1 percent, respectively). Some scholars argue, however, that women play the central role in communicating religious traditions within the family. Moreover, women have compensated for the lack of official leadership positions through a variety of means. For example, a large number of Mexican American *curanderas,* and Puerto Rican *espiritistas* are women, who, in effect, exercise alternative forms of religious power.

Pentecostalism has been particularly known for allowing women to become leaders. Maria Atkinson (1879–1963), who is regarded as the founder of the Church of God in Mexico, was very active in the U.S.-Mexican borderlands. She initially had great authority, but lost much of it to men she helped to train. One could also mention Ana María Falcon García, a pastor of the largest church (Willimantic, Connecticut) in the Iglesias de Dios Pentecostal denomination; but mainline Protestant denominations also have made some notable appointments—for example, the Reverend Altagracia Pérez, the first Hispanic female minister of the Episcopal Church.

As more women become educated, some groups, such as "Las Hermanas," which formed in Los Angeles in the 1970s, may seek to retain their Catholic identity while engaging in spiritual and political activities in their own sacred spaces. Latina theologians, such as Ada María Isasi-Díaz, María Pilar Aquino, Jeanette Rodríguez, and Daisy Machado, have developed a "mujerista theology," which centers on empowering women. Other women, such as Gloria Anzaldúa, the author of *Borderlands,* and Ana Castillo, the author of *So Far from God* (1996), use literature to express their own brands of spirituality.

Conclusion

The encounter between Christianity and non-Christian traditions that has shaped the Latin American religious experience has assumed new forms in the United States. While Catholicism remains a strong institutional presence, U.S. Latinos have increasingly opted for the large number of other choices available in the United States. In part, this is owing to increased education and movement into new socioeconomic levels. In the future, Latino identity will probably not be tied to Catholicism in the way it once was. At the same time art, health care, literature, music, politics, and other cultural components will continue to be recontextualized by the U.S. Latino religious experience. Indeed, U.S. Latino religion is undergoing a monumental evolution that may provide one of the most interesting narratives in the history of religion.

RELATED ARTICLES

Altares; Anzaldúa, Gloria; Bible in Spanish; Catholicism; Crypto-Jews; Curanderismo; Espiritismo; Health; Islam; Jesuits; Jewish Life; Laviera, Jesús; Literature; Mormonism; Music, Classical; Music, Popular; Protestantism; Santería; Spirituality; Virgen de Guadalupe; Virgen de la Caridad del Cobre; Virgen de Montserrate.

FURTHER READING

Avalos, Héctor, ed. *Introduction to the U.S. Latina and Latino Religious Experience*. Boston: Brill, 2004.
Bettinger-López, Caroline. *Cuban-Jewish Journeys: Searching for Identity, Home, and History in Miami*. Knoxville: Univ. of Tenn. Press, 2000.
De La Torre, Miguel A., and Edwin D. Aponte. *Introducing Latino/a Theologies*. Maryknoll, N.Y.: Orbis, 2001.
Díaz-Stevens, Ana María, and Anthony M. Stevens-Arroyo. *Recognizing the Latino Resurgence in U.S. Religion: The Emmaus Paradigm*. Boulder, Colo.: Westview Press, 1998.
Dolan, Jay P., and Gilberto Hinojosa, eds. *Mexican Americans and the Catholic Church, 1900–1965*. Vol. 1, Notre Dame History of Hispanic Catholics in the U.S. Notre Dame, Ind.: Univ. of Notre Dame Press, 1994.
Dolan, Jay P., and Jaime R. Vidal, eds. *Puerto Rican and Cuban Catholics in the U.S., 1900–1965*. Vol. 2, Notre Dame History of Hispanic Catholics in the U.S. Notre Dame, Ind.: Univ. of Notre Dame Press, 1994.
Dolan, Jay P., and Allan Figueroa Deck, S. J., eds. *Hispanic Catholic Culture in the U.S.: Issues and Concerns*. Vol. 3, Notre Dame History of Hispanic Catholics in the U.S. Notre Dame, Ind.: Univ. of Notre Dame Press, 1994.
González, Roberto O., and Michael LaVelle. *The Hispanic Catholic in the United States: A Socio-Cultural and Religious Profile*. New York: Northeast Catholic Pastoral Ctr. for Hispanics, 1985.
Isasi-Díaz, Ada María, and Fernando F. Segovia, eds. *Hispanic/Latino Theology: Challenge and Promise*. Minneapolis, Minn.: Fortress Press, 1996.
Sandoval, Moisés. *On the Move: A History of the Hispanic Church in the United States*. Maryknoll, N.Y.: Orbis, 1990.

HECTOR AVALOS

REPUBLICAN PARTY

The U.S. Republican Party's stance on issues of race and ethnicity has been complicated since the early days of its existence. The party that emerged to oppose the spread of slavery into new U.S. territories yet did not necessarily support equality between the races has had an equally complicated relationship with Latinos, who have been members of the party since the 19th century. On one hand, Republican presidents have been responsible for the expansion of colonialism and paternalism in the Western Hemisphere. On the other hand, by some accounts, Republicans have made the most organized and concerted effort to reach out to Latino voters in recent elections.

Latinos' relationship with the Republican Party is equally complicated. While Latinos express a measure of social conservatism, this more traditional ideology does not necessarily translate into uniform support for the Republican Party. Additionally, there are noticeable ethnic differences in partisanship among Latinos; Cuban Americans, in particular, identify predominantly with the Republican Party. Typical analyses of Cuban American partisanship attribute this identification to foreign policy concerns that emanate from the forced exile of Cubans to the United States after Castro's revolution. While these concerns are real and do explain Cuban American partisan identification in part, other, political factors have influenced Cuban American participation in Republican Party politics, particularly in South Florida.

Latinos tend to have a more diverse partisan identification than their African American peers. According to the 1992 Latino National Political Survey, about three-fifths of the Latinos surveyed (who were Mexican, Puerto Rican, and Cuban American) identified as Democrats, while a little over a quarter of Latinos identified as Republicans. (As a point of reference, over 80 percent of African Americans identified themselves as Democrats.) There are also class differences in partisanship within the Latino community, as more wealthy Latinos are more likely to identify themselves as Republicans.

Partisan identification by each ethnic group is very different, however. Mexican and Puerto Rican Americans identified more strongly with the Democratic Party (66 percent and 70 percent, respectively), while 70 percent of Cuban Americans identified themselves as Republicans—with nearly half of all Cubans identifying as strong Republicans. Again, class and ethnic identity can also interact with ethnicity to influence partisan identification. Juan Gómez Quiñones (1990) writes of Mexican American Republicans: "Usually, Mexican participation in the Republican Party has been part of the conservative sector of the community, coming from upper and middle income sectors, professionals, highly educated and often, but not always, notably assimilated persons."

Other studies have tried to gauge partisan identification among other Latino immigrants. According to the National Latino Immigrant Survey, one-third of non-Puerto Rican, non-Cuban and non-Mexican Latinos surveyed indicated that they would be Republicans if they were citizens. Among Mexican immigrants, only half indicated that they would be Democrats if they were American citizens.

Cuban American identification with the Republican Party is largely attributed to the foreign policy orientation of Cuban Americans, who support candidates who take a strong anti-Castro stance regarding Cuba. The group began to look to the Republican Party to support the defeat of Castro after the Kennedy administration failed to overthrow Castro during the Bay of Pigs invasion. In fact, many Cuban Americans felt that the Kennedy administration betrayed them during the invasion when the administration did not protect the exiled Cuban liberators from capture.

However, domestic considerations may have influenced Cuban American partisanship as well. Many Cubans settled in South Florida, particularly Dade County, which had a strong Democratic Party but a weak Republican Party. From a pragmatic perspective, it was easier to break into the leadership structure of the Republican Party than the Democratic Party. Because of Cuban American participation in the Dade County Republican Party, the party became extremely competitive within the region; by the mid-1990s, almost half of all the members of the state legislature from Dade County were Cuban American Republicans, and Dade County was represented by two Cuban American Republican members of Congress, Ileana Ros-Lehtinen (elected 1989) and Lincoln Díaz-Balart (elected 1992).

It is thought that many more Cubans and other Latinos should be inclined to identify with the Republican Party because of its conservative platform. Latinos indicate that they support traditional values, such as opposition to abortion and homosexuality; are more likely than Anglos to support the death penalty; and are perceived to be more religiously observant than Anglos. The Republican Party platform supports similar ideals. However, survey analysis indicates that Latinos are concerned about other issues as well, and those views may explain the more Democratic orientation of non-Cuban Latinos. In particular, Latinos express a belief that government should do what it can to help people meet their material needs; Republicans have historically been advocates of smaller government. Such a belief in a responsive federal government informs Latino support of taxes to improve education and the environment, among other things, and could help direct non-Cuban Latinos toward the Democratic Party.

The Republican Party has also had some difficulty making inroads into the Latino community because some of the policies it espouses run counter to the interests of Latino voters. Lewis Gould notes that since the 1960s, the party's desire to recruit Latino members has been countered by a desire to appeal to a white base that joined the party at that time in part because they thought civil rights were advancing too quickly or because they thought the 1964 Civil Rights Act gave the federal government an unconstitutionally large amount of enforcement power. This notion of conflicting goals was evident in the policy orientations of two U.S. governors. In 1994, California governor Pete Wilson jump-started his campaign during his reelection bid by running on an anti-immigrant platform. This platform included support for Proposition 187, which would deny illegal immigrants access to social services in California. One of the most famous images of that campaign was a commercial featuring nighttime footage of people (whom the viewer was to assume were Mexican) sneaking across the California border. The commercial began with the line, "They keep coming." In contrast, Texas governor George W. Bush, convinced that a strong relationship with Mexico promoted the Texas economy, sought good relations with Mexico and supported bilingualism during his term of office.

In addition, U.S. foreign policy toward Central and South America is probably not the most significant area determining the partisanship of non-Cuban Latinos. The Latino National Political Survey noted that while 70 percent of Cuban Americans supported increased U.S. involvement in Central American affairs, less than 60 percent of Puerto Ricans and less than 40 percent of Mexican Americans took the same stance.

The Republican Party, however, is the party that is most clearly identified with interventionist policies in Central and South America. From President Dwight Eisenhower's support of the overthrow of José Arbenz Guzmán in Guatemala to the Reagan administration's support of the Contra rebels in Nicaragua to President George H. W. Bush's overthrow of Manuel Noriega in Panama, Republican presi-

dents have taken a leading role in opposing and sometimes replacing leftist regimes in Latin America.

Despite the challenges facing Republicans in persuading Latino voters to commit to their party, the party has had some notable success in wooing voters. In addition to the fact that a larger proportion of the Latino population identifies as Republican when compared to African Americans, and that a large portion of the Latino immigrant population seems poised to identify and vote Republican when they become citizens, there are a number of Latino Republicans who indicate that they are converted Democrats who changed their partisan identification. One-fourth of all Latino Republicans were once Democrats.

The partisan conversion rate and the general conservative orientation of Latino voters indicates that

© YESSIKA VIVANCOS/AP/WIDE WORLD PHOTOS

New York State governor George Pataki with actress Carla Pinza, left, and Roberto Clemente, Jr., during the launch of the Amigos de Pataki rally for reelection, 2002.

there is some room for the Republican Party to mount a viable effort to recruit partisans within the Latino community, and for over 30 years the party has made efforts to reach out to Latino voters. Quiñones notes that in the 1968 elections, the Republican Party made a concerted effort to diminish the Mexican American vote for the Democratic Party. By 1972 the party had developed a concerted strategy to win Latino votes. The Nixon administration made a point of highlighting Mexican American appointees, and it created a Cabinet-level committee, the Cabinet Committee on Opportunities for Spanish Speaking People, out of the old Inter-Agency Committee on Mexican American Affairs. These efforts were effective; 30 percent of Latino voters voted for Richard Nixon in 1972, which was twice the rate that voted for Republican congressional candidates.

By 1988, targeting Latino voters was a fixed priority of the Republican Party. According to Federico Subveri-Vélez, the Republicans had a more centralized plan to reach out to Latino voters than the Democrats did. In the 1988 election, the George H. W. Bush campaign opted for a media strategy that was developed in Ronald Reagan's reelection campaign in 1984, in which they would "reach [Latinos] in English, but . . . convince them in Spanish" (Hispanic Victory Initiative '84). The campaign ghostwrote editorials for prominent Latino columnists and strategically placed them in Latino newspapers. They generated their own news stories, which were sometimes picked up verbatim by the Latino press. The campaign also produced four English-Spanish commercials. Three of the ads focused on issues such as jobs, education, the prominent role that Latinos would play in a Bush administration, and the notion of opportunity generally. The final ad featured Columba Bush, the daughter-in-law of George H. W. Bush (and wife of Jeb Bush, who would become governor of Florida). In this ad, she suggested to Latino voters that they could trust George H. W. Bush as president because he personally understood the plight of Latino people.

In the 2000 election, Columba Bush's son George Prescott Bush filled the same role for his uncle George W. Bush in his presidential bid. George W. Bush, who was governor of Texas when he ran for the presidency, enjoyed favorable ratings among Latino voters in Texas. For the national campaign, George P. Bush appeared in a television ad where he proclaimed pride in his Latino heritage and noted that there was a candidate with the same name as his. In addition to having his telegenic nephew campaign for him, George W. Bush and the Republican Party appointed Latinos to other prominent roles in the campaign. For instance, Congressman Henry Bonilla from Texas, the only other Latino Republican in Congress, served as one of the co-chairs of the 2000 Republican National Convention and later as an adviser to the Bush-Cheney 2000 campaign.

While the Republican Party worked to win Latino voters and to recruit Latino partisans, those who identified with the party were relatively active. Despite the fact that there are fewer Latino Republicans than there are Latino Democrats, Latinos have historically donated more money to the Republican Party than to the Democratic Party. This is largely due to the fact that prominent Cuban American Republicans donate money to the Republican Party because of the party's stance against Castro.

George W. Bush's victory in the 2004 presidential election demonstrated the Republican Party's success in reaching out to the Latino community. According to the exit polls used by many major news organizations, Bush received 44 percent of the Latino vote (however, the William C. Velasquez Foundation, which conducted exit polling among Latinos in 14 states, reported that Bush had received 31.4 percent of the Latino vote). While this was less than the 53 percent that his Democratic opponent, John Kerry, received, Bush's performance among Latinos was nine percentage points higher than it had been in 2000 and was the best performance for a Republican presidential candidate among Latinos since exit polling begain in 1972.

Increased support among Latinos probably helped Bush secure victory in "battleground" states. In New Mexico, for example, exit polls indicated that Bush's share of the vote was 12 percentage points higher than it had been in 2000. Scholars and analysts attributed increased Latino support of the Republican ticket to voters' concerns about moral issues (abortion and same-sex marriage were among the most frequently cited) and terrorism. Latino voters who listed these issues as their chief concerns overwhelmingly voted for Bush.

RELATED ARTICLES

Congress, United States; Cuban Americans; Democratic Party; Political Parties; Politics, Latino; Voting.

FURTHER READING

DeSipio, Louis. *Counting on the Latino Vote: Latinos As a New Electorate.* Charlottesville: Univ. of Va. Press, 1996.

Gould, Lewis L. *Grand Old Party: A History of the Republicans.* New York: Random House, 2003.

McClain, Paula, and Joseph Stewart, Jr. *Can We All Get Along? Racial and Ethnic Minorities in American Politics.* Boulder, Colo.: Westview Press, 1995.

Montejano, David. "On the Future of Anglo-Mexican Relations in the United States." In *Chicano Politics and Society in the Late Twentieth Century.* Ed. by David Montejano. Austin: Univ. of Tex. Press, 1999.

Moreno, Dario. "The Cuban Model: Political Empowerment in Miami." In *Pursuing Power: Latinos and the Political System.* Ed. by F. Chris García. South Bend: Univ. of Notre Dame Press, 1997.

Quiñones, Juan Gómez. *Chicano Politics: Reality and Promise, 1940–1990.* Albuquerque: Univ. of N.Mex. Press, 1990.

Subveri-Vélez, Federico A. "Republican and Democratic Mass Communication Strategies: Targeting the Latino Vote." In *From Rhetoric to Reality: Latino Politics in the 1988 Elections.* Ed. by Rodolfo de la Garza and Louis DeSipio. Boulder, Colo.: Westview Press, 1992.

ANDRA GILLESPIE

RESTAURANTS

As a marker of cultural identity, the food we eat and how it is prepared can often pinpoint our heritage or country of origin, and restaurants, whether they are fast-food or full-service establishments, represent a public place where one can be linked to his or her culture. For Latinos living in the United States, eating establishments have played an important role in helping to preserve ties to the community. Across the country, many restaurants double as cultural centers and serve as beacons to recent immigrants, particularly men who have crossed into the United States alone and who seek them out to find their footing in the United States, as well as longtime residents and U.S.-born Latinos who do so to maintain their cultural identity. Eating establishments have served in this capacity since Latinos first began migrating to the United States, or, as in the case of Mexico, they are the legacy left behind when Mexico lost much of its territory to the United States in 1848 as a result of the Treaty of Guadalupe Hidalgo.

Reflecting the history of other ethnic cuisines in the United States, that of Latin America frequently first hit the streets in the form of independent street vendors selling traditional delicacies. In the 1850s, tamales, enchiladas, tortillas, and a variety of other Mexican food items were being peddled in San Francisco and throughout the Southwest, and tamale vendors were also selling on the streets of New York City in the late 1800s. The most widespread and familiar of Latino cuisines is still that from Mexico, with Mexican food outlets now found nationwide, despite obvious clustering throughout the southwestern states. What started with pushcarts in the street has evolved into a plethora of Mexican or Tex-Mex restaurants ranging from limited-service to fine-dining establishments.

The introduction of other Latino food establishments mirrors the trends of migration into the United States, and the proliferation of certain kinds of ethnic cuisines in specific areas logically parallels settlement patterns. In the early 1900s Puerto Ricans began arriving in New York City, their numbers increasing significantly after World War II and during the Great Migration between 1946 and 1964. Puerto Rican entrepreneurs established bodegas (small grocery stores) and modest eateries, including *chuchifritos* (snack food stands), to provide the community with links to its homeland. After the assassination of dictator Rafael Leónides Trujillo in 1961, Dominicans began flooding into New York City, bringing their foods with them and setting up restaurants in their communities. Although Cubans were represented in the United States earlier, the majority came after the Cuban Revolution in 1959. This resulted in an explosion of Cuban *cafeterías* (restaurants) and *cafetines* (espresso bars), especially in Miami, as well as Chino-Cubano restaurants, notably in New York City.

Other Latino eating establishments also are found throughout the United States. Colombian, Argentinean, Ecuadorian, Venezuelan, and Peruvian restaurants have found a foothold. The number of Central American restaurants also is growing largely in those areas where Salvadorans, Guatemalans, and Hondurans have settled.

The restaurant industry is the biggest private-sector employer in the United States and the most labor-intensive of all retail-trade industries. It is also the single largest employer of immigrants in the United States, relying heavily on workers from Mexico, Central America, and other Latin American countries. Given the very high turnover of labor, job opportunities are constant.

The number of Latinos employed in dining establishments and food preparation and food service jobs continues to increase as the Latino population increases. But this has represented a double-edged sword for Latinos; despite the fact that jobs in the industry are an entry point for Latinos to join the U.S. workforce, most jobs are unskilled, pay low wages, and provide few, if any, benefits. Many require little command of the English language. A significant percentage of employees are undocumented immigrants whose reluctance to demand better wages and benefits helps keep wages low. However, for those who are able to take advantage of the opportunities offered by the industry, there is a chance to move up: the restaurant industry employs more minority managers than any other industry. In addition, eating establishments serve as a way for Latinos to own their own piece of the American pie. Restaurants—from corner *taquerías* (low-end taco stands) to full-service dining establishments—are one type of business most often selected by Latino entrepreneurs. According to the 1997 Economic Census, published in 2001 by the U.S. Census Bureau, the number of Latino-owned eating and drinking establishments more than doubled between 1992 and 1997, and their numbers have grown more than three times faster than all other restaurants.

Just as food unites a people and highlights its culture, it also serves as a way for people to experience a cuisine and a culture other than their own. Latino dining establishments in the United States play an important role in American society because Latinos represent the largest minority group in the United States, and their culinary traditions have had the greatest impact on U.S. dining habits. As diners become familiar with Latino foods, they also learn more about Latinos and their culture.

The best example of how Latino cuisine is transforming U.S. dining preferences is seen in the case of Mexican food outlets. As a category, Mexican restaurants represent one of the fastest growing and most profitable groups of ethnic restaurants in the United States, expanding out of the barrios and into the mainstream. Growth is across the board, from fast- to full-service food establishments, and encompasses those that specialize in Mexico's many regional cuisines to those that cater as well as to more Americanized tastes.

Non-Latinos also have recognized the money-making potential of Latino food restaurants. A classic example is that of the fast-food franchise Taco Bell. In 1962 founder Glen Bell recognized that by Americanizing the food and applying clever packaging and marketing, the sale of Mexican cuisine could be very lucrative. Taco Bell was acquired by PepsiCo in 1978 and today makes up part of YUM! Brand, Inc. As of summer 2004, there were more than 6,500 Taco Bell restaurants in the United States. At the end of 2003, Taco Bell system sales reached $1.6 billion in company revenues and $3.8 billion in franchise sales.

As U.S. diners acquire a taste for new foods and ingredients, ethnic restaurants continue to grow, with Latinos contributing their traditional foods to the pot. Another manifestation of this trend is the growing popularity of "fusion" food through which diverse ingredients and cooking techniques are combined to create new dishes. Chefs across the country have mined Latino recipes, food products, and food preparation methods to increase the appeal of fusion cooking. They have turned to the fruits, vegetables, and other ingredients used in Latin American cooking to create a new Latino-inspired cuisine called Nuevo Latino.

RELATED ARTICLES

Business; Cuisine; Cuisine, California; Cuisine, Cuban; Cuisine, Dominican; Cuisine, Mexican; Cuisine, Nuevo Latino; Cuisine, Puerto Rican; Cuisine, South American; Cuisine, Spanish; Cuisine, Tex-Mex; Fast Food; Labor.

FURTHER READING

Gabaccia, Donna R. *We Are What We Eat: Ethnic Food and the Making of Americans.* Cambridge: Harvard Univ. Press, 1998.

Hooker, Richard J. A. *Food and Drink in America: A History.* Indianapolis: Bobbs, 1981.

Kittler, Pamela Goyan, and Kathryn Sucher. *Food and Culture in America: A Nutrition Handbook.* New York: Van Nostrand Reinhold, 1989.

Knauer, Lisa Maya. "Eating in Cuban." In *Mambo Montage: The Latinization of New York.* Ed. by Agustín Laó-Montes and Arlene Dávila. New York: Columbia Univ. Press, 2001.

Pérez y González, María E. *Puerto Ricans in the United States.* Westport, Conn.: Greenwood Press, 2000.

Pilcher, Jeffrey M. *¡Que vivan los tamales! Food and the Making of Mexican Identity.* Albuquerque: Univ. of N.Mex. Press, 1998.

KATHARINE A. DÍAZ

RETABLOS

Mexican *retablos* are small paintings that portray a prominent religious figure or illustrate the real-life story of a miracle that has been granted in response to prayer. The Spanish word *retablo* has its origin in the Latin *retro tabula,* referring to religious paintings associated with the altar. Although the roots of the *retablo* can be traced back to Spanish colonialism as well as to pre-Columbian indigenous religious practices, Mexican *retablos* developed to a high point during the 19th century, as paintings on inexpensive tin plates became affordable for middle- and working-class Mexicans. The artistic form and religious content of Mexican *retablos* were originally inspired by European Catholicism and have evolved over time in response to local dynamics, influenced by indigenous Mesoamerican culture and successive waves of cultural exchange and immigration. Today, some *retablos* are still being produced and older pieces are collected as folk art. The form and content of *retablos* have had a significant effect on other kinds of Mexican art as well as on Chicano art in the United States. For scholars today, Mexican *retablos* capture ways of thinking that might otherwise be lost.

Retablos became popular at a time of protracted sociopolitical turmoil. During the 19th century, independence movements, civil wars between rival political factions, and invasions by the United States and France destroyed much of the old regime. The very practice of Catholicism in Mexico and the role of the Catholic Church were intensely debated from the 1820s on, as the pro-secular, liberal state clashed with conservative political groups. During this period *retablos* served as a means for the Mexican people to continue practicing their religion in ways that were meaningful. Collectors and scholars have gathered together impressive numbers of these modest paintings, which make the genre accessible to future generations. New Mexico State University maintains the largest collection of 19th- and 20th-century Mexican *retablos* in the United States.

Historian Ramón Gutiérrez suggests a useful terminology that distinguishes "religious *retablos*" from "votive *retablos*." The religious *retablo* (*retablo santo*) is a portrait of a religious figure and is used for personal devotion in the home. The votive *retablo* (*retablo ex voto*) portrays an experience of divine intervention in a human life and is placed in a public shrine (*ex voto* meaning "from a vow or promise" in Latin). Depending on geographic region, religious *retablos* are also called *láminas, imágines, pintadas,* or *santos,* although *santo* can also refer to a carved figurine. Votive *retablos* are sometimes called *milagros.* Votive *retablos* painted on tin plates (approximately 10 by 14 inches; 25 by 35 cm) are one of many kinds of votive offerings (food, flowers, personal ob-

© LEE FOSTER/BRUCE COLEMAN INC.

Woman surrounded by *retablos* in a store in the Spanish Market, Santa Fe, New Mexico.

jects, photographs, and so on). The *retablo* artist is typically anonymous and untrained.

Both kinds of *retablo* paintings have their roots in the religious iconography imported and imposed by the Spaniards. Anthropologist Jorge Durand and sociologist Douglas S. Massey argue that while both religious *retablos* and votive *retablos* adopted the same artistic medium in Mexico, they sought different ends, employed contrasting styles and aesthetic principles, and developed along distinct trajectories as cultural phenomena. In the religious *retablo,* the orthodox rendering of a religious figure served as a focal object in the home altar. By contrast, the votive *retablo* is itself a ritual: the painting is commissioned to complete a vow, it records the testimony of a granted prayer, and its placement in a public shrine makes it an individual offering to the deity. In the postconquest and early colonial periods, Spanish clergy used canonical paintings of saints and other religious figures, situated around the church altar, for evangelization. Spanish clergy also commissioned didactic paintings for the church altars that included priests in the image (typically giving thanks). Over time in New Spain, both kinds of *retablo* paintings came to be adopted for use in the home, first at the initiative of elite *criollos* (American-born Spaniards) who commissioned works by trained artists who painted with oils on canvas, wood, or copper. It was not until the 19th century, however, with the advent of industrial technology that could produce inexpensive tin sheets, that members of the mestizo middle class, and eventually members of the working class, began to purchase *retablos* painted by anonymous artists. The incorporation of tin sheeting into *retablo* painting in the early 19th century fostered a dramatic proliferation of the popular art form.

Religious *retablos* are portraits of a sacred personage. Examples include San Francisco de Paula, La Sagrada Familia (the Holy Family), and La Virgen de Guadalupe. In Mexican religious *retablos,* Catholic holy figures are recognizable through the reproduction of orthodox renderings of costumes and attributes (objects and incidents) that are distinctive to each figure. Artists copied available images (paintings in churches, engravings in books, and carved figures) to create acceptable *retablo* paintings. According to the dictates of the Catholic Church, these paintings, featured in home altars, were to be treated as icons (it was the model and not the image that was to inspire faith). Thus careful reproduction of the church's official iconography, not artistic originality, was most important.

The iconography that appears in religious *retablos* reflects the rich complexity of the Catholic iconography that Spaniards imported to New Spain, which was significantly influenced by the cultures of various European territories that the Spanish empire controlled at different times (Flanders/Belgium, Italy, the Basque provinces, Portugal, and so on). Precedents for the veneration of sacred images were well established among the numerous ethnic peoples of preconquest Mexico, who worshipped a pantheon of deities. Although saints imported by Spanish clergy continued to be important in New Spain and Mexico, Catholic iconography and rituals were influenced by local events and precedents. (The most important example of this is the confluence of the Virgin Mary and the indigenous Tonantzin in the Virgin of Guadalupe, who later became Mexico's patron saint.) Still, orthodox Catholic iconography (the Council

of Trent, 1545–1563, defined a reformed Catholic theology in response to the challenge of the Protestant Reformation) prevailed in vice-regal New Spain and postindependence Mexico. Religious *retablos* painted on tin were produced from roughly 1820–1920, and in those 100 years the genre remained relatively static. By the end of the 19th century, higher-quality lithographs printed on inexpensive paper came to dominate the market for icons for use in home altars.

Votive *retablos* represent scenes of divine intervention in the lives of pious Catholics. The Catholic practice of placing votive offerings in a pilgrimage church can be traced back to the Holy Roman Empire (c. 800–1800s). At that time the Latin initials *VFGA* were inscribed on the offering (*votum fecit gratium accepit,* "made a vow and received a grace"). In the Mexican votive *retablo,* this same process, whereby the believer engages directly with the deity, is acted out, without intervention from a priest. In the votive painting, the artist interprets the client's testimony. Unlike the religious *retablo,* which disallows deviation from the canonical image, the votive *retablo* reveals a syncretism of multiple elements, including the artist's personal, stylistic, and regional influences as well as the client's preferences and instructions. In contrast to other kinds of votive objects (anatomical charms, personal objects, photographs, and other kinds of offering practices, notably books of miracles), what makes tin-plate votive paintings distinctive is that the form captures specific information about the social circumstances and religious values of individual believers.

Unlike religious *retablos,* which are portraits, votive *retablos* are landscapes featuring distinct sections (typically horizontal), with an area for text and portions for particular kinds of visual images. Typically, the top section contains the image of the sacred figure, floating in space and unaffected by gravity in the physical world. The middle section portrays the physical world, juxtaposed to the sacred. Here the artist renders a pictorial narrative of events related by the believer (the person in question has typically suffered a serious illness, injury, or other misfortune). In the bottom section, an inscription records the words and sentiments of the believer and reinforces the message conveyed by the images, and typically identifies the name of the votary, their residence, and the date of the event (if not the artist's name). Votive *retablos* usually contain a full range of bright colors (unlike religious *retablos,* which feature subdued, even dark, colors). Conventions for rendering space and time are typically distorted to emphasize the emotion of the event and the significance of divine intervention. Scholars of this form of art assert that the popularity and historical artistic development of votive paintings in Mexico distinguishes them from votive *retablos* and other forms of votive art that developed in Europe and in the rest of Latin America.

Mexican artists of the 19th and 20th centuries explored themes of Mexico's colonial heritage, including Catholic religious themes such as the veneration of Guadalupe and countervailing themes of indigenous cosmologies. When one considers the work of prominent Mexican artists such as the 19th-century illustrator José Guadalupe Posada, early modernist painter Angel Zárraga, muralist Diego Rivera, and most notably the painter Frida Kahlo, it becomes clear that the votive *retablo* has exerted more influence than religious *retablos* as a form of art and popular culture. By experimenting with the genre of votive *retablos* in their art, Mexican artists have extended the life of the genre while they comment on popular culture, politics, and Mexican national identity. Some of Kahlo's best-known works incorporate the stylistic conventions of the votive *retablo,* but as opposed to the anonymous *retablo* artist, Kahlo portrayed herself as an eminently mortal heroine. For example, in *Self-Portrait on the Borderline* (1932) Kahlo portrays herself on the border between the United States and Mexico in the style of a votive *retablo,* testifying to her perception about the two cultures and her identity with *mexicanidad.* Using the votive *retablo* style, the atheist Kahlo replaces Catholic iconography with a cosmic sun and moon dyad, and yet she presents herself as the agent who makes the choice about which culture is more authentic. Thus, Kahlo uses the votive *retablo* form to explore her Mexican cultural identity, and she presents her vision with a candor and originality that continues to engage Mexicans and Mexican Americans today.

From the late 1960s on, both Chicano and Chicana artists have engaged Mexican religious themes as part of their social critique and cultural self-definition. Chicano artists made visible the new Chicano nationalist identity that called for resisting oppression and strengthening rural and urban communities, and some Chicana artists criticized not only the oppressiveness of the Anglo culture but also the oppression of women within the Chicano community and the Chicano movement. In a process that artist Melesio Casas called "iconic friction," Chicano and Chicana artists experimented with blending neoindigenism and popular Mexican Catholicism to document and interpret religious practices and culture in the Chicano community. For example, Carmen Lomas Garza's landscapes allude to both religious and votive *retablos* as she portrays how Chicano families carry out rituals in their everyday lives. In *Curandera* (1977), Lomas Garza included a home altar with a religious *retablo* in the background, even as the central action of the painting is a faith healing ceremony. In another example of Chicano syncretism, Chicana artist Yolanda López created a self-portrait of herself as Guadalupe (*Portrait of the Artist as the Virgin of Guadalupe,* 1978). López's Chicana-feminist portrait of herself, vibrantly healthy and striding forward in running shoes while garbed in Guadalupe's raiment, blends the vernacular of the votive *retablo* (testimony of a miracle) with the religious *retablo* (portrait of a saint or self).

The Mexican *retablo* is a significant cultural form that has evolved over time, and it appears that this trend will continue as the U.S.-Mexican borderlands develop. Durand and Massey have charted new territory by documenting the proliferation of votive *retablos* among Mexican migrants to the United States. These *retablos* go beyond the traditional subject matter found in votive *retablos* to address new issues specific to the migrant experience: making the journey, legal problems, narco-traffic, homecoming, and so on. While religious *retablos* fell out of use by the early 20th century (replaced by machine-made prints), votive *retablos* have been a dynamic form of popular religious expression for more than 100 years. For Catholics and non-Catholics, for Mexicans and Mexican Americans, votive *retablos* tell the story of the people from their own perspective, and they allow other valuable insight into social and cultural identity.

RELATED ARTICLES

Art, Folk; Catholicism; Religion.

FURTHER READING

Durand, Jorge, and Douglas S. Massey. *Miracles on the Border: Retablos of Mexican Migrants to the United States.* Tucson: Univ. of Ariz. Press, 1995.

Gifford, Gloria Fraser. *Mexican Folk Retablos.* Albuquerque: Univ. of N.Mex. Press, 1992.

Griswold del Castillo, Richard, Teresa McKenna, and Yvonne Yarbor-Bejarano, eds. *Chicano Art: Resistance and Affirmation, 1965–1985.* Los Angeles: Wight Art Gallery, Univ. of Calif. at Los Angeles, 1991.

Herrera, Hayden. *Frida Kahlo: The Paintings.* New York: HarperCollins, 1991.

Montenegro, Roberto. *Retablos de México/Mexican Votive Paintings.* Mexico, D.F.: Ediciones Mexicanas, 1950.

Zarur, Elizabeth Netto Calil, and Charles Muir Lovell, eds. *Art and Faith in Mexico: The Nineteenth-Century Retablo Tradition.* Albuquerque: Univ. of N.Mex. Press, 2001.

CARMEN NAVA

RHUMBA

Rhumba is a word that arose in the 1930s, simultaneously possessing three distinct but interrelated meanings: First, the word itself was an Anglicization or Americanization of the Spanish word *rumba*; second, it was a shorthand label used particularly in the United States, Great Britain, and France for the entire spectrum of popular music and dance in Cuba as well as in other Caribbean countries; third, it became an actual dance form, created in the United States, England, and France during the 1930s, loosely based on the way Cubans and other people throughout the Caribbean danced socially. The similar-

© ALFRED EISENSTAEDT/TIME AND LIFE PICTURES/GETTY IMAGES

Patrons dancing to a rhumba as Ecita and her orchestra perform at New York City's Stork Club in 1944.

sounding rumba genre refers to the Cuban secular singing and dancing music that traces its origins to the Congolese, the African ethnic group most influential in Cuban music.

On April 26, 1930, the Don Azpiazu Havana Casino Orchestra introduced mainstream America to Cuban music at the Palace Theater in New York City, ushering in the Rhumba Era both in the United States and around the world. People fell in love with Cuban music. It was novel, exotic, lively, and danceable. Over time they were exposed to such popular Cuban song forms as *danzón, son, guaracha, guajira,* and bolero. However, the word that took hold in the non-Cuban public consciousness to define this newly discovered music and dance fashion was *rumba*. In Cuba, the word *rumba* generally meant a "party" (or, alternatively, a secular folkloric genre of music). American and other foreign tourists visiting Cuba no doubt heard the word *rumba* being used by Cubans when speaking about music and dance. The assumption developed that rumba must be the name of the social dance Cubans were doing.

Outside Cuba, the word *rumba* was, of course, "foreign." To make it more accessible to their public, British and American journalists soon created the Anglicized or Americanized term *rhumba* to describe this exciting new phenomenon (based on the notion that if a Spanish word such as *ritmo* becomes *rhythm* in English, the word *rumba* must then translate to *rhumba*). From time to time, there has been speculation that the word *rhumba* was actually coined by knowledgeable musicians as a term of derision for Latin music that had been watered down to suit foreign tastes; however, this hypothesis is not supported by tangible evidence.

As the Rhumba Era unfolded during the 1930s, a new dance craze also swept the United States, Great Britain, France, and other countries outside Cuba. The dance was itself called the "rhumba" and was reputed to be an authentic representation of the rumba as it was danced in Cuba. An ongoing series of highly charged literary exchanges—often known among the participants as the "rhumba wars" and carefully documented in dance publications of the time—occurred among American, British, and French "dance experts" to determine who had "discovered" the most authentic version of the Cuban rumba. History has shown, of course, that what these "experts" were attempting to emulate—in a highly elaborate, ornate misinterpretation—was a rather simple way in which Cubans—as well as people from countries all over the Caribbean, and members of the Latino community in the United States—were dancing socially to the popular music of the time (including *son, guaracha,* and *guajira*). Cubans themselves, in fact, were known to call what they were doing *el sistema cubana de bailar* (the Cuban way of dancing).

In the United States today, the word *rhumba* has largely fallen out of fashion, being replaced, when used at all, by its original counterpart, *rumba.* Currently, yet another catchword, salsa, is being employed to describe Cuban music and its offspring. The rather highly embellished dance form called rhumba, which was spawned during the 1930s, has long been recognized as a product not of Cuba, but of non-Latino dance academies.

RELATED ARTICLES

Dance; Music, Popular; Rumba.

FURTHER READING

Daniel, Yvonne. *Rumba: Dance and Social Change in Contemporary Cuba.* Indianapolis: Ind. Univ. Press, 1995.

Roberts, John Storm. *Latin Jazz: The First of the Fusions; 1880s to Today.* New York: Schirmer Bks., 1999.

Roberts, John Storm. *The Latin Tinge: The Impact of Latin American Music on the United States.* 2d ed. New York: Oxford Univ. Press, 1999.

Steward, Sue. *¡Música!: Salsa, Rumba, Merengue and More: The Rhythm of Latin America.* San Francisco: Chronicle Bks., 1999.

FRAN CHESLEIGH

RICARDO, RICKY. *See* ARNAZ, DESI.

RIVERA, CHITA

Born: January 23, 1933; Washington, D.C.

Chita Rivera is one of the most heralded Broadway performers. A distinguished dancer, singer, and actress, Rivera has garnered five Tony nominations and two Tony awards for best actress in the musicals *The Rink* and *Kiss of the Spider Woman.* In 2002 she received the Kennedy Center Honors, marking the first time a Latino received the esteemed award.

Rivera was born Dolores Conchita Figueroa del Rivero to Puerto Rican parents. Her father, Pedro Julio Figueroa, was a musician who played for the Navy Band; he died when Rivera was only seven years old. Soon thereafter her mother, Katherine Anderson del Rivero, put her in ballet classes, where

AP/WIDE WORLD PHOTOS

Chita Rivera in the musical stage production *Kiss of the Spider Woman,* in Los Angeles.

Rivera's talent for dance was first discovered. She so impressed her teachers that she earned the chance to audition for George Balanchine's American School of Ballet in New York. She was promptly accepted.

It was not long before she was wooed by the lights of Broadway, where she debuted in 1952 in the chorus of the musical *Call Me Madam.* Her talent and aggressive style of dancing caught the attention of some of the foremost choreographers and producers on Broadway, including Hal Prince, Jerome Robbins, and Bob Fosse. She went on to star in the shows *Guys and Dolls, Can-Can, Seventh Heaven,* and *Mr. Wonderful.* Her 1957 portrayal of Anita in the first production of *West Side Story* catapulted her to stardom. The musical about two star-crossed lovers, a (white) American boy and a Puerto Rican girl, and the racial rivalries between their friends and family was particularly poignant for Rivera, the daughter of Puerto Rican immigrants. Her performance in this role was distinctive. As Hal Prince noted, "If you look at tapes of 'America' you will see a kind of sharp, clean, defined performing that is common to very few people. You can be a star with looks and personality, but Chita also has the technique."

Moving on from her success in *West Side Story,* Rivera was featured in Broadway productions and national and international tours. Among them were *Born Yesterday, The Rose Tattoo, Call Me Madam, Sweet Charity, Kiss Me Kate,* and the first production of Fosse's *Chicago,* starring Gwen Verdon. The dancer Jacques d'Amboise described Rivera's dance style as "aggressive and passionate." "She attacks her steps. And she has her own thing, her signature. It's like Streisand, you know it's *her.*"

Rivera's spectacular career was interrupted when in 1986 her car crashed into a taxi in New York. Her leg was severely damaged and required nearly a year to mend. The accident, while slowing her down for some time, did not end her career. She starred in the physically demanding *Spider Woman* role just seven years later, at the age of 60. Based on a novel by the Argentine writer Manuel Puig, the musical brought new accolades to Rivera, whose vitality did not seem to have diminished.

In 2003 Rivera starred on Broadway in a revival of the musical *Nine,* based on Federico Fellini's film *8 1/2.* No stranger to cinema, Rivera continued to make appearances in film, including a cameo spot in the 2002 film version of *Chicago.* She had one daughter with director Tony Mordente, Lisa Mordente, who has followed in her mother's musical footsteps as a singer, dancer, and choreographer. A source of pride among Latinos, Chita Rivera is a model of unquestionable charisma and talent in Hollywood and on Broadway. A handful of the characters she has portrayed were Hispanic and her portraits are endearing but also complex.

RELATED ARTICLES

Dance; Film; Theater; *West Side Story.*

FURTHER READING

Trescott, Jacqueline. "For Chita Rivera, A Career With Legs." *Washington Post* (Sunday, December 8, 2002).

Reyes, Luis, and Rubie, Peter. *Hispanics in Hollywood, A Celebration of 100 Years in Film and Television.* Hollywood, Calif.: ifilm Pubs., 2000.

SELECTED WEB SITE

Chita Rivera. www.chitarivera.com

JOSEPH TOVARES

RIVERA, DIEGO

Born: December 8, 1886; Guanajuato, Mexico
Died: November 24, 1957; Mexico City, Mexico

Diego Rivera was arguably the most important of the Mexican muralists. He was also an easel painter, a printmaker, a notable collector of pre-Columbian art, and an advocate of popular traditions. Rivera married painter Frida Kahlo (1907–1954) in 1929; they divorced in 1939 and remarried in 1940.

After studying at the San Carlos Academy (1896–1905), Rivera interacted with many leading artists in Europe, producing 200 works during his remarkable cubist phase. His first Mexican mural was *Creation* (1922–1923), a strange hybrid painted in wax encaustic. After learning the true fresco technique, he painted over 100 major panels at the Ministry of Education (1923–1928), including narratives illustrating revolutionary *corridos* (ballads). In the process, Rivera destroyed or inhibited the work of his fellow muralists. Rivera's greatest work is *The Liberated Earth* (1926–1927) frescoed in a former chapel in Chapingo. Rivera's early murals make direct allusions to the Italian Renaissance: they herald a national rebirth that was social, political, and cultural. His nationalistic imagery exalted indigenous peoples, common laborers, and popular customs. Rivera replaced traditional religious symbols with emblems that expressed his fervent Marxism (he had visited the Soviet Union in 1927). The artist also painted frescoes at the Health Ministry (1929), the National Palace stairway (1929–1930; 1935), and the Cortes Palace, Cuernavaca (1930–1931).

Rivera garnered prestigious mural commissions in the United States; he was honored, as well, by retrospective exhibitions in San Francisco (1930) and New York (1931). He painted three frescoes in the San Francisco Bay area in 1931: the Pacific Stock Exchange, the California School of Fine Arts (now the San Francisco Art Institute), and a mural at the Stern residence (now at the University of California at Berkeley). Rivera had been enamored of technology since childhood; as a Marxist he believed that industrialization was a prerequisite for revolution. His *Detroit Industry* at the Detroit Institute of Arts (27

Mexican artist Diego Rivera working on a mural in New York City, 1933.

panels painted in 1932–1933) draws parallels between the evolution of life and technology. Attacked by both the Left and the Right, Rivera sought to elevate political content in his next fresco, *Man at the Crossroads* (Rockefeller Center, New York, 1933). Though Abby Aldrich Rockefeller (wife of John D. Rockefeller, Jr.) had encouraged Rivera to express his political convictions, the Rockefeller Center's managing agent opposed the fresco. Objections were made to a portrait of Lenin, and work was halted. General Motors Corporation canceled Rivera's next commission, signaling the end of capitalist patronage. Rivera painted a radical history of the United States for the New Workers School in New York City in 1933 (all panels since dispersed or destroyed). The unfinished Rockefeller Center mural was destroyed in 1934, thwarting a plan to move it to the Museum of Modern Art (cofounded by Abby Rockefeller). On returning to Mexico, Rivera painted a revised replica (Palace of Fine Arts, Mexico City, 1934) that depicts John D. Rockefeller, Jr., as a rapacious and diseased man. In 1936 Rivera secured political asylum for Leon Trotsky. They were visited by surrealist leader André Breton in 1938. Trotsky wrote the *Manifesto for a Free and Revolutionary Art,* signed by Breton and Rivera. Rivera's surrealism-influenced easel paintings are among his best.

The artist's notable later murals include *Pan-American Unity* (now at City College, San Francisco, 1940), *Dream of a Sunday Afternoon in the Alameda Park* (1947–1948), the *Lerma Waterworks* (1951), and *The History of Medicine in Mexico* (1953). Rivera bequeathed three art-filled studios to Mexico: the Frida Kahlo Museum in Coyoacán (notable for its collection of popular arts) and the twin modernist studios in San Angel and Anahuacalli (an intended studio-mausoleum that contains the bulk of his nearly 60,000 pre-Columbian objects).

RELATED ARTICLES

Art, Popular; Charlot, Jean; Kahlo, Frida; Muralism; Painting; Posada, José Guadalupe.

FURTHER READING

Charlot, Jean. *The Mexican Mural Renaissance 1920–1925.* New Haven, Conn.: Yale Univ. Press, 1963.

Favela, Ramón. *Diego Rivera: The Cubist Years.* Phoenix, Ariz.: Phoenix Art Mus., 1984.

Helms, Cynthia, ed. *Diego Rivera: A Retrospective.* Detroit: Detroit Inst. of Arts, 1986.

Herrera, Hayden. *Frida: A Biography of Frida Kahlo.* New York: Harper and Row, 1983.

Hurlburt, Laurance P. *The Mexican Muralists in the United States.* Albuquerque: Univ. of N.Mex. Press, 1989.

Wolfe, Bertram D. *Portrait of America by Diego Rivera.* New York: Covici Friede, Pubs., 1934.

Wolfe, Bertram D. *The Fabulous Life of Diego Rivera.* New York: Stein and Day, 1963.

RUBÉN CORDOVA

RIVERA, TOMÁS

Born: December 22, 1935; Crystal City, Texas
Died: May 16, 1984; Riverside, California,

Tomás Rivera's success as a writer and university administrator was a result of his philosophy of life, his well-defined objectives, and his strong interest in the welfare of his people. As a boy he had been told by his maternal grandmother that writing and art were the most important things in life. However, as the son of migrant workers (Florencio Rivera-Martínez and Josefa Hernández-Gutérrez), he had to conquer tremendous odds in order to be educated and to fulfill his desire to become a teacher and writer.

After completing high school in his hometown, he attended Southwest Texas Junior College at Ubalde. Wishing to become a teacher, he enrolled

---

THE LOST YEAR

That year was lost to him. At times he tried to remember and, just about when he thought everything was clearing up some, he would be at a loss for words. It almost always began with a dream in which he would suddenly awaken and then realize that he was really asleep. Then he wouldn't know whether what he was thinking had happened or not.

It always began when he would hear someone calling him by his name but when he turned his head to see who was calling, he would make a complete turn and there he would end up—in the same place. This was why he never could discover who was calling him nor why. And then he even forgot the name he had been called.

One time he stopped at mid-turn and fear suddenly set in. He realized that he had called himself. And thus the lost year began.

Excerpt from *. . . y no se lo tragó la tierra//And the Earth Did Not Devour Him* by Tomás Rivera, translated by Evangelina Vigil-Piñón (1987).

---

at Southwest Texas State University, in San Marcos, where he received a B.A. in English in 1958 and an M.Ed. in administration in 1964. After teaching for several years in the Texas public schools, he went to the University of Oklahoma, Norman, where he completed a Ph.D. in 1969 with a dissertation about León Felipe, the famous Spanish poet exiled in Mexico.

Rivera had married Concepción Garza in 1958. They had two daughters and one son. He taught in San Antonio public schools from 1958 to 1960; at Sam Houston State University, Huntsville, from 1969 to 1971; and at the University of Texas, San Antonio, from 1971 to 1973. He had several administrative positions at the University of Texas, El Paso, from 1973 to 1979, the year he was appointed chancellor at the University of California, Riverside, where he remained until the year of his death.

As a writer Rivera became famous in 1971 with the novel . . . *y no se lo tragó la tierra/ . . . And the Earth Did Not Part,* which won the first prize offered by the Quinto Sol (Fifth Sun) publishing house of Berkeley, California. Upon its appearance, with an English translation by Herminio Ríos C., it became an immediate success and its author a celebrity among Hispanic readers (it was translated in 1987 by Evangelina Vigil-Piñón as *And the Earth Did Not Devour Him.*

In this novel Rivera gives expression to a vital theme for Chicanos: the hardships endured by migrant workers. Not less important, however, is its fragmented structure, made up of 12 independent stories (one for each month of the year) integrated into a harmonious unit by means of a frame consisting of 2 additional stories, the first and the last, which serve to give the 12 stories the structure of a novel. In the frame Rivera introduces the theme of the lost individual in search of an answer to the meaning of life. His dream is a dream inside a dream, a dream that can be confused with reality. At the same time it helps the young narrator understand himself.

In an interview Rivera said the purpose of creating his literary works was to express his love for people. But his writings, as well as his personal achievements in the educational field, have also served as a model for young Latinos and Latinas. He has had a great influence on those wanting to become writers.

RELATED ARTICLES
Literature, Mexican American.

FURTHER READING
Bruce-Novoa, John. "Tomás Rivera." In *Chicano Authors, Inquiry by Interview.* Austin: Univ. of Tex. Press, 1980.
Hinojosa-Smith, Rolando, et al., eds. *Tomás Rivera, 1935–1984: The Man and His Work.* Tempe, Ariz.: Bilingual Review 1988.
Olivares, Julián, ed. *International Studies in Honor of Tomás Rivera.* Houston, Tex.: Arte Público Press, 1986.
Sommers, Joseph, and Tomás Ybarra-Frausto, eds. "The Narrative: Focus on Tomás Rivera." In *Modern Chicano Writers: A Collection of Critical Essays.* Englewood Cliffs, N.J., 1979.

LUIS LEAL

ROCK-EN-ESPAÑOL

With its foreign roots and strains of rebellion and hedonism, rock music was long suppressed in many Latin American countries. As many governments began to relax their authoritarian grip in the late 1980s, however, the backbeat made up for lost time. By the early 2000s, many critics and fans believed that the most innovative rock in the world was rock-en-Español.

Rock, of course, originally rose in the mid-1950s out of an interracial stew that could be described as three parts rhythm and blues (R&B), two parts pop, and one part country. Elvis Presley, with talent in all three areas, quickly became known as the "King of Rock." The new genre's heavy African American influence dismayed many older whites, who heard R&B's bawdy lyrics and saw Presley's hip-swivels and feared that culture, morals, and race hierarchies were about to drastically change.

In Mexico, artists such as Enrique Guzmán and Los Hooligans began covering American rock hits to great success. At the time, Mexico's authoritarian government feared that rock's association with rebellion, illustrated in movies such as *The Blackboard Jungle,* would provoke gang culture and crime. Leaders were also worried that rock would sap Mexican identity. The government, using its vast power over media and business, worked quickly to clamp down on the trend. Times remained tough for Mexican rock acts through the early 1980s, and most of the groups that did survive, such as Fest and Three Souls in My Mind, performed in English. Cuba also was a lost cause, since Fidel Castro, who seized power in 1959, had banned rock music sung in English.

Interestingly, it was a California-born Chicano, Ritchie Valens, who in 1958 realized the power of fusing roots music with rock, in his hit version of the traditional *son jarocho, La Bamba*. In the United States, Chicano groups continued experimenting with bilingual rock, with some of their material catching fire at the national level—including such 1960s prom-rock classics as Sonny and the Sunglows's *Talk to Me* and Rene and Rene's *Lo Mucho Que Te Quiero*.

Mexican-born guitar legend Carlos Santana was next with his 1970 hit *Oye Cómo Va,* written by Tito Puente, known as the "king of mambo." Santana's version only contained nine words, but the song made the "top 10" and his version remains a rock classic. At the fringes of rock, the Spanish vocal-harmony group Mocedades scored a fluke U.S. top-10 hit in 1974 with *Eres Tú.*

Meanwhile, in Argentina progressive rock briefly flourished in the early 1970s, thanks to a Frank Zappa–like figure named Charly García, who sang and played keyboards with Serú Girán and Sui Generis. However, a military junta that took power in the late 1970s turned the environment considerably colder, and music in English went underground in 1982 during and after Argentina's disastrous invasion of the Falkland Islands and its subsequent defeat by Great Britain.

As mass communications, cable and satellite television, and freer trade practices made suppressing foreign music more trouble than it was worth for most Latin American governments, the reemergence

Two members of the Spanish rock group Maná play at the Universal Amphitheater during their 1998 Sueños Líquidos tour.

of rock-en-Español took on a stronger Latin flavor; this time the groups sang in Spanish. Argentina's Soda Stereo and Chile's Los Prisioneros became South American favorites with their jangly, Britpop-derived hooks combined with a distinctly South American social consciousness, one that railed against suppression of freedoms. Rock was making up for lost time.

Simultaneously, in Mexico, Los Caifanes and Maldita Vecindad were pioneering a homegrown scene that fused the backbeat with Latin roots music such as the Colombian *cumbia* rhythm. Maldita Vecindad sang in support of illegal Mexican immigrants, while Los Caifanes incorporated abstract lyrics sprinkled with Aztec mysticism. Three Souls in My Mind had become El Tri and by the 1980s was performing hard rock in Spanish.

The East Los Angeles band Los Lobos soared to number one in the United States in 1987 with their version of *La Bamba,* recorded for the Ritchie Valens biopic of the same name. Playing a blues-based fusion of rock and Latin rhythms, Los Lobos had been loved by critics and album-rock fans for years. Its pop success was fleeting, but the group cared little for mainstream success and preferred to continue with its substantive musical experimentations rather than try for more top-40 success. Los Lobos's legacy includes the success of a San Angelo, Texas–based group, Los Lonely Boys, whose guitar-fueled, laid-back *Heaven* scored multiformat airplay (pop, country, and Latin) during 2004.

The Latin American creative renaissance continued to flourish into the 1990s with Guadalajara, Mexico's, Maná, whose memorable riffs, romantic lyrics, and Latin touches, including the Andean flute, helped Latinos claim rock as their own. Maná went on to duet with Santana for the Grammy-winning cut *Corazón Espinado* from Santana's 1999 comeback album *Supernatural,* which sold over 21 million copies in the United States alone.

Mexican experiments with rock-rap fusions were not far behind those in the United States, and in 1997 Mexico City's Molotov finally dared to do what the Mexican government had feared in the 1950s—come up with an irresistibly catchy, irrepressibly vulgar, and unmistakably antigovernment masterpiece, *¿Dónde Jugarán las Niñas?,* whose title mocked the softer Maná's 1993 album *¿Dónde Jugarán los Niños?* The government at first attempted to keep Molotov's compact disc out of stores, but with backing by major label Universal and an expec-

tation of coming political plurality and openness among Mexico's youth, the album was unstoppable.

Political changes in Latin America and the Caribbean ushered in cultural changes. In 2000 Mexico's PRI (Institutional Revolutionary Party), which after 71 years in control was at the time was the longest continuously ruling party in world, was finally thrown out of office by the election of opposition candidate Vicente Fox; and even in Cuba a statue of John Lennon was erected, although the country's music industry remained under tight state control. Latin-rock fusions continued to be popular in the early 21st century, with Aterciopelados and Juanes finding inspiration in traditional Colombian music, Orishas combining rap with earthy Cuban beats, and Argentina's Mosca Tse Tse fusing rock with samba and tango. Other groups, including Chile's La Ley and Miami's Volumen Cero, sounded more Anglo-American, but scaled the charts anyway with their irresistible melodies and aggressive beats.

As immigration to the United States rose to near-record levels through the 1990s, a strong indie rock-en-Español scene blossomed in Los Angeles with groups such as Cábula, Satélite, and Hijos del Sol; however, the genre's top sellers, including Maná, Jaguares, and Molotov, had all cut their teeth in Mexico. After decades in the shadows, rock-en-Español had evolved into an open-minded, creative genre that constantly incorporated new ideas from around the world but succeeded in maintaining its Latin identity.

RELATED ARTICLES

Music, Popular; Vocalists, Popular; Santana, Carlos; Valens, Ritchie.

FURTHER READING

Broughton, Simon, et al., eds. *World Music: The Rough Guide.* London: Rough Guides, Ltd., 1994.
Kanellos, Nicolás, ed. *The Hispanic Almanac: From Columbus to Corporate America.* Detroit: Invisible Ink Press, 1994.
Reyes, David, and Tom Waldman. *Land of a Thousand Dances: Chicano Rock 'n' Roll from Southern California.* Albuquerque, N.M.: Univ. of N.Mex. Press, 1998.

RAMIRO BURR
DOUG SHANNON

RODEO

The rodeo is a public competition in which contestants participate in standardized events such as bareback bronco and bull riding, team roping, steer wrestling, and calf roping. In national competitions, however, events for women are limited to barrel racing on horseback. The word *rodeo* comes from the Spanish verb *rodear,* to surround or round up.

Rodeo began in the early days of the Spanish colonization of what was to become the southwestern part of the United States. During the late 1700s and early 1800s, when the missions and *ranchos* were established throughout the region, cattle-raising flourished as the means of supplying beef and leather to the Spanish territories. There was a great need for skilled horsemen to handle the herds as they made their way to markets. In the early days, especially before the U.S. war with Mexico in 1847, most of the horsemen were *vaqueros,* Spanish or Mexican cowboys who brought to the Southwest the various breeds of horses that had been introduced to the Americas by the Spanish. Among these breeds were

Jerry Díaz of San Antonio, Texas, waves his sombrero as his horse takes a bow during the Mexican Rodeo Extravaganza in Denver, Colorado.

the Andalucians, which had been brought to Spain during the Arab occupation. Many of these horses escaped into the wild, transforming American Indian culture and eventually becoming the working horse of the American cowboy.

After the Mexican territories, which included most of the present southwestern United States, became part of the United States at the end of the war in 1848, American cowboys began to work alongside the *vaqueros* in the large *ranchos* of the West, learning many of the techniques and traditions of Spanish and Mexican horsemanship. The influence of both the Spanish language and culture became part of the cowboys' everyday life on the cattle ranches of the West.

Much of the language that is associated with the American cowboy and the folklore of the West has its origins in the Spanish language and the Spanish and Mexican traditions of horsemanship. The *rancho* became ranch; the words *lasso* and *lariat* came from the Spanish *laso* and *la reata.* The name for the leather chaps worn by cowboys came from the Spanish *chaparreras.* The cowboy's horse was the mustang, from the Spanish *mestengo* (stray, or wild), and the cowboy tamed the bronco from the Spanish word meaning *wild* or *rough.* If the cowboy got into trouble with the law, he was sent to the hoosegow, from *juzgado* (a tribunal), or to the calaboose, from *calabozo* (jail).

It was, however, after the end of the U.S. Civil War in the 1860s that the cattle ranches spread throughout the West and the ranks of the cowboys grew. Many of these American *vaqueros* worked for the large cattle barons, driving herds across the western plains to the stockyards in the growing cities of the West. But with the advent of the railroads, the open rangelands were fenced off and cattle cars began to carry beef to markets in the East. This reduced the demand for labor and many cowboys eventually saw their lifestyle undergo significant change.

There had always been competition among cowboys and *vaqueros* in the skills, such as roping cattle and breaking broncos, that are used in ranching. As employment decreased for the cowboy, a more formal form of competition began to emerge in towns throughout the West. This friendly competition between cowboys was sometimes called a rodeo and it provided an opportunity for cowboys to supplement their incomes by winning prize money.

In the early years of the 20th century, those cowboys who had, in essence, become professional rodeo performers began to see a need to establish rules and regulations for their own safety and to guarantee fair competition. The formation of the Professional Rodeo Cowboy's Association (PRCA) was believed to have occurred in 1936 when competing cowboys at a rodeo in the Boston Gardens (Massachusetts) staged a walkout over a dispute about prize money. They had originally called themselves the Turtle Association for having stuck their necks out. In 1945 they formally adopted the PRCA name.

Today, rodeos are sanctioned by PRCA and enjoy great popularity. Latinos make up some of the approximately 170,000 fans who have been attending the National Finals Rodeo in Las Vegas in recent years. The television cable network ESPN broadcasts rodeo finals regularly to as many as 13 million viewers. Cowboys from Australia, Canada, Brazil, and Mexico join U.S. cowboys in high-stakes competition at events throughout the country, with many communities hosting annual rodeos as significant events in their cultural calendars, usually accompanied by large parades during their fiesta days. Also alive and well in the Southwest are *charriadas,* the Mexican version of the rodeo in which *charros* (elegant *vaqueros*) compete in a variety of events where their horsemanship is on display.

Latino *vaqueros* continue to participate in modern rodeos and to work on today's cattle ranches. While helicopters, jeeps, and pickup trucks are commonly used on many ranches, the cowboy or *vaquero* on horseback continues to be a crucial part of ranching. Anglo and Latino cowboys together learn the skills of ranching, and usually the best of them compete against one another in modern rodeos.

The success of rodeos today, however, is accompanied by a significant degree of controversy over what animal rights groups consider to be the cruel treatment of the rodeo stock used in these events. Critics claim that while the rodeo is promoted as the "rough and tough" display of human skill and courage in dominating wild animals in the tradition of the Old West, the shows are in fact displays of the cruel treatment of animals for "greed and profit."

Animal rights groups note that rodeo animals are not aggressive by nature but are provoked into displays of wildness by the use of electric prods, caustic oils, and other devices such as cinched straps on horses and bulls to make them buck. Every year dozens of animals die as a result of injuries suffered in the rodeo arena. While cowboys also suffer many injuries, critics note that the cowboys volunteer for the competition while the animals have no choice. Because of the popularity of rodeos today and the attention focused on rodeos by animal rights groups, government officials have stepped up their efforts to make sure that animals are protected as much as possible.

RELATED ARTICLES

Horsemanship and Horse Racing; Sports in Latino Life.

FURTHER READING

Bannon, John Francis. *The Spanish Borderlands Frontier 1513–1821.* 1970. Reprint. Albuquerque: Univ. of N.Mex. Press, 1974.

Billington, Ray Allen. *America's Frontier Heritage.* 1974. Reprint. Albuquerque: Univ. of N.Mex. Press, 1993.

Fredriksson, Kristine. *American Rodeo: From Buffalo Bill to Big Business.* College Station: Tex. A&M Univ. Press, 1985.

Pitt, Leonard. *The Decline of the Californios: A Social History of the Spanish-speaking Californians, 1846–1890.* 2d ed. Berkeley: Univ. of Calif. Press, 1998.

Wooden, Wayne S., and Gavin Ehringer. *Rodeo in America: Wranglers, Roughstock and Paydirt.* Lawrence: Univ. Press of Kans., 1996.

RAYMOND J. GONZALEZ

RODRÍGUEZ, ALBITA

Born: circa 1962; Havana, Cuba

Vocalist, composer, and guitarist Albita Rodríguez (better known since the mid-1990s as Albita) was born to a couple of *punto guajiro* (a rural musical genre) singers from the central Cuban region of Las Villas. Albita began singing in public with her parents at age 16. Slowly but surely she started to fill concert halls and theaters, becoming the new generation's Celina González (grand dame of Cuba's *música guajira,* or country music) by placing a modern image on the old rural traditions. Her recording debut, *Habrá música guajira,* (There Shall be Country Music, 1988) was one of her label's biggest sellers.

From 1991 to 1993 Albita resided in Colombia, where she recorded a couple of albums, *Si se da la siembra* (If the Field Grows) and *Cantaré* (I Shall Sing), which sold throughout Latin America. In spring 1993, at the height of their pre-U.S. career, Albita and her band decided to expand their artistic horizons and painstakingly made it to the U.S.-Mexico border to seek political asylum in El Paso,

Texas. Shortly thereafter they arrived in Miami on tickets paid by for by the Florida radio station WQBA, which had heard of the group's ordeal. Since the early 1960s defection of Sonora Matancera, no other Cuban group had managed to defect collectively.

Soon Albita attracted unprecedented attention in Miami, moving from a cult cabaret show at Little Havana's now-defunct Centro Vasco to the fashionable restaurant and club Yuca in South Beach. She packed both venues, night after night, with every imaginable segment of the south Florida population, as well as large numbers of European and Latin American tourists.

In 1994 Albita was signed to Emilio Estefan's Crescent Moon label. Repackaged in an androgynous image of tailored white suits, two-toned shoes, and slicked-back blonde hair, she became the darling of every jet-setting celebrity in Miami, from Madonna to Sylvester Stallone to Gianni Versace to Liza Minelli.

As a protégé of Miami's leading Latin entertainment entrepreneur, Albita made three albums from 1995 to 1998 for Crescent Moon: *No se parece a nada* (There's Nothing Like It) *Dicen que . . .* (They Say That . . .) and *Una mujer como yo* (A Woman Like Me). These were well received by most critics but their sales decreased successively as she strayed from her role as the keeper of the *música guajira* flame to that of a commercial Pan-Caribbean chameleon. She eventually emerged with dyed platinum hair and ample décolletage, in an apparent attempt to satisfy the expectations of her traditionalist Latin fans.

After a two-year hiatus, during which her record company and half of the band deserted her, she returned with red hair, flowing skirts, and a new record (*Son*, 2000) that reaffirmed the suitability of her gutsy contralto to both dramatic ballads and popular dance music.

RELATED ARTICLES

Music, Popular; Vocalists, Popular.

FURTHER READING

Díaz Ayala, Cristóbal. *Cuando Salí de La Habana/1898–1997: Cien años de música cubana por el mundo* (When I Left Havana/1898–1997: A Hundred Years of Cuban Music Around the World). San Juan, Puerto Rico: Fundación Musicalia, 1998.
Sweeney, Phil. *The Rough Guide to Cuban Music*. London: Rough Guides, 2001.

LUIS TAMARGO

RODRÍGUEZ, RICHARD

Born: July 31, 1944; San Francisco, California

Born in San Francisco, Richard Rodríguez is primarily an essayist and television and radio commentator who focuses on American culture. The opinions in his books, which are published to great acclaim, do not always proceed according to politically correct lines, and he is considered by some Latinos to be a symbol of opposition in the world of facile identity politics. That reaction has had the result of making his views a permanent part of discussions on U.S. Latinos, which have generally served to show the weakness of the arguments that are marshaled against him. Whatever controversy his work evokes, Rodríguez is a widely recognized, wonderful prose stylist in English, capable of drawing convincing ethical and social lessons from what in lesser Latino talents becomes predictable sentimentality.

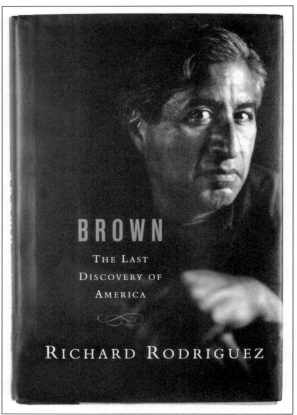

Cover of Richard Rodríguez's book on Latino history, *Brown: The Last Discovery of America.*

HUNGER OF MEMORY

But then there was Spanish. *Español*: my family's language. *Español*: the language that seemed to me a private language. I'd hear strangers on the radio and in the Mexican Catholic church across town speaking in Spanish, but I couldn't really believe that Spanish was a public language, like English. Spanish speakers, rather, seemed related to me, for I sensed that we shared—through our language—the experience of feeling apart from *los gringos*. It was thus a ghetto Spanish that I heard and I spoke. Like those whose lives are bound by a barrio, I was reminded by Spanish of my separateness from *los otros, los gringos* in power. But more intensely than for most barrio children–because I did not live in a barrio—Spanish seemed to me the language of home. (Most days it was only at home that I'd hear it.) It became the language of joyful return.

Excerpt from *Hunger of Memory: The Education of Richard Rodríguez* by Richard Rodríguez (1982).

Rodríguez's first book, *Hunger of Memory: The Education of Richard Rodríguez* (1982), which is widely used in high school and college courses, and the essays collected in *Days of Obligation: An Argument with My Mexican Father* (1992) and *Brown: The Last Discovery of America* (2002) can be examined as part of an ongoing autobiography. In these works memory gives the author a sense of self, continuity, history, and a coming to terms with the Latinicity that had initially befuddled his reconciliation of comedy and tragedy as a U.S. Latino.

If there is wide disagreement among some Latinos regarding how to negotiate Rodríguez's stance, it may be because *Hunger of Memory* sees the loss of ethnicity as a by-product of a privileged education such as the one Rodríguez received (at Stanford and Columbia universities and at London's Warburg Institute). The implication might be drawn that privileged academic training should enhance Latino ethnicity, but in Rodríguez's view this only leads to the ghettoizing of one's life. In the frequently moving *Days of Obligation,* he adds fuel to the fire by positing that affirmative action and bilingual education are not panaceas for social wrongs. Paradoxically,

he seeks the same valuing of individuality that his Latino cohort is still struggling to achieve, on its own terms. In *Days of Obligation* essays such as "Mexico's Children" actually have the impact of some of Octavio Paz's best work.

Latino diversity is now making room for Rodríguez's ideas, and his marginality—as a gay Mexican American who is devoutly Catholic (explored in "The Latin American Novel" in *Days of Obligation*)—is actually not very different from that of many other Latinos. In his role as a cultural commentator on PBS's *News Hour with Jim Lehrer,* he is open about his sexuality. In that regard *Brown,* on the surface about the "browning" of America, is more the distilling of metaphors about erotic discoveries. Full of profound soliloquies, *Brown* also argues that Mexico does not really thrive on multiculturalism, that Latinos can be racists, and that the United States is no longer racially split along black and white lines. These arguments may be hard to tolerate for some, but they are finding more acceptance with the present demographic changes across the United States; thus the importance of Rodríguez's work cannot be slighted.

RELATED ARTICLES

Literature, Mexican American.

FURTHER READING

Castro, Juan E. de. "Richard Rodríguez in 'Borderland': The Relocation of the Discourse of Mestizaje." In *Mestizo Nations: Culture, Race, and Conformity in Latin American Literature.* Tucson: Univ. of Ariz. Press, 2002.

Decker, Jeffrey Louis. "Mr. Secrets: Richard Rodríguez Flees the House of Memory." *Transition* 61 (1993): 124–33.

Fine, Laura. "Claiming Personas and Rejecting Other-Imposed Identities: Self-Writing as Self-Righting in the Autobiographies of Richard Rodríguez." *Biography* 19, no. 2 (Spring 1996): 119–36.

Fogelquist, Jim. "Ethnicity, Sexuality and Identity in the Autobiographies of Richard Rodríguez." In *Double Crossings/ EntreCruzamientos.* Ed. by Mario Martín Flores and Carlos von Son. Fair Haven, N.J.: Colección Academia, 2001.

Limón, José E., ed. "Richard Rodríguez: Public Intellectual." *Texas Studies in Literature & Language* 40, no. 4 (Winter 1998): 389–459.

Rivera, Tomás. "Richard Rodríguez' *Hunger of Memory* as Humanistic Antithesis." *MELUS* 11, no. 4 (Winter 1984): 5–13.

Stavans, Ilan. "The Journey of Richard Rodríguez." *Commonweal* 120, no. 6 (March 26, 1993): 20–24 [review of *Days of Obligation*].

WILL H. CORRAL

Gonzalo Rubalcaba performs during the 37th annual Grammy Awards show.

RUBALCABA, GONZALO

Born: May 27, 1963; Havana, Cuba

Composer and keyboardist Gonzalo Julio González Fonseca Rubalcaba (better known as Gonzalo Rubalcaba) is a third-generation star of one of Cuba's most celebrated musical dynasties. He is the son of Guillermo Rubalcaba, a widely known pianist and bandleader, and the grandson of Jacobo Rubalcaba, a famous trombonist and composer, whose immortal *danzónes* (late-19th-century Cuban musical genre) include *El Cadete Constitucional* and *Linda Mercedes*.

Originally drawn to the drums, Rubalcaba commenced classical piano studies by the age of nine, at the Amadeo Roldán Conservatory. After earning his degree in music composition from Havana's Escuela Nacional de Arte and collaborating with various prominent Cuban bands (Orquesta Cubana de Música Moderna, Orquesta Aragón, Los Van Van, among others), he began to record and tour abroad with his own electro-acoustic Grupo Proyecto, credited for revitalizing the *danzón* genre by replacing the tradi-

tional strings with jazz-oriented horns on the historic session *Mi gran pasión* (*My Great Passion,* 1987; Messidor). By the early 1990s he started to work regularly with his Cuarteto Cubano, an eclectic quartet known to effectively adapt, without prior notice, to the demanding structure of his meticulous arrangements.

During the 1990s—along with Paquito D'Rivera, Arturo Sandoval, Chucho Valdés, and other musical luminaries—Rubalcaba contributed significantly to the rapid growth in the new wave of Cuban influence in modern jazz. In 1996, after spending a few years in the Dominican Republic, he was able to finally migrate to the United States, the birthplace of jazz, in order to pursue his artistic dreams without hindrance. As reflected in his extensive solo discography, Rubalcaba's style has alternated between avant-gardism and extemporization from a base of standards.

Disciplined is an important adjective to remember when talking about Rubalcaba's music; even his most turbulent solos possess a reasonable and structured logic. As the grandson of a *danzón* catalyst and prodigal son of a cha-cha icon, he knows how to frame his improvisations to make every silence, every slapping chord sound surprising. He has taken elements threading modern jazz and cycled them through his own creative Cuban idiosyncrasy.

In 2002 Rubalcaba won a Grammy Award in the Latin jazz category for his seventh Blue Note album (*Supernova;* 2001), in which he addressed the orchestral potential of the grand piano, seasoned to his unconventional taste with select electronic keyboards.

RELATED ARTICLES

Jazz; Music, Popular.

FURTHER READING

Acosta, Leonardo. *Raíces del jazz latino: Un siglo de jazz en Cuba* (Roots of Latin Jazz: A Century of Jazz in Cuba). Barranquilla, Colombia: La Iguana Ciega, 2001.

Chediak, Nat. *Diccionario de jazz latino* (Dictionary of Latin Jazz). Madrid: Fundación Autor, 1998.

Holston, Mark. "Profile: Gonzalo Rubalcaba." *Jazziz* (February-March, 1992): 78–80.

Mandel, Howard. "Gonzalo Rubalcaba: Ballads beyond Borders." *Jazztimes* (September 1991): 39.

LUIS TAMARGO

RUBIROSA, PORFIRIO

Born: January 22, 1909; Santo Domingo, Dominican Republic

Died: July 5, 1965; Paris, France

Porfirio Rubirosa was a Dominican diplomat and polo player, although he was better known for his love exploits and his fame as playboy of the international jet set. When Rubirosa was six, his father, a general, received a diplomatic assignment and the family moved to Paris, where Rubirosa grew up and developed a liking for its nightlife. In 1928, when Rubirosa was performing poorly in school, his father sent him back to the Dominican Republic. There, dictator Rafael L. Trujillo (who ruled the Dominican Republic between 1930–1961), asked Rubirosa in 1932 to join the Dominican army as a lieutenant. Once in the army the young Rubirosa met Flor de Oro, Trujillo's eldest daughter, and after a brief romance they were married in December 1932. Being Trujillo's son-in-law propelled Rubirosa's rise to prominency. He was promoted in the army, named a congressman, and appointed to the country's foreign service. In 1936 the Rubirosas moved to Europe, where the marriage floundered as Porfirio reintegrated himself in Paris's active nightlife. Flor de Oro eventually returned to the Dominican Republic, where she obtained a divorce decree. The separation briefly soured relations between Rubirosa and Trujillo, but by 1939 the dictator was requiring the former's services, since his son and pregnant daughter-in-law were going to Paris. Shortly thereafter, Trujillo himself visited Paris where Rubirosa showed him a good time, and his star began to rise once more.

World War II and the German occupation of France complicated things for Rubirosa, who at the time was dating French actress Danielle Darrieux. He spent some months in a German prison castle for foreign diplomats; after his release in 1942 he married Darrieux. The marriage lasted throughout the war, but with the liberation of Europe, Rubirosa went back to his active lifestyle and the marriage ended in 1947. He was soon remarried, to heiress Doris Duke, the wealthy owner of American Tobacco Company and publishing businesses. The marriage was short lived, but it added to Rubirosa's growing fame as a playboy and seducer of the rich and famous. His divorce from Duke was followed by a torrid, well-publicized romance with Hollywood star Zsa-Zsa Gabor, which went on and off for several years. In 1953 he married Barbara Hutton, another wealthy woman, but the marriage lasted only three months. He then revived his love affair with Gabor, and even tried to make a movie with her, but the U.S. government denied him a working permit, given the fact that he was legally a Dominican diplomat. His rocky relationships with women of means and fame made of Rubirosa a prime target for gossip columns, where he was reviled for apparent incidents of physical abuse against women. On the other hand, many of these columnists also wondered about his "secret" to success in love, and they helped develop his "Latin lover" mystique (even propagating the rumor that Rubirosa used secret potions made from exotic tropical plants that allowed him to make love for hours). In 1956 Rubirosa married—for the last time—Odile Rodin, a 19-year-old French actress. She abandoned her acting career for him, and they moved to Santo Domingo. Rubirosa continued working for the Trujillo dictatorship as a diplomat until the collapse of the regime in 1961, shortly after the assassination of the dictator. He returned to France, where he lived for a few more years, dying in Paris on July 5, 1965, after losing control of his Ferrari sports car and crashing into a tree. Porfirio Rubirosa died the way he had lived—in the fast lane. Since his death he has become something of a macho icon in the Dominican Republic, where he has become known as the "first Dominican playboy."

RELATED ARTICLES

Dominican Americans; Machismo.

FURTHER READING

Clase, Pablo. *Rubi: La vida de Porfirio Rubirosa* (Rubi: The Life of Porfirio Rubirosa). Santo Domingo: Cosmos, 1979.

Collado, Lipe. *La impresionante vida de un seductor: Porfirio Rubirosa* (The Impressive Life of a Seductor: Porfirio Rubirosa). Santo Domingo: Editora Collado, 2001.

Peña Rivera, Víctor A. *El playboy Porfirio Rubirosa: Su vida y sus tiempos* (Playboy Porfirio Rubirosa: His Life and Times). Miami: V. A. Peña-Rivera y Asociados, 1991.

Rubirosa, Porfirio. *Mis memorias* (My Memoirs). Santo Domingo: Letra Gráfica, 2000.

ERNESTO SAGÁS

RUIZ DE BURTON, MARÍA AMPARO

Born: 1832; Loreto, Baja California
Died: 1895; Chicago, Illinois

María Amparo Ruiz de Burton, the first-known Mexican American to write novels (two) in English, was born in 1832 in Loreto, Baja California, to a prominent landowning Californio family; her grandfather had served as the governor of Baja and owned vast tracts of land around Ensenada. However, the family met the same fate as did the other California landholding gentry (known as Californios) who lost control of the area during the Mexican-American War (1845–1848), when the U.S. army occupied Baja and forced the surrender of its citizens. At the war's close, María and her mother took advantage of the terms of the Treaty of Guadalupe Hidalgo to move north to Monterey and become U.S. citizens. In 1849 María married Henry S. Burton, a West Point graduate and captain in the U.S. Army. She was thought to have been very beautiful, and some have conjectured that she was the subject of the popular song *The Maid of Monterey,* a romantic ballad sung by Mexican war veterans in the early days of the state. Her marriage to Burton—a "California" to an Anglo, a Catholic to a Protestant—flouted the conventions of the time; for some it also demonstrated the contradictions of her life and Mexican American identity. Having witnessed the U.S. invasion of her land, she nonetheless later married a captain of the invading army; the fact that she had traveled in the elite social circles of her time, was a published writer, fluent in English and in Spanish, and a landowner did not prevent her from suffering the social dislocation and economic hardships that had devastated many other Californios, and she met an impoverished end in Chicago in 1895, after fruitless attempts to gain legal rights in U.S. courts to her inheritance in Ensenada and her ranch in California.

Ruiz de Burton's writings reflect her complex reality. Her first-known work was a comedy based on the adventures of Miguel de Cervantes's character, Don Quixote; her first novel, *Who Would Have Thought It?,* published in Philadelphia in 1872, is a biting, controversial satire of the northeastern culture she witnessed during the ten years she spent living in the East with her husband and children. The novel is set during the Civil War and Reconstruction era and challenges the area's hypocrisy, materialism, and Anglocentrism. By the time she had written the novel, the author was a widow and had returned to San Diego, California, to find the property she and her husband had purchased, Rancho Jamul, occupied by American squatters. The land struggles that she and other Californio families experienced after U.S. annexation with unscrupulous squatters, an unsympathetic court system, and monopoly capitalism in the form of the railroad industry are fictionalized in her subsequent novel, *The Squatter and the Don* (1885), published anonymously as "C. Loyal," an abbreviation of "Loyal Citizen," a 19th-century method of closing official letters in Mexico. Modern critics find the melodramatic novel—a romance between the children of two families, an aristocratic California and an Anglo—problematic for its portrayal of the upper classes on both sides as dignified and the working classes as grasping and unethical. Her novels are notable nonetheless for their unique perspective on issues of race, gender, class, power, and colonialism in 19th-century America.

RELATED ARTICLES

Californios; Literature, Mexican American.

FURTHER READING

Aranda, José F., Jr. "Contradictory Impulses: María Amparo Ruiz de Burton, Resistance Theory, and the Politics of Chicano/a Studies." *American Literature: A Journal of Literary History, Criticism, and Bibliography* 70, no. 3 (1998): 551–579.

Fisher, Beth. "The Captive Mexicana and the Desiring Bourgeois Woman: Domesticity and Expansionism in Ruiz de Burton's *Who Would Have Thought It?*" *Legacy: A Journal of American Women Writers* 16, no. 1 (1999): 59–69.

Goldman, Anne E. "Who Ever Heard of a Blue-Eyed Mexican?" In *Recovering the U.S. Hispanic Literary Heritage.* Vol. 2. Ed. by Erlinda Gonzáles-Berry and Chuck Tatum. Houston, Tex.: Arte Público Press, 1996.

Gonzáez, John M. "Romancing Hegemony: Constructing Racialized Citizenship in María Amparo Ruiz de Burton's *The Squatter and the Don.*" In *Recovering the U.S. Hispanic Literary Heritage.* Vol. 2. Ed. by Erlinda Gonzáles-Berry and Chuck Tatum. Houston, Tex.: Arte Público Press, 1996.

McCullough, Kate. "María Amparo Ruiz de Burton's Geographies of Race, Regions of Religion." In *Regions of Identity.* Stanford, Calif.: Stanford Univ. Press, 1999.

Sánchez, Rosaura, and Beatrice Pita. "Introduction." *The Squatter and the Don.* Houston, Tex.: Arte Público Press, 1992.

Sánchez, Rosaura, and Beatrice Pita. "Introduction." *Who Would Have Thought It?* Houston, Tex.: Arte Público Press, 1996.

Sánchez, Rosaura, and Beatrice Pita, eds. *Conflicts of Interest: The Letters of María Amparo Ruiz de Burton.* Houston, Tex.: Arte Público Press, 2001.

MARGARITE FERNÁNDEZ OLMOS

RUMBA

Rumba is a secular lyrical and dance genre that traces its origins to the Congolese, the African ethnic group most influential in Cuban music. In the 18th century African slaves and Afro Cubans living in urban slums or semirural areas near sugar plantations, specifically in Matanzas province, created this complex of Cuban drum rhythms—played on either drums or boxes, with accompanying chants and dances—for social gatherings. Rumba starts with an attention-getting introduction called *diana* (reveille). A chorus response follows and a soloist begins to tell a story, with social and even philosophical asides. There are three basic rumba styles: *yambú, columbia,* and *guaguancó. Yambú,* most likely the oldest style, is slower than the other two—the steps and gestures of the dancers imitate old people—and there is no *vacunao,* when male and female partners suddenly press together connoting sexual union, as there is in the other two rumba styles. The *columbia* is sometimes danced alone by a man who gestures athletically while holding a machete (cane knife) in each hand,

passing the knives closely along different parts of his body. The *guaguancó* is more conducive to extensive lyrics by the soloist, with the chorus intervening with a refrain.

Although sometimes persecuted by the authorities as part of policies curtailing African cultural remnants in slaves and free Afro Cubans, the rumba prevailed. At the beginning of the 20th century, it was adapted by the *bufo* Cuban theater (minstrel shows) as the musical ending for short dialogues by comic characters such as *el gallego* (Spaniard), *el negrito* (black man), and *la mulata* (mulatto girl), with accompaniment by a small orchestra using a timpani drum as percussion.

Gradually nightclubs began to feature a more elaborate kind of rumba designed for American tourists. This version is called *la rumba teatral,* or theatrical rumba. Moreover, when the Cuban *son* was introduced in Europe and America, it also was called *rumba,* as the latter was already familiar to American visitors to Cuba and was easier to pronounce than *son,* often confused with the word *song.* In the 1940s the frequent presence of Cuban *rumberas* (female rumba dancers) in Mexican and Argentinian movies spread the rumba around the American continents. Then, in the 1950s, Cubans rediscovered the real

© JOHN LOENGARD / TIME AND LIFE PICTURES/GETTY IMAGES

Director George Abbott and instructor Lilyan Martin dance the rumba on a Miami, Florida, beach.

rumba, particularly the *guaguancó,* and the genre was performed by groups such as Los Muñequitos de Matanzas and Los Papines.

Rumba dances were introduced to the United States during World War I and by the 1930s and 1940s were a part of the country's dance hall rhythms, along with other Latin dances such as the mambo and conga. The Xavier Cugat Band played a large role in popularizing rumba with dance crowds. After the U.S. embargo on Cuba was enforced in the 1960s and *rumberas* on the island disappeared, some Cuban drummers living in the United States, such as Mongo Santamaría and Patato Valdés, kept the *guaguancó* alive as part of their repertoire of Afro-Cuban music. Santamaría created such songs as *Chango Drums and Chants* and *Yambú,* while Valdés recorded *Patato and Totico* and *Ready for Freddy.* In the 1970s rumba became a part of the salsa movement.

Meanwhile, in Cuba the rumba kept a low profile during the first 20 years of the revolution. When the government lessened its negative attitude toward Afro-Cuban cultural representations in the 1980s the rumba made a comeback. It is now alive in its native country and is a well-known cultural export.

RELATED ARTICLES

Afro-Latino Influences; Dance; Music, Popular; Rhumba.

FURTHER READING

Acosta, Leonardo. "The Rumba, the Guaguancó, and the Tío Tom." In *Essays on Cuban Music: North American and Cuban Perspectives.* Ed. by Peter Manuel. Lanham, Md.: Univ. Press of Am., 1991.

Daniel, Yvonne. *Rumba: Dance and Social Change in Contemporary Cuba.* Bloomington: Ind. Univ. Press, 1995.

Martínez Rodríguez, Raúl. "La rumba en la provincia de Matanzas." In *Panorama de la música popular cubana.* Ed. by Radamés Giro. Havana, Cuba: Editorial Letras Cubanas, 1996.

Moore, Robin D. *Nationalizing Blackness: Afrocubanismo and Artistic Revolution in Havana, 1920–1940.* Pittsburgh: Univ. of Pittsburgh Press, 1997.

CRISTÓBAL DÍAZ-AYALA

S

SAINT AUGUSTINE

The oldest permanent settlement in the United States, Saint Augustine is thus the first U.S. Hispanic settlement. In 1565 the great Spanish admiral Pedro Menéndez de Avilés, the last in a long line of Spanish would-be conquistadors of Florida, settled present-day Saint Augustine, which had been, up to that time, an important center for the Timucuan Indians. Soon after, Menéndez followed through on his objective of destroying a French Huguenot settlement, Fort Caroline, 40 miles (65 km) north of Saint Augustine along the Saint Johns River in today's Jacksonville. By this conquest, Menéndez established Spanish hegemony over Florida.

Spain administered its Florida colony from Saint Augustine from that time until 1763, when the Iberian nation lost it to the British following the Seven Years' War. Twenty years later, through military accomplishments and diplomacy, Spain regained control of Florida and again administered the colony from Saint Augustine.

In the First Spanish Period (1565–1763), Florida was a problematic, impoverished colony, which disappointed Spain's empire builders, who expected to find gold there, as well as to secure the Florida Straits against the incursions of pirates preying on Spanish treasure ships. Although neither expectation was realized, Florida, specifically Saint Augustine, the lone settlement of any consequence in the colony, did offer many "firsts": the first orange trees were cultivated there; the first black slave community was situated in Saint Augustine by the late 1500s; the beginnings of a cattle "industry" appeared near Saint Augustine. Spain ruled Florida, through a governor appointed by the mother country, from Saint Augustine. Florida and Saint Augustine received sustenance from the annual *situado,* a subsidy from the viceroy of New Spain in Mexico City. Otherwise the struggling colony, whose population in 1600 stood at only around 700, almost all of whose members were residents of Saint Augustine, would have been unable to sustain itself economically.

Saint Augustine's troubles stemmed from widespread disease that killed many settlers, storms that inflicted great damage on the settlement, underproducing farms, and periodic sacks and raids from pirates and adventurers. Exacerbating the problems of the settlement was a rising conflict between Spain and England, which led to British raids into Florida in the early and mid-1700s. To guard the settlement, Spanish authorities in Saint Augustine erected, from the late 1500s to the late 1600s, nine forts overlooking the harbor on the Matanzas River, an inlet from the Atlantic Ocean. Each of these wood forts was destroyed, prompting the Spanish to build a stone fort, the Castillo de San Marcos, which took decades to complete and millions of dollars to build. Finally, in the early 1700s, the Castillo, with its 10-foot (3-meter) walls, made of native coquina stone, was completed—and just in time to help the residents of Saint Augustine endure an attack and protracted siege from a British military force. Despite the ever-present danger of British attempts to control Saint Augustine and Florida, the Spanish endured until they lost the colony through a broader war and peace treaty in 1763.

The high point of Spanish control over Florida in the First Spanish Period was its success in converting thousands of native Floridians to Christianity in the 17th century. In 1674, the peak year of Spanish Florida missions, Franciscans administered 32 missions stretching across northern Florida with more than 13,000 Christianized Indians living in or nearby them. The missionaries taught Indians carpentry, weaving and other crafts, agriculture, and, most important, how to read and write. Sadly, by the beginning of the 1700s, the missions had closed, following

a new round of fighting between Spaniards and Indians and the growing conflict between Spain and England.

After the British interregnum, 1763–1783, Spain regained Florida and initiated the Second Spanish Period, 1783–1821. Spain attempted to administer its colony again from Saint Augustine in a more enlightened fashion in that era, inviting peoples of other faiths and ethnic groups to settle there, but settlers were few, and Spain's grip over its troublesome colony weakened further from Indian raids and British machinations, including the latter's attempts to sever East Florida from Spain and establish a separate colony there. Finally, after Andrew Jackson led a pu-

The taking of Saint Augustine, Florida, by Sir Francis Drake on June 7, 1586. This 1588 engraving is the earliest engraved view of a U.S. city.

nitive expedition against Indians and British in northwest Florida, in 1817—an action known as the First Seminole War—Spain, with its control now minimal, decided to sell Florida to the expansion-minded United States. In 1821 a lengthy, complicated era of negotiations ended with the sale of the colony to the United States, with no payment made to Spain but with the United States's relinquishment of the $5 million in damage claims by Americans against Spain.

After more than 200 years, Spanish rule over Florida had ended. But the era of Spanish Saint Augustine remains alive today in a city with many Spanish colonial structures, singular and otherwise, still standing, along with a profusion of Spanish surnames among residents of the ancient city.

RELATED ARTICLES

Colonial Period; Florida; Spain.

FURTHER READING

Bushnell, Amy T. *The King's Coffer: Proprietor of the Spanish Florida Treasury, 1565–1702.* Gainesville: Univ. Press of Fla., 1981.

Deagan, Kathleen. *Spanish St. Augustine: The Archaeology of a Colonial Creole Community.* New York: Acad. Press, 1983.

Lyon, Eugene. *The Enterprise of Florida: Pedro Menendez de Aviles and the Spanish Conquest of 1565–1568.* Gainesville: Univ. Press of Fla., 1976.

Waterbury, Jean Parker. *The Oldest City: St. Augustine: Saga of Survival.* St. Augustine, Fla.: St. Augustine Hist. Soc., 1983.

PAUL S. GEORGE

SAINTS

The strong, widespread devotion expressed for saints in Latin American countries and among various Latino communities in the United States goes back to the evangelization processes immediately after the arrival of Spaniards in the Americas in 1492. Spanish colonization was a twofold process. On the one hand, it was a political enterprise; Spain, the first modern European empire, took possession of the government of its American colonies. On the other hand, Spanish colonizers promoted a complex process of religious conversion. It can be argued that the religious teaching of American indigenous groups was not solely an act of true humanity under the claim of spreading the "joys" of the Gospels; scholars have pointed out many ways in which social and political

institutions depended on religious control of the native peoples to maintain them as marginal groups.

The Roman Catholic faith had a distinctive influence on Latin American religious belief systems, particularly at the levels of popular, or folk, practices. The fusion of Catholic traditions observed in Spain and the numerous, diverse indigenous customs would create unique practices that today characterize the Roman Catholic Church of Latin America. One of the most important characteristics of the Latin American and of the Latino Roman Catholic faiths is the indisputably key role of saints in both the institutionalized church rituals and in popular belief systems or traditions.

Using graphic terms, the earliest Spanish chroniclers described Native American religious traditions as barbaric, including extreme practices of human sacrifices and ritual cannibalism. These behaviors would facilitate the imposition of the church's role in acculturation of the indigenous to European religious systems and the native peoples' incorporation into a subservient social and political structure. Religious conversion became, therefore, an integral part of the conquest, and Catholic dogma became synonymous with acceptable behavior, in line with the Spanish patterns of Western civilization. Roman Catholic priests, Dominicans, and Franciscans arrived in considerable numbers after Columbus's second voyage, in 1493, and they created a complex campaign of evangelization. The forced conversion of indigenous peoples into the Catholic faith, mandated by Pope Alexander VI in 1493, was a central component of the political campaign of the conquest—so much so that some critics argue that the wars against American native groups were fought under platforms of religious ideology. In any case, imposition of Christian belief led to conversions and also to radical changes in the indigenous communities' social fabric. One important element in the conversion process was the use of images of saints as didactic, concrete examples of proper Catholic behavior.

Priests' testimonial accounts of their experiences and their creation of dictionaries of the native languages provide documentation of native religious practices, including records of rituals and of oral legends. One example is the work of Bernardino de Sahagún, a Franciscan priest who arrived in Mexico in 1529 as part of a religious contingent. In 1540 Sahagún had started to transcribe the Nahuatl phonemes into the Spanish alphabet, a task that allowed him to transcribe local indigenous legends, history, and religious customs. This was the beginning of the *General History of the Things of New Spain,* a compilation of 12 books written in Nahuatl and in Spanish, transcribed between 1578 and 1580.

In the process of evangelization the use of the saints gave priests opportunities to communicate basic tenets of the Catholic Church. The native peoples' religious practices were based on rich oral traditions in support of beliefs in multiple characters of supernatural nature. Thus the saints' hagiography, or life stories, came to support Roman Catholic dogma, stressing, in particular, characteristics that made for a good citizen, one servile to the wishes of both the church and of imposed political institutions.

The influence of devotion to saints at official and popular levels is noticeable today among the Latino communities in the United States. The connection is historical, especially in the Southwest, where the

THE GRANGER COLLECTION

St. Francis of Assisi in Meditation (circa 1639); oil on canvas by Francisco de Zurbaran.

Spanish government had established flourishing missions, such as the one founded in 1769 in San Diego, California. The church had an important role in the education of native populations. Under the leadership of Fray Junípero Serra, 21 missions provided evangelical and manual instruction to natives in an area extending north from San Diego to San Francisco de Solano (north of San Francisco), some 600 miles (970 km) away. A statue to Fray Serra in San Francisco's Golden Gate Park is a testimony to his intensive missionary work, which led to the development of notable cities. Today these missions—among them, San Juan de Capistrano, which Serra founded in 1776—are romantic representations of clashes among the Spanish, native American, and Mexican cultures, and which in turn characterize the modern Chicano, or Mexican American, culture of the Southwest.

The Franciscans' emphasis on the arts, music, and the performing arts provided distinctive artistic production for local religious traditions. Among the craft works are the *santos,* or wooden carvings of saints, which were central icons in mission churches and are today found in Latino homes. This type of religious carving is an important folk art in New Mexico, where *santeros,* or saint makers, follow the ancient traditional forms introduced by missionaries beginning in the late 18th century. The carvings are done in two forms: a freestanding figure, sometimes placed into a *nicho,* or on a wooden structure resembling a building, usually a church; and a *retablo,* a wooden panel displaying painted scenes of saints and their miraculous lives.

The cult of saints was at the heart of the evangelization of indigenous groups. During the earliest stages, and in order to overcome the linguistic barriers, the saints acted as concrete images of expected and proper Catholic behavior. Thus the representation of saints, as well as major biblical figures, played a paramount role in rituals intended to attract native people into the Catholic faith. A return to the early Christian church's practice of learning by imitating is clear in the oldest surviving carvings. For example, a number of the earliest *santos* are representations of key biblical moments, particularly those of the New Testament. Examples of the most common carvings are of Mary, in her multiple facets, as tender mother of the Baby Jesus and as a suffering witness of her son on the way to his death. Other popular images were of Joseph, as a humble father and teacher of

Christ the Savior, and of the apostles who became the ultimate teachers of the Christian faith.

Today the cult of the saints continues to be part of strong popular belief among the Latino population. Saints are present in the names of major cities throughout the southwestern United States, such as San Francisco and Los Angeles, a reminder of the missionary past of that area. For the city of Santa Fe in New Mexico, named after the theological concept of faith, the patron saint is Saint Francis of Assisi. Indirect institutionalized influence can also be seen in the New Mexico National Guard's adoption of the Holy Child of Atocha, a representation of the Baby Jesus Christ, as its patron saint.

The devotion of saints has had colorful influences on popular traditions. For instance, some worshippers attribute supernatural powers to certain saints. Folk belief attributes to Saint Anthony the power to find lost objects, and he is also thought to provide husbands for women who have lost hope of "locating" a suitable mate. In the latter case, a prayer will not suffice, however; since Saint Anthony must be enticed to perform, women tell the saint that they will keep his statue sitting upside down until he fulfills the request for a husband. Another unusual custom is practiced by some homeowners wanting to sell their house quickly; they bury an image of Saint Joseph (patron of, among other things, the home) outside of the house, and only when the house is sold will the homeowner disinter the image in gratitude for the favor fulfilled.

The cult of the saints has, however, an important role beyond folklore in modern Catholic rituals. The Virgen de (Virgin of) Guadalupe, patron saint of Mexico and of the Americas, is the best example of faith in a miraculous apparition that has been welcomed into both popular belief systems and institutionalized rituals. The history of the Virgen de Guadalupe goes back to the beginning of the conquest and colonization of Mexico, when in 1531, some 11 years after the fall of Tenochtitlán, the Aztecs' imperial capital, the Aztec Indian convert, Juan Diego, saw an apparition of the Madonna. Unlike the religious images imported by the Spanish priests and actively used in the evangelization process, the Virgen stands out for two reasons. First, she appeared to an Indian and, according to the legend, spoke to him in his indigenous language. Second, her miracle, a reproduction of her image on Diego's *tilma* (cloak

or poncho) was that of a dark-skinned Madonna surrounded by an icon of interest to local native groups.

The apparition of the Virgen has been historically challenged as a fraud. The coincidences that the apparition took place on a hillside with a strong connection to Aztec religious practices, that the Virgen is depicted as a indigenous woman, and that she chose to appear to a native peasant seem to point to an organized effort to facilitate the conversion of indigenous groups into the Catholic faith. The extended devotion to "la Virgen morena," the dark-skinned Madonna, as she is affectionately known throughout Latin America, has a strong appeal among sectors of the lower classes, particularly among peasant groups. Evidence of the strength of devotion to her was the canonization of Juan Diego as a saint in 2002, by Pope John Paul II, in an impressive ceremony in the Basilica of Guadalupe in Mexico City. Diego became the first canonized saint of indigenous background in the history of the Roman Catholic Church.

Another significant activity related to popular devotion of saints is the tradition of building altars in public and private spaces. Examples of public display of religious devotion are numerous, ranging from the placement of images of saints, particularly of Madonnas, outside homes, to offerings of various kinds, including flowers, fruits and candles. Although not associated with saints, the placement of crosses at locations of fatal traffics accidents is also a common tradition among Latino communities.

The best-known activity associated with altar making is the feast of the Day of the Dead. Following the Catholic celebration of All Saints' Day (November 1), the church remembers, on November 2, all dead family members, including ancestors and people of national and international note. This celebration, while of great importance in most Latin American countries and in Latino communities, is most especially observed in Mexico and in Mexican American centers. At the core of the celebration is the detailed and sophisticated construction of altars, with elements that reveal the influence of indigenous religious belief systems.

Aside from its profound religious significance, the worship of saints and the public manifestations of religious beliefs among Latino communities have social and political ramifications. First, these beliefs serve as activities that provide cohesion to various economically divided migrant groups. Thus the reverence of the Virgen de Guadalupe among Mexican Americans transcends racial and social barriers and unites an otherwise fragmented community. Virgen-related folktales are also inspiration for the arts, her image often prominent in street murals in urban areas of the U.S. Southwest.

The Virgen as a dynamic religious icon has transcended the limits of Mexican culture. Around her image, Latinos have incorporated issues related to their struggles as immigrants. This sociopolitical element in devotion to her is an important contribution to the development of a U.S. Latino subculture. Like teachings of the saints, the Virgen de Guadalupe's original religious message to the underclass continues alive among the migrant groups, who frequently struggle in extreme economic conditions. The message now goes beyond the original religious context to include fair treatment under Christian ethical codes.

RELATED ARTICLES

Catholicism; Diego, Juan; Missions; Religion; Retablos; Virgen de Guadalupe.

FURTHER READING

Carmichael, Elizabeth, and Chloë Sayer. *The Skeleton at the Feast: The Day of the Dead in Mexico.* Austin: Univ. of Tex. Press, 1997.

Dries, Angelyn. *The Missionary Movement in American Catholic History.* Maryknoll, N.Y.: Orbis Bks., 1998.

Frank, Larry. *A Kingdom of Saints: Early Retablos of New Mexico.* Santa Fe, N.Mex: Red Crane Bks., 1993.

Griffith, Jim. *Saints of the Southwest.* Tucson, Ariz.: Rio Nuevo Pubs., 2000.

RAFAEL OCASIO

SALAD. *See* SPANISH AMERICAN LEAGUE AGAINST DISCRIMINATION.

SALAZAR, RUBÉN

Born: March 3, 1928; Ciudad Juárez, Mexico
Died: August 29, 1970; Los Angeles, California

An intellectual figure in the Chicano movement whose early, tragic death interrupted a promising career, Rubén Salazar was a columnist and a journalist both in print and television. He covered the Vietnam War in 1965 and was bureau chief for the *Los Angeles Times* in Mexico City—the first Mexican American ever to take such a major role in any U.S. newspaper. He was kidnapped in Panama and held for a time by antigovernment terrorists.

As a schoolboy Salazar moved from Ciudad Juarez, Chihuahua, Mexico, across the Rio Grande into Texas, and he went to high school there. He was reported to be a Boy Scout. Salazar was fluent in Spanish and English, and was a good student. In the early 1950s he joined the army, and after his tour of duty ended, he received a bachelor's degree in journalism from the University of Texas. His degree led to his first reporting job at the El Paso *Herald Post*. If he had not been politicized before, his days as a beat reporter in southwest Texas radicalized him. He covered the suffering of the Mexican American community in the barrios, institutions, and prisons around El Paso. This focus on the struggles of *la raza,* the Mexican American people, followed him through his journalistic postings in California. He moved up the ladder, from a Santa Rosa paper to the *San Francisco News*, then to the powerful newsroom of the *Los Angeles Times*.

After serving as a foreign correspondent for the paper, Salazar returned to Los Angeles and was assigned the Chicano beat. *Raza* consciousness was on the rise, the civil rights struggles of the 1960s now igniting protests and upheavals in Aztlán. Salazar was able to launch a regular column in the paper, documenting these troubled times. His occasionally incendiary language brought him unwelcome attention from local law enforcement and the Federal Bureau of Investigation. His bosses at the paper began to encourage him to tone down his use of rhetoric.

In 1969 Salazar was offered the position of news director at KMEX, the Spanish-language television station. Suddenly he was in a position to reach millions of Chicanos through the nightly news, while maintaining his controversial column in the *Times*.

In 1970 a large march was scheduled by the National Chicano Moratorium for the Los Angeles area. The news media covered the march, in which 30,000 civil rights protesters walked from Belvedere Park to Laguna Park. Salazar was on hand to give the Chicano perspective. The march was tumultuous, and the police made a strong showing. What happened to Salazar remains in contention—some claim it was part of a conspiracy to silence what was perceived by some as his dangerous and powerful voice. Others have argued that it was an unfortunate accident precipitated by the threat posed by the event itself. Whatever the cause, Rubén Salazar en-

The Death of Ruben Salazar by Frank Romero.

tered a café on Whittier Boulevard, and Los Angeles Sheriff's Department officer Tom Wilson stepped inside and fired a tear-gas grenade launcher, hitting Salazar in the head with a 10-inch (25.4-cm) gas canister. In the words of writer Hunter S. Thompson, he "blew Salazar's head off." The killing was ruled a homicide, but Wilson was never prosecuted.

Symbolically, Salazar's death had an element of martyrdom. It has been immortalized in novels by Manuel Ramos and Lucha Corpi, paintings by Frank Martínez, documentaries such as *Chicano!,* and in music and other artistic forms. In 1971 he received a posthumous Robert F. Kennedy Journalism Award. The Rubén Salazar Library can be found in Santa Rosa, where he had his beat. There are scholarships and educational awards in his name throughout the United States.

RELATED ARTICLES

Chicanismo; Chicano Movement; Journalism; Los Angeles; National Chicano Moratorium of Vietnam.

FURTHER READING

Anonymous. *In Memoriam: Rubén Salazar.* Los Angeles, Calif.: Regeneración, 1970.
García, Mario T., ed. *Rubén Salazar: Border Correspondent.* Berkeley: Univ. of Calif. Press, 1995.
"Rubén Salazar. " *La Voz de Aztlán.* Heroes of La Raza Series 1, no. 3 (January 31, 2000).
Stavans, Ilan. *Bandido: The Death and Resurrection of Oscar "Zeta" Acosta.* Evanston, Ill.: Northwestern Univ. Press, 2003.
Thompson, Hunter S. *The Great Shark Hunt: Strange Tales from a Strange Time.* New York: Summit Bks., 1979.

LUIS ALBERTO URREA

SALSA

Salsa is not a musical genre; it is a way, a mode, of making Latin music. As a sauce, it reminds one of the different ingredients in it, but the taste is unmistakable—different. As with any sauce, it is capable of infinite changes, as long as one adds or omits some of its components. Thus jazz, American rhythm and blues, pop, *plena, bomba, guaguancó,* and many other forms of Latin American music have been added in different combinations.

Cuban dance music in Latin American and American cities with big Latin communities started to decline after 1960 because of the revolution in Cuba and the subsequent U.S. embargo of Cuba. The influence of the mambo, the cha-cha, and the *pachanga* was still evident during the 1960s, but New York slowly took the place of Cuba as the creator of new music and dance forms. *Charangas* such as Johnny Pacheco and Charlie Palmieri were experimenting with other instruments; in Puerto Rico, Cortijo and his combo, with its singer, Ismael Rivera, introduced innovations in traditional *bomba* and *plena* music. Much experimentation resulted in new genres that combined Afro-American and American pop music in the mid-1960s: Ray Barreto with the watusi, Joe Cuba with the bang bang, Richie Ray and Bobby Cruz with the *jala-jala*, and Pete Rodríguez with the boogaloo. With the closing of the Palladium, smaller clubs came to the fore. New labels—Alegre, Tico, Cotique, and one founded by Dominican musician Johnny Pacheco and a young lawyer, Jerry Masucci—sprang up and snapped up new talents. Latin jam sessions, or *descargas*, were also popular. Arsenio Rodríguez, legendary Cuban *tres* player and composer, was also around, adding another ingredient: the *guaguancó*, a rumba form, often with lyrics extolling the merits of some of Havana's poorer quarters (barrios).

Latins in New York and Puerto Rico were trying "to cook" something new in music. Salsa, or sauce, had been used by Cuban *sonero* Ignacio Piñeiro in 1928 as the title for a song, *Echale salsita* (Pour Sauce in It) but in a culinary sense. In New York in 1935 Antonio Machín recorded *El amor de mi guajira*, with lyrics such as *sigan ustedes en su salseo* (keep on with your festivities). *Salseo* was commonly used in Cuba as a synonym for "festivities." In 1962, when Cuban musician Pupi Legarreta recorded an album titled *Salsa Nova*, he used the name in connection with the music he was playing. An album recorded by Federico y su Combo Latino in Venezuela in 1966 was titled *Llegó la salsa* (Salsa Has Arrived). The word *salsa* had been used since 1962 by a Venezuelan DJ (disc jockey), Fidias Escalona, in his program *La hora del sabor, la salsa y el bembé*.

Only when the Fania label produced a concert at Cheetah cabaret in 1971, and used *salsa* on the album cover of "Our Latin Thing," was the name *salsa* applied to the new music being produced in New York. Izzy Sanabria used *salsa* in his magazine *Latin New York*. The name caught on quickly. Soon, new albums, instead of naming genres such as *son, son montuno,* and so on, simply had the titles of the songs, and the composers. The word *salsa* might be used

in the title of the album or in the songs themselves. If it came from Fania, it was understood that it was salsa.

Salsa is a mixture of something old, something new, something borrowed, and something blue. The old Cuban *son* was the root, but new elements were added—completely different arrangements, richer rhythm patterns, new subjects for the lyrics, new dance steps. Although the original format for salsa, the *charanga,* was borrowed from Cuban music, considerable innovations were made—trombones were added, electric piano and bass, conga, and so on. The blue tinge was found in the frequent references to the "barrio," "slavery," or other adversities.

Fania had the best groups: Johnny Pacheco, Larry Harlow, and the portoricans (Puerto Ricans) Ray Barreto, Willie Colón, Roberto Roena, and singer Hector Lavoe. Later, Fania added two Cuban *soneros* (singers): Justo Betancourt and Monguito. By 1971 the label also had the singers Pete "El Conde" Rodríguez, Adalberto Santiago, Cheo Feliciano, Santitos Colón, and Ismael Miranda, all portoricans. Other labels had important figures like Eddy and Charlie Palmieri, Richie Ray, and Bobby Cruz, his singer. When a woman's voice was needed, Fania got the Cuban veteran Celia Cruz in 1974, who was, until her death in 2003, "the queen of the salsa." Also in 1974, Fania signed the Panamanian Rubén Blades. With pioneers such as Mon Rivera, Cortijo and his combo with singer Ismael Rivera, Sonora Ponceña and Gran Combo bands, Puerto Rico was immediately part of the salsa wave. Other bands came from New York—Roena, Willie Rosario, Tommy Olivencia and Johnny el Bravo—as did the most important composer of this first stage of salsa, Tite Curet Alonso. The Cuban singer La Lupe was also a major addition. An era of big concerts began, and the best of the Fania roster was packed into the Fania All Stars group and toured in some cities in the Caribbean, especially Caracas where salsa caught on quickly. By 1973 Venezuela had an important salsa orchestra, Dimensión Latina, and a few years later one of the great stars of salsa—Oscar D'León and his band. Until about 1970, salsa was in its formative stage, using mainly the *son* and other genres (*guaracha,* mambo, and bolero and, later on, *plena, bomba,* and many others) but with a different style, innovative arrangements, a more aggressive sound, provided mostly by the trombones, and new rhythm combinations with the use of congas, *pailas,* and bongos (the trinity of Afro-Cuban percussion instruments). Dancers in New York and Puerto Rico were creating new steps to go with the new music. The lyrics either were about love, almost always with "machist" tinges, or about the barrio, its ambiance and characters, with critical overtones, especially with composers Blades and Tite Curet.

By 1980, salsa was also present in different parts of the Caribbean, especially Colombia and Panama. Cuba was claiming that salsa was nonexistent, that it was just another name for the *son.*

Arrangers were important to salsa since its beginnings. Often an album's cover would have the titles of the songs and the names of the arrangers but not the composers. Many of the arrangers were less talented than orchestras, thus orchestras began to sound very much alike. In addition, the plague that had attacked other genres, including jazz, struck: singers became more important than bands. Consequently, instrumental solos, large fast *montunos,* were replaced by slower versions; singers like Tito Rojas, Tito Nieves, Gilberto Santarrosa, and José Alberto "El Canario" came to the forefront. Salsa orchestras found Europe, becoming especially popular in Spain, Holland, Sweden, Finland, and Germany. Even Japan got its own orchestra, La Luz. Salsa fans were divided between the "salsa dura" with fans from mostly the lower-middle or working class, and "salsa romantic" with fans coming from the middle class and the wealthy. Salsa romantic often had erotic content, and thus has also been called "salsa cama" (bed salsa).

While developing in places other than New York, there emerged five principal schools or salsa styles: New York, Puerto Rico, Venezuela, Colombia, and Cuba. The island nation, after fighting salsa for many years, accepted it, but added the adjective *cubana.* Salsa cubana made the marketing of Cuban music in Europe easier. During the 1960s and 1970s, salsa had little competition from other Latin music forms, but by the 1980s merengue from Santo Domingo, pop Spanish-style music, rock in Spanish, the Nueva Trova from Cuba, *vallenato* from Colombia, and some other forms had become contenders in the European market. Salsa learned to share with all of them. Instead of being salsa-only artists, some, including La India and Marc Anthony, have developed eclectic repertoires. The five schools of salsa are all transnational. Cuba's artists are really playing *songo* and *timba* under the name of salsa cubana. Salsa's social and political importance help to unite Latins, to make them aware of their problems, hopes, and dreams. Salsa also acted as a dike to protect Latin music from the rock wave that almost covered the world in the 1960s. No other Latin music has become internationally known and played so quickly. The other well-known Latin genre, the bolero, took almost half a century to gain international recognition, even with the help of its prevalence in the Mexican movies. Salsa reached all of the Americas in less than a decade. After conquering Venezuela and Colombia, salsa took over Panama and the Dominican Republic, Peru, and then the rest of Central America except Mexico, which took more time to assimilate salsa. Other South American countries, however, were never conquered by salsa.

RELATED ARTICLES

Afro-Latino Influences; Blades, Rubén; Bugalu; Colón, Willie; Cruz, Celia; Dance; Music, Popular; Palmieri, Charlie; Popular Culture.

FURTHER READING

Báez, J. C. *El vínculo es la salsa.* (Salsa Is the Bond) Caracas, Venezuela: Dirección de Cultura VCV, 1989.

Boggs, V. W. *Salsiology.* New York: Excelsior Publ., 1992.

Gómez, José Manuel. *Guía Esencial de la Salsa.* Valencia, Spain: Editorial La Máscara, 1995.

Manuel, Peter. *Popular Musics of the Non-Western World.* New York: Oxford Univ. Press, 1988.

Quintero Rivera, Angel G. *Salsa, sabor y control! Sociología de la música "tropical."* Havana, Cuba: Casa de las Américas, 1998.

Rondón, César Miguel. *El libro de la salsa. Crónica de la Música del Caribe Urbano.* Caracas, Venezuela: Editorial Arte, 1980.

Ulloa, A. S. *La Salsa en Cali.* Cali, Colombia: Editora U.P.B., 1989.

Waxer, Lise. *Situating Salsa—Global Markets and Local Meaning in Latin Popular Music.* New York: Routledge, 2002.

Waxer, Lise. *The City of Musical Memory—Salsa, Record Grooves, and Popular Culture in Cali, Colombia.* Middletown, Conn.: Wesleyan Univ. Press, 2002.

CRISTÓBAL DÍAZ-AYALA

SALT OF THE EARTH

A strike by miners in Grant County, New Mexico, more than a half century ago resonates today for its militancy and the issues it raised. The workers' struggle, however, would be a mere footnote in American labor history were it not for a film, *Salt of the Earth,* based on the strike, made by Hollywood leftists, some of them blacklisted for their political beliefs. Almost all of them Mexican American, the 150 strikers belonged to the International Union of

Mine, Mill and Smelter Workers (Mine-Mill) local number 890 (local #890), and the company they worked for was Empire Zinc, a subsidiary of New Jersey Zinc.

The strike began on October 17, 1950, with economic issues. Mine-Mill had been expelled from the Congress of Industrial Organizations (CIO) the previous year for its refusal to disavow communist ideology. With the strike still not settled by the following June, Empire Zinc told rank-and-file Mine-Mill members that it planned to reopen with strikebreakers, politely called replacement workers. The company secured a Taft-Hartley injunction prohibiting strikers from blocking access to the plant, and paid for sheriff's deputies to arrest picketers.

Mine-Mill local #890 met the evening of June 12. Two points of view surfaced: damn the injunction—let's fight to the bitter end—and our coffers are low, we're broke, they got us beat, let's settle for what we can get. Then a third suggestion came from the floor—why not let the Ladies' Auxiliary take over the picket line? The restraining order addressed only the strikers; it said nothing about their wives. Thus their logic was impeccable: the women would walk the line for the strikers, would keep the scabs out and the mines closed, and no one would be breaking the law.

The notion had been floated informally, but now out in the open it had the power of a single bolt of lightning crackling through the window. Women on a picket line? The more skeptical of the laborers, 30-year-old shop steward Juan Chacón among them, resisted the idea. What of possible violence? Sheriff's deputies? Company "goons"? Scabs? Who'll take care of the kids and clean the house? You're not experienced strikers—you're ladies. You'll quit after a day or two. Better for us to go down fighting than have ladies do it for us.

Others were not so quick to condemn. While they allowed that women walking the line might prove disastrous, they reasoned that this was their only alternative and that they would know its effectiveness only if they gave it a try. Further, they argued that the women had supported them, so it was right for the women to become a fuller part of the community. Local #890 called for a vote. The women would walk the line the next morning.

Initially the women were to picket for one day only, but it soon became clear that they would stay as long as needed. Their children joined them after

school. The men took care of home chores and watched the strike drama play out from a nearby hillside.

Some women were carted off to jail, and others took their place. Confrontations started soon. The sheriff shot canisters of tear gas into the women's line to clear the way for strikebreakers. The cry "¡No les dejan pasar!" (Don't let them through!) went up, and when the wind finally blew the fumes away, the wives had held their line. Some new hires simply drove in, seriously injuring a few women. Whenever possible, women clustered around strikebreakers' cars and ripped out the wiring, rocked the cars until they turned over, punctured tires, or pummeled the driver and tossed Mexican mace—ground chili peppers—in their eyes. Women who had never worn pants outside the home came dressed for action.

Union demands were not changed, but the women, now full partners in the strike, insisted that Empire provide hot running water in their company housing, since the company had furnished it for its Anglo miners. Arrests were common, with deputies plucking women out of the line and tossing them in jail. Other unions around the country sent support money and food, the Ladies' Auxiliary, fueled by a sense of righteousness and momentum, assumed the vanguard in the struggle.

The strikers felt they had history with them. Some saw the dynamics of larger forces at work. The Communist party, whose influence in Mine-Mill was significant but not dominant, helped shape local #890's decision making, yet when the local was red-baited, its members rose to defend their leadership, trusting its decisions.

By Christmastime New Jersey Zinc felt the losses from its New Mexico subsidiary. In January 1952 Empire agreed to negotiations, and, after nearly 15 months, the walkout ended with a new contract. Hot running water flowed soon thereafter.

Paul Jarrico, a Hollywood screenwriter and producer who had refused to testify before the House Un-American Activities Committee (HUAC), learned of the strike while vacationing in New Mexico and, once back in Los Angeles, told his two partners in a newly formed independent production company about it. One partner, screenwriter Michael Wilson, had, like Jarrico, refused to testify before HUAC. The other, director Herbert Biberman, having been publicly labeled a Communist, had recently been released after six months in prison for refusing to discuss his political inclinations with HUAC. The three agreed to pursue a movie shot on location in Grant County, with the Mine-Mill as a partner and with the local mining community allowed to influence the screenplay.

Will Geer took the role of the wizened sheriff who carried out the mining company wishes. The role of the union president's wife, Esperanza, whose personal growth and personal dignity symbolizes the community's sense of struggle, went to Rosaura Revueltas, an actress from a highly cultured Mexican family. The leading role of the union president went to the newly elected president of local #890, Juan Chacón. Most of the roles of miners and their families were played by the miners themselves and their families.

Shooting began in January 1953, but during the second week of February, a Hollywood trade journal reported, "Reds are shooting a feature length Anti-American racial issue propaganda movie." A labor columnist then wrote that the shoot was "not too far from the Los Alamos Atomic proving ground" and that "carloads of Negroes" were brought in for a scene involving mob violence. Neither was remotely true, but following on this was a piece in *Newsweek* headlined "Reds in the Desert." California congressman Donald Jackson denounced the film-in-progress on the floor of the House of Representatives as "designed to inflame racial hatreds." He asked Hollywood and Washington to keep it out of movie theaters, which elicited a reply from Howard Hughes of RKO: "If the motion picture industry—not only in Hollywood, but throughout the United States—will refuse these skills (processing, soundtrack, dubbing, editing facilities, etc.), the picture cannot be completed in this country."

Meanwhile the U.S. Immigration and Naturalization Service arrested Revueltas and deported her. At the beginning of March the filming itself was attacked; shots were fired, and an armed mob stormed filming in front of the union hall in Bayard, New Mexico, tossing down a camera and breaking it. Vigilantes met at a nearby American Legion Hall and warned, "Get out of Grant County or go out in black boxes." *The El Paso Herald-Post* congratulated the vigilantes "in their determination to clear away the pink overcast from their beautiful country."

Editing, the music track, and processing was carried out clandestinely throughout Southern California, and in spite of all these hardships, by the beginning of 1954 *Salt of the Earth* was complete. It is a period piece, black and white, often moving, occasionally awkward, but full of dignity, integrity, and humane values. It never achieved general release.

The tendency in assessing *Salt of the Earth* generations later is to magnify its content, yet part of its appeal lies in its durability. The mining camp is frozen in time, but the powerful themes are timeless. Equality for women and Mexican Americans entwines with collective bargaining, each drawing strength from the other. The movie remains a staple in university classes focusing on McCarthyism, the women's movement, cinema, and labor history. In the 1990s it was broadcast nationally on PBS (Public Broadcasting Service) and eventually became available in conventional video stores. An opera based on the movie, called *Esperanza,* with a libretto by playwright Carlos Morton, premiered in Madison, Wisconsin, in 2000. And in Grant County, miners no longer take zinc from the land where the original "Salt" strike took place. Many of the underground shafts are flooded, and the concentrator has since been demolished. In 1998 the Phelps Dodge Company purchased the remains of the old Empire Zinc facility.

The militant Mine-Mill finally voted itself out of existence in 1966; its locals, including #890, joined the United Steel Workers of America. By 2000 #890's membership had dropped precipitously, partly because so much mining had been automated, but also because the labor movement that once dominated Grant County in its "Salt" days had decelerated to a crawl.

RELATED ARTICLES

Film; Labor.

FURTHER READING

Biberman, Herbert. *Salt of the Earth: The Story of a Film.* Boston: Beacon Press, 1965.
Lorence, James J. *The Suppression of "Salt of the Earth": How Hollywood, Big Labor, and Politicians Blacklisted a Movie In Cold War America.* Albuquerque: Univ. of N.M. Press, 1999.
Miller, Tom. *Jack Ruby's Kitchen Sink: Offbeat Travels through America's Southwest.* Washington, D.C.: Natl. Geographic Soc., 2000.
Revueltas, Rosaura. *Los Revueltas; Biografía de una familia* (The Revueltas; Biography of a Family). Mexico City: Grijalbo, 1980.
Wilson, Michael, and Deborah Silverton Rosenfelt. *Salt of the Earth.* Old Westbury, N.Y.: Feminist Press, 1978.

TOM MILLER

SALVADORAN AMERICANS

Salvadorans started immigrating to the United States in the early 1980s, fleeing the civil war in their country. One of the newest and largest Latino groups in the United States, Salvadoran Americans are the largest single Central American national group and the fourth largest Latino community in the United States, with population estimates ranging, in the late 1990s, from 607,000 (U.S. 1997 Census) to press figures of over 1 million. The great majority arrived during the Salvadoran civil war from 1979 to 1992, and some have been granted political asylum, while the vast majority have an undocumented legal status. Salvadoran Americans concentrate in several metropolitan cities. Their presence has rapidly diversified the Latino community in cities such as Los Angeles (with more than 50 percent of the Salvadoran American population); Washington, D.C., and Houston (with more than 10 percent each); San Francisco; Austin, Texas; and New York City.

Demographic data on Salvadoran Americans are difficult to obtain, owing both to the nature of the community and to the Immigration and Naturalization Service's (INS's) statistics on Central Americans, which represent only a fraction of the population because INS provides no data on undocumented or second- and third-generation Salvadorans. Up-to-date information about Salvadoran Americans is scarce, and non-Latinos often confuse them with the more numerous Mexican Americans. Many Salvadoran immigrants entered the United States without legal immigration papers (escaping the violence of the civil war in their country and leaving without any documents), and the fear of deportation has kept them away from the agencies that provide official counts. Numerous Salvadorans who filed claims for political asylum have been unsuccessful; despite the political situation in El Salvador, the United States granted political asylum to only 213,539 between 1981 and 1990 (the Salvadoran civil war). During the 1991–2002 period, 277,391 Salvadorans were granted legal residence in the United States.

El Salvador is the smallest Latin American country (8,260 sq mi, or 21,390 sq km) and the most densely populated, with an estimated population of 6.3 million in 2002. The country is bounded on the south by the Pacific Ocean, on the west by Guatemala, and on the north and east by Honduras. The vast majority of people are of mixed indigenous and Spanish descent (mestizos). Spanish is the official language, and Catholicism the prevailing religion (the name El Salvador, in fact, means the Savior in Spanish). There is, however, substantial activity by evangelical Protestant groups.

Before the arrival of the Spaniards, El Salvador was inhabited by the Pipils, descendants of the Aztecs and the Toltecs of Mexico, who had arrived in the 12th century. The indigenous population of Pipils and other native Americans declined tremendously in El Salvador after the Spanish occupation in the mid-1500s. El Salvador remained part of the Spanish captaincy of Guatemala until independence in 1821. Between 1923 and 1839 El Salvador joined the Central American Federation with four other states (Costa Rica, Nicaragua, Honduras, and Guatemala). After the dissolution of the federation (1839), the country was plagued by frequent interference from the dictators of neighboring countries at the same time it began to attract British and American investments in its mines and coffee plantations. An oligarchy known as the Fourteen Families developed, and it gained control of practically all the country's land and wealth by the early 1900s. The island nation has been characterized by an extreme gap between the rich and the poor.

The primacy of coffee cultivation in the economy took hold in the second half of the 19th century, with the economy and the government very vulnerable to fluctuations in the world market price for coffee. In 1931 Maximiliano Hernández Martínez, capitalizing on discontent caused by the collapse of coffee prices, led a coup. His dictatorship lasted until 1944, after which there was chronic political unrest, and despite the democratic structure of the country, El Salvador has been under military dictatorship for most of its history. By the late 1960s the country's relationship with Honduras deteriorated, which resulted in a border clash in 1967 and a short war in July 1969, and it was only in 1992 that an agreement settling the border controversy with Honduras was signed.

In the 1970s El Salvador's inequitable social system and economical problems led to social and political unrest. There was popular discontent with the feudal way of life, and peasants, workers, students, as well as the clergy poured into the streets in mass protests. In 1979 Gen. Carlos Humberto Romero, the last in a series of presidents whose elections were denounced by many as fraudulent, was overthrown by a military junta. This resulted in yet another military coup and the beginning of government-supported "death squads" that terrorized the whole country. Murders, *desaparecidos* (the "disappeared ones"), and other terrorist acts continued, leading to a full-scale civil war between the government—that is, the military—and the guerrilla resistance of the leading opposition group, the FMLN (Farabundo Martí National Liberation Front).

During the 12 years of civil war (1980–1992), an estimate of 75,000 Salvadorans were killed and hundreds of thousands displaced. The civil war in El Salvador is considered one of the most violent and prolonged in the history of Central America, and notwithstanding the nation's continuing human rights abuses, the Salvadoran government received U.S. military and economic aid. In 1980 Archbishop Oscar Romero, an outspoken critic of the government, was assassinated while celebrating Mass; this crime was condemned all over the world, raising public awareness and prompting yet another wave of refugees fleeing the country. By the middle of the 1980s, some 500,000 Salvadorans had been internally displaced, and as many as 750,000 had fled El Salvador; the combined figure represents well over 20 percent of the population of the country at that time (estimated at 5,000,000).

In 1989 Alfredo Cristiani, leader of the right-wing ARENA (National Republican Alliance) party was elected president, but the excesses and abuses continued or worsened until 1991, when the Cristiani government, with help from the United Nations, negotiated with the FMLN. In January 1992 a peace treaty was signed between the two parties, ending the bloody 12-year civil war. The FMLN demobilized and participated in the postwar 1994 elections, which resulted in the presidency of Armando Calderón Sol, the ARENA candidate, but which also marked the beginning of the FMLN in government (it won several seats in the National Assembly). The ARENA party remained in power with the election of Francisco Guillermo Flores Pérez to the presidency in 1999. In March 2000, however, the FMLN won the greatest number of seats in the National Assembly, although not enough to control the legislature. The army was apparently restrained, and terrorism and violence seemed to have disappeared. A major program was put in place to transfer land (80 percent of which was concentrated in the hands of the wealthy) to former combatants. However, progress

in implementing reforms and rebuilding the economy was slow and was further hindered by several natural tragedies. A major hurricane (Hurricane Mitch) severely hit El Salvador in 1998 and in early 2001 two earthquakes—a month apart—struck central El Salvador, killing about a thousand people and leaving many homeless. Also in 2001 El Salvador adopted the U.S. dollar as its official currency. Today the country is still struggling to rebuild its shattered economy and heal the social wounds of the civil war.

Researchers calculate that as many as 850,000 Salvadorans lived in the United States by the middle of 1980s. Their immigration was minimal until the beginning of the island's civil war in 1979. Between 1980 and 1990, Salvadorans from all social classes fled the country; wealthy people left the country fearing death or injury and the loss of property, and middle-class Salvadorans escaped the economical crisis that the civil war brought about, but the vast majority of the refugees were displaced peasants who had to leave their communities after their villages had been destroyed by Vietnam-style, scorched-earth tactics. The trends of emigration continued at the same pace for most of 1980s, so that, according to estimates, a third or more of all Salvadorans were living outside the country by the signing of the peace accords in 1992. During the 1980s, 214,000 Salvadorans were admitted as legal immigrants to the United States, and it is estimated that between 300,000 to 500,000 crossed the border during the first three years of the civil war. Most refugees were poor peasants who could not meet legal immigration requirements but were desperate enough to escape from their country that they risked all kinds of danger in search of a safe place to live. The Reagan administration at that time refused to grant the Salvadorans refugee status, claiming that they were simply looking for better economic opportunities, a decision reflecting the U.S. tradition of favoring people who were leaving Communist or Socialist countries (such as Cuba during Fidel Castro or Nicaragua during the Sandinista government) rather than nations that had received the support of the United States during civil strife (such as Guatemala or Chile).

In the early 1980s the sanctuary movement was founded by Jim Corbett and other concerned Americans who helped newly arrived refugees by creating a network of safe houses. About 300 religious congregations took part in this movement, assisting more than 300 refugees and raising the public consciousness about their plight. Numerous private organizations joined in these efforts, helping refugees with emergency housing, social services, legal aid, English classes, and job training. The Central American Refugee Center (CARECEN) in Los Angeles is a good example of a nonprofit organization that has helped Salvadorans and Central Americans with legal, social, cultural, and economic issues. Other agencies include Clínica del pueblo in Washington, D.C.; the Central American Resource Center in Austin, Texas; and Casa El Salvador in Chicago.

On arriving in the United States, Salvadorans often look for Latino barrios, where they can share the language and culture and where housing is inexpensive. Ethnic neighborhoods with Salvadoran *pupuserías* (restaurants) and markets are famous in these cities. Salvadoran Americans are among the poorest Latino groups, with one-fifth of families living in poverty in 1989. This situation is directly linked to their undocumented status in the United States and their low socioeconomic status in El Salvador; many come from poor rural areas where they had no access to schools (only one-third of those age 25 had finished high school by 1990). The two major occupations among the Salvadoran community during the last census were service and operators or laborers, with only 6 percent in managerial and professional positions. In areas with a significant Salvadoran population, parades to celebrate Independence Day and hometown associations are common. Hometown associations raise money for community projects in El Salvador, such as the construction of roads, parks, or churches. Except for the large Salvadoran communities of Los Angeles, Salvadoran Latino communities are products of narrower immigration patterns (for example, most of the people in Washington, D.C., have come from the small town of Intipucá; similarly, most Salvadorans living on Long Island, New York, come from towns in the northeast part of El Salvador).

Salvadoran Spanish shares with other Central American varieties of Spanish (such as Honduran or Nicaraguan) the use of the familiar second-person pronoun *vos* with the accompanying verb forms (for example, *vos tenés, querés, hacés,* and so on) with nearly total exclusion of *tú.* They also use *va* as a discourse marker similar to "you know" in English. Some rural varieties of Salvadoran Spanish use the preposition *hasta* (until) to mark the beginning of an event, as in "¿Hasta cuándo viene Juan?" (When is

Juan coming?). The majority of Salvadorans migrated to the United States from rural regions and possessed very little school literacy in Spanish. Large numbers of Salvadoran children started entering the U.S. school system and were placed in transitional bilingual education classes, often surrounded by Mexican children. Salvadoran children coming predominantly from rural areas were less familiar with any kind of formal schooling than were their Mexican classmates, who were mostly from urban origins, and they were behind their grade level. Furthermore, most bilingual materials focused mainly on Mexican vocabulary, and Salvadoran children simply could not understand the items in questions (for example, Mexican Spanish will use *chamaco* [child] and *lana* [money], while Salvadoran Spanish will use *cipote* [child], *pisto* [money]). The Salvadoran community in the United States is demographically and socially significant and, as more people acquire legal immigration status and better working conditions, they will be able to participate more fully in the different arenas of society.

RELATED ARTICLES

Bilingual Education; Coffee; Politics, Latino; United States–Central America Relations.

FURTHER READING

Argueta, Manlio. *One Day of Life.* Tr. by Bill Brow. New York: Vintage, 1991.

Argueta, Manlio. *Cuzcatlán donde bate la mar del sur* (Cuzcatlán, Where the Southern Sea Pounds). Honduras: Guaymuras, 1986.

Argueta, Manlio. *Magic Dogs of the Volcanoes* (Los perros mágicos de los volcanoes). Ill. by Elly Simmons, tr. by Stacey Ross. San Francisco: Children's Press, 1990.

Ferris, Elizabeth. *Uprooted!: Refugees and Forced Migrants.* Cincinnati: Friendship Press, 1998.

Lipski, John. *Latin American Spanish.* London: Longman, 1994.

U.S. Immigration and Naturalization Service. *Statistical Yearbook of the Immigration and Naturalization Service, 2002.* Washington, D.C.: USGPO, 2002.

SELECTED WEB SITE

Bureau of the Census.
http://www.census.gov/population/www/socdemo/foreign/foreign98.html

M. CECILIA COLOMBI

SAN ANTONIO

San Antonio, Texas, is one of the oldest settlements in the southwestern United States. The history of the city dates to the founding of the mission of San Antonio de Valero—now known as the Alamo—near the San Antonio River in 1718; The mission was moved to its present site in 1724. The Alamo was one of three mission founded by Franciscan missionaries Antonio de San Buenaventura Olivares as a response to French encroachment on the northern border of what was then New Spain. In 1731, 15 families from the Canary Islands arrived and established the town of San Fernando de Béxar across the river from mission San Antonio de Valero and its attached presidio, San Antonio de Béxar.

San Antonio remained a small outpost on the Spanish, and later Mexican, frontier until the early part of the 19th century. After Mexico won its independence in 1821, settlers from the United States—working closely with Texas Mexican, or Tejano, leaders—began migrating to the Mexican province. By 1830 more than 30,000 U.S. settlers were resident in Texas. The Tejano population numbered just 4,000. Within a few years Texas—among other regions of Mexico—was in open rebellion against Mexican president Antonio López de Santa Anna and his strong central government. By 1836 much of Texas—including many Tejano leaders—opted to fight for secession from Mexico. San Antonio was the scene of the most famous battle in that war. On March 6, 1836, Santa Anna and several thousand men stormed the Alamo, killing the nearly 200 defenders inside, among them several Tejanos; more than 600 Mexican soldiers also died. The Mexican victory at the Alamo was followed by defeat at San Jacinto; Texas then declared itself the Republic of Texas. The resulting Mexican-American War was ended with the Treaty of Guadalupe Hidalgo (1846–1848), by which Mexico lost much of its northern territory.

Between 1836 and 1848, declining economic activity, diminished resources, and political instability caused a decline in San Antonio's population. But economic stagnation gave way to more prosperous times after the town became a central terminal in Texas's developing cattle industry.

Increasing cattle production and distribution was made possible by what historian David Montejano calls a "peace structure." According to Montejano

the peace structure, which maintained a certain level of continuity in the changing social order of Texas, evolved as Anglo elites usurped positions of the ruling Tejano families. While subordination of the Tejano population in general, and the lower classes in particular, was taking hold, elite Anglos and Tejanis often intermarried and continued ranching, mostly in the rural areas of south Texas.

The peace structure did not extend to small urban areas like San Antonio. Although relations between San Antonio's elite Tejano and Anglo families were cordial, the vast majority of San Antonio's Tejanos were treated as second-class citizens. The city, on the edge of the frontier and at a crossroads of the cattle trails, was dependent on Mexican labor for the success of the transportation industry and small-scale mercantile trading in the area. Nevertheless, the Mexican community continued to lose status and became increasingly more segregated. The late 1880s saw the eventual erosion of the peace structure by the establishment of new social customs and economic practices and a different attitude about cattle and the land.

In response to their increased social and economic isolation, Tejanos in San Antonio organized against local efforts at segregation, for example, ordinances that restricted them from socializing in public areas. They also organized for increased political representation and, in the 1880s, pressured the Democratic Party to give their concerns a place on the local party platform.

The rapid and intense social changes that occurred in San Antonio between 1875 and 1900 were the result of increased labor specialization, the introduction of wage labor, the transition to industrialization, and the emergence of capitalism as the dominant economic mode.

After 1900 the Tejano community in San Antonio became increasingly isolated, experiencing the effects of Jim Crow laws in their daily lives. The first two decades of the century were especially harsh, partly because of the arrival of thousands of immigrants from Mexico fleeing civil strife brought on by the Revolution. These immigrants, many of whom were professionals, however, gave fresh impetus to a growing Mexican presence in politics, business, and the arts.

Between 1920 and 1960, San Antonio's Mexican American community became a significant force in the city. From Spanish-language entertainment, journalism, the performing arts as well as the presence of local community leaders developing strategies to fight segregation, racism, and unequal educational and economic participation, Mexican Americans emerged as critical social actors. Key leaders from LULAC (League of United Latin American Citizens) and the American GI Forum came from the city, as did local leaders like Emma Tenayuca, a labor activist who assisted the pecan shellers during their strike in 1938. An active and viable arts community, located at several key theaters, especially the Alameda, hosted performers from Mexico and Latin America as well as local artists.

Organizations and leaders emerged in the 1960s and 1970s and continued the efforts of earlier arrivals. The Mexican American Legal Defense and Educational Fund was started in San Antonio in 1968 by a local attorney; the late Willie Velásquez founded the Southwest Voter Registration Education Project in 1974. In the 1970s, Ernesto Cortez, after training as an organizer with the Industrial Areas Foundation, returned to San Antonio and became the first organizer of Communities Organized for Public Service, an organization based on the Saul Alinsky model of social action that has become an important political and social force for urban Mexican Americans. Others, including Judge Mike Machado and Archbishop Patrick Flores, played critical roles in transforming the political landscape of the city.

White flight and continued Mexican immigration made the city even more Mexican in the mid-to-late 1900s; Anglos in San Antonio became a numerical minority, and, in the 1980s, for the first time in more than a century, the city elected a "Mexican" mayor—Henry Cisneros. Today the city uses its Mexican past as a selling point. San Antonio is the number one tourist destination in Texas, with the city hosting many conventions. On any given weekend *conjunto* and Tejano music blare from loudspeakers and the aroma of sizzling fajitas fills the downtown air. The Guadalupe Cultural Arts Center—funded in part by the city—and other cultural institutions and events are a testament to San Antonio's undeniable Mexican roots.

RELATED ARTICLES

Alamo, Battle of the; Missions; Texas.

FURTHER READING

Cruz, Gilbert. R. *Let There Be Towns: Spanish Multiple Origins in the American Southwest, 1610–1810.* College Station: Tex. A&M Univ. Press, 1988.

de la Teja, Jesús F., and John Wheat. "Bexar: Profile of a Tejano Community, 1820–1832." *Southwestern Historical Quarterly* 89, no. 1 (1985): 7–34.

De León, Arnoldo. *The Tejano Community, 1836–1900.* Albuquerque: Univ. of N.Mex. Press, 1982.

Flores, Richard R. *Remembering the Alamo: Memory, Modernity, and the Master Symbol.* Austin: Univ. of Tex. Press, 2002.

García, Richard. *Rise of the Mexican American Middle Class.* College Station: Tex. A&M Univ. Press, 1991.

Johnson, David R. "Frugal and Sparing: Interest Groups, Politics, and City Building in San Antonio, 1870–1885." In *Urban Texas: Politics and Development.* Ed. by C. Miller and H. T. Sanders. College Station: Tex. A&M Univ. Press, 1990.

Matovina, Timothy M. *Tejano Religion and Ethnicity, San Antonio, 1821–1860.* Austin: Univ. of Tex. Press, 1995.

Montejano, David. *Anglos and Mexicans in the Making of Texas, 1836–1986.* Austin: Univ. of Tex. Press, 1987.

Poyo, Gerald E., and Gilberto M. Hinojosa. *Tejano Origins in Eighteenth-Century San Antonio.* Austin: Univ. of Tex. Press, 1991.

Rosenbaum, Robert J. *Mexicano Resistance in the Southwest: The Sacred Rights of Self-Preservation.* Austin: Univ. of Tex. Press, 1981.

Stewart, Kenneth L., and Arnoldo De León. *Not Room Enough: Mexicans, Anglos, and Socio-economic Change in Texas, 1850–1900.* Albuquerque: Univ. of N.Mex. Press, 1993.

RICHARD FLORES

SAN DIEGO, PLAN DE

The Plan de San Diego called for Mexican Americans to rebel against Anglos and to establish an independent republic in the United States Southwest. Written and dated at the town of San Diego, Texas, on January 6, 1915, this proclamation issued a call for a general uprising on February 20, 1915. Nine signatories called for the formation of a Liberating Army of Races and Peoples composed of Mexican Americans, blacks, and Japanese to join the fight for "Equality and Independence" from Anglo domination. The supporters of the Plan de San Diego intended to execute all white males over 16 years of age.

The origins of the Plan de San Diego remain unclear. Anglo-European authorities found the document in the possession of a Mexican American, Basilio Ramos. On December 13, 1915, a federal grand jury issued an indictment against Ramos and eight other revolutionaries for conspiracy to levy war against the United States.

The authorship of the document and military sponsorship of the insurrections have not been confirmed. According to Ramos, the document was smuggled into the Monterrey prison where the conspirators were jailed. On his release, Ramos carried a signed copy of the document to Matamoros, Mexico, and later across to Brownsville, Texas, to begin recruiting for the insurrection. He was captured by Francisco Villa's army and was turned over to U.S. federal authorities.

Some theories suggest the Plan was drafted by W. M. Hanson, a supporter of the Mexican president (by coup) Victoriano Huerta, to instigate conflict between the various political factions vying for power in Mexico. Others have argued that it was authored by Mexican Americans to liberate the Southwest. Most historians consider the Plan to have been part of a broader conspiracy authored by Huerta to carry out his counterrevolution, and recent interpretations suggest that Huerta's followers initiated the Plan and later involved Mexican president Venustiano Carranza. The raids ended with the recognition of Carranza's government by Washington, D.C., on October 19, 1915.

A second plan was reissued in July 1915, a Manifesto to the Oppressed Peoples of America. The release of the new plan was accompanied by a series of raids in the lower Rio Grande Valley. Although no specific political objectives were articulated by the border revolutionaries, controversy continues to exist surrounding these incidents. It has been suggested that the revolutionaries operated from the Mexican side of the border and that they were followers of Carranza. One of the revolutionaries was Luis de la Rosa, a former deputy sheriff in Cameron County, Texas; another, Ancieta Pizaña, was a Carrancista (supporter of Carranza) and the second in command of the uprising.

Although the goals of the conspiracy would have been difficult to implement, the Plan de San Diego had important repercussions for relations between Mexico and the United States and relations between Mexicans and Anglos along the border. One consequence was the U.S. government's increased patrol of the border, and its fortification of the number of Texas rangers to 50. On June 18, 1916, President Woodrow Wilson federalized the national guards of Texas, New Mexico, and Arizona to patrol the U.S.–Mexico border. Between July 1915 and July 1916, rebels carried out 30 raids into Texas, and U.S. law enforcement agents shot, hanged, or beat to death 300 "suspected" Mexicans. Rebels killed 21 Anglo-Europeans during the same period. The militarization of the border reached a high of 35,000 U.S. soldiers stationed at the border and relations between Mexico and the United States and between Mexicans and Anglos along the border remained tense for several decades.

RELATED ARTICLES

Politics, Mexican American; Southwestern United States, Anglo Immigration to.

FURTHER READING

Acuña, Rodolfo. *Occupied America: A History of Chicanos.* 4th ed. New York: Longman, 2000.

Gomez-Quinonez, Juan. "Plan De San Diego Reviewed." *Aztlán: Chicano Journal of the Social Sciences and the Arts* 1 (Spring 1970): 124–132.

Harris, Charles H., III, and Louis R. Sadler. "The Plan of San Diego and the Mexican–United States War Crisis of 1916: A Reexamination." *The Hispanic American Historical Review* 58 (August 1978): 381–408.

Harris, Charles H., III, and Louis R. Sadler. *The Border and the Revolution.* Las Cruces, N.Mex.: Ctr. for Latin Am. Studies/Joint Border Res. Inst., N.Mex. State Univ., 1988.

Smith, Michael M. "The Mexican Secret Service in the United States, 1910–1920." *The Americas* 59, no. 1 (July 2002): 65–85.

ARCELA NUÑEZ-ALVAREZ

SAN DIEGO REVOLT

The San Diego revolt of November 5, 1775, at Mission San Diego de Alcalá symbolized the resistance of Native Americans against the arrival of Spanish colonists in Alta California. After approximately six years of conflict between the Kumeyaay people, the native population in the San Diego area, and Spaniards, Native Americans organized a well-orchestrated revolt against Spaniards. Kumeyaay people set fire to the oldest mission in California. The Kumeyaay rebels killed Father Luis Jayme and two other Spaniards and forced the Spanish to seek refuge at the nearby military fortress or *presidio*.

The animosity Native Americans felt toward Spaniards arose from the treatment of the former by the latter and from the threat posed by the Spanish settlers. San Diego was the birthplace of Christianity on the West Coast. Following the founding of the mission in 1769, missionaries and soldiers began the

Hispanization of Native Americans who had lived in this area for thousands of years. Relations between Spaniards and Native Americans were characterized by conflict. Beginning in 1771, missionaries carried out the "spiritual conquest," or conversions, and attempted to persuade Native Americans to relocate near the mission. By 1775 close to 500 Native Americans had been baptized. These efforts, however, were met with strong resistance from the native people. In addition to the intensification of religious conversion efforts, rapes of Indian women were also reported. Furthermore, Spanish soldiers grazed cattle on native fields and grasslands, thereby harming the agricultural activities of native communities. Other reports indicated Kumeyaay fear of captivity was also a motive for the conflict between natives and Spaniards. These factors most likely played a role in the outbreak of the San Diego revolt.

On November 5, 1775, a group of natives from at least 15 villages attacked the mission. After the attack, the native rebels retreated. The revolt appears to have been organized and carried out by southern Kumeyaay-Tipai shamans and leaders. As well as recruiting supporters from their own ranks, they traveled from village to village inciting the indigenous residents, relying on traditional village alliances. They sought to seek redress of grievances perpetrated by Spaniards against particular clans.

The San Diego revolt complicated the missionary efforts in southern California. After the revolt it took the friars one and one-half years before resuming their efforts. Father Junípero Serra returned in 1777 to begin rebuilding the mission. Thirteen alleged leaders of the revolt were jailed under the supervision of Lieutenant Ortega and Captain Rivera, and several prisoners were sent into exile in Baja California.

Tension between Spaniards and Kumeyaay continued, however, the result of the clash of two cultures. Despite the tensions, Father Serra reestablished the mission according to the specifications of an army fort and reinstated the conversions of local natives. The mission was the least economically successful of all the California missions, but the "spiritual conquest" was successful. In 1797 the mission reported 565 baptisms, 1,405 souls converted to Christianity, and 50,000 acres (20,200 sq ha) of land area under the control of the mission. Furthermore, the mission owned 20,000 sheep, 10,000 head of cattle, and 1,250 horses. By 1821, when Mexico gained its independence from Spain, the mission enjoyed some stability.

After the Mexican-American War (1846–1848), the mission of San Diego was used for artillery and cavalry. In 1892 the mission was transformed into a school for Native American children, and in 1931 the mission was rebuilt and preserved. It continues to be an active Catholic Church and is a historical landmark symbolizing the arrival of Europeans on the Pacific Coast and the struggle of native people to maintain their way of life.

RELATED ARTICLES

California; Indian Wars; Indigenous Heritage; Missions; Serra, Junípero.

FURTHER READING

Carrico, Richard L. "Sociopolitical Aspects of the 1775 Revolt at Mission San Diego de Alcalá: An Ethnohistorical Approach." *The Journal of San Diego History* 43, no. 3 (1997).

Costo, Rupert, and Jeannette Henry Costo. *The Missions of California: A Legacy of Genocide.* San Francisco: Am. Indian Hist. Soc. Indian Historian Press , 1987.

Hurtado, Albert L. *Intimate Frontiers: Sex, Gender, and Culture in Old California.* Albuquerque: Univ. of N.Mex. Press, 1999.

Mancall, Peter C., and James Hart Merrell. *American Encounters: Natives and Newcomers from European Contact to Indian Removal, 1500–1850.* New York: Routledge, 2000.

Pourade, Richard F. *The Explorers.* San Diego: Union-Tribune Publ., 1960.

Weber, Francis J. *The Proto Mission: A Documentary History of San Diego De Alcalá.* Hong Kong: Libra Press, 1980.

ARCELA NUÑEZ-ALVAREZ

SANDOVAL, ARTURO

Born: November 6, 1949; Artemisa, Cuba

As illustrated throughout some 20 solo recordings, the Cuban trumpeter, percussionist, and composer Arturo Sandoval has mastered the disciplines of jazz, classical, and Cuban music with an equal degree of authority. Born in Artemisa, a small town near Havana, Sandoval started playing music at the age of 13 with a local *son* septet. After experimenting on many instruments, he settled on the trumpet. From 1964 to 1967 he studied classical trumpet at Havana's Escuela Nacional de Arte, where he came under the influence of Luis Escalante, one of the best classical trumpeters in all of Cuba. In 1967 Sandoval joined the groundbreaking, all-star big band called Orquesta Cubana de Música Moderna. By this time he was

© JACQUES LOWE/RETNA

Jazz great, trumpeter Arturo Sandoval.

dom" (1991) on the GRP label. It appears that his U.S. discography as a bandleader has been studiously designed to showcase the exiled horn-man's facility with everything from Clifford Brown's bop to Hummel's trumpet concerto to Cuba's *son* and *danzón* traditions. Since his defection Sandoval has won four Grammy Awards and increased his classical performances worldwide, including collaborations with the National Symphony Orchestra, Los Angeles Philharmonic, Pittsburgh Symphony, London Symphony Orchestra, Oklahoma Symphony, and Atlanta Symphony Orchestra, among others. His trumpet playing can also be heard on the soundtracks of various Hollywood movies (*Havana, Mambo Kings,* and *The Perez Family,* among others).

Although he is better known as the most influential Latin jazz trumpeter of our time, Sandoval revealed his lifelong romance with the piano on the CD (compact disc) appropriately titled *My Passion for the Piano* (2001; Crescent Moon/Columbia). Moreover, on other occasions he showed his ability on the flugelhorn, combining the consistent fluidity of a Clark Terry with the dazzling speed of a Freddy Hubbard. Sandoval's life story was portrayed by Andy Garcia in the HBO (Home Box Office) original movie *For Love or for Country: The Arturo Sandoval Story* (1999), filmed in Miami, at the height of the Elían González controversy.

RELATED ARTICLES

Jazz; Music, Classical; Music, Popular.

FURTHER READING

Acosta, Leonardo. *Raices del jazz latino: Un siglo de jazz en Cuba* (Roots of Latin Jazz: A Century of Jazz in Cuba). Barranquilla, Colombia: La Iguana Ciega, 2001.

Birnbaum, Larry. "Cubano Bopper and the Mambo King." *Downbeat* (June 1993): 16–21.

Charres, Rafael. "Arturo Sandoval: A Man with a Horn and a Purpose." *Rhythm Music Magazine* 3, no. 9 (1994): 46–48.

Chediak, Nat. *Diccionario de jazz latino* ("Dictionary of Latin Jazz"). Madrid: Fundación Autor, 1998.

Diaz Ayala, Cristobal. *Cuando salí de La Habana, 1898–1997: Cien años de música cubana por el mundo* (When I Left Havana, 1898–1997: A Hundred Years of Cuban Music around the World). San Juan, Puerto Rico: Fundación Musicalia, 1998.

LUIS TAMARGO

fascinated with jazz and truly idolized Dizzy Gillespie and Clifford Brown. In 1974 he became one of the main improvisational firebrands of Irakere, which soon became Cuba's most important jazz band. Irakere's late 1970s and early 1980s recordings for CBS (Columbia Broadcasting System) and Milestone acquainted many North Americans with Sandoval's uncanny ability in the higher register of his instrument.

Sandoval left Irakere, however, in 1981, to organize his own band, with the pianist Hilario Durán as musical director. For a decade he combined this work with high-profile collaborators, recording with Dizzy Gillespie on the highly acclaimed LP (long-playing record) *To a Finland Station* (1982; Pablo). It was while touring in 1990 with Gillespie's United Nation Orchestra that he requested political asylum at the U.S. embassy in Rome.

Sandoval resettled in Miami, where he became a professor at Florida International University. Shortly afterward he recorded his U.S. debut "Flight to Free-

SANTA ANNA, ANTONIO LÓPEZ DE

Born: February 21, 1794; Jalapa, Veracruz, Mexico
Died: June 21, 1876; Mexico City, Mexico

The destiny of Antonio López de Santa Anna was historically linked with the fates of two nations, the United States and Mexico. He was born Antonio López de Santa Anna Pérez de Lebrón, in Jalapa, in what is now the state of Veracruz, Mexico. His parents were respected and of Spanish background, his father a colonial official and army officer. Santa Anna left school early and became a military cadet as a teenager.

With Mexican independence in 1821, Santa Anna, a rising military leader, pledged support to new Mexican emperor Augustín de Iturbide. The emperor was toppled when opponents—then including Santa Anna—revolted, and he later died by firing squad. In the following years a series of governments forced their way to power with Santa Anna's military backing. As one regime lost favor, the wily general would switch sides, joining the opposing forces. By these means, his first term as *el presidente* ("the president") began in 1832. Most of his terms in power were despotic.

Mexico at this time included what would later become the American states of the Southwest: Texas, New Mexico, Utah, Nevada, and California. But in 1836 Santa Anna faced rebellious "Texans" demanding independence. In the Battle of the Alamo, thousands of Santa Anna's soldiers overwhelmed rebels holed up in an old mission building; prisoners were executed. The self-styled "Napoleon of the West" then led his forces toward a smaller Texas force commanded by Sam Houston near San Jacinto. As the Mexicans rested in camp on April 21, 1836, the Texans took them by surprise. A bewildered Santa Anna was captured on foot in civilian clothes. *El presidente* was now a prisoner, an end to hostilities was negotiated, and the rebels proclaimed a Texas Republic. Santa Anna returned to Mexico in humiliation. He was exiled to Havana in 1845, after yet another stint in power.

Mexican tempers flared when an expanding United States annexed Texas in 1845. Tensions mounted until the U.S. declared war on Mexico on May 13, 1846, after a skirmish at the disputed Texas-Mexico boundary. American authorities let Santa Anna slip through a naval blockade and back into Mexico, hoping he would reach a settlement with the U.S. once in power, according to historians. But once there, he quickly organized armies in defense. The general—popular again—marched to Mexico City to halt General Winfield Scott's invasion force. But the Americans defeated his armies and occupied the city on September 14, 1847. The next year almost half of Mexico's territory was ceded to the United States in the Treaty of Guadalupe Hidalgo. It was a devastating blow to national pride. Despite this, Santa Anna remained at the helm of Mexican affairs until 1855, when he was overthrown by new nationalists who sent him into exile for the last time. He was largely forgotten and ignored on his return to Mexico in 1874. Santa Anna died at age 82, still believing himself the savior of his country.

RELATED ARTICLES

Alamo, Battle of the; United States–Mexico Relations.

FURTHER READING

Callcott, Wilfred Hardy. *Santa Anna: The Story of an Enigma Who Was Mexico.* Norman: Univ of Okla. Press, 1936.
Costeloe, Michael P. *The Central Republic in Mexico, 1835–1846.* Cambridge: Cambridge Univ. Press, 1993.
Krauze, Enrique. *Mexico: Biography of Power.* New York: HarperCollins, 1997.
Olivera, Ruth R., and Crété, Liliane. *Life in Mexico under Santa Anna 1822–1855.* Norman: Univ of Okla. Press, 1991.
Richmond, Douglas W., ed. *Essays on the Mexican War.* College Station: Tex. A&M Univ. Press, 1986.
Santa Anna, Antonio Lopez de. *The Eagle: The Autobiography of Santa Anna.* Austin, Tex.: Pemberton Press, 1967.
Singletary, Otis A. *The Mexican War.* Chicago: Univ. of Chicago Press, 1960.
Wharton, Clarence R. *El Presidente: A Sketch of the Life of General Santa Anna.* Houston, Tex.: C. C. Young Printing Co., 1924.
Wilentz, Sean, ed. *Major Problems in the Early Republic 1787–1848.* Lexington, Mass.: D. C. Heath, 1992.

E. MARK MORENO

SANTA BÁRBARA, PLAN DE

A 154-page document including a manifesto, an outline of political action, strategies for campus organizing, and guidelines for creating Chicano studies departments, the Plan de Santa Bárbara was promulgated by the University of California at Santa Barbara (UCSB) in 1969. The Chicano Youth Liberation Conference, organized by the Crusade for Justice in Denver, on March 30, 1969, catapulted the Chicano civil rights movement to the national civil rights scene. Following the Denver conference, the Chicano Council on Higher Education (CCHE), a collective of students, faculty, staff, and community activists, met at the UCSB in mid-April to formulate a Chicano plan of higher education.

The CCHE exposed the condition of Chicanos as undereducated and disenfranchised within the educational system and proposed a plan to dismantle their marginalization. The blueprint called for implementation of the following initiatives:

(1) admission and recruitment of Chicano students, faculty, administrators, and staff;

(2) a curriculum program and an academic major relevant to the Chicano cultural and historical experience;

(3) tutorial programs and support services;

(4) research programs;

(5) publication programs; and

(6) community cultural and social action centers. These initiatives were intended to diversify the staff and curriculum, democratize the access to higher education, enrich cultural awareness, and promote community development.

The philosophy behind the Plan was rooted in "the just struggle" and analysis of the "community's strategic needs." The manifesto reaffirmed the use of the term *Chicano* as a positive term of cultural identity. The Plan cited racism and discrimination as the main obstacles to realizing the "American Dream," pointing out that Mexicans were "suppliers of cheap labor." Therefore, the CCHE offered the state of California recommendations to improve educational access and opportunities.

Defining political action as a means of influencing the decision-making process of institutions such as education, the Plan de Santa Bárbara provided a working ideology of Chicanismo, a concept that invoked cultural pride and self-awareness, and it assigned Chicano students with the task of disseminating information and mobilizing resources to enhance educational opportunity. The student activists were charged with creating a "network of activists who will respond as a unit to oppression and racism" and with promoting cultural awareness. Under the umbrella organization of the Movimiento Estudiantil Chicano de Aztlán (MEChA), a student organization, students were assigned the roles of leaders and educators. The Plan suggested programs and services to bridge the gaps between Chicano communities and institutions of higher education. To this end,

the Plan recommended that members from community agencies serve on programs related to Chicanos, that community centers offer courses, and that colleges and universities diversify their academic and nonacademic personnel.

In the area of community development, students were given five major responsibilities:

(1) policing social and governmental agencies to ensure culturally proficient delivery of programs and services;

(2) conducting research on the economic and credit policies of businesses in Mexican communities to ensure implementation of legal and ethical codes;

(3) carrying outreach to middle school and high school students;

(4) providing public information and education resources; and

(5) exposing discrimination and racism against Chicanos. Fulfillment of these objectives was intended to facilitate the progress and development of the Mexican community.

Despite the positive outcomes originating from the Plan, critics have pointed out several weaknesses, one critique maintaining that the Plan proposed a narrow vision for Chicano studies. Current debates regarding the original purpose, philosophy, relationship between academy and community, and ethnic identity will influence the future of Chicano studies and the interpretation of the original aspirations in the Plan de Santa Bárbara.

RELATED ARTICLES

Chicanismo; Chicano Movement; Politics, Mexican American.

FURTHER READING

Chicano Coordinating Council on Higher Education. *El Plan de Santa Bárbara; A Chicano Plan for Higher Education.* Santa Barbara, Calif.: La Causa Pubs., 1971.

Gómez-Quiñonez, Juan. *Chicano Politics: Reality and Promise, 1940–1990.* Albuquerque: Univ. of N.Mex. Press, 1990.

Maciel, David, and Isidro D. Ortiz. *Chicanas/Chicanos at the Crossroads: Social, Economic, and Political Change.* Tucson: Univ. of Ariz. Press, 1996.

Muñoz, Carlos, Jr. *Youth, Identity, Power: The Chicano Movement.* New York: Verso, 1989.

Rochin, Refugio I., and Dennis Nodín Valdés. *Voices of a New Chicana/O History.* East Lansing: Mich. State Univ. Press, 2000.

ARCELA NUÑEZ-ALVAREZ

SANTA FÉ, NEW MEXICO.

Circa 1840 American engraving of a wagon train entering Santa Fe, New Mexico.

SANTA FE EXPEDITION

The Santa Fe Expedition of 1841 was an ill-fated venture on the part of the Texas Republic to seize eastern New Mexican settlements and capitalize on the trade that swelled the Santa Fe Trail. Texas president Mirabeau B. Lamar was intent on reducing the substantial debts of the young republic as well as staking Texas's claim to surrounding territories. Without legal sanction, Lamar sent a group of commission-ers, merchants, and militiamen to carry out the annexation. State senator José Antonio Navarro was among them.

Navarro was reluctant to participate, however. Perhaps to facilitate communication with the area's indigenous Mexican population, Lamar personally persuaded Navarro to join the group. With misgiv-ings, Navarro accepted the appointment in the hopes that he would be able to protect the indigenous peoples if they did come under Texas rule. Poor provisions, attacks by Native Americans, and faulty navigation soon caused the expedition to falter. Leaving Texas in mid-June of 1841, the group did not arrive at its destination until nearly four months later.

Expecting to be welcomed by the local populace, the expeditionary force was surprised when the Mexican government, under the leadership of Governor Manuel Armijo, dispatched militia to Santa Fe to arrest them. The Texans had sent an advance party to Santa Fe that included Captain William G. Lewis. Having met with the Mexican militia, Lewis turned traitor and assisted the Mexicans with the surrender of the remaining party. Not a single shot was fired.

Navarro and the others were taken prisoner and marched to Mexico City. Of special importance to Mexican president Antonio López de Santa Anna was Navarro's punishment. Calling him the "vilest of traitors," Santa Anna had Navarro placed under extra security and sentenced to life imprisonment. The U.S. government was able to have most of the expeditioners freed; Navarro, however, was at the mercy of the Mexican president.

While Navarro remained in prison, his home was invaded twice by Mexican troops. Relations between Anglos and Tejanos in San Antonio and elsewhere in Texas quickly deteriorated as a result. When American soldiers descended on San Antonio to aid in fighting the Mexicans, they made no distinction between Tejanos and Mexican aggressors. Rumors of Mexican insurrection and treason spread through Texas and caused Anglos in San Antonio to threaten the life of the former revolutionary hero Juan N. Seguin.

In 1844 Navarro escaped from prison, and a British vessel took him first to Cuba and New Orleans before finally arriving in Texas. His affiliation with the Santa Fe Expedition and his subsequent imprisonment added to his reputation—he was one of the signers of the Texas Declaration of Independence.

The failed Santa Fe Expedition was indicative of the tension between Mexico and the United States in the mid-19th century. In 1846 Texas was admitted as a state to the United States and soon thereafter entered the Mexican-American War. This war, settled by the Treaty of Guadalupe Hidalgo in 1848, resulted in the ceding of both New Mexico and California to the United States.

RELATED ARTICLES

Guadalupe Hidalgo, Treaty of; New Mexico; Southwestern United States, Anglo Immigration to.

FURTHER READING

Crisp, James Ernest. "Anglo-Texan Attitudes toward the Mexican, 1821–1845." Ph.D. diss., Yale Univ., 1976.

Matovina, Timothy M. "Between Two Worlds." In *Tejano Journey, 1770–1850.* Ed. by Gerald E. Poyo. Austin: Univ. of Tex. Press, 1996.

Matovina, Timothy M., and David R. McDonald, eds. *Defending Mexican Valor in Texas: Jose Antonio Navarro's Historical Writings, 1853–1857.* Austin, Tex.: State House Press, 1995.

Montejano, David. *Anglos and Mexicans in the Making of Texas, 1836–1986.* Austin: Univ. of Tex. Press, 1987.

DESIRÉE GARCIA

SANTANA, CARLOS

Born: July 20, 1947; Autlán de Navarro, Mexico

Carlos Santana, musician, guitar virtuoso, and Latino rock icon, was the fourth of seven children born to José and Josefina Santana. The son of a violinist, Santana's first instrument was the violin and his first musical exposure was mariachi. Eventually, he would fall in love with the guitar and rock and roll.

The family moved to Tijuana, Mexico, in 1955 when Santana was 8, and in 1962, when he was 15, they moved to San Francisco. He returned to Tijuana and performed with a local band, The TJs, at a local strip club. Before the move to San Francisco, Santana had already begun playing music in Tijuana on the street and in clubs and was determined to follow in his father's footsteps and become a professional musician. His parents, however, were concerned for their young son, and a year later Carlos, escorted by his mother and oldest brother, Antonio, rejoined his family in northern California.

By this time Santana was listening to the music of blues musicians like T-Bone Walker and B. B. King, and Latin jazz artists such as Tito Puente and Mongo Santamaria. Living in San Francisco in the early 1960s, he was exposed to the growing music scene. He spent time at local clubs, occasionally getting a chance to play. Santana's big break came in 1966, when he stepped in to jam with the guitarist Mike Bloomfield at the Fillmore West, owned by the concert promoter Bill Graham.

So impressed was Graham with this young musician that he gave Santana and his group, the Santana Blues Band, a chance to perform at the Woodstock

Carlos Santana (*right*) performing at the Woodstock music festival in 1969.

music festival in 1969. There, Santana's Latin rhythms, accentuated by conga drums and the timbale and mixed with blues and bold guitar solos, established his band as a new sound in rock and roll.

The song *Evil Ways,* written by Peter Green, would be the band's first hit from its debut album, *Santana,* in 1969. The next year the band released *Abraxas,* which contained two hits, *Black Magic Woman* and the infamous *Oye Como Va,* by Tito Puente. The album would become a quadruple-platinum seller.

Over the years Santana's style evolved to incorporate jazz while still remaining loyal to his Latin and blues roots. In 1995 he released a four-CD (compact disc) compilation of his work titled *Dance of the Rainbow Serpent.*

Santana received his first Grammy Award in 1988 for Best Rock Instrumental Performance for his solo record *Blues for Salvador.* And he experienced a renaissance in 1999, when he released his 36th album, *Supernatural.* The album scored platinum sales 14 times, and in 2000 Santana took home eight more

Grammy Awards, including Record of the Year and Song of the Year.

Santana parlayed his tremendous success into the creation of the Milagro Foundation for arts education. The foundation is supported by private donations as well as from a portion of the sales of Santana's women's shoe line, Carlos, which was launched in 2000. He was included in the Hollywood Rock Walk in 1996, and in 1998 he and the original Santana Blues Band were inducted into the Rock and Roll Hall of Fame.

For his work in the Latino community, Santana received a Golden Eagle Award from Nosotros in 1997, an Alma Award in 1999 from the National Council of La Raza, and a Latino Spirit Award in 2003 from the Latino Caucus of the California Assembly. On August 30, 2004, Santana was honored as the 2004 Latin Recording Academy Person of the Year. Gabriel Abaroa, president of the academy, called the musician "an extraordinary human being, musician and activist who has made a global impact on music and culture."

In 2002 Santana released the album *Shaman.* He has been married since 1973; he and his wife, Deborah, have three children.

RELATED ARTICLES

Music, Popular; Puente, Tito; Rock-en-Español.

FURTHER READING

Leng, Simon. *Soul Sacrifice: The Santana Story.* London: Firefly Pub., 2000.

Menard, Valerie. "The Man behind the Music: Carlos Santana Sends a Message of Hope to Fellow Latinos." *Hispanic* (March 1996): 19–22.

Fong-Torres, Ben. "He Wails for the World." *Parade* (March 20, 2003): 4–5.

SELECTED WEB SITE

Carlos Santana. www.santana.com

VALERIE MENARD

SANTERÍA

Santería, also referred to as Regla de Ocha (the religion, order, or rule of the orisha) is—with Regla de Palo, and the Abakuá Secret Society—one of the major Afro-Cuban religious practices. It is a religion based on the traditions of the enslaved Yoruba-speaking groups from Africa—a group that predominated on the island in the final stages of the Cuban slave trade—combined with the imposed Roman Catholicism of the Spanish colonists and settlers. In Cuba during the colonial period, the Catholic Church sponsored institutions, *cabildos,* that were based on the mutual aid confraternities or religious brotherhoods, common throughout Europe in the Middle Ages, that organized to assist one another and to honor their patron saint. The African population in Cuba, excluded from white confraternities, were permitted to govern and organize their own, to plan communal feasts, dances, and carnival processions, and to help members in need. Replacing families and institutions that had been lost in slavery, these *cabildos* also provided a structure for enslaved Africans to evolve their alternative religious systems. They became the site for the syncretic process between Catholicism and the African traditions by which Africans and their descendants transformed imposed institutional structures to support their own African cultural and religious practices—which would give rise eventually to the Afro-Cuban religions. Borrowing from Catholic discourse, Africans and their descendants reinterpreted it in terms of their own religions.

The saints, Jesus Christ, and the Virgin Mary were identified with African gods or ancestors who, in return for sacrifices, would protect or assist blacks in their daily lives. Debate exists about the actual degree of syncretism between Catholicism and African worship, as most devotees clearly distinguished between the two: the slaves danced before a Catholic altar, but their chants and entreaties were actually addressed to African divinities. Though the condition of slavery obscured or eliminated certain African rituals that were replaced or combined with Catholic ceremonies, African religious traditions survived nevertheless and predominate in practices that thrive in the present day. Of the three major Afro-Cuban religions practiced in Cuba today, Santería, or Regla de Ocha, is the most widespread, although there is much commingling among the practices, which demonstrate a significant degree of syncretism among them. In addition, all of the Afro-Cuban religious practices are, in fact, more than religions; they affect a wide area of the culture encompassing language, art, music, pharmacology, and psychotherapy.

Worshippers are called *santeros,* for they venerate the Yoruba deities—*orishas*—which are also referred to as *santos* since they were syncretized with Catholic saints. Beneath the supreme creator in the Yoruba hierarchy—Olodumare—is the pantheon of *orishas,* spirits created in some cases prior to the creation of

© COLIN BRALEY/REUTERS/LANDOV

A resident of Miami's Little Havana district is blessed by a Santería high priest (*babalao*) before a dove is sacrificed in a cleansing ceremony.

human beings, and others who were human at one time and evolved into deities because of some remarkable quality. *Orishas* intercede in the daily lives of humans and, if appeased, can help humankind. They are messengers and embodiments of *aché*, a spiritual command and vital force that permeates all aspects of life and motivates the world both sacred and profane; the propagation of *aché* in rituals and ceremonies is believed to bring balance, well-being, and harmony. Since the *orishas* in Cuba were referred to by the Spanish word *santos,* this led to naming the practice Santería, the worship or way of the saints.

The *orishas* are spiritual entities that have been anthropomorphized and identified with a force of nature and an aspect of human character or personality. For nearly every *orisha* there is a corresponding Catholic saint based on associations made by the slaves between the mythology of the *orishas* and attributes or qualities identified with the saints, particularly as perceived in the iconographic representation of the latter in the statues and chromolithographs that were an important element of popular colonial Catholicism and religious instruction. The hagiographies of the saints that described their lives and legacies would bring to mind characteristics that could be associated with a particular *orisha.* Thus the popular and powerful Yoruba *orisha* of fire and thunder, Changó, for example, was identified in Cuba with the patroness of Spanish artillery, Santa Bárbara, because of her representation in chromolithographs dressed in red—Changó's symbolic color—and her identification with the thundering artillery cannons. An alternative explanation takes into account the legends surrounding Santa Bárbara's pagan father who, to separate her from the Christians, had her locked in a tower. Upon discovering her Christian faith, her father gave her up to the authorities where she was condemned to death for her faith and beheaded with a sword—one of Changó's attributes. As one version of the legend also states that her father was struck by lightning, her association with Changó becomes even clearer.

If their specific origins are varied and complex, so too are the *orishas'* Christianized representations, which vary from one locale to the next within a particular country, and from country to country within the African diaspora. These variations are based on historical and environmental factors; *orishas* changed as a result of their transplantation to the New World and in their adjustment to the various regions of the diaspora and as a result have numerous *caminos*—avatars, aspects, paths or roads, identities, forms, or manifestations. *Orishas* are also protean and multifaceted in character: Eleguá, the messenger deity who opens or closes paths, indicates the crossroads (the future), and must be propitiated before any other *orisha,* is a mischievous trickster. Among the other more well known and worshiped deities are Ogún, the *orisha* of war, iron, the instruments of work, minerals, the mountain, and the forge, a warrior and blacksmith; Yemayá, the great universal mother and deity of maternity and fertility, of the sea and saltwater, who gave birth to all of the *orishas* as well as to the sun and the moon; Obatalá, the god of purity and justice who represents truth, purity, peace, and compassion and has several male and female aspects, who is also the archetypal spirit of creativity; Ochún, Santería's Aphrodite, the deity of rivers, freshwaters, gold, representing female sensuality, love, beauty, and sexual desire, and who is identified with Cuba's patron saint, the Virgen de la Caridad del Cobre; Oyá, a female warrior deity who often fights at the side of Changó, mistress of lightning, the wind, and gatekeeper of the cemetery; Orula, the deity and master of divination; Babalú Ayé, Saint Lazarus for the Christians, the crippled *orisha* who heals and preaches good habits, receiving the veneration of all. While their principal forms can have a Catholic equivalent, each *orisha* may have several forms, which helps to explain the variety of Christianized representations in Cuban Santería and other Creolized practices.

To obtain their *aché, orishas* must be propitiated through an *ebó*—sacrifice-offering spell—which has the double purpose of honoring the deities and communicating *aché* from spiritual being to human. The sacrifice can range from a simple offering of fruit, candles, food, or flowers appropriate to the attributes of a particular *orisha* to, for a serious problem and if so indicated in divination, a blood sacrifice involving a specific sacrificial animal. *Orishas* are identified with specific numbers, foods, and plants used in their worship, and explicit chants, drum rhythms, dance movements, and sacred narratives of their lives and relationships. Thus spiritual work to venerate Ochún, for example, would be done using her number and attributes: five yellow candles and cakes, amber beads, and so on, are required to obtain Ochún's *aché.* The offering is then transformed into *aché* to carry out the needs of the petitioner.

The primary representation of the *orishas* is found in the *otanes,* or sacred stones, that are typically kept in a soup tureen and "fed" with the blood of sacrificed animals and ritual liquid so that in and through the *otanes* the *orisha* can drink up nourishment in the form of *aché.* The sacred stones summon the *orishas* to come down and take possession of their spiritual children in ritual practices to communicate with them and confirm that they accept their sacrifices. Elements of a here-and-now, crisis-oriented religion, the herbs, stones, amulets, necklaces, and other ritual objects used in worship are vital for achieving its magical or healing purposes. Humans, it is believed, can find balance and peace holistically by maintaining personal, social, and cosmic harmony, living in accord with their destiny (discovered through divination), proper character, appropriate behavior, and a relationship with and worship of the *orishas.*

After the abolition of slavery in the late 19th century and the elimination of the traditional *cabildos,* house temples headed by initiated *santeros* and *santeras* emerged to continue the tradition for the next generations and to form a spiritual family in the religion. Gradually a range of Cubans of all backgrounds and classes were drawn to the religion, despite the repression and social derision attached to the African-based practice. The various waves of Cuban exiles to the United States after the Cuban revolution in 1959, called by some the "second diaspora" of Yoruba religion, has created challenges and served to inspire and create a pan-diaspora tradition of the *orishas* beyond the borders of Cuba and beyond the Cuban exiles themselves. The preservation, maintenance, and revelation of the religion's secrets and mysteries (tightly guarded for years for the protection of the practice from nonsympathetic and openly hostile forces, and even from those considered nominally sympathetic) has been the task of courageous and devoted priests and priestesses who have handed down the knowledge of the religion's mysteries orally for generations.

It is claimed that the first *babalao,* or high priest, arrived in the United States in 1946. Prior to the 1959 Cuban revolution, godparents took their godchildren to Cuba to be initiated; the first initiations in the United States took place in the 1960s. The lack of a ritual infrastructure—the necessary ritual resources, especially the herbs that were purchased in the "botanical gardens" of New York City's barrio (precursors to the *botánicas* seen in major cities today),

the lack of ritual specialists of initiation and of the sacred *batá* drums and initiated drummers—delayed the reconstitution of Afro-Cuban religious practice in the United States. Exile and the displacement of the devotees of the *orishas* to a new foreign culture had once again tested the adaptability of an old tradition in a new environment. In its transplantation outside of Cuba, and particularly to the United States, Santería blended with Puerto Rican Espiritismo in such areas as New York and New Jersey, begetting what some refer to as "Santerismo," which was adopted by a significant non-Cuban population in the United States and Europe. Santería/Regla de Ocha has in recent years, become identified by many who study African diasporic cultures as the *orisha* tradition, a term that encompasses the various approaches to *orisha* worship in Africa and throughout the world, and the ethnic diversity, social composition, and ritual practices of contemporary Santería/Regla de Ocha houses. In the United States, most Santería/Regla de Ocha houses include a mosaic of people from Latin America, North America, and the English- and French-speaking Caribbean.

For Cuban exiles, however, Santería has taken on a special meaning: an alternative medical system, a support system, and a coping mechanism for dealing with the stress of exile and immigration, eliminating the feelings of guilt resulting from such dramatic life changes; and a way of expressing cultural identity in a foreign society without the socioeconomic and racial restrictions that some might have encountered in their homeland. Once again, the religion serves to substitute for lost kin, severed ties, and a missing sense of belonging. Always flexible, the Afro-Cuban religions change with their travels, adapting to a new population and a new environment, winning a new legitimacy for ancient practices that have not simply survived but flourished in a modern world.

RELATED ARTICLES

Afro-Latino Influences; Catholicism; Cuban Americans; Religion; Saints; Spirituality.

FURTHER READING

Fernández Olmos, Margarite, and Lizabeth Paravisini-Gebert. *Sacred Possessions: Vodou, Santería, Obeah, and the Caribbean.* New Brunswick, N.J.: Rutgers Univ. Press, 1997.

Fernández Olmos, Margarite, and Lizabeth Paravisini-Gebert. *Creole Religions of the Caribbean: An Introduction from Vodou and Santería to Obeah and Espiritismo.* New York: N.Y. Univ. Press, 2003.

González-Wippler, Migene. *Santería: The Religion.* New York: Harmony Bks., 1989.

Murphy, Joseph M. *Santería: African Spirits in America.* Boston: Beacon Press, 1993.

Stevens, Anthony M., and Ana María Díaz-Stevens, eds. *An Enduring Flame: Studies on Latino Popular Religiosity.* New York: Bildner Ctr. for Western Hemisphere Studies, 1994.

Vélez, María Teresa. *Drumming for the Gods: The Life and Times of Felipe García Villamil, Santero, Palero, and Abakuá.* Philadelphia: Temple Univ. Press, 2000.

MARGARITE FERNÁNDEZ OLMOS

SARDINAS, ELIGIO. *See* KID CHOCOLATE.

SCHOMBURG, ARTHUR

Born: January 24, 1874; Puerto Rico
Died: June 10, 1938; Brooklyn, New York

A legendary bibliophile and collector of black folk art as well as a member of the generation of intellectuals in New York City that came to be known as the Harlem Renaissance, Arturo Alfonso Schomburg grew up in Santurce, Puerto Rico's capital. His father was a mestizo merchant with German heritage, and his mother a black midwife from the island of St. Croix, in the Virgin Islands. With this mixture, he identified himself as an "Afroborinqueño," part African and part Puerto Rican.

Schomburg attended the Instituto Popular in San Juan, Puerto Rico, and St. Thomas College in St. Thomas, Virgin Islands. After his fifth-grade teacher observed that "Black people have no history, no heroes, no great moments," he decided to devote his life to the catalog and study of African artifacts. Decades later, already an integral part of the New York City scene, Schomburg would announce: "The American Negro must rebuild his past in order to make his future. Though it is orthodox to think of America as the one country where it is unnecessary to have a past, what is a luxury for the nation as a whole becomes a prime social necessity for the Negro. For him, a group tradition must supply compensation for persecution, and pride of race the antidote for prejudice. History must restore what slavery took away, for it is the social damage of slavery that the present generation must repair and offset."

Moving to New York City in 1891, Schomburg lived on the Lower East Side. He attended night school at Manhattan Central High School and soon got involved with Cubans and Puerto Ricans in the city. It was the eve of the Spanish-American War, and his sympathies were with the colonized people of the Caribbean Basin. Along with other prominent Hispanic intellectuals of the time, such as José Martí and Eugenio María de Hostos, he fought for the independence of Cuba and Puerto Rico through Las Dos Antillas (The Two Antilles) club, which he helped organize. Through his travels to New Orleans, Seville, the Caribbean, and elsewhere, he consolidated a collection of some 10,000 items, including books (slave narratives, in particular), manuscripts, etchings, almanacs, journals, and pamphlets.

Schomburg married three times, the first time to Elizabeth Bessie Hatcher from Staunton, Virginia. They had three sons, Máximo Gómez, Arthur Alfonso, Jr., and Kingsley Guarionex. After she died in 1900, he married Elizabeth Morrow Taylor from Williamsburg, North Carolina. She too died, leaving two young sons, Reginald Stanfield and Nathaniel José. And around 1914 he married Elizabeth Green, a nurse, with whom he had three more children: Fernando, Dolores Marie, and Plácido Carlos. All of Schomburg's children except the last three lived with their maternal relatives.

In 1911 Schomburg cofounded the Negro Society for Historical Research, an entity devoted to black history. A couple of years later he was inducted into, and later presided over, the American Negro Academy. Eventually, he became a curator at Fisk University's Negro Collection. As an essayist, he collaborated on W. E. B. Du Bois's journal *Crisis* and on Alain Locke's anthology *The New Negro: An Interpretation* (1925), among scores of other works. Subjects of his writing are the Puerto Rican artist José Campeche, the Haitian freedom fighter Toussaint L'Ouverture, and the Afro-Cuban general Antonio Maceo. Although these and other profiles and articles are still in need of a comprehensive, annotated anthology, a handful are available in Flor Piñeiro de Rivera's *Arthur A. Schomburg: A Puerto Rican's Quest for His Black Heritage.* A biography of Schomburg by Elinor Des Vernay Sinnette appeared in 1989.

Schomburg's lifelong collection was presented to the New York Public Library's Division of Negro History in 1926 through a $10,000 grant from the Carnegie Foundation. He himself curated it. Today the collection is part of the Schomburg Center for

Research in Black Culture. It comprises almost 6 million items, including photographs, films, audio recordings, and institutional archives. Today much of the Center's records are available online.

At the dawn of World War II, at Schomburg's memorial, on June 8, 1939, Charles Spurgeon Johnson's celebrated his legacy stating that his collection was a visible monument to the life's work of Arthur Schomburg. It stands for itself, quietly and solidly for all time, a rich and inexhaustible treasure store for scholars and the public alike, the materialization of his foresight, industry, and scholarship.

RELATED ARTICLES

Afro-Latino Influences; African Americans, Influence and Relations; Libraries and Archives; Literature, Puerto Rican on the Mainland.

FURTHER READING

Piñeiro de Rivera, Flor, ed. *Arthur A. Schomburg: A Puerto Rican's Quest for His Black Heritage.* Foreword by Ricardo E. Alegría. San Juan, Puerto Rico: Centro de Estudios Avanzados de Puerto Rico y el Caribe, 1989.

Porter, Dorothy Burnet. *North American Negro Poets: A Bibliographical Checklist of Their Writings, 1760–1944.* Hattiesburg, Mo.: Bk. Farm, 1945.

Roy-Féquière, Magali. "Afro-Puerto Rican Radicalism in the United States: Reflections on the Political Trajectories of Arturo Schomburg and Jesús Colón." In *Focus en foco: Race and Identity.* New York: Centro de Estudios Puertorriqueños, Hunter College, 1996.

Sinnette, Elinor Des Vernay. *Arthur Alfonso Schomburg, Black Bibliophile and Collector: A Biography.* New York and Detroit, Mich.: New York Public Lib./ Wayne State Univ. Press, 1989.

Sinnette, Elinor Des Vernay, et al., eds. *Black Bibliophiles and Collectors.* Washington, D.C.: Howard Univ. Press, 1990.

Stavans, Ilan. *The Hispanic Condition: The Power of a People.* New York: Rayo/HarperCollins, 2001.

SELECTED WEB SITE

Africa Within.

www.africawithin.com/schomburg/schomburg.htm

ILAN STAVANS

SCHOOL DESEGREGATION

The issue of school desegregation was one of the preeminent civil rights issues of the late 20th century. The primary argument in favor of creating diverse, desegregated schools lies in the knowledge that segregated schools serve to reproduce inequalities in society. Issues of school equity are notoriously complicated and have been addressed through multiple approaches, often emphasizing different issues.

School desegregation as a means to improving educational opportunities for all children is arguably one of the most important ways through which the struggles for equity as well as excellence in education have been addressed.

Public education in the United States has always been seen as a means to "level the playing field." Public schools are supposed to afford children from all social and ethnic backgrounds access to a strong education and can become the foundation for further study at the university level, thus opening the door to more opportunities in the workforce. In the case of Latinos, these struggles have been and continue to be remarkably complex. The fight for equal access to quality schools is always characterized in terms of race and socioeconomic status and parallels the civil rights struggles of the African American community in many respects. For Latinos, however, this struggle frequently takes on additional dimensions, most notable among these, the effects of linguistic differences and immigration status on educational opportunity.

Segregation in schools as well as other forms of racial and ethnic discrimination have two manifestations. De jure segregation refers to policies upheld by legal precedents, such as the "Jim Crow" laws that sought to maintain a separation of the races. Examples of de jure segregation include redlining in housing developments, differential lending practices with respect to minority groups, and the earlier practices of school, military, and social segregation based on the doctrine of "separate but equal." The latter was supported by early court rulings, in particular, *Plessy* v. *Ferguson,* which allowed states to maintain segregated schools providing that the facilities within the institution were of equal quality. In contrast, de facto refers to segregation that results from social and economic conditions, such as racism, income disparities, and xenophobia. Such material and ideological conditions fuel cultural divides and many times result in spontaneously occurring segregated neighborhoods. This creates a vicious circle, since segregation continues to fuel the differences that could be cited as the initial cause for residential and hence school segregation. De facto segregation is not upheld by any legal precedents but is often targeted for reform through legal measures and social interventions, such as busing or affirmative action policies in hiring. These policies seek to change the nature of racial and ethnic divides in communities, schools and the workplace, thereby forcing communities that may not have any actual knowledge of one another to interact.

Several key rulings frame the struggle for education equity and school desegregation: *Plessy* v. *Ferguson, Mendez* v. *Westminster,* and *Brown* v. *Board of Education. Plessy* was a case argued in the Supreme Court in 1896. Homer Plessy, a man of mixed African and European descent, was jailed for taking a Louisiana train and sitting in a section reserved for whites, thus violating a statute that forbade the mixing of races in public spaces that had been racially designated. The resulting lawsuit established that practices enforcing "separate but equal treatment" do not necessarily contribute to discrimination. This ruling opened the doors to widespread separation of the races in the public domain; public transportation (including buses), drinking fountains, eating establishments, and schools, all were subjected to this treatment under the doctrine of separate but equal.

In 1946 Gonzalo and Felicita Mendez and others sued Orange County, California, for discrimination in the public schools, claiming that their children and over 5,000 others were forced to attend inferior "Mexican schools" based on their ethnic or racial identity. The ruling in *Mendez* v. *Westminster* was in favor of the Mendezes and their co-suitors, and was upheld in the 9th Circuit Court of Appeals in San Francisco on June 14 of that same year. Then-governor of the state of California Earl Warren subsequently overturned all remaining discriminatory statutes allowing school segregation in the California Education Code. The monumental court case became part of the historical legacy of desegregation rulings that came to a fore in the influential case *Brown* v. *Board of Education.* In 1953 Warren, now chief justice of the Supreme Court, used the *Mendez* ruling as the basis for the case, which, through unanimous decision, overturned the earlier *Plessy* decision, abolishing all de jure school segregation in the United States. Serving as the pivotal case for all civil rights legislation to follow, the *Brown* ruling mandating that "separate is not equal" is frequently seen as the case that changed the face of racial discrimination and segregation in public education in the United States.

The legal structures that worked to maintain inequality in the United States became the targets of the civil rights movement and were, by and large, overturned. However, the occurrence of de facto segregation—segregation not enforced by any legal means—is far from resolved, and in fact there exists evidence that in many parts of the country the incidence of severely segregated communities is again reaching crisis levels. De facto segregation of Latinos is long-standing and complex. In the Southwest many states granted legal rights to "Hispanics" during negotiations following the Louisiana Purchase and the Spanish-American War. Hence, in California, for example, Californios—mostly wealthy landowners of Spanish heritage who held large estates in California at the time of its incorporation in the United States—were granted equal legal status with other Americans, making them the first non-Anglos with equal rights under the law. Despite what may appear to have been early acceptance of Latinos in the United States, the actual practice of integrated communities did not follow from this legal reality. In the Southwest, Mexican immigrants and Mexican Americans, whether native to the actual geographic territory or more recent immigrants, have not enjoyed the same access to schooling as their Anglo counterparts.

Tracking of national trends indicates that the segregation of African Americans in schools dropped off significantly in the 1960s and continued to decline until the 1980s, when a reversal began to slowly take place. In contrast, school segregation of Latinos has continually grown worse since the 1960s, when this type of data began to be collected. By the late 1990s, data showed that over 70 percent of all Latinos in the United States would probably attend a school with a majority Latino population. The segregation of racial and ethnic communities today is more likely to result from economic disparities as well as linguistic differences that often play upon existing racial and ethnic stereotypes. Moreover, Latino communities may appear to some in the mainstream population as "foreign" entities resistant to assimilation and therefore unwilling to "become American."

Factors such as race, class, and perceived immigrant status contribute to increasingly segregated public schools in many areas of the country, and while the dynamics of race and class or socioeconomic status in the United States is complex, schools with high concentrations of impoverished students also tend to be the most highly segregated schools; they are most frequently located in neighborhoods with highly segregated housing. Low-income families tend to be less well educated than their higher-income counterparts and face a limited choice in housing options. Further exacerbating the situation is that in many school districts across the country, school funding is tied, at least partially, to property values, a portion of property taxes generally being allocated to fund local schools; therefore, the problem of school funding and the resulting drop in school resources is complicated by the existence of these property-value-based funding mechanisms. Low-income communities must live in less expensive residential areas generating fewer tax-based revenues, which results in neighborhood schools with fewer locally generated resources. Poor communities also have fewer financial resources with which to develop and enhance the resources of neighborhood schools independent of local funding structures, that is, direct donations of cash and volunteer time to, for example, the school PTA (Parent-Teacher Association). These two economic realities combine and result in schools that are underfunded.

Due to these budget constraints, schools in low-income neighborhoods many times are able to offer only essential programs that maintain the minimal state educational requirements, and schools located in such neighborhoods are often forced to drop programs such as physical education, music, extracurricular activities, and, in many areas, even science. In turn, schools with limited class offerings are not considered academically desirable, a condition further aggravated by the difficulty many impoverished districts face in recruiting highly qualified teachers. The interplay of the social and economic dynamics resulting in segregated or depressed housing (or both), poverty, and lack of access to quality education creates a vicious circle that severely limits the potential of education in racially and economically segregated schools to increase the life opportunities of those living in low-income communities. Naturally, all these challenges to excellence and equity in education are especially severe in markedly segregated Latino communities with a high percentage of low-income residents.

The issue of linguistic resources in schools with a high percentage of nonnative English-speaking populations has been another challenge for educators in the United States. In 1968 the Bilingual Education Act attempted to improve educational access by mandating the implementation of bilingual programs throughout the United States. These programs sought to address the inequity of all-English classrooms for language minority populations. It has been argued

and supported in the courts that if a child is unable to understand the curriculum content presented in the classroom, then that child is in effect being denied access to education. Legislation and the courts in the 1960s and 1970s supported the position that the lack of linguistic resources in schools, in areas with a high language-minority population is a type of discrimination against these populations. This position was developed and upheld through various provisions in the 1964 Civil Rights Act, which banned discrimination on the bases of race, class, or national origins. Based on the Civil Rights Act, the 1974 Supreme Court decision *Lau* v. *Nichols* introduced the idea of equity in educational access as also essentially tied to native language instruction.

Although the courts have continually upheld the rights of language minority children to equitable education, the various proposals and legislation never strongly mandated the form these types of linguistic support programs would take. Traditional bilingual education programs have varied greatly in the amount of time given students before being "mainstreamed" into English-language classrooms, the degree to which the native language is used for instruction, and the amount of development of the native language that is encouraged. Some very strong bilingual programs, such as dual immersion programs, feature a complex but effective linguistic mixture of native English speakers and nonnative English speakers. This program is quite effective at promoting the development of both English and the native language within a school population that includes students from both linguistic groups. In contrast, early- and late-exit bilingual programs separate non-English speakers from English speakers in an attempt to support academic and language development as students transition to English. At some schools throughout the country, these types of bilingual programs have been criticized for furthering segregation between linguistically diverse populations of students within the same school.

The effect of these debates among Latinos in the United States has played into the continued problem of segregation in the schools. Some Latino populations throughout the country remain highly supportive of bilingual education programs and look to the development of Spanish as a means of preserving cultural integrity. At the same time, many Latinos feel that bilingual programs have excluded their children from educational opportunities and highly rigorous academic coursework and have further segregated and stigmatized Latinos. The trend since the passage of the No Child Left Behind Act in 2002 is against bilingual education programs. The English First movement has been gaining ground with some Latino support, with backers of the movement successfully passing propositions doing away with bilingual education in several states, including California, Arizona, and Massachusetts. Whether the elimination of bilingual programs will increase equity in education remains to be seen. Initial studies indicate that the civil rights struggles for educational equity in the United States are far from over. Schools and neighborhoods are increasingly segregated, and the federal education legislation of 2002 has taken steps that roll back legislation hard won in the past.

RELATED ARTICLES

Bilingual Education; Civil Rights; Congress, United States; Education; *Mendez* v. *Westminster School District*; Supreme Court, United States.

FURTHER READING

Arroyo, Luis L. *A Bibliography of Recent Chicano History Writings, 1970–1975.* Bibliographic and Reference Series. Los Angeles: Chicano Studies Ctr., Univ. of Calif. at Los Angeles, 1975.
Hochschild, Jennifer. *The New American Dilemma: Liberal Democracy and School Desegregation.* New Haven, Conn.: Yale Univ. Press, 1984.
Massey, Douglas, and Nancy Denton. *American Apartheid: Segregation and the Making of the Underclass.* Cambridge, Mass.: Harvard Univ. Press, 1994.
Orfield, Gary. "Turning Back to Segregation." In *Dismantling Desegregation: The Quiet Reversal of Brown v. Board of Education.* Ed. by Gary Orfield et al. New York: New Press, 1996.
Wells, Amy S., and Robert Crain. *Stepping over the Color Line: African American Students in White Suburban Schools.* New Haven, Conn.: Yale Univ. Press, 1997.
Wollenberg, Charles. *All Deliberate Speed: Segregation and Exclusion in California Schools, 1855–1975.* Berkeley: Univ. of Calif. Press, 1976.

JILL PINKNEY PASTRANA

SCIENCE

The number of Latinos who are professional scientists is relatively small. This is because access to institutions of higher learning has proven elusive for this minority. Also, the educational system in Latin America is not known for encouraging students to enter the field. Consequently, students with a Hispanic background seeking degrees in the sciences often face a wide range of socioeconomic obstacles, including quality of education, immigration status, language proficiency, and discrimination. Still, a number of pioneering Latino scientists have made important contributions to their respective areas of knowledge—medicine, physiology, physics, chemistry, biology, space research, and technology, among others.

Door Openers

A native of Spain, Severo Ochoa became a U.S. citizen in 1956 and went on to become a respected biochemist and educator. With Arthur Kornberg, he received the 1959 Nobel Prize in physiology or medicine for the synthesis of ribonucleic acid (RNA). His contributions to science have opened doors to our understanding of genetics.

In 1980 Baruj Benacerraf of Harvard Medical School received the Nobel Prize for medicine or physiology. A native of Caracas, Venezuela, Benacerraf shared his honor with his two colleagues, Jean Dausset and George D. Snell, "for their discoveries concerning genetically determined structures on the cell surface that regulate immunological reactions."

Mario Molina, a native of Mexico and a graduate of the Massachusetts Institute of Technology, won the Nobel Prize in chemistry in 1995. Molina and his two colleagues, Paul Crutzen and F. Sherwood Rowland, received the award for their work in atmospheric chemistry, particularly concerning the formation and decomposition of ozone.

Luis Walter Alvarez, a native of San Francisco, became the first American-born Latino to receive the Nobel Prize in 1968 when he won the award for his work in the field of physics. A decade later Alvarez and his geologist son, Walter Alvarez, achieved even greater fame when they developed the meteorite theory to explain the extinction of the dinosaurs 65 million years ago. The two scientists had detected unusually high levels of the rare element iridium in rocks dating back to the end of the dinosaur era. They correlated the presence of this rare element with the impact of a devastating meteorite that caused widespread extinctions in a short period of time.

Like the Nobel Prize winners, Latinos involved in America's space program are squarely in the media's limelight because they are forging a new path for others to follow. In the process they become role models. One woman who has earned the respect and admiration of many Americans is Ellen Ochoa, the first Hispanic female astronaut. Ochoa, a native of California, graduated from San Diego State University and subsequently received her doctorate degree in electrical engineering from Stanford. In 1990 Ochoa was selected by the National Atmospheric and Space Administration (NASA) to become an astronaut. Since 1991 she has been on four spaceflights. In addition to her professional accomplishments, Ochoa has become actively involved in community outreach, encouraging young Latinas and Latinos to major in the sciences.

Sid Gutiérrez, a native of Albuquerque, New Mexico, became a NASA astronaut in June 1985. Gutiérrez received a bachelor of science degree in aeronautical engineering from the United States Air Force Academy in 1973. He has taken part in two shuttle missions and has received numerous engineering awards, as well as the Congressional Hispanic Caucus Award.

Born in Lima, Peru, Carlos Ismael Noriega is one of many South Americans who came to the United States to follow his dreams. Graduating from high school in Santa Clara, California, Carlos attended the University of Southern California and received his commission in the United States Marines. In 1994 Noriega was selected by NASA to begin training and evaluation. Taking part in spaceflights in 1997 and 2000, he logged more than 461 hours in space, including three space walks.

Toward a Wider Representation

Data about Latino students in the sciences for the early years of the 21st century are still to come. But some numbers are available for part of the 1980s and most of the 1990s. From 1983 to 1997 Latino Americans received only 2.2 percent of all STEM (science, technology, engineering, and mathematics) doctoral degrees earned by U.S. citizens. These doctorates earned by Hispanics were primarily in the fields of life sciences (47 percent), physical sciences (33 percent), and engineering (20 percent). In 1997 Latinos earned only 3.7 percent (or 1,028) of all Ph.D. degrees received by American citizens in all of the disciplines.

NASA has roughly 2,000 Hispanic employees, many of them in the electronic, aeronautical, and space engineering fields. Out of 109 NASA astronauts, 8 are of Hispanic descent. In an effort to encourage more students to pursue science careers, in October 2003 NASA began publishing a newsletter, *El Noticiero de NASA*. At the same time, NASA

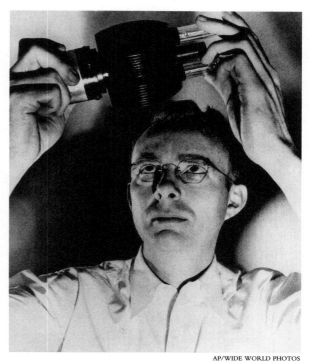

AP/WIDE WORLD PHOTOS

Luis Walter Alvarez, developer of the radar Ground Controlled Approach system, which helps guide airplanes through fog.

hosted a conference at the University of Texas–Pan American in Edinburg, Texas, to give students an opportunity to explore careers relating to science and mathematics.

Some of the greatest concerns about Latino participation in the sciences are reserved for the medical profession. In New York, for example, Latinos account for 15 percent of the state population, but make up only 4 percent of practicing physicians. According to the University of California at Los Angeles (UCLA) School of Medicine, out of 74,345 licensed physicians in California in 1999, only 3,578 were Latino. In other words, in a state in which Latinos made up almost 30 percent of the population at the time, only 4.8 percent of physicians were Latino.

This problem has been of concern to several professional organizations. The Interamerican College of Physicians and Surgeons (ICPS) was founded in 1979 to promote cooperation among Hispanic physicians in the United States and to advance their professional and educational needs. Today the ICPS is the largest association of Hispanic physicians in the nation, with a membership exceeding 39,000.

As a means of increasing the number of Latino students entering all the scientific fields, several organizations have been established to reach out to students when they are still young and to provide them with a strong incentive to take the physics, calculus, chemistry, and mathematics classes that are essential to achieving a science degree in college.

Since the poverty level of some Latino families may represent an impediment to a science education, many organizations have been established in various parts of the country with the expressed purpose of helping Latino students overcome the various obstacles that stand between them and a science career. Some organizations arrange for the students to receive scholarships and grants that will help pay for college and postgraduate studies.

Latinos in Science (LIS) was organized by in 1991 by a group of students at the University of California at Riverside. LIS uses community service to promote the natural, physical, and social sciences as a viable alternative for young Latino and Latina students in high school. It has also created the Science Awareness and Mentor Program to reach Hispanic children at the elementary school level. Periodically members of the program visit local elementary schools and give science presentations to sixth graders. These presentations are designed to introduce young students to college life and give them academic encouragement.

The Society of Latino Engineers and Scientists (SOLES) was established as a student organization dedicated to promoting engineering as a viable career option for Latino students. Representatives of SOLES actively recruit high school students and encourage them to go into the field of engineering. The Mexican American Engineering Society was founded in 1974 as a nonprofit, tax-exempt organization with the goal of bringing more Hispanic Americans into the technical and scientific fields. In 1989 the organization changed its name to the Society of Mexican American Engineers and Scientists (MAES). Its members provide motivation and mentoring to students to help them in their scientific and engineering studies. In addition, MAES has assisted many students in securing financial aid for education and finding employment.

The Society for the Advancement of Chicanos and Native Americans in Science (SACNAS) was founded in 1973 and has evolved into a national organization with members spread throughout the United States. The membership of SACNAS includes science professors, industry scientists, kindergarten through grade-12 educators, and students. The mission of SACNAS is to encourage Chicano, Latino, and Native American students to pursue graduate education and obtain the advanced degrees necessary for research and teaching careers.

The Center for the Advancement of Hispanics in Science and Engineering Education (CAHSEE) is a national educational and scientific nonprofit organization founded by Latino scientists and engineers to help talented Hispanic science and engineering students to achieve academic excellence and professional success. Through several of their programs, CAHSEE tries to increase the number of Hispanics who enter and complete graduate programs in mathematics, science, and engineering and ultimately become scientists.

The Association for Puerto Ricans in Science and Engineering (ASPIRA) was founded in 1961 by Antonia Pantoja and a group of Puerto Rican educators. ASPIRA takes its name from the Spanish verb *aspirer* (to aspire). Originally, Pantoja and her colleagues created ASPIRA in order to address the exceedingly high dropout rate and low educational attainment of Puerto Rican youth. They were convinced that the best way to help Puerto Ricans escape the cycle of poverty was to focus on the education of young people. ASPIRA provides leadership training, career and college counseling, financial aid, scholarship assistance, and cultural activities as a means of developing self-esteem and pride in the cultural heritage of Puerto Rican students. Since its establishment, ASPIRA has grown into a national association with statewide associate organizations in several states.

Probably the most effective means of encouraging students in grammar school and high school to enter the science fields is to provide them with impressive role models. Many Latinos who have achieved recognition in their scientific fields have been willing to donate some of their time to community outreach. Loyda Martínez received a bachelor degree in computer sciences at the College of Santa Fe in New Mexico and went on to become a network manager for the management division of the Los Alamos National Laboratory (LANL). She has become actively involved in community outreach services to inspire young Hispanic students to embrace a scientific curriculum in their high school and college studies.

Rosalee Montoya-Read was program development officer for the Cancer Research and Treatment Center at the University of New Mexico Health Sciences Center. With over ten years of fund raising and public relations experience, Montoya-Read was active within the Hispanic community advocating for increased awareness and access to programs that benefit the Latino community.

RELATED ARTICLES

Alvarez, Luis; Education, Higher; Medicine; Molina, Mario; Ochoa, Ellen; Technology.

FURTHER READING

Cid, Carmen R. *Perspectives on Latina Issues: Problems and Solutions: Focus on Latinas in Science.* http://awis.org/m_02sumlat.html

Díaz-Sprague, Raquel. *Perspectives on Latina Issues: Problems and Solutions: Reflections on Issues Faced by Latinas in Science.* http://awis.org/m_02sumreflect.html

González, K. P., et al. "Understanding the Nature and Context of Latina/o Doctoral Student Experiences." *Journal of College Student Development* 42 (2001): 563–570.

Medina, C., and G. Luna. "Narratives from Latina Professors in Higher Education." *Anthropology and Education Quarterly* 31 (2000): 47–66.

Quintana-Baker, Maricel. "A Profile of Mexican American, Puerto Rican, and other Hispanic Stem Doctorates: 1983 to 1997." *Journal of Women and Minorities in Science and Engineering* 8 (2002): 99–121.

Sanderson, A. R., et al. *Doctorate Recipients from United States Universities: Summary Report 1999.* Chicago: Natl. Opinion Res. Ctr., Univ. of Chicago, 2000.

Zannos, Susan. *Latinos at Work: Careers in Science and Medicine.* Bear, Delaware: Mitchell Lane Pubs., 2001.

SELECTED WEB SITES

CAHSEE. http://www.cahsee.org/about/index.htm

JOHN P. SCHMAL

SCULPTURE

Sculpture was the primary monumental art form of pre-Hispanic Mesoamerica, and the sculptural traditions of Latin America and the Hispanic United States have a 3,000-year history of artistic achievement. In the first decades of Spanish colonization, 1520–1580, pre-Hispanic and European sculptural forms blended into a hybrid now called the Indo-Christian style. Indo-Christian monumental sculptures were primarily in the preferred indigenous stone medium, but when Spanish devotional sculptures, of carved wood and often polychromed and gilded, arrived in the New World in the 1500s, both stone sculpture—usually found as architectural decoration—and poly-chromed wooden images began to be produced in Latin America.

In the 1600s and 1700s, exports of Spanish sculpture, including the works of the finest Sevillian ateliers, such as that of Juan Martínez Montañés (1564–1649), provided models for the development of local schools, among which those of Mexico, Guatemala, and what is now Ecuador achieved particular success. In Guatemala and in Quito, Ecuador, poly-chromed sculpture manifested East Asian influences, including technical details such as lacquering and stylistic elements from Chinese, Japanese, Philippine, and Indian carved ivories brought across the Pacific on the Manila galleons. A measure of the technical sophistication and artistic power of Mexican sculpture in the mid-1600s may be taken from the anonymous statue of San Felipe de Jesús in the Mexico City cathedral, in which a combination of severe geometric forms and explosive baroque compositional elements creates a haunting but sumptuous artistic experience. In the last half of the 1600s, Mexican sculptors and joiners such as Salvador de Ocampo (1665–1732) and his father-in-law, Tomás Xuárez (1650–1724), the latter of indigenous descent, not only produced works of sculpture but also functioned as contractors installing the huge gilded *retablos,* or altar ensembles, that would continue to be such an important aspect of Latin American art in all areas throughout the 18th century, in the stylistic explosion called *churrigueresque,* or the "second baroque."

South America also produced many sculptors of note in the 18th century, almost all of them working principally in polychromed wood, although we have mention of other media as well. In Quito, Bernardo de Legarda (c. 1700–1773) and Manuel Chili, called "Caspicara" (fl. 1750–1800), led the school; their contemporary in Santa Fe de Bogotá, Colombia, was Pedro Laboria (1700–1770). In Cuzco, Bolivia, Melchor Huamán created devotional images in the mid-1700s, while in Lima, Peru, Baltazar Gavilán made both religious and secular works, such as his 1743 equestrian monument to the Spanish king Philip V, which was destroyed in an earthquake in 1746. The best-known South American sculptor of the 18th century is, however, the Brazilian Antônio Francisco Lisboa, called "O Aleijadinho" ("the Cripple"; 1738–1814). His sculptural ensembles in wood and stone, such as the exterior statues at the church of Bom Jesus (1796) in Congonhas, Brazil, present an expressionistic style that he and his followers elaborated.

The early modern period, 1780–1900, began with the establishment of art academies throughout Latin America, many of which continue to function today. In Mexico the Valencian neoclassical sculptor-architect Manuel Tolsá (1757–1816) arrived in 1791 and began to train the subsequent generation of Mexican sculptors, such as Pedro Patiño Ixtolinque (1774–1834), who brought neoclassical academic sculpture into the Republican period. Academic forms tended to dominate outdoor monuments and similar large commissions during the 19th century, with immigrant sculptors from Europe often being brought in. Of more interest to Latino culture, however, are the popular sculptural forms, such as the painted terra-cottas, popular devotional ensembles, and polychromed, small-scale religious sculptures called *santos* or *bultos,* produced throughout Latin America into the early 20th century, with special interest in the centers in Puerto Rico, Guatemala, northern Mexico, and what is now the southwestern United States. In New Mexico the *santero* tradition has continued unbroken from the 18th into the 21st century and forms a major part of contemporary artistic production. A constant source of inspiration for the *santeros* are the large-scale polychromed sculptures that were created in the 18th and 19th centuries for the altars of colonial churches in Texas, New Mexico, Arizona, and Southern California.

The prominence of Mexican mural painting in the early 20th century tended to push monumental sculpture somewhat to the side of the cultural map. Outside Mexico, however, 20th-century Latin American artists made significant contributions to postwar sculpture internationally. In particular, from the 1940s through the 1970s, Atlantic South America nurtured a vital school of nonfigurative abstract sculpture, closely allied to European modernism but also keenly aware of developments in the United States. Among many artists in this group, we may cite Jesús Soto of Venezuela (born 1923); Lygia Clark (1920–1988) and Hélio Oiticica (1937–1980) in Brazil; Eduardo Díaz Yepes (1910–1978) and Germán Cabrera (1903–1990) in Uruguay; and Raúl Lozza (born 1911) and Gyula Kósice (born 1924) in Argentina. The subsequent generation of Latin American sculptors carried this creative explosion into the 21st century.

The work of one Mexican modern sculptor, Francisco Zúñiga (1912–1998), does provide an important bridge between Latin American and United States sculptural traditions. Zúñiga was born in Costa Rica and worked principally in Mexico, but his sculptures, drawings, and prints were avidly collected in the United States, particularly in the Southwest, where he inspired many followers and imitators. His subject matter is popular, consisting almost exclusively of indigenous Mexican women, and he worked with traditional materials, such as bronze, in a style descended from Aristide Maillol and other 20th-century classicists.

In the 1960s and 1970s, Nuyorican (New York City Puerto Rican) artists such as Rafael Montañez Ortiz (born 1934) and Rafael Ferrer (born 1933), working in the dominant pop art (neodada) and conceptual art movements, provided a Hispanic presence in New York City exhibitions of contemporary sculpture. A noted teacher and social activist, Ortiz was the founding director of El Museo del Barrio. Also active in New York, from 1966 to 1971, was the Texas artist Luis Jiménez (born 1940), whose painted fiberglass sculptures are arguably the best-known Latino art objects of the late 20th century. (It is significant that Jiménez's *Vaquero* [1990, casting; model, 1980], was chosen as the signature piece of the Smithsonian American Art Museum in Washington, D.C.).

Other contemporary Hispanic sculptors in the United States have worked in a wide variety of media and styles. The *santero* tradition of northern New Mexico lives in the works of artists such as Félix A. López (born 1942), Luis Eligio Tapia (born 1950), and Nicholas Herrera (born 1964), while artists such as Amalia Mesa-Baines (born 1943) use Mexican and Chicano popular devotional traditions, including house shrines, *ofrendas,* (offerings) and tabernacles for the Day of the Dead, as the starting point for modernist ensembles, a tradition taken into more abstract forms by Rudy Fernández (born 1948).

In contrast, the stone sculptures of Jesús Bautista Moroles (born 1950) are completely nonobjective. Moroles, who describes himself as a granite carver, creates totemic stone monoliths or site-specific abstract public monuments, which, except for the occasional reminder of pre-Columbian forms, are almost entirely within the international modernist tradition rather than overtly "Hispanic" in their visual references. In the nascent 21st century, scores of younger U.S. Hispanic artists have chosen sculpture as their expressive medium and, like the slightly older

Sculpture entitled *Vaquero* by Luis Alfonso Jimenez, Jr., fiberglass and epoxy (cast 1990).

generation of Jiménez and Moroles, have felt free to work in a wide variety of idioms.

FURTHER READING

Ades, Dawn, et al. *Art in Latin America: The Modern Era, 1820–1980.* New Haven, Conn.: Yale Univ. Press, 1989.

Bayón, Damián, et al. *History of South American Colonial Art and Architecture.* New York: Rizzoli Intl. Pubns., 1989.

Beardsley, John, and Jane Livingston, with an essay by Octavio Paz. *Hispanic Art in the United States: Thirty Contemporary Painters and Sculptors.* New York and Houston: Cross River Press/Abbeville Press/Houston Mus. of Fine Arts, 1987 [published to accompany the exhibition].

Burke, Marcus B. *Pintura y Escultura en Nueva España: El Barroco* (Painting and Sculpture in New Spain: The Baroque). Mexico City: Grupo Azabache, 1992.

Cancel, Luis R., ed. *The Latin American Spirit: Art and Artists in the United States, 1920–1970.* New York: Bronx Mus. of the Arts/Abrams, 1988 [exhibition catalog].

Mexico, Splendors of Thirty Centuries. New York and Boston: Metropolitan Mus. of Art/Bulfinch Press, 1990 [exhibition catalog].

Oettinger, Marion, Jr. *Folk Treasures of Mexico: The Nelson A. Rockefeller Collection.* New York: Abrams, 1990.

Quirarte, Jacinto. *The Art and Architecture of the Texas Missions.* Austin: Univ. of Tex. Press, 2002.

Sullivan, Edward, ed. *Latin American Art in the Twentieth Century.* London: Phaidon Press, 1996.

Sullivan, Edward, ed. and curator. *Brazil: Body and Soul.* New York: Guggenheim Mus., 2001.

Toussaint, Manuel, and E. Wilder Wiesmann, ed. and tr. *Colonial Art in Mexico.* Austin: Univ. of Tex. Press, 1967.

MARCUS BURKE

SELENA

Born: April 16, 1971; Lake Jackson, Texas
Died: March 31, 1995; Corpus Christi, Texas

A leading singer of Tejano music and a tragic symbol of Latino crossover ambition, Selena, as she was commonly known, was born Selena Quintanilla-Pérez near Houston. She began singing in her family's restaurant at the age of six. When the restaurant was forced to close in the early 1980s, and Selena and her family moved to Corpus Christi, her career started to take shape—she, her older sister Suzette, and her brother Abraham (A.B.) formed the group Selena y los Dinos. Abraham played bass and composed; Suzette played the drums; Chris Pérez joined later as lead guitarist. Soon the group was focusing on Tejano music, and, in 1986, at age 15 Selena was named Female Vocalist of the Year and Performer of the Year at the annual Tejano Music Awards. By the mid-1990s she had risen as a solo star to the top of the Tejano market with her amazing fusion of the Mexican *cumbia,* keyboard-fueled dance hooks

© BARBARA LAING/TIME LIFE PICTURES/GETTY IMAGES

Memorial to Tejano singer Selena Quintanilla.

and spices of pop and R&B (rhythm and blues). Through her catchy tunes and party spirit, Selena's influence spread far beyond Tejano fans, winning followers in Mexico, Latin America, and eventually in the U.S. Top 40 scene. Along the way she became an idol for a generation of young women pursuing their artistic dreams.

The first few years were tough, recording on a series of independent labels that produced albums but little chart success. Tejano (Spanish for "Texan") music is dance music that arose during the 1950s by combining folksy accordion border music with jazz, big band, and other influences. Selena's brand of Tejano incorporated *cumbia*—the bouncy Colombian rhythm. She also recorded ballads and romantic, pop-infused polkas. Selena first scored on the charts in 1989 with a cover of *La Bamba.* In 1990 she signed with EMI Latin and her debut album, *Ven Conmigo,* began her rise with radio-friendly material, largely written by A.B., backed by vocalist Pete Astudillo and keyboardist Ricky Vela.

She possessed a soulful soprano, was physically attractive, and was in constant motion on stage. Sometimes performing in provocative clothing such as a black bustier, she was sometimes compared to Madonna. The R&B shadings in her vocals owed something to disco queen Donna Summer—Selena loved to sing Summer's *On the Radio* in concert. Despite these influences, Selena (always under the watchful eye of her father) preferred a wholesome sexiness, rather than in-your-face eroticism.

Many fans and critics consider *Amor Prohibido* (1994) both Selena's best album and one of the best Tejano albums of the 1990s. It produced hit singles: the *cumbia* title track, reggae-flavored *Bidi Bidi Bom Bom,* mariachi bolero *No Me Queda Más,* and the hip-hop fusion *Techno Cumbia.* The album was incredibly deep, a rare achievement in the Tejano market, whose albums tend to be singles-oriented and released on tight deadlines. Other cuts that received extensive club and radio play included the mariachi-*cumbia Si Una Vez* and the brassy, Colombian-influenced story-song *El Chico del Apartamento 512,* with "512" a sly reference to Corpus Christi's then area code. Tejano's weakness is its simplistic, generic lyrics; Selena and her songwriting team overcame this stereotype with songs that painted vivid, poetic portraits of barrio life (*La Carcacha,*) and relationships gone wrong (*La Llamada* and *No Me Queda Más*).

On April 2, 1992, just two weeks before her 21st birthday, she married guitarist Chris Perez, who had joined the band in the late 1980s. The sky seemed the limit for Selena, who still lived in her hometown of Corpus Christi. SBK Records signed her to an English pop deal in 1994 and she set out to record her crossover breakthrough, working with renowned producer K.C. Porter. On March 31, 1995, a former fan club president, Yolanda Saldívar, shot and killed Selena at a Corpus Christi hotel. The family suspected that Saldívar had been taking fan club money for personal use. Saldívar was convicted of murder and sentenced to life in prison.

The others' lives took various turns; Perez and girlfriend Vanessa Villanueva had a daughter, Cassie, in 1998; the couple married in 2001. Perez re-emerged musically in 1999 with the rock-en-Español-flavored Chris Perez Band. The group disbanded in 2003, and he began playing guitar for Kumbia Kings, a highly successful group formed by his former brother-in-law A.B. in 1998. The group's pop/*cumbia*/hip-hop fusions were not unlike Selena's music, and during concerts A.B. paid tribute to his sister with a Selena medley.

In any case, Selena's *Dreaming of You,* released that summer, posthumously fulfilled her dream, with Top 40 hits *I Could Fall in Love* and the title track. Selena was also remembered with the 1997 biopic *Selena,* which established Jennifer Lopez's career as an actress. It grossed $35 million in North America. Lopez's role foreshadowed her own stellar music career. Selena's influence remained strong as young female artists entered the Tejano and regional Mexican music scene, formerly a male bastion. Scores of them openly admitted their admiration of her pioneering Tejano-pop fusions. Selena's albums and greatest hits collections continue to sell briskly years after her death.

RELATED ARTICLES
Music, Popular; Vocalists, Popular.

FURTHER READING
Burr, Ramiro. *The Billboard Guide to Tejano and Regional Mexican Music.* New York: Billboard Bks., 1999.
Patoski, Joe Nick. *Como la Flor.* Boston: Little, Brown, 1997.
Richmond, Clint. *Selena!* New York: Avon Pocket Bks., 1995.
Stavans, Ilan. "Santa Selena." In *The Essential Ilan Stavans.* New York: Routledge, 2000.

RAMIRO BURR
DOUG SHANNON

SEMINOLE WARS

When Andrew Jackson defeated the Maskoki in what is now known as the Creek War of 1813–1814, a number of the most determined warriors took their families and sought refuge in Spanish Florida. There they merged with members of other tribes as well as with escaped slaves from the southern states. The nucleus of this group called themselves *yat siminoli,* or the free people, and it was not long until the Americans started referring to all the descendants of this group as Seminoles.

Because Spain could not afford to properly patrol Florida's long northern border, some Americans moved south across that border to settle on the rich northern Florida lands. The concept of Manifest Destiny was used to justify such appropriation, coupled with the common belief that Spain and England were actively supporting and encouraging the Florida Seminoles to raid southern farms and plantations.

The British, who had formerly had brief possession of Florida, was also a presence in the area.

Lacking adequate resources, Spain was unable to oust the British, stop their military activities, or even force their ships to leave Gulf Coast anchorage. American officials, believing that Spain was in concert with the British, became increasingly angry with the Spanish representatives for not defending the border, for not stopping the Seminole raids, and for not stopping the protection openly offered to escaped slaves by the Seminole. A number of conflicts and even minor skirmishes resulted as southern Americans used force to bring impose their will.

"Old Andy," as Jackson was known, decided to settle the problem by taking direct action against the Spanish colony. With no official orders or sanction, he organized a private army and invaded Spanish Florida, burning several towns, capturing escaped slaves, and even having two British citizens hanged for inciting the Seminoles to war. This long series of events, now known as the First Seminole War (1817–1818), bolstered Jackson's reputation as an Indian fighter, made him the first governor of Florida, and politically helped to propel him into the White House in 1829.

In 1821 Spain ceded Florida to the United States, but conflict did not end. A number of treaties were then negotiated between the United States and the Seminoles, the Treaty of Moultrie Creek (1823) including the Treaty of Payne's Landing (1832), along with talks and meetings. U.S. Indian agents and tried to force the Seminoles to sell their pigs and cattle, return all runaway slaves, and relocate west of the Mississippi River to Indian territory. As president, Jackson pushed through Congress the Indian Removal Act, which affected the Seminoles in 1835.

This attempt at relocation sparked the Second Seminole War (1835–1842). The U.S. government committed almost $40 million to force the Seminoles out of Florida. The Second Seminole War was the only Indian War in which the army, navy, and marines engaged in joint operations. Unlike the famous Trail of Tears (1838) in which several thousand Cherokee were relocated, the removal of the Seminoles started earlier and lasted 20 years longer. The Third Seminole War was fought between 1856 and 1858 as Seminoles left in Florida continued to fight.

During the Second Seminole War, Osceola emerged as the Seminole leader; he planned the strategy for a number of successful battles against five U.S. generals, killed the U.S. Indian agent, punished any who cooperated with the whites, and was the national symbol of the Seminoles' defiance. His capture while under a flag of truce offered by General Thomas Jesup remains one of the blackest marks in American military history. A larger-than-life character, Osceola is surrounded by numerous myths; his 1838 death in a Charleston, South Carolina, prison was noted on front pages of newspapers around the world.

A number of famous men fought in the Seminole Wars: in addition to Jackson and Jesup the list includes Zachary Taylor, Oliver O. Howard (the Christian general), Edmund Gaines, and Richard Keith Call. All risked their lives attempting to fight the Seminoles in an area where dysentery and malaria were common. One U.S. soldier wrote that, "if the Devil owned both Hell and Florida, he would rent out Florida and live in Hell." William S. Harney, who later fought in the Indian wars in the West, learned military tactics fighting the Seminoles, as did

Contemporary wood engraving depicting white settlers being massacred during the Second Seminole War.

Winfield Scott, who reorganized the entire army based on tactics he had learned from the Seminoles.

The Seminole fought the United States in its first guerrilla war, using the natural terrain against their enemies and fighting in flexible units that could disappear in a moment. Only after spending an additional $20 million and having 1,500 soldiers die did President John Tyler cease operations against the Seminoles, who were the undefeated—no surrender ever took place.

The reverberations in Latino consciousness of the Seminole Wars are many. Those Chicanos and Puerto Ricans on the mainland who view their countries as colonized by the United States often call attention to the Seminole Wars as an example of American oppression of its own. In that sense, the wars have helped solidify a political and spiritual alliance between Latinos and Native Americans.

RELATED ARTICLES

Florida; Indian Wars; Indigenous Heritage.

FURTHER READING

Laumer, Frank. *Massacre!* Gainesville: Univ. Press of Fla., 1968.

Porter, Kenneth W. *The Black Seminoles.* Gainesville: Univ. Press of Fla., 1996.

Tebeau, Charlton W. *A History of Florida.* Coral Gables, Fla.: Univ. of Miami Press, 1971.

ARTHUR E. CHAPMAN

SERRA, JUNÍPERO

Born: November 24, 1713; Majorca, Spain
Died: 1784; Mission Carmel, California

A polemical figure of the colonial period whose missionary work was based on the premise that indigenous peoples needed support and also discipline to become "civilized," Fray Junípero Serra was born Miguel José Serra into farming family on the Spanish island of Majorca. He attended a school run by Franciscan monks, and at age 16 he joined the order, taking the name Junípero. He went on to earn a doctor of theology degree, teach philosophy, and become known on the island for his inspired sermons.

Serra worked at the university until, at age 36, he asked for and was granted a post in the New World. Serra likely saw missionary work in the Americas as a tremendous opportunity to spread the teachings of his beloved church.

LIBRARY OF CONGRESS

Statue of Fray Junipero Serra, Monterey, California.

After his ship landed at Vera Cruz, Mexico, Serra decided to walk the 200 miles (320 km) to the capital. His personal religious practice incorporated mortification of the flesh (deliberate infliction of physical discomfort) and during the trip he hurt his leg badly. For the rest of his career, he often walked long distances, enduring considerable pain and becoming well known as an especially devout priest. Serra also regularly fasted, beat his chest, and flogged himself with a scourge.

In Mexico Serra helped with the administration of the College of San Fernando and served as a missionary to a band of Native Americans. He learned their language and translated the catechism, but also used harsh methods, including burning villages, to coerce them into church-run missions. Serra believed that priests were spiritual fathers who, must both care for and impose discipline on their "children." While the methods of the missionaries may appear cruel by modern standards, Serra often intervened to prevent even worse treatment by soldiers. By almost any reckoning, indigenous peoples under Spanish rule fared better than those in the path of U.S. settlers migrating west.

In 1767 Serra was appointed as the new head of the missions in Baja California. A year later he was ordered north with Captain Gaspar de Portolá's expedition to secure Alta California for Spain as a defensive action to limit Russian claims to the region. Serra established the first mission in present-day San Diego in 1769. During Serra's administration, nine missions were founded, as far north as San Francisco. The system eventually expanded to include 21 sites and secured California as part of the Spanish empire.

For California Native Americans, as for those in Mexico, life at the missions was hard. Many were compelled to convert and relocate to mission lands. Priests required new converts to learn Catholic doctrine, wear European clothes, and work on the farms that supported the missions. Priests did not hesitate to have disobedient converts flogged. In 1780 the governor of California described the conditions of the mission Indians as "worse than slaves." In the six decades that the missions operated, as many as 100,000 Native Americans died, mostly from disease.

Serra personally presided at the conversion of more than 5,000 Native Americans and headed the mission effort until his death at Mission Carmel, near Monterey, California, in 1784. In 1821 the newly independent Mexico secularized the missions, and they fell into disrepair. After a number of restoration efforts, some missions are back in use as churches and others as tourist attractions.

Fray Serra remains a controversial figure, beatified by Pope John Paul II for his devotion and missionary work, and reviled by many indigenous peoples in California for the cultural destruction the mission system brought.

RELATED ARTICLES

Catholicism; Colonialism; Indigenous Heritage; Missions; San Diego Revolt.

FURTHER READING

Couve de Murville, M. N. L. *The Man Who Founded California: The Life of Blessed Junípero Serra.* Ft. Collins, Colo.: Ignatius Press, 2000.

Palóu, Francisco. *Palóu's Life of Fray Junípero Serra.* Translated and annotated by Maynard J. Geiger. Washington, D.C.: Academy of Am. Franciscan Hist., 1955.

Sandos, James A. "Junípero Serra's Canonization and the Historical Record." *American Historical Review* 93 (December 1988): 1253–1269.

Serra, Junípero. *Writings of Junípero Serra.* Ed. by Antonine Tibesar. 4 vols. Washington, D.C.: Academy of Am. Franciscan Hist., 1955–1966.

Tinker, George E. "Junípero Serra." In *Missionary Conquest: The Gospel and Native American Cultural Genocide.* Ed. by George E. Tinker. Minneapolis, Minn.: Fortress Press, 1993.

P. SCOTT BROWN

SEXUALITY

Latino sexuality in the United States is affected by multiple layers of cultural controversy. On one level, mainstream discussions of Latinos routinely refer to their high fertility rates. If *immigration* is a term with constant relevance to debates about Latinos in the United States, so too is its twin, *fertility*. As recently as March 2004, a Harvard professor, Samuel P. Huntington, argued in *Foreign Policy* that Latinos posed a threat to the United States's cultural integrity in part because their high birthrates showed no sign of slowing down. The fact of Latinos' tendency to have more children than their Anglo counterparts naturally reflects back on questions of Latino sexuality. Is there something distinctive about the way Latinos have sex? Do they have it more often than other groups? Do they start earlier and pursue sexual relations with less precaution? The answers to each of these question is too complicated to narrow down to a mere yes or no, and many Latinos are ambivalent about how to answer them.

On another level, partly but not entirely related to the sociological reality of their high fertility rates, Latinos have been subjected to a great deal of stereotyping in popular culture. Many stereotypes hinge on the widespread belief that they are more sexually inclined than Anglo-Americans. Myths of the "Latin lover" and the "Latin spitfire"—male and female archetypes of Latino passion—are not entirely hurtful, since they imply that Latino bodies are essentially beautiful and particularly capable of giving pleasure to their partners. For example, Cesar Romero, Desi Arnaz, Rita Moreno, and Carmen Miranda—while fair objects of criticism by Latinos concerned with the stereotypes to which these notables contributed in the 1940s, 1950s, and 1960s—were nonetheless symbols of Latin passion. Countless devotees (of many different heritages) found pleasure in watching them perform. When placed in the context of a country such as the United States, with its history of puritanical repression, a visually provocative people believed to be less restrained in sensual matters can at times be welcomed with open arms. Latinos and

Latinas in various circumstances have embraced these images and used them to their advantage, whether to attract sexual partners or, in the case of performance artists such as Selena, Jennifer Lopez, and Ricky Martin, to market their talents by appealing to an audience's natural sexual desires. Like all stereotypes, however, they can become limiting or exaggerated and can inevitably backfire.

To be characterized as a Latin lover or a spitfire would not be as negatively consequential were not the United States heir to a long tradition of Western dualism that celebrates mental or spiritual purity while distrusting carnal urges. One can trace back to the Greek philosophers Socrates and Plato a distinct belief that the human body is a force for corruption and that its passions diminish the strength of the human spirit. The concept of Platonic "dualism" does not merely view the mind and the body as separate entities; it also moralizes the separation by valuing the former at the expense of the latter. Since sexuality is so difficult to process through pure mental abstraction, and because it is ultimately a physical field of activity carried out in the realm of the body, sex is tainted within dualism as dirty, inferior, and most important, anti-intellectual. For this reason, Plato's *Symposium* dictates that ultimate enlightenment must come through a human being's ability to transcend and therefore overcome his or her lust for the bodies of others. This assumption rests on the belief that one cannot think clearly when one is having sex or trying to seduce someone else. Platonic dualism was particularly distrustful of heterosexuality after Socrates, in the *Symposium,* posited the highest form of love as an asexual attachment between close friends of the same sex. Many of Plato's adherents would, as a result, romanticize friendship among men and would hold a generally grim view of women, relating maleness to the mind and femaleness to the body.

With the introduction of Christian theology, and particularly the writings of Saint Paul, dualism and its distrust of sexual passion would be translated into the more absolutist dualism of good and evil. With the advent of a globally imposed monotheism under the reign of Roman emperor Constantine (4th century A.D.), the body and its sexual desires became tied inextricably to evil, temptation, and corruption. Conversely, mental and spiritual activity was viewed as clean, holy, and redemptive. Saint Paul's letters in the first century, for example, exhorted Christians to deliver their bodies to the Lord as a living sacri-fice. Since the body died but the soul continued after death, Christianity's emphasis on everlasting life tended to view entrance into heaven as a reward for self-restraint in sexual matters. "Love" and "lust" became permanently distinguishable and defined in opposition to each other. Paul's famous disquisition on love in Corinthians 1:13 seeks to enshrine love as *agape,* or a purely spiritual form of inspiration, ultimately pointed toward God through the earthly medium of other people. *Eros,* the kind of love that feeds on bodily desires and manifests itself in carnal contact, was a corruption of *agape* and had the potential, if indulged, to prevent a Christian soul from entering heaven.

Although the fear of sexuality would increase and decrease at various points in the history of Christendom, for the most part the ironclad distinction of holy love and evil lust would remain consistent. Lust became one of the seven deadly sins, while love, often translated into English as desexualized "charity," became one of the three theological virtues alongside faith and hope. It was sexuality that marked the borderline between lust, the sin, and love, the theological virtue. As a result, human beings who were sexually defined—as hot-blooded, sexy, seductive, tempting, queer, horny, deviant, or any of a number of labels—were usually targeted by church leaders as evil.

Both Latin America and North America inherited the dualism that Christians originally inherited from the ancient Greeks. While Latin America is predominantly Catholic and North America predominantly Protestant, both sides of the Western Hemisphere are overwhelmingly Christian, and their cultures, with some variations, are imbued with Christian fears of sexuality. Although the myths of the Latin lover and the Latin spitfire might suggest that Latinos transported a lax attitude toward sexuality from their nations of origin, such a conclusion would be erroneous. The dominant Catholic cultures of virtually all Latin American nations construe sexual excess as unholy and associate sex with sin and guilt, unless it is sanctioned by the familiar religious blessing of marriage.

For Latinos, the specters of sin and guilt are not distributed equally across the sexes, and also tend to be aligned with gender-specific values of *marianismo* for women and machismo for men. *Marianismo* ostensibly dictates that women should remain virgins until after marriage. It also places a premium on women's sexual attractiveness and creates contradictory expectations of Latina women, who are encouraged to incite sexual desires in their male counterparts but not to satisfy them. This "virgin-whore complex" of incompatible gender values collides, moreover, with the expectations of Latino males under the system of machismo. Machismo, often misconstrued in North American culture as a belief that men should have and indulge rampant libidos, in reality values the ability of males to manage their sex lives with authority and control. This control means that men should be confident and resourceful enough to obtain sexual partners, while also strong enough to shield their partners from the competing interests of other men. The ideal Latino man also chooses his sexual partners wisely, distinguishing effectively between "good" girls, who have not been promiscuous, and "bad" girls, whose reputations are tarnished by too many past lovers. The emphasis is still on the Greco-Christian tradition of controlling sexual urges, containing them within repressive social strictures, and protecting one's spiritual essence from the dangers of unbridled lust. Machismo, like *marianismo,* is also in large part based on the male's and female's ability to subordinate sexual activity to their proper roles within the family. While both men and women are praised for being, respectively, sexually potent and sexually desirable, their sexual games must be organized in some modality that will not embarrass or endanger their families. A man must provide a respectable home for his children, and a woman must uphold good Catholic virtues in addition to passing them on to her children. Insofar as having many sexual partners risks corrupting or undermining the integrity of the family, Latino men are not encouraged by the machismo of their culture to be wild and indiscreet with their sex lives, as it is often incorrectly believed by North Americans.

The high fertility rates among Latinos, in fact, can be partly (but not entirely) traced to the community's Catholicism. Contraception and abortion carry with them, in a Christian rubric, the stigma of sexual excess; they imply that sex can exist purely for its own sake rather than for the sake of cementing marriage and producing children in accordance with the spiritual dictates of their deity. While succumbing to lustful urges might be a sin, many Latinos who have been raised religiously fear that using contraception or practicing abortion would be even worse, because it would be accommodating essentially guilty pleasures with a premeditated desire to shield oneself from the consequences.

North Americans may have a tendency to overlook the guilt and shame that Latinos associate with sex when they characterize them as hot-blooded or passionate. Some theorists have proposed that the myth of the Latin lover and the spitfire stems from North Americans' desires to find an object on which to project their own suppressed sexual desires, rather than from a real difference in the way Latinos relate to their eros. Carl Jung, a psychoanalytic scholar of the 20th century, formulated a model of the "shadow," the shadow being the dreamy projection of Western man's suppressed urges, notably sexual and violent ones, onto a darker-skinned counterpart. For instance, Jung recorded dreams in which he envisioned an African "savage" standing next to him, who slew people toward whom Jung himself felt hostile. By contemplating these strange images, he concluded that every person had a shadow hidden in his or her unconscious, who committed forbidden acts without sullying the person's own sense of innocence. It is possible, as some postcolonial theorists have suggested, that the Latin lover and the Latin spitfire have no basis in reality at all, and are the mere shadows of the ambivalent sexual urges that North Americans want to act on but must repress, in order to find acceptance in a society with essentially Puritan sexual mores.

If the Latin lover and the spitfire are the Jungian shadows of repressed North American lust, then these myths are constantly reinforced by social realities linked to urban poverty. Since Latinos in the United States are more likely to be poor and less likely to have an economically beneficial education, and since they often live in major urban centers, they are plentifully represented in the ranks of prostitution and pornography. The research of feminist scholars has long established a link between poverty and sex-based industries. Most women who sell their sexual talents as prostitutes, erotic performers, or pornographic models do so because they are poor, not necessarily because they enjoy being sexual objects. While a handful of celebrated Latina pornographic stars like Vanessa del Rio might rise to the level of cultural icons, most Latinas who enter sex-based industries end up contributing to the lascivious clichés about Latino sexuality without extracting long-term benefits. To a certain extent, therefore, it is understandable that North Americans would entertain notions about Latina women as lurid, sexually available, and more willing to experiment than their Anglo counterparts. Insofar as poor Latinas exchange sex for payment out of a need to survive, they are more compelled or constrained to experiment than are women who have no such need.

The stigma of prostitution affects not only the female half of Latino sexuality. As the North American gay movement became more vocal after the Stonewall Inn revolt of 1969 in New York City, and fought for more visibility after the AIDS (acquired immune deficiency syndrome) crisis took hold in the 1980s, there was an increase in the visual representation of homosexuality at all levels of culture, from Broadway plays to pornography. While some Latino men took prominent roles in the gay movement, it was impossible to stop an increasingly powerful gay community from reproducing much of the racial exploitation prevalent in straight American society. A cottage industry of gay pornography featuring Latino men grew rapidly in the 1980s and 1990s, accompanied by the continuing popularity of gay vacation spots in various hubs of Latin America, from Puerto Rico to Brazil, where North American gays could fulfill taboo sexual tastes with local male prostitutes more freely than they could in North American cities. Even at the level of mainstream films, images of gay Latinos with uncontrollable libidos popped up with increasing frequency, and the archetype of the flaming Latin homosexual was an established cliché. In gay neighborhoods such as Chelsea in New York City or South Beach in Miami, moreover, there are subcultures of Latino male prostitution not unlike the Latina streetwalkers who haunt inner cities.

Despite the common experience of sexual exploitation in the United States, and despite the dualistic guilt imposed both by their Latin American origins and by the puritan roots of their new home country, many Latinos and Latinas still enjoy healthy sex lives. Notwithstanding the problematic stereotypes, there are cultural differences inherent in Latino and Anglo sensibilities about bodily contact, perhaps best symbolized by their means of expressing affection in nonsexual settings. It is common for Latino men and Latina women who are friends to kiss one another on the cheek when they see each other, with much more closeness than the often-mocked "air kissing" of Anglo salutations. Latino men, while typically wary of physical interactions that could cast doubts on their heterosexuality, can often embrace or touch

each other's bodies in ways that bourgeois North Americans find discomforting. It is also not hard to notice that Latinos are more comfortable with physical proximity than Anglos and do not need as large a "safe zone" between their bodies and the bodies of strangers or acquaintances in places such as movie theaters, trains, elevators, and the like.

An important cultural difference between Latinos and the Anglo mainstream, and one that poses particular challenges in the fight against AIDS, is that the boundary between gay and straight is more firmly drawn in the United States than in Latin America. In Latin America homosexual behavior is more likely to be carried out in secret and does not as readily indicate that a person will refrain from getting married. In the early 21st century, attitudes have been changing in Latin America, where gay movements in places such as Brazil and Mexico have adopted many of the sexual definitions from North American movements and some activists are working to carve out a separate gay community.

In North America there is a widespread impetus to connect a person's sexual orientation with a social identity. People who feel attractions to the same sex are, in North American vocabulary, deemed gay and lesbian. In Latin America, where homosexuality is not discussed as openly, it is much more common for a person to have occasional sexual encounters with the same sex while still maintaining a standard marriage and remaining indistinguishable from the general population. There are men and women in Latin America who commit themselves to a strictly homosexual lifestyle, but this choice severely restricts them in a way it would not in parts of North America, and many of their compatriots would dismiss their lifestyle as bizarre or self-destructive. Most Latin Americans who choose to declare a strictly homosexual lifestyle have to exist on the fringes of society and receive little protection from abuse, violence, or ostracism. Hence bisexuality is an unspoken reality for many Latin Americans.

Because of the different implications of same-sex attraction in the two halves of the Western Hemisphere, Latinos occupy a confusing place in the sexual culture of the United States. Inheriting a cultural mindset that prefers a secret bisexuality to an open homosexuality, they migrate into a country that prefers the reverse. They are raised in a culture that allows more intimate physical contact, and then must function in a culture that tends to equate most forms of physical contact with a sexual advance. This may confuse a Latino or Latina who engages in casual contact with the same sex without any intention of giving up on the opposite sex, only to discover that in U.S. society their brief encounter has identified them "gay" or "lesbian."

Other social factors make Latinos particularly susceptible to such confusion. Since Latinos of both sexes have a higher rate of incarceration, for instance, they are more likely to be exposed to same-sex encounters designed to compensate for the absence of the opposite sex. In the Latino classic *Down these Mean Streets,* Piri Thomas chronicles his sexual confusion as a young Puerto Rican man whose friends encourage him to sodomize transvestites to prove his manliness. Later, in prison, peers expect him to engage in relations with fellow inmates. Thomas is constantly uncertain about the implications of his actions. At first he is satisfied to believe that he is a homosexual only if he engages in intercourse, but in prison he begins to fear that even that distinction will not protect him from becoming addicted, in a sense, to men if he plays the active role in sodomy. He views homosexuality as a looming addiction akin to his dependence on heroin and, in order to avoid compromising his masculinity, chooses to abstain from any sex in prison at all. Yet many of the other inmates Thomas describes have sexual relationships with other men in prison, while still claiming not to be homosexuals.

In addition to the high rate of incarceration, the high concentration of Latinos in poor urban areas plays a role as well. Gays and lesbians tend to congregate in large cities, and as such, Latinos who disproportionately grow up in those same large cities are likely to be exposed to queer subcultures before reaching an age when they are in a position to understand them fully. Adolescence, during which all individuals struggle to carve out a sexual identity, is fraught for urban Latinos with a range of influences beyond their maturity level. One such influence is the established subculture of gay and lesbian communities.

The disconnect between U.S. and Latin American sexual categories, combined with the distinctive Catholic attitudes about sex held by most Latinos, makes it particularly difficult to combat AIDS in the Latino community. While intravenous drug use might explain part of the high incidence of AIDS among Latinos and Latinas, sexual contact is also a factor.

Just as the shame about using contraceptives contributes to a high fertility rate, it also leaves Latinos highly vulnerable to sexually transmitted diseases. To prepare for a sexual encounter by buying a contraceptive beforehand implies a level of premeditation for a carnal act that their religion deems sinful, leading many to choose the lesser of two evils, which is to commit the sin and accept the consequences with no protection. Since homosexual and bisexual men are at particularly acute risk for contracting HIV (human immunodeficiency virus), a main educational goal of health-care workers has been to disseminate information about safer sex to the gay male community. Unfortunately, this information cannot always reach Latino men who have sex with other men. Latinos are more likely to consider themselves straight despite occasional homosexual encounters. They are also likely to consider such encounters off-limits for discussion with other people, since affairs with other men carry a double guilt, offending both Catholic injunctions against sex in general and macho taboos against playing the woman's role for another man in illicit sex acts like sodomy or fellatio. The result of the double guilt is too often silence and an avoidance of the very gay-oriented places where health-care workers are most likely to disseminate badly needed information about safe sex.

In conclusion, Latinos in the United States have often been defined in popular culture in sexual terms. Most sexual stereotypes about Latinos are mixed, involving some positive and some negative effects. Some of the stereotypes are based on North American fantasies about Latinos; others are based on Latinos' fantasies about themselves, and still others are based on reality.

RELATED ARTICLES

Family; Feminism; HIV/AIDS; Homosexuality, Female; Homosexuality, Male; Love, Latino Conceptions of; Machismo; Marianismo; Marriage; Stereotypes and Stereotyping.

FURTHER READING

Bacarisse, Pamela, ed. *Carnal Knowledge: Essays on the Flesh, Sex, and Sexuality in Hispanic Letters and Film.* Pittsburgh: Ediciones Tres Rios, 1991.

Balderston, Daniel, and Donna J. Guy, eds. *Sex and Sexuality in Latin America.* New York: N.Y. Univ. Press, 1997.

González, Ray, ed. *Muy Macho: Latino Men Confront Their Manhood.* New York: Anchor Bks., 1996.

Guttman, Matthew, ed. *Changing Men and Masculinities in Latin America.* Durham, N.C.: Duke Univ. Press, 2003.

Huntington, Samuel P. *Who Are We? The Challenges of America's Identity.* New York: Simon & Schuster, 2004.

Lavrin, Asuncion, ed. *Sexuality and Marriage in Colonial Latin America.* Lincoln: Univ. of Nebr. Press, 1989.

Paternostro, Silvana. *In the Land of God and Men: Confronting Our Sexual Culture.* New York: Dutton, 1998.

Schiffer, Jacobo. *Public Sex in a Latin Society.* New York: Haworth Hispanic/Latino Press, 2000.

Taylor, Diana, and Juan Villegas, eds. *Negotiating Performance: Gender, Sexuality and Theatricality in Latin/o America.* Durham, N.C.: Duke Univ. Press, 1994.

Thomas, Piri. *Down These Mean Streets.* New York: Vintage, 1997.

Twinam, Ann. *Public Lives, Private Secrets: Gender, Honor, Sexuality, and Illegitimacy in Colonial Spanish America.* Stanford, Calif.: Stanford Univ. Press, 1999.

ROBERT OSCAR LÓPEZ

SIDA. *See* HIV/AIDS.

SINARQUISTA MOVEMENT

The Sinarquista movement, or *sinarquismo,* begun in 1937 in León Guanajuato, Mexico, was founded by José Antonio Urquiza Septién and a group of loyal supporters. Also known as the UNS (Unión Nacional Sinarquista; National Synarquist Union), it attracted a broad base of support, from urban professionals to the rural poor who vowed support for the original goals of the Mexican Revolution and protection of the Catholic Church. The word *sinarquismo* was a contraction of the two Spanish words *sin* (without) and *anarquismo* (anarchy)—"orderly" or "with authority."

Although loosely based on Falangist (Spanish fascist) ideology, the movement remained largely a peaceful source of political opposition to the PRI (Partido Revolucionario Institucional; Institutional Revolutionary Party) founded after the Mexican Revolution. According to its founder Urquiza Septién, *sinarquismo* could be defined simply as *el bien que quiero para mí es el bien que quiero para los demás* ("the well-being I want for myself is the well-being I want for everyone else"). The *Manifesto of the Sinarquista Organizing Committee,* published in June 1937, describes *sinarquismo* as a way of life, a spiritual attitude, and a manner of working on problems of common concern. *Sinarquismo* as an ideology was disseminated through literature, conferences, Synarquist schools, and civic acts. In 1944 a group split from the UNS to form the PNS (Partido Nacional Sinarquista; National Synarquist Party), a political party that attempted to implement the ideology of the Sinarquista movement.

Sinarquistas organized Mexicans in the United States as well, ostensibly for the reclamation of, and respect for, the borderland territories taken by the United States government in 1848. In the 1940s, relying on the racism and discrimination faced by Mexicans in the United States, the media and the U.S. government claimed that Sinarquistas hoped to interrupt the Allied war effort in Europe and domestically. *Sinarquismo* became a popular media topic in the United States, especially in Southern California during the Sleepy Lagoon Trial of 1942 and the Zoot Suit Riots in 1943, as a cause for racial discord and altercations, although no evidence of this connection was ever found. By 1941 the Sinarquista movement claimed more than 500,000 followers in Mexico and, by 1944, more than 900,000.

In 1942 California historian Carey McWilliams estimated Sinarquista movement followers to be between 2,000 and 4,000 in the United States. During 1941–1942, Sinarquista meetings were reported to have been held in California, Texas, Indiana, Illinois, New York, and Colorado. Support for the movement came from Father Charles E. Coughlin and the National Union of Social Justice in Michigan, as well as other pro-Catholic organizations in California and Texas. Other organizations, such as the Congress of Industrial Organizations, denounced *sinarquismo,* particularly as a detriment to the Allied war effort.

The Sinarquista movement still exists and continues to express faith in the Mexican nation and protest against self-interested politicians, foreign intervention, secular education, and social injustice.

RELATED ARTICLES

Catholicism; Mexican Americans; Mexican Revolution; Mexico.

FURTHER READING

García, Mario T. *Mexican Americans: Leadership, Ideology, and Identity, 1930–1960.* Yale Western Americana Series. 1989. Reprint, New Haven, Conn.: Yale Univ. Press: 1991.

Johnson, Kenneth F. "Ideological Correlates of Right Wing Political Alienation in Mexico." *The American Political Science Review* 59, no. 3 (September 1965): 656–664.

McWilliams, Carey. *North from Mexico: The Spanish Speaking People of the United States.* New ed. New York: Praeger, 1990.

Michaels, Albert L. "The Crisis of Cardenismo." *Journal of Latin American Studies* 2, no. 1 (May 1970): 51–79.

SUSAN MARIE GREEN

SLEEPY LAGOON CASE

On the morning of Sunday, August 2, 1942, José Díaz, 22 years old, was found lying on a dirt road near Sleepy Lagoon, a water-filled gravel pit in rural Los Angeles. When Díaz died later that day at a local hospital, the swimming hole frequented by Mexican American youth banned from segregated public pools became the site of a murder mystery that captured the attention of the entire city. Although the exact circumstances surrounding his death were never determined, investigators established that Díaz had attended a party at a nearby ranch the previous night where Mexican American youths from the 38th Street neighborhood initiated a brawl with other partygoers. The Los Angeles Police Department (LAPD) immediately blamed the incident on the increasing threat posed by Mexican American *pachuco*, or zoot suit, gangs in the city, known for their style of long coats and baggy pants. The LAPD proceeded to round up more than 600 Mexican American youths for questioning, jailed the entire group known as the 38th Street Club, and subsequently charged 22 youths with having a hand in the death of Díaz.

The ensuing trial was biased against the defendants. Not only were many of the defendants and witnesses subject to police violence, but Judge Charles Fricke denied the defendants their constitutional right to consult with their attorney, did not allow them to change clothes or cut their hair despite spending months in jail, and consistently referred to them as "gangsters." The prosecuting attorney even argued to the jury that all Mexicans were cowards and naturally inclined to violence. In January 1943, in what was the largest mass conviction in California history, 17 of the boys were found guilty of second-degree murder, assault, or criminal conspiracy. Despite the lack of any evidence connecting even one of them to the murder, 10 were sent to San Quentin Prison, where they remained for nearly two years until their release on appeal.

During and after the trial, local authorities used the case as an excuse to heighten surveillance of Mexican Americans. Conflict between the LAPD and the Mexican American community intensified as youths were apprehended on sight for the mere suspicion of criminal behavior; in addition, police brutality continued unabated. Increasingly seen as enemies of the state, Mexican American youths became the focus of grand jury investigations, citywide patrols, and increasing hostility from the general public. The growing anti-Mexican sentiment was encapsulated by the grand jury testimony of Lieutenant Edward Duran Ayers of the Los Angeles Sheriff's Department, who argued, in essence, that Mexican American youth were bloodthirsty animals that needed to be caged for the safety of law-abiding citizens.

Throughout the trial and appeal, mainstream newspapers in Los Angeles, including the *Times,* the *Herald Express,* and the *Daily News,* similarly conflated Mexican American youth with criminal behavior. During 1942 and 1943, headlines were dominated by allegations that Mexican American youth were violent gangsters, drug users, and sexual predators. More a product of sensationalistic journalism and overzealous policing than any real rise in crime, the propaganda campaign blamed cultural inferiority and an abundance of idle time to make juvenile delinquency a problem unique to Mexican Americans. Mexican American youth, such reports claimed, were responsible for undermining the American war effort by disrupting peace on the home front and failing to contribute to war production industries.

In the midst of the growing animosity toward Mexican Americans following the verdict, several organizations mobilized to free the defendants on appeal and fight against the mistreatment of the city's Mexican American residents. Including Mexican American professionals such as lawyer Manuel Ruiz and labor organizer Josephina Fierro de Bright; prominent white social activists such as Carey McWilliams and Alice McGrath; African American community leaders such as Charlotta Bass, who owned and edited the *California Eagle* newspaper; and even Hollywood stars such as Orson Welles, the Sleepy Lagoon Defense Committee (SLDC) was formed to expose the trial's unfairness and support the defendants during their imprisonment. The SLDC tried to gain sympathy for the defendants by distributing pamphlets about the case, holding rallies, fund-raising, and claiming that racial discrimination hurt the war effort. Other groups such as the Citizens Committee for Latin American Youth (CCLAY) followed suit by establishing Boy Scout troops, Police Athletic Leagues, and after-school programs in an effort to decrease juvenile delinquency. Despite their important critiques of law enforcement strategies and plans to limit juvenile delinquency, many of these groups pushed their own assimilationist agenda for Mexican Americans and failed to confront the popular notion that Mexican American youth were biologically and culturally inferior. Although discrimination against Mexican American youth and youth of color continued to be a major problem, the SLDC and its supporters realized victory in October 1944 when the Second District Court of Appeals overturned the convictions of the Sleepy Lagoon defendants and they were freed.

Generating a powerful conviction among many Americans of the need to defend the United States from internal enemies as well as foreign, the Sleepy Lagoon case had a tremendous impact on the history of Los Angeles, Mexican Americans, and the United States. Fears that Mexican American youth were being organized by fifth-column fascists and communists inflamed wartime xenophobia that demonized youth of color and eventually led to the Zoot Suit Riots in June 1943. The racialization of juvenile delinquency soon spread to other metropolitan areas, as Mexican American and African American youth in New York, Detroit, and elsewhere were similarly blamed for raising crime rates and disrupting the war effort. The trial also mobilized the Mexican American community in ways previously unseen, connected them to a larger web of multiracial liberalism, and helped fuel the growing political force of Mexican Americans in the United States. Perhaps most important, the Sleepy Lagoon case illustrates how the activities of youth played an important role in shaping public policy during World War II. Ultimately, the Sleepy Lagoon case demonstrates that more recent debates around gang warfare, racial biases in the penal system, and the criminalization of youth of color in the United States are not something new; rather, they have a long history.

RELATED ARTICLES

Crime and Latinos; Discrimination; Los Angeles; Pachuco; Stereotypes and Stereotyping; Zoot Suit Riots.

FURTHER READING

Endor, Guy. *The Sleepy Lagoon Mystery.* Los Angeles: Sleepy Lagoon Defense Committee, 1944.

Escobar, Edward J. *Race, Police, and the Making of a Political Identity: Mexican Americans and the Los Angeles Police Department, 1900–1945.* Berkeley: Univ. of Calif. Press, 1999.

Mazón, Mauricio. *The Zoot-Suit Riots: The Psychology of Symbolic Annihilation.* Austin: Univ. of Tex. Press, 1984.

Pagan, Eduardo. "Sleepy Lagoon: The Politics of Youth and Race in Wartime Los Angeles, 1940–1954." Ph.D. Dissertation, Princeton University, 1996.

Sánchez, George. *Becoming Mexican American: Ethnicity, Culture and Identity in Chicano Los Angeles, 1900–1945.* Oxford: Oxford Univ. Press, 1993.

SELECTED WEB SITES

Public Broadcasting Company. *Zoot Suit Riots, American Experience.* www.pbs.org/wgbh/amex/zoot/index.html

LUIS ALVAREZ

SOCCER

The growth of American soccer is a relatively recent phenomenon—essentially beginning in the second half of the 20th century—and intrinsically connected to the patterns of immigration and acculturation in the United States, especially that of first- and second-generation Latinos. While the term *soccer mom* became a political catchword in the 1990s for a white, affluent suburban demographic, the influence of Latino culture on American soccer has been a critical factor from the beginning, and at all levels—from youth and amateur leagues in cities and suburbs across the country to professional leagues and the U.S. national teams.

Since the American Youth Soccer Organization (AYSO) first began its nationwide youth league in 1964, a unique breed of soccer (as opposed to *fútbol*) has been created, combining a variety of styles and influences. Soccer has been the fastest-growing high school sport since the mid-1990s; and it, perhaps more than any other sport, has become a principal player in the debate over America's multicultural identity.

AYSO was not the only league to play a major role in introducing soccer to the United States. Latino leagues have grown up as well, often side by side with immigrant communities in and around cities such as Los Angeles, Chicago, Miami, and New York. In Flushing Meadows Park in Queens, New York, or in Red Hook, Brooklyn, leagues of South American and Central American teams jostle for space on weekends with fans, food vendors, and sound systems creating a distinctly Latin festival atmosphere. Often these leagues are a way of maintaining connections to old traditions while creating new ties to American cities. The Liga Latina, for example, in Contra Costa, California, began in 1993 and spread over the next five years as the Latino population jumped by more than 20,000. Similar Latino youth leagues crisscross Southern California, where about 1 million people play amateur soccer, while other leagues thrive elsewhere, particularly throughout the Southwest and the East Coast. In New York the Latino influence is especially pervasive. Spanish radio and television stations carry matches of the Mexican and South American leagues and Spanish-language newspapers, such as *el diario,* follow the local action as well. (The Copa America tournament,

broadcast from Peru in the summer of 2004, drew overflow crowds in the restaurants of Jackson Heights, Queens, when it was broadcast live on Univisión.)

The history of the intersection of American soccer and the Latino impact on a professional level begins with the short-lived but highly influential North American Soccer League (NASL) of the late 1970s and early 1980s—and its most famous team, the New York Cosmos. For a few short years an American soccer team rivaled the New York Yankees in star appeal, box office, and pure drama. A

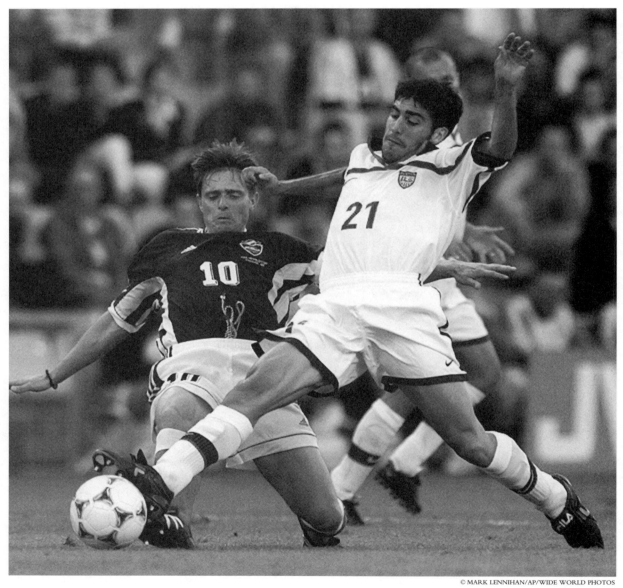

© MARK LENNIHAN/AP/WIDE WORLD PHOTOS

Dragan Stojkovic of Yugoslavia (*left*) and Claudio Reyna of the United States during a 1998 World Cup Group F soccer match in Nantes, France.

United Nations of international stars, the Cosmos's fortunes first rose on the strength of the Brazilian Pelé, who came to the United States in the mid-1970s in the twilight of his legendary international career. Soon, however, the team became a who's who from Europe and Latin America: Carlos Alberto and Marinho from Brazil; Roberto Cabanas and Julio Cesar Romero from Paraguay; as well as Giorgio Chinaglia from Italy and Franz Beckenbauer from Germany.

The NASL certainly anticipated the overwhelming appeal of American soccer, particularly in drawing crowds from its immigrant fans (the Cosmos regularly filled the 70,000-plus Giants Stadium in New Jersey, becoming a soccer mecca for carpooling crowds, heavily Spanish-speaking, from across New York's tristate area). But it ran out of steam in the early 1980s, leaving American soccer to develop from grassroots youth leagues, largely suburban, sprouting up across the country. The fruits of these youth programs, as well as the high level of collegiate soccer, were finally realized when the United States hosted the 1994 World Cup. The men's national team, with its Uruguayan-born captain Tab Ramos, captured the attention of the rest of the world and even sportscrazed Americans as it advanced to the second round before losing to Brazil 1–0 on July 4. In staging the 1994 World Cup, which played to sold-out crowds from California to Texas, from Massachusetts to New Jersey, Americans got their first real taste of the ecstasy and pageantry of this sport.

In the afterglow of the tournament, the next American professional league was born in 1996: Major League Soccer (MLS). A more modest enterprise than the NASL, and with a lot more homegrown players, MLS nevertheless improved on the tradition of marrying American soccer with Latin American stars and style. The Colombian great Carlos Valderrama came to play for the Miami franchise, quickly becoming a fan favorite. Jorge Campos, the flashy Mexican goalkeeper, also joined the league, as did the Bolivian striker Marco Etcheverry and Mexican idol Luis Hernandez (adding scoring power to the Los Angeles Galaxy in 2000 to the delight of overwhelmingly Latino capacity crowds). In fact, MLS has been reaching out more than ever to its heavily Latino fan base. In 2002, 30 percent of those attending MLS games were Latino, while 20 percent of the players had Latino backgrounds. Nine of the league's ten teams also broadcast games on Span-

ish radio and television, and plans were under way for the Mexican team Chivas to join the league. It is truly a "New Soccer Nation," as the MLS ad campaign proclaims.

The U.S. men's national team became more competitive internationally in the 1998 and 2002 World Cup matches. Led by captain Claudio Reyna (born in Argentina but, like Tab Ramos, raised in New Jersey), the U.S. men's team effectively became the powerhouse in its region (Caribbean, North and Central America), with a fierce rivalry developing with the Mexican team, which the U.S. team eliminated in the 2002 World Cup. (The Mexican film *Y Tu Mamá También* gives a biting but comic perspective on Team America.) Of course, the world's most glamorous team at the start of the 21st century is the Spanish Real Madrid, with such international stars as Ronaldo, Roberto Carlos, Luis Figo, Zinedine Zidane, and David Beckham. The search continues across North America for the first real American star to bring the U.S. game to a higher level—a player who will fuse the athletic American style with the technique, instincts, and joy of a Latin American player. American soccer, with its hybrid identity rooted in an immigrant past, might just prove to be the most American sport of all.

RELATED ARTICLES

Sports in Latino Life.

FURTHER READING

Bellos, Alex. *Futebol: The Brazilian Way.* New York: Bloomsbury, 2002.

Foer, Franklin. *How Soccer Explains the World: An Unlikely Theory of Globalization.* New York: HarperCollins, 2004.

Galeano, Eduardo. *Soccer in Sun and Shadow.* New York: Verso, 1998.

Kapuscinski, Ryszard. *The Soccer War.* New York: Penguin, 1991.

Markovits, Andrei S., and Steven Hellerman. *Offside: Soccer and American Exceptionalism.* Princeton, N.J.: Princeton Univ. Press, 2001.

Morales, Ed. *Living in Spanglish: The Search for Latino Identity in America.* New York: St. Martin's, 2002.

SELECTED WEB SITES

U.S. National Soccer Team Players Association. http://www.ussoccerplayers.com

World Soccer. http://www.worldsoccer.com

American Youth Soccer Organization. http://www.soccer.org

ANDERSON TEPPER

SON

Son is an original Cuban song form, which has become the foundation for the popular music that is today called salsa. Developed in the province of Oriente during the late 19th century, *son* is generally regarded as the first truly Cuban song form, as well as the first to successfully integrate musical elements from both Spanish and African origins. While *danzon,* Cuba's national song form (of Spanish colonial origin), is considered a product of the highly sophisticated, upper-class urban (generally white) populace, *son* was born in the rural countryside. It is regarded as the music of the working class (often black or of mixed racial origins).

In its early stages a *son* group might have featured one or two guitars, supported rhythmically by percussion instruments such as *claves* and maracas, and perhaps a *botija* (earthenware jug) serving as a bass instrument. One or more *soneros* (lead singers) in the group would improvise lyrics and be backed up by a *coro* (chorus of two or more singers) in a call-and-response pattern. Typically, the *sonero* might choose to criticize community politics, poke fun at a neighborhood personage, or even question the fidelity of a local citizen's wife. It became commonplace for such sessions to end badly, often developing into major riots. In time, *soneros* learned to tone down their insults, and the form gradually gained widespread popularity throughout Cuba.

By the early 1920s many *son* groups had expanded, becoming *sextetos.* These groups now consisted of *tres* (a six- or nine-string instrument native to Cuba), guitar, *marimbula* (African-derived thumb piano), *claves,* maracas, and bongos. The most famous of these ensembles was the Sexteto Habanero, which had developed from an early *son* group called Trio Oriental. The instrumentation of *sextetos* was further changed later in the 1920s, with the replacement of the *marimbula* by a string bass and with the addition of a cornet or trumpet—in order to offer a more powerful melodic sound. Thereafter, such groups were known as *septetos.* Of these, the most famous was undoubtedly Septeto Nacional, under the musical direction of Ignacio Piñeiro. One of Piñeiro's well-known compositions, *Echale Salsita,* is often cited as the first instance in which the word *salsa* was used to characterize Cuban-derived Latin music.

Toward the end of the 1930s, the composition of *son* groups changed once more, with the addition of a piano (often as a replacement for the *tres*), along with one or more additional trumpets to strengthen the overall sound. Groups containing such augmented instrumentation were called *conjuntos.* The *tresista* (*tres* player) Arsenio Rodriguez led one of the best-known *conjuntos* of the time, eventually adding a *campana* (cowbell) and *tumbadora* (conga drum) to his group. The addition of these percussion instruments literally revolutionized the sound of the *conjunto,* and formed the true foundation for what we recognize today as the salsa band.

Rodriguez popularized one of the many hybrid forms of *son,* the *son montuno,* which adds a driving, continuous rhythm pattern to the last part of the song. Other hybrid forms of the *son,* which became popular over time, include *son-pregon, afro-son,* and *son-guajira.*

RELATED ARTICLES

Afro-Latino Influences; Danzon; Music, Popular; Salsa.

FURTHER READING

Gerard, Charley, and Marty Sheller. *Salsa: The Rhythm of Latin Music.* Gilsum, N.H.: White Cliffs Media, 1989.

Roberts, John Storm. *The Latin Tinge: The Impact of Latin American Music on the United States.* New York: Oxford Univ. Press, 1999.

Steward, Sue. *Musica!: The Rhythm of Latin America; Salsa, Rumba, Merengue and More.* San Francisco: Chronicle Bks., 1999.

FRAN CHESLEIGH

SOSA, SAMMY

Born: November 12, 1968; San Pedro de Maris, Dominican Republic

Major league baseball star Samuel Peralta Sosa was raised in a poor household with parents Lucrecia Sosa and Bautista Montero, his two sisters, and four brothers. As a child Sosa could not afford a bat and a glove. According to a legend he himself fostered, he made a glove out of milk cartons, a bat out of a tree branch, and a ball out of a rolled-up sock with tape around it. Anything was done to play baseball, or *pelota,* as it is called in Spanish.

At 14 Sosa picked up his first real bat and played in several small leagues in Santo Domingo. When he reached 16, scout Omar Minaya signed him with the Texas Rangers, giving him a signing bonus of

© BETH A. KEISER/AP/WIDE WORLD PHOTOS

Sammy Sosa of the Chicago Cubs, watches his 62d home run of the 1998 season sail over the wall in a game against the Milwaukee Brewers.

$3,500. Sosa generously sent $3,300 back to his mother to help support the family and bought himself a bicycle.

In his first year in the major leagues, 1989, Sosa struggled with a .238 batting average and a single home run for the season. He was sent to the minor leagues several times and then traded to the Chicago White Sox. His struggle continued during his three-year stay with the White Sox, averaging just .240 at bat, with many strikeouts. The White Sox sent Sosa back to the minor leagues and then traded him to the Chicago Cubs in 1992.

In his first full year (1993) as a Cub, Sosa hit 33 home runs, knocked in 93 RBIs (runs batted in), and was on his way to becoming an All-Star. In 1998 he made history when he finished the season with 66 home runs—breaking the 37-year-old record of 61 once held by Roger Maris—and was named the National League's Most Valuable Player.

Sosa instantly became a household name and a hero to many, especially to those from the Dominican Republic. He was honored with parades and celebrations for his accomplishments during the 1998 season. After the season Sosa went home to face a severe crisis. Hurricane George had ravaged the Dominican Republic, leaving over 100,000 homeless, without food and shelter. Sosa played a major role in providing aid to the victims of the hurricane by supplying food, water, and shelter, and by forming the Sammy Sosa Foundation.

In 1999 Sosa continued his torrid hitting and became the only player to hit over 60 home runs in two different major league seasons. During the 2000 season he proved that he remained one of the top sluggers in baseball when he hit 50 home runs with a career-high batting average of .320. And in 2003 he reached another milestone when he became the 18th player in baseball history to hit 500 career home runs, also becoming the first Latino to ever do so. But soon thereafter Sosa's reputation as a home run hitter came into question when umpires found cork in his shattered bat during a game. Sosa, who said he used that bat for batting practice and had not intended to use it during a game, was immediately ejected and served a seven-game suspension. Sosa and his wife, Sonia, have four children, Keysha, Kenya, Sammy, Jr., and Michael.

RELATED ARTICLES

Baseball; Dominican Americans; Sports in Latino Life.

FURTHER READING

Gentile, Derek. *The Complete Chicago Cubs.* Black Dog & Leventhal Pubs., 2002.

Pare, Michael A. *Sammy Sosa.* In *Sports Stars* (Series 5). Gale Group, 1999.

Sosa, Sammy, and Breton Marcos. *Sammy Sosa: An Autobiography.* Warner Bks., 2000.

SELECTED WEB SITE

Latino Legends in Sports. www.latinosportslegends.com

OZZIE GONZALEZ

SOUTH CAROLINA

The first Spaniards probably arrived in the region that would become South Carolina as early as 1514, but the first Spanish settlement was not established until 1526 near present-day Fort Winyall. A Spanish settlement was also established at Santa Elena in 1566, near present-day Parris Island. This city served as the capital of Spanish Florida from 1568 to 1576, when attacks by Native Americans forced a brief evacuation. The Spaniards returned in 1577, rebuilding Santa Elena. However, in 1587, English raids forced the evacuation of Santa Elena; the Spanish settlers moved to Saint Augustine in present-day Florida, leaving the South Carolina coast in the hands of their European rivals.

South Carolina, named by the British in honor of King Charles I of England, became an American state on May 23, 1788. For the better part of the next two centuries, the Palmetto state was home to a very small Latino community. Until the 1980s South Carolina's Spanish-speaking population was primarily made up of Puerto Ricans and Cubans. In the 1980s, however, larger numbers of Mexicans and Central Americans began taking jobs in South Carolina's agricultural industry.

In 1990 the number of Latinos living in South Carolina was tallied at 30,551. The next ten years saw the population increase by 379 percent to 95,076, representing 2.4 percent of the state's total population. At least 52,871 of these were of Mexican heritage, representing 55.61 percent of the total Latino population and 1.3 percent of the state population. Puerto Ricans, numbering 12,211, made up 12.84 percent of the Hispanic population; Cubans numbered only 2,875 in 2000, a mere 3 percent of the state's Latino population.

The counties with the largest numbers of Hispanics and Latinos in 2000 were Greenville—14,283; Richland—8,713; Beaufort—8,208; and Charleston—7,434. The counties with the highest percentages of Latinos were Saluda—7.3 percent; Beaufort—6.8 percent; Jasper—5.8 percent; Newberry—4.2 percent; and Greenville—3.8 percent.

The increased numbers of Latinos arriving in South Carolina prompted government officials to review specific services in order to meet the unique needs of this population. Acercamiento Hispano de Carolina del Sur was established in Columbia in 1995 to promote the well-being of members of the Hispanic community, especially migrant and seasonal farmworkers. In addition, the South Carolina Hispanic/Latino Health Coalition was founded to help

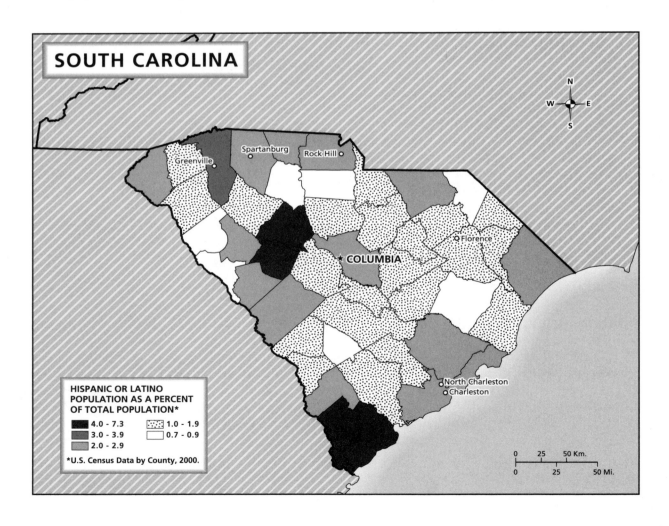

the Latino community overcome barriers to obtaining appropriate health care.

Irma Santana, a citizen activist of South Carolina, founded the Columbia-based Hispanic Outreach of South Carolina. Santana, as director, has campaigned to organize Latino participation in the electoral process. At the beginning of the 21st century, Latino political representation in South Carolina was nonexistent. However, with the Latino population expected to reach 316,000 by the year 2010, Hispanic representation in political process is certain to be realized.

RELATED ARTICLES

Immigration, Latino; Politics, Latino.

FURTHER READING

Armas, Genaro C. "Hispanic Population Surges, Led by South, West." *Las Vegas Review-Journal,* September 18, 2003.

Clark, Elmer Talmage. *The Latin Immigrant in the South.* Nashville, Tenn.: Cokesbury Press, 1924.

Ivers, Larry E. *British Drums on the Southern Frontier: The Military Colonization of Georgia, 1733–1749.* Chapel Hill: Univ. of N.C. Press, 1974.

Montgomery, Bob, and Dale Perry. "State's Hispanic Population Tripled." *The Greenville News,* March 15, 2001.

Murphy, Arthur D. et al. *Latino Workers in the Contemporary South.* Athens: Univ. of Ga. Press, 2001.

Quattlebaum, Paul. *The Land Called Chicora: The Carolinas under Spanish Rule, with French Intrusions, 1520–1670.* Gainesville: Univ. of Fla. Press, 1956.

SELECTED WEB SITES

Acercamiento Hispano de Carolina del Sur.
http://www.schispanicoutreach.org/
South Carolina Hispanic/Latino Health Coalition.
http://www.schlhc.org/

JOHN P. SCHMAL

SOUTHWESTERN UNITED STATES, ANGLO IMMIGRATION TO

Anglo immigration to the Southwest began a historical relationship both contentious and cooperative with Latino society. Latino life experiences included dependence on their own particular organizations for survival in a society that challenged their culture. Anglo technological advancements in agriculture, mining, rail transport, and foreign-funded capitalism and foreign policies affected Latino life and cultures, creating Anglo-Latino relations that were sometimes tense and at other times focused on the same goals.

In the middle of the 1700s, French traders from Illinois and Louisiana began to penetrate New Mexico in an effort to initiate trade. Anglo traders and mountain men were some of the first entrants into Mexico's northern frontier that later became the U.S. Southwest. In 1821 William Becknell, a trader, made his way into Santa Fe, New Mexico, where he was welcomed and traded profitably. He returned to Missouri, and the news of his experience spread. Soon, Becknell, Stephen Cooper, and others led trading expeditions to Santa Fe. Missouri senator Thomas Hart Benton was instrumental in getting Congress to pass an act on March 3, 1825, for military protection of the trade caravans. With Mexico's granting permission for a survey to Santa Fe in 1826, the Santa Fe Trail became a trade route between Missouri and New Mexico. Business enterprises of both countries cooperated in trade negotiations and commerce. The effect on the region—influx of household goods and equipment, and solidifying business relations with the United States—was immediate. New Mexico had earlier opened trade routes to Chihuahua, Sonora, and California, Mexico. This economic relationship between the United States and Mexico would continue to expand, culminating in the North America Free Trade Agreement (1994).

New Mexico, including present-day Arizona, had been part of Mexico's Provincias Internas, which incorporated the whole of what is today the U.S. Southwest. After Mexico gained its independence from Spain in 1821, the Provincias became Mexico's northern territory. Mexico was accommodating Anglo-Americans who sought to trade or settle in its territories. Stephen Fuller Austin acquired a land grant from the Mexican government to settle in Texas in 1823 and founded the colony of San Felipe de Austin. Mexico gave hundreds of land titles to Anglo-American settlers. In addition, the Mexican government provided for further colonization through agents authorized by Mexican state contracts. Texas's Anglo population grew rapidly, creating friction around culture, language, and political views with Latino populations. A colonizer agent (*empresario*) named Hayden Edwards led a revolt and declared a Republic of Fredonia and called for all "Americans" to join his cause. The "Americans" who settled in Mexican territory had been expected to be loyal Mexican subjects. Laws enacted by the Mexican government had rubbed Texas colonists the wrong way, and the constitution of 1835, which replaced the federalist Mexican government with a centralist one, led Texans to declare an independent republic. Ten years later Texas was annexed by the United States. United States president James K. Polk desired land for economic development, the establishment of a railroad to the West Coast, and national expansion and settlement; these desires resulted in further U.S. intrusions into Mexico's northern territory. This led to the Mexican-American War of 1846–1848, which resulted in Mexico ceding its northern territories to the United States under the terms of the Treaty of Guadalupe Hidalgo.

The news of discovery of gold in California on the land of John S. Sutter, a Swiss immigrant, quickly spread throughout the country and Anglo-Americans rushed to California to seek their fortunes. The avalanche of English-speakers affected the outnumbered Californios (Spanish-speaking Californians) adversely—the Anglos squatted on private lands, challenged the titles of land grants, were violent, passed restrictive legislation, and often jumped the Spanish-speaking miners' mine claims. Nevertheless, Californios in California's state constitution of 1849 were able to secure a degree of protection in the form of support for biculturalism and bilingualism. But within 30 years all semblance of constitutional, cultural, and language protections ended in the public schools, courts of law, and public administration.

Throughout the Southwest, Mexican Americans occupying lands under titles granted from the Mexican and Spanish governments and Articles VIII and IX of the Treaty of Guadalupe Hidalgo lost most of the land titles to legal strategies that placed the lands in the hands of Anglos and in the U.S. public domain. For example, Congress was pressured by state politicians to pass the Land Act of 1851 for California and to create in 1891 the Court of Private Land Claims for New Mexico, Colorado, and Arizona. In regard to Pueblo common lands, the case of *United States* v. *Sandoval* in 1897 rejected New Mexico Pueblo claims to common lands held and used for livelihood for more than two and half centuries.

The Anglo-American immigrants had come to the Southwest to conquer militarily, trade, mine gold, acquire land to settle, and farm or ranch. Hundreds of thousands of Anglo-Americans arrived and quickly outmatched Latinos in population, soon dominating the political and legal processes, controlling the economy, and promoting their culture and social mores. The violation of Latino cultural norms and political

rights by the majority Anglo-American population provided Mexican Americans with the motivation for establishing community organizations to fight back. With specific social, economic, and political objectives—political equity and equality—locally, regionally, and nationally these organizations gave Latinos the only recourse for redress and the exercise of political influence. These *mutualistas* (mutual aid) groups were the forerunners of modern day nonprofit organizations like the League of United Latin American Citizens, founded 1929 in Corpus Christi, Texas, and the American GI Forum started in Texas after World War II to look out for the interests of Latino veterans. Latino veterans also formed American Legion posts and carried out projects to end discrimination that had previously kept Latinos out of public places such as swimming pools and movie theaters. Latinos continued to struggle against pay differentials and to end real estate restrictions prohibiting Latinos from purchasing homes in certain areas. National organizations that actively address community political issues of Hispanic populations include the Mexican American Legal Defense and Education Fund (MALDEF) and the National Council of La Raza, both founded in 1968. Latinos traditionally joined labor unions in mines and smelters and participated in strikes.

Anglo-American immigration to the Southwest accelerated the development of mining, ranching, and farming industries, transformed the used of natural resources, and speeded the integration of the western economy with that of the eastern United States and Europe. The resulting need for labor was answered by Mexican workers immigrating into the Southwest, providing a workforce that expanded with the growth of the United States economy. Latinos and Anglos engaged in many cooperative efforts in building the Southwest.

RELATED ARTICLES

Arizona; Guadalupe Hidalgo, Treaty of; Homestead Act; Manifest Destiny; Mutual Aid Societies; New Mexico; San Diego, Plan de; Santa Fe Expedition; Texas.

FURTHER READING

Acuña, Rodolfo. *Occupied America: The Chicano's Struggle toward Liberation.* San Francisco: Canfield Press, 1972.

Bancroft, Hubert Howe. *History of Arizona and New Mexico 1530–1888.* Albuquerque, N.Mex.: Horn & Wallace, 1962 [a facsimile of the 1889 edition].

Bender, Averam B. *The March of Empire: Frontier Defense in the Southwest 1848–1860.* Lawrence: Univ. of Kans. Press, 1952.

Faulk, Odie B. *Land of Many Frontiers: A History of the American Southwest.* New York: Oxford Univ. Press, 1968.

García, Chris F., and Rudolph O. de la Garza. *The Chicano Political Experience: Three Perspectives.* North Scituate, Mass.: Duxbury Press, 1977.

Gonzales, Sylvia Alicia. *Hispano American Voluntary Organizations.* Westport, Conn.: Greenwood Press, 1985.

Kruszewski, Z. Anthony, et al., eds. *Politics and Society in the Southwest, Ethnicity and Chicano Pluralism.* Boulder, Colo.: Westview Press, 1982.

Meier, Matt S., and Feliciano Ribera. *Mexican Americans/American Mexicans: From Conquistadors to Chicanos.* New York: Hill & Wang, 1993.

SANTOS C. VEGA

SPAIN

The role the Spanish empire played in the 16th century in the colonization of the Americas—and in particular the territories that form the United States today—left a lasting mark on Latino identity and culture. Despite the animosity toward *lo español* among the Hispanic population, the influence is unquestionable in all areas—from religion to language, from psychology to politics, from gender relations to culinary tastes. To understand that influence it is crucial to look at the intertwining history: at one point Spain controlled a large portion of American land, but by the end of the 19th century, its military and political fortunes across the Atlantic Ocean were in tatters. Spain nevertheless left a deep legacy.

The Iberian Invasion

Spain had been fighting the Muslim occupation for nearly eight centuries when the kingdoms of Aragón and Castile, united by the marriage of their monarchs, the Catholic Ferdinand and Isabel, completed the reconquest of Spain in 1492. That same year Christopher Columbus began his first voyage that would land him in a world unknown to Europeans. Columbus became the flag bearer of the expansionist policy of Castile. While Aragón expanded eastward, Castile did so westward toward the new continent. The year 1492 saw published the first grammar of the Spanish language, written by scholar Antonio de Nebrija of the Universidad de Salamanca. In its prologue Nebrija suggested that "language has always been a companion of empire."

Oxford historian Salvador de Madariaga once commented that the spirit of Spanish ambition defined the battalion of men who crossed the sea in search of adventure, power, and recognition. The first Spanish explorer to set foot on the part of the North American continent that would become the United States was Ponce the León, who, in 1513, on Easter day, landed in what would become the state of Florida, which became the starting point for a long process of exploration and settlement. On the other side of the continent, in what would become the state of California, 30 years would pass before the first Spanish explorer set foot on the shore of San Diego Bay. In 1542 Juan Rodríguez Cabrillo set off under orders from the viceroy of the New Spain, to explore the northern areas.

In the east Alonso Alvárez de Piñeda led the early explorations, including an expedition in 1519 that went from Mexico, followed the contour of the Gulf, up to the Mississippi Delta. Another explorer who ventured into the southeastern parts of the United States was Hernando de Soto, whose 1542 expedition took him from Florida to the edge of the Mississippi River near where Memphis, Tennessee, would later arise. He died there. In 1565 the explorer Pedro Menéndez de Avilés founded the town of Saint Augustine, the first Spanish settlement in Florida, establishing a chain of forts along Florida's eastern coast to guarantee that supplies could reach all settlements by sea.

Cabrillo first explored the western part of the continent in 1542; he sailed from Baja California and found the huge natural port of San Diego. When he died on the journey north, he was replaced by his pilot, Bartolomé Ferrelo, who continued up the Oregon coast before returning in 1543 to the port of Navidad.

In the late 20th and early 21st centuries—using Fray Bartolomé de Las Casas as an example—historians and others have accused the Spanish of genocide in the Americas. Certainly the Iberian colonizers destroyed much of the flora, fauna, and indigenous peoples. They were not alone, however; a whole European concept of the world and their proper place within it allowed those excesses. Spanish colonization of North America took three centuries to complete. For scholarly purposes, its spread is divided into four distinct geographic areas: Florida, Louisiana, Texas, and California, all of which had administrative autonomy.

Florida. Intensive and continuing efforts began by Jesuit priests to convert the indigenous peoples of the area to Christianity. Franciscan friars started their

missionary work in Florida just ten years after the Jesuits. In 1586 Sir Francis Drake, a British seafarer, conquered and burned Saint Augustine; throughout the 17th century, although sometimes impeded by sporadic attacks by Native Americans, Spanish colonization continued in Florida. By the 1680s San Marcos de Apalache (now, St. Marks) was a fort and a settlement of consequence. Pensacola was permanently resettled in 1698. The French captured Pensacola in 1719; however, it was soon returned to Spain after the French entered into an alliance with Spain in an effort to contain the English on the continent. The French also occupied the Gulf Coast west of Pensacola. The British managed to conquer Pensacola, and the Spanish recovered the city in 1781. Two years later the British returned Florida to Spain. In 1819 American secretary of state John Quincy Adams and Spanish minister Luis de Onís reached an agreement, ratified by both nations only in 1821, by which Spain gave the United States title to East and West Florida.

Louisiana. Louis Juchereau de St. Denis founded Fort St. Jean Baptiste, present-day Natchitoches. The first permanent settlement in Louisiana was established in 1712. Only in 1769 did Spanish governor Alejandro O'Reilly gain firm control of Louisiana for Spain. O'Reilly divided the province into 12 districts (posts) and 22 ecclesiastical parishes. The system of posts died with the end of Spanish rule, but parishes persisted as the primary county-level administrative unit under territorial and state governments. The 1779 war between Spain and Britain affected Louisiana—Spanish governor Bernardo de Gálvez conducted a surprise attack on the British fort at Baton Rouge and captured the outpost. As a result, the West Florida parishes were returned to Spanish rule. Spain returned the Louisiana territory west of the Mississippi to France by the secret Treaty of San Ildefonso in 1800 to avoid the colony's continued drain on Spain's treasury.

Texas. The first explorer to reach the area was Alvar Núñez Cabeza de Vaca, who was shipwrecked in 1529 on what today is Galveston Island. For six years he explored the Texas interior on his way back to Mexico. In search of the fabled Seven Cities of Cibola, Francisco Vásquez de Coronado led an expedition in 1540–1542 into the present southwestern United States and across northern Texas. Settlement began along the Texas coastline but it was unsuccessful. Not until the 18th century did Spain establish Roman Catholic missions in Texas; along with the missions, it established the towns of San Antonio, Goliad, and Nacogdoches, which were the first successful cities in Texas; however, the Gutierrez-Magee expedition, leaving from Louisiana, moved successfully against Spanish rule in Texas in 1812.

California. The main settlement process employed by Spanish in California was the establishment of missions. Fray Junípero Serra, a Spanish Franciscan, arrived in California in 1769, founding California's first nine missions and serving as father-president of the mission system. An ambitious colonial administrator, José de Gálvez, arrived in New Spain in 1765. Gálvez conceived and ordered what came to be called the "Sacred Expedition," a push to extend Spanish settlement northward to Alta California. Gálvez hoped that the success of the expedition would lead to his appointment to higher colonial office. The first city to be established was San José, founded in 1777. It was followed in 1781 by El Pueblo de Nuestra Señora la Reina de los Angeles del Río de Porciúncula, also known as Los Angeles.

African American founding families made up more than half of the original settlers of Los Angeles. The local government of the pueblos consisted of an *alcalde,* or mayor, and a city council known as the *ayuntamiento.* No records survive of the actual founding of Los Angeles on September 4, 1781. By 1784 the settlers had replaced their first crude huts with more substantial adobe houses and laid the foundations for a church and other public buildings. Six years later the pueblo had grown to 141 persons, of whom 80 percent were under age 16. In the fields around the pueblo grazed 3,000 head of cattle. By 1820 the pueblo had increased to about 650 resi-

dents, the largest civilian community in Spanish California. One of the most active figures in the Spanish exploration of the California interior was Lieutenant Gabriel Moraga; between 1805 and 1817 Moraga led several expeditions into the Central Valley. He visited and named such prominent geographical features in the interior as the Sacramento River (named for the Holy Sacrament), the San Joaquin River (named for Saint Joseph), and the Merced River (named for Our Lady of Mercy). Moraga named Mariposa for the butterflies seen in the area, and Calaveras for its many skulls. In 1821 Mexico took charge of California from the Spanish. Mexico would govern California until the Treaty of Guadalupe Hidalgo in 1848, the terms of which ceded California to the United States.

The Events surrounding 1898

Spain lost its influence in the Caribbean Basin at the end of the 19th century as a result of the Spanish-American War, a conflict that involved the United States in a fight against the Spanish in Cuba, Puerto Rico, Guam, and the Philippines. The conflict took place and was resolved relatively quickly, and it marked the end of Spain as a colonial world power.

In January 1897 both William Randolph Hearst's *New York Journal* and Joseph Pulitzer's *New York World,* through sensational reporting on the insurrection in Cuba, helped strengthen anti-Spanish sentiment in the United States. Cuban rebel Adolfo Rodríguez was executed by a Spanish firing squad; the event was reported by Richard Harding Davis in an article entitled "Death of Rodríguez" in the *New York Journal.* On October 8, 1897, Karl Decker of the *Journal* reported on the rescue of Cuban Evangelina Cisneros from a prison on the Isle of Pines.

In March 1897 William McKinley was inaugurated as president of the United States; Theodore Roosevelt was named assistant U.S. secretary of the navy. In August Spanish prime minister Antonio Cánovas was assassinated, prompting a change in government and causing increased chaos in Spain and its military institutions. On the first day of 1898, Spain granted limited autonomy to Cuba, thus giving the island government some active representation in the Spanish legislature. On February 15, the U.S.S. *Maine* exploded in Havana harbor, which put Spain and the United States onto the path to war.

At the end of March a "Report of U.S. Naval Court of Inquiry" found the explosion on the *Maine* to have been caused by a mine; however, the Spanish denied any involvement, claiming that the sinking of the *Maine* was done to start the war. The United States issued an ultimatum to Spain to end its presence in Cuba. Although Spain did not accede to the demand in its reply of April 1, 1898, Spanish governor-general Blanco in Cuba did suspend hostilities against the Cuban rebels.

In April the U.S. Congress agreed to President McKinley's request for intervention in Cuba, but without recognition of the Cuban government. The American fleet left Key West, Florida, for Havana to begin a blockade of the principal ports on the north coast of Cuba and at Cienfuegos. Spanish minister of defense Segismundo Bermejo had sent instructions to Admiral Cervera to proceed with his fleet from the Cape Verde Islands to the Caribbean, Cuba, and Puerto Rico. War was formally declared between Spain and the United States on April 25.

In June U.S. marines landed at Guantánamo, Cuba, and, by July 17, Santiago, the last bastion of Spanish resistance, had surrendered to American troops. The next day the Spanish government, through the French ambassador to the United States, Jules Cambon, sent a message to President McKinley requesting a suspension of hostilities and the start of negotiations to end the war. Juan Manuel Sánchez y Gutiérrez de Castro, Duque de Almodóvar del Río, as Spanish minister of state, sent a telegram to the Spanish ambassador in Paris telling him to negotiate a suspension of hostilities as a preliminary step to final negotiations.

The Treaty of Paris was ratified on April 11, 1899. The treaty ended hostilities between the two countries and included the purchase of the Philippines and the annexation of Guam and Puerto Rico. Spain was out of the region and the United States was in.

The 20th Century

By the early part of the 20th century, Spain would exercise influence on the United States only through its Latino population. Spain's role as a colonizer was over, and it became a European country without world power or political influence. As Spain fought a civil war and endured the subsequent dictatorial regime of General Francisco Franco before again achieving democracy, it continued to send small numbers of immigrants to the United States. In the 1920s, for instance, a total of 28,958 Spaniards resettled north of the Rio Grande. By the 1960s the number had doubled but was still minute in comparison with other Hispanic groups, among them Puerto Ricans and Mexicans.

The three central characteristics of Hispanics north of the Rio Grande—Catholicism, an Iberian domestic outlook, and the Spanish language—all point in the direction of Spain. As a result of centuries of colonization, the Spanish-American War, and Catholicism, a deep anti-Spanish feeling had found its way into all levels of American society. The attempt by Anglo-Protestant culture to erase traces of Spanish influence throughout Florida, Texas, and California, denigrating the Spanish language, and disregarding the history of places and names, was never fully successful. Now the demographic growth of the Latino community is making Hispanic culture dominant again.

More than 100 years after 1898, Spanish is still widely used throughout the United States. Instead of disappearing like other immigrant tongues, it is actually expanding its reach, thanks in large part to bilingual education and affirmative action programs. The Spanish government has invested in programs and cultural organizations such as the Cervantes Institute; the objective of these programs is to quietly support efforts to safeguard and perpetuate the Spanish language. As a result, interest in things Iberian is on the rise—Spanish theater, film, and dance are frequently featured in major American metropolitan centers.

Many scholars have noted that the 1992 Spanish commemoration of the quincentennial of Columbus's arrival in the Bahamas was an attempt to renew Spanish cultural influence in the Americas. In that year the Spanish government officially apologized to the Jews for their expulsion from the country. It also opened its arms to the United States in recognition of the cultural impact both countries have had on world history. The Spanish government commissioned numerous monographs on Spanish colonization, released films, and organized concerts and literary events.

RELATED ARTICLES

Colonialism; Colonial Period; Columbus, Christopher; Cuba; Cuisine, Spanish; Explorers and Chroniclers; Mexico; Missions; Spanish in the United States.

FURTHER READING

Blackmar, Frank Wilson. *Spanish Colonization in the Southwest.* Baltimore: Johns Hopkins Univ., 1890.

Blackmar, Frank Wilson. *Spanish Institutions of the Southwest.* Baltimore: Johns Hopkins Press, 1891.

Bolton, Herbert Eugene. *The Colonization of North America.* New York: Macmillan, 1920.

Bolton, Herbert Eugene. *The Spanish Borderlands; A Chronicle of Old Florida and the Southwest.* New Haven, Conn.: Yale Univ. Press, 1921.

Castro, Américo. *The Structure of Spanish History.* Tr. by Edmund L. King. Princeton, N.J.: Princeton Univ. Press, 1954.

Chávez, Thomas E. *Spain and the Independence of the United States: An Intrinsic Gift.* Albuquerque: Univ. of N.Mex. Press, 2002.

Edwards, Jill. *Anglo-American Relations and the Franco Question, 1945–1955.* New York: Oxford Univ. Press, 1999.

Thomas, Hugh. *Rivers of Gold: The Rise of the Spanish Empire.* New York: Knopf, 2004.

Whitaker, Arthur Preston. *The Spanish-American Frontier: 1783–1795; The Westward Movement and the Spanish Retreat in the Mississippi Valley.* Boston: Houghton Mifflin, 1927.

CÉSAR ALEGRE

SPANGLISH

Also known as espanglés and inglañol, Spanglish is a hybrid way of communication much in vogue in the United States at the dawn of the 21st century. It is used by a wide variety of people, primarily, although not exclusively, by Latinos, and it is also widespread in various regions of Latin America and the Iberian Peninsula. The reaction to Spanglish is mixed; people either dislike it intensely because it represents for them the impurity of mixing nationally defined languages (English and Spanish), or they embrace it passionately as a symbol of the emergence of a new hybrid, mestizo culture north of the Rio Grande.

Although the media often portray Spanglish as a recent phenomenon, in truth it has a long and rich history. Its roots are traceable as far as back as the Treaty of Guadalupe Hidalgo (1848), when, after the American War with Mexico, two-thirds of the Mexican territory was sold to the United States for $15 million. Those territories were mostly inhabited by Spanish-speaking dwellers who suddenly found themselves exposed to English and an Anglo-Protestant way of life. In newspapers and legal documents of the period, there are traces of Spanglish words and syntactical formulations.

The next moment of intense linguistic experimentation was the Spanish-American War of 1898, when Spain finally ceded its colonies in the Caribbean Basin. Cuba and Puerto Rico entered the orbit of influence of the United States, thus embarking—each of them in a different fashion—in a cultural life that made English an integral part of it.

It is difficult to establish precisely how many people use Spanglish, as well as when and how often they use it every day. Unquestionably, it is used on a regular basis in Puerto Rico and the U.S.-Mexico border region. But it is also heard in major urban centers—among them, Miami, New York City, Los Angeles, San Antonio (Texas), Chicago, Dallas, Boston, and Albuquerque (New Mexico). Its primary spaces are the home, the street, the community center, the classroom, and the office.

Interdisciplinary studies have established that Spanglish speakers can be bilingual (English and Spanish) and also monolingual (either English or Spanish). They belong to different social strata: low-income workers, middle-class professionals, upper-class entrepreneurs, and so on. This means that Spanglish is defined neither by class nor by ethnicity or other ancestral grouping. Latinos and other speakers of every background use it.

The three verbal strategies of Spanglish speakers are: (1) code-switching, that is, the free travel from English to Spanish and vice versa ("Yo went to la store"); (2) automatic and simultaneous translation (for example, expressions such as "Te llamo pa'trás!"); and (3) the coining of new terms (*marqueta* for market, *grincar* for green card, *rufo* for roof). Depending on where geographically and temporally Spanglish speakers might use it, the syntactical foundation is either English or Spanish.

The exponential growth of the Latino community in the United States and its influence worldwide has made major corporations realize the value of Spanglish. In 2002 Hallmark Cards launched a new line of cards in Spanglish. Taco Bell has used it in television and radio commercials. Even the U.S. Army resorts to it in graphic ads seeking to recruit Hispanics soldiers. In large part, the growth of Spanglish itself is the result of factors such as an unabated Hispanic immigration to the United States, the triumphs and pitfalls of bilingual education, the spread of multiculturalism as an ideology, and globalization as a cultural pattern at the beginning of the 21st century.

As more detailed scholarship accumulates, it is clear that there is not one Spanglish but a whole variety. Each Latino national group has its own version. Thus there are Pocho, Pachuco, and Chicano

---

Don Quixote de la Monda: First Parte, Chapter Uno

In un placete de La Mancha of which nombre no quiero remembrearme, vivía, not so long ago, uno de esos gentlemen who always tienen una lanza in the rack, una buckler antigua, a skinny caballo y un greyhouse para el chase. A cazuela with más beef than mutón, carne choppeada para la dinner, un omelet pa' los Sábados, lentil pa' los Viernes, y algún pigeon como delicacy especial pa' los Domingos, consumían tres cuarers de su income. El resto lo employaba en una coat de broadcloth y en soketes de velvetín pa' los holidays, with sus slippers pa' combinar, while los otros días de la semana él cut a figura de los más finos cloths. Livin with él eran una housekeeper en sus forties, una sobrina not yet twenty y un ladino del field y la marketa que le saddleaba él caballo al gentleman y wieldeaba un hookete pa' podear. El gentleman andaba por allí por los fifty. Era de complexíon robusta pero un poco fresco en los bones y una cara leaneada y guanteada. La gente sabía that él era un early riser y que gustaba mucho huntear. La gente say que su apellido was Quijada or Quesada–hay diferencia de opiníon entre aquellos que han escrito sobre el sujeto––but acordando with las muchas conjecturas se entiende que era really Quejada. But all this no tiene mucha importancia pa' nuestro cuento, providiendo que al cuentaro no nos separenos pa' nada de las verdá.

Excerpt from *Spanglish: The Making of a New American Language* by Ilan Stavans (2003).

---

forms of Spanglish, as well as other versions, including Cubonics, Nuyorican, and Dominicanish. This is not surprising, since Spanish in Latin America is not homogeneous; each country has its own distinct type (Ecuadorian Spanish, Peruvian, Venezuelan, and so forth). As immigrants from the Hispanic world move to the United States, they bring with them their own national type, which in turn influences the way Spanglish evolves. But the multiplicity of Spanglish is also defined by location: Chicano Spanglish in El Paso, Texas, is different from Chicano Spanglish in Portland, Oregon.

There are many other hybrid languages in the world—for example, Portuñol (a mix of Portuguese and Spanish spoken in the border area of Spain and Portugal as well as in Brazil and Venezuela, among other South American countries) and Franglais (a cross between French and English, spoken on both sides of the English channel, in the Caribbean, and in parts of Africa). But Spanglish is a far more complex verbal way of communication, used by a huge number of speakers (more than the total population of Spain or Argentina).

Some specialists argue that Spanglish is but a middle step in the process of English language acquisition. This would mean that as soon as Latinos abandoned Spanish completely and became fully fluent in English, Spanglish would disappear. These specialists use as evidence the experience of previous immigrants to the United States. Among Jewish immigrants from Russia and Eastern Europe, for instance, Yiddish gave way to Yinglish, which in turn gave way to English.

Now, roughly a century after the first Yiddish-speaking Jewish immigrants arrived on American shores, the vast majority of American Jews speak no Yiddish. A similar pattern was followed by German and Italian immigrants, among others.

This argument is flawed. Hispanic immigration, for one thing, has been constant for over a century and does not show signs of diminishing. In addition, the closeness of the immigrant's old home (Mexico, Guatemala, Puerto Rico, the Dominican Republic, and so on) and the relatively inexpensive travel fares make mobility between it and the United States relatively easy. This means Spanish does not disappear from the linguistic landscape as other immigrant languages have done.

Another major influence in the spread of Spanglish in the United States is the media; no other immigrant group has ever had two major, native-language television networks like Latinos have— Univisión and Telemundo. The number of Spanish-language radio stations countrywide is gigantic. And Latinos have numerous print outlets, with three veteran yet increasingly influential ones at the lead: *el diario/LA PRENSA* (New York City), *El Nuevo Herald* (Florida), and *La Opinión* (Los Angeles).

Spanglish was already on the airwaves in the 1950s in English-language TV shows such as *I Love Lucy,* and it has become prevalent in *The George Lopez Show, The Brothers Garcia, Dora the Explorer,* and other programs. For Spanish-language TV programs such as *Sábado Gigante* and *El show de Cristina,* Spanglish is a necessity.

Comedians and performance artists have also made use of it. Guillermo Gómez-Peña has designed his monologues (such as *The Warrior of Gringostroka*) in Spanglish since the 1990s. John Leguizamo (*Spic-O-Rama: A Dysfunctional Comedy*) and Josefina López (*Real Women Have Curves*), among others, have incorporated it as well.

Spanglish has as its favorite outlets music and the Internet, where a special variety known as Cyber-Spanglish is ubiquitous. In music the strength and vivacity of Spanglish is astonishing. Individual singers as different as Juan Luis Guerra, Rubén Blades, and Gloria Estefan and music groups such as Cypress Hill, Aventura, Los Tigres del Norte, and Los Super Seven use Spanglish to reach out to their fans. (Often the lyrics are transcribed in their CD booklets.) Lyrics to hip-hop, rock, salsa, *bachata*, and meringue as well as rap use Spanglish to reflect on the experience of Latinos in the United States.

There are already scores of novels, short stories, poems, essays, and memoirs written in Spanglish. These include Susana Chávez-Silverman's *Killer Crónicas*, Ana Lydia Vega's "Pollito Chicken," Rosaura Sánchez's "Jac-in-the-bag," Giannina Braschi's *Yo Boing*, Gloria Anzaldúa's "Chicano Spanish," and Tato Laviera's "AmeRícan." Other authors—among them, Junot Díaz, Christina García, Richard Rodríguez, Rubén Martínez, Juan Felipe Herrera, and Rosario Ferré—make reference to it in their work.

Spanglish has also made its way into the American academy. As an undergraduate course, the language was first taught in 2000. The first translation into Spanglish of chapter one of *Don Quixote of La Mancha* by Miguel de Cervantes was published in Barcelona in 2002 (it is included in the book *Spanglish: The Making of a New American Language* [2003]). And the first international and interdisciplinary conference on Spanglish took place in April 2004 at Amherst College in Massachusetts.

A controversial language, Spanglish is debated along ideological lines. In the United States, opponents argue that it is a block in the road to Latinos' full assimilation into the melting pot. These opponents also believe that Spanglish is proof that bilingual education was a half-baked language-learning system. Supporters counterargue that Spanglish is not an obstacle but, instead, the stepping stone to a new culture, part Latino and part Anglo.

© HECTOR MATA/AFP/GETTY IMAGES

Sign on the side of a coffee shop in Los Angeles mixes the Spanish word *café* with a Spanish phonetical translation of the English word *donuts*.

Outside the United States, especially in the Spanish-speaking world (and with Spain as the leader), the argument is different. There the belief is that the purity of the Spanish language is disappearing as a result of Spanglish and that something needs to be done quickly. Several members of the Royal Academy of the Spanish Language in Madrid and its 40 branches in the Hispanic world publicly decry the dissemination of Spanglish.

Dictionaries of Chicano Spanglish, Cubonics, New Mexican Spanglish, and other varieties have been published since the 1970s. In 2003 a 6,000-word lexicon gathering Spanglish words and expressions from different national backgrounds was published. These attempts, along with the literary and maybe the Internet manifestations listed previously, show that this way of communicating is in the process of some sort of standardization. From the oral to the written form, Spanglish often shows up in the classified section of newspapers, and instruction manuals and other how-to publications.

It is anyone's guess what the future holds for Spanglish. Will it be even more extensively used that it already is? Will it affect the morphological and syntactical structure of Spanish and English? Will it cease to be a sum of dialectical exercises and become a fully codified, standard language? Will works of art written in it need to be translated into English or Spanish to be understood by non–Spanglish users?

RELATED ARTICLES

Bilingual Education; Bilingualism; Caló; Cubonics; Dominicanish; Spanish in the United States.

FURTHER READING

Acosta-Belén, Edna. "Spanglish: A Case of Languages in Contact." In *New Directions in Second Language Learning, Teaching and Bilingual Education.* Ed. by M. Burt and H. Dulay. Washington, D.C.: TESOL, 1975.

Barreto, Amílcar A. *Language, Elites, and the State: Nationalism in Puerto Rico and Quebec.* Westport, Conn.: Praeger, 1998.

Chávez-Silverman, Susana. *Killer Crónicas.* Madison: Univ. of Wis. Press, 2004.

Cruz, Bill, et al., eds. *The Official Spanglish Dictionary.* New York: Fireside, 1998.

Gómez-Peña, Guillermo. *Warrior for Gringostroika: Essays, Performance Texts, and Poetry.* Introduction by Roger Bartra. St. Paul, Minn.: Graywolf, 1993.

Gómez-Peña, Guillermo, et al. *Codex espangliensis: From Columbus to the Border Patrol.* San Francisco: City Lights Bks., 2000.

Leguizamo, John. *Spic-O-Rama: A Dysfunctional Comedy.* New York: Bantam, 1994.

Ramos, Jorge. *The Other Face of America: Chronicles of the Immigrants Shaping Our Future.* Tr. by Patricia J. Duncan. New York: Rayo/HarperCollins, 2002.

Rodríguez, Richard. *Hunger of Memory: The Autobiography of Richard Rodríguez.* Boston: David R. Godine, 1982.

Stavans, Ilan. *Spanglish: The Making of a New American Language.* New York: Rayo/HarperCollins, 2003.

ILAN STAVANS

SPANISH AMERICAN LEAGUE AGAINST DISCRIMINATION

Founded in Miami in 1974, the Spanish American League Against Discrimination (SALAD) works to reduce and eliminate discrimination against persons of Hispanic descent. Organized as an individual membership organization composed largely of Cuban Americans, SALAD has had only six presidents during its 30 years of existence. Past presidents have included nationally known figures such as Eduardo Padrón, currently president of Miami-Dade Community College, and Manny Díaz, the mayor of Miami. Since 1985 local attorney Osvaldo N. Soto has headed the organization. The commitment of leaders to be both proactive and reactive to community needs has been emphasized over institution building and maintenance. SALAD has no permanent offices nor sizable staff; neither does it have a Web site or a publication outlet. Yet it is a nationally well-known and respected organization, as evidenced in its coalition action with LULAC (League of United Latin American Citizens), El Consejo Nacional de La Raza, and the NAACP (National Association for the Advancement of Colored People) to improve educational opportunities for minorities, and its collaboration with the Jewish American Committee to advocate for bilingual education.

Unlike many Latino civil rights groups, SALAD has generally relied on negotiation and public opinion as its principal tools rather than litigation and confrontation. This can be partially explained by the dominance of Cuban Americans and other Spanish speakers in Miami-Dade County; people of Hispanic origin form the majority not only in Miami but also in Miami-Dade County. The 2000 U.S. Census enumerated 700,000 Cubans in the county and 600,000 other Hispanics, or 57.3 percent of all residents. Furthermore, Cuban Americans are well known as an unmeltable minority for whom acculturation and assimilation are not a collective aspiration. Given their majority position it is understandable that SALAD relies on negotiation to gain incremental concessions. Since the 1990s they have had the collective capacity to outvote other racial and ethnic groups and have infrequently needed to be adversarial to achieve their goals.

Three campaigns have distinguished the organization. Best known is the campaign to rescind a 1980 "English Only" ordinance in Miami-Dade County. In 1976 the County Commission declared the county bilingual. Government agendas were published in English and Spanish throughout the 1970s. With the arrival of 125,000 Cubans by way of the Mariel boat lift, the resulting social disruption made English Only a popular idea that was easily passed by the County Board of Commissioners prohibiting expenditure of public funds on the use of languages other than English. A coalition including the local Chamber of Commerce was organized and staffed by Osvaldo Soto of SALAD to promote the idea of "English Plus," which accepted English as the official language but acknowledged the economic and cultural benefit of a multilingual society. In 1993 the newly elected Latino majority of the County Board of Commissioners unanimously revoked English Only and their action survived legal challenges.

A second issue in the early years of SALAD was the struggle to desegregate the Miami-Dade County Metro Police Department. SALAD leaders negotiated agreements with the county manager and later with the city manager to open opportunities to minorities on a proportional basis.

In a third major campaign, SALAD negotiated with the city of Miami Beach to desegregate its workforce. All three of these actions resulted in more equitable representation of Latinos In recent years SALAD has taken a less active role in community life, waiting to be approached for endorsements or substantive matters rather than taking campaigns to the public. While the prestige of the group remains, it may be that majority status has dampened the need for the organization.

RELATED ARTICLES

Bilingual Education; Civil Rights; Discrimination; Inter-Latino Relations; Miami; Politics, Latino.

FURTHER READING

Capaldi, Nicholas, ed. *Immigration: Debating the Issues*. Amherst, N.Y.: Prometheus Bks., 1997.
Grenier, Guillermo J., and Alex Stepick. *Miami Now!: Immigration, Ethnicity, and Social Change*. Gainesville: Univ. Press of Fla., 1992.
Portes, Alejandro, and Alex Stepick. *City on the Edge: The Transformation of Miami*. Berkeley: Univ. of Calif. Press, 1993.

HOLLY ACKERMAN

SPANISH AMERICANS

The term *Spanish Americans* refers to persons originally from Spain who live for a time in the United States. Although this group within Latino society has not had a major impact on contemporary American culture, their early influence as conquistadors, explorers, and missionaries is still felt in the United States, especially in the Southwest where the Spanish and their descendants developed the colonial infrastructure. The persistence late into the 20th century of the term *Spanish* for Spanish-speaking peoples resident in the United States attests to the enduring influence of Iberian language and culture.

Spain lost most of its empire in the late 18th and early 19th century, and Mexico won independence in 1821, resulting in many Spanish Americans becoming U.S. citizens through the purchase of Louisiana from France (1803), the annexation of Florida (1819), the annexation of the independent Republic of Texas (1846), and, in 1848, after the Mexican-American War, the forced sale by Mexico of California, Arizona, New Mexico, Utah, and Colorado, which had been Spanish territory until 1821. Well into the 20th century, some Creole (full-blooded Spanish born in the Americas) citizens of the United States attempted to maintain Spanish customs and dress; their efforts are exemplified in the works of Cleofas Jaramillo and Nina Otero Warren. Spanish folktales, collected by ethnographer Juan Rael in oral sessions in the 1930s, persisted among descendants of Spanish colonists well into the 20th century in the Southwest. Spanish iconography also still exists in the United States, particularly in small churches of the Southwest.

In addition to those of Spanish descent who had long lived in North America, in the late 19th century a small group of Spanish intellectuals migrated to the United States; among them was George Santayana, whose literary criticism, philosophical writings, and memoirs made him the best-known Spanish intellectual of his time. In the same generation, Rodolfo Cortina had a great deal of influence through his books on Spanish-language learning and his editing of anthologies of Spanish literature. Another influx of Spanish Americans came after the annexation in 1898 of the territories of Guam, the Philippines, and Puerto Rico, when these Spanish colonies became U.S. territories and their inhabitants citizens of the United States. The writer Federico Garcia Lorca spent a brief time in New York City, which resulted in the scathing *A Poet in New York* (1940); Felipe Alfau, who produced the novels *Locos* (1930) and *Chromos* (1990), lived for over 50 years in the New York area, where he was a translator and wrote for an earlier incarnation of *el diario/LA PRENSA*. In addition, a number of Spanish authors have written fiction about the United States, including César Antonio Molina, Javier Marías, and Eduardo Mendoza.

Several migrations to the United States from depressed areas in Spain were the result of adverse political circumstances in early-20th-century Spain, including the dictatorships of Primo de Rivera (1923–1931) and Francisco Franco (1939–1975). Significant numbers of Basques immigrated to the United States from northern Spain; according to the 2000 U.S. Census, about 58,000 Basques are current U.S. residents, one of the largest constituencies of Spanish Americans. Another contingent that migrated to the United States was a group of intellectuals and scholars who were threatened by the Franco dictatorship; members of this group were encouraged by the involvement of volunteer American fighters in the Lincoln Brigades, which fought alongside republicans in the Spanish Civil War (1936–1939). This connection was chronicled in the 1984 film *The Good Fight*. Those scholars and intellectuals who joined American institutions of higher learning became an integral part of the educational system and Spanish studies tradition of the United States.

During the 1980s and 1990s, the Spanish government encouraged the study and appreciation of Spanish culture through the funding of institutions in the United States. At New York University, the government established the Juan Carlos I Center for Iberian Studies, which quickly developed an impressive series of public programs in which Spanish writers and intellectuals came to the United States for brief periods to teach and lecture. In 2003 the Spanish government reopened the Cervantes Institute, its showcase cultural center, in a Manhattan, New York, landmark series of small buildings after a $12 million renovation.

The appearance of popular Spanish personalities has also increased the visibility of Spanish Americans. In film, the director Pedro Almodóvar, the actor Antonio Banderas, and the actress Penelope Cruz have often been featured in magazines, on television, and in newspaper gossip columns. High-end Spanish cuisine has also become more well known in the United States through the influence of Catalan chef Ferran Adriá of El Bulli, where many American chefs have apprenticed and whose techniques have been featured in both restaurants and in cooking magazines and newspapers. Young Spanish restaurateurs have begun to open *cocina nueva* (new cooking) restaurants to capitalize on this popularity.

According to the latest data from the Spanish government, the number of Spanish people living in the United States has increased significantly. In 1995, Spaniards living in the United States numbered 20,193, and by 2002 their numbers had increased to 42,359. Despite this increase, Spanish Americans remain a minority within the Latino population in the United States.

RELATED ARTICLES

Alfau, Felipe; Architecture, Spanish Colonial; Californios; Cuisine, Spanish; Immigration, Latino; Literature; Spain.

FURTHER READING

Altman, Ida. *Emigrants and Society: Extremadura and America in the Sixteenth Century.* Berkeley: Univ. of Calif. Press, 1989.

Díaz, Beatriz. *Todo negro no igual: Voces de emigrantes en el barrio bilbaíno de San Francisco* (Everything Black Isn't Equal: Immigrant Voices in the Bilbao Neighborhood of San Francisco). Barcelona, Spain: Virus, 1997.

Sánchez Alonso, Blanca. *Las causas de la emigración española, 1880–1930* (The Causes of Spanish Emigration, 1880–1930). Madrid, Spain: Alianza, 1995.

SELECTED WEB SITES

Españoles en USA.
  http://www.spainemb.org/laboral/espusa.htm

CÉSAR ALEGRE

SPANISH-AMERICAN WAR

Many North American history books limit discussion of the 1898 Spanish-American War to the brief 114-day armed conflict between U.S. armed forces and Spain in Cuba, the Philippines, and Puerto Rico. Victory brought the United States colonial possessions in the Pacific and the Caribbean, including the Philippines, Guam, Puerto Rico, and, after a brief occupation, control over a nominally independent Cuba via the 1901 Platt Amendment. During the war the United States also formally annexed Hawaii, which it had occupied in 1893. Thus, the war involved the destinies of peoples in the Pacific and Caribbean, and, ultimately, Latino populations in the United States.

For Cubans the U.S. declaration of war against Spain came as an intervention in their ongoing war with Spain for independence (1895–1898). Furthermore, that conflict formed part of Cuban attempts at gaining independence from Spain going back to 1868 and the Ten Years' War. Therefore, the "Spanish-American" war could be named the "Spanish-Cuban-American War"; however, since it also led to the Philippine-American War at the turn of the 20th century—usually referred to as the "Philippine Insurrection"—perhaps "War of 1898" is more appropriate.

The North American public had followed the Cuban war of independence closely. Many sympathized with Cuba's attempt to separate from Spain, while others hoped that the United States would become a world power, extending its reach into Latin America and Asia in much the same way that European nations were engaged in colonial ventures in Africa and Asia. Before the U.S. Civil War, the nation had engaged in expansionism directed at contiguous continental territories occupied by Native Americans, Mexico, and European nations, including Great Britain and Spain. American policymakers from Thomas Jefferson to James Buchanan repeatedly declared the desire to acquire Cuba. Expansionist projects, including unofficial filibuster expeditions modeled to some degree on the Texas movement, peaked during the presidency of James Polk and the Mexican-American War (1846–1848). Southern slaveholding interests desired Cuba as a possible slave state to achieve parity with free states in the North. Annexation appealed to some Cuban planters fearful of the abolition of slavery on the island. The relative weakness of the United States vis-à-vis Great Britain stymied extraterritorial ambitions for much of the 19th century. American policy preferred the maintenance of Spanish control of Cuba until such time that it could be ceded to the United States.

On October 10, 1868, a group of wealthy landowners in eastern Cuba launched an uprising, the Grito de Yara. They freed their own slaves, advocating gradual abolition in Cuba with compensation to

owners for their loss of property. A similar movement in Puerto Rico had already revolted in the Grito de Lares. The insurrection was initially successful in eastern Cuba, attracting poor whites, blacks and mixed-race rural people; eventually the insurrection extended to the center of the island. Spain moved to suppress the rebellion, successfully in the case of Puerto Rico, but leading to a decade of protracted warfare in Cuba. Eventually Spain defeated the Cuban separatists because of little unity of purpose between planters and other groups, and between whites and blacks; thus the insurrection could not be sustained across the entire island. Isolated in eastern Cuba, the revolt ultimately failed, but not before a group of rebels led by the Afro-Cuban general Antonio Maceo refused Spain's terms that neither abolished slavery nor guaranteed Cuba's independence.

Rebellions against Spanish authority were frequent as the 19th century progressed, but without unity they were doomed to failure. Cuba remained a colony of Spain, but much of its economy became oriented toward North America as direct U.S. investment expanded in the latter decades of the century. In 1892 José Martí, a Cuban intellectual, writer, and poet living in exile in the United States, founded a new independence movement: the Cuban Revolutionary Party (PRC) among Cuban American tobacco workers in Tampa, Florida. Martí had been imprisoned during his youth for criticizing Spanish colonialism, and he emerged as a tireless advocate for independence and national unity. He was also a critic of elements of North American society that urged circumspection in Cuba's relations with its powerful, possibly domineering, neighbor. Martí organized a new uprising in Cuba, incorporating officers, including Maceo and Máximo Gómez, from the earlier failed effort, and support from Cuban communities in American cities and on the island itself.

The Cuban War of Independence began on February 24, 1895, in the eastern province. Leaders, including Maceo, Gómez, and Martí, landed on the coast and moved inland to insurgent camps. In one early battle on May 19, 1895, Martí was killed. The Cuban insurgents organized an irregular army and invaded Cuba's prosperous western sugar provinces by October. The Cuban army carried war to all parts of the island, unlike in the previous conflict where a fortified line had isolated the insurrection in the east. The insurgents used guerrilla strategies against Span-

THE BATTLE OF
SAN JUAN HILL

RICHARD HARDING DAVIS
tells in the OCTOBER SCRIBNER'S how San Juan Hill was captured. His story of the battle is fully illustrated.

CAPTAIN ARTHUR H. LEE
the British Military Attaché, gives a thrilling account of the fight of the Regulars at El Caney. Illustrated with photographs by the author.

SURRENDER OF SANTIAGO
an illustrated article by J. F. J. Archibald, a correspondent present at the event.

Many other interesting features.

OCTOBER SCRIBNER'S
NOW READY   PRICE, 25 CENTS

Advertisement for an edition of *Scribner's* magazine that features articles on the Spanish-American War.

ish forces, frequently targeting agrarian areas. This strategy deprived the colonial metropolis of funds, tied down Spanish troops, incorporated unemployed and displaced persons into the rebel forces, and struck at many of the wealthiest interests in Cuba. To quell the revolt, Spain dispatched a large conscript army under the command of General Valeriano Weyler. The Spanish commander enacted a population removal strategy, known as "reconcentration," to deprive the insurgents of rural support.

Reconcentration forced rural Cubans into Spanish-controlled cities and towns and also led to outbreaks of disease, hunger, and overcrowding as urban areas were ill-prepared for the rural influx. Many sided with the rebels rather than move to the towns. The U.S. press, in a bid to attain ever-larger readership, presented sensationalist accounts of what was, by any standards, a cruel war. The destruction of

U.S. properties and the failure of Spain to suppress the revolt or obtain a peace agreement prompted changes in Washington's policy toward Cuba and Spanish control. The public demanded action, while the PRC in New York and Washington urged recognition of the provisional Cuban government.

By late 1897 Maceo had been killed and the insurgency appeared weakened in western Cuba, but victory eluded Spain. Much of Cuba had been laid waste. Spain recalled Weyler and changed strategy by opting to extend autonomy to the island in the hopes of bringing the insurgents to the negotiating table. Thirty years of struggle had not disposed the Cuban independence forces to accede to Spanish demands; they sensed that victory was attainable and decided to continue to fight. Spaniards and pro-Spanish groups on the island rioted against the prospect of self-rule, which led the United States to send much of its Atlantic squadron to Key West, Florida, and the battleship U.S.S. *Maine* to Havana in January 1898 "to protect the lives and property of American citizens" resident there.

The U.S. government urged Spain to cede control of Cuba or, at minimum, allow the United States to intercede in the conflict. A cease-fire between the Cubans and Spaniards proved elusive, however. In the midst of the unfolding crisis in Cuba, the *Maine* exploded in Havana harbor on February 15, 1898, killing more than 260 sailors aboard. The cause of the explosion remained a mystery, and the source of considerable controversy, but at the time a naval inquiry board ruled that the cause had been deliberate action and that Spain was responsible. What is certain is that the United States reeled from the news of the tragedy and rallied to the battle cry "Remember the *Maine*! To hell with Spain!"—reminiscent of "Remember the Alamo!" from the war with Mexico. The disastrous event clearly had deep significance during the War of 1898, but its designation as a cause of the conflict tends to overlook deeper tensions between the United States and Spain over Cuba.

On April 11, 1898, President William McKinley requested that the U.S. Congress authorize military intervention in the ongoing war in Cuba. Congress approved, but added the Teller Amendment that rejected U.S. attempts to "exercise sovereignty, jurisdiction, or control [of Cuba] . . . except for the pacification thereof." By April 22, 1898, the U.S. fleet had imposed a blockade of certain ports in Cuba, an act of hostility according to international law. Spain declared war on the United States, whereupon the U.S. Congress reciprocated, changing the date of the declaration of war to the beginning of the blockade.

The U.S. Army organized a fifth corps in Tampa, Florida, and readied for an invasion of Cuba. The military had never undertaken such a large operation across a body of water and supply shortages, confusion, and inadequate equipment and weapons marked the effort. The first major battle occurred on May 1, 1898, when Commodore George Dewey sailed with the U.S. Asiatic squadron from Hong Kong to Manila in the Philippines after the declaration of war. He destroyed the antiquated Spanish fleet at anchor in an overwhelming American victory. Troops were dispatched from San Francisco, taking over Guam en route. The United States also annexed formerly independent Hawaii. United States forces became involved in a three-year war against Filipinos who had hoped for independence rather than the imposition of U.S. authority. That conflict would prove far bloodier than the battles waged against Spain in Cuba.

United States troops landed on the east coast of the island where Cubans had cleared and protected the invasion beaches in June 1898. The U.S. Navy bottled up Spain's Atlantic fleet in Santiago de Cuba harbor, while U.S. ground forces marched on the outskirts of the city, which was ringed by Spanish fortifications and protected by the Cuban army. American soldiers, including the "Rough Riders" volunteer cavalry unit led by presidential hopeful Theodore Roosevelt, captured San Juan Hill and the fort of El Caney on July 1, 1898, after daylong battles. Santiago de Cuba lay within artillery range, which forced the Spanish fleet to attempt to break out of the harbor. On July 3, the U.S. fleet annihilated the Spanish ships in a running battle along Cuba's southern coast. With yellow fever and other diseases threatening both U.S. and Spanish forces, and the prospect of a lengthy siege, the Spanish commander surrendered his 22,000 troops to U.S. general William Shafter on July 17, 1898.

The United States had secured the cooperation of the Cuban forces, and their presence prevented Spain from reinforcing its garrisons or effectively maneuvering against the North Americans. Relations between the United States and the Cuban forces deteriorated, however, as the United States intended to occupy Cuba and sideline the independence army in negotiations. The Cuban military was ragged and poor, its ranks filled with black and mixed-race soldiers, and its officer corps included many people of color in leadership positions. The U.S. Army of the time had segregated units all led by white officers. Given the racist attitudes of the white supremacist United States, relations often soured between the Cubans and the North Americans. When the U.S. command left Spaniards in positions of authority and refused to allow Cubans under arms into cities, General Calixto García wrote a strong letter of protest to Shafter and resigned his position.

Cubans were not consulted in armistice negotiations or about the Treaty of Paris, convened after the United States had seized Puerto Rico in late July. In December Spain transferred sovereignty of Cuba, Puerto Rico, the Philippines, and Guam to the United States. In the case of Puerto Rico, U.S. troops began military occupation that set the stage for future colonial control. Military occupation of Cuba lasted from the start of 1899 to May 20, 1902, when Cuba became independent. The Teller Amendment and strong nationalist sentiment prevented direct acquisition of Cuba, but a form of control over the island's affairs was found in the Platt Amendment.

The Platt Amendment proved to be the price for ending the occupation in 1902. The amendment was passed by U.S. Congress and imposed on the Cuban Constitutional Convention in 1901. It prohibited the Cuban government from making treaties or accepting loans without prior U.S. approval, thus the United States controlled Cuba's foreign relations. It authorized American intervention where necessary for the "maintenance of a government adequate for the protection of life, property, and individual liberty." It also leased to the United States the naval base at Guantánamo Bay. The amendment was bitterly condemned but ultimately approved by the Cuban Congress. It was to remain in force until it was abrogated in 1933 by the Ramón Grau San Martín government and dropped by U.S. president Franklin D. Roosevelt in 1934.

Thus the Spanish-American War dramatized the emergence of the United States as a world power of global reach and an overseas empire. It involved the destinies and histories of Cuba and Puerto Rico with North America, and underlay relations between the Hispanic Caribbean and the "colossus of the north" into the 20th century.

An important outcome of the war was the political and social linking of the annexed territories to the United States and the resulting demographic changes both to the islands and the mainland. Although Cuba soon gained its independence, Puerto Rico remained a U.S. possession; the Jones Act in 1917 recognized Puerto Ricans as U.S. citizens. Before World War I, the Puerto Rican population on the mainland numbered about 20,000; after World War II and such labor programs as Operation Bootstrap, the Puerto Rican population grew markedly, reaching almost 1 million by the late 1960s. On the island, Puerto Rican educational systems were modified to reflect the new status, English became a de facto second language, and the dollar became the island's currency. At the beginning of the 21st century, Puerto Rico's political status continues to be questioned both on the island and on the mainland.

RELATED ARTICLES

Colonialism; Cuba; Cuban Americans; Martí, José; Mexican-American War; Military, U.S.; Philippines; Puerto Rico; Spain.

FURTHER READING

Ferrer, Ada. *Insurgent Cuba: Race, Nation, and Revolution, 1868–1898.* Chapel Hill: Univ. of N.C. Press, 1999.

Foner, Philip S. *The Spanish-Cuban-American War and the Birth of U.S. Imperialism.* 2 vols. New York: Monthly Review Press, 1972.

Guerra y Sánchez, Ramiro. *La expansión territorial de los Estados Unidos a expensas de España y de los países hispanoamericanos.* Havana: Editorial de Ciencias Sociales, 1973.

LaFeber, Walter. *The New Empire: An Interpretation of American Expansion, 1860–1898.* Ithaca, N.Y.: Cornell Univ. Press, 1963.

Offner, John L. *An Unwanted War: The Diplomacy of the United States and Spain over Cuba, 1895–1898.* Chapel Hill: Univ. of N.C. Press, 1992.

Pérez, Louis A., Jr. *Cuba between Empires, 1878–1902.* Pittsburgh, Penn.: Univ. of Pittsburgh Press, 1983.

Pérez, Louis A., Jr. *The War of 1898.* Chapel Hill: Univ. of N.C. Press, 1998.

Poyo, Gerald E. *With All and for the Good of All: The Emergence of Popular Nationalism in the Cuban Communities of the United States, 1848–1898.* Durham, N.C.: Duke Univ. Press, 1989.

Santiago, Roberto, ed. *Boricuas: Influential Puerto Rican Writings, An Anthology.* New York: Ballantine Bks., 1995.

Schoultz, Lars. *Beneath the United States: A History of U.S. Policy towards Latin America.* Cambridge, Mass.: Harvard Univ. Press, 1998.

Wagenheim, Karl, and Olga Jiménez de Wagenheim. *The Puerto Ricans: A Documentary History.* Princeton, N.J.: Markus Wiener Pub., 1994.

DAVID C. CARLSON

SPANISH HARLEM

Spanish Harlem, East Harlem, and El Barrio are the different monikers given to the oldest Puerto Rican settlement in the continental United States; it is located between East 96th and East 125th Streets, between the East River and Fifth Avenue in the borough of Manhattan in New York City. Spanish Harlem's boundaries are likely to fluctuate depending upon whom and when you ask. Over the decades, as the borders of the neighborhood have shifted, so have the residents. Between the late 1800s and the turn of the 20th century, East Harlem was inhabited by German, Irish, Jewish, and Italian immigrants and by African Americans. For the majority of the 20th century, however, East Harlem was known as a Puerto Rican enclave. No discussion on Puerto Ricans in the United States can occur without talking about East Harlem. While Puerto Ricans have migrated to other cities in the United States and to other parts of New York City, East Harlem is the nation's most widely studied and best-known Puerto Rican neighborhood.

A noticeable Puerto Rican migration to New York City—"the Pioneer Migration"—extended from 1900 to 1945. Puerto Ricans started to establish a *colonia* (a locale in an urban area heavily populated by Puerto Ricans) in East Harlem by setting up visual markers that denoted their permanency in this community; they opened bodegas (grocery stores), published Spanish-language newspapers, opened restaurants, and established political organizations. In 1918 the Socialist Party opened its first continental U.S. Puerto Rican branch in East Harlem. Another socialist group, Alianza Obrera Puertorriqueña (Puerto Rican Workers Alliance), was located in Spanish Harlem and boasted such members as Bernardo Vega, author of *Memoirs of Bernardo Vega* (1977; written in 1940); Jesús Colón, author of *A Puerto Rican in New York, and Other Sketches* (1961); and Luis Muñoz Marín, who would govern Puerto Rico from 1948 until 1964. This politically active *colonia* was strongly reminiscent of its home country. Although other *colonias* were established in New York City, flourishing businesses and institutions made East Harlem the center of the Puerto Rican world in the city. The neighborhood was also starting to be known as the Barrio Latino, and it became the destination for new migrants to New York City. This influx caused tensions among European immigrants who still lived in East Harlem, ultimately leading to the "Harlem Riots" of July 1926, when they assaulted the Puerto Rican residents.

The largest surge of Puerto Rican migration, estimated at approximately 34,000 persons a year, occurred between 1946 and 1964 during the "the Great Migration" period. The large increase in the number of Puerto Ricans migrating, especially to East Harlem, led to nonresidents of the neighborhood seeing the neighborhood as solely Puerto Rican. Consequently, East Harlem was made infamous by the countless sociological, anthropological, and literary texts that focused heavily on the rising "slum" culture of El Barrio. The neighborhood's economic decline, the exodus of European immigrants, the increase in violence and drug abuse/trafficking came to be associated with and blamed on the influx of Puerto Ricans.

Two of the most widely known books that come out of this era are Oscar Lewis's *La Vida* (1966) and Piri Thomas's autobiography *Down These Mean Streets* (1967). Both deal with issues that were plaguing the neighborhood. Thomas chronicles the day-to-day violence he experienced; he engaged in gang violence, robberies, and drug use. The intensity of drug abuse among Puerto Rican migrants has marked their (im)migration experience as different from that of other ethnic groups that came before them. Consequently, El Barrio, in the popular imagination, has frequently been reduced to a crime-ridden, drug-infested neighborhood, especially because so many scholars and writers have promoted this image of the neighborhood.

In the late 1960s and early 1970s, all these issues were still plaguing the residents of El Barrio. In response, a group of mostly Puerto Rican college

© RALPH MORSE/TIME LIFE PICTURES/GETTY IMAGES

Young boys playing a street game in New York City's Spanish Harlem.

students who thought changes were needed formed the Young Lords Party. In the summer of 1969 the Young Lords started the Garbage Offensive in Spanish Harlem because the Sanitation Department did not pick up the garbage in the neighborhood. The Young Lords, along with the residents of East Harlem, started sweeping the garbage from the streets and piled it up so no traffic could pass, thus forcing the Sanitation Department to pick up the garbage. Also, we see how El Barrio remained the center of the Puerto Rican community in New York in that the Young Lords chose to launch their offensives from there.

At the beginning of the 21st century, Spanish Harlem is again in flux: numerous revitalization efforts are aimed at alleviating social problems, and non–Puerto Rican immigrants have increased in the neighborhood. The area is becoming increasingly populated with Mexicans, Dominicans, and other immigrants from Latin America. Although the ethnic groups are changing, permanent fixtures show the lasting effect of Puerto Rican presence in El Barrio: on East 106th Street and Lexington Avenue stands the Julia de Burgos Cultural Center, named after the renowned Puerto Rican poet who died on the streets of East Harlem; on Fifth Avenue, El Museo del Barrio, founded in 1969 by a group of Puerto Rican educators, activists, and artists, stands at 104th Street; and each June, a parade on Fifth Avenue is attended by Puerto Ricans and non–Puerto Ricans who have come to celebrate the legacy of Puerto Ricans in Nueva York.

RELATED ARTICLES

Barrio, El; New York City; Puerto Ricans on the Mainland; Puerto Rican Young Lords; Washington Heights.

FURTHER READING

Duany, Jorge. *The Puerto Rican Nation on the Move: Identities on the Island and in the United States.* Chapel Hill: Univ. of N.C. Press, 2002.

Korrol, Virginia E. Sánchez. *From Colonia to Community: The History of Puerto Ricans in New York City.* Berkeley: Univ. of Calif. Press, 1994.

Perez y Gonzalez, Maria E. *Puerto Ricans in the United States.* Westport, Conn.: Greenwood Press, 2000.

Sexton, Patricia Cayo. *Spanish Harlem: Anatomy of Poverty.* New York: Harper & Row, 1965.

IVELISSE RODRIGUEZ

SPANISH IN THE UNITED STATES

The Hispanic presence and the Spanish language have a long history in North America, predating the arrival of the Pilgrims in the New England area. The Spanish language, which was brought to the continent by the Spanish explorers and conquistadores, has been continuously spoken in what is now the United States longer than any other European language. The first English-speaking settlement, Jamestown, in what would eventually become the United States dates to 1609. In contrast, the earliest Spanish explorations of the continent date to the 16th century.

By 1565, for instance, Pedro Menéndez de Avilés and his men had already founded the city of San Agustín (Saint Augustine) in what is now Florida. It is the oldest European-founded city in the United States, and its founders' language was Spanish. Even before Menéndez de Avilés, Spaniards were already venturing throughout the continent, discovering and laying claim to rivers, mountains, and new territories for Spain and its empire. These Spanish explorers encountered different indigenous cultures and languages, new wildlife and flora, new sights and treasures in many parts of the North American continent. As early as 1513, Juan Ponce de León, usually remembered for his desire to find the mythical "Fountain of Youth," laid claim to the territory he would call La Florida (later, the state of Florida). In 1519 he went on to explore the area that is south Texas today while also exploring parts of the Carolinas; he and his group founded Peñiscola (Pensacola, Florida, today) in the same year. In other regions, Juan de Oñate founded the Misión de San Gabriel in New Mexico in 1598.

Spanish language and culture in North America thus dates to the times of the Spanish explorers in North America, when the West was part of Mexico and Mexico was a Spanish colony. The names of many states bear witness to this history: Colorado, Nevada, Texas, Arizona. The word *California* is a particularly literary example: the name, which refers to an enchanted and beautiful land, comes from a medieval novel of chivalry, *Amadís de Gaula,* that the explorers would have been familiar with. In California, 21 Spanish missions were established throughout that land; many of them eventually became major cities such as San Diego, San Francisco, and Los Angeles. In fact, countless town and street names in the United States reflect our Spanish history.

The Treaty of Guadalupe Hidalgo (1848), which ended the Mexican-American War (Mexico lost more than half its territory to the United States) had linguistic ramifications. Upon the signing of the agreement, Mexican nationals found themselves no longer living in their own country but in the United States, which, by treaty, took over Mexican territory. One of the many protections that the treaty was supposed to offer Mexicans who lived in the newly acquired American land was the right to continue using the Spanish language. Along with oft-broken promises concerning property rights, this linguistic right was not always respected.

Nevertheless, the Spanish of the Southwest was able to survive, as was the Spanish of what is today the state of New Mexico, a region that offers an interesting case in the history of the Spanish language in the United States. New-Mexican Spanish (formally described by pioneering linguist Aurelio Espinosa as early as 1909 and more recently studied and mapped by University of New Mexico professors

Garland Bills and Neddy Vigil) to this day represents a unique and archaic variety of U.S. Spanish. It is in danger of being lost forever—a victim of the economic factors that pull young people away from rural communities and of mass media's successful infiltration into even the most remote areas.

A very small minority of Spanish speakers in the United States can trace their families' presence to the time of Spanish explorations and settlements in California, Texas, and New Mexico—most Latinos arrived more recently. The Mexican Revolution (1910), for example, engendered a great wave of immigration north as Mexicans sought refuge from the violence in their country. The search for a safe haven continued throughout the 20th century with revolutions, wars, and unrest spurring Latin Americans to move north to the United States. Economic factors have been and continue to be the primary motivator for Spanish-speaking immigrants; immigration has been encouraged or discouraged by the need for cheap labor in the United States.

After English, the Spanish language is the second most spoken language of the United States, with Lati-

© WILLY SPILLER/BRUCE COLEMAN INC.

Signs in Spanish and English in Los Angeles.

nos representing the second largest ethnic and linguistic minority group in the country. One-half of the Latino population of the United States lives in California and Texas. States that have more than 1 million Hispanic residents include New York, Florida, Illinois, Arizona, and New Jersey.

The most recent U.S. Census (2000) offers figures and updates (2002) that show that the Latino population (more than 35.3 million) surpassed the African American population (34.6 million) sooner than predicted. The 2000 census also revealed the extraordinary variety that exists in the Latino population: approximately 66 percent of Latinos were of Mexican national or ethnic background, 9 percent were Puerto Rican, and 4 percent were Cuban. Central and South Americans together made up 15 percent of the total. These numbers help us to understand the various cultural and linguistic influences on the U.S. Latino population.

The 1980 census estimated the Latino population to be around 14 million. In just 20 years Latinos have more than doubled their numbers and now make up approximately 14 percent of the population of the United States. Although cities like Los Angeles, New York, Miami, and Chicago experienced the greatest growth in Latino population, and other "Hispanic" cities like San Diego and Houston continued to show increases, a new trend has become evident—the Latino population is growing in Georgia (in Atlanta and its suburbs, for example) and in other parts of the South (including North Carolina and Alabama). As Robert Suro of the Pew Hispanic Center and Audrey Singer of the Brookings Institution Center on Urban and Metropolitan Policy report in "Latino Growth in Metropolitan America" " . . . the Latino population is rapidly evolving and that its demographic impact on the nation is changing quickly. Significant concentrations of Latinos are no longer confined to a few regions such as Southern California or the Southwest, or only to a few cities like New York and Miami. Instead, in the coming years, Latino population growth will most impact communities that had relatively few Latinos a decade ago."

Myths and misconceptions about Latinos and the Spanish that is spoken in the United States abound. One typical misconception is that Latinos are all pretty much alike and that they all speak a nonstandard form of Spanish or what many refer to as "Spanglish." This term, referring to the mixing of English and Spanish, or the alternation of linguistic codes, known in linguistics as code-switching phenomena, can have negative or derogatory associations.

What is obvious to linguists is that the centuries of contact between English and Spanish have permitted each language to influence the other. Because English is the de facto official language, the language of the majority of the country, and the language of business and the professions in general, we can more easily observe how English affects Spanish—borrowings from English, loan shifts, and utterances that are in Spanish but use code switching expressions, idioms, or grammatical structures that have been transferred from English usage. Examples: "Mamá, ya llegó el *rufero*; dice que él puede arreglar el *liqueo*, pero que te tiene que *llamar p'atrás* para decirte qué día puede venir con su *troca* y su ayudante para poner el *tar* en el *hole* que encontró en el *rufo*."

In reality, the Spanish spoken in the United States reflects many Latin cultures and the many linguistic varieties of its speakers, who use it in various contexts and with different degrees of proficiency. As the majority of Latinos are Mexican or of Mexican American background, much of the Spanish spoken north of the Rio Grande reflects varieties of Mexican and Mexican American Spanish, particularly in states heavily populated by this heterogeneous group—California and Texas, for example.

Puerto Rican Spanish on the mainland, also heavily influenced by daily contact with English, is found mostly in the largest enclaves in metropolitan areas like New York, Chicago, and Boston; Puerto Ricans, like Mexican Americans and Cuban Americans, also reside all over the United States, not just in the barrios of New York City or Chicago. Cubans and Cuban Americans are found primarily in Miami, but considerable numbers live in Union City, New Jersey; many who had been relocated in the early 1960s to Illinois and California returned to Miami upon retirement. The decades of the 1980s and 1990s witnessed, in addition to the three major Spanish-speaking groups, significant immigration (legal and illegal) from Central and South American countries. Nicaraguans, Salvadorans, Guatemalans, Chileans, and, more recently, Colombians and Argentines, are the Spanish-speaking South Americans most likely to come to the United States. In Miami, for example, the discerning ear can hear in one day characteristics of Caribbean Spanish, Cuban American Spanish, or Puerto Rican Spanish.

A significant percentage of third- and fourth-generation Latinos, particularly those of Mexican American background in a city like Los Angeles, tend to use more English in their daily lives, and many Latinos in the United States sometimes lose some, if not all, of their ability to understand and speak Spanish. Other Latinos in the United States have managed to maintain their proficiency in Spanish to varying degrees despite efforts of groups like U.S. English to have English made the official language of the United States and despite the overwhelming economic, social, and cultural predominance of English. Additionally, the alternating of the two languages adds more complexities to English-Spanish/Spanish-English bilingualism, giving rise to varieties of Spanish that come in contact with those of American English (such as African American vernaculars and varieties of regional American English).

How are Latinos able to nurture their Latino roots and keep their Spanish-language abilities despite the Official English movement, a post-9/11 anti-immigrant political atmosphere, and antibilingual education forces? One answer lies in the important role language plays in preserving cultural heritage, not only by way of home and community interaction in Spanish, but also through mass media, entertainment, and advertising. Bilingualism and culture, always connected, also help foster and strengthen a feeling of identity and belonging to a group. In addition, in some American cities—Miami, for example—Spanish-English bilingualism confers significant and documented economic benefits.

The news and entertainment world and the Latino media, including advertising, play crucial roles as access to Spanish-language television, radio, and print media becomes more widespread. The world of "crossover" and successful bilingual artists such as Linda Ronstadt (in the 1960s), Enrique Iglesias, Shakira, and Gloria Estefan reaches young and older audiences alike as well as Latinos and non-Latinos in the United States.

Spanish newspapers and magazines, radio broadcasting, Internet search engines, and Spanish-language television programming (including cable and satellite services) like those of Univisión and Telemundo, Venevisión, Telefutura, and Azteca América now reach millions of households. Univisión even beats its English-language news program competitors in

New York, Los Angeles, and Chicago, which constitute the top three television markets. Latino buying power—now approximately $600 billion and growing by 8.7 percent every year, double the pace of non-Latinos—is projected to increase to 9.4 percent of the national total by 2007. In addition, given the growing wealth and population of the Latino community, the Latino media are likely to expand even further.

Clearly, as the Latino population already here keeps increasing annually as children are born, and as the continuing influx of new immigrant native speakers of Spanish act as linguistic and cultural "booster shots," Spanish-language survival and growth in the United States are assured. The continuing influx of Spanish-speaking immigrants helps counteract some of the language change, shift, and loss that occurs naturally with the passing of generations, and this has been documented and discussed by numerous linguists.

The Latino population, thus, is a heterogeneous linguistic population that demonstrates varying degrees of English-Spanish bilingualism and varying degrees of monolingualism in Spanish or in English. Levels of Spanish-language proficiency vary tremendously throughout regions of the country, within single school districts, from family to family, and even among siblings in a family. The multiple factors that can affect Spanish-language development include but are not limited to these: length of residence in a Spanish-speaking country before coming to the United States, socioeconomic level, education, Spanish-language use at home and in the community, language attitudes at home as well as at school and in the community, media and community support or lack thereof, experience with reading in Spanish at an early age, and access to bilingual education programs that are not solely meant as transitional programs into an all-English curriculum. Other factors that come into play in terms of Spanish-language maintenance involve issues of cultural background, national identity, race and ethnicity, socioeconomic and legal status (documented or undocumented), and the level of literacy and schooling.

The United States is the fourth largest Spanish-speaking country in the world after Mexico, Spain, and Colombia. Policy and educational planning were surely influenced by the Latino community and the Spanish language in international trade and business. More important, Spanish speakers in the United

States will take part in the history, the politics, the economy, the mass media, public health, the courts, and the public and private education systems in the United States. In the 21st century the idea of the "melting pot" does not seem to fit what we observe happening with the Latino population. This group adapts to the American English-speaking culture and language, but still manages to maintain a Latino identity and retain its particular national and cultural roots. At the same time, as a reaction to conservative anti-immigrant movements, the complex and diverse Latino population has also become unified as a result of its struggles for a political voice. Latino identity may not ensure Spanish-language oral proficiency or literacy, but after centuries of English and Spanish coexisting in the United States, Spanish remains viable and will continue to evolve and meld with English.

In the last 25 years, we have witnessed increased interest by Spanish-language professionals in trying to meet the pedagogical and linguistic needs of their Spanish-speaking students, particularly at the secondary and college levels. Although Spanish has normally been taught in the United States as a foreign language, when the numbers of Spanish-speaking students increased dramatically in the 1970s and 1980s, professional associations (for example, the American Association of Teachers of Spanish and Portuguese—the AATSP; the American Council for the Teaching of Foreign Languages—or ACTFL; and the Center for Applied Linguistics—CAL), instructors and publishers began to take note and to play a pivotal role in bringing pedagogical, curricular, and policy issues related to the teaching of Spanish as a heritage language into consideration. The needs were then and remain clear: Search for new methods for teaching Spanish language and culture to Latino bilingual learners (more commonly referred to today as heritage language learners); call for a variety of appropriate materials (Miami-Dade County schools alone have over 100,000 Spanish for Native Speakers, or SNS, students, in grades K–12; and improve the preparation of novice teachers of Spanish and the professional development of experienced teachers. The heritage language instruction movement in Spanish is part of a larger heritage languages initiative that includes indigenous groups. It gained initial momentum in the 1990s via national conferences, publications, and resolutions, and a movement calling for the preservation and development of minority languages as resources that need to be developed for professional and personal use as well as for the security and domestic well-being of the United States. The U.S. Bureau of the Census projects that by 2025 the Latino population will increase from 35 million to 61 million, or 18 percent of the entire U.S. population. The addition of undocumented persons would make the projection much higher; consequently, Spanish-language use will continue to grow.

While writings on Spanish in the United States first started appearing in the 19th century, only in the 20th century did they begin to be published as serious academic writings in linguistics. Aurelio Espinosa began to publish in 1909 what would later be a series of writings on the Spanish of New Mexico (before it was a state). Today the study of Spanish in the United States is flourishing, with a number of publications (reference volumes, special journal issues, hundreds of journal articles on many aspects of bilingualism and Spanish in the United States) as well as an established conference—El Español en los Estados Unidos/National Conference on Spanish in the United States. Formerly an annual linguistics conference, this conference is now held at different universities every two years. Several other national and international Hispanic language and bilingualism studies conferences and symposia are held each year.

RELATED ARTICLES

Bilingual Education; Bilingualism; Caló; Cubonics; Dominicanish; Newspapers and Magazines; Onomastics; Radio; Spanglish; Television; Toponymy.

FURTHER READING

Boswell, Thomas D. "Demographic Changes in Florida and Their Importance for Effective Educational Policies and Practices." In *Research on Spanish in the U.S.* Ed. by Ana Roca. Somerville, Mass.: Cascadilla Press, 2000.

Kreeft Peyton, Joy, et al., eds. *Heritage Languages in America: Preserving a National Resource.* Washington, D.C.: Center for Applied Linguistics and Delta Systems, 2001.

Lipski, John M. "Back to Zero or Ahead to 2001? Issues and Challenges in U.S. Spanish Research." In *Research on Spanish in the United States.* Ed. by Ana Roca. Somerville: Cascadilla Press, 2000.

Roca, Ana, ed. *Research on Spanish in the United States: Linguistic Issues and Challenges.* Somerville, Mass.: Cascadilla Press, 2000.

Roca, Ana, and M. Cecilia Colombi, eds. *Mi Lengua: Spanish as a Heritage Language in the United States.* Washington, D.C.: Georgetown Univ. Press, 2003.

Sánchez, Rosaura. *Chicano Discourse.* Rowley, Mass.: Newbury House, 1983.

Silva-Corvalán, Carmen. *Language Contact and Change: Spanish in Los Angeles.* Oxford: Clarendon Press, 1994.

Suro, Robert, and Audrey Singer. *Latino Growth in Metropolitan America: Changing Patterns, New Locations.* Survey Series. (Census 2000, July 2002). Washington, D.C.: Brookings Inst./Pew Hispanic Ctr., 2002.

Valdes, Guadalupe, and Michelle Geoffrion-Vinci. "Chicano Spanish: The Problem of the 'Underdeveloped' Code in Bilingual Repertoires." *Modern Language Journal* 82 (1998): 473–501.

Zentella, Ana Celia. *Growing Up Bilingual.* Malden, Mass.: Blackwell, 1997.

SELECTED WEB SITE

U.S. Census Bureau Population Projections. http://www.census.gov/population/www/projections/natproj.html

ANA ROCA

SPIRITUALITY

As Latinos migrated to the United States, they brought their religious customs and perpetuated them. Popular religious expressions, such as home altars, pilgrimages, lighting candles in church, novenas, blessings, *promesas,* and so forth are so widespread that a reported 77 percent of Puerto Ricans and 76 percent of Mexicans engage in these practices.

Being Latino means being religious in varying degrees. Although the majority of Latinos are considered Catholic, the religious experiences of Latinos are not so neatly categorized. Latinos often syncretize religious rituals—mixing religious practices that in the United States are seen by many as fundamentally in opposition, for example Santería, which is often erroneously characterized and dismissed as voodoo, and Catholicism. Another example can be found in the patron saint of Cuba, La Virgen de la Caridad (Our Lady of Charity), whose name in Catholicism is an invocation of the Virgin Mary; in Santería she is known as Oshun, an *orisha,* who is the patron of love and the river. Latinos may participate in a religion like Santería wholeheartedly, may engage only in certain practices while still seeing themselves as part of a "traditional" religion, or may not be at all involved in Santería. Someone of Mexican origin, for instance, might be a devout Catholic but also go to a *curandera,* a female healer, who uses folk medicine to treat ailments. For Latinos, this conflation of icons or engaging in religious practices outside of one's principal religious identity is not contradictory. Latin Americans and Latinos, however, have found that a great gulf exists between how they view their Christian practices and beliefs and those

dictated by various church officials in the United States.

The way that Catholicism is practiced in Latin America differs markedly from its practice in the United States. Catholicism in the United States centers on attending Mass and participating in church activities; in Latin America, church attendance was not always possible, thus it became nonessential to proving that one was a religious person. Various studies confirm that religion is very important to the majority of Latinos, but they do not consider attending services proof of their commitment.

Initially, many immigrants to the United States tried to attend church since the church is an institution common to their native land and adopted land. But Latin Americans soon realized that their religious behavior was viewed as wrong. The Catholic Church in the United States wanted to extirpate these elements from Latinos' religious practices. In the United States this has led to much misunderstanding between Latino Catholics and the church hierarchy, which had set up a "right or wrong" paradigm dealing with Latinos. A more fruitful course for the Catholic Church and others would have been to regard religious affiliation of Latinos as a continuum, rather than as an either/or classification.

A specific example comes from research done on Cuban practices as noted in Thomas A. Tweed's book *Our Lady of Exile: Diasporic Religion at a Cuban Catholic Shrine in Miami* (1997). Research shows that in pre-1959 Cuba, more than half of Cubans had never seen a priest, which was interpreted as Cubans not being very religious. Cubans, however, express show their spirituality and religiosity by having relationships with the African *orishas* and the Catholic saints. Cuban homes are adorned by religious figures, especially statuettes of the La Virgen de Caridad. Cubans, like many other Latin Americans, celebrate *fiestas patronales*—each patron saint has a feast day assigned to her or him and a festival usually occurs on that day. Another form of worship typical of Latin America is participation in religious pilgrimages. Thus spiritual belief is expressed in various ways, but expression is not limited to what is considered acceptable by the religion's hierarchy.

Through their religious traditions, Latinos have shown that nonecclesiastical practices are fundamental to the way they express their spirituality and religious beliefs. Some of the spiritual practices Latinos engage in include public displays of rituals, *fiesta patronales,* keeping altars in their homes, and wearing black during periods of mourning.

Joseph P. Fitzpatrick's *Puerto Rican Americans: The Meaning of Migration to the Mainland* (1971) studies the religious experience of Puerto Ricans in the United States. The religious framework that he uses is applicable to other Latino groups as well. He puts forth the concept of a *pueblo,* which is used to signify both the town and the community. For the Spaniards to have imposed their colonial rule on the indigenous inhabitants of Puerto Rico, they had to establish that the individual existed only within the realm of the community—no space was allowed for an individual who did not want to be part of the community and conform to its norms. In addition, communities could exist only if God was a part of it—the Spanish used this idea to impose both their religion on the indigenous peoples of Latin America and to colonize them. An individual, however, could claim to be religious just by being part of the community. Thus anyone could consider her- or himself to be religious without necessarily going to church because they were part of the *pueblo* and God was ever-present and ubiquitous.

Another way that spirituality and religion are expressed and experienced in Latin America is by the individual's engaging with the spirit world. Fitzpatrick says that all cultures colonized by the Spaniards have the concept of *personalismo*—an individual has a close, personal relationship with God, invoking the Virgin Mary and numerous saints in times of trouble and in thanks. The individual who engages in *personalismo* builds home altars, lights candles, and prays to particular saints. She or he also carries images of the saints in processions and makes promises to the saints. The individual, in turn, expects her or his prayers to be answered by the saints. Within this tradition of *personalismo,* familiar terms are used to address the saints. For example, the terms *compadre* and *padrino* both mean, in this context, "godfather." The relationship between godparents and parents within Latino cultures is exceedingly important, carrying much responsibility and respect. Godparents are carefully chosen because if the parents die, then the godparents must take care of the children. Thus the use of these terms to address the saints confirms that the relationship is *personalismo* and is very respectful, filled with trust, and exemplary of what it means to practice one's faith. There is no one "right" way to worship; rather the way one worships depends on the needs of the individual. Those who engage in *personalismo* do not have to attend church to have a relationship with God or the saints; such relationships exist outside of these constructs and are based in the home.

Another manifestation of *personalismo* can be found in Mexican American culture. This version of *personalismo* has been named by scholars such as Virgil Elizondo as *religión casera* (home-based religion) and "*abuelita* (grandmother) theology" by Gilbert Cadena. Home-based spiritual practices are taught and passed on by family matriarchs. The focus of these spiritual practices has been on what can be accomplished at home, what occurs outside of the home—official church ceremonies—get considerably less attention. About half of the Mexican Americans and Mexicans living north of the Rio Grande in the first half of the 20th century had religious altars in their homes; while this figure may have decreased over the decades owing to acculturation, the image of a Mexican American with an altar at home remains a popular one. These home-based spiritual practices emphasize the use of sacred objects: rosaries, medals, candles, relics, holy water, and scapulars. Prayers, devotions, triduums, and worship of saints are also central to home-based spirituality. Statues of saints are commonly found in homes; necklaces with medals having an image of a saint are also worn. These are used to ward off harm; promises, typically of a pilgrimage, are made to the saints in exchange for grating a petition. A devotion to saints rather than the worship of God or Jesus is common in Mexican and other Latino groups. Saints are perceived as being much more accessible and are also known for performing miracles and having special powers.

Marianismo refers to the worship of the Virgin Mary. Each ethnicity worships the Virgin Mary differently and gives her different names. To Puerto Ricans, the Virgin Mary is known as La Milagrosa (The Miraculous One); to Cubans, La Virgen de la Caridad; and to Mexicans, La Virgen de Guadalupe (Our Lady of Guadalupe).

Our Lady of Guadalupe is the most important figure in Mexican American spirituality. Because Mary was human, she is seen as more accessible than God; because she is a mother, she has became the figurative mother of the Mexican people providing maternal love, especially during difficult times. Every Mexican church contains a shrine to the Virgin. An important procession to honor La Virgen de Guadalupe started in East Los Angeles in 1927 and has become an annual event. After the procession there was usually a fiesta, which, like the procession, served to reinforce the spiritual beliefs of this community. La Virgen's image has often been used when Mexican Americans have protested a social injustice.

La Virgen de Caridad is the center of spiritual worship within the Cuban exile community in Miami. For many, La Virgen de Caridad is synonymous with Cuba; thus religious worship is tied to a sense of patriotism and nationhood. She is also called La Virgen Mambisa (the Revolutionary Virgin) because she was venerated during the wars for independence in the 19th century. Today those who pray to her often pray that one day Cuba will be free of communism. Because she was discovered as an icon floating in the Bay of Nipe attached to a piece of wood that said "Yo Soy la Virgen de la Caridad" (I am Our Lady of Charity), her legend has been recast so that she now is seen as the first Cuban refugee at sea. Because of her importance to the exile community in Cuba, the Catholic Church in Miami aided in having a shrine built in her honor.

Marian devotion is important to the spiritual life of Latinos; the linking of the image of Mary with the idea of the nation has helped Latinos in the United States maintain an ethnic identity—not abandoning their Latino identity in an attempt to assimilate and assume an "American" identity.

Latinos engage in various public displays of their faith, some of which have been disavowed by the Catholic Church because they were found to be not in keeping with its theology. Nevertheless, Latinos have not abandoned these displays; rather they are proud of their religious practices and are adamant about maintaining them.

One of the most recognizable public displays of spirituality among Mexican Americans is the Día de los Muertos (Day of the Dead)—the day set aside to honor the dead. Traditionally celebrated on November 1, participants spend several days before and after this date making preparations and several days actually venerating their dead. Various activities—attending Mass, having a procession with elaborate floats and costumes, and worshipping at altars at home and at church—emphasize the indigenous elements of Mexican culture. The procession commences with the beat of Aztec drums and features Aztec dancers in feathered headdresses and beaded dress. The staples of such celebrations are *calavera* (skull) images and *cempoaxóchitl* (marigolds). *Calaveras* are the emblematic image—miniature skulls are placed on altars and floats with papier-mâché skulls are ever present; in addition, people dress up in skeleton-inspired costumes. Procession attendees can often be seen with bouquets of orange marigolds—the customary flowers used in the *ofrendas* (altars for the deceased). The flowers are ideal for these celebrations because it is thought that their strong odor and intense color help lure back the spirits of loved ones.

Mass is celebrated on the Day of the Dead. A traditional altar, which is often elaborate, detailed, and multitiered, is set up in the church. Some of the objects often found on these altars are marigolds, *calavera* masks, *pan de muertos* (sweet bread fashioned into images of skeletons and *calaveras*), *papel picado* (tissue paper cut and shaped into traditional designs), and photos of dead family members or other loved ones. At the Mass a "Book of Names" is passed around so those gathered can enter the names of those who have died. The book is placed on the altar after having been blessed by the priest.

Prior to the 1970s, the celebration of Día de los Muertos in the United States occurred in private; activities were limited to the construction of and veneration at home altars and visits to the cemetery. Gradually, celebrations shifted to more public venues, exemplifying the integration and acceptance of certain nonecclesiastical practices into the practices of the Catholic Church.

A ubiquitous type of public display of religious and spiritual beliefs among Latinos is the *fiesta patronal* (feast day celebrations for a patron saint). An example of a *fiesta patronal* is the Fiesta de San Juan that took place in New York City for many years.

As with other immigrant groups, when Puerto Ricans started migrating to the United States, the Catholic Church was both an introduction to their new society and a source of comfort. The Catholic Church did try to meet the needs of the Puerto Rican community. Priests learned Spanish and studied the culture. Most important, the Catholic Church started an annual festival in the customary Puerto Rican fashion of *fiesta patronoles*. Rather than seeking to destroy the folk traditions of Puerto Ricans, the church decided to build on these traditions to try to forge a better relationship with Puerto Ricans, and thus started the Fiesta de San Juan to honor Saint John the Baptist, the patron saint of Puerto Rico. The festival usually occurred in June, on the Sunday closest to June 25, the feast day of Saint John the Baptist. Festivities in New York City featured a procession, a sermon, then a Mass, the awarding of the San Juan Medal, activities for children, an arts component with dance troupes and music, and other activities.

Some scholars believe that this holding on to "popular" religious practices is a method of cultural resistance. If that is the case, then these public displays of spiritual or folk beliefs also serve to further solidify a rejection of what is normative for the Catholic Church and help build group identity in unfamiliar and often hostile territory.

The cultural clashes between Latinos and the Catholic Church in the United States persist. Just as Latinos have been transnational (im)migrants, in that they, for the most part, have kept their cultural traditions or begun new traditions based on those of their home country, they have continued to maintain their spiritual and religious practices. Latinos have resisted through low church attendance, remaining steadfast to their traditional beliefs, practicing their religious beliefs at home, and converting from Catholicism to other denominations.

Also, how the indigenous (for example, African) religions have been viewed in the United States has been flawed. Santería in the United States has been misunderstood and been misrepresented as something sinister. Even though Latino Catholicism has been syncretized with indigenous practices, syncretism in the United States has come to mean an inferior brand of Catholicism from the outset. With any interaction between U.S. Catholics and Latino Catholics, there has been the continual insistence on eliminating any traditions that U.S. Catholics deem inappropriate or contrary to the "right" way of practicing Catholicism. Regardless, folk or African-based religions have continued to proliferate in the United States. Indicative of how normative these practices are is the *botaníca*, a store that sells religious icons, herbs, ritual instructions—it is a common part of any Puerto Rican neighborhood in Puerto Rico and in the United States. The Cuban exile community has an enormous number of *botanícas* in Miami, more so than in Cuba. Mexican Americans also have *botanícas* where *curanderas* practice their spiritualism. Puerto Ricans are also involved in *espiritismo*—spiritualism, which claims that an individual can contact the dead, who can be called on to aid the individual.

Some scholars believe that a change in Latino practices is inevitable. For example, scholar Virgilio Elizondo believes that all the cultures that have an impact on Mexican Americans will lead to a new type of religion, to a "second *mestizaje*." An example is provided by Timothy Matovina and Gary Riebe-Estrella in *Horizons of the Sacred: Mexican Traditions in U.S. Catholicism* (2002). They maintain that the racial prejudice Mexican Americans face in the United States caused them to respond in specific ways. For example, the image of Our Lady of Guadalupe was used in a procession to counteract the prejudice Mexican Americans faced in San Antonio, Texas. Latino spirituality and religion seem to be moving toward a heightened veneration of the spiritual elements of Latino faith. What also needs to be noted is that if a greater shift toward the nonecclesiastical occurs, then the Catholic Church in the United States will be faced anew with the very elements that they had tried to eliminate.

RELATED ARTICLES

Botanícas; Catholicism; Compadrazgo; Cuban Americans; Curanderismo; Espiritismo; Exile; Marianismo; Mexican Americans; Puerto Ricans on the Mainland; Religion; Santería; Virgen de la Caridad del Cobre; Virgen de Guadalupe.

FURTHER READING

Díaz-Stevens, Ana Maria. *Oxcart Catholicism on Fifth Avenue.* Notre Dame, Ind.: Univ. of Notre Dame Press, 1993.

Dolan, Jay P., and Allan Figueroa Deck, eds. *Hispanic Catholic Culture in the U.S.: Issues and Concerns.* Notre Dame, Ind.: Univ. of Notre Dame Press, 1994.

Dolan, Jay P., and Gilberto M. Hinojosa, eds. *Mexican Americans and the Catholic Church, 1900–1965.* Notre Dame, Ind.: Univ. of Notre Dame Press, 1994.

Fitzpatrick, Joseph P. *Puerto Rican Americans: The Meaning of Migration to the Mainland.* Englewood Cliffs, N.J.: Prentice-Hall, 1971.

Matovina, Timothy, and Gary Riebe-Estrella, eds. *Horizons of the Sacred: Mexican Traditions in U.S. Catholicism.* Ithaca, N.Y.: Cornell Univ. Press, 2002.

Stevens-Arroyo, Anthony M., and Gilbert R. Cadena, eds. *Old Masks, New Faces: Religion and Latino Identities.* New York: Bildner Ctr., 1995.

Stevens-Arroyo, Anthony M., and Ana María Díaz-Stevens. *Recognizing the Latino Resurgence in U.S. Religion.* Boulder, Colo.: Westview Press, 1998.

Tweed, Thomas A. *Our Lady of the Exile: Diasporic Religion at a Cuban Catholic Shrine in Miami.* New York: Oxford Univ. Press, 1997.

IVELISSE RODRIGUEZ

SPIRITUAL PLAN OF AZTLÁN

The *Spiritual Plan of Aztlán* (*El Plan Espiritual de Aztlán*) is a social manifesto written by Chicanos in the late 1960s with roots in the folklore concerning Aztlán. Aztlán is understood to be the original land of the Aztecs prior to their move south to conquer Central Mexico. In Nahuatl the word *Aztlán* is translated as "the land to the north" or "the land of the white reeds." The location of Aztlán is vague, but many believe it existed in the United States, in the valley of the lower Colorado River and beyond. At the heart of the politicized use of the term *Aztlán* is the legend that suggests that Aztec Emperor Motecuhzoma (in Spanish, Moctezuma; anglicized Montezuma) prophesied the rising up of his descendents into a rekindled and renewed life, thereby restoring the Aztecs to prominence.

The prophetic vision attributed to Motecuhzoma provided the foundation for the use of Aztlán as a concept of liberation during the Chicano Liberation Youth Conference, at which the *Spiritual Plan of Aztlán* was adopted as a resolution. Conference attendees included representatives from large and small Chicano student organizations as well as other groups, such as the Puerto Rican Young Lords. At the conference held in Denver at El Centro de la Crusada in March 1969, 3,000 Chicanos gathered to address the question, "Where do the barrios' youth, the students, the rural Chicanos, the campesinos fit into the Chicano movement?" and, subsequently, to proclaim the fruition of the vision of Motecuhzoma. The conference addressed social revolution and cultural identity with panel discussions about organization, self-defense, protest planning, and cultural production. Inspired by the working-class labor-union organizing of César Chávez and led by the origin-seeking ideologies and barrio culture concerns of Rodolfo "Corky" Gonzáles, attendees declared themselves a nation, a union, and the reemergence of Aztlán. Within a context of a developing black power movement and nationwide protest against violation of human rights and the Vietnam War, the conference was a welcome opportunity for almost 1,500 youth to address growing concerns for Chicano communities. The ethnocentric, radical determination to gain respect and autonomy espoused by leaders like Gonzáles called for a plan to develop a Chicano national consciousness. Gonzáles, who had assisted in the writing of political manifestos on behalf of Chicanos in the poor peoples' campaign of the 1960s, brought a militant rhetoric to the *Spiritual Plan of Aztlán*. He provided a redefinition of Chicanismo and led in the proclamation of Aztlán as the southwest homeland of Chicanos. In the manifesto, Gonzáles articulated the necessity for unity, a separate political entity for Chicanos, collaboration across class lines, and a desire to maintain connection to the working class and its values.

The *Spiritual Plan of Aztlán* rejects current sociopolitical and economic conditions of Chicanos and articulates a specifically nationalist agenda for an autonomous Chicano community. Aztlán envisioned a reshaped identity that connected Chicanos to Aztec cultural roots and history and provided a legendary foundation for a nationalist consciousness to use in overcoming oppression. The Plan's preface acknowledges the historical heritage and invasion of Mexican territories; the proclamation demands a united brotherhood and sets Chicanos in direct opposition to, and independent from, mainstream colonialist America. The Plan also maintains that commitment to its ideologies leads to complete liberation from American racism and exploitation and expresses a desire for self-reliance and control of neighborhoods and systems operating within them, including economies, cultures, and politics.

The four points of the *Spiritual Plan of Aztlán* include detailed commentary on nationalism, organization goals, action, and the achievement of liberation. It suggests nationalism as the unifying philosophy for the liberation struggle. The Plan's seven organizational goals are as follows:

- develop unity across all circumstances and professions toward liberation;
- achieve economic self-determination and commit to gaining control over resources and skills, including ownership of community land. It suggests that the community should embrace humanism, reject materialism, and embrace nationalism and the organizations that protect Chicano interests as the guarantors of economic responsibility;
- realize that education is fundamental to community growth and commit to maintaining community authority in schools;
- insist on "restitution" for historical manipulation, exploitation, and denial of fundamental human rights through community institutions;
- commit to the defense of Chicano interests;

- set standards for the artistic production of La Raza and adopt values that are counter to materialism and that encourage unity; and
- form an independent political party, "La Familia de La Raza," to operate as a political manager for *raza* (race) interests and to place political pressure on the two-party system.

The third section sets forth six goals for a nationalist plan of action:

- distribute and present the Plan in every possible venue;
- engage in mass student demonstration in honor of Mexican Independence on September 16th in a national walkout of classes until educational institutions revise all aspects of their programs to meet community needs;
- insist on defense against oppressive occupation;
- nationalize and organize the community toward application of the Plan;
- uphold cooperative community efforts for economic self-determination; and
- create La Familia de la Raza to operate at all political levels.

The fourth and final point of the Plan is a statement of the desire for liberation and freedom to control the cultural, social, and economic decisions and activities of the community's institutions, peoples, judgments, and labor. The Plan ends stating that, "El Plan de Aztlán is the Plan of Liberation!" The Plan's effect was felt almost a decade later and provided a foundation and reference for other groups' organizational and philosophical planning, including the Familias Unidas, a group of activists in the Texas Chicano Movement. Families Unidas use the Plan's vision in its efforts to alter the lives of poor Robstown, Texas, residents. The Plan continues to be at the heart of sociopolitical programming and activism on campuses across the United States, in the work of groups such as Movimiento Estudiantil Chicano de Aztlán (MeChA), through nationalist organizations such as the Nation of Aztlán, and in various social-justice oriented Latino journals and newspapers.

RELATED ARTICLES

Aztlán; Chicanismo; Chicano Movement; Gonzáles, Rodolfo; Movimiento Estudantil Chicano de Aztlán; Nahuas; Politics, Mexican American.

FURTHER READING

Acuña, Rodolfo. *Occupied America: A History of Chicanos.* 5th ed. New York: Longman, 2003.

Anaya, Rudolfo A., and Francisco Lomelí. *Aztlán: Essays on the Chicano Homeland.* Albuquerque: Univ. of N.Mex. Press, 1991.

Anzaldúa, Gloria. *Borderlands/La Frontera: The New Mestiza.* San Francisco: Aunt Lute, 1987.

Chávez, John R. *The Lost Land: The Chicano Image of the Southwest.* Albuquerque: Univ. of N.Mex. Press, 1984.

García, Ignacio. *Chicanismo: The Forging of a Militant Ethos among Mexican Americans.* Tucson: Univ. of Ariz. Press, 1997.

Valdéz, Luis, and Stan Steiner, eds. *Aztlán: An Anthology of Mexican American Literature.* New York: Alfred A. Knopf, 1972.

HELANE D. ADAMS

SPORTS IN LATINO LIFE

From the earliest days of the republic, sports have had an important place in the lives of most Americans. Many Latinos are avid fans. In fact, the large influx of Latin American immigrants to the United States in the second half of the 20th century has resulted in a remarkable revolution in American sports. Latinos have transformed American sports through their passion and loyalty. But most of all, they have transformed American sports through their sheer numbers.

Sports have always been recognized as an important avenue to help children to channel their energy constructively. Training for sports activities develops coordination and improves physical fitness. Physical fitness, in turn, promotes a sense of well-being that can influence the self-esteem and pride of a young person of any ethnicity.

From early childhood many young Hispanics across the United States are encouraged to participate in a wide variety of sports, often getting their first sports experience when their parents enroll them in church sports programs during their preschool years. When they reach grade school, sons are often encouraged by their parents to become involved in school-sponsored sports activities, such as baseball, football, or basketball.

Other Latino children become involved in neighborhood soccer and football, or join Little League baseball teams. For young Chicano boys in the barrios of California and Texas, playing neighborhood soccer may play a crucial role in keeping a child from gang activities or illegal drug use. For a rare few gifted and talented Latinos, involvement in sports can represent a ticket to fame and fortune in professional sports.

For adult Latinos sports occupy an equally important position. For many Latino adults in the United States, spectator sports engender great passion and excitement. Fiercely loyal to the home team, the Latino spectator can become very passionately involved in the intricacies of the game and the personalities of favorite players.

When national origins come into play—as they frequently do—the spectator's enthusiasm and competitive feeling becomes an expression of national pride and ethnic loyalty. In fact, many Mexican American neighborhoods in California have organized soccer leagues, a number of them representing the native states of their players.

The issue of Latino Americans and their attachment to certain sports is complex because Latinos are not a homogenous group of people and may belong to any one of two dozen ethnic groups. Although each of these ethnic groups has brought its own cultural preferences and tastes to America, they all share a great passion for sports.

When Cubans, Puerto Ricans, Salvadorans, Dominicans, or northern Mexicans arrive anywhere in the United States, they bring with them a passion for baseball. For these immigrants, baseball is not just a sport, but a cultural tradition that helps them to maintain a connection to their homelands. In most cases, a strong loyalty to hometown and neighborhood teams is maintained for a lifetime.

Although baseball is popular with some Latino ethnic groups, the vast majority of immigrants who come from South America, Central America, Spain, and Mexico are avid soccer fans. For Latin Americans, no sport incites more passionate feelings. With roots stretching back many centuries, soccer gradually spread from Europe to South America, North America, and Africa. The World Cup games in Uruguay in 1930 became a stepping-stone for the dominance of South American teams in the sport. This dominance continues to be a source of immense pride for South American immigrants living in the United States.

Known throughout Latin America as *fútbol,* soccer—to many Hispanics—represents a way of life that crosses all borders. Although each Latin American country has embraced the sport as an integral element of its own culture, no one ethnic group can claim soccer as its own unique creation and practice.

When Latin Americans immigrate to the United States, they bring their passion for *fútbol* with them.

The media have helped American Latinos follow their favorite national teams and players by airing the contests on Univisión, Fox Sports, and World Español. These broadcasts permit soccer fans to come together in homes, cantinas, and community centers to watch the games and share the camaraderie and emotions that soccer stirs in most Latin Americans.

Through these social gatherings, *fútbol* has become the bond that helps many American Latinos to maintain emotional, social, and cultural links to their Latin American roots. At the same time, soccer represents an instrument of confrontation between nationalities and ethnic groups. Even after living in the United States for several decades, a naturalized citizen, originally from Latin America, will often maintain a fanatical allegiance to his or her home country's team. This fierce loyalty is a hallmark of Latin American soccer. In pointing out the passion and zeal that soccer incites in its many fans, historians have cited the July 1969 "Fútbol War," in which El Salvador invaded neighboring Honduras after a qualifying round of the World Cup championship. This war claimed almost 4,000 casualties.

The competitive nature of soccer reaches new heights when Mexico's soccer team comes north to play the U.S. men's national team. In these competitions, thousands of Mexicans and Mexican Americans show up to cheer the visitors and boo the American team. From 1937 to 1980 Mexico won 24 matches in a row. In the last decades, however, many of the matches have been excruciatingly close, providing spectators with a thrilling display of neighborly rivalry and professional brinkmanship.

The Major League Soccer (MLS) organization of the United States has come to recognize that the growing Hispanic population in some areas is a financial gold mine. Starting in 2001, the MLS made a concerted effort to embrace the Latino community by organizing Hispanic Heritage Nights (HHN). Designed as a series of 10 or 12 games held each year in conjunction with regularly scheduled league games, Hispanic Heritage Nights celebrate Hispanic heritage through culturally appropriate foods and music.

In Los Angeles County, where almost 50 percent of the residents were Hispanic in 2003, the MLS awarded a franchise to Mexican businessman Jorge Vergara, the owner of the Mexican powerhouse team Chivas de Guadalajara. The new team was given the name Chivas USA and was scheduled to begin playing in 2005 at the Home Depot Center

© ROB TRINGALI/SPORTSCHROME USA

New Jersey Devils hockey player Scott Gomez on the ice.

in Carson, California, sharing its home field with the Los Angeles Galaxy soccer team in what would become the first MLS intracity rivalry in the United States.

Soccer role models include Hugo Perez, a native of El Salvador, who was raised in Southern California and joined the North American Soccer League's Los Angeles Aztecs before moving on to the Tampa Bay Rowdies and San Diego Sockers. Perez was elevated to the status of superstar when he played for the United States at the 1984 Olympics and 1994 World Cup.

Fernando Clavijo, a native of Uruguay, started his professional career in his home country but moved to the United States in 1979, where, at the age of 22, he joined the America Soccer League. During the 1980s Clavijo became one of the top players in the history of the Major Indoor Soccer League (MISL). He was named an All-Star 12 times, and in 1990 the MISL dubbed him its "Player of the Decade" for the 1980s.

Without a doubt, baseball is one of the most popular Latino sporting events in the United States. For more than a century, Cubans and Puerto Ricans have shared the American passion for the sport. In fact, the first Latin American to play baseball in the United States was the Cuban Esteban Bellan, who started playing in 1871. The first Latinos to play in the major leagues arrived in 1902, 45 years before Jackie Robinson broke baseball's color barrier. Between 1902 and 1947, Robinson's rookie year, at least 45 Latinos—most of them Cubans—played in the major leagues.

Since 1990 the baseball franchises have invested much time and effort in sending scouts to Latin America to discover potential talent for America's favorite pastime. Because of this aggressive recruitment of Latin America youth, the number of Latino players in Major League Baseball has increased dramatically. In 1990 Latinos made up 13 percent of major league players; by 1997 that number had increased to 24 percent, surpassing the number of African American ballplayers (17 percent).

In the 2002 season the 849 major league players included 74 Dominicans, 36 Venezuelans, 36 Puerto Ricans, 16 Mexicans, 11 Cubans, and 6 Panamanians. Another 33 players were Americans of Latino heritage. In all, 221 players—or 26 percent of all big-league players—were of Latin American descent, and many of these players have received Most Valuable Player awards and other honors.

Two individuals epitomize Latino pride in baseball: Roberto Clemente and Sammy Sosa. Although hundreds of Latinos have made their marks in Major League Baseball, Clemente and Sosa are the most respected. Clemente, born in Carolina, Puerto Rico, in 1934, played for the Pittsburgh Pirates from 1955 to 1972. His life was cut short at the age of 38 on December 31, 1972, when he died in an airplane crash while taking food and relief supplies to earthquake-torn Nicaragua. As a ballplayer Clemente was exciting to watch; as a Latino legend his image has inspired new generations of Hispanic youth to follow in his footsteps.

In more recent years, Sammy Sosa has fired the imagination of Latino youth in both the United States and Latin America. During the 2003 baseball season, the Chicago Cubs star hit 40 home runs in his sixth straight season, closing in on Babe Ruth's seven-year streak with the New York Yankees (1926–1932).

The importance of Latino participation in spectator sports has become so significant that Spanish-language television programs have taken steps to provide a wealth of sports news to their Latino viewers. In the first few years of the new millennium, the National Football League (NFL), the National Hockey League (NHL), and the National Basketball Association (NBA) have all launched marketing campaigns specifically aimed at the Hispanic community, both in the United States and in Latin America.

Although Latino participation in professional basketball has been very limited, Eduardo Najera of the Dallas Mavericks has gained fame for his rebounding and scoring abilities. A native of Meoqui in the Mexican state of Chihuahua, Najera is only the second Mexican-born player to join the NBA and has become one of Mexico's most famous sports celebrities. In 2003, *La Opinión,* a Spanish-language newspaper in the United States, partnered with the NBA in publishing *NBA en Español,* a special supplement that focused on the steadily growing Latin presence in basketball.

The NHL has also taken steps to attract a Latino audience to hockey—particularly difficult because of the few Hispanic players in the NHL. In 2004 the league had only three Hispanic players: Scott Gomez of the New Jersey Devils, Bill Guerin of the Dallas Stars, and Raffi Torres of the Edmonton Oilers. Gomez, a native of Alaska, gained recognition as the only Hispanic NHL first-round draft pick in 1998. Gomez was with the Devils when they won the Stanley Cup in 2000.

In 2004 Cuban American goaltender Al Montoya from Glenview, Illinois, was selected by the New York Rangers as the sixth overall choice in the NHL entry draft. The entry of more Latinos into the sport has thrilled Hispanic fans in California and Texas, where a considerable fan base of Chicanos has been developing since the 1980s.

On April 11, 1999, the premier Spanish-language media company in the United States, Univisión Communications, introduced *República Deportiva* to a predominantly Hispanic audience. Hosted by the popular television personality Fernando Fiore, *República Deportiva* initially made headlines for its innovative approach to sports reporting. Set in a neighborhood "sports bar" atmosphere, *República Deportiva* gives its viewers the latest sports news and covers the most important international sporting events.

Fiore is assisted by Rosana Franco, Spanish-language television's foremost female sportscaster. *República Deportiva* has been credited with putting the fun back into sporting events, emphasizing the lighter and amusing side of sports. In response to its overwhelming success, the program was eventually expanded from a one-hour live broadcast to that of two hours and has commanded respectable Nielsen ratings.

In 1997 Fox Sports en Español began providing comprehensive sports coverage, including games from six soccer leagues, four baseball leagues, four sports anthology programs, two sports news programs, professional boxing, and National Association for Stock Car Auto Racing (NASCAR). Fox Sports en Español, the only 24-hour Spanish-language network in the United States, has earned very strong ratings for its sports coverage.

In late January 2003 the U.S. Census reported that the Hispanic population had become the largest ethnic group in the United States. Numbering 37 million, Latinos now represented almost 13 percent of the American population. Other studies conducted around the same time revealed that Hispanic consumers had become the largest purchasers of online tickets for entertainment-related events. As a result, RazorGator and other ticket agencies made determined efforts to provide friendly and expert bilingual customer service representatives to serve their Hispanic customers.

American football was originally developed from the English game rugby. Despite its popularity with mainstream Americans, most Latinos did not develop a strong identification with the sport during most of the 20th century. Such lack of interest may have been attributable, in part, to the lack of Latino football superstars. A truly American sport with authentic American roots, football has attracted many assimilated Hispanic Americans, who give it the same devotion and commitment as Anglos and African Americans have.

According to a 2002 study, 70 percent of Hispanics questioned said they were fans of the National Football League. When questioned about their interest in football, some explained that their love of football has made them feel "more American." In recent decades, several Latino football players, such as Jim Plunkett and Anthony Muñoz, have become role models for young Latinos interested in the sport. Nevertheless, in 2003 the NFL still had only 17 Latino players, representing less than 1 percent of the entire league. San Francisco 49ers quarterback Jeff Garcia and Kansas City Chiefs tight end Tony Gonzalez were among the best-known NFL players of Latin origin.

The NFL has made concerted efforts to reach out to Latinos through Spanish-language radio and television. One-third of NFL teams now carry their games in Spanish, including the Oakland Raiders,

Dallas Cowboys, and New York Jets. NFL commissioner Paul Tagliabue has stated that marketing to Hispanics would be a "league priority."

The American passion for auto racing found its expression in the 1948 founding of NASCAR, which began a slow but steady ascent to popularity through the 1970s and 1980s. By the 1990s NASCAR had become another one of America's favorite spectator sports. According to ESPN, however, only 1.4 percent of NASCAR fans in 1995 were of Hispanic heritage.

By 2001 the number of Hispanic NASCAR fans had increased by 631 percent, to 10.2 percent of the total fan base. This new enthusiasm has been attributed to the emergence of notable Latino race-car drivers. In 1999 HRT Motorsports was established as the first Hispanic owned, sponsored, and driven NASCAR racing team. The goal of HRT was to create a new fan base within NASCAR by enlisting several well-known Latino auto-racing heroes, including such drivers as Carlos Contreras and Roberto Guerrero.

In 2000 NASCAR reached out to minorities by establishing a Diversity Council. Composed of drivers, team owners, and corporate sponsors, it presently has 36 members. Through the efforts of the Diversity Council and Fox Sports Español, NASCAR has begun to effectively target the Hispanic audience.

Televised boxing is and has been a major draw for Latino audiences since the 1990s. But the appeal of boxing to Hispanic Americans goes back more than a century to the barrios of California. During the early 20th century, professional boxing provided Mexican Americans in California with an important source of entertainment. In fact, boxing became so popular in California that matches involving Chicano boxers drew crowds from afar, even from the northern Mexican states of Baja California and Sonora.

As boxing fans, many Mexican American Californians developed a strong sense of solidarity with their brothers south of the border. Aurelio Herrera was the most famous boxer of the early 20th century. Although he was born in San Jose, California, in 1876, Herrera was dubbed "The Mexican" by the Anglo-American and Spanish-language presses of the time. This designation served to heighten the competition among boxers of different ethnic origins.

Herrera's boxing career lasted from 1898 to 1909, and his matches drew thousands of spectators. After his retirement Herrera was replaced by other Chicano boxers. Joe Rivers and Joe Salas, both with roots deep in the Los Angeles Hispanic community, came to the forefront of boxing in the second decade of the 20th century and aroused the same passion and excitement that Herrera had.

In 1924 Salas made all Latinos proud when he traveled to Paris to take part in the eighth Olympics. By the time they ended, Salas had captured the silver medal in the flyweight division and become the first Latino to win an Olympic medal for the United States. Herrera and Salas paved the way for such renowned boxers as the Los Angeles native Oscar de la Hoya.

De la Hoya's grandfather, Vicente de la Hoya, had been an amateur boxer in Durango, Mexico. In his own amateur career, Oscar won 223 bouts and lost only 5. He inspired millions of Latino fans when he won the gold medal for boxing in the 1992 Olympics in Barcelona, Spain.

Several Spanish-language networks have made a point of covering up-and-coming boxing talent. Such boxing events draw great interest, especially from Mexican Americans and Puerto Ricans. Both Mexico and Puerto Rico have rich boxing traditions that go back many decades. As a result, Mexican and Puerto Rican boxers have fought many important fights against each other. On occasion the media have trumpeted the legendary boxing rivalry as a means of attracting viewers. For some boxing fans this sports rivalry is a catalyst for national pride and adds a certain flavor to the events.

For decades American golf was regarded as a sport of upper-class Anglo-Americans. But several Latino golfers have helped to change that perception. Lee Treviño, a native of Dallas, broke new ground as the first Latino superstar in golf when he won the United States Open in 1968 and back-to-back British Opens in 1970 and 1971. In 1981 Treviño was inducted into the World Golf Hall of Fame. His success in golf was mirrored by Nancy Lopez, a Mexican American native of California, who rose to new heights with women's golf and was inducted into the Golf Hall of Fame in 1987.

The publicity surrounding Lopez's success in golf would influence a generation of aspiring Latina sports stars. For many decades most young Latinas in the United States were reluctant to become involved in school-sponsored sports activities. As a result, Hispanic women were all but absent from the ranks of female sports superstars well into the 1980s.

Many sociologists have attributed this phenomenon to complex, deeply rooted cultural taboos. Numerous teenage Hispanic girls were raised with the belief that participation in competitive sports was unfeminine—a gender-based stereotype that many Latin American immigrants brought to the United States. A large number of Latina teenagers believed that the aggression required in most sports was inappropriate, and the lack of support from male family members reinforced their discomfort. To complicate matters, some experts also cite social pressures, ethnic and cultural traditions, poverty, and the high incidence of obesity and diabetes among Hispanics as other contributing factors.

From the earliest years of the 20th century well into the 1970s, most Americans had their own reservations about the participation of women in competitive sports. But in 1975 Congress enacted Title IX, which prohibited sexual discrimination in federally funded education programs. This government action opened the doors of competitive sports to all American women. Finally, in the 1980s, some of the taboos against young Latinas and their involvement in sports started to diminish, especially in the more assimilated Mexican American communities of the Southwest.

The participation of Latinas in sports was a slow and gradual process. Latino parents—more assimilated and educated than previous generations—began to encourage their daughters to participate in various competitive sports. In many parts of the United States, Latinas are now proudly taking their place on the playing fields, sometimes competing against their own brothers and cousins.

Recent sociological studies, in fact, have pointed out that Latina teenagers who become involved in soccer, basketball, or other sports are less likely to drop out of high school, get pregnant, or become single mothers. In addition, Latina athletes—especially those from rural schools—were more likely than nonathletic Hispanics not only to improve their academic standing in high school but also to go on to attend college.

However, the strongest motivator for young Latina athletes is the emergence of many Latina sports stars. Lisa Fernandez, a native Californian of Cuban and Puerto Rican heritage who started pitching at the age of seven, became the most recognizable softball player in the country, in large part because of her amazing performances on the University of California, Los Angeles, Bruins team and with the 1996 U.S. Olympic team, which won a gold medal.

The sight of Latina women winning medals for their country at the Olympics paints an indelible picture in a young Latina athlete. The success of tennis stars Gigi Fernandez and Mary Jo Fernandez—bronze and gold medals, respectively, for the United States in the 1996 Olympics—inspired new generations of Latinas. Speed skater Jennifer Rodriguez won two speed-skating bronze medals in the 2002 Olympics.

Latinos are changing the face of American sports. Originally, many Latin American immigrants carried their dedication to soccer and baseball to American shores, while mainstream Anglo-America continued its devotion to football, basketball, and baseball. Numerous Latinos brought their skills, passion, and loyalty to the United States, but, at some point, their children begin to assimilate. While the sons and daughters of Latin American immigrants have maintained many ties to their ancestral cultures, they have also begun to broaden their horizons. Hispanic Americans are expected to play a significant role in the evolution of American sports during the first decades of the 21st century.

RELATED ARTICLES

Auto Racing; Baseball; Basketball; Boxing; Bullfighting; Canseco, José; Clemente, Roberto; de la Hoya, Oscar; Fencing; Golf; Horsemanship and Horse Racing; Kid Chocolate; Lopez, Nancy; Olympic Games; Rodeo; Soccer; Sosa, Sammy; Tennis; Wrestling.

FURTHER READING

Burgos, Adrian, Jr., "Learning America's Other Game: Baseball, Race, and the Study of Latinos." In *Latino/a Popular Culture.* Ed. by Habell-Pallán, Michelle, and Mary Romero. New York: N.Y. Univ. Press, 2002.

Longoria, Mario. "Latino Olympic Moments." *VISTA: The Magazine for All Hispanics* 11, no. 6 (April 1996).

Longoria, Mario. *Athletes Remembered: Mexicano/Latino Professional Football Players, 1929–1970.* Tempe, Ariz.: Bilingual Review Press, 1997.

Menard, Valerie. "Careers in Sports." *Career Role Models for Young Adults. Latinos at Work Series.* Bear, Del.: Mitchell Lane Pubs., 2002.

Rodríguez, Gregory S. "Boxing and the Formation of Ethnic Mexican Identities in 20th-Century Southern California." *La Prensa de San Diego* (Nov. 12, 1999).

Shinn, Christopher A. "Fútbol Nation: U.S. Latinos and the Goal of a Homeland." In *Latino/a Popular Culture.* Ed. by Habell-Pallán, Michelle, and Mary Romero. New York: N.Y. Univ. Press, 2002.

Wendel, Tim. *The New Face of Baseball: The One-Hundred Year Rise and Triumph of Latinos in America's Favorite Sport.* New York: HarperCollins, 2003.

JOHN P. SCHMAL

STEREOTYPES AND STEREOTYPING

Where do stereotypes or labels come from? Can they be altogether eliminated or are they an essential feature of human psychology? And what function do stereotypes play in a multiethnic society like the United States? What are the stereotypes that non-Latinos have of Latinos, and, conversely, what kinds of stereotypes do Latinos have of non-Latinos? This two-part entry explores the issue of labeling.

ANGLO STEREOTYPING OF LATINOS

Anglo labels for and attitudes toward Latinas and Latinos, although continually evolving, are unusually clear in U.S. culture. In the mid-1800s the pejorative term *greasers* first came into use in California and the Southwest for those of Mexican appearance. Its origin is uncertain; some suggest that the term came from Mexican laborers in the Southwest greasing their backs to unload cargo, while others suggest that it may derive from the similarity between Mexican skin color and grease or even from the presupposition that Mexicans are unkempt and unclean. Later its use expanded to encompass Peruvian and Chilean miners during California's Gold Rush and ultimately to anyone of Spanish origin. Hollywood embraced the greasers label in the era of silent films with such titles as *The Greaser's Gauntlet* (1908), *The Girl and the Greaser* (1913), *The Greaser's Revenge* (1914), and, simply, *The Greaser* (1915).

By the 1940s Mexicans and Mexican Americans in Los Angeles were labeled *pachucos* or "zoot suiters." Perhaps the *pachuco* reference derived from the city of Pachuca in the state of Hildago in central Mexico. *Zoot* grew out of urban jazz circles in the 1930s as a reference to clothing or performance in an outrageous style, and *zoot suits* referred specifically to the extravagant outfits worn by urban Latino youth in Los Angeles. The 1943 Zoot Suit Riots, in which off-duty servicemen and other Anglos stormed barrio neighborhoods to strip and beat *pachucos,* were thus named.

Immigrants from Mexico and other Central and South American countries were labeled "wetbacks," "aliens," and "illegals" as the U.S.–Mexico border was fortified against entry by undocumented immigrants. Mexican immigrants and Mexican Americans sometimes are referred to disparagingly as "beaners," presumably for their staple diet, as well as the diet-based derogatory references to Mexicans as "chilies" or "tamales." Puerto Ricans, particularly those in New York City, acquired their own degrading label, "spic," which, like most labels, eventually came to represent Latinos of all origins. The origin of *spic* is disputed—some suggest a derisive reference to the accent-thick response "don't speak English"; others claim the term "spic" is an acronym for those of Spanish, Indian, and colored origin. Still others say it derives from the term *Hispanic.*

Used by the government to categorize Latinos, the label *Hispanic* has an uncertain history, both in its origin and the circumstances leading to its official adoption by the U.S. government. Allegedly created by the British, the term *Hispanic* derives from *Hispaña* or *Hispania* and is thus rooted in the legacy of Spain's colonization of the Americas. From the early 1900s, cultural and civic organizations in the United States sometimes used this label, but its adoption by the U.S. government in the 1970s helped to galvanize opinion for and against it. Although a majority of Latinos seem comfortable with either, some view the "Hispanic" label as representing an Anglo vision of assimilation, while others view the "Latino" label as expressing a political statement of cultural preservation akin to the Chicano identification embraced by some Mexican American activists. Despite the sometimes negative political and cultural connotations of these labels, most would agree they do not rise to the derogatory level of labels such as "greaser" and "spic."

Some Anglo attitudes toward Latinos are often negative and have had significant social and legal consequences. Anglos frequently view Latinos as criminally inclined—hot tempered, violent, and thieving, gang members adept with a switchblade knife, and drug smugglers, dealers, and users.

Some Anglos also consider Latinos to be lazy, drunken, and inclined to frequent *siestas.* Further, some Anglos believe them to be overwhelmingly recipients of welfare, users of social services, and a drain on resources. An early-1990s survey found that three of four Anglos felt that Latinos were more likely than whites to prefer welfare. Studies have also confirmed that Anglo-Americans tend to overestimate dramati-

A parody of a California driver's license depicting an undocumented Mexican immigrant.

cally the number of Latinos collecting welfare benefits in the United States. Related to this perception, Anglos believe that Latinos are passionate and preoccupied with sex (the "Latin lover" image). Accordingly, some Anglos perceive Latinas as excessively fertile.

Latinos are seen as unintelligent or as less intelligent than Anglos, who often equate having Spanish as one's primary language as a marker of lower intelligence. Union organizer César Chávez recounted that a teacher once hung a sign around his neck reading, "I am a clown, I speak Spanish." In 1996 a candidate for Washington State's top education post declared Spanish as "the language of doormen, dishwashers, and fruit pickers." A February 2003 comic advice column in *Vanity Fair,* "Ask Dame Edna," referred to the Spanish language as unintellectual and as the language of domestic servants and leaf blowers. In 1995 a Texas judge overseeing a child custody dispute chastised a Latina mother for speaking Spanish to her five-year-old daughter, ruling that the child "will only hear English" in the home because learning the Spanish language would relegate her to being ignorant and to the life of a housemaid.

Many Anglos consider Latinos to be foreigners, often based on their use of the Spanish language or their speaking English with an accent. In 1996 Congressman Luis Gutierrez, a Puerto Rican born in Chicago, was unrecognized and denied admission to the nation's Capitol by a security aide who told him to "go back to the country where you came from," presumably because his daughter and niece were carrying small Puerto Rican flags. Anglos regard Latinos, immigrants and native-born alike, as unwilling to assimilate by learning English and otherwise adopting the mores of U.S. society. For example, some Anglos doubt the patriotism of Latinos; a 1990 survey found that over half of whites believed Latinos to be less patriotic than whites. Anglos, further, do not trust Latinos.

Anglos have also considered Latinos to be dirty, disease-ridden, unclean, and unsanitary (the "dirty Mexican"). Using the caption "Wetbacks Bring Insects," one 1950s magazine warned of the supposed health threat posed by Mexican immigrants. In 1994 a Michigan radio station announced that the winner of its mock Cinco de Mayo "contest" would receive his or her own personal Mexican, but that bathing and delousing of the Mexican would be the winner's responsibility.

The images held by many Anglos, and the one conveyed by the mass media, are simultaneously one of an animal (unclean, subhuman, unintelligent) and one of an alien, inhuman being. The familiar labels in American society and media for undocumented Latino immigrants—"illegal aliens" and "wetbacks"—further dehumanize them. With headlines such as "Three Suspected Illegal Immigrants Die," or "Seven Illegal Migrants Die in Snowstorm," newspaper accounts of Latino migrants who succumbed to heat, cold, or other hazards while entering the United States elicit the same public compassion as that for criminal suspects killed in police shoot-outs.

Latinos are commonly associated with dogs in the United States. Until recently, some Southwest taverns posted signs such as "No Mexicans or Dogs Allowed." During the height of the public sensation over the talking Chihuahua in Taco Bell restaurant commercials, one Internet joke site even proclaimed the Taco Bell Chihuahua as "The World's Smartest Mexican."

Overall, Anglos view Latinos as near the bottom of the social ladder. A 1989 survey asking questions about 58 ethnic groups in the United States found that all Latino groups listed were ranked 49th or lower in "perceived social standing," with only Gypsies ranking lower than Mexicans and Puerto Ricans. Indeed, the fictional survey ethnic group "Wysians" outranked all the Latino groups.

The longevity of these derogatory labels and attitudes is striking. Most of these stereotypes date to the 19th-century Southwest. For example, a Texas newspaper editorialized in 1871 about the lack of sanitation among Mexican residents, suggesting that Mexicans lived in the same fashion as their pigs. A 1940 public opinion poll in the United States revealed that Anglos viewed Latinos as "quick-tempered," "backward," "lazy," and "ignorant," rather than "progressive," "honest," or "intelligent." Over the years Anglo perceptions have shown some fluidity. As socioeconomic and political forces have demanded—for example, when U.S. industries needed cheap labor to replace those workers fighting in World War II—media images and public perceptions of Latinos softened. During this time a Hollywood self-censorship organization removed from film scripts and film titles many ethnic slurs. When those

wartime labor pressures eased, however, the federal government launched the oppressive Operation Wetback deportation program, thus contributing to the perception of Latinos as subhuman "wetbacks" or "illegal aliens" that is still dominant throughout segments of the public. Negative depictions also returned to Hollywood.

Attitudes of Anglos toward Latinos have long been reflected in, or perhaps even driven by, mass media and popular culture. For example, treacherous *bandidos,* robbing and killing indiscriminately, populated the era of silent film in Hollywood. The Hollywood rural *bandido* gradually gave way in the 1960s and 1970s to the urban Latino gang member (the "*vato loco*"), and to the Latino drug dealer. Popular songs in the 1940s (*Mañana [Is Soon Enough for Me]*) and the 1960s (*Speedy Gonzales*) depicted Latinos as womanizing, as lacking initiative, and as living in squalor. In addition to the media's overwhelmingly negative portrayals, Latinos continue to be relatively absent from films as well as from prime time television.

Anglo labels for and attitudes toward Latinos may differ based on such factors as skin color, gender, and immigration status. Negative perceptions—inability or unwillingness to assimilate, laziness, and lack of intelligence—are heightened as the skin color of the Latino subject darkens. As applied to Latinos, the stereotype of the Latin lover is a romanticized image, as reflected by the adulation of popular singers such as Enrique Iglesias and Ricky Martin, and of former Hollywood actors Gilbert Roland, Ricardo Montalban, and Fernando Lamas. By contrast, Latinas are regarded by Anglos and portrayed in the media in less flattering terms as sexually indiscriminate, overly fertile, and even as prostitutes.

Recent Latin immigrants are often perceived differently from native-born Latinos. These immigrants might be seen as more reluctant to assimilate and more determined to receive public assistance.

Anglo attitudes toward Latinos are frequently similar to their views of other racial and ethnic groups, for example, African Americans, Asian Americans, and Native Americans. Some Anglos regard African Americans as violent, involved with drugs, lazy, preferring welfare to employment, unintelligent, and criminally inclined; they perceive Native Americans as treacherous as well as prone to alcoholism and reliance on welfare. Some Anglo attitudes toward Asian Americans are derogatory: Asians are foreigners, incapable of assimilation, disloyal and traitorous, and carriers of disease.

Many Anglo concepts of Latinos are false, exaggerated, or otherwise constructed unfairly. Regarding crime, Latinos are arrested and convicted for crimes at rates disproportionate to their percentage of the population and to the rate for Anglos. Rather than serving as evidence of some inherent criminal character, however, these statistics reflect the roots of much crime in poverty as well as the youth of the Latino population—more than one-third of Latinos in the United States are under the age of 18 and three in ten of these youth are poor (compared with fewer than one in ten white children living in poverty). In addition, arrest rates and conviction rates are to some extent a product of the targeting of Latinos by law enforcement and prejudicial treatment by prosecutors and juries.

Latinos are disproportionately involved with gangs—a 1997 study concluded that 5 out of 100 Latino boys aged 12 to 16, and 2 out of 100 Latina girls aged 12 to 16 belonged to a gang in the last year (by comparison, only 2 out of 100 Anglo males in this age group were involved with gangs). Still, the number of Latino youth participating in gang activity is neither overwhelming nor defining of a people. Rather, like crime, gang involvement stems from factors such as poverty, under- and unemployment, and cultural ostracization.

Although the welfare participation rate of Latinos exceeds that for Anglos, Anglos tend dramatically to overestimate the number of Latinos who receive welfare. A nationwide study in 1999 revealed that more than one-third of the respondents believed that half of citizen or documented resident Latinos in the United States received welfare. The actual numbers are substantially lower.

Latina fertility rates exceed those for Anglo women. Among Latinas, birthrates are highest for Mexican Americans, who average 3.2 births, nearly twice the rate of non-Hispanic white women. Birthrates have declined dramatically among women in Mexico—having averaged seven children in 1965, Mexican women average only 2.4 today. Mexican American birthrates are expected to follow suit. High birthrates among Mexican American women stem from poverty, religious scruples against contraception and abortion, and a lack of education. In contrast to public perception, Latinas are no more sexually active than Anglo women. A 1997 national study found that 19 percent of Latinas aged 12 to 16 had engaged in sex during the previous year, compared with 20 percent of white girls.

The speaking of Spanish instead of English contributes to the perception that Latinos are unwilling or unable to assimilate. U.S. senator Alan Simpson once remarked that the mastery of the English language by Spanish-speaking immigrants appeared to be less rapid and complete than for other groups. Author and former presidential candidate Pat Buchanan has written that millions of Mexican immigrants have no desire to learn English. Showing the falsity of these perceptions are studies demonstrating the desire of Latino immigrants to learn English and, in addition, their ability to learn English as fast as or faster than past Anglo immigrant groups arriving from Europe. One study revealed that more than nine in ten ethnic Mexican, Puerto Rican, and Cuban Latinos agreed or strongly agreed that U.S. citizens and residents should learn English. A separate survey of Mexican immigrants concluded that 93 percent believed that residents of the United States should learn English. Although the traditional pattern of English-language acquisition by immigrants to the United States has spanned three generations (the second generation is bilingual, English dominates by the third generation), one study points to a two-generation pattern of English language acquisition by Latinos.

Intelligence testing in the early to mid-1900s consistently found that Mexican children scored below Anglo children. Further, statistics of educational attainment of Latinos in the United States reflect a large gap between Anglos and Latinos. For example, only 57 percent of Latinos in the United States aged 25 and over are high school graduates, while the graduation rate for non-Hispanic whites is more than 88 percent. The national high school dropout rate for Latinos is twice that of blacks and more than three times the rate for white children. Although some observers blame Latino ethnicity and culture for these disparities, the root causes are mainly institutional—gross disparities in school funding and teacher competence, language barriers, attitudes and expectations of teachers, and poverty at home.

Perceptions of Latino unintelligence illustrate the strong, sometimes circular, relationship between societal attitudes and institutional subordinating structures. Attitudes help drive institutional inequities, as Anglos flee urban schools based on false and negative perceptions of the communities of color they leave behind. At the same time, institutional discrepancies can drive societal attitudes—underfunded, substandard schools contribute to high dropout rates that perpetuate stereotypes of Latinos as lacking intelligence.

Perceptions of Latinos as dirty and disease-ridden stem, too, from poverty and also from substandard housing conditions. Latino migrant workers crowd into substandard housing out of economic necessity rather than from some character flaw or sense of enjoyment.

The pervasive reach of derogatory labels for and attitudes toward Latinos results in the establishment of poor self-images among Latinos, particularly youth, who are bombarded with negative images in mass media. These demeaning media portrayals, replicated in schoolyard jokes and societal derision, shape Latino children's opinions about their social and self-worth, causing humiliation, isolation, and despair. Internalizing these negative attitudes and oppression causes self-hatred and cultural hatred. This cultural hatred has prompted some Latinos to target others who oc-

© JIMMY DORANTES/LATIN FOCUS

Crossing sign featuring a caricature of a Mexican with maracas and a sombrero.

cupy an equally subordinate or an inferior place in the pecking order of American society, leading to inter- and intra-ethnic and racial tensions. For example, tensions exist between Latino immigrants and later-generation Latinos over such flash points as jobs, culture, and class. Indeed, a 1992 survey revealed that more than three of four Mexican Americans felt there were too many immigrants.

Additionally, Anglo attitudes toward and labels for Latinos influence their legal treatment. Some connections are more obvious, such as the Official English or English Only laws and initiatives in a majority of states that, at minimum, declare English as the state's official language. These English-language laws are a response to the perception that Latinos and certain other groups, particularly recent immigrant groups, are reluctant or unable to learn English. Anti-Spanish-language forces have targeted bilingual education that aims to teach students English while not sacrificing their proficiency in other substantive subjects, which are therefore taught in Spanish or other languages. Citizen initiatives have undermined bilingual education programs in California, Arizona, and Massachusetts. Another obvious connection existed between Anglo attitudes and the adoption by voters in 1994 of California's Proposition 187 (now largely invalidated by the courts), which implied a view of Latino immigrants as overly fertile and too reliant on welfare by cutting off state social services and public education resources to undocumented immigrants and their children. Numerous other examples exist of the relationship between attitudes and legal consequences for Latinos. The recent rulings against affirmative action by courts and citizen initiatives on outlawing affirmative action in the states of California and Washington are driven, in part, by perceptions that Anglo applicants are treated unfairly.

Latinos fare worse than Anglos at every stage of the criminal justice system—from racial profiling that draws on preconceptions of Latino criminal tendencies and searches of Latino suspects for drugs or other criminal involvement, to disproportionate sentencing of those Latinos convicted of crimes. Fatal encounters between police and Latino suspects have been fueled by perceptions of Latinos as aggressive and dangerous, requiring nothing short of deadly force. The stereotyping of the Latino defendant no doubt influences juries. In 1996 a Texas prosecution expert went so far as to suggest to a jury that they could infer "future dangerousness," an aggravating circumstance that justifies the death sentence, from the Latino heritage of a convicted murderer.

Anglos have also taken vigilante action against Latinos. In the Southwest, patrols by armed ranchers aim to intercept undocumented immigrants near the U.S.–Mexico border. In the 1980s mock State Game Commission guidelines for hunting and killing "wetbacks" were circulated nationally as a joke. Authorizing an open season on the "Southwestern Wet Back (known locally as Mexican, Greaser, Grease Ball, Spic, Mex, or Low Rider)," these mock rules declared it unlawful to shoot "wetbacks" in taverns where the bullet could "ricochet off the grease and injure a civilized white person," and prohibited setting "traps" in welfare offices.

Employers throughout the United States have adopted policies prohibiting the speaking of languages other than English in the workplace. Private businesses, such as restaurants and taverns, have also imposed English-only rules on their customers. These anti-Spanish-language policies reach into the home, with examples such as a Florida cooperative apartment building that voted to deny admission to non-English speakers to keep out "undesirables," and a San Jose, California, landlord who refused to rent apartments to Spanish speakers who could not speak English.

Often regarded as subhuman, Latinos have been exposed to a variety of health risks by the government and private actors. Among them are the coercive sterilization, until the 1970s, of more than one-third of the women in Puerto Rico of childbearing age, as well as the navy bombings on the Puerto Rican island of Vieques, finally discontinued in 2003, that contaminated the island, increased infant mortality rates, and caused health problems for residents. Just as the U.S. government chose to test its dangerous military weapons where Latinos live, private companies tend to site their hazardous-waste-producing or storage facilities near Latinos and other racial and ethnic minorities, a practice known as environmental racism.

Will Anglo attitudes about Latinos improve? The prospects are dim. Some scholars trace negative stereotypes at least as far back as United States expansion during the 1800s, when such attitudes helped justify the usurpation of parts of the Southwest that culminated in the Mexican-American War (1846–1848). The steady immigration of Mexicans and Cubans to the United States—and Puerto Ricans relocating to the mainland—suggests that the Latino experience may differ from that of early 1900s immigrants from southern and eastern Europe. Those European immigrants and their descendants, once classified by other Anglos as nonwhite, substantially escaped the "subhuman" label once the pace of immigration slowed. Given the proximity of Central and South American nations, the continued labor demands of U.S. industry, and the economic instability in Latin America, high rates of immigration are likely to continue—leaving in place negative Anglo attitudes that lump native Latinos and immigrants together.

RELATED ARTICLES

Advertising; Discrimination; Film; Nativism; Radio; Television.

FURTHER READING

Bender, Steven W. *Greasers and Gringos: Latinos, Law, and the American Imagination.* New York: N.Y. Univ. Press, 2003.

De León, Arnoldo. *They Called Them Greasers: Anglo Attitudes toward Mexicans in Texas 1821–1900.* Austin: Univ. of Tex. Press, 1983.

Delgado, Richard, and Jean Stefancic. "Images of the Outsider in American Law and Culture: Can Free Expression Remedy Systemic Social Ills?" *Cornell Law Review* 77 (1992): 1258.

Padilla, Laura M. "'But You're Not a Dirty Mexican': Internalized Oppression, Latinos and Law." *Texas Hispanic Journal of Law and Policy* 7 (2001): 59.

Rodríguez, Clara E., ed. *Latin Looks: Images of Latinas and Latinos in the U.S. Media.* Boulder, Colo.: Westview Press, 1998.

Román, Ediberto. "Who Exactly Is Living *La Vida Loca*? The Legal and Political Consequences of Latino-Latina Ethnic and Racial Stereotypes in Film and Other Media." *Journal of Gender, Race and Justice* 4 (2000): 37.

STEVEN W. BENDER

LATINO STEREOTYPING OF ANGLOS

The use and misuse by Latinos of epithets for Anglos generally derives from a sense of otherness, often supported by the subordinate status of the Latino in the United States. Such terms tend to be derogatory but, with time and widespread use, can often lose the power of racial and ethnic anger; though, even as they become less hostile, their underlying history can still cast them in terms of alienation and anger.

Among Latinos the word most often used for Anglos is *gringo* (or the feminine *gringa*). Although the Anglo pejoratives for Latinos—*greaser, spic, wetback,* and *illegal alien*—are almost always demeaning, the *gringo* reference is sometimes humorous, other times intended to be or taken to be derogatory, and some-

times is meant to be merely descriptive of Anglos. As with the Anglo terms *greasers* and *spics* directed at Latinos, the origin of the term *gringo* is disputed. One account attributes *gringo* to "green coats," a reference to the green jackets worn by U.S. soldiers during the Mexican-American War. Although rejected by etymologists, one supposition is that the term *gringo* derived from the song *Green Grows the Grass* (other sources title the song as *Green Grow the Rushes* or *Green Grow the Lilacs*), supposedly sung by U.S. soldiers during the war. Latino writer Pedro Malavet suggests instead that as early as the 18th century, *gringo* was being used in Spain as a variation of the word *griego* (Greek) as a reference to anyone who spoke a foreign language. Under this version of its origin, *gringo* is analogous to the familiar Anglo saying "It's Greek to me," itself derived from the Latin *graecum est.*

Despite the likely benign origin of *gringo* as a descriptive reference to a foreigner, many Anglos regard the term as derogatory. At one extreme, the Web site for a U.S. white nationalist group labels *gringo* as a racial epithet equivalent to racist slurs for African Americans, Latinos, and Vietnamese. In *A Chicano Manual on How to Handle Gringos* (2003), Latino writer José Angel Gutiérrez remarked that not all Anglos are gringos, as *gringo* connotes only a bad, racist Anglo. Yet many Latinos use the term descriptively for all Anglos rather than as a slur. César Chávez is said once to have publicly decried as "gringo justice" a city council decision in California that closed a park where his farmworker organizational meetings were being held. He later said it was the only time he could recall using the term *gringo* in anger.

Gutiérrez also has suggested that *gringo* is more an attitude than a nationality, race, or ethnicity. Indeed, African Americans, Asian Americans, and other groups might be regarded and referred to as gringos in some settings. The *gringo* reference, however, is used by Latinos particularly to describe fair-haired persons of northern European descent.

Other slang terms among Latinos for Anglos include *blanquitos* and *gabachos,* as well as *los güeros* (those white people) and *bolillos* (white bread). *Gabacho* connotes an imperialist. According to one account, its usage originated in Spain as a reference to the French. Carrying a similar connotation, Latinos may also label Anglo Americans as *yanquis*—Spanish for "Yankees." Indeed, even Mexican Americans or other Latinos who are regarded as overly assimilated might be called *gabachos* or *pochos* by both Mexican nationals and by other Latinos in the United States as a derogatory reference. *Pocho* has several literal meanings, including to be cut off, as if from one's roots. Some might even label a highly assimilated Latino a gringo.

Latino attitudes toward Anglo Americans range from dismissive to implacable. At one end of the spectrum is the view, shared by African Americans, that Anglos possess no rhythm and cannot dance. Other attitudes are more substantial and include the view of Anglos as monolingual; by contrast, many Latinos are fluent in both Spanish and English and perhaps in an indigenous language, such as the Mixtec language of some Mexican immigrants from Oaxaca, Mexico. One riddle among Latinos asks the name for a person who speaks three languages (polyglot), two languages (bilingual), and only one language (the answer—gringo).

Related to this perception is the broader view of Anglos as obsessed with assimilation. Anglo spokespersons and U.S. laws help foster this perception. Latinos are accused by Anglo politicians and others of being unwilling or unable to assimilate into U.S. culture, for example, the speaking of English. One of Pat Buchanan's 2000 presidential campaign television advertisements targeted Latinos, suggesting that immigration was "out of control" and asking voters whether they "ever miss English?" About half the states have laws that declare English the state's official language. This modern English Only movement was spurred by Anglo activists in Dade County, Florida, reacting to the rapidly growing Cuban American community. Bilingual education—the offering of instruction for substantive subjects in Spanish and other non-English languages while students learn English—has come under attack in California and other states, which have passed laws mandating all-English classrooms. Several employers have banned Spanish and other non-English languages in the workplace. Tavern owners have outlawed the speaking of Spanish in some bars, and residents of a Florida cooperative apartment building even voted to deny residency to non-English speakers.

Some Latinos, however, maintain that Anglos fail to accept or value Latino culture. Unless that culture is packaged as Latino-lite, as with fast-food tacos, the liquor-industry-commodified holiday Cinco de Mayo, or watered-down, cross-over pop songs such as Ricky Martin's *Livin' la Vida Loca,* Latino culture is often seen by Anglos as threatening and subversive. Images in media of Latinos carrying Mexican flags in protest of the anti-immigrant initiative Proposition 187 in California were cited by some commentators as instigating a backlash among Anglo voters. When, after years of hit pop recordings in English, Linda Ronstadt, a Latina, toured in 1987 to support her first Spanish-language recording, *Canciones de mi padre,* hecklers chanted "English, English," and one journalist observed a concertgoer stomping toward the exit shouting "Remember the Alamo, Mex!" To cite another example, the mainstream media depict the Santería religion, practiced by some Cuban Americans and other Latinos, as ritualistic and barbaric.

Additionally, some Latinos have suggested that Anglo culture is bland and would profit from the spice found in Latino culture and that of other groups. For example, Latino artist and author José Antonio Burciaga has written about the painful experience of being served "bland, gringo military food" while in the U.S. Air Force. Latino author Alfredo Vea captured this sentiment in his novel *La maravilla* (1993) when he contrasted the rich mestizo (Spanish and Indian) roots of a Latino character of Yaqui Indian heritage to the culture of the *gringos* who have no "stories" or "tribe," and whose "campfire" is their television.

Regarding family, a 1990s study of Mexicans and Mexican Americans in the United States revealed their perception that Anglos were much colder to their children than were Latinos. Similarly, some Latinos bristle at the practice of Anglos placing their elderly parents in nursing homes rather than caring for them in their own homes, believing that the Anglo practice disrespects the elderly.

Latinos regard themselves as group and community oriented—as willing to sacrifice individual success for community advancement. By contrast, Latinos perceive Anglo culture as one of rugged individualism and survival of the fittest. Moreover, some Latinos view Anglos as overly materialistic and wasteful. For example, in 1900, Uruguayan author José Enrique Rodó wrote that compared with the materialism of North America, South Americans were more spiritual. Related to this conception is what one Latina writer called the Anglo belief in exceptionality—that Anglos have imagined themselves as a special creation able to triumph as a people over any adversity and as possessing a manifest destiny. Remarking on this conception of Anglo exceptionalism, Mexican novelist Carlos Fuentes has pointed out a lack of fatalism among Anglos. He contrasts this attitude to that of the Mexican imagination that is influenced by Catholicism and Aztec beliefs that place an individual's destiny beyond human control.

The most widespread perception of Anglos held by Latinos is that of the racist Anglo. Many Latinos view Anglos as prejudiced, as discriminating against them, and U.S. institutions as unjust. A 1996 poll of Latino immigrants revealed that eight in ten felt that they were treated with racism or contempt by Anglos. Reflecting the perception held by Latinos of U.S. institutions, a 1992 survey conducted for the California Judicial Council found that a majority of Latinos believed that U.S. courts do not ensure racial fairness. In his book *Gringo Justice* (1987), Latino scholar Alfredo Mirandé discussed the double standard of justice in the United States for Chicanos on the losing side and Anglo-Americans on the winning side.

Latino media reflect this conception of Anglos as racist. Several Latino media productions portray the gringo as a racist, regarding Latinos as subordinate and inferior and as discriminating against them in schools and the workplace. For example, Latino director Gregory Nava's film *Selena* (1996) depicts the refusal of a Texas beachfront club owner to audition Selena's then youthful father's vocal group because they are "a bunch of Mexicans." Directed by Latino Edward James Olmos, the film *American Me* (1992) suggests the animosity of Anglos toward Latinos in 1940s Los Angeles by having an Anglo streetcar passenger change seats because a Latina sits next to him. In Latino Ramon Menendez's film *Stand and Deliver* (1988), the lead character, a Latino high school teacher, accused Advanced Placement testing officials with racism when they questioned the test scores of his barrio students. In his 1987 film *La Bamba,* Latino director Luis Valdez included a racist Anglo father who prevented his daughter from dating Mexican American rocker Ritchie Valens (Valenzuela). Latino authors, playwrights, and activists have also depicted Anglos and Anglo institutions as racist, as have some Latino musicians. For example, the Latino band Ozomatli has denounced police brutality in the Latino community, and the late Puerto Rican Miguel Piñero's play *Short Eyes* mocked justice in the white man's court as justice for "just us" white people. Leg-

endary Chicano lawyer and author Oscar "Zeta" Acosta wrote in his narrative *The Revolt of the Cockroach People* (1973) that gringos regard the Chicano as a "lowdown cockroach." Chicano poet and activist Rodolfo "Corky" Gonzáles proposed *El Plan Espiritual de Aztlán* in 1969, a blueprint for Chicano liberation that contends that the brutal gringo invaded Chicano territory and that this foreigner *gabacho* exploited Chicano riches and destroyed Chicano culture.

These Latino conceptions of the Anglo as racist are of long standing. For example, a famous *corrido* (street ballad) of the Great Depression—"Los deportados" (The Deported Ones)—contended that Anglos were "very bad fellows," treating Mexicans coming to the United States to work as migrant workers "without pity" and as bandits. That many Latinos regard them as racist and discriminatory may surprise Anglos; indeed, a 1994 survey determined that most Anglos do not believe they act on any prejudice or that they discriminate against Latinos. Yet the Latino perceptions of many Anglos as racist and of Anglo institutions as unjust are grounded in historical experience in criminal, education, legal, political, and other arenas of U.S. society.

Latino attitudes that hold U.S. institutions to be unfair are particularly acute with regard to law enforcement. In the U.S. criminal justice system, Latinos (and blacks) are disproportionately targeted for traffic stops and searches for criminal activity—a practice known as racial profiling. For example, the U.S. Customs Service disproportionately targets Latinos and blacks in its searches of airport travelers for drug possession or drug trafficking (43 percent of travelers searched in 1998). But the actual rates for finding contraband that year revealed that only 2.8 percent of those Latinos searched had contraband, as compared with a "hit" rate of 6.7 percent for Anglo travelers searched. A study by the Texas Department of Public Safety concluded that Latino motorists, once stopped, were twice as likely to be searched by Texas state troopers as were Anglo motorists. Further, Latinos often are the target of police brutality in confrontations with law enforcement. In one of many national incidents, in April 2001, at least 25 Portland, Oregon, police officers responded to a hospital's call to restrain an unruly Latino patient. When he armed himself against the police officers with a metal rod pulled from a door, the brigade of officers killed him. Once arrested and convicted, Latinos receive disproportionately heavy sentences. A study in 2002, for example, found that a Latino youth arrested for drug offenses but never before detained would spend more than twice as much time incarcerated (306 days) as an Anglo youth in the same circumstances (144 days).

Apart from their treatment in the criminal justice system, the experience of Latinos in other settings supports the impression of many Latinos that Anglos and Anglo institutions are unjust and discriminatory. Often Latinos occupy the lowest rung of the employment ladder, with disproportionately few employed in management positions. Thus, for many Latinos, Anglos are seen as their uncompassionate bosses and company owners—as the *patrón* and the *jefe*. Substandard wages, intolerable working conditions, and dilapidated housing are common for farmworkers, the majority of whom are Latino, further reinforcing the negative images of Anglos as oppressive company owners and employers.

In the U.S. public school system, Latinos have a history of segregation in California and the Southwest that excluded many Latinos from Anglo schools. Further, Mexican American students were once subjected to flea and lice inspections by school officials fearful of the stereotypical "dirty Mexican." The Spanish language has never been welcome in the U.S. classroom. Schoolchildren have been routinely disciplined in Texas and elsewhere for speaking Spanish in the classroom or on school grounds. Today the states of Arizona, California, and Massachusetts have enacted citizen initiatives that prohibit Spanish and other non-English languages in classroom instruction. Standardized testing penalizes Latino students when admissions officials in college and graduate school programs rely unduly on test scores that disadvantage students for whom English is a second language. Property tax limitations in some states cripple public schools in their ability to properly educate youth of color and to compete with private schools educating Anglo students.

Latinos have suffered discrimination in housing and labor markets, as well as in other settings. Restrictive covenants among residential owners also, in effect, barred the sale of property to Mexicans in some areas of the Southwest. According to a 2002 survey, 31 percent of Latinos responded that they, or a family member or close friend, had experienced discrimination because of their racial or ethnic background (by contrast, only 13 percent of Anglos

responded affirmatively). As determined by the same survey, 14 percent of Latinos responded they had not been hired or promoted because of their race or ethnic background (the figure was 8 percent for Anglos). Forty-five percent of Latino respondents answered that they were treated with less respect than were other people (23 percent for Anglos); 41 percent of Latino respondents received worse service than other people did in restaurants or stores (18 percent for Anglos); and 30 percent were called names or insulted (18 percent for Anglos).

Latino candidates for office are treated shabbily in the political arena. In the 2001 Los Angeles mayoral race, James Hahn stormed from behind in the polls on the strength of media ads that depicted his rival, Latino Antonio Villaraigosa, as a friend of drug dealers, and perhaps even a drug user himself. These ads juxtaposed the chopping of cocaine and images of a crack pipe with statements such as "Los Angeles can't trust Antonio Villaraigosa." In the 2002 Texas gubernatorial campaign, incumbent Republican Rick Perry ran ads against Latino rival Tony Sánchez that spotlighted the connection between the savings and loan association owned by the Sánchez family and the laundering of money for Mexican drug smugglers. In California's recall election of 2003, media and other critics of gubernatorial candidate Cruz Bustamante suggested that his association with the Latino student group MEChA during college made him a potential terrorist and a threat to unity. Earlier, during a 2002 campaign for Oregon's highest education post, radio personalities suggested a candidate's mere Latina ethnicity called into question her loyalty and citizenship and therefore her ability to serve in public office.

Latinos are frequently victims of hate crimes in the United States. Vigilante violence by Anglos against Latinos has a long history, with scores of lynchings and mutilations of Mexicans in Texas in the 1800s. Latino immigrants are still a common target for vigilante violence, such as that administered on Long Island in September 2001 by two skinheads who lured two Latino migrant workers and nearly beat them to death with a posthole digger and a knife. Border violence against Latinos by Anglo vigilantes is unrelenting. In one incident, while target shooting, a San Diego–area gunman suggested to his friends, "Let's shoot some aliens," and fired his high-powered rifle into the hills, killing a 12-year-old Mexican boy crossing the border with his family.

Latinos believe that Anglos are prejudiced against them because of their experiences with Anglos and their overwhelmingly negative attitudes. Typically, Anglos regard Latinos as criminally inclined, as drug smugglers and drug users, as ruthless gang members, as collectors of welfare, as unintelligent, as reluctant or unable to assimilate, and as dirty, disease-ridden, and unsanitary. More generally, Anglos tend to perceive Latinos as foreigners and as interlopers—and as less than human. Negative images of Latinos dominate mainstream Anglo media—television, television news, and films. These negative conceptions of Latinos by Anglos and Anglo media have significant legal and societal consequences. By contrast, the perceptions of many Latinos that Anglos are racist and discriminatory have less legal and societal significance because Latinos have such slight political, financial, and legal clout. Anglo hate crimes against Latinos have been rampant throughout the modern history of the United States; Latino hate crimes against Anglos, however, seem to have been less organized and less sustained. Nevertheless, some criminal Latino rebellion against Anglos is evident. One example is found in the origin of the Mexican *bandido* image, which derived from some Mexicans reacting to their physical, legal, political, cultural, and social displacement in the U.S. Southwest during the Mexican-American War and its aftermath. Another is violence between Puerto Rican and Anglo gangs in New York that resulted in the infamous 1959 stabbing of two white teens in a New York City playground by Salvador "Capeman" Agron and other Puerto Rican gang members who mistook their victims for rival Irish gang members.

Given the broad racial, religious, political, and other differences among Latinos, their perceptions of Anglos, themselves a greatly varied group, are across the spectrum. Still, considerable opinion and historical evidence support Latinos' opinion that Anglos and Anglo institutions are biased against them. Can this concept be changed? A first step would be the elimination of stereotypical depictions of Latinos from media, particularly the virulent depictions of Latino immigrants spouted by commentators on hate radio and elsewhere. But efforts to change Anglos' opinions of Latinos are insufficient to breach institutional barriers that cause Latinos to question the integrity of the criminal justice system and other U.S. institutions. For example, instead of eradicating bilingual education with citizen initiatives, our educational system must consider how to include Latino voices in deciding how best to educate non-English-speaking children. Local police, too, must respect Latino voices and engage with the community around enforcement practices, for example, antigang policing. Only by including Latino voices in solving local and national problems, rather than blaming Latinos and other communities of color for social ills, will Anglo-Americans overcome the perception among numerous Latinos that their participation in charting the future of the United States is unrespected and undervalued.

RELATED ARTICLES

Advertising; Discrimination; Film; Nativism; Radio; Television.

FURTHER READING

Bender, Steven W. *Greasers and Gringos: Latinos, Law, and the American Imagination*. New York: N.Y. Univ. Press, 2003.

Lazos Vargas, Sylvia R. "Deconstructing Homo[geneous] Americanus: The White Ethnic Immigrant Narrative and Its Exclusionary Effect." *Tulane Law Review* 72 (1998): 1493.

Malavet, Pedro A. *Puerto Rico: Cultural Nation, "American" Colony*. New York: N.Y. Univ. Press, 2004.

Mirandé, Alfredo. *Gringo Justice*. Notre Dame, Ind.: Univ. of Notre Dame Press, 1987.

Wildman, Stephanie M., et al. *Privilege Revealed: How Invisible Preference Undermines America*. New York: N.Y. Univ. Press, 1996.

STEVEN W. BENDER

STONEWALL MOVEMENT

The Stonewall Riot or Stonewall Revolt has been seen as the cornerstone of the modern lesbian, gay, bisexual, and transgender (LGBT) movement, but the crucial participation of Latinos and Latinas and other people of color has often been downplayed in the popular imagination. The revolt happened outside of a Mafia-controlled bar called the Stonewall Inn on Christopher Street in Greenwich Village, New York City, on June 28, 1969.

After a routine police raid, the regular patrons of the working-class bar (which included many African American and Latin American drag queens) resisted arrest and attacked the police, leading to three days of street fights and protests. One of the participants, Sylvia Lee Rivera (1951–2002, née Ray Rivera), was a Bronx-born, half Puerto Rican, half Venezuelan drag queen who later went on to form part of the Gay Liberation Front and Gay Activist

Alliance. In 1971 Rivera and her best friend Marsha P. Johnson, an African American drag queen, established Street Transvestite Action Revolutionaries, or STAR, a shelter for homeless gay and transgender youth on the Lower East Side of New York City. According to Phillip Vélez, "Rivera remained involved in the gay liberation movement until 1973 when she and other transgender activists were not allowed to speak at the annual Christopher Street Liberation Day Parade (now called the Heritage of Pride Parade), commemorating the Stonewall Riot." After a period of relative invisibility, Rivera once again became notorious in New York state politics in the late 1990s for her advocacy for equal rights for transgender individuals, specifically working toward the passage of the Sexual Orientation Non-Discrimination Act (SONDA). The historian Martin Duberman has extensively documented Rivera's life in his book *Stonewall,* and the Center for Lesbian and Gay Studies of the City University of New York established a prize for transgender scholarship in honor of Rivera in 2001. Nigel Finch's feature-length independent film *Stonewall* (1996) has as its central character a fictionalized version of Rivera called La Miranda, played by Guillermo Díaz.

Another Nuyorican transgender individual who participated in the Stonewall revolt is Cristina Hayworth, a Puerto Rico–based activist best known for obtaining the permits for the first official Lesbian and Gay Pride parade on the island, held in 1991 in San Juan (the actual first "parade" was a caravan of cars that went from Plaza Las Americas to Luquillo Beach in 1974).

The impact of Stonewall has been felt strongly in the United States and Latin America and serves as inspiration for many; organizational efforts in Puerto Rico in the 1970s, for example, have been referred to as "echoing Stonewall" by filmmaker and scholar Frances Negrón-Muntaner. Latino lesbian and gay activists in New York City have called their historic participation in the 1989 National Puerto Rican Day Parade (after an absence of ten years) as "our Stonewall." Their absence is an indication of homophobia in the Latino community and their distance from the white gay community. The Stonewall revolt is celebrated every year in New York City and around the globe in gay or LGBT pride parades, usually in June.

RELATED ARTICLES
Discrimination; Homosexuality, Female; Homosexuality, Male.

FURTHER READING
Duberman, Martin. *Stonewall.* New York: Plume, 1994.
Negrón-Muntaner, Frances. "Echoing Stonewall and Other Dilemmas: The Organizational Beginnings of a Gay and Lesbian Agenda in Puerto Rico, 1972–1977." *Centro Journal* 4, no. 1 (1992): 77–95; 4, no. 2 (1992): 98–115.

LAWRENCE LA FOUNTAIN-STOKES

SUGAR

As a social and agricultural product, sugar occupies a significant position in Latin American and U.S. Latina and Latino histories. Conversely, Latin America and the Latino diaspora do have and have had significant roles in the global history of sugar. Sugar's monoculture in some Latin American contexts has profound implications for Latino cultures, as it is intricately linked to histories of colonization, slavery, production, consumption, nationalism, and culture.

The main producers of sugar in Latin America are Mexico, Cuba and the Dominican Republic in the Caribbean, Guatemala in Central America, and Brazil, Colombia, and Argentina in South America. In the United States, Louisiana and Florida are the major sugar-producing states, followed by Hawaii and Texas.

In the early 1990s Brazil emerged as the world's largest producer of sugar, with India as its largest consumer. After Brazil, the next four largest sugar exporters are the European Union, Australia, Thailand, and Cuba.

Sugar, or sucrose, is found naturally in all plants as a product of photosynthesis through which plants turn solar energy into food. Sugarcane (*Saccharum officinarum*) and sugar beet (Beta vulgaris) plants are most commonly used for commercial sugar production because of their high quantities of sucrose. Sugarcane has six known species. Cane stalk, the common source of sugar in most Latin American countries, is a tropical grass that grows 10–20 feet (3–6 meters) high. Sugarcane is not native to the Americas, yet it has become an integral part of Latin American and North American food cultures.

The origin of sugarcane is a subject of debate. Some historians locate the domestication of sugarcane in New Guinea and trace its dissemination through India, the Philippines, and possibly Indonesia. Sugarcane was introduced to Latin America by European colonizers mainly as a crop for export to European and later North American consumers. Some historical narratives claim that the first sugarcane plant was brought to the Americas by Christopher Columbus, to Spain's colonized islands of the Caribbean.

The first cane juice squeezed in Latin America was most likely extracted by indigenous methods. In Cuba, local production of sugar products with the indigenous *cunyaya* cane-pressing device was replaced by European methods of mass production. Beginning in the 16th century, sugar plantations and mills owned and controlled by colonizers began to produce large quantities of sugar for export.

Sugar's role in Latin America is multidimensional and demonstrates shifting economic, social, and cultural processes. The ecological, human, and climactic conditions of the Caribbean area and parts of Latin America made these regions attractive to colonizing and enslaving powers for the production of sugar. European colonialism thus attempted to appropriate Latin American land and resources to create a monopolistic, monocultural sugar-plantation model. Even during the height of sugar production, however, other agricultural products, including coffee, tobacco, timber, and indigo, continued to be produced for export.

Sugar production in Latin America increased to satisfy demand for sweetness emerging in colonial Europe. Documents record shipments of sugar exported from the Americas to Europe from the early 1500s. The British Caribbean began intensive sugar monoculture (exclusive cultivation of a single species, commonly found in modern agriculture) by the late 18th century. In the 18th and 19th centuries, the "sugar revolution" was said to have taken hold of the Hispanic Caribbean. Sugar, alongside various other agricultural products, played a role in British and Spanish hegemony in the "sugar colonies" of the Caribbean.

Race, gender, and class demographics of Latin America and people of Latina and Latino descent have been affected by sugar through colonization and slavery. The cultivation and production of sugar involves labor-intensive seasonal work. To accomplish profitable sugar cultivation, Europeans subjected indigenous populations in the Caribbean and many areas of Latin America to violent conquest, battle, slavery, overwork, disease, and slaughter. The majority of the intensive labor on sugar plantations and sugar mills of the Caribbean and other regions of Latin America was done by enslaved people forcibly taken from Africa and transported to the Americas.

Sugar plantations and mills played significant roles in slavery. These plantations bred traditions of resistance and active rebellion. Slave uprisings on sugar plantations evidence the more visible ways in which those enslaved contested their status as slaves and organized to overthrow their enslavers. Scholars have begun to research the ways in which enslaved women and men defied their condition through subtle acts of daily resistance.

Scholars have called attention to the heterogeneity of both the enslaved and enslaving classes involved in sugar plantations and sugar mills. In Cuba, for example, the majority of sugar and tobacco plantation slaves were Africans. Populations of mulatto, Chinese, Irish, English, Moorish, Berber, indigenous peoples, and people of mixed race were also exploited as slaves or indentured servants for the cultivation and production of sugar. The demographics of sugar workers demonstrated the complex histories of colonization, rape, enslavement, and *mestizaje* in the Americas. In the 21st century many of those working in sugar cultivation and production are descendants of enslaved peoples.

Scholars continue to debate the imperial ambitions that brought the sugar industry and slavery to its height in the Hispanic Caribbean. In the 19th century the production of sugar came to be increasingly mechanized through the inventions of the Industrial Revolution. The introduction of the steam engine in the early 1800s resulted in the gradual replacement of sugar mills previously powered by water or horsepower. Sugar trade was transformed by transportation by rail and ship.

In the 20th century U.S. economic and military intervention in Latin America increased. North American economic intervention in Latin America drastically influenced the production of sugar. International sugar markets, shaped by production, consumption, prices, and trade, are strongly affected by U.S. economic hegemony (predominance of ideas exercised by a dominant or privileged social group). Also, U.S. tariffs and quotas for sugar affect Latin American markets, contributing to complex interactions between competing sugar-producing nations.

Sugar plays a role in negotiations between governments, most notably seen in U.S.-Cuban relations.

What is the role of sugar quotas as a method to maintain U.S. hegemony in Latin America? After the 1959 Cuban revolution (in which Fidel Castro overthrew the Batista regime, took power, and became communist) the United States suspended Cuban sugar imports in July 1960, blocking roughly 80 percent of Cuban exports to the United States. The Soviet Union rapidly agreed to purchase sugar previously sold to the U.S. market. In addition, in the late 1950s to early 1960s, Presidents Dwight D. Eisenhower and John F. Kennedy signed sugar quota agreements with the Dominican Republic. While the United States entered into agreements with the Dominican Republic, aimed at bolstering liberal economic policies, it also provided an opportunity for the Dominican Republic to negotiate for preferential trade agreements.

Technology and globalization influence the changing role of sugar as the product continues to figure prominently in the economies of many Latin American countries. Economic policies in the 21st century are increasingly characterized by free trade agreements and sugar tariff-rate quotas. Economic issues surrounding sugar are frequently centered on disputes between Latin American nations and bodies such as the United States, the European Union (EU), and the World Trade Organization (WTO) with regard to "free trade" agreements such as NAFTA (North American Free Trade Agreement) and CAFTA (Central American Free Trade Agreement). Disputes have arisen regarding U.S. sugar subsidies, labor, and environmental issues and their effect on Latin American development.

Sugarcane requires tropical and subtropical climates, making certain regions of Latin America and the United States prime for sugar cultivation. With a growing season of 12 months, sugarcane requires intensive labor, fluctuating temperatures, and rainfall to mature. The production of sugar creates a seasonal work system of intensive field and mill production within a short period and is frequently accompanied by months of economic insecurity for sugar workers.

Processing removes bagasse (fibrous residue remaining after extracting the juice from sugarcane), molasses, and sediment. Different methods are used to extract juice and refine crystals for sugar products. Generally, this process involves pressing sugarcane to extract juice, boiling the juice to crystallize sugar, spinning in a centrifuge to separate crystals from syrup, washing and refining to remove the brown color and nonsugar elements, and crystallizing, drying, and packaging for consumption.

Sugar is consumed in many forms, including multiple types of granulated sugars, brown sugars, and liquid sugars. Sugar is commonly sold as brown, white, turbinado, molasses, syrup, loaf, and powdered sugar. Sugar is an important ingredient in many Latin American foods including pastries and confections such as *pan dulce* (Mexico) regional cakes, candies, *dulce de leche*, *bizcocho*, *flan*, and beverages such as *agua de canela*. Liquors distilled from sugarcane, including *aguardiente*, *guarapo* (quechua), brandy, and rum, figure into Latino food cultures.

Sugar is a major ingredient in numerous imported products and popular recipes and is used as a sweetener for drinks. In addition to food products, sugar is used in processing fuel, paper, wallboard, cattle fodder, and fertilizer. Scholars are beginning to assess the ways in which the rise of artificial sweeteners influences commercial sugar production and global sugar markets. Despite these trends, worldwide sugar production has experienced consistent growth since the mid-1990s largely because of the impact of Brazil as a producer and an exporter.

In complex ways, cultivation, refinement, and consumption of sugar contributed to shifting constructions of national identity. Scholars posit that sugar's taste and color qualities are not unrelated to social constructions of gender, race, class, and sexuality. In colonial European and Latin American discourses, sugar and sweetness came to be gendered as female and subsequently associated with domestic docility. In the 17th century, sugar appeared frequently in British colonial cookbooks, which increased demand for sugar and solidified its cultural associations.

Scholars have linked the social significance and economic value of sugar to symbolically embedded race and class connotations in constructions of national identities. Through the refinement process, sugar's coloring changes from dark to light. Sugar begins brown in its form as molasses and through whitening processes achieves its whitest, most refined and economically expensive states. The price and social value of the most refined and whitened crystallized sugar have been analyzed in relation to European constructions of whiteness and domestic "femininity." Molasses and brown sugar have been linked to intersecting gender, race, class, and sexual stereotypes in the figure of the mulatta.

In 1947 the Cuban scholar Fernando Ortiz published *Cuban Counterpoint: Tobacco and Sugar,* which analyzed the dynamic between "masculine" tobacco and "feminine" sugar in relation to the historical complexities of Cuba. Ortiz tied the agricultural and industrial developments of these products with the foreign economic interests that forcibly changed the history of Cuba. Considering land, machinery, labor, and money, Ortiz examined the history of these two products and their involvement in Cuban national identity.

Cultural discourses on sugar exhibit themselves in many Latin American and U.S. Latino contexts. Colonial cigar and cigarette labels frequently featured engravings of sugar mills and plantations. In Cuba, the emergence of literary traditions including *poesia negra* and *poesia mulata* intertwined racial connotations and national narratives of sugar. Representations of sugar figure in Latino and Latin American popular culture including music and regional idioms. Sugar also figures symbolically in some Afro-Latino spiritual traditions. Latino musicians use of the word *azucar* testifies to sugar's visibility in popular cultural discourses. Sugar continues to contribute to complex and shifting ideologies that involve constructions of race, class, gender, and sexuality in U.S. Latino and Latin American contexts.

RELATED ARTICLES

Agriculture; Business; Chocolate; Cuba; Cuisine; Dominican Republic; Health; Labor; Mexico.

FURTHER READING

Aparicio, Frances R., and Susana Chávez-Silverman. *Tropicalizations: Transcultural Representations of Latinidad.* Hanover, N.H.: Univ. Press of New England, 1997.

Hall, Michael R. *Sugar and Power in the Dominican Republic: Eisenhower, Kennedy, and the Trujillos.* Westport, Conn.: Greenwood Press, 2000.

Kutzinski, Vera M. *Sugar's Secrets: Race and the Erotics of Cuban Nationalism.* Charlottesville: Univ. of Va. Press, 1993.

Mintz, Sidney W. *Sweetness and Power: The Place of Sugar in Modern History.* New York: Viking, 1985.

Ortiz, Fernando. *Cuban Counterpoint: Tobacco and Sugar.* Tr. by Harried De Onibs. New York: Knopf, 1947.

Sandiford, Keith A. *The Cultural Politics of Sugar: Caribbean Slavery and Narratives of Colonialism.* Cambridge: Cambridge Univ., 2000.

Shepherd, Verene A. *Slavery without Sugar: Diversity in Caribbean Economy and Society since the 17th Century.* Gainesville: Univ. Press of Fla., 2002.

USEFUL WEB SITES

The Sugar Association. http://www.sugar.org/
Sugar: World Markets and Trade. www.fas.usda.gov/htp2/sugar/1999/november/coverpage.htm
United States Department of Agriculture (USDA). http://www.fas.usda.gov/

JANIVA CIFUENTES-HISS

SUPERSTITIONS

In its literal and most universal meaning, *superstition* signifies an allegedly irrational belief or ritualistic practice with an assumed but erroneous causal relationship. A belief in supernatural forces underlies superstitious behavior. In general, superstitious practices or rituals are intended to attract good luck while warding off bad luck. At the same time, superstition may also include accessing gifts of healing or fortune-telling as well as the ability to curse an enemy with death or bad luck. Superstition may also entail the presumed supernatural powers of amulets or magical charms, such as a "lucky" rabbit's foot. In all cases, the emphasis on cosmic forces (good and bad) underscoring superstition render it inextricably connected to broader religious and cultural contexts. Many Latino superstitions fall into the following three main categories: intermediaries, illnesses, and supernatural spirits.

The subjective nature of superstition is greatly compounded when the term is applied to the beliefs and traditions of underrepresented racial and ethnic communities within the United States. Thus the concept of superstition cannot be adequately explored without considering critically the historical role of European colonialism and, more recently, Western modernization in Latin America. Latino superstitions serve their communities in two main ways: offering "knowable" ways to explain the apparent randomness of good and bad fortune; and expressing a mestizo cultural consciousness in which both European and indigenous traditions are validated.

In its conquest of the Americas, Europe asserted not only physical domination over the indigenous populations but also ideological domination. Hence European religion, social structure, and values were affirmed, while those of indigenous peoples were subverted and dismissed as "primitive" and "superstitious." In the tradition of European Catholicism, Franciscan order priests and friars, who played central roles in the conversion of countless indigenous peoples, condemned spirituality that emphasized sensory experience; Christian spirituality was deeply suspicious of the body and instead promoted stoic—even ascetic—worship. That Europe placed value in rationality and empirical knowledge only further denigrated cultural expressions that found and honored mystery in the natural world.

This tension between European and indigenous spirituality continues and lies at the heart of defining *superstition*. Chicana writer Gloria Anzaldúa explores this conflict in her seminal work *Borderlands/La Frontera* (1987). After a discussion about the legendary figure of *la llorona,* she states, "Back then, I, an unbeliever, scoffed at these Mexican superstitions as I was taught in Anglo school." Later, she highlights more explicitly the role of white—or European—rationality upon the consciousness of the mestizo: "Like many Indians and Mexicans, I did not deem my psychic experiences as real. . . . I allowed white rationality to tell me that the existence of the 'other world' was mere pagan superstition. I accepted their reality, the 'official' reality of the rational, reasoning mode." Thus, hundreds of years after the conquest of the Americas by Europe, Latino culture continues to struggle with two cultural traditions.

The folkloric aspects of superstition make research a formidable challenge. As Rafaela G. Castro points out, unlike "high culture" or "elite culture," which is transmitted "through formal channels, such as music academies, universities, and other established institutions," folk culture is "transmitted among a group of people face-to-face on a daily basis, from generation to generation." Thus documentation on superstition is limited. At any rate, these superstitions vary greatly—from spiritual intermediaries to folk illnesses and remedies to the manifestation of supernatural entities.

With regard to intermediaries, there is widespread belief among Latino cultures about the power of both *curanderas* and *brujas*. While these two figures are often confused and their services blurred, distinct differences exist between them. In many cases, Western medicine has viewed the rituals, practices, and the role of the *curanderas* (female healers) and *curanderos* (male healers) as ignorant superstition. But in fact these criticisms suggest a lack of knowledge regarding what *curanderismo* actually entails. *Curanderas* serve an important role in the Latino community as healers whose holistic methods acknowledge a bond

between the mind and the body. Combining deep religious faith (mostly from the Catholic tradition), natural herbal remedies, and folk wisdom, *curanderismo* quintessentially represents Latino culture in its mixture of indigenous and European roots. While the figure of the *curandera* is profoundly respected within the Latino community and, in many cases, is quite effective in administering treatment, some methods and purported remedies clearly do fit the category of blatant superstitions. Hence it is important to distinguish between popular cultural folklore practiced by the legitimate *curandera*—that is, in the words of Aurelio M. Espinosa, "efficacious," from *remedios supersticiosos,* or superstitious remedies "which are evidently based on mere ignorant superstitions." Here is a brief sampling of some *remedios supersticiosos* provided by Espinosa's research of New Mexican folklore in the early 20th century:

(1) For warts: One takes a small rag and makes a knot in it. Then one goes to a road-crossing and throws it away. The first person who happens to pass by will grow a wart, and the other one loses it.

(2) For any female disease: Ashes and urine are mixed together with garlic, and this is applied to all parts of the body by making crosses with it.

(3) For wounds or cuts: They are carefully bandaged with rags of men's clothing.

(4) For sunstroke: A glass of water is placed on the patient's head. When the water boils, the ailment is gone.

In the above list the linkages between ailment and remedy seem nonexistent. Nevertheless, at least one of the superstitious remedies underscores its mestizo nature since Christian crosses are made of herbal (garlic) substances and administered to the afflicted.

Curanderas are at times confused with the less generously regarded *brujas*. The belief in *brujas* (witches) and *brujería* (witchcraft) is widespread and well documented. This superstition holds that witches are capable of casting as well as lifting spells that may inflict illness, cause infatuation (love potions), and generally wreak havoc on their victims. Among the witch's magical repertoire is the ability to shape-shift into animals, the most prevalent form being the *tecolote* (owl). Shape shifting helps the witch to execute spells and to evade capture, rendering her (or him) all the more fearful.

Brujería has manifested itself in the rise of "psychic surgery" as a method of healing and exorcising evil. This practice has been discredited by both medical professionals as well as magicians. To perform the procedure, the practitioner—who sometimes, but not always, identifies himself as a *brujo*—first lays his shirtless patient down, face up, and proceeds to miraculously pull out tumors or other malevolent internal growths with his bare hands. No surgical instruments are used to create incisions in the patient's skin. Skeptics of psychic surgery claim that animal blood, and blood-soaked matter—like uncooked bacon or chicken—are strategically "pulled" out of the body by a sleight of hand to create the appearance of freshly extracted tumors. Sometimes metallic screws or nails are "extracted" instead. Afterward, psychic surgery patients are often told that the origins of their ailments—whether from physical pain such as backaches, or emotional pain such as depression—stem directly from a witch's spell.

While psychic surgery is a relatively recent remedy-phenomenon, one of the oldest and most pervasive illness-related superstitions throughout much of Latin America is *el mal ojo*, also called *mal de ojo*. *Mal ojo*, or "evil eye," is a condition most often suffered by children and is the result of exorbitant admiration or attention through the act of "eyeing." The affliction may be intentionally or unintentionally passed to its victim. Folklorist George M. Foster explains that "Unintentional eyeing can be guarded against by the cautious admirer adding 'God bless you,' or some such phrase, and slapping or touching the child." He also points out that in some parts of Latin America coral and religious charms are believed to ward off the "magical causation" of the evil eye. When contracted, symptoms appear flulike with severe fever cited most often. Treatments for *mal ojo* vary; nevertheless, rituals performed by *curanderas* appear to be among the more popular.

Other Latino superstitions regarding illnesses include *mal aire* and *susto*. *Mal aire* (bad or evil air) contains both literal and figurative meanings, as the air can refer to cold currents that spread illness or bad spirits that invade the body and bring ill fortune. The Latino condition called *susto* (fright or shock) is said to occur if one witnesses or experiences a traumatic event; for example, the loss of a loved one or an act of violence. The most severe result of this condition is soul-loss. Treatment for *susto* involves calling on supernatural powers for the return of the lost spirit. More specifically, Ozzie G. Simmons has noted that often such rituals take place at midnight and make use of chants along with the patient's clothing.

Aside from intermediaries who channel cosmic forces, Latino superstition also recognizes direct contact with certain supernatural spirits. In particular, *la llorona, chanes,* and *duendes* constitute spiritual figures who reveal themselves physically to community members from time to time. *La llorona* (the sobbing woman) is discussed at length by Anzaldúa, who traces her roots to pre-Columbian female deities. Likening *llorona* to the indigenous goddess *Cihuacoatl*, Anzaldúa explains that she "howls and weeps in the night, screams as if demented . . . [and] brings mental depression and sorrow." In many versions her wailing stems from her agonizing regret for the killing of her own children. She appears most often before children who disobey their parents by wandering off at night.

Chanes (water spirits), too, represent a danger to children. They reside in bodies of water and threaten children who disregard their mothers' admonitions about staying clear of the water. To mitigate the danger posed by *chanes*, Castro points out that mothers may leave food at the water's edge as an offering to the menacing spirits. In addition, specific chants may be repeated along with the child's name to inoculate her from the *chanes'* spells.

The elfin *duendes* are less widely known. According to Espinosa, the role of the *duende* is to frighten and otherwise frustrate lazy individuals. In her research on Chicano folklore, Castro also points out that "*duendes* are believed to be the spirits of dead ancestors who return to invade a house and cannot be removed." On the other hand, should a family properly accommodate a *duende* with comfort and provisions, then the *duende* may in turn provide help around the house instead of agitating family members.

Although numerous Latino superstitions are pervasive throughout most of Latin America and the southwestern United States, many Latinos dismiss superstitions as most prevalent among rural people of the lower social classes. When discussing witchcraft, for example, Latino folklorist Aurelio Espinosa attributes such "ideas and beliefs [to] the New Mexican *lower classes*." Furthermore, in her definition of *creencias* (folk beliefs), Castro also notes that "witchcraft, superstitions, and folk illnesses" are "traditionally associated with uneducated and peasant cultures." Nevertheless, she wisely points out that while many of these beliefs are associated with peasant culture, "folk beliefs are found among all peoples, rural and urban." In addition, social critics, including Anzaldúa, emphasize the social role that certain legendary narratives—like superstitions—affirm. For example, Anzaldúa notes that "stories of the devil luring young girls away and having his way with them discouraged us [Chicanas] from going out." Hence she identifies how gender roles, and in particular the value of female virginity, are perpetuated in the circulation of particular narratives. *Duendes,* too, seen in this light serve to encourage industry and a strong work ethic, as it is only the lazy and unkempt who need fear them. Thus Latino superstitions serve not only to offer an order to the apparent randomness of good and bad luck, but also to validate mestizo cultural heritage and cultural values.

RELATED ARTICLES

Brujería; *Botanícas*; *Curanderismo*; Folklore, Caribbean American; Folklore, Mexican American; Health.

FURTHER READING

Anzaldúa, Gloria. *Borderlands/La Frontera.* San Francisco: Aunt Lute Bks., 1987.

Castro, Rafaela G. *Dictionary of Chicano Folklore.* Santa Barbara, Calif.: ABC-CLIO, 2000.

Espinosa, Aurelio M. "New-Mexican Spanish Folk-Lore." *The Journal of American Folklore* 23 (October–December 1910): 395–418.

Foster, George M. "Relationships between Spanish and Spanish-American Folk Medicine." *The Journal of American Folklore* 66 (July–September 1953): 201–217.

Simmons, Ozzie G. "Popular and Modern Medicine in Mestizo Communities of Coastal Peru and Chile." *The Journal of American Folklore* 68 (January–March 1955): 57–71.

CHRISTY FLORES

SUPREME COURT, UNITED STATES

The Supreme Court's rulings on cases involving Mexicans and Puerto Ricans are representative of two ideologies that inform the Court's treatment of Latinos in the United States. The Court's opinions involving Mexican Americans have traditionally addressed questions regarding the social, economic, and political status of Latinos in the United States. In contrast, Court opinions concerning Puerto Rico have reaffirmed the marginalization and exclusion of Puerto Ricans and other citizens or persons residing on the island. This entry will provide a brief introduction to some of the debates that have shaped the relationship between Latinos and the Supreme Court in the United States.

The Supreme Court of the United States is composed of nine judges. The president, with the advice and consent of the Senate, traditionally nominates these justices. To date, Benjamin N. Cardozo (served on the Court from 1932 to 1938) has been the only Supreme Court justice with clear Hispanic heritage, his parents having been born in Spain. Although various presidents in the late 20th and early 21st century considered Latino judges for filling vacancies on the bench, none has yet nominated a Latino judge to the High Court.

The Court renders decisions on cases that raise questions arising from disputes over constitutional provisions, an act of Congress, and or international treaties to which the United States is a party. Most legal disputes, such as those involving criminal offenses, are resolved in state courts. The Court generally hears cases that rise up from lower courts of appeals or circuit courts, disputes between and among states, or disputes between states and the federal government. Since 1925, the Court has relied on a special certification process to select cases it wants to hear. The Court will usually issue a *writ of certiorari* to hear a case if four justices vote to hear a case. The Court's rulings are presumed to be the final interpretation of the Constitution and, by extension, the guiding rules for all interpretations of law.

In 1966 the Supreme Court ruled in *Miranda* v. *Arizona,* a case involving a Mexican immigrant accused of murder, that police officers must give certain warnings to a suspect before his or her statements made during interrogation could be admitted as evidence. On June 26, 2000, the Court held in *Dickerson* v. *United States* that Miranda warnings have "become embedded in routine police practice to the point where the warnings have become part of our national culture." Thus, Court rulings involving Latinos have contributed to the formation of a larger national culture and have shaped the contours of numerous precedent-setting interpretations of constitutional provisions. Similarly, the experience of Latinos in the United States has been informed by numerous Court rulings that seek to define limits of state actions affecting Latinos and other citizens or persons in society. One important area of law that has helped define the relationship between the Constitution, Latinos, and society has been the Fourteenth Amendment's equal protection clause.

Prior to the adoption of the Reconstruction Amendments—Thirteenth (1865), Fourteenth (1868), and Fifteenth (1870)—citizenship was generally reserved for "free white males." The Reconstruction Amendments abolished slavery (Thirteenth); extended citizenship rights as well as the equal protection of the laws to all persons born or naturalized in the United States (Fourteenth); and prohibited disenfranchisement of race, color, or previous condition of servitude. Notwithstanding these amendments to the Constitution, the Supreme Court endeavored to restrict their progressive implementation in the United States by interpreting their provisions very restrictively—emphasizing procedures and eventually a "color-blind" interpretation of the law.

Moreover, states generally adopted Jim Crow laws that institutionalized various forms of segregation. In *Plessy* v. *Ferguson* (1897) the Court established that segregation was constitutional if the state guaranteed "separate but equal" facilities to blacks and other "nonwhites." Because immigration laws were racialized, immigrants from Latin America were often treated as nonwhites, and Latinos were generally subject to forms of segregation and discrimination similar to those imposed on blacks. Not until the 1950s, as a direct result of the civil rights struggles, would the Supreme Court adopt a more progressive and expansive interpretation of the Reconstruction Amendments. The Court's innovative interpretation of the equal protection clause of the Fourteenth Amendment opened many of the doors that have enabled Latinos to become an integral part of the United States polity.

Juan F. Perea suggests that the Supreme Court began to consider questions of discrimination against Mexican Americans in *Hernandez* v. *Texas* (1954). This case addressed the systematic exclusion of Mexican Americans from juries. The defendant, Pete Hernandez, claimed that by systematically excluding Mexicans from becoming members of a jury that would hear his case, the trial court was depriving him of a jury of his peers, and, by extension, he was denied the equal protection of the law. According to Perea this was the first time that the Court recognized that this ethnic group constituted a minority group for equal protection purposes. The Court reasoned that excluding jury members on the basis of their national origin (for example, Mexican), like dis-

crimination on the basis of race or color, constituted a violation of the equal protection clause. This ruling is especially important because the Supreme Court made efforts to transcend the "two-class theory" that was premised on a black-white racial paradigm and further recognized that Mexicans, and by extension Latinos, had been subject to discrimination and other forms of segregation.

Later the Court rendered its opinion in *Brown* v. *Board of Education* (1954), repudiating the "separate but equal" body of law that rested on earlier interpretations of the Constitution. The Court basically established that to deny black children access to "white" public schools was a denial of the equal protection of the law. The Court further concluded that educational facilities available to blacks and whites were inherently unequal and that such state-sponsored segregation was unconstitutional. Although this ruling opened the door for many Latinos to receive quality public education, states like Louisiana continue to implement school policies that seek to undermine the mandates arising from the *Brown* decision.

Notwithstanding the promise of *Brown* to end segregation in public schools, the Court would eventually render other opinions that undermined *Brown*'s progressive principles. With *San Antonio Independent School District* v. *Rodríguez* (1973), the Court validated a school funding system that effectively created separate and unequal schools for predominantly poor Mexican communities and their more affluent neighboring school districts populated by a majority of white residents. Under the Texas school funding plan, property taxes provided the basis for most of the funds available to public schools. Thus, in communities where the residents were mostly wage earners and of Mexican heritage, the funds available for the public school system were substantially lower than in suburbs populated by a majority of whites with higher incomes.

Mexican American parents challenged the Texas system of public school funding by arguing that it discriminated against Latino children because it did not provide additional resources comparable to those available to students in wealthier school districts. Notwithstanding the Court's acknowledgment of the effects of disparate funding, the Court concluded that the "class" in question was "not saddled with such disabilities, or subjected to such a history of purposeful unequal treatment, or relegated to such a position of political powerlessness as to command extraordinary protection from the majoritarian political process." The Court reasoned that Latinos could overcome their condition of poverty in a capitalist system, and therefore no steps were required to protect the poor. This ruling effectively enabled states to create multiple-tier public education systems in which poor Latinos would not received the same kind of education available to the children of affluent parents. Because a significant number of Latino children are sons and daughters of immigrants, they often live in poor communities with few resources and low property taxes.

In 1974, however, the Court addressed the relationship between proficiency in English, segregation, and the equal protection clause in *Lau* v. *Nichols.* The Court ruled that the failure of the San Francisco school system to provide English-language instruction to students of Chinese ancestry who did not speak English or to provide them a other adequate instructional procedures denied them a meaningful opportunity to participate in public education programs and, by extension, violated the Civil Rights Act of 1964, which bans discrimination on the basis of race, color, or national origin in any program or activity receiving federal financial assistance. This ruling has enabled the creation of numerous bilingual education programs, English as a second language (ESL) courses, and total immersion programs in K–12 schools. More important, this opinion made federal funding contingent on an effort to desegregate schools and to enable non-English-speaking children to become a part of the nation.

In the late 20th and into the 21st century, the Supreme Court rendered a number of rulings that affect the status of Latinos in the United States in distinct ways. Perhaps the most relevant opinions address questions of immigration. The Supreme Court has been deciding cases that limit due process rights of immigrants in the workplace as well as in immigration proceedings. Moreover, the attacks of September 11, 2001, have heightened the Court's support of the Bush administration's immigration policies. These policies have had their harshest effect on immigrants crossing the U.S.–Mexico border.

In a 1990 opinion, *U.S.* v. *Verdugo-Urquidez,* the Court legitimized the kidnapping, by U.S. officials, of a Mexican doctor who had allegedly participated in the torture and murder of a U.S. Drug Enforcement Agency agent. This ruling has given constitu-

tional protections to U.S. government agents who are engaged in the apprehension of suspected criminals operating outside of U.S. borders. Not only did this opinion allow agents of the U.S. government to carry out missions in Latin America, including the kidnapping of foreign nationals, but also made it clear that kidnapped suspects were not entitled to the same constitutional protections afforded U.S. citizens.

The Supreme Court's treatment of Puerto Ricans continues to be informed by a series of opinions rendered at the turn of the 19th century known as the "Insular Cases," which declared that U.S. citizens residing in Puerto Rico are only entitled to the "fundamental rights" afforded by the Constitution. For example, according to the Court's position in *Balzac* v. *Porto Rico* (1922), U.S. citizens residing on the island are not entitled to trial by jury. In addition, the Court's rulings on the status of Puerto Rico provide the legal justification for the treatment of the detainees held at Camp X-Ray at Guantánamo Bay, Cuba, during the U.S. "war on terror" in the early 2000s.

RELATED ARTICLES

Affirmative Action; Civil Rights; Law Enforcement; *Mendez* v. *Westminster School District.*

FURTHER READING

Perea, Juan F., et al., eds. *Race and Races: Cases and Resources For A Diverse America.* St. Paul, Minn.: West Group, 2000.

CHARLES R. VENATOR SANTIAGO

SWEATSHOPS AND INFORMAL WORKERS

The term *informal,* used when describing work or the economy, refers to income-generating activity that is outside the legal regulatory system of government. Informal workers range from self-employed microentrepreneurs to sweatshop employees whose employers pay less than legal minimum wage or avoid Social Security contributions, or both, to home-based sweatshops wherein production is subcontracted. Many sweatshop workers are undocumented immigrants, a large proportion of whom are female, and are paid by piece rate, earning hourly wages below the legal minimum wage. Their vulnerabilities open these workers to exploitative relationships.

Research on informal labor began with studies that the International Labour Organization (ILO) spon-

© MARK RICHARDS/PHOTOEDIT

Female workers in a garment factory.

sored in African countries. The term spread in use to many developing countries in Asia, Africa, and Latin America where people struggle economically to support themselves outside the formal, regulated workforce. In Mexico and the rest of Latin America, official and independent research studies document that at least a quarter to a third of the labor force supports itself through informal means. Mexico, which generally counts small businesses with five or fewer employees as informal, claims extremely low official unemployment figures because its labor surveys ask questions about work for pay in a recent unit of time; thus informals count as employed. The U.S. Census has underestimated informality, a consequence of research strategies that ask about primary rather than all earned incomes. The Peruvian economist Hernando de Soto links the huge informal sector to a critique of the swollen state and the over-bureaucratization of regulations and business licenses.

Informal economies have often been linked to preindustrial, premodern economies as well as to poverty, although increasingly researchers see links between informal work, the globalized economy, and global cities. Garment factories, for example, subcontract with informal home-based workers and sweatshops to compete in the global economy. Because of the grand theory linking economic development and informality, few studies have been done in industrialized countries such as the United States, or about Latino populations therein. (This essay will not treat crime, such as drug trafficking, sex work, and gambling, as informal work, although some studies link those phenomena.)

Historians have uncovered how immigrants earn through informal labor, whatever their country of origin. Studies of Latino street vendors, some of them recent immigrants, have been conducted in large cities such as Los Angeles, New York, Chicago, and El Paso, Texas. Self-employed entrepreneurs can make a livelihood for themselves and their families, although with difficulty owing to local government regulations and license fees. Studies have also focused on enclave economies, where more prosperous immigrants or "native-born" Latinos recruit workers from their homeland or place of national origin. In Miami, for example, Cuban Americans recruit heavily based on cultural identity, although the pay in sweatshop contexts is no less exploitative than if employers were non-Cuban. Studies of maids, gardeners, farmworkers, and construction day laborers, most of whom could be considered informal workers, stress ease of entry but low earnings and limited-to-nonexistent fringe benefits.

At the mostly Latino U.S.-Mexico border, informality flourishes with an incidence in low- to middle-income neighborhoods of one in three. Yet for these quintessential "free traders," the North American Free Trade Agreement (NAFTA) burdened, rather than benefited, borderlanders (*fronterizos*).

Changes in immigration and welfare laws enacted in 1996 bore heavily on workers who supported themselves informally. To obtain Social Security benefits, for example, workers had to prove that they earned in 40 quarters, a complicated way of requiring ten years in the documented, formal workforce. Some maids found it difficult to secure proof of employment over decades from employers who did not pay the minimum wage or neglected to make Social Security contributions, for employers did not want to put themselves at risk.

There has been debate about appropriate economic policies concerning the informal workforce. Some seek to eliminate informality in order to regulate and protect all work, benefits, and taxes. Others seek to recognize and support informality, providing loans to microentrepreneurs, for example, while gradually formalizing work at particular size or earnings levels. Informality will likely continue, however, whatever the policy strategy.

RELATED ARTICLES

Business; Labor; Maquiladoras.

FURTHER READING

De Soto, Hernando. *The Other Path.* New York: Harper, 1989.

Fernandez-Kelley, et al. "Economic Restructuring in the United States: Hispanic Women in the Garment and Electronics Industries." In *Women and Work: An Annual Review.* Ed. by Barbara Gutek, et al. Beverly Hills, Calif.: Sage Pubns, 1988.

International Labour Organization (ILO). *Employment Incomes and Inequality.* Geneva: ILO, 1972.

Moore, Joan, and Raquel Pinderhughes, eds. *In the Barrios: Latinos and the Underclass Debate.* New York: Sage Pubns., 1993.

Portes, Alejandro, et al., eds. *The Informal Economy: Studies in Advanced and Less Developed Countries.* Baltimore: Johns Hopkins Univ. Press, 1989.

Roberts, Bryan, ed. *International Journal of Urban and Regional Research* 18 (1994) [special issue on informality].

Sassen, Saskia. *Cities in a World Economy.* Thousand Oaks, Calif.: Pine Forge Press of Sage, 1995.

Staudt, Kathleen. *Free Trade? Informal Economies at the U.S.-Mexico Border.* Philadelphia: Temple Univ. Press, 1998.

KATHLEEN STAUDT

TAÍNO

In the pre-Hispanic era, the Arawaks gradually invaded and dominated the Antilles Islands; by the time the Europeans arrived in 1492, the Arawak were firmly established in Jamaica, the Bahamas, eastern Cuba, and, to some extent, in Florida. Taíno, the name given to the group by the Spanish conquistadors, is derived from *nitayno,* meaning "gentleman," "sir," "landowner." Use of the term *Taíno* to refer to the entire indigenous population of the western Caribbean began to be widespread only at the beginning of the 20th century. During the previous century, each island had its own name for its pre-Columbian peoples: Borincanos and Borinqueños in Puerto Rico; Siboneyes in Cuba; Haitianos and Quisqueyanos—Haitians and Dominicans, respectively—in Hispaniola; Xamayquinos in Jamaica. As a unified, living people, the Taíno have been extinct since the 18th century (the 1778 census is the last to include a category for "Indios"), but in recent years this group has become a symbol of the Caribbean's, particularly Puerto Rico's, rich and far-reaching heritage.

Archeological discoveries affirm that when the Spanish arrived, the Taíno were using instruments of stone, shell, bone, or hard wood, tools that were symmetrical, well-constructed, polished, and decorated. The dominant craft was pottery, including vessels, dishes, and other tools and domestic items. Other artisan crafts included basket making, weaving, and making fishing equipment and hammocks.

The Taíno also ornamented their bodies. They lived in *bohíos,* rectangular structures built with palm wood, the roofs patched with clumps of guano from the same tree. Villages were strategically placed "*a dos aguas,*" near two sources of water, at least one potable. Contrary to the poor hygiene of the subsequent European invaders, the Taíno kept quite clean. The *bohíos* surrounded a large open space called a *batey,* which was used for communal gatherings and festivals.

The people were of medium stature with copper-toned skin and straight, black hair that they kept trimmed. The most striking physical characteristic of the Taíno was the artificial flattening of the front of the cranium. The gentle and agreeable climate permitted the Taíno to go naked, except for married women, who wore a type of short skirt called a *nagua.* They covered their skin with ornamental unguents that possessed magical or social meaning as well as protected them from the sun and tropical insects.

After abandoning the nomadic life, the Taíno developed practices of agriculture, fishing, hunting, and gathering. They maintained a simple organization of tribal castes divided into three strata. The greatest authority was the *cacique,* who belonged to the highest caste (*nitainos*) of the nobles and military chiefs. A *behique* cared for the tribe's spiritual life as well as serving as doctor, sorcerer, and seer; he, his family, and his apprentices and assistants belonged to the *bohitihus* class. The productive, laboring class was called *naborias.*

The Taíno are known for having developed the ritual of *areíto,* an expression of music, dance, song, poetry, and religious liturgy that was a form of education—of keeping alive legends, history, traditions, and customs. Verses recounted aloud told the heroic deeds of ancestors and the evolution of the Taíno. The entire community participated in the *areíto,* and everyone dressed up for the special event.

In the Antilles the indigenous populations did not strongly resist contact with the Europeans, and the Taíno were treated cruelly by the Spanish conquistadors, who eventually caused their extinction, and with them all the history of their society. Their labor was replaced by African slaves. Although the Taíno did not leave a deep footprint in the Caribbean, one of their lasting contributions was linguistic—a number of Taíno terms are still in use today, including: *maíz* (corn), *ceiba* (silk-cotton tree), *mamey* (an orange-fleshed tropical fruit), *maní* (peanut), *manatí* (manatee), *bohío* (round hut), *yagua* (royal palm tree), *maraca* (gourd-like musical instrument), *hamaca* (hammock), *batey* (yard area), and the most well-known—Cuba.

During the political and cultural tumult of 1960s and 1970s, Caribbean Americans, particularly in the U.S. Northeast and Midwest, began to show increased interest in Taíno culture, studying and identifying with this indigenous group. By the 1980s a "Taíno revival" was in full swing and tribal "councils" were created across the country, often connected to sister organizations in the Caribbean, including Nación Taína, Taíno del Norte, and the Taíno Intertribal Council of New Jersey. This revival paralleled other movements Caribbeans joined that emphasized particular ethnic or religious roots—such as Afrocentrism and the Nation of Islam. Those focused on Taíno culture, however, have been more involved in advocacy work, and protecting the environment and the rights of all Native Americans. One result of the resurgence of interest in this population was the exhibition Taíno Pre-Columbian Art and Culture from the Caribbean at the Museo del Bar-

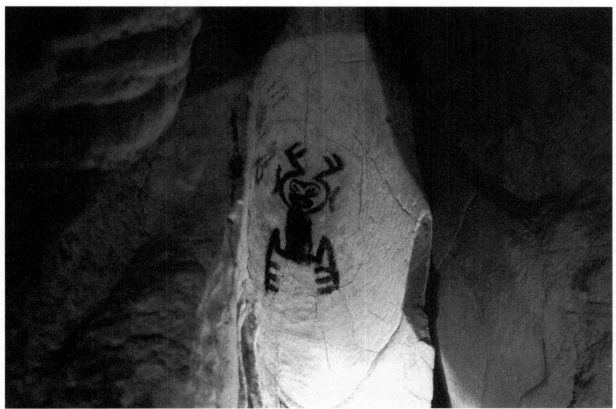

Pre-Columbian drawings left by Taíno peoples decorate a cave in San Cristóbal, Dominican Republic.

rio in New York City in late 1997 through early 1998.

RELATED ARTICLES

Afro-Latino Influences; Cuba; Indigenismo; Indigenous Heritage; Puerto Rico.

FURTHER READING

Colón, Cristobal. "Carta de Colón en que da Cuenta del Descubrimiento de América." (Letter from Columbus in Which He Recounts the Discovery of America) México, Imprenta Universitaria, 1939 [facsimile edition of Latin text published in Rome in 1493, with Castilian translation].

Haslip-Viera, Gabriel, Arlene Dávila, et al. *Taíno Revival: Critical Perspectives on Puerto Rican Identity and Cultural Politics.* Princeton, N.J.: Markus Wiener Pubs., 2001.

Ramos Gómez, Luis J. Valladolid. "Cristóbal Colón y los Indios Taínos: de Octubre de 1492 a Diciembre de 1494." (Christopher Columbus and the Taíno Indians: From October 1492 to December 1494) *Cuadernos Colombinos* 18. Valladolid: Casa–Museo de Colón/Seminario Americanista de la Universidad de Valladolid, 1993.

Wilson, Samuel M. *The Indigenous People of the Caribbean.* Gainesville: Univ. Press of Fla., 1997.

MAGALY LLORO
Translated by Jennifer M. Acker

TAOS REBELLION

On May 13, 1846, President James K. Polk declared war on Mexico following a skirmish between U.S. and Mexican troops in Texas. Using the concept and slogan "manifest destiny," the U.S. government invaded and occupied New Mexico, the majority of California, and parts of northern Mexico. Colonel Stephen Watts Kearny was charged with leading the Army of the West on this mission, without provoking large-scale uprisings among Mexican citizens en route.

On August 15, 1846, Kearny and his troops reached Las Vegas, New Mexico, unopposed. Addressing residents in the plaza, Kearny promised to protect the people, their property, and religion if they vowed allegiance to the U.S. government. Accorded grudging acceptance, Kearny then prepared to march to Santa Fe, expecting resistance along the way at Apache Canyon.

For reasons that are not completely documented, Mexican governor Manuel Armijo fled to Mexico at the last minute, leaving the way clear for Kearny's troops to enter Santa Fe on August 18. Despite Kearny's efforts to assure the local populace that his troops meant them no harm, fear and resentment were widespread as were rumors started by the clergy

and wealthy citizens who opposed the occupation. After establishing a legal code and civilian government under Governor Charles Bent, Kearny left for California. Once Kearny had departed, local opposition grew. A group of Mexicans and Native Americans conspired to retake the government, but word got out in late fall and the leaders of the conspiracy were arrested or fled. Governor Bent thought that the resistance was quelled and decided to travel to his home in Taos. On January 19, 1847, Mexican rebels and Taos, led by Pablo Montoya and Tomasito Romero, broke into Bent's home, scalped and killed him and as many other American sympathizers as they could find in Taos and the surrounding towns. When the news of the massacre reached Santa Fe, several companies of American troops and some local volunteers (about 500 men) marched north and engaged the enemy (about 1,500 men) in the Rio Grande canyon south of Taos. Routed by the Americans' superior arms and artillery, the rebels withdrew to Taos and then to the Pueblo of Taos where they were defeated. Speedy trials and executions of the conspirators ended the Taos Rebellion. Whether the revolt grew out of the earlier plot in Santa Fe or whether it had been festering independently since the beginning of the occupation six months earlier remains unknown. Either way, as an observant American officer wrote at the time, "A people conquered but yesterday could have no friendly feeling for their conquerors who had taken possession of their country, changed its laws and appointed new officers, principally foreigners" (Beck; *New Mexico: A History of Four Centuries.* Rowdy and racist American soldiers who referred to Mexicans as "greasers" added to the insult of invasion, and many local citizens also were angry at Armijo's betrayal and the ease with which Kearny's entry into New Mexico was accomplished.

The unsuccessful Taos Rebellion marked the end of indigenous armed resistance to occupation, but it did not end the nuevomexicanos efforts to maintain their language, culture, and political power under U.S. territorial rule and even after the granting of statehood in 1912.

RELATED ARTICLES

Colonialism; Indigenous Heritage; Mexico; New Mexico.

FURTHER READING

Beck, Warren A. *New Mexico: A History of Four Centuries.* Norman: Univ. of Okla. Press, 1962.

Ellis, Richard N. *New Mexico, Past and Present: A Historical Reader.* Albuquerque: Univ. of N.Mex. Press, 1971.

McNierney, Michael, ed. *Taos 1847: The Revolt in Contemporary Accounts.* Boulder, Colo.: Johnson Pubs., 1980.

Simmons, Marc. *New Mexico: An Interpretive History.* Albuquerque: Univ. of N.Mex. Press, 1988.

DORIS MEYER

TATTOOS

In José Antonio Villareal's classic Chicano novel *Pocho* (1959), the police suspect the protagonist, Richard Rubio, and his friends of participating in gang activity. In an effort to confirm his suspicions, the questioning officer inspects Richard's hand for the "*pachuco* mark," a tattoo of a cross with radiating lines that was the sign of Chicano street gangs. The scene dramatizes a key moment in tattoo history in which U.S. attitudes toward the practice were shifting rapidly as Chicanos began to make a distinct contribution to the art form.

Between the two world wars, the tattoo enjoyed social acceptance in the United States. The primary recipients of tattoos were military men heading off to war who had their bodies inscribed with patriotic images or had the names of their mothers and sweethearts emblazoned on their flesh. Tattoos rapidly declined in acceptability following World War II and became associated with such subcultures as bikers, sailors, and Chicanos. The last association was heightened during the 1940s and 1950s, when the zoot suit riots in Los Angeles brought several aspects of Chicano gang culture to the attention of the American masses.

Chicano tattooing developed in the barrios of Arizona, California, New Mexico, and Texas. Aside from its gang associations, Chicano tattoo art introduced several aesthetic and technical innovations. Mainstream U.S. tattooing used electric tattooing machines with five or more needles that produced heavy dark lines. In contrast, Chicano tattoos were usually applied by hand with a single needle using India ink. Additionally, Chicano tattoos were almost always rendered only in black, unlike the red, blue, green, and black tattoos applied in other sectors.

Chicano tattoos were also distinguished by the archive of images they drew from. Commonalities between Chicano tattoos and Mexican muralism are readily apparent. As is evident in the pachucos' use of a cross, Catholic symbols proliferate in Chicano tattooing. The Virgin of Guadalupe and Christ figures are among the most popular images. Wearers of such tattoos often remark that they are protective images. Noted Chicana writer Sandra Cisneros is tattooed with the Virgin of Guadalupe in the lotus position, which she refers to as the "Buddhalupe." Images from Mexican folklore, including *calaveras* (skeletons) and exotic, sexualized *charras,* are also common.

While these images convey Mexican solidarity, a number of more local images convey allegiance to a community, family, or gang. Neighborhood names are often tattooed in Old English script; low-rider or car club affiliations are also favorites. One familiar image from low-rider culture is the mustached *vato loco* (crazy) with sunglasses and a low-brimmed hat. Among gang tattoos, the best known is the one representing Nuestra Familia, one of the oldest and most notorious Chicano gangs. The Nuestra Familia tattoo exists in two variations: a sombrero with a

© JOHN CASTILLO/LATIN FOCUS

Latino man with a religious scene tattooed on his back.

165

bleeding dagger or the dagger alone accompanied by the letters NF.

Nuestra Familia was a gang founded in the California prison system. Given the association of tattooing with gang culture, it is not surprising that tattooing became a dominant mode of expression within prison walls, despite the disapproval of prison officials. Chicano artists were important contributors to prison tattoo communities, often using sewing needles and cassette players that had been modified to act as makeshift electric tattooing machines. They developed images that told the story of an inmate's crimes and gang affiliations. A knife and skull, for instance, designated a killer, while a cross branded a thief, and a gun an armed robber. A tear near the outer edge of the eye signified that the person had killed while in prison.

Religious images are frequent in prison tattooing and, as is the case in Chicano street culture, are regarded as protective images that will ensure the safety of the prisoner. In one notable variation, prison religious images are often shown behind prison door bars. Birds, a symbol of freedom, are also common, as are roses, which are regarded as a symbol of beauty and as a reminder of the female sexuality that is unavailable during incarceration. Despite animosity between different racial gangs in prison, Chicano artists are often enlisted to tattoo members of other gangs. This results in surprising situations in which, for instance, Chicano artists produce racist slogans for the bodies of white supremacists.

In the 1970s and 1980s Chicano tattooing practices became more mainstream. Jack Rudy and Charlie Cartright opened a tattoo parlor, Good Time Charlie's Tattooland, in East Los Angeles. Rudy and Cartright were the first professional tattooists to specialize in Chicano-style tattooing. In the 1970s they were joined by Chicano tattooist Freddy Negrete, a legend in the tattooing community. Negrete was named Tattooist of the Year in 1980 by the National Tattoo Association. Negrete developed a finely detailed style that has sometimes been referred to as "photo-realist." His work can be seen in the Hollywood films *Blade* (1998) and *Con-Air* (1997).

Chicano tattooing's use of a single needle and its fine-line technique make it a much more time-consuming process than other tattooing methods. Nevertheless, by the 1980s Chicano tattooing had become the basis for a number of emergent styles and trends within the mainstream U.S. tattooing community.

In this period, tattooing was once again embraced by the American middle classes. In addition to bearing tattoos done in the Chicano style, these later middle-class consumers also made use of images such as the Virgin of Guadalupe and Old English script that had been closely associated with the Chicano tattoo tradition.

Chicano tattooing benefited from the counterculture that was flourishing on the West Coast in the 1960s and 1970s. Tattooing on the East Coast, especially in New York City, developed in a less-welcoming environment. In 1961 New York City government officials banned tattooing in response to a hepatitis scare. Many tattoo parlors continued to operate covertly until tattooing was again declared legal in 1997. Such clandestine operations closely affiliated tattooing with various underground cultures in New York as well as with crime. However, the ban drove out many of the innovative and cutting-edge tattooists from the New York City metropolitan area. Modern tattooing developed in the European, working-class immigrant communities of New York City's Bowery neighborhood in the 1890s, much more closely tying the white working classes to tattooing than was the case in the West. Newspaper articles and crime reports identifying Puerto Ricans and Dominicans with distinguishing tattoos (especially the cross) demonstrate that Latinos chose tattoos through the period of the ban, and the appearance of Spanish-surnamed victims of the fatal viral hepatitis that precipitated the ban in the early 1960s reveals Latino participation in New York tattoo culture. The ban on tattooing combined with a history that connected the practice with a number of immigrant communities in the city created an environment that was less hospitable to the kinds of innovation seen in Chicano tattooing.

RELATED ARTICLES
Fashion; Gangs; Graffiti; Popular Culture.

FURTHER READING
Atkinson, Michael. *Tattooed: The Sociogenesis of a Body Art.* Toronto: Univ. of Toronto Press, 2003.

DeMello, Margo. *Bodies of Inscription: A Cultural History of the Modern Tattoo Community.* Durham, N.C.: Duke Univ. Press, 2000.

Govenar, Alan. "The Variable Context of Chicano Tattooing." In *Marks of Civilization.* Ed. by Arnold Rubin. Los Angeles: Museum of Cultural History, Univ. of Calif., 1988.

Hall, Douglas Kent. *Prison Tattoos.* New York: St. Martin's Press, 1997.

Lueck, Thomas. "On the Tattoo Map, It's the Sticks." *New York Times.* (May 16, 1998): B1.

Steward, Samuel M. *Bad Boys and Tough Tattoos: A Social History of the Tattoos with Gang, Sailors, and Street-Corner Punks, 1950–1965.* New York: Haworth Press, 1990.

WILLIAM E. ORCHARD

TECHNOLOGY

The technological advances made since the 1970s have transformed our lives, how we access information, and how we study and work. The two driving forces behind these changes have been the personal computer and the Internet. Technological literacy has become a requirement to be economically successful. For example, studies have found that both computer and Internet use are positively correlated with career development (online job postings and applications) as well as benefits in interpersonal (e-mail), financial (electronic banking), and political communication.

The rapid development of the Information Age in the United States has threatened to create a "digital divide" between those groups that are proficient in the use of the new technologies and those that are not. Latinos as an ethnic group fall into the latter category; their lack of participation in the current information society puts them at risk of becoming a social underclass. With most jobs requiring at least some computer skills, the current economy disfavors those who lack access to and knowledge of technology. As a result, people who are employed are more likely to be both computer and Internet users: in 2001, employed Americans used computers (73 percent) and the Internet (65 percent) significantly more often than those without employment (41 percent and 37 percent, respectively). More political and community efforts are necessary to bridge the digital divide for Latinos in the United States.

The growth of electronic commerce and other transactions on the Internet have increased the demand for workers with information technology (IT) skills. The number of highly skilled IT jobs such as computer engineers and system analysts is expected to more than double between 1996 (874,000 jobs) and 2006 (1.8 million positions). In addition, the demand for programmers, database administrators, and network technicians is projected to grow by 118 percent through 2006. These IT jobs have higher-than-average salaries and can be expected to attract many young people. According to numbers released by the National Science Foundation, Latinos held only 4 percent of IT jobs. This low number is likely related to the fact that Latinos are not graduating from academic-degree-granting computer science programs: they earn less than 6 percent of the bachelor's degrees granted in computer science, only 3 percent of the master's degrees, and about 1 percent of the doctoral degrees in computer science.

Several studies undertaken by the National Telecommunications and Information Administration (NTIA) have found that Latino households make less use of the new technologies than most other ethnicities. The 2000 NTIA report revealed that computer ownership was slightly higher in Hispanic households (33.7 percent) than in African American homes (32.6 percent). However, both groups fell well below the national average of 51 percent. As for more general computer use, data from the 2002 report by the U.S. Department of Commerce, indicated that Latinos (48.8 percent) used computers less frequently than African Americans (55.7 percent), Caucasians (70 percent), and Asian Americans and Pacific Islanders (71.2 percent). Statistics are similar for Internet use. According to the 2000 NTIA report, only 23.5 percent of Hispanic and African American households had an Internet connection, compared with the national average of 41.5 percent. Internet use was highest for Asian Americans (58.8 percent) followed by Caucasians (46.1 percent). By 2002, Internet use had increased across all ethnic groups but mainly for African Americans and Latinos. However, Internet use by Latinos (31.6 percent) was still the lowest among all ethnicities, when compared with African Americans (39.8 percent), Caucasians, and Asian Americans (both approximately 60 percent).

The 2002 report from the U.S. Department of Commerce also described how education level relates directly to both computer and Internet use rates. The study found that adults who had not graduated from high school had a computer use rate of 17 percent and an Internet use rate of 13 percent. Latinos with some college education reported higher usage of computers and the Internet than Latinos with only a high school education. Only 56 percent of Latino students graduate from high school, thus the explanation for lower engagement with technological advances by Latinos.

Because computers are still absent in many Latino households, many Latino children rely on public institutions to learn, access, and effectively use the new technologies. Schools and public libraries, in particular, have become venues for the use of computers and the Internet. In 2002, 39 percent of Latino children relied solely on schools to use computers, while only 11 percent of Caucasian and 15 percent of Asian children did so. Almost 14 percent of all Latinos use public libraries to access the Internet, and about one-third of the Latino children who can use the Internet at school, but not at home, make frequent use of public libraries to connect to Internet resources. Because of the less convenient access, overall Internet use by Latino children (48 percent), lags behind that of African American children (52 percent), and Caucasians and Asian Americans (both at least 79 percent).

Many Latino children use computers at school, thus schools that offer access to modern technologies can play a very important role in bridging the digital divide, especially in less affluent districts. Just making the technology available in classrooms is not enough because children need instruction in effective use. Consequently, teacher training and support staff are essential; many schools with limited resources, however, reallocate their small technology funds to address other needs, such as bilingual education, that are considered more pressing. Absence of technology resources denies poor children educational opportunities often taken for granted in wealthier classrooms. In addition, students of all eco-

nomic levels must be given adequate instruction from trained staff. Studies have found that children from less affluent households often end up doing drill-and-practice exercises at school (and noneducational games at home), while their more affluent counterparts spend their computer time on more creative and intellectually stimulating activities.

To address the Latino lag in the adoption of computers and the use of the Internet, understanding the factors that contribute to the problem is crucial. The 2000 NTIA report claimed that the differences in technology use were not solely attributable to the lower education or the lower income level of Latinos—these two factors only accounted for half of the difference in Internet use. Ethnicity was responsible for the other half. Other factors included age and health: computers and the Internet are used less frequently by older people and by those with disabilities. Also, single-parent families as well as families living in rural areas generally lag behind. Nonetheless, 39 percent of Latinos stated that the costs associated with computer ownership and Internet access were the primary reason for not participating in these new technologies. However, familiarity with the tools also plays a role: people who use computers and access the Internet at work also use these technologies at home, regardless of income.

In addition to socioeconomic factors, cultural issues also appear to affect Internet and computer use. A comparison of households with an annual income of $75,000 or less has shown that Latinos in this group are less likely than Caucasians to own a computer or to access the Internet. These differences may be rooted in the attitudes that ethnicities have toward technology in general. For example, Caucasians have higher self-reported skills than Latino Internet users. Some Latinos express concern about the time computer use takes away from the family, as well as the presence of pornography on the Internet. In addition, many Latinos mention the difficulty of learning new technologies, even when they are willing to learn. Some have suggested that language may be a barrier for Latinos who want to improve their computer skills or access Internet content. Efficient operation of computers obviously requires at least basic literacy, but a 2002 report by the U.S. Department of Commerce also found that the use of the Internet among Latinos was affected by the primary language spoken at home. Only 14 percent of Latinos who spoke Spanish at home used the Internet, whereas

© RICK GOMEZ/MASTERFILE

Young woman doing her homework using a laptop computer

38 percent of Latinos who spoke English at home went online. Finally, because Latinos have not yet become a large online population, much of the content available on the Internet is not geared to their cultural interests and concerns and therefore fails to attract new Hispanic Internet users.

In the mid-1990s, U.S. leaders realized that many groups, including Latinos, had been left behind in the technological and economic boom because of a lack of access to computers and the Internet and insufficient skills. The U.S. Department of Commerce commissioned a series of reports that described the growing gap between people of different socioeconomic levels, education, age, sex, race and community (urban or rural). This series of revolutionary reports, *Falling through the Net,* was published in 1995, 1998, 1999, and 2000. It provided invaluable information for defining the socioeconomic characteristics of the digital divide in the United States. Partly based on the information contained in these reports, President Bill Clinton implemented a series of measures to make technology more accessible to the public. The Schools and Libraries Universal Service Fund was created as part of the Telecommunications Act of 1996 to ensure all that schools and libraries in the United States have affordable access to the Internet. Three other programs were also implemented during the Clinton administration. The Home Internet Access Program allocated $50 million to bring low-income and single-parent households online. The Technology Opportunity Program (TOP) provided $45 million in matching funds for state and local governments to extend the use of technology to nonprofit organizations and the general public. Finally the Community Technology Centers (CTC) promoted the development of model programs that demonstrate the educational effectiveness of technology in rural areas as well as economically distressed communities.

After the release of the 2002 report by the U.S. Department of Commerce, the administration of George W. Bush announced plans to eliminate funding for the TOP and CTC programs. The new administration suggested that the private sector should be responsible for supporting programs to close the digital divide. In addition, the Bush administration preferred to use the term *digital opportunity* instead of *digital divide.*

Many Latinos are not participating fully in the new information technologies. For example, the Pew survey found in 2002 that the majority of the Latino population (56 percent) was not online. However, the survey also showed that Latinos are motivated to go online. More than half of Latino nonusers expressed the desire to go online, compared with 62 percent of the Caucasian nonusers, who claimed that they will never go online. Bridging the digital divide thus appears possible. Two key factors will be the decreasing price of owning a computer and better instruction in the schools. A larger Latino online population will lead to more culturally attractive content (if only from advertisers) and, in turn, garner more users. Once Latino children are comfortable using the new tools, they are more likely to expand on this knowledge in college and later obtain IT jobs. Then they can truly start making their own contributions to the development of the Information Age and help shape the future.

RELATED ARTICLES

Business; Education; Education, Higher; Internet.

FURTHER READING

Atewell, Paul. "The First and Second Digital Divides." *Sociology of Education* 74 (2001): 252–259.

Chandler, Alfred, and James W. Cortada, eds. *A Nation Transformed by Information. How Information has Shaped the United States from Colonial Times to the Present.* New York: Oxford Univ. Press, 2000.

García, Oscar, and Roscoe Giles. *Researching Foundations on Successful Participation of Underrepresented Minorities in Information Technology.* National Science Foundation, 1999. www.cise.nsf.gov/cns/cwardle/it_mnor/ itminorities_final_report.pdf

Hacker, Kenneth L., and Robert Steniner. "The Digital Divide for Hispanic Americans." *The Howard Journal of Communications* 13 (2002): 267–283.

Kuttan, Appu, and Laurence Peters. *From Digital Divide to Digital Opportunity.* Lanham, Md.: Scarecrow Press, 2003.

SELECTED WEB SITES

Computing Research Association. "The Supply of Information Technology Workers in the United States." (1999) www.cra.org/reports/wits/cra.wits.html

Digital Divide Network. www.digitaldividenetwork.org/content/sections/index.cfm

National Telecommunications and Information Administration. "Falling Through the Net" (2000, 1999, 1998, 1995). www.ntia.doc.gov/ntiahome/digitaldivide/

New York State Forum. Government Information Focus. "The Digital Divide: Understanding and Addressing the Challenge." www.nysfirm.org/pubs/reports/index.asp

Pew Internet and American Life Project. "The Ever-Shifting Internet Population: A New Look at Internet Access and the Digital Divide 2003." www.pewinternet.org/reports/toc.asp?Report=88

Tomás Rivera Policy Institute. www.trpi.org

U.S. Department of Commerce. "A Nation Online: How Americans Are Expanding Their Use of the Internet" (2002) www.commerce.gov/

Willhem, Anthony. "Buying into the Computer Age." www.cgu.edu/inst/aw1-1.html

ALICIA MUÑOZ SÁNCHEZ

TEJANO

Like American country, blues, and rock 'n' roll, Tejano music is an original music form that has produced a rich legacy. Originating along the Texas-Mexico border, Tejano's roots go back to the dawn of the recording industry. Spanish for "Texan," Tejano represents the fusion of two disparate Mexican American genres of the mid-20th century—*conjunto* and Tejano, also known as *orquesta Tejana*. The more popular form is Tejano, a modern, urban splinter of *conjunto,* that incorporates more instruments, especially keyboards, and borrows heavily from other music forms: rock, country, and the pop look—leather or blue jeans, fog machines, and big sound.

Conjunto music may not get the national spotlight as often as Tejano, but the genre has been around longer. *Conjunto* originated in southwest Texas in the late 1800s when German, Czech, and Polish immigrants brought the accordion to the area. Early practitioners such as the late Narciso Martínez, Valerio Longoria and Santiago Jiménez, Sr., merged the lively strains of the accordion and European dance forms, for example, the waltz, with Mexican *rancheras* and boleros. *Conjunto* is folksy and acoustic, influenced by the rural, agrarian Southwest landscape. It developed into a basic four-piece band with the accordion as the lead instrument just prior to and after World War II. *Conjunto* relies heavily on the polka and the Polish *redowa* rhythms.

Sax player Alberto "Beto" Villa (1915–1986), born in Falfurrias, Texas, was the father of Tejano. By the mid-1950s he was the most successful and prolific Mexican American bandleader in the Southwest, with hits including *Rosita* and *Monterrey*. During the first half of the 20th century, few musicians, even the top performers, were able to give up their regular jobs. They often picked crops during the day, following harvests from the Rio Grande Valley up to the Pacific Northwest and upper Midwest. Some of them stayed and raised families in places like Michigan and Washington, and Tejano and *conjunto* maintain pockets of strong local followings in those states. Urban musicians also worked day jobs—Jiménez worked for years as a janitor. In mid-20th century south Texas, educational opportunities for Hispanics were scant.

Living legends in modern *conjunto* include accordionist Flaco Jiménez, a multiple Grammy winner; Grammy nominees Esteban Jordan and Santiago Jiménez (Flaco's brother); and the perennial favorite, Mingo Saldivar. Flaco Jiménez has served as *conjunto* music's chief ambassador to the American music mainstream. Playing accordion on Ry Cooder's album *Chicken Skin Music* (1976), the hit Buck Owens and Dwight Yoakam duet *Streets of Bakersfield* (1988) and the Rolling Stones' *Voodoo Lounge* album track *Sweethearts Forever* (1994), Jiménez has been the go-to musician for adding Tex-Mex flavor to pop and rock music. His contribution to *Streets of Bakersfield,* a country-music smash, was particularly noteworthy, as musically it was a Tejano and *conjunto* song in every way—only the lyrics were in English.

In the 1990s neotraditional groups, including Los Desperados, the Hometown Boys, Los Palominos, and Jaime y Los Chamacos enjoyed success playing in a simple down-home style. For *conjunto* fans, of course, the big celebration comes each May in the form of a five-day outdoor concert series, the Tejano Conjunto Festival in San Antonio, Texas, which showcases the music's pioneers and young turks.

In the 1940s and 1950s the *orquesta Tejana* movement was taking shape in south Texas towns and cities. Favored by the Mexican American middle class, this genre borrowed from the Cuban ballroom sound, American big band, and jazz. Some *conjunto* fans mocked it as "high-tone," which came to be spelled in phonetic Spanish as *jaiton,* while *orquesta* mavens dismissed *conjunto* as cantina music. Although the genres were rivals and in some ways opposites, they were destined to collide and produce a new musical strain.

In 1954 Isidro "El Indio" López, who played the guitar and sax and had recorded with *orquestas* and *conjuntos,* sang for a recording session that combined the Juan Colorado Orchestra's big band sound with accordion. This session created the fusion of *conjunto* and *orquesta* that led to modern Tejano. López formed his own orchestra in 1956 and toured successfully using the new hybrid sound, scoring hits such as *Nuevo Contrato* and *Emoción Pasajera*. However, the music was not yet known as Tejano. It was called *música alegre* or Mexican music. In the 1960s other hybrid artists emerged such as Sunny Ozuna, Little Joe and the Latinaires, Roy Montelongo, and Freddie Martínez, acts that were smaller than the traditional *orquestas* but still featured horn sections.

In the 1970s, with the emerging Chicano civil rights movement, artists began to combine a variety of rhythms and express a social consciousness. One of those top artists, Little Joe, born in 1940 in Temple, Texas, was influenced by *conjunto* and *orquesta,* but also by rhythm and blues, rock, country, and salsa. In 1970, he covered the traditional folk song *Las Nubes,* a song about struggle and ambition that resonated with farmworkers who were trying to organize for better wages and Mexican Americans in general who had had enough of discrimination.

Other influential hits followed. The San Antonio–based Royal Jesters used sax and electric guitar and recorded the pride anthem *Soy Chicano* ("I Am Chicano") in 1972. The lyrics included the lines "soy Tejano" and "soy Mexicano," helping to foster a Tejano identity and popularizing the term *Tejano.*

While these songs expressed a social awareness, the original *conjunto* topical song form, *corrido,* had largely faded, although it continued to thrive in the related *norteño* genre. In the Rio Grande Valley town of Edinburg, Roberto Pulido rose in the mid-1970s by incorporating sax and accordion, a template that resurrected López's innovation and would be used by artists like David Lee Garza y los Musicales, Emilio Navaira, and La Tropa F.

The decade also saw the emergence of pop-leaning Tejano groups, Houston's La Mafia and Brownsville's Mazz, who used impressive sound-and-light shows while dressing and preening like rock stars. The groups had also adopted the *cumbia* rhythm, which originated in Colombia and had, by the 1970s, become a popular step in Mexico and Central America.

Another sign of Tejano's ascendance was the inaugural Tejano Music Awards ceremony, held at San Antonio's Henry B. González Convention Center in 1981. Approximately 1,500 fans attended. As Tejano's popularity grew in the 1980s, major labels began to pay more attention. In 1986, Little Joe signed with CBS Discos, becoming the first Tejano act to sign with a major label.

The multinational labels also wanted to maximize their investments by signing artists who would sell well internationally. They encouraged the Texas-based artists to appeal to the broader Latin market

© LEONEL MONROY/LATIN FOCUS

Musicians from the Tejano band Grupo Intocable.

by titling their albums in Spanish (many of them gave English titles to their records, although nearly all the songs were in Spanish). Tejano artists had long met skepticism in interior Mexico, where their Spanglish dialect was viewed with suspicion. But with free trade and technology making the world smaller, groups like La Mafia (signed to Sony Discos) and Mazz (on EMI Latin) were able to make it big south of the border. Both groups added more ballads to their repertoire to seem less "regional" and tailored their live sets depending on where they were playing—more polkas for Texas, and more tropical *cumbias* and ballads in central Mexico. By the early 1990s, the Tejano Music Awards were being held in San Antonio's cavernous Alamodome to crowds in excess of 25,000.

A youthful band called Selena y Los Dinos emerged in the late 1980s, specializing in sunny, keyboard-fueled *cumbias* with sing-along choruses and touches of reggae. The Corpus Christi–based group scored early 1990s hits like *La Carcacha* and *Como la Flor*. The lead singer, Selena, was shot and killed on March 31, 1995, by her former fan club president Yolanda Saldivar, who had been accused of embezzling funds from the band. The loss of Tejano's biggest star coincided with a slowdown in the general Tejano market. Labels had gone on a signing binge and were now overburdened with no-name or copycat acts. Believing that Tejano was losing its creative edge, young fans began to drift to hip-hop or *norteño*, which were (rightfully) seen as having more socially conscious lyrics. Several groups in the mid-1990s began incorporating an edgy new sound—a fusion of *norteño* and Tejano, as exemplified by such hybrid artists as Intocable, Michael Salgado, Bobby Pulido (Roberto's son), and Grupo Control.

In the new millennium, Tejano has returned to its pre-1990s gold rush, with many artists back on independent record labels, doing their own marketing and booking. The Tejano Music Awards no longer required the Alamodome's space and were held at a large San Antonio club, with attendance down to about 3,000. While it was a tough letdown, the adversity was likely to engender a create-or-get-out ethic that would spur creativity and lay the foundation for a new revival in the cyclical genre.

RELATED ARTICLES

Music, Popular; Selena; Vocalists, Popular.

FURTHER READING

Burr, Ramiro. *The Billboard Guide to Tejano and Regional Mexican Music.* New York: Billboard Bks., 1999.

Mendoza, Lydia. *Lydia Mendoza: A Family Autobiography.* Houston, Tex.: Arte Público Press, 1993.

Peña, Manuel. *The Mexican American Orquesta: Music, Culture, and the Dialectic of Conflict.* Austin: Univ. of Tex. Press, 1999.

RAMIRO BURR
DOUG SHANNON

TELENOVELAS

The *telenovela* is the most popular kind of program on Spanish-language television, drawing millions of loyal viewers and attracting millions of dollars in advertising. Although considered soap operas by many, the *telenovelas* watched by U.S. Latino audiences are quite different from their English-language counterparts in both form and presentation. The structure of the typical *telenovela* is different from its English-language cousin in its defined length. U.S. soaps often go on for years and characters on them often depart the series, returning years later to new storylines. The typical *telenovela,* however, lasts only several intense months. Most of these series consist of 180–200 episodes.

The history of the *telenovela* dates to the 1950s, when television first made inroads into Latin America. Cuba was an early producer of *telenovelas*; Cuban producers were closely aligned with U.S. advertisers eager to expand into the Latin American market that Hollywood had demonstrated could produce enormous profits. By the 1980s, the number of producers had grown tremendously. Mexico, with its tradition of prolific film production, was the leader, but Argentina, Venezuela, and Brazil were also producing and distributing *telenovelas* internationally, including to the United States, where the Hispanic market was catching the attention of advertisers.

The programming strategies employed by broadcasters of *telenovelas* differ greatly from the approach taken by U.S. networks. Mainstream English-language soap operas are broadcast primarily during the day. But the largest U.S. Spanish networks, Telemundo and Univisión, position their *telenovelas* at night—during prime time hours—a sign of their importance to the broadcaster. For Spanish-language broadcasters, *telenovelas* are central to their overall programming.

Telenovelas, very popular with both men and women, are among the most profitable programs, earning consistently high ratings for their broadcasters. In the late 1980s, the Telemundo Network, in a programming strategy against its rival Univisión, opted not to present *telenovelas* in the evenings and saw its ratings drop severely as a result. Today, U.S. Latino consumers have an opportunity to view *telenovelas* at different times of the day, on a variety of media outlets—traditional broadcast, cable, and dish services. There is even talk of offering *telenovelas* on the Internet. In the United States the *telenovela* has become the stuff of water cooler and lunchroom conversations for many Latinas and Latinos. The relatively high number of Latin American producers assures a steady supply programs.

Melodrama is a key component of the *telenovela,* with the central characters in the stories often a romantically involved couple. The source of dramatic tension in the programs usually stems from obstacles to their union. *Telenovelas* traditionally relied on simple storylines, but as the *telenovela* developed and the number of producers expanded, the traditional form evolved. The melodrama remains, but audience sophistication demanded thornier issues. The once-taboo subjects of sex, race, and class have become dominant themes in contemporary *telenovelas*. Another important change occurred as a result of competition from upstart *telenovela* producers in Venezuela and Brazil. In Mexico, *telenovelas* were exclusively taped on soundstages, but Venezuelan and Brazilian *telenovelas* raised the production bar by shooting episodes on location, forcing Mexican producers to do the same.

The leading producer of *telenovelas* seen in the United States is Televisa, a Mexican television company and the largest producer of Spanish-language television programs in the world. For years Televisa, controlled by Mexican media magnate Emilio Azcárraga, had a stranglehold on the U.S. Spanish-language market because it owned SIN, the Spanish International Network and SIN's "owned and operated" U.S. stations. Azcárraga was for a time considered the wealthiest man in all of Latin America. The relationship between SIN and Televisa was understandably close, and the network relied heavily on its Mexican parent for programming—especially for *telenovelas*. In 1986, however, the Federal Communications Commission forced the sale of SIN, finding the network to be in violation of a U.S. law that

© JIMMY DORANTES/LATIN FOCUS

Actors in a *telenovela.*

prohibits a foreign company from owning U.S. television stations. SIN was bought by Hallmark Cards, which changed the name of the network to Univisión.

Hallmark Cards distanced itself from Televisa and drastically changed the way Univisión acquired programming. Fully half of its shows were produced in the United States, including a *telenovela.* But the Hallmark era was short-lived. Unable to make an adequate return on its investment, Hallmark sold the network to a syndicate headed by television mogul Jerry Perenchio, a former partner of producer Norman Lear in the production company that developed *The Jeffersons.* The other members of the syndicate that bought Univisión were the Venezuelan billionaire Cisneros brothers and, ironically, Emilio Azcárraga and Televisa. Perenchio retained a 50 percent stake in the company to avoid foreign ownership issues. Despite significant protests by U.S. Latino groups, the sale was approved.

Following the sale of Univisión, Spanish-language programming produced in the United States declined. Acquiring programming from Televisa and other Latin American producers proved to be cheaper than producing it domestically. But the U.S. Latino market has proven too powerful to ignore and the networks have responded: Univisión presented a *telenovela—Dos Mujeres*—that featured a story set on the U.S.-Mexican border and, perhaps more important, included a U.S. Latino character, played by the well-known Latino actor Erik Estrada. In 2002 Univisión chief Jerry Perenchio announced *Te Amaré en Silencio,* a U.S.-produced *telenovela.*

The only other major source of *telenovelas* produced in the United States is the Telemundo network. Established to compete with Univisión for the booming Latino market, Telemundo was created by investors Saul Steinberg and Henry Silverman in 1986. The two men started by acquiring stations and then moved into production. According to Patricia Constantakis-Valdés, by 1991 more than 50 percent of Telemundo's programming was produced in the United States. Among its U.S.-produced shows was *Angélica Mi Vida,* based on the lives of Latinos in the United States. In 1996 Telemundo formed an alliance with Groupo Azteca in Mexico to coproduce programming for its U.S. audience. Given the dominance of Televisa in Mexico, Globo in Brazil, as well as Argentine and Venezuelan producers, U.S.-produced *telenovelas* are unlikely to have much opportunity for export and large-scale production.

Because of efficiencies in the production of *telenovelas* in Mexico and other countries, the U.S. Latino audience has been largely denied television that reflects its own cultural space. Nevertheless, the genre remains hugely popular and may serve a larger purpose. Vicki Mayer, in the study "Living Telenovelas/Telenovelizing Life: Mexican American Girls' Identities and Transnational Telenovelas" points out that for some Mexican American girls in San Antonio, Texas, *telenovelas* are a way to maintain a connection to Mexico. These and other studies suggest that these serialized television presentations serve a special purpose for Latinos struggling to carve out a cultural identity within a white-dominated society. The retention of language, for instance, is cited as one reason Latino viewers watch *telenovelas.*

RELATED ARTICLES

Film; Television.

FURTHER READING

Barrera, Vivian, and Denise D. Bielby. "Places, Faces, and Other Things: The Cultural Experience of Telenovela Viewing among Latinos in the United States." *Journal of Popular Culture* 34, no. 4 (Spring 2001).

Mayer, Vicki. "Living Telenovelas/Telenovelizing Life: Mexican American Girls' Identities and Transnational Telenovelas." *Journal of Communication* (September 2003).

JOSEPH TOVARES

TELEVISION

Until relatively recently Latinos were largely absent from the small screen. With the exception of Desi Arnaz on I Love Lucy, their contributions to society were rarely seen in American living rooms. But not anymore. Today, Latinos play an increasingly important role in television as viewers, producers, and actors. This entry looks at Latinos and television from two views. First, the history and development of Spanish-Language Television in the United States, followed by Latinos in English-Language Television.

SPANISH-LANGUAGE TELEVISION IN THE UNITED STATES

The creation and development of Spanish-language television in the United States is the result of several interrelated factors, of which the most prominent are the growth and increased purchasing power of the Spanish-speaking population, changes in federal regulations, such as making available UHF (ultra-high-frequency) channels for television transmissions, and technological innovations, including satellite communication. The three largest Spanish-language television networks currently operating in the United States, Univisión, Telemundo, and Azteca América, are, to a large extent, the result of the interaction of these factors.

In examining the development of Spanish-language television in the United States, it is important to keep in mind the geographic area where Spanish-language television first found success—the Southwest. This region had been, until about the mid-1800s, Spanish and then Mexican territory. Then and now these lands had a significant number of Spanish-speaking residents. In the second half of the 20th century, the number of Spanish-speaking residents in the United States grew dramatically. For example, in 1961 the U.S. Census counted just under 7 million Latinos, about 4 percent of the national population. The majority of them were of Mexican ancestry and resided in the Southwest. By 1990 the U.S. population of Latinos numbered 26 million, almost 10 percent of the population. By 2002, the Bureau of the Census reported 34.5 million Latinos in the United States. Much of this growth is attributable to immigration, both legal and undocumented.

The wealth of the U.S. Latino community has also increased. The number of Latinos who are members of the middle class has increased steadily since

World War II. Latino buying power was estimated to be about $440 billion in 2004 and is projected to grow to almost $1 trillion by the end of the decade. Latinos in the United States are considered to be an attractive audience by media managers because, as one media executive put it, they are "the wealthiest Hispanics in the world."

Changes in government policies, such as the Federal Communications Commission (FCC) making available UHF channels for the transmission of television signals, also helped promote Spanish-language television. The use of satellite technology to synchronize the schedules of network owned and affiliated stations gave the Spanish International Network, today known as Univisión, a more efficient system of program distribution and helped consolidate the Latino audience for national advertisers.

In 1955 the first Spanish-language television station in the United States—KCOR-TV in San Antonio, Texas—went on the air. Before KCOR-TV was launched, however, entertainers and managers had negotiated for television airtime on English-language stations or part-time Spanish-language stations. They saw potential in the Spanish-language audience.

Spanish-language television programming in the United States started soon after English-language television programming went on the air. Entrepreneurs in the Mexican American community, or those with close ties to the Mexican American community, began to explore the possibility of exploiting the new technology of television by buying time from English-language television stations and programming that time with Spanish-language content. This arrangement of buying one or two hours of airtime, or "blocks," is known as "brokering." The blocks of time purchased from station owners were generally the hours when viewership was low, early Saturday afternoons, for example. Selling time to Latino entrepreneurs relieved station owners of having to spend money to buy programming for parts of the day that did not attract a large English-language audience. At the same time producers of Spanish-language programs did not have to pay station owners the large sums required to reach audiences during prime-time viewing hours. Another incentive for station owners to sell time for Spanish-language programming was the Federal Communications Commission's requirement that broadcasters serve the public interest. By selling an hour or two of airtime

every week for live, Spanish-language programming that featured local talent, the stations could satisfy this FCC requirement.

Among the first brokered Spanish-language television programs was *Buscando Estrellas*. In 1951 Mexican-born José (Pepe) Pérez del Río approached Pioneer Flour Mills in San Antonio and suggested that it sponsor a Spanish-language television program that would showcase local talent. The variety and talent-search program produced by del Río was broadcast live on Sunday afternoons on KERN-TV, Channel 5 (today KENS-TV). The program, which remained on the air for three years, is important because it gave artists and entertainers from Texas and Mexico exposure to a mass audience in a language it could understand and see performers with whom it could identify.

Buscando Estrellas was recorded on film and sent to television stations in Texas cities, including Harlingen, Laredo, and Corpus Christi. As had been done with KERN-TV, time was also brokered from English-language stations in those cities.

The host of *Buscando Estrellas,* del Río, went on to host a Mexican cinema program, *Cine en Español,* also on KERN-TV, which aired from 1956 to 1961. *Cine en Español* showed films from Mexico, Spain, and Argentina.

Anecdotal evidence exists that at about the same time a similar process for getting Spanish-language television programs on air was being initiated on the East Coast. Two radio personalities, Don Pessante and Don Méndez, began hosting what may have been the first U.S.-Latino-oriented television entertainment programs when they brokered time from local English-language television stations to air their entertainment programs. The first Spanish-language television broadcast in the United States may have occurred in the early 1950s when *El Show Hispano* aired over then-commercial station WATV, Channel 13, in New York; it ran for about two years. The program consisted of music, skits, and a 15-minute newscast.

In the 1960s Spanish-language programming on English-language television stations made its appearance in cities with significant numbers of Spanish-language residents. Los Angeles, Houston, Miami, Phoenix, Tucson, and Chicago all had television stations that aired some Spanish-language programs. The pattern of development was similar in all these cities. A local company would sponsor an hour-long program that featured musical acts and skits. Many of these programs were produced by individuals with experience in radio.

Univisión Network

The Spanish International Network (SIN), which changed its name to Univisión in 1987, started airing in the United States over KCOR-TV, Channel 41, in San Antonio, Texas, in 1955. Its broadcast "day" was from 5:00 P.M. to midnight. The station depended heavily on television programs and films from the studios of Emilio Azcárraga in Mexico City.

Channel 41 was on the UHF band that had been authorized to operate for television broadcasting by the FCC in 1952. Prior to this FCC ruling, television sets made in the United States could receive only very high frequency (VHF) broadcast signals. During the early days of television the three major networks, the American Broadcasting Company (ABC), the Columbia Broadcasting System (CBS), and the National Broadcasting Company (NBC), encouraged the production of television sets that could receive only VHF signals, the frequency they used to transmit their own broadcast signals. In 1952, however, the FCC ruled that both VHF and UHF frequencies could be used to transmit television signals. This ruling made more channels available and created a need for more programming for those channels. However, anyone who wanted to receive programs transmitted through UHF channels had to buy a converter box that allowed for the reception and decoding of UHF signals. Although the FCC ruling that UHF could be used to transmit television signals was made in 1952, not until 1964 did the FCC requirement that all manufacturers of television sets include both VHF and UHF tuners in the sets go into effect. Before 1964 many English-language stations using UHF frequencies found competition against established VHF stations difficult because viewers were unwilling to pay extra for the UHF converter box. Many Spanish-speaking viewers, however, were willing to buy UHF boxes because no alternatives existed for them.

Raúl Cortéz, who was behind KCOR-AM, the first Spanish-language radio station in the United States, was also the first owner of KCOR-TV, which had a program schedule consisting of variety and entertainment programs that showcased talent from Mexico. The programs were often carried simultaneously by both KCOR-AM and KCOR-TV. The rest of the television broadcast schedule consisted of films and recorded programs from Mexico.

A major problem for the owners and managers of KCOR-TV was advertising. Many companies and advertising agencies were hesitant about buying time on the Spanish-language station. In the early days of television, Latino viewers were not counted by ratings services such as Neilsen Media Research. According to Emilio Nicolás, the first general manager of KCOR-TV, during the 1940s and 1950s many Latinos preferred to downplay their heritage. Blatant discriminatory practices and assimilationist politics encouraged a "melting pot" philosophy rather than a "multicultural" approach to ethnic identity. Such an environment made measuring the Latino audience for Spanish-language television particularly difficult, which, in turn, made it almost impossible for the station to contract with major advertisers. Cortéz sold the station to an Anglo organization, which took the call letters KUAL. Similar problems in contracting with major advertisers continued to plague the new owners.

In 1961 KUAL-TV was sold to Mexican media baron Don Emilio Azcárraga Vidauerreta, the man behind Mexico's radio and television systems, who changed the station's call letters to KWEX. Azcárraga's purchase was the first step in extending his communications empire into the United States. Eventually Azcárraga, together with his son, Emilio Azcárraga Milmo, and U.S. business partner René Anselmo, would develop the Spanish International Network (SIN) in the United States.

One problem the new company had to address was the FCC's restriction on foreign ownership of broadcast entities. In 1962 SIN purchased station KMEX-TV, Channel 34, in Los Angeles; Azcárraga got around the restrictions on foreign ownership by forming the Spanish International Communications Corporation (SICC), which was run by René Anselmo, who was from Boston and of Italian and Chilean ancestry. SICC was financed by Azcárraga, who legally owned only 20 percent of the company. Unlike ownership of a broadcast license, which limits foreign ownership, television networks have no such restriction. Azcárraga and Anselmo established the Spanish International Network, which bought programs from Azcárraga's television studios in Mexico City and distributed them to SIN and its affiliated stations in the United States. SIN also began selling commercial time for the network's stations. Thus, shows from Azcárraga's studios in Mexico City kept programming costs down, while the strategy of selling commercial time on the network was attractive to a number of major advertisers. This business arrangement proved to be quite lucrative because programming produced in Mexican pesos earned profits in U.S. dollars.

In 1968 New York station WXTV, Channel 41, was added to the network. In the early 1970s stations WLTV, Channel 23, in Miami and KFTV, Channel 21, in Fresno-Hanford were purchased. Other stations, in San Francisco and Phoenix, owned by SICC/SIN partners were also added to the network. Television stations in Albuquerque, Chicago, Corpus Christi, Houston, and Sacramento, which had no previous corporate ties to SIN, became affiliated with the network. In Mexico, SIN's parent company, Televisa, S.A., owned several stations along the Mexican border, which served viewers in the U.S. stations in Juárez, Mexicali, Nuevo Laredo, and Tijuana all broadcast their signals to viewers in the Mexico and U.S. borderland area.

In 1972, with the death of Azcárraga Vidaurreta, his son, Emilio Azcárraga Milmo, took over the family enterprise. Under his leadership SIN became the first television network to distribute programs by way of satellite. This important technological innovation, along with low-power satellite repeaters located in smaller Spanish-language markets, helped SIN cut costs and increase efficiency. The SIN network also centralized the process of buying airtime and in this way reduced the cost of reaching the Latino audience.

Until 1976 all television networks recorded programs on videotape and sent those videotapes from one affiliated station to another. A station would air the tape and send it on to the next station. Often tapes were lost, damaged, or arrived late. Human error also sometimes caused the wrong program to air. National advertisers could not be guaranteed that their ads would run as planned. When the SIN network began to use satellite technology to distribute programming, confidence of national advertisers that their ads would run as scheduled increased.

At the same time that SIN was broadcasting by way of satellite, Azcárraga Milmo and some other investors reorganized Telesistema Mexicano, which had been formed in the mid-1950s in Mexico, and renamed it Televisa. The purpose of Televisa was to produce and distribute live, Spanish-language programming to Spanish-speaking audiences around the world, but especially to the U.S. Spanish-speaking audience.

In 1979, as cable television franchises spread across the country, SIN began to pay cable operators to carry its signal into subscribers' homes. The FCC also gave the SIN network the go-ahead to operate several low-power television stations with signals that cover an area 10 to 15 miles (16 to 24 km) from the point of transmission.

By the early 1980s Spanish-language television stations under the SIN/SICC umbrella were reaching 3.3 million Latino households in the United States. In 1980, however, the FCC had brought action against SICC after the Spanish Radio Broadcasters Association accused SICC of being under foreign control, a violation of FCC rules. Two proceedings followed: a stockholder derivative suit first filed in 1976 and the FCC inquiry into foreign ownership and control. In 1986 a legal ruling against SICC ordered the network to sell its stations to a U.S.-based organization. Hallmark Cards stepped in to buy the stations. In 1987 SIN and SICC were renamed Univisión. Eventually, Hallmark, together with First Capital, an investment group, came to own the SIN network and several of its affiliated stations.

In 1992 Univisión was once again up for sale. This allowed Televisa to reenter the U.S. television market; Televisa was careful to follow FCC rules on foreign ownership. The majority owner, holding 50 percent of the Univisión Network Partnership, was Hollywood producer A. Jerrold Perenchio, who had previously owned Spanish-language television stations (see below). Televisa owned 25 percent of Univisión while the Venezuelan Cisneros Grupo de Compañías (CGC), owned the other 25 percent. Perenchio also owned 75 percent of the Univisión Station Group, the actual stations that made up the network, while Televisa and Venevisión each owned approximately 12 percent, to conform with foreign ownership restrictions.

Univisión is exploring new avenues to keep the company at the forefront of delivering news and entertainment to viewers around the world. In 2002 Univisión.com was targeting Latinos who are online with news and information but later focused on delivering only entertainment. The largest markets for Latinos online are New York and Los Angeles, each with about 1.6 million Latinos online and Miami, with just over 700,000 Latinos online.

Univisión also launched the television network Telefutura, which targets a younger Latino audience. Galavision Network, another Univisión property, offers cable subscribers news, sports, and entertainment programming. In the summer of 2002, Univisión also announced a proposed $3.5-billion merger with Hispanic Broadcasting Corporation, finalized in 2003. This merger combines the nation's largest Spanish-language television company with the largest Spanish-language radio company.

Telemundo

In 1986, Saul Steinberg, chairman of the board and chief executive officer of Reliance Capital Group, and Henry Silverman bought John Blair & Company, which owned television stations in Miami and San Juan, Puerto Rico. This was the beginning of what would eventually become Telemundo Group, Inc. With the corporate buyout of John Blair & Company, the Reliance Capital Group found itself with two television stations in predominantly Spanish-language markets, WSCV-TV, Channel 51, in Miami and WKAQ-TV, Channel 2, in San Juan. Station WSCV-TV had been an English-language subscription station, while WKAQ-TV had been part of the Fundación Angel Ramos, a media conglomerate that transmitted programming to affiliated stations throughout Puerto Rico.

This network, however, actually began in 1985, when Reliance bought into Estrella Communications, Inc., a company that had been established for the purpose of buying KBSC, Channel 52, in Los Angeles. That station was owned by Columbia Pictures and Jerrold Perenchio, who set it up in the late 1970s to compete against television station KMEX-TV. Station KBSC-TV split its broadcast schedule between English-language and Spanish-language programming, offering 95 hours of programming per week in Spanish. Most of the Spanish-language programming was supplied by Imevisión, the Mexican government's troubled TV Channel 13. The Reliance Capital Group bought part of KBSC-TV in 1985 and changed the call letters to KVEA-TV. By the end of 1986, Reliance had bought out the remaining stockholders and thus became the sole owner of the television station. In 1986 Capital Reliance Group also bought station WNJU-TV in New Jersey, which served the New York metropolitan area.

Telemundo continued to grow and develop as it bought more stations in the United States. In 1987 it acquired National Group Television, Inc., which owned and operated station KSTS-TV, Channel 48, which aired in the San Jose–San Francisco viewing area. The following year it bought KTMD-TV, Channel 48, in Houston. WSNS-TV, Channel 26, in Chicago became a Telemundo affiliate. Previously, WSNS-TV had been affiliated with Univisión. In 1990 Telemundo entered the San Antonio market by purchasing a majority of the stock of Nueva Vista, the company that owned KVDA-TV, Channel 60, in that market. With these television stations, Telemundo started the 1990s with potential access to 80 percent of the Latino households in the United States.

Initially Telemundo aired *telenovelas,* or soap operas, entertainment programs, and variety shows provided by WKAQ-TV in Puerto Rico and programs from Mexico, Venezuela, Brazil, Argentina, and Spain. *Telenovelas,* however, made up almost two-thirds of the prime time schedule. The *telenovela Angélica, Mi Vida* was produced in Puerto Rico and was designed to appeal to a diverse Latino market by weaving together the stories of Mexican, Puerto Rican, and Cuban families.

In July of 1988 Telemundo launched "MTV Internacional" a one-hour version of MTV programming. The show was distributed to teenage audiences in Latin American countries. By January of 1992 the Telemundo Group controlled a network that included six full-power stations and four low-power stations. In addition, 6 full-power and 16 low-power stations were affiliated with the network. The network's signal was carried by several cable companies that served 14 of the 50 states and the District of Columbia. Across the border, three stations in Tijuana, Juárez, and Matamoros transmitted to San Diego, California, El Paso, Texas and McAllen–Brownsville, Texas, respectively. Relying on the satellite *Spacenet II,* by 1992 the Telemundo network group could reach 84 percent of U.S. Hispanic households.

In 1997 Telemundo was bought by Sony and Liberty Media for $750 million. The NBC network, which is owned by the General Electric Company, bought Telemundo in 2001 for $2.7 billion. Thus, NBC became the first English-language television network to invest in the growing Latino television market.

Launched in the fall of 2001, Mun2 (pronounced "mundos") is Telemundo's effort to reach a younger

Latino audience. The cable network offers Latino music, talk shows, game shows, and comedy.

TV Azteca

A later entry into Spanish-language television in the United States is Azteca América, a wholly owned subsidiary of TV Azteca, S.A. de C.V., the second largest producer of Spanish-language television programs in the world. Launched in 2000, Azteca América planned to begin broadcasting by the end of that year; however, its competitors, Univisión and Telemundo, began an aggressive campaign to buy stations and sign up affiliates, attempting to block the entry of Azteca América into the U.S. market. Nevertheless, in 2004 Azteca América consisted of stations in 24 markets that could reach 60 percent of the U.S. Latino population. To attract the lucrative national advertising accounts a network must reach a threshold of at least 70 percent of the Latino audience.

Azteca América was specifically set up by TV Azteca to enter the U.S. Latino market; TV Azteca distributes its library of video programs to its stations in the United States. Many of these *telenovelas* were produced for Telemundo at TV Azteca's digital production facility in Mexico City. The other Azteca América partner, Pappas Telecasting Companies of Los Angeles, is the largest private owner of television stations in the United States. Initially, Azteca América had been relying primarily on low-power stations in secondary cities located in the western United States. One important exception to this pattern was the purchase of station KAZA-TV in Los Angeles. Later, Azteca América added stations in markets such as Houston, San Francisco–Oakland–San Jose, and Santa Barbara.

Investors and Spanish-language television owners and managers are following closely the development of Azteca América. Some investors believe that the continued growth and increased wealth of the Latino community can support at least three Spanish-language television networks. Others believe that splitting the Latino audience three ways will only reduce the profits of all three networks.

Concern has also been voiced about taking money away from the English-language networks. Since its inception, Spanish-language television owners and managers have complained that their audiences have been undervalued. As the Latino audience in the United States continues to grow in both numbers and buying power, the Spanish-language networks can be expected to increase the cost of reaching this segment of the population. This increase will pull advertising dollars away from the English-language networks.

Conclusion

The growth of Spanish-language television in the United States was the result of a combination of factors: the increase in the Latino population, government regulations such as the FCC ruling to allow UHF frequencies for television broadcasting, and changes in technology, such as satellite communication. These factors provided the foundation upon which entrepreneurs built Univisión and Telemundo and that allowed the third Spanish-language network in the United States, Azteca América, to enter the market. With the growth and development of the Internet, many television networks, including Spanish-language television networks, are exploring ways to reach audiences through that medium. No one can predict where such efforts will lead, the only certainty is that as the Latino population in the United States grows in numbers and wealth, as it has since the 1950s, owners of mass media will find ways to serve that community.

RELATED ARTICLES

Film; Telenovelas; Stereotypes and Stereotyping.

FURTHER READING

Gutiérrez, Félix. "Mexico's Television Network in the United States: The Case of Spanish International Network." In *Proceedings of the Sixth Annual Telecommunications Policy Research Conference.* Ed. by H. S. Dordick. Lexington, Mass.: D.C. Heath, 1979.

Rodríguez, América. *Making Latino News: Race, Language, Class.* Thousand Oaks, Calif.: Sage, 1999.

Sinclair, John. *Latin American Television: A Global View.* New York: Oxford Univ. Press, 1999.

Subervi-Veléz, Frederico A., et al. "Mass Communication and Hispanics." In *Sociology Volume of the Handbook of Hispanic Cultures in the United States.* Ed. by F. Padilla. Houston, Tex.: Arte Público Press, 1994.

RAÚL DAMACIO TOVARES

LATINOS IN ENGLISH-LANGUAGE TELEVISION

In 1999 the National Council of La Raza (NCLR) called for a boycott of the major networks—ABC, CBS, NBC, and Fox—over the issue of underrepresentation of Latinos in broadcast television. The NAACP (National Association for the Advancement of Colored People) joined the effort, which included former congressmen Esteban Torres and Norman Mineta. Torres said that the "goal of the boycott is to achieve a 'long-lasting, verifiable agreement that will create a rapid inclusion of minorities in programming as well as ownership.'" The boycott, termed a "Brown Out" by the NCLR, was in response to a Screen Actors Guild study that found Latinos had a 2 percent visibility on prime-time television, although they made up 11 percent of the population.

The issue of underrepresentation of Latinos on television is as old as the industry itself. Against tough odds, however, many Latinos—dating back to the 1950s—had managed to carve out a piece of real estate in what Newton Minnow, chairman of the Federal Communications Commission, would later call "the vast wasteland." The first Latino to achieve success on television was Desi Arnaz. No Latino since has come close to matching his accomplishments. Desiderio Alberto Arnaz III was born in Santiago, Cuba, in 1917 and by 1935 had started his career in show business performing with the Xavier Cugat band. In 1939 he got a part in a Broadway production and the next year met and married Lucille Ball. Ten years later Arnaz and Ball convinced reluctant CBS executives to green-light the *I Love Lucy* show for the 1951–1952 season. The show was a big hit and ran through 1957. But Arnaz and Ball's genius was in the production techniques for and distribution of the program. The series was shot on film using as many as four simultaneous cameras, thus assuring a high-quality archive. In exchange for a reduced salary, the prescient Arnaz negotiated a deal that gave their company, Desilu, ownership of the programs once they had aired. The quality of the content and the post-broadcast ownership made reruns and syndication possible. According to B. R. Smith, writing for the Museum of Television History Web site, Desilu eventually resold the rights to *I Love Lucy* to CBS for more than $4 million, which allowed the couple to start a television empire. Arnaz is still considered a visionary in the production and business of television.

Latinos did appear on television in the 1950s. The most successful was Duncan Renaldo and Leo Carillio in *The Cisco Kid*. The program ran from 1950 to 1955 and filmed more than 150 half-hour episodes. Other Latino actors also worked in television during this time, mostly in Westerns: *Gunsmoke*, *Wagon Train*, *Cheyenne*, and *Bonanza* all had Latino actors in small roles. Most were stereotypical characters—*bandidos*, peons, and hot-tempered women. According to Luis Reyes and Peter Rubie in *Hispanics in Hollywood*, Ricardo Montalban, Fernando Lamas, and Rita Moreno all worked in television during the 1950s and managed on the small screen to escape the stereotyping that was so prevalent in the movies. Montalban told *TV Guide* in 1970 that "It is to television that I owe my freedom from the bondage of the Latin Lover image. Television came along and gave me parts to chew on. It gave me wings as an actor." Montalban's experience was the exception; for many Latino actors, television brought little but the usual demeaning roles. Latina actors, in particular, had difficulties finding meaningful roles in the early years of television.

The 1960s and 1970s saw a slight increase in the number of Latino actors as television executives explored the urban United States as a setting for television series. *Barreta*, *Kojak*, *Hill Street Blues*, and *Hunter* hit the airwaves with the occasional Latino actor. But Latino cops in these crime genre series were few and far between. Most Latinos on these series were victims and criminals. Reyes and Rubie in *Hispanics in Hollywood* point out, however, that a number of Latino actors during this time did not necessarily play Latino characters. Among them was Italian Puerto Rican Joe Santos, who played a detective on *The Rockford Files*, the English Mexican Lynda Carter, the star of *Wonder Woman*, and the German Mexican Catherine Bach, who had the role of Daisy Duke on the *Dukes of Hazard*. Rita Moreno gave one of the most memorable performances by a Latina actor playing a non-Latina—the veteran actress had a recurring role as Rita Capkovic, a Polish prostitute, on *The Rockford Files*. Moreno, who had already won an Oscar, a Tony, and an Emmy, picked up her second Emmy for her role in an episode titled "The Paper Place" in 1978.

Latinos were not only succeeding on screen; behind the camera Latinos were also making inroads—notably on the Public Broadcasting Service (PBS). *The Ballad of Gregorio Cortéz* and *Seguin* were both produced in 1982 and received critical acclaim. *The Ballad of Gregorio Cortéz* was written by Víctor Villaseñor and starred Edward James Olmos, Pepe Serna, and Rosana DeSoto. *Seguin* was directed by Jesús Treviño and produced by Severo Pérez. Both aired on the PBS series American Playhouse. Although both were well-received, they were not without critics. Américo Paredes, the legendary folklorist and the author of the book upon which *The Ballad of Gregorio Cortéz* was based, was unhappy with the final cut and distanced himself from the film. *Seguin* was criticized for its overly romantic, one-dimensional view of Tejanos.

In the 1980s and 1990s Latinos made small advances as a few actors secured recurring roles on popular prime-time series. Among the most notable was Jimmy Smits in *NYPD Blue*, and Héctor Elizondo in *Chicago Hope*. While neither Smits nor Elizondo was a lead character, they were both regulars on the series and perhaps more important, the actors played the parts of professionals—Smits a detective and Elizondo the head of surgery at a major hospital. Smits, whose parents are from Puerto Rico and Suriname, is a classically trained actor. He told writer Jae-Ha Kim of the *Chicago Sun Times,* "I think that television is beginning to reflect the cur-

rent change of society's attitude toward minorities. Not all Latinos are gang members or drug pushers, and television is beginning to come around and present us in another light. Hopefully my character won't be one of the few minority role models on television."

Elizondo is the son on a Basque father and a Puerto Rican mother. Like Smits, he was born and raised in New York. But Elizondo was considerably older and had witnessed the Latinization of the city from the 1940s onward. Unlike many other Latino actors, Elizondo managed to avoid stereotypes, playing non-Latino roles for most of his career. He had a successful run on the stage before he moved to film. Elizondo appeared in a number of television programs including *Columbo, Kojak,* and *All In The Family*. He starred in the four-hour miniseries *Burden of Proof* and worked on a number of public television projects as well.

TALLER DE TELEVISION INFANTIL

Illustration of the characters from *Plaza Sesamo,* the Spanish-language version of the popular children's program *Sesame Street*.

In 1994 Elizondo assumed the role of Dr. Philip Watters, the head of surgery on the show *Chicago Hope*. The character of the stoic Watters earned the actor an Emmy in 1997. Elizondo credits other Latino actors who came before him. Among his heroes are Desi Arnaz, Ricardo Montalban, and Rita Moreno.

Other Latino actors also found success on television during this time. Mexican American actor Edward James Olmos found new fame playing Lieutenant Castillo on the hit series *Miami Vice,* and Puerto Rican Jon Seda won a coveted recurring role as detective Paul Falsone on the critically acclaimed *Homicide: Life on the Streets.*

As the United States entered the new millennium the story of Latinos on television came full circle. For the first time since Desi Arnaz starred in *I Love Lucy*, a Latino was once again the star of a network series—the *George Lopez Show*. In addition, a series orphaned by CBS was adopted by PBS and became the first Latino drama in the history of broadcast television—*American Family*.

ABC / THE EVERETT COLLECTION

Cast of the *George Lopez Show*, from left to right, Valente Rodriguez, Belita Moreno, Masiela Lusha, Luis Armand Garcia, George Lopez, and Constance Marie.

The creators of the *George Lopez Show* were careful to construct a Latino family that would have broad appeal—Lopez plays a Mexican American and Constance Marie plays his Cuban American wife. According to Lopez, "this show is not about a Mexican, but about a man who wants to be a better person." The program and its network, ABC, were hailed for bringing a Latino-themed series to prime time. ABC gave the *George Lopez Show* what no other Latino-themed show on network television has had in three decades—a chance. "We hope the *George Lopez Show* is just the beginning of a new era for Latinos on prime-time network television," stated Raúl Yzaguirre, NCLR President.

PBS touted *American Family* as the "the first drama series ever to air on broadcast television featuring a Latino cast, and the first original prime time American episodic drama on PBS in decades." The series assembled a cast of marquee Latino talent including Edward James Olmos, Constance Marie, Yancey Arias, Jesse Borrego, Patricia Velásquez, Kate del Castillo, Raquel Welch, Esai Morales, and Sonia Braga. The series was created by Academy Award–nominated director Gregory Nava (*El Norte, Selena*). The series is about an American family living in Los Angeles that happens to be Latino, according to Nava. *American Family* is distinctly Latino—and Mexican American—and is set in a well-known Chicano barrio. As a result *American Family* was perceived as a regional series by some PBS stations. Some station programmers, fearful of low ratings, disregarded the PBS common-carriage rule and ran the series at other than the national feed times.

UCLA media scholar Chon Noriega suggests that the *George Lopez Show* and *American Family* were born out of the Brown Out protest of 1999. That was the year that the major networks introduced 26 new, all-white, prime-time series. The outrage that followed was channeled into an organized and historic effort to bring economic pressure to bear on the television networks. Whether the effort will have a long-term effect on the character of the television landscape remains to be seen. Broadcasters remain slaves to ratings. The most successful Latino in television history remains Arnaz. He and his partner, Ball, delivered high audience numbers to advertisers from 1951–1957.

The full benefits of the Brown Out are not yet apparent. Although some training programs and internships resulted from pressure on the networks and may prove beneficial in the future, years are likely to pass before a critical mass of Latinos working in network television can make their presence felt. "It would be naive to say that a week's boycott would change the behavior of television networks overnight," said one Latino scholar, "but it does make them think about these things."

RELATED ARTICLES

Arnaz, Desi; Film; *I Love Lucy*; Moreno, Rita; Olmos, Edward James; Stereotypes and Stereotyping; Telenovelas; Theater.

FURTHER READING

Noriega, Chon. "Prime Time for Latinos." *UCLA Today.* www.today.ucla.edu/2002

Reyes, Luis, and Peter Rubie. *Hispanics in Hollywood: An Encyclopedia of 100 Years in Film and Television.* Hollywood, Calif.: Lone Eagle Pubs., 2000.

Smith, B. R. *Desi Arnaz.* Museum of Broadcast Communications.
http://www.museum.tv/archives/etv/A/htmlA/arnazdesi/arnazdesi.htm

JOSEPH TOVARES

TENNIS

Originally known as lawn tennis (different from court tennis, its ancient parent game), tennis originated in England in the 19th century. It was first played in America in 1874.

Long dominated by western Europeans, Americans, and Australians, it was not until the mid-20th century that nonwhite players, including some from south of the Rio Grande, began to reach the upper echelons of the game. It was only then that Latinos from the United States, including such players as Pancho Gonzáles and Pancho Segura, came to prominence.

Richard "Pancho" Gonzáles was born in Los Angeles to Mexican parents. While he never took any formal tennis lessons, the tall and agile Gonzáles captured the amateur U.S. National Championship in 1948. He performed the same feat again, and turned professional, the next year. Gonzáles was barred from playing at Wimbledon, one of the world's premier tennis tournaments, during the prime of his career owing to a change in the rules regarding the commingling of professionals and amateurs. But in 1969, the first year that open—that is, professional—tennis came to Wimbledon, the 41-year-old Pancho took the title in the longest match the tournament had

© BOB DEAR/AP/WIDE WORLD PHOTOS

Pancho Gonzáles on Center Court at Wimbledon, 1969.

ever seen. Many believe that with his powerful serve and incredible court coverage, he could have won many more titles had he been given the chance.

A contemporary, and sometimes rival of Gonzáles was Ecuadorian American Pancho Segura, who won the U.S. Professional Championships from 1950 to 1952, beating Gonzáles in 1951 and 1952. Although Segura only played in one Wimbledon event, he went on to coach tennis superstar Jimmy Connors to his first titles.

Latinas from the United States have not fared as well in the sport. The dominant women players have been Americans and Europeans, although some players from Spanish-speaking countries, such as Mary Joe Fernández of the Dominican Republic (who went on to a successful career as a tennis commentator after retiring as a player) and Gabriela Sabatini of Argentina, have distinguished themselves through notable careers. Rosemary Casals, a Salvadoran American, was one-half of the most dominant women's doubles teams of the late 1960s and early 1970s; with Billie Jean King she won the doubles title at Wimbledon in 1967, 1968, 1970, 1971, and 1973. The team took the U.S. National Championship in 1967 and the U.S. Open doubles championship in 1974. Casals also won the U.S. Open doubles, with other partners in 1971 and 1982.

Tennis is popular among Latinos. A 1990 survey by American Sports Data, Inc., showed that 12 percent of Latinos play it recreationally, while another survey by the Sports Media Index found that by 1993, 26 percent of Latinos regularly watched tennis on television.

RELATED ARTICLES
Sports in Latino Life.

FURTHER READING
Danzig, Allison, and Peter Schwed, eds. *The Fireside Book of Tennis.* New York: Simon and Schuster, 1972.
Grimsley, Will. *Tennis, Its History, People and Events.* Englewood, N.J.: Prentice Hall, 1971.

SELECTED WEB SITE
History of Tennis.
http://www.cliffrichardtennis.org/planet_tennis/history.htm

AARON BRITT

TEXAS

According to the 2000 U.S. Census, somewhere between 5 and 7 million Mexican-descent people resided in Texas. These numbers amounted to about one-third of the state's estimated 20 million inhabitants. Some demographers believe that by the year 2030, owing both to reproduction and further immigration from Mexico, Mexican Americans will become the majority group in the Lone Star State. The fact that Mexican Americans constitute a conspicuous component of the Texas population is not surprising, for their ancestors set foot there long before the arrival of Anglo-Americans.

The history of Mexican-origin people in the state began when a Spaniard, Alvar Núñez Cabeza de Vaca, and three other explorers shipwrecked in 1528 just off the Texas coast on what is modern-day Galveston Island. When he returned to New Spain in 1536, Núñez Cabeza de Vaca hinted of precious minerals existing in lands north of where he had traveled. But subsequent expeditions in search of wealth in the hinterlands yielded nothing of consequence. Royal authorities thus neglected its far northern regions (among them Texas) until the 1680s, at which time French activity prompted them to reconsider their policy of inattention. By the early decades of the 18th century, the Spanish crown had established numerous missions, several *presidios* (military garrisons), and three civilian settlements in Texas. About 1800 the Spanish-Mexican population in the province numbered about 5,000.

Change followed rapidly for Tejanos between 1800 and 1836. In September 1810 Father Miguel Hidalgo y Costilla led an independence crusade in Mexico, an act that in Texas produced civil turmoil when troops dispatched by royal officials punished and chastised those Tejanos who had supported the Hidalgo rebellion. In 1821 Mexico agreed to have Stephen F. Austin settle American families in Texas, a decision that ultimately miscarried for the newly independent country. On March 2, 1836, the Anglo-Texans declared Texas independent from Mexico, and on April 21, 1836, they defeated Mexican forces under Antonio López de Santa Anna. With this victory, Anglos created the Republic of Texas and assumed control of all governing institutions.

The Texas Constitution of 1836 (establishing the Republic of Texas) bestowed citizenship on those living in Texas at the time of the state's declaration of independence (March 2, 1836), among them Texas Mexicans, and the state constitution of 1845 recognized Tejanos as having the same status. Old-line families such as those of José Antonio Navarro (of San Antonio) and Santos Benavides (from Laredo) fared well under the new political order, but for most other Mexicans the letter of the law and reality seldom corresponded. In the aftermath of the Texas war for independence in 1836, Anglos moved into vacated properties left behind by Tejanos who had fled to safety in Louisiana or Mexico during the war, initiating years of legal struggles by Tejanos who fought to regain lost lands. A similar pattern of land conflict occurred in south Texas during the 1850s as Anglos arrived there in significant numbers after the

TEXAS—POPULATION BY HISPANIC ORIGIN, 1980 TO 2000

Census Year	Total Population	Percent	Hispanic Origin (of any race)	Percent
2000	20,851,820	100	6,669,666	32.0
1990	16,986,510	100	4,339,905	25.5
1980	14,229,191	100	2,985,824	21.0

Source: U.S. Census Bureau, 2000, 2002.

war with Mexico (1846–1848), creating resentment among the old Mexican inhabitants of the region. Mexicans, furthermore, despised the manner by which Anglos supplanted them in political office and the ease by which Anglos came to dominate local economic activity.

The inevitable result was racial animosity throughout the state. In 1857 violence broke out in the Goliad region in an episode known as the Cart War; Anglo freighters attacked Mexican cartmen underbidding the Anglos' higher charges, and they destroyed many of the carts and killed several Mexicans. In Brownsville, Juan N. Cortina led an opposition drive against the Anglo interlopers, but his popular rebellion ended in defeat at the hands of Texas Rangers and the U.S. military. In San Patricio (near modern-day Corpus Christi), a court ordered the legal hanging of Chepita Rodríguez, a woman convicted on questionable evidence of killing a white man at her home. During the 1870s Mexicans fell

victim to racial strife in the trans-Nueces region as Anglos implicated the local Mexican population in cattle rustling operations orchestrated from Mexico. The Salt War of 1877 in the El Paso Valley represented still another episode of racial animosity; it started because Anglos sought a monopoly of local salt beds on which Mexicans relied for their livelihood.

HISPANIC OR LATINO AND RACE TEXAS, 2000

Total Population	20,851,820	100.0%
Hispanic or Latino (of any race)	6,669,666	32.0%
Mexican	5,071,963	24.3%
Puerto Rican	69,504	0.3%
Cuban	25,705	0.1%
Other Hispanic or Latino	1,502,494	7.2%
Not Hispanic or Latino	14,182,154	68.0%

Source: U.S. Census Bureau, 2000.

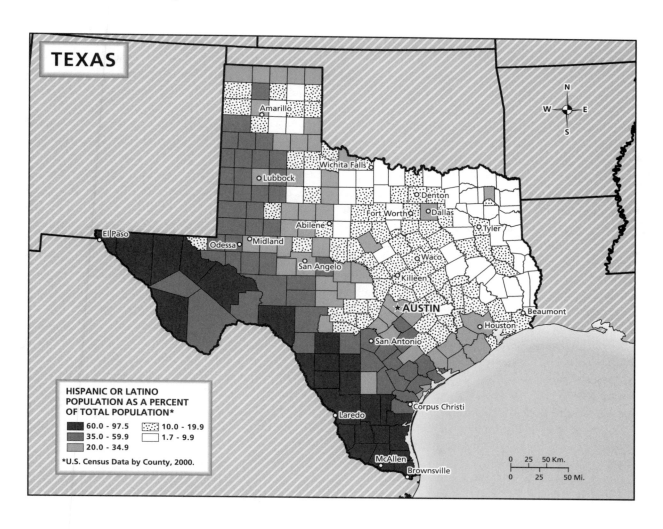

Rapid change occurred for the Texas Mexican community (which totaled approximately 277,231 in 1910) in the 40-year period from 1880 to 1920. First, the state pulled away from its long-standing frontier leanings and lunged toward urban modernity. A farm revolution in south Texas, still the region with the heaviest Mexican American concentration, accompanied the change. With it came uncertainty, for the new farm society undercut the long-standing ranching order on which many depended. Segments of the Texas Mexican community resisted the change and turned for support to the old and familiar. In Brooks County, for instance, people confidently relied on folk healer (curandero) Don Pedrito Jaramillo, since he represented tradition amid rapid change. People in Karnes County (and throughout south Texas, for that matter) rallied to the aid of Gregorio Cortéz, his heroics in eluding a posse chasing him down (for having killed a peace officer, in self-defense) having recalled earlier times when few questioned Tejano range prowess. In 1915 many throughout south Texas gave aid and succor to paramilitia groups (propounding the Plan de San Diego) engaged in warfare against Anglos blamed for the farm revolution that had wrought havoc on old Texas Mexican communities.

A second factor that engendered change in the old Texas Mexican communities during the era between 1880 and 1920 was immigration from Mexico. No one can precisely determine the number of people who struck north from Mexico toward Texas, but some sources place the figure at about 71,000 in 1900 and 250,000 in 1930. The new arrivals made their way into the old established towns along the border, including El Paso, and those in the interior such as San Antonio and Corpus Christi, but also nascent Hispanic communities in Houston and the northwest Texas frontier. In entering older communities the immigrants momentarily disrupted Mexican American acculturation, not only by invigorating the Tejanos' Mexican heritage, but by forcing Tejanos into reassessing their nationalism. For several decades during the late 19th century and early 20th century, many colonias (neighborhoods) housed residents who leaned toward the cultural and national allegiance of Mexico instead of the United States. In this atmosphere many found appealing the ideas advanced by Mexico's liberal Ricardo Flores Magón (who set up offices in Texas in 1904) and his Partido Liberal Mexicano (PLM). Among such supporters was Sara Estela Ramírez of Laredo, who publicly campaigned in behalf of the PLM's opposition to Mexico's president, Porfirio Díaz, and in favor of the party's defense of workers' rights, both in Mexico and the United States.

A good many Mexican Americans, however, were never swayed by the presence of the immigrants. Either born or raised in the United States, they had received their educations in Texas, established careers or businesses there, had been influenced by the nation's call on all Americans to assist in the World War I effort, or felt comfortable with themselves as bicultural individuals. Their ranks included attorneys J. T. Canales and Alonso Perales, educators such as J. Luz Saenz, and journalists such as the Idar family (Nicasio, Clemente, and Jovita) of Laredo. This contingent of Mexican Americans (collectively referred to as "Tejano Progressives" by historians) very much admired U.S. institutions and actively pursued constructive means to improve conditions for the general Tejano population. In 1911, for instance, Tejano Progressives organized the Primer Congreso Mexicanista in Laredo to address serious issues (among them inferior schooling, violence, land loss, and segregation) impeding Tejano progress. Their struggles would gain momentum after World War I, and more particularly by the 1930s.

The Orden Hijos de América (Order of Sons of America), their initial effort (in 1921) to launch a statewide network designed to ameliorate conditions for Mexican Americans, faltered. More successful was the organization's successor, the League of United Latin American Citizens (LULAC, 1929), which included among its leadership the lawyers Alonso Perales and M. C. Gonzáles, businessman Ben Garza, and teacher J. Luz Saenz. LULAC addressed issues pertinent to the native-born or naturalized populace (Mexico-born residents could appeal to the Mexican consul in case of problems) and thus stressed citizenship, patriotism, education, and political interest. Local LULAC councils held night classes to teach English, good conduct, and duty to country. They fought against segregation and challenged any implication that Mexican Americans were nonwhite. Also fighting LULAC battles in the 1930s were Mrs. J. C. Machuca of El Paso and Alice Dickerson Montemayor of Laredo, both of whom concerned themselves with the status of women.

Outside the ranks of LULAC, others engaged in equally important struggles, among them Eleuterio

Escobar, who in 1934 organized the School Improvement League in San Antonio to get school officials to focus on the dismal conditions that plagued the district's segregated Mexican schools. Also in San Antonio, Emma Tenayuca, a 22-year-old native of the city, led a strike of pecan shellers in 1938, demanding from management pay increases for workers and physical improvements in the workplace. The strikers won concessions, although their gains proved fleeting as management modernized and no longer had use for the old labor force.

Many Tejanos answered the country's call to defend democracy overseas during World War II. In the military, servicemen gained respect for their fighting spirit and experienced a world more tolerant than the one they knew in the Texas urbanscape and farm towns. Upon their discharge they expected a changed society, but such was not the case. Jim Crow traditions hardly faded in the postwar era, and white society still viewed Mexicans as undeserving of equal treatment. This reality was made evident to Tejanos in the insult inflicted on the family of Félix Longoria, a Three Rivers, Texas, native who had fallen in action fighting in the Philippines. When the government returned his body in 1949, the local funeral home at Three Rivers refused to handle Longoria's remains. Both veterans and citizens rallied behind protests led by Héctor P. García of Corpus Christi, and the result of the episode was an energized American GI Forum, a civic organization founded by García in 1948.

The GI Forum and LULAC thus became the leading advocates and defenders of Mexican American rights during the 1950s and 1960s, by which time the Texas Mexican population reached a figure higher than 1 million. Many of the men and women in the forefront of the crusade sought to overturn old obstacles in the path of ethnic progress. They included prewar activists such as Perales, M. C. Gonzáles, George I. Sánchez of the University of Texas, and the younger generation represented by García, Gus García, and Henry B. González of San Antonio, and John Herrera and Félix Tijerina of Houston. Together the two organizations challenged violations to Mexican American rights, such as educational segregation and racial discrimination. In 1954 the two organizations won a historic victory when the U.S. Supreme Court in *Hernández* v. *Texas* ruled that Mexican Americans were in fact the victims of a long history of discriminatory treatment. Starting

in 1948 and continuing through the 1950s, LULAC and the GI Forum won several court cases that ended (at least theoretically) a wide range of improper practices in Texas schools. LULAC undertook other means to help Mexican American children with their education. Tijerina, for one, founded the Little School of the 400, which targeted preschoolers and tried to teach them 400 English words before they entered the first grade.

The post–World War II period obviously featured more than just political activity. Labor unionism persisted, although most strikes ended in failure, since management and antiunion sentiments in the state proved too tenacious for discontented workers. As to identity, the 1950s became years of accelerated acculturation, for mass culture captivated many of the young and the schools augmented their bicultural preferences. At the university level, pioneering academic works on Mexican Americans gained unprecedented attention as three professors at the University of Texas either continued their publishing records or began them. Carlos Eduardo Castañeda, the great historian raised in Brownsville, wrote on early Tejano history; George I. Sánchez remained an authority on Mexican American education; and Américo Paredes launched his long-standing association with the University of Texas as a renowned folklorist.

During the 1960s Mexican Americans joined the larger crusades to change the status quo across America. One way to make a difference, many GI Forum and LULAC leaders believed, was to help John F. Kennedy win the presidential election of 1960. To that end, Héctor García and others founded "Viva Kennedy" clubs. Aiding Kennedy gain the White House, many believed, would strengthen ties to national figures, and Kennedy might well reciprocate for Hispanic assistance by appointing Mexican Americans to high offices or by seeing to it that Democratic monies were channeled to support Mexican American civil rights causes. Association with the Kennedy name would give Mexican Americans political legitimacy within the Democratic Party in Texas and hasten political victories at the local and state level.

Although Kennedy won, disappointment followed, since the expected rewards from the Kennedy administration did not materialize. So García and like-minded leaders established the Political Association of Spanish-Speaking Organizations (PASO) to maintain the political intensity of the moment. But

PASO proved to be ineffective, and by the mid-1960s membership and faith in it were on the wane. The Viva Kennedy movement thus passed off the historical stage, but not before leaving a mark. As García had hoped, Mexican Americans did form ties with national Democrats, especially during the Lyndon Johnson presidency, and both the Texas Democrats and Republicans took notice of Mexican American voting potential. PASO had further acted as an inspiration for younger protoactivists or as a training ground for them.

Bolder action in the attempt to gain the elusive equality for Mexican Americans came from the Chicano generation of the 1960s and 1970s. As PASO waned, the Mexican American Youth Organization (MAYO) surfaced. Founded in 1967 by José Angel Gutiérrez and a handful of social reformers, MAYO hoped to improve on older ways of solving age-old problems such as poverty, substandard education, police harassment, and lingering discrimination.

Inspiration for Gutiérrez and his outlook came from several sources, among them the many social movements of the 1960s, but more directly from the labor struggles led in California by César Chávez and from efforts in New Mexico by Reyes López Tijerina to reacquire lost land grants. What roused MAYO most immediately were the reverberations of the farmworkers' march that occurred during the summer of 1966. Compelled to dramatize their problems in light of indifference from employers and government, farmworkers from the Rio Grande Valley decided on a 290-mile (490-km) march to Austin, where they hoped to get the legislature to heed their needs. But Governor John Connally met the marchers in New Braunfels, Texas, and there informed them he would call no special session to hear their concerns. The outrage that accompanied the farmworkers' mistreatment produced the Texas version of the "Chicano movement," led initially by MAYO.

The Chicano *movimiento* (as it is called in Spanish) involved several elements within the Texas-Mexican community, although the leadership consisted primarily of students, both college and high school, the majority of whom came from backgrounds in the barrios or from the migrant-farmworker stream. Most knew firsthand a life of poverty and the limited opportunities available to those of Mexican descent, but, given their educations, understood American fair play. Their militant rhetoric borrowed from the thinking of other discontented

groups protesting American inequities in the 1960s, although it was more intimately grounded on their experience of growing up as Mexican Americans. They visualized a society for Mexican Americans in which their heritage would be celebrated, while no doubt would exist as to their allegiance to American society and politics. Groups as diverse as farmworkers and intellectuals found the call to action appealing.

MAYO remained the leading force behind the movement from the late 1960s until the early 1970s. In the town of Crystal City, José Angel Gutiérrez engineered a political coup that won for the newly formed Raza Unida Party (RUP) seats in the city council and on the school board. Crystal City became a model to be duplicated throughout south Texas, and MAYO followers joined RUP in the cause to gain political advantage elsewhere. At his point MAYO declined in importance, and RUP came to head the "militant" phase of the *movimiento*. The party reached a high-water mark in 1972, when it ran Ramsey Muñiz for governor, advancing a platform that offered solutions to inadequacies in the educational system, gerrymandering, police harassment, and women's rights, among other problems. Muñiz lost, although he gained 6 percent of the total vote, a margin almost large enough to cause the defeat of the Democratic candidate.

RUP, however, was not the only player in the movement. Middle-class organizations such as LULAC and the GI Forum joined in, though their strategy involved using acquaintances with state and national leaders to force a response from government. Women advanced their own agenda, wishing to overturn the image of women as mainly homemakers and wanting to find answers to problems associated with gender. To that end, Chicanas held the Conferencia de Mujeres por La Raza (National Chicana Conference) in Houston in 1971. The Texas farmworkers constituted still another element within the *movimiento*. Represented by Antonio Orendain, they voiced the need for improved wages, benefits to match those of urban workers, and the right to organize collectively.

For numerous reasons the *movimiento* lost force by the mid-1970s. Several causes explain its exhaustion, among them the scarcity of cash to finance political campaigns, infighting, harassment by law authorities, and, significantly, a reluctance by the general population to accept the left-of-center platform of the militants. In its wake, however, the movement

© JAKE SCHOELLKOPF/AP/WIDE WORLD PHOTOS

Texas state senator Eddie Lucio, Jr., with a replica of the battle flag used by Texans at the Battle of Gonzáles in 1835.

left many with a renewed pride in being "Mexican," old issues pushed to the political forefront, and an energized leadership (although a more moderate one) prepared to carry on the banner in behalf of ethnic advancement.

Among those who practiced the politics of moderation in the post-Chicano era were the members of LULAC, who spoke for some 3 million Tejanos living in the state as of 1980. LULAC leaders took their role as advocates for Mexican American issues seriously during the Ronald Reagan era, but did so by networking with high-powered government officials and forming partnerships with large corporations willing to finance ethnic causes. The most prominent Mexican American figure during the 1980s and 1990s was Henry Cisneros, who served as mayor of San Antonio during the late 1980s and then as secretary of urban and housing development during the Bill Clinton presidency 1993–2001. Cisneros did not advocate ethnic-specific politics, but his administrations nonetheless sought to help out

the less fortunate in society, among them Mexican Americans, with whom he identified.

Despite their more careful rhetoric, Mexican American leaders during the last decades of the 20th century understood their duty to Mexican American voters, for it was a Mexican American electorate that generally accounted for their position. In efforts to improve life for their constituents, therefore, they negotiated alliances with those able to lend a hand to Tejano issues, among them church groups, African Americans, labor unions, and liberal Democrats. They fought to fend off efforts detrimental to the Mexican American community, such as insistence on at-large elections, on speaking "English only," or on eliminating affirmative-action programs. Outrage accompanied the Fifth Circuit Court of Appeals's decision in *Hopwood* v. *Texas* (1996) that the manner of admitting minority groups into the University of Texas law school was unfair. Mexican Americans entertained the old dreams of seeing Hispanic communities achieve greater participation in the world of politics and having Mexican Americans play a deciding role in the country's destiny. These objectives were among those advanced by the Southwest Voter Registration, Education Project (SVREP), established in 1974. Its founder, Willie Velásquez, saw the SVREP as a vehicle by which Mexican American voters could be mobilized and more Mexican American officials could be elected who thereby would be able to uplift the many living with daily misfortune.

Among those whose circumstances politicians sought to ameliorate were literally thousands (anywhere from 50,000 to 150,000) of migrant farm laborers (*campesinos*) who had come out of the farmworkers' march of 1966 and the Chicano movement with little to show. Actually, the *campesinos* organized their own farmworkers' movement for better working conditions during the 1970s and 1980s, led by Tony Orendain of the Texas Farm Workers Union (TFWU) and Rebecca Flores Harrington of the United Farm Workers union (UFW). But starting in the early 1980s, Mexican American legislators succeeded in passing various laws beneficial to farm laborers, among them one compelling farmers to tell migrants about the use of pesticides in the fields where the *campesinos* worked and another forcing better wages. Despite such strides, problems persisted into the 1990s; including stiff opposition by growers and their conservative spokespersons in government.

The federal census of 2000 counted people of Mexican descent in all sections of the state. South Texas remained a kind of homeland for Tejanos, but the border areas from Laredo to El Paso contained majority populations of Mexican Americans, and the interior counties of west Texas gained more Mexican-descent citizens. San Antonio, once considered the Hispanic capital of Texas, gave way to Houston in 2000 as the "Hispanic Mecca of Texas." Indeed, the Hispanic population (which included Central Americans, Cubans, Puerto Ricans, and other Hispanic groups) in the "Bayou City" constituted more than one-third of the entire city's inhabitants.

The growing Tejano population still grappled with many of the older problems that had historically afflicted them, such as poverty, educational lag, and underrepresentation in local and state governments. But they now increasingly joined the march of events unfolding in the early 21st century. Many from Texas went to Washington to work in the George W. Bush administration, among the most

prominent being Alberto R. Gonzáles, the White House counsel. In November 2002, Mexican Americans rallied behind the banner of Tony Sánchez, the Democratic candidate for governor from Laredo, though in a losing effort. In the Iraqi War of March 2003, hundreds of Mexican American men and women took part in the military offensive, some of them suffering injuries or losing their lives in combat.

Meanwhile, the newer generation had begun enjoying a standard of living unknown to their parents and grandparents. More than 40 percent of Tejanos belonged to the middle class as of the year 2000. Tejanos were now visible in the corporate sphere, in the medical and legal professions, in higher education, in the music industry, in the media, and in many other esteemed places. Despite these grand strides into the world of mainstream America, Mexican-origin culture remained as vibrant as ever. The Spanish language, regard for Mexican holidays (Cinco de Mayo or Diez y Seis de Septiembre), religious observations, ethnic foods, Tejano music, as well as many traditional customs retained their vigor. Almost unknown to Anglo society, Tejano culture became the focus of widespread interest following the tragic killing of the Tejano music queen Selena (Quintanilla Pérez) in 1995. As it focused on her untimely death, the media publicized the world in which she had been raised and the community that had made her a star. Coverage of her tragedy pointed to aspects of being Mexican American in modern times; like many Tejanos, Selena was a native-English speaker. Moreover, American pop culture had shaped her own music; she had functioned comfortably in both Tejano and Anglo environments.

Acculturation threatens to neutralize and dilute Hispanic culture in Texas, but continuing immigration from Mexico forestalls such a process. Much like everyone else, Mexican American Tejanos place faith in the American dream.

RELATED ARTICLES

Alamo, Battle of the; American GI Forum; Austin; Border, United States-Mexico; Cuisine, Tex-Mex; El Paso; Guadalupe Hidalgo, Treaty of; Homestead Act; League of United Latin American Citizens; Mexican Americans; San Antonio; Selena; Southwestern United States, Anglo Immigration to; Tejano; Texas Rangers; Three Rivers.

FURTHER READING

Acosta, Teresa Palomo, and Ruthe Winegarten. *Las Tejanas: 300 Years of History.* Austin: Univ. of Tex. Press, 2003.

Alonzo, Armando. *Tejano Legacy: Rancheros and Settlers in South Texas, 1734–1900.* Albuquerque: Univ. of N.Mex. Press, 1998.

Arreola, Daniel D. *Tejano South Texas: A Mexican American Cultural Province.* Austin: Univ. of Tex. Press, 2002.

De la Teja, Jesús F. *San Antonio de Béxar: A Community on New Spain's Northern Frontier.* Albuquerque: Univ. of N.Mex. Press, 1995.

De León, Arnoldo. *Mexican Americans in Texas: A Brief History.* Arlington Heights, Ill.: Harlan Davidson, 1999.

García, Ignacio M. *Hector P. García: In Relentless Pursuit of Justice.* Houston, Tex.: Arte Público Press, 2002.

García, Richard A. *Rise of the Mexican American Middle Class: San Antonio, 1929–1941.* College Station: Tex. A&M Univ. Press, 1991.

Montejano, David. *Anglos and Mexicans in the Making of Texas, 1836–1986.* Austin: Univ. of Tex. Press, 1987.

Navarro, Armando. *La Raza Unida Party: A Chicano Challenge to the U.S. Two-Party Dictatorship.* Philadelphia: Temple Univ. Press, 2000.

San Miguel, Guadalupe, Jr. *"Let All of Them Take Heed": Mexican Americans and the Campaign for Educational Equality in Texas, 1910–1981.* Austin: Univ. of Tex. Press, 1987.

ARNOLDO DE LEÓN

TEXAS RANGERS

The precursor to the Texas Rangers, a law enforcement organization, was formed in the 19th century in what became the state of Texas. Throughout their long history, the men known as Rangers have won the admiration of many Texans while incurring the enmity of many others. In all periods Rangers reflected society's demand for law and order. Its early years explain the Rangers' no-nonsense approach to law and order, a trait still associated with the organization.

The earliest force dates to 1823, when Stephen F. Austin hired several "rangers" to protect his new colony from Indian attacks. In 1835, on the eve of the revolt against Mexico, the fledgling Republic of Texas officially created a unit later called the Texas Rangers (the bands of volunteers had previously been called by many names, such as mounted gunmen and scouts). It consisted of 56 men organized into three companies, each headed by a captain and two lieutenants. The number of Ranger companies fluctuated after Texas became a state in 1845, depending on the need for their services and the state's usually limited budget. The greatest danger came from Indian attacks. Ranger strategy against Indians, according to one Ranger's wife, was simply to run down the Indians and kill them. Rangers were effective because of their superior tracking skills, knowledge of the local terrain, and give-no-quarter methods; thus punitive expeditions by Rangers and the U.S. Army ended this danger by the 1880s.

Prior to statehood, the region that included Texas had been claimed by Spain in 1691, falling to Mexico in 1821. Mexico allowed U.S. citizens to settle in Texas, but the steady influx of Southern Anglos and their slaves eventually alarmed the Spanish Mexican population. Thus, because slavery and the appropriation of land caused problems, Mexico outlawed slavery in 1829, and Mexicans sometimes aided slaves in their flight to Mexico. At least one Ranger company invaded the country to retrieve runaway slaves. The Mexican War (1846–1848) and the U.S. Civil War (1861–1865) involved the Texas Rangers in different capacities. In 1846 Rangers gained a national reputation for their fierce campaigns in Mexico, and their conduct there, which included killing Mexicans without provocation, was so ruthless that Mexicans called them *los diablos Tejanos* (the Texas devils) and General Zachary Taylor requested that no Rangers be sent to him.

During the Civil War and the immediate postbellum period, Ranger activities were at a low level. Many Rangers enlisted, as individuals, in the Confederate Army, while others remained in Texas to handle local problems. For example, the Cortina War, which began in 1859 and continued for several years, engaged Rangers and U.S. troops. The conflict stemmed from tense racial relations between Mexican and Anglo-Texans in south Texas. Both politically and economically the minority Anglo population dominated Mexican Texans. In this setting Juan Cortina emerged as a defender of oppressed Mexicans, even leading large guerrilla forces during his revolt. The cycle of violence that ensued cost several lives, Mexican and Anglo, and extensive damage. Many in south Texas feared both Cortina and the Rangers. Another racially charged episode, the Salt War, occurred in west Texas over salt deposits near El Paso. Mexicans from both sides of the border had enjoyed communal use of the mineral until Charles Howard acquired control of the salt bed in 1877 and charged for its use. Howard killed an adversary, Mexicans killed Howard, and Rangers killed several Mexicans. Additional Ranger activities to maintain law and order included expeditions against army deserters during the Civil War and against other marauders who plagued Texas. In the 1870s Rangers intervened in bloody feuds and tracked down many outlaws, including Sam Bass and John Wesley Hardin.

Rangers' duties increased sharply when the violent unrest accompanying the Mexican Revolution of 1910 spread into south Texas. Some Mexican Texans joined Mexican revolutionaries and fought on both sides of the border. The long-term economic discrimination against Mexican Texans contributed to their collusion with Mexican nationals. In 1915 a bold irredentist plot called the Plan of San Diego was discovered in Texas. It was a call to arms for Mexicans and Mexican Americans to establish a new republic after reclaiming land lost by Mexico in the Mexican War. The 1917 Zimmermann telegram from Germany to Mexico during World War I added further doubts, unfairly, about the patriotism of Mexican Americans. Both the U.S. Army and the Rangers attempted to suppress the violence in south Texas that had claimed many Anglo lives. American forces crossed the U.S.-Mexico border, as did Mexican revolutionaries. Rangers (called pejoratively *rinches* by Mexican Texans) as well as vigilante groups killed hundreds, perhaps thousands, of Mexican Texans, frequently by lynching, and drew national criticism. State representative J. T. Canales of Brownsville, Texas, called for an investigation of the Rangers in 1919. His demand for reforms, however, had limited success.

Rangers provided valuable services in the next decades. In the 1920s they helped to enforce Prohibition, control Ku Klux Klan violence, and curb lawlessness in new oil boomtowns. In 1929 the Great Depression resulted in state budget cuts that reduced the Rangers to 32. In 1935 the Department of Public Safety (DPS) was created, consisting of the Rangers, Highway Patrol, and a Headquarters Division. The new DPS updated its laboratories and investigative methods, and the Rangers, although modernized, lost much of their traditional individualism. The civil rights movements of the 1960s and 1970s presented other challenges. Instead of confronting Indians, Mexican revolutionaries, or bootleggers, Rangers encountered Mexican Texans in their attempts to become enfranchised, as in Crystal City in 1963, or to obtain fair wages, as in 1966, when farmworkers in south Texas struck for higher wages. The Rangers harshly enforced Texas's antilabor laws, some of which were later declared unconstitutional, and beat strike organizers and participants. Negative national media coverage detailed the violation of the civil rights of Mexican Texans and described the Rangers' intervention as being on behalf of local political and business leaders.

The vast, nearly hagiographic literature by and about the Texas Rangers perpetuates their fame and makes it difficult to separate fact from myth. It is certain, however, that the Rangers are living legends who have served their society in different capacities since the 1830s. Despite past demands by critics for it to be abolished, the organization is an integral part of Texan identity and is even protected from dissolution by Texas statute. The reformed law enforcement agency consists of college-educated officers who are trained in state-of-the-art investigative techniques, and just as important, the Texas Rangers agency, whose members totaled 116 in 2003, includes more minority officers and has added female officers to its force. Texas society has changed greatly since the 1830s, as has the elite law enforcement agency known as the Texas Rangers.

RELATED ARTICLES

Cortéz, Gregorio; Discrimination; Law Enforcement; Mexico; Southwestern United States, Anglo Immigration to; Texas.

FURTHER READING

Procter, Ben. *Just One Riot: Episodes of Texas Rangers in the 20th Century.* Austin, Tex.: Eakin Press, 1990.

Samora, Julian, et al. *Gunpowder Justice: A Reassessment of the Texas Rangers.* Notre Dame. Ind.: Univ. of Notre Dame Press, 1979.

Texas Senate and House. *Proceedings of the Senate and House in the Investigation of the Texas State Ranger Force.* Austin: s.l. s.n., 1919.

U.S. Commission on Civil Rights. Texas State Advisory Committee. *Civil Rights in Texas: A Report* [Austin?]: 1970.

Webb, Walter Prescott. *The Texas Rangers: A Century of Frontier Defense.* Boston and New York: Houghton Mifflin Co., 1935. Reprint with a forward by Lyndon B. Johnson. Austin: Univ. of Tex. Press, 1965.

WEB SITE

Texas Ranger Hall of Fame and Museum. http://www.texasranger.org

LINDA J. QUINTANILLA

THEATER

Spanish-language theater groups in the United States have performed on stage since the second half of the 19th century. After 1850, Spanish-language folk theaters, tent theaters, vaudeville acts, and professional companies from Spain and Latin America traveled the country by wagon and rail, stopping at cities and settlements to perform anything from burlesque comedies to romantic melodramas. New York, Los Angeles, and San Antonio, Texas, grew into the three major centers for Spanish-language theater, and each city offered theater houses with their own repertory companies, as well as separate establishments for touring dramatic groups.

By the start of the 20th century, Spanish-language vaudeville dominated the Hispanic theater, limiting the potential for the rise of a serious Latino theater movement. The advent of the motion picture industry drew attention away from American professional theater as a whole, yet few films appealed to Latino audiences. In the years between the Great Depression and the beginning of American participation in World War II, neighborhood amateur theatrical groups performing plays as fund-raising enterprises for community projects replaced professional stage repertories as the preeminent source of Spanish-language and English-language Latino theater in the United States.

The end of World War II was followed by unprecedented prosperity in the United States, as well as mass waves of migration from Latin America. Cuban, Puerto Rican, and Mexican immigrants settled throughout the United States, expanding preexisting Latino communities concentrated in urban settings such as Los Angeles, New York, Chicago, and Miami. The influx of Latin American people and culture reinforced and reconfigured Latino cultural growth in the United States. Old-world traditions merged with the realities of the American Latino experience and, as Hispanic communities reestablished themselves in their respective regions, a number of amateur and professional theater troops carrying distinct Latino identities began to appear. Making the transition from a source of entertainment to a method of cultural expression, theater was becoming homegrown, taking on a new consciousness that reflected the unique background and experiences of Latinos in the United States.

Contemporary Latino theater was only in its embryonic stages when, in the late 1960s and early 1970s, waves of Latin American artists, writers, and intellectuals emigrated to the United States from countries including Argentina, Chile, and Uruguay. Escaping the violent and repressive military regimes that seized power in their homelands, these educated people brought with them formal training in the arts

---

A LITTLE SOMETHING TO EASE THE PAIN

Cacha: Well, our Paye's here early!
Clara: My Paye! (Paye and Tatín try to speak at once. They laugh.)
Tatín: Paye-Paye!
Paye: It's nice to be called Paye again!
Dilia: What do they call you . . . ?
Paye: My friends, Carlos.
Cacha: Ay!
Tatín: Should we call you Carlos?
Paye: No! No! Paye's fine. It's just fine. It's just that no one's called me Paye in so long. Even the family in Jamaica. Once when I was there for Christmas, Papa called me Paye by mistake and Alexandra nearly choked on her milk. She thought it was the funniest thing since Aunt Sophie fell into Uncle Solomon's grave. (Tatín looks puzzled.) They were lowering him in. Oh. you should've been there! She had been wailing: "Solomon, take me with you! Don't leave me, Solomon!" Then as she fell, she started screaming, "Draw me out! Will you get me outta here!" (Everyone bursts into laughter but Tatín.) Everyone was laughing so hard they didn't have the strength to get her out of the hole. And Uncle Elías, he slipped in the mud and fell in too! (More laughter.)

Excerpt from *A Little Something to Ease the Pain* by René R. Aloma (1980).

and experience in professional urban theater that many rising U.S. Latino playwrights lacked. The exile of professional Latin American theater also coincided with the American civil rights movement, which radically transformed the notion of theater as an institution, challenging socially conscious playwrights and repertories to explore new themes, spaces, and techniques. The coalescence of these two influences dramatically affected the evolution of Latino theater. The genre broadened to encapsulate two facets of Latino identity: the political activism that arose in response to the conditions faced by Hispanic communities in the United States, and the ethnoracial implications of being defined as a "minority" by the dominant Anglo culture. One performance piece that reflected the development of Latino theater in the 1960s and 1970s was Osvaldo Dragún's one-act play *El hombre que se convirtió en perro* (The Man Who Became a Dog), a Chicano work that critiqued the inhuman working conditions of capitalism and commented on issues of race consciousness.

El Teatro Campesino and Chicano Theater

Modern theater, understood as a form of secular amusement, is known to be a European phenomenon that developed in Christian societies, as well as in Japan during the Hun dynasty. (Jews and Muslims are known not to have theater until the advent of the Enlightenment.) Although religious rituals also involve some sort of theatrical representation, the indigenous people of the Americas—in epicenters such as Macchu Picchu and Tenochtitlán in particular—were not exposed to the concept of theater until after 1492, when missionaries used the stage as a venue for purposes of indoctrination. More specifically, Spanish missionaries looked to theater as a way to introduce the notions of Western religion, using drama as a significant method for the conversion of indigenous peoples to Catholicism. As a result of this hybrid cultural past, Chicano theater in the United States reflects a dual heritage that includes Spanish and Catholic tradition as well as indigenous myth and ritual. This evolution has produced unique Chicano cultural and allegorical models of semimystical theater such as the auto-sacramental, *La Pastorela*, and passion plays.

Professional and commercial Mexican theatrical influences entered the United States with traveling theater companies in the late 19th century. One such company traveled by ship, stopping to perform at major cities along a section of the West Coast from San Francisco to Mazatlan, and another repertory performed lyric and dramatic works along the Mexican border from Laredo to Los Angeles. The Mexican Revolution of 1910 led to the establishment of numerous large colonies of Mexican immigrants throughout the United States, and soon after coast-to-coast theatrical circuits kicked off nationwide tours made possible by the advent of rail transportation.

In the 1930s, repatriation programs designed to deport Latin American immigrants living in the United States drastically reduced the populations of Mexican communities in California, the Southwest, and the Midwest, displacing many Mexican stage artists and playwrights and shrinking the audience for Hispanic plays. However, post–World War II immigration repopulated these communities and bolstered the development of Chicano artistic expression.

The history of contemporary Chicano theater begins with the genre's most prominent institution, El Teatro Campesino. Founded as a folk-theater group in 1965 in Delano, California, by Luís Miguel Valdéz, El Teatro Campesino initially functioned as a part of the United Farm Workers of America (UFW), a union led by César Chávez comprising mostly Chicano and Filipino farmworkers from the vineyards of the San Joaquin valley. The purpose of the theater group was to inform farmworkers about the union's goals, assist in recruiting new members, and to publicize the farmworkers' cause. Valdéz recruited farmworkers to develop "agitational" performance pieces and to serve as actors. Because they possessed only minimal funding and had to quickly create pieces that were functional and adaptable to issues the union faced, El Teatro Campesino used no scripts or scenery and relied on only the simplest props, sometimes as basic as signs hanging around the necks of actors to indicate their characters, such as *esquirole* (scab) and *patroncito* (grape-grower boss).

El Teatro Campesino mixed traditional Mexican music and singing with burlesque comedy to create biting satires meant as propaganda against the grape-grower bosses and as a call to action for the audience. Valdéz and the Teatro catered their plays to the Mexican American farmworker community, performing pieces that incorporated elements from their cultural heritage, such as *caló* (Spanish slang), folk narratives, and Mexican mythology. The plays also contained influences from the Mexican *carpas,* or vaudeville tent shows that toured the American

Southwest as early as the 19th century. To relate to and unify the Chicano farmworkers, El Teatro Campesino used folkloric symbols and allegorical figures such as Superstition, Death, and the Sun. The company's performances aimed to empower Mexican American farmworkers by connecting contemporary Chicano life to the legacy of pre-Columbian Mexico. Semimystical and always agitational, El Teatro's brand of theater established the template for contemporary Chicano dramatics.

In its years working with the UFW, El Teatro Campesino employed two types of performance pieces, the *acto* (skit) and the dramatized *corrido* (ballad). *Actos,* one-act, 15-minute skits, provided the Teatro a simple format from which it could quickly and effectively transmit direct and succinct messages to the farmworkers. *Actos* characteristically involved simple and straightforward plots, where the roles of protagonist and antagonist were clearly defined and problems were resolved with uncomplicated solutions. Valdéz also chose to perform *actos* in the grassroots theater because they required few resources. *Actos* could be written quickly, required few cast members and little financial backing, and could be performed with minimal rehearsal and production time. Like much of what was done by the union, the *actos* were collective efforts. Even on the Teatros's fledgling stages, Valdéz encouraged all members of the company to participate in writing and producing the performances. El Teatro Campesino also performed dramatized traditional Mexican *corridos* (ballads). *Corridos* were similar to *actos* in that they adapted themselves well to the Teatro's minimal resources; and because folk ballads told a story, they translated well to the stage.

The professionalization of El Teatro Campesino, and the first steps toward developing a Chicano theater movement, began in 1967 when the Teatro split from the UFW and formed its own institution, El Teatro Campesino Cultural, a farmworkers' cultural center in Del Rey, California. While maintaining its ties to the struggles of the grape workers and the UFW, El Teatro Campesino diversified its repertoire, performing *actos* that addressed broader issues affecting the Chicano communities throughout California. The company took on a new role as it began to perform to urban, multicultural audiences. El Teatro Campesino became the cultural ambassador of the Mexican American community through bilingual performance pieces, including *Soldado Razo*

(Buck Private) and *La Carpa de los Resquachis* (The Tent of the Underdogs), which delivered Mexican culture, history, and social and political concerns to a diverse audience.

Throughout the 1970s El Teatro Campesino explored fresh types of theater art and created elaborate and professional pieces that went beyond the *acto* and *corrido* to explore more experimental techniques to address themes of Chicano politics, culture, and identity. It became apparent that El Teatro Campesino had entered the mainstream when, in that decade, Valdéz and the Teatro began touring the United States, Mexico, and Europe, performing their traditional *actos*, as well as full-length plays written by other Latino playwrights.

El Teatro Campesino has come a long way since its humble beginning in 1965. It has become a nationally and internationally recognized performing arts groups, and various of its projects have garnered critical and commercial success. The greatest legacy of El Teatro Campesino, however, is the *acto*, a theatrical form that has served as the predecessor and the backbone to the corpus of work that now constitutes the basis of all Chicano drama.

Valdéz's role in bringing El Teatro Campesino and Chicano theater as a whole to such a level of maturity and attention cannot be overstated, and many consider him the innovator of theater for the Chicano people. In 1978 the Mark Taper Forum in Los Angeles commissioned Valdéz to write *Zoot Suit*, an award-winning play based on the true story of a group of young Chicano men involved in the Sleepy Lagoon murder trial that occurred during the 1940s in Los Angeles. After the play's 46 successful weeks on stage in Los Angeles, its run on Broadway failed and was terminated after only 58 performances. Valdéz directed the movie version in 1981 featuring Edward James Olmos as the flamboyant El Pachuco.

Chicano theater has also matured on other fronts. Playwrights including Carlos Morton, author of *The Many Deaths of Danny Rosales* and *Johnny Tenorio*, have established themselves internationally. Their work is often staged in regional theaters in cities such as Los Angeles, El Paso, and Chicago.

Puerto Rican Theater in New York

New York City is the center of Puerto Rican population and cultural expression in the continental United States; thus the city has provided the setting for the birth and maturation of contemporary Puerto

Actors celebrate during a production of *Zoot Suit*, a play produced by Luis Valdéz.

Rican Latino theater. New York City also boasts one of the richest and most extensive heritages of professional and commercial theatrical activity in the world, and the effects of operating in such a developed yet competitive market have had both beneficial and detrimental implications for Puerto Rican drama. The bases of contemporary Puerto Rican theater, however, are the dramatic techniques, use of music, modes of interaction and expression, mimetic gestures, and narrative formats established by both "high" theater and popular theater in Puerto Rico.

Like theater in the Spanish-ruled regions of California and the Southwest in the colonial period, the tradition of professional Puerto Rican theater found initial expression during the 18th century in biblical and moral dramas and processions that were organized by, and centered on, the Catholic Church. The island's theatrical activity increased as Puerto Rican theater troops performed Spanish classics during ecclesiastical or political events, such as the arrival of an archbishop or the coronation of the Spanish monarch. From this tradition of "high" theater came sporadic secular theater groups, including traveling theaters that staged Spanish works, as well as plays written by native dramatists for an increasingly bourgeois audience. Aiming to reproduce this established drama for a less affluent demographic, amateur theaters emerged in even the smallest towns across the island, performing in makeshift theaters and *zaguanes*, interior patios of city tenements converted into stages for a theater of *charlatanería* (buffoonery).

Like Chicano theater, contemporary Puerto Rican theater is rooted in labor activism. Its union ties also reach back to Puerto Rico, where Eduardo Conde, a member of the *zaguán* theater of Old San Juan and organizer of the Federación de Trabajadores Puertorriqueños, referred to his experience as a dramatist to construct a proletarian theater within the labor organization. Puerto Rican actors and playwrights brought with them to the United States when they emigrated from the island the traditional amateur stagecraft utilized by the workers' union and other nonprofessional troupes, and these theatrical customs melded with practices and traditions already established by 19th-century traveling Spanish-language troops that had performed to Hispanic audiences in

New York for decades. Contemporary Puerto Rican theater in the United States began as a continuation of these myriad spheres of Hispanic theatrical activity.

In New York City after World War II, Puerto Rican immigrants established their own communities within the city, and in 1953 a group of actors staged René Marqués's *La Carreta* in the community-based Hunts Point Palace. Written by a Puerto Rican author, *La Carreta* told the story of postwar migration and the effects on Puerto Rican families and culture of life in the United States. For Puerto Rican theater, the play represented an unprecedented dramatic consciousness, as audiences immediately recognized that the story *La Carreta* told was their own. The performance was the first installment of a corpus of performance pieces that became the foundation of contemporary Puerto Rican theater. From this original production two focal points of contemporary Puerto Rican theater were established—the Teatro Rodante Puertorriqueño (Puerto Rican Traveling Theater) and the Nuyorican theater movement on the Lower East Side of Manhattan in New York City.

The Puerto Rican Traveling Theater was the creation of Miriam Colón, a well-known Puerto Rican actress and director, who founded the theatrical company with the assistance of the Shakespeare Festival's Mobile Unit after producing in 1965 a second staging of *La Carreta* starring Raúl Julia. Conceived as an organization that would support and develop Puerto Rican theater in the community, the Traveling Theater initially staged professional performances of works that were created by established island dramatists, and later the organization began producing plays written by Puerto Rican American playwrights from New York.

Recognizing the demand for more diversity in the New York drama circuit and wishing to expand Puerto Rican theatrical expression, the company began performing Spanish-language plays translated into English for non-Latino audiences. Likewise, the Traveling Theater periodically staged samples of European and North American theater in both languages. Since its inception the Traveling Theater has presented quality professional drama that reaches out to broader audiences while remaining relevant to the Puerto Rican community. Besides *La Carreta*, some notable productions include dramatizations of short episodes of the New York experience by Pedro Juan Soto, and the theatrical presentation of poems by New York writers such as Pedro Pietri, Papoleto Meléndez, and Piri Thomas. Today, the company owns its own theater and operates a traveling unit and drama school.

The second focal point of contemporary Puerto Rican theater in New York is the Nuyorican theater movement of the Lower East Side. Professional theatrical activity in the area was pioneered by two organizations, the Puerto Rican Bilingual Workshop, founded by Carla Pinza in 1973, and the Nuyorican Poets' Cafe, formed in 1974 by poet Miguel Algarín and a group of writers and artists who called themselves Nuyorican in recognition of their identities as Puerto Rican New Yorkers.

Aiming to capture the harsh conflict and conditions of oppression that they felt characterized Puerto Rican reality, Nuyorican playwrights such as Miguel Piñero and Papoleto Meléndez spearheaded a body of work that attempted to capture the living drama of Nuyorican daily life. Piñero's play *Short Eyes*, which dramatizes the destructive effect of the United States prison system on inmates, won the New York Drama Critics Circle Award for Best American Play of the 1973–1974 season. Inspired by the commercial success of *Short Eyes*, Algarín and affiliates of the Open Theater conducted the Nuyorican Writers' and Actors' Workshop in 1974, a program that later grew into the Nuyorican Theater Festival, featuring works such as Lucky Cienfuegos's *America Congo Mania* and Piñero's *Side Show*.

In addition to these two founding companies, today the Nuyorican theater movement incorporates a variety of dramatic institutions such as Aquarius, the Latin Insomniacs, the Family, and Teatro Otra Cosa. These groups have encouraged playwriting as an imperative of theatrical work, and each individual company has employed its own unique style to address an assortment of issues that relate to the generalization of Puerto Ricans born or raised on the mainland. The existence of multiple independent creative movements within Nuyorican theater adds to the diversity of contemporary Puerto Rican theater and ensures that mainstream acceptance of the professional side of the genre will not lead to the sacrifice of the social and political consciousness that characterize popular or grass-roots Puerto Rican dramatics.

ANNA IN THE TROPICS

Marela: What are you planning to read to us?
Juan Julian: First, Tolstoy, *Anna Karenina.*
Marela: *Anna Karenina.* I already like the title, Is it romantic?
Juan Julian: Yes, quite romantic.
Marela: Ah, *Anna Karenina* will go right to Cheché's heart. The poor man. He won't be able to take it.
Juan Julian: I could pick another book. I've brought many.
Conchita: No, read *Anna Karenina* if that's the book that you chose.
Marela: He needs to listen to another love story and let the words make nests in his hair, so he can find another woman.
Ofelia: And how do you like Tampa so far, Juan Julian?
Juan Julian: Well, I . . . I . . . It's very . . . It seems like it's a city in the making.
Ofelia: That is is. We are still trying to create a little city that resembles the ones we left back in the island.
Juan Julian: It's curious, there are no mountains or hills here. Lots of sky I have noticed . . . And clouds . . . The largest clouds I've ever seen, as if they had soaked up the whole sea. It's all so flat all around. That's why the sky seems so much bigger here and infinite. Bigger than the sky I know back home. And there's so much light. There doesn't seem to be a place where one could hide.

Excerpt from *Anna in the Tropics* by Nilo Cruz (2003).

Latina Theater

From the beginning of the contemporary Latino theater movement, Latinas have participated both on stage and backstage in a multitude of capacities. However, the rise of Latina playwrights in the mid-1980s proved to be the true catalyst for the birth of Latina theater, a hybrid genre that embodies both Hispanic and feminine discourse. Plays written, directed, or produced by Latina dramatists inevitably bear characteristics shared by generalized Latino theater. However, the Latina theater movement has carved out a niche of its own thanks to Latina playwrights who create plays, often with female protagonists, that strive to retell history in a way that empowers women.

Until the mid-1980s there were only three major Latina playwrights: Dolores Prida, María Irene Fornés, and Estela Portillo. Although now considered the vanguard of the Latina theater movement, these early dramatists lacked a historically established space into which to insert themselves and their work—the overall concept of Latina playwriting and "Latinidad" were only in their embryonic stages, and many Hispanic women involved in drama identified themselves along ethnic and nationalist lines rather than as Latinas. However, the commercial success of Latina novelists, the artistic maturation of female members of regional theaters, and the professionalization of playwriting as more Latinas choose to advance their education in theater have all played influential roles in setting the stage for Latina theater.

With the exception of Estela Portillo's volume *Sor Juana and Other Plays* (1983), it was not until the 1990s that Latina playwrights such as Fornés, Prida, and Cherríe Moraga began to publish anthologies of plays written by Latinas. These dramatic pieces addressed previously taboo subjects such as the female body, as well as engaged a variety of questions and issues concerning gender relations, marginalization, and sexuality. Foremost, Latina theater uses theatrical expression to focus on dramatizing the identity of women to a wide audience.

Latino Theater Present and Future

Contemporary Latino theater is an ever-evolving art, whose diversity has grown exponentially since it first began to flourish in the 1960s and 1970s. Although many of the founding institutions of the movement still exist, previously ethnic- or nationalist-specific theaters now incorporate plays written by Latino playwrights from cultural or national roots other than their own. Since 1990 the various entities that practice Hispanic drama—companies representing a multitude of ethnic and regional variations as well as distinct styles and ideologies—have gradually united into a Pan-Latino theater movement, greater in breadth and depth, that now reaches out to a much wider audience. Theatrical events such as the 2003 Latino Festival at Chicago's Goodman Theater and the Miami Hispanic International Theater Festival exemplify the efforts of Latino playwrights to bring their stories together as various dramatic expressions of a similar American experience. The result is a Latino theater movement that is networked and less rigidly compartmentalized, but still rich in diversity and representative of a broad spectrum of backgrounds and personal histories.

The movement's styles and characteristics have also been adapted to meet the circumstances of Latino communities, the trends of conventional theater, and the demands of an expanding audience. While Spanish-language theater in Latin America and the United States serves as the heritage and foundation of contemporary Latino theater, from its inception the genre has often been a linguistically hybrid phenomenon, operating in both Spanish and English. In recent years, however, Hispanic playwrights have shifted more and more to writing English-language scripts only, a transition that reflects both a change in the Latino community and a desire among Hispanic dramatists to reach a broader audience. In addition, dramatists of all types have attempted to move away from the clichés that characterize Latino theater—magical realism, the suffering mother, the machismo father—to create a theater movement that is entirely self-determined, made rich with meaning rather than laden with stereotypes.

The commercial success of stage works such as *Forever Tango* and John Leguizamo's *Freak,* and the critical praise acquired by Nilo Cruz's Pulitzer Prize winning *Anna in the Tropics,* indicate that there is potential for large-scale professional Hispanic theater works to attract substantial audiences from both inside and outside the Latino community. However, the Broadway failure of *Zoot Suit* and other Latino-oriented plays have rendered investors cautious of Hispanic projects, despite whatever acclaim they may glean in smaller venues.

One of the primary obstacles facing professional Latino theater today is the paucity of Hispanic audiences throughout the country. With a tendency to gravitate toward plays written by playwrights from their own ethnic or national group, Hispanic theatergoers have yet to constitute a base-audience large enough to sustain grand-scale Latino productions. However, many established theater companies have begun to include English-language plays by contemporary Latino dramatists in their seasons. In addition to enriching and entertaining non-Latino audiences, professional Hispanic theater productions are cultivating a Latino audience while bringing Latino social patterns, internal conflicts, traditional culture, and political and social concerns to the public sphere.

Popular theaters and unconventional theater companies also continue to do work that inspires social action. In Latin America after World War II, a radical type of theater appeared in impoverished countries such as Brazil, Mexico, Venezuela, and Argentina that sought to bring theater to the masses and to use it as a tool for political awareness. Theorists and directors including Augusto Boal organized guerrilla theater groups. An age of street theater and improvisational traveling performances was born. That approach had an impact on Latinos in the United States. Guillermo Gómez-Peña, Coco Fusco, Nao Bustamante, Migdalia Cruz, Enrique Chagoya and other *performeros,* as performance artists became known, created a movement of outrageous theater that dealt with social issues. Similarly, groups such as Culture Clash explored major historical events from a strictly non-Anglo perspective.

RELATED ARTICLES

Alfaro, Luis; Farmworkers Movement; Feminism; Fornés, María Irene; Gomez-Peña, Guillermo; Literature; Loisaida; Nuyorican Poets Cafe; Pachuco; Piñero, Miguel; Sleepy Lagoon Case; Thomas, Piri; Valdéz, Luis; *West Side Story*; Zoot Suit Riots.

FURTHER READING

Castro, Rafaela G. *Chicano Folklore: A Guide to the Folktales, Traditions, Rituals and Religious Practices of Mexican Americans.* Oxford: Oxford Univ. Press, 2001.

De la Roche, Elisa. *¡Teatro Hispano!: Three Major New York Companies.* New York: Garland, 1995.

Feyder, Linda, ed. *Shattering the Myth: Plays by Hispanic Women.* Houston, Tex.: Arte Público Press, 1992.

Kanellos, Nicolás, and Jorge A. Huerta, eds. *Nuevos Pasos: Chicano and Puerto Rican Drama.* Houston, Tex.: Arte Público Press, 1989.

Montoya, Richard, Ricardo Salinas, and Herbert Sigüenza. *Culture Clash: Life, Death, and Revolutionary Comedy.* New York: Theater Communications Grp., 1998.

Roman, David. "Latino Performance and Identity." *Aztlán: A Journal of Chicano Studies* 2 (Fall 1997), 151–168.

Sandoval-Sánchez, Alberto, and Nancy Saporta Sternbach, eds. *Puro Teatro: A Latina Anthology.* Tucson: Univ. of Ariz. Press, 2000.

Svich, Caridad, and María Teresa Marrero, eds. *Out of the Fringe: Contemporary Latina/Latino Theatre and Performance.* New York: Theater Communications Grp., 2000.

ADAM JUDE GONZÁLES

THOMAS, PIRI

Born: September 30, 1928; New York, New York

With his novelized autobiography, *Down These Mean Streets*, Piri Thomas set the parameters for a genre that has been closely identified with the Puerto Rican diaspora novel. Set in the streets of the ghetto (most often in El Barrio—East Harlem—but also, on occasion, in the South Bronx), *Mean Streets* dwells on the effects of poverty, privation, and prejudice on a young man. The final positive outcome of *Mean Streets* endows it and the genre with the possibility of achieving an archetypical quality—turning the protagonist into a hero who triumphs over his troubles.

Born John Peter Thomas in New York City's Spanish Harlem, Piri Thomas was the eldest of the four surviving children born to a Cuban father and a Puerto Rican mother, both of whom had immigrated to New York. (Piri was the nickname his mother gave him.) His parents raised their children in El Barrio, but at one point moved to Long Island in an attempt to give them a better life. Nevertheless, Piri succumbed to the violence of the streets. In 1950 he was wounded in a shoot-out with the police in the course of an armed robbery. He was sent to Sing Sing prison and was later moved to Comstock, Great Meadows Correctional Institution, spending a total of seven years in prison.

While incarcerated, Thomas read and educated himself. Once free, he began to write about his experiences and was aided in publication by Angus Cameron, an editor from Knopf. *Down These Mean Streets* was published in 1967 to considerable critical and popular acclaim. It made the *New York Times* Best-Seller List, a first for a book written by a Puerto Rican. It was a classic autobiographical coming-of-age novel about a black Hispanic boy who is confused about his identity in terms of race and ethnicity and who responds with violence to the violence that surrounds him.

When Thomas left prison he worked with Youth Development Incorporated, trying to help young people avoid addiction and violence, using his own story as a deterrent. The notoriety that his first novel brought garnered him an invitation to Puerto Rico, where he lectured at Interamerican University and was active in antidrug programs. He lived in Puerto Rico on three different occasions. Nevertheless, his work was little-known on the island. In 1983 Thomas, who lectured frequently in universities and colleges, moved to San Francisco with his wife, Suzanne Dod Thomas, who translated *Down These Mean Streets* into Spanish in 1998.

After publishing his first book, Thomas wrote *Savior, Savior, Hold My Hand* (1972), also autobiographical; *Seven Long Times*, a prison memoir (1974); and *Stories of El Barrio* (1978). He has written several plays, among them *Las calles de oro* (The Golden Streets), which was produced and performed in 1972 by Myriam Colón's Puerto Rican Traveling Theater.

In 1964 a documentary of his work with street gangs, *Petey and Johnny*, was produced by Drew Associates. It was awarded first prize in the Festivale dei Popoli in Florence, Italy. Another, *The World of Piri Thomas*, written and narrated by Thomas himself, was directed in 1968 by Gordon Parks and produced by National Educational Television.

He has also produced several recordings of his poetry recited against a backdrop of Latin jazz played by, among others, Carlos "Patato" Valdéz, with Greg Landau as producer. He calls them "wordsongs."

Down These Mean Streets made the American reading public aware, for the first time, of a different dimension to the phenomenon of Puerto Rican migration. The only other widely known effect of that migration on the arts had been rather negative: the portrayal of New York Puerto Ricans in the Leonard Bernstein–Stephen Sondheim musical *West Side Story*, which opened on Broadway in 1957.

Down These Mean Streets adopted an autobiographical form already familiar to American readers through the then-recent work of African American authors such as Claude Brown and his *Manchild in the Promised Land* (1965) and Alex Haley's *The Au-*

ALIEN TURF

Sometimes you don't fit in. Like if you're a Puerto Rican on an Italian block. After my new baby brother, Ricardo, died of some kind of germs, Poppa moved us from 111th Street to Italian turf on 114th Street between Second and Third Avenue. I guess Poppa wanted to get Momma away from the hard memories of the old pad.

Excerpt from *Down These Mean Streets* by Piri Thomas (1967).

tobiography of Malcom X (1965). These also were stories of prejudice and discrimination against migrants who came from the South who were technically U.S. citizens but lived in urban ghettos amid difficult conditions. The 1960s were, in fact, a time when books with dramatic and shocking content reflected the growing public opinion about and public policy toward the rights of African Americans.

Thomas's book, however, differs in important ways. The crucial issue is not being discriminated against because of his skin color, but the choice that the protagonist must make between racial or ethnic identification. The subtle differences between the two that are present in American society are played up in Thomas's novel. In the years covered by *Down These Mean Streets,* to identify with a Hispanic group could accrue some advantages over the identification of a person as black. The story thus became a search for the best way—or the most authentic way—in which an "outsider" could assert himself within American society. This theme had rarely been sounded before in American literature or, for that matter, in Puerto Rican literature.

Down These Mean Streets, moreover, dwelled on immigrant Hispanic families' domestic relationships concerning the issue of color. In addition, it showed the ways in which immigrants sought—unsuccessfully, for the most part—to achieve the "American Dream" and the differences between the parents' and the children's experiences and expectations. It focused, above all, on a young boy's life in the streets and the ways in which he interacts with his peers within a difficult, violence-ridden environment while devising ways to get ahead. Thomas transformed the usual rags-to-riches or rags-to-doom theme of this kind of story into a journey of increasing self-awareness and personal liberation despite external circumstances. Thus it transcends the typical ghetto story or the prison memoir.

Form and language contribute to the book's effectiveness. The city of New York and its Spanish ghetto come alive with a particular intensity. Thomas's literary language is a powerful tool—a strong street language, full of curses that parallel—with their violence—the unsavory realities of the characters. Thomas's skillful use of Spanish terms anchors the narrative to a particular time, place, and social milieu. Immensely vital, even shocking, and, at the same time, hauntingly rhythmical, his writing is the book's biggest asset. The book piques the senses: we can

feel, smell, touch, and hear as the protagonist feels, smells, touches, and hears. The book comes alive with his experiences, which are seen from a highly effective double perspective. On the one hand, the protagonist looks at his life and its surroundings with a cold-eyed, unsentimental, sharp focus while, on the other hand, the author infuses his narrative with a particular understanding and even tenderness not only for what is described but also for the child who is remembered as he then was.

None of Thomas's later books reached the heights and depths of *Down These Mean Streets.* Some cover similar territory and all have a more documentary quality that lacks the particular poetry of his first book, which has become a true classic of Puerto Rican diaspora writing. Among the novels that have continued the genre, with variants, two of the most important are Edwin Torres's *Carlito's Way* (1975) and *Spidertown* by Abraham Rodríguez, Jr. (1993).

RELATED ARTICLES

Literature, Puerto Rican on the Mainland; Theater.

FURTHER READING

Aparicio, Frances. "From Ethnicity to Multiculturalism: An Historical Overview of Puerto Rican Literature in the United States." In *Handbook of Hispanic Cultures in the United States: Literature and Art.* Ed. by Nicolás Kanellos and Claudio Esteva-Fabregat. Houston, Tex.: Arte Público Press, 1993.

Barradas, Efraín. "Isla entre dos islas: Nota sobre la estructura narrativa de *Down These Mean Streets* (Island Between Two Islands: Note on the Narrative Structure of *Down These Mean Streets).*" In *Partes de un todo* (Parts of a Whole). Río Piedras: Editorial de la Universidad de Puerto Rico, 1998.

Flores, Juan. "Puerto Rican Literature in the United States: Stages and Perspectives." In *Divided Borders. Essays on Puerto Rican Identity.* Houston, Tex.: Arte Público Press, 1993.

Hernández, Carmen Dolores. "Piri Thomas." In *Puerto Rican Voices in English: Interviews with Writers.* Westport, Conn.: Praeger, 1997.

Stavans, Ilan. "Race and Mercy: Piri Thomas." In *Conversations with Ilan Stavans.* Tucson: Univ. of Ariz. Press, 2005.

CARMEN DOLORES HERNÁNDEZ

THREE RIVERS

In 1949 south Texas, most Mexican Americans attended inferior schools, lived in substandard housing, and benefited little from public services. Bigotry took the form of Anglo paternalism—as long as the Mexican American stayed within well defined but seldom spoken bounds, little trouble ensued. Certainly such was the case in Three Rivers, a town of about 2,000 approximately halfway between San Antonio and

Corpus Christi. The Guadalupe Longoria family was better off than many of its neighbors because Mr. Longoria was a skilled carpenter and fence builder who was employed regularly by Anglos and who often hired neighbors to work for him.

Félix Longoria, born in 1924, grew up working for his father and also for nearby oil field operations. At age 18 he married Beatrice Moreno. Two years later, in November 1944, Félix enlisted in the U.S. Army and said good-bye to Beatrice, their young daughter Adela, and Three Rivers. Eight months later, on Luzon Island in the Philippines, young Félix Longoria was killed in action and buried in a temporary military cemetery.

In late 1948 the army notified Beatrice, by then living with her parents in Corpus Christi, Texas, that her husband's remains could now be shipped home. Where did she want them sent? She decided on Three Rivers and went to arrange a wake at the Manon Rice Funeral Home, the only such facility in town. Beatrice was urged by the mortician to use the Longoria family house instead, because "the whites would not like it." She returned a day later after receiving further inquires from the War Department about the disposition of Félix's remains. The funeral home director repeated that he would not host the wake because of white opinion, but he agreed to help with a wake at the small, now vacant and ill-equipped house Beatrice and Félix had lived in after their marriage. Back in Corpus Christi, Beatrice told her family, whereupon her sister Sara, involved in community affairs, thought to enlist the aide of Héctor P. García, an activist doctor. Just months earlier García had formed the American GI Forum, a group dedicated to helping Mexican American and other war veterans gain their lawful benefits.

García called funeral home owner Tom Kennedy in Three Rivers and was told, "I have to do what the white people want." García countered by pleading patriotism—the deceased was a veteran, "Doesn't that make a difference?" Kennedy replied that it didn't. "You know how the Latin people get drunk and lay around all the time. . . . I don't dislike the Mexican people but I have to run my business. . . ."

García notified a sympathetic Corpus Christi journalist, then sent 17 telegrams to the national press and to officials in Washington, D.C., and Austin. When U.S. Senator Lyndon B. Johnson read García's telegram at his Capitol Hill office, he immediately exclaimed, "By God, we'll bury him in Arlington!" He wrote to Beatrice, "This injustice and prejudice is deplorable." Within days newspapers across the United States and deep into Latin America knew of the case.

At two P.M. February 16, 1949, Félix Longoria was buried with full military honors at Arlington National Cemetery. The Longoria family was present, as well as Lyndon Johnson and White House, State Department, and Mexican Embassy officials.

It was classic Johnson, writes his biographer Robert A. Caro, who saw the entire drama as encompassing Johnson's honorable sympathy for the underdog as well as his uncanny ability to exploit a circumstance to his great political advantage. When Johnson's considerable Texas Anglo support strongly disapproved of his action, he distanced himself somewhat. In Three Rivers, near the confluence of the Atascosa, Frio, and Nueces rivers, Anglos insisted that funeral home owner Tom Kennedy had simply been misunderstood, that race had never been a problem in Three Rivers.

The dilemma's rapid resolution astonished and exhilarated Mexican Americans throughout Texas and elsewhere, and gave the American GI Forum an enormous boost. It did likewise for García, who became a protégé of Johnson's. As for Johnson, when he campaigned in south Texas for re-election in 1954, he was greeted by, "¡Olé Johnson, Olé Johnson! ¡Tres Ríos, Tres Ríos, Tres Ríos!"

RELATED ARTICLES

American GI Forum; Discrimination; Texas.

FURTHER READING

Caro, Robert A. *The Years of Lyndon Johnson: Master of the Senate.* New York: Alfred A. Knopf, 2002.

Carroll, Patrick J. *Félix Longoria's Wake.* Austin: Univ. of Tex. Press, 2003.

Pycior, Julie Leininger. *LBJ & Mexican Americans: The Paradox of Power.* Austin: Univ. of Tex. Press, 1997.

TOM MILLER

TIJERINA, REIES LÓPEZ

Born: 1926; Falls City, Texas

A Pentecostal preacher born to cotton-pickers in Falls City, Texas, Reies López Tijerina was one of the most distinguished leaders of the Chicano movement of the late 1960s and early 1970s. The numerous provisions of the Treaty of Guadalupe Hidalgo (1848) affected many people in the decades that followed its ratification, but almost 120 years would pass before it would be presented in court by a New Mexico firebrand, López Tijerina, as a resounding reminder of its provisions. The terms of the treaty that Tijerina drew on were those that protected the culture and property rights that had been in effect in Mexico to continue under U.S. rule. Most land grant claims had been eroded and erased, adjudicated and legislated out of existence, and, in general, rendered less valuable than the parchment they were written on. Many protested this treatment in court early on, usually individually and occasionally with others, but not until the mid-1960s did Tijerina's militant movement—whose purpose was to reclaim the seized land from governments and current owners and return it to the descendants of the original land grantees—force consideration of these guarantees.

Centered in northern New Mexico, the Alianza Federal de las Mercedes (Federal Alliance of Land Grants) had Tijerina as its leader. He used the Treaty of Guadalupe Hidalgo as the foundation for his declarations.

Tijerina's followers lived mostly in Rio Arriba County—an expanse of fairly low population and very high poverty. For generations prior to U.S. acquisition of present-day New Mexico, many inhabitants followed Spanish law, which allowed them use of ancestral lands, both communal and family. Federal agencies usurped much of this land in the 20th century, leading to ill will in relation to property and related concerns. Two events precluded conventional redress of grievances: a 1960 federal court decision giving Congress, not the courts, jurisdiction over treaty interpretation, and a 1966 New Mexico state finding that "There is little historical validity to any of [the Aliancista] claims."

Combining the land issue with health, education, and general welfare concerns, on October 16, 1966, Tijerina and the Alianza made the bold move of occupying the Echo Amphitheater campground in the Kit Carson National Forest, which had been part of an 18th-century Spanish estate. The occupation lasted one week. Although authorities subsequently set up barriers, Tijerina and others returned to again take over the land, an act for which they were soon arrested.

The following spring some landowners in Tierra Amarilla County suffered acts of sabotage and violence that were blamed on Aliancistas; haystacks and farm buildings were burned, fences were cut, animals set free. The Alianza announced a meeting for June 3, 1967, at Coyote, New Mexico, a gathering that the county district attorney, Alfonso Sánchez, tried to stymie by blocking access to the town and arresting on charges of unlawful assembly those who got by the barricades. Eight Aliancistas were arrested and jailed. Two days later Tijerina and some followers, all armed, set out to free their imprisoned comrades and make a citizen's arrest of Sánchez. Their surprise attack on the Tierra Amarilla courthouse wounded a deputy sheriff superficially and a state trooper critically. Tijerina, unaware that the eight had been released on bond, went into hiding, but a couple of armed colleagues took two hostages as shields to escape the area.

Eventually the National Guard and other law officers spread out through the thickets, arroyos, and hills of the county searching for Tijerina and other Aliancistas. On June 10 Tijerina was captured. In December 1968 he successfully defended himself in court for his part in the raid; a jury found him not guilty on three charges. Tijerina was not so fortunate in his arrests and trials resulting from other incidents, and in the following years he was in and out of jail on a wide range of charges stemming from his personal audacity and political militancy; these convictions were for assault and false imprisonment.

Tijerina gained respect for his extensive land grant research in the United States and Mexico as well as for his willingness to meet with elected officeholders. He formed alliances with Martin Luther King, Jr., and other civil rights leaders of his day. *Corridos* (ballads) mythologized Tijerina and the Aliancistas, but years after the infamous courthouse raid, by which time he had mellowed in his attitude on race and instead considered class as the main social impediment, he ruefully acknowledged, "We traded justice for food stamps. We accepted powdered milk instead of justice."

Tijerina moved to the state of Michoacán, Mexico, in the mid-1990s, making infrequent trips to the States. In October 2003, with diabetes rendering his legs almost useless, Tijerina visited Albuquerque, New Mexico, to receive a Lifetime Achievement Award at the De Colores Hispanic Culture Festival.

RELATED ARTICLES

Chicanismo; Chicano Movement; Civil Rights; Guadalupe Hidalgo, Treaty of; New Mexico.

FURTHER READING

Blawis, Patricia Bell. *Tijerina and the Land Grants.* New York: Intl. Pubs., 1971.

García, Mario T. *Memories of Chicano History, the Life and Narrative of Bert Corona.* Berkeley: Univ. of Calif. Press, 1994.

Gonzáles, Carolyn. "The Tijerina Archive at the University of New Mexico—Visionary or Villain?" *Hispanic Outlook in Higher Education* 12; no. 14 (April 22, 2002): 8.

Nabokov, Peter. *Tijerina and the Courthouse Raid.* Berkeley, Calif.: Ramparts Press, 1970.

Rosales, F. Arturo. *Testimonio: A Documentary History of the Mexican American Struggle for Civil Rights.* Houston, Tex.: Arte Público Press, 2000.

Tijerina, Reies López. *They Called Me "King Tiger": My Struggle for the Land and Our Rights.* Tr. by José Angel Gutiérrez. Houston, Tex.: Arte Público Press, 2000.

TOM MILLER

TOBACCO

Tobacco has been commercially produced in North America since John Rolfe began farming the crop at the Jamestown colony in 1612. While attempts to farm tobacco had occurred as far north as Connecticut and as far west as California, truly successful production was possible only in the southeastern United States, where it became a cornerstone of state and local economies. Today, significant production is limited to 16 states, with North Carolina and Kentucky accounting for approximately 70 percent of all tobacco grown in the United States.

For the first few years of commercial cultivation, farm labor was supplied by the farm owner and other colonists who were paid for their efforts. Tobacco is a labor-intensive crop and a permanent, cheap workforce was necessary. For more than 200 years slaves labored on tobacco farms and plantations. After slavery was abolished following the U.S. Civil War, the inexpensive labor required to work large tobacco farms disappeared, and tobacco farmers were once again forced to rely on family members and a few paid workers to cultivate and harvest their crops. Change began in the 1970s; since the 1980s, the Latino influence on tobacco farming has steadily increased with higher rates of ownership and greater numbers of temporary and seasonal laborers. The Latino farm laborer has become the mainstay of the tobacco workforce, representing over 80 percent of all hired tobacco farmworkers in North Carolina and Kentucky.

The number of farms in the United States declined as the nation moved from its rural roots toward a more urban society. Between 1982 and 1997, farm ownership decreased 14.7 percent. Latinos, however, have moved in the opposite direction—overall farm ownership increased 71.3 percent (from 16,183 farms to 27,717 farms) over the same period. The trend was even more pronounced in the tobacco industry, where the number of Latino-owned tobacco farms doubled between 1982 and 1997. Eighty percent of the increase occurred in just the five years between 1992 and 1997 (from 225 to 405 tobacco farms).

Three percent of all farms in the United States grow tobacco, but tobacco farms constitute less than 1.5 percent of all Latino-owned farms in the United States. However, in the states where tobacco is grown, the percentage of Latino-owned tobacco enterprises is significant. In particular, 40.7 percent of all Latino-operated farms in Kentucky and 34 percent of all Latino-owned farms in North Carolina were involved in tobacco production in 1997.

While farm ownership among Latinos in the United States is on the rise, the largest Latino contribution to farming is the employment of nonimmigrant temporary and seasonal migrant farmworkers. Migrant farmworkers relocate each season to obtain agricultural employment. These workers may move from state to state as they work on different crops at different times of the year and may be documented (legal) workers or undocumented (illegal) workers. For more than 50 years, the documented foreign migrant farmworkers have been employed in the United States under one of two programs, the Bracero Program and the H–2A Program. However, the majority of agricultural workers in the United States are believed to be undocumented.

Since the beginning of the 20th century, U.S. agricultural producers have depended on a foreign workforce, mostly Mexican, for a significant percentage of their temporary labor. From 1942 through 1964, migrant agricultural workers from Mexico generally worked legally in the United States under the Bracero Program. Established initially to meet World War II labor shortages, the program provided approximately 5 million workers in its 22-year existence, peaking at more than 400,000 workers in the mid-1950s. While a few of the *Braceros* were employed in the tobacco fields, they were never a significant percentage of that workforce.

Since 1964 the only legal temporary foreign agricultural worker program in the United States has been the H–2A guest-worker program. First authorized in 1952 as the H-2 program, H-2A is a foreign labor certification program that allows agricultural producers to hire nonimmigrant temporary workers when the producers can demonstrate that there is a shortage of U.S. workers who are willing, able, qualified, and available to perform the duties at the time and place required.

The number of workers entering the United States under the H-2A program is significantly fewer than under the Bracero Program, but the effect on the tobacco industry is much greater. Historically, the H-2A program was used mainly to bring Jamaicans into Florida to cut sugarcane, but with increased mechanization of the sugarcane industry, tobacco has become the primary utilizer of H-2A labor. In 2001 a total of 47,686 H-2A visas were issued, with almost one-quarter of them granted for work on tobacco farms in North Carolina (9,000) and Kentucky (2,700). According to the USDA Economic Research Service, in 1997 tobacco farms employed 62 percent of all H-2A temporary workers.

To participate in the H-2A program, a potential employer must be able to show that there are insufficient numbers of U.S. residents available to perform the work and that the wages and working conditions of Americans in similar employment will not be adversely affected by the hiring of temporary employees. Additionally, if at any time before the season is half over a qualified American worker applies for employment, the H-2A employer must hire the American worker even if a temporary foreign worker must be released.

If H-2A certification is granted by the U.S. Department of Labor, the tobacco farmer can then offer a written employment contract to a foreign worker who can work only for that farmer for the extent of the contract. The offered contract must spell out the conditions for migrant farm labor, including the hours of work required (usually either or seven or eight per day), wages, housing, and transportation reimbursements. The wages offered must be the highest of the prevailing wage for the particular crop, the state or federal minimum wage, or the "adverse effect wage rate." Under conditions set by the program, the tobacco producers are also required to provide the workers with three-quarters of the number of hours in the job offer or pay the worker for any shortfall. This is referred to as the "three-quarters" guarantee. Overtime is permitted and should be paid at one-and-one-half times the regular hourly

© JOSE GOITIA/AP/WIDE WORLD PHOTOS

Cuban singer Francisco "Compay Segundo" Repilado smokes a cigar he rolled himself, in Havana, Cuba, 2001.

rate of pay. The employer must provide or pay for the worker's housing and provide worker's compensation for on-the-job injuries. If housing is provided, the structures should meet federal safety and health standards.

The H-2A provisions also include protections against unwarranted retribution on workers who report violations of the contract. However, since the H-2A worker is tied to one employer during the length of the contract, most H-2A workers are reluctant to report any violations, fearing that they will lose their jobs or will not be hired in the future.

Since the end of the Bracero program, foreign farmworkers have increasingly had to work in the United States illegally. However, because of the fear of deportation, a precise count of the undocumented workforce (agricultural or nonagricultural) is not possible. In 2000 the Immigration and Naturalization Service estimated that 7 million illegal aliens were living in the United States, with the Pew Institute estimating that 58 percent of undocumented workers were employed in agriculture. Estimates of undocumented farmworkers generally range from 25 percent to 75 percent of the workforce, with the National Agriculture Workers Survey concluding that 52 percent of farmworkers in 1997 were working illegally in the country.

Although the number of illegally employed farmworkers in the tobacco industry is undoubtedly significant, the relative success in employing H-2A workers has probably resulted in smaller percentages of undocumented foreign workers in the tobacco fields. However, just as with agricultural workers in total, the number of illegally employed tobacco farmworkers is unknown. Therefore the tobacco farmer's dependence on the undocumented worker cannot be quantified.

President George W. Bush proposed a change in the guest-worker program that would give temporary legal status to millions of illegal immigrants in the United States by allowing undocumented persons already working in the United States to obtain a work visa. Anyone wishing to immigrate through the program would need to have a job offer from an employer willing to sponsor him or her for the period of the visa. The visa could be valid for up to three years, but once the visa expired, the guest worker would have to return to his or her home country. As presently proposed, these temporary visas could not be adjusted to "green cards," or permanent residency. Although the proposal is controversial, tobacco producers are generally supportive. Many farmers believe that implementing the proposal would broaden the farm labor pool by allowing undocumented immigrants who were previously afraid to seek employment to do so without risking deportation. The program would also lessen fears associated with the hiring of possible undocumented workers at planting and harvest times when labor shortages force farmers to use whatever labor they can find.

Other proposals that endeavor to change current immigration and temporary foreign worker policies are at various stages of the legislative process. These proposals include the Land Border Security and Immigration Improvement Act, introduced in July 2003 by Senator John McCain and Representatives Jim Kolbe and Jeff Flake, and the Hagel–Daschle Immigration Reform Act of 2004, introduced by Senators Tom Daschle and Charles Hagel.

Through contact with pesticides, fertilizers, and the tobacco plant itself, tobacco fieldworkers find themselves at greater risk of developing many health problems, including nicotine poisoning, respiratory illnesses, skin and eye disorders, infertility, and possibly cancer.

The most commonly reported illness among tobacco farmworkers is "Green Tobacco Sickness." Attributed to acute nicotine poisoning and most commonly characterized by headaches, nausea, vomiting, and dizziness, the illness tends to occur "after exposure to wet tobacco leaves in the morning while plants are still covered with dew or after a rain" when the nicotine is more easily absorbed through the skin. The sickness may affect over 40 percent of tobacco field-workers during the course of a summer. According to a study performed by Wake Forest University Baptist Hospital in Winston-Salem, North Carolina, symptoms of the sickness have been reported since the 1970s. However, the condition has been exacerbated in recent years by decreased spacing between the tobacco plants, which has increased production but also increased exposure for the worker. The Wake Forest study found that fears of job loss and the inability to afford lost wages cause most workers to attempt to treat themselves. Therefore, "only 9 percent sought medical treatment and 7 percent lost work time."

According to the General Accounting Office, in 2003 more than 25 million pounds of pesticides were used in tobacco production, ranking the crop sixth among all agricultural commodities in the amount of pesticides applied per acre in the United States. As a result, dermatitis (skin problems) and eye problems are very common among tobacco farmworkers, who often find themselves in close contact with these pesticides while bending down to work on the crop. In a study of 41 families in North Carolina and Virginia, where at least one member was employed in tobacco, food, or Christmas tree production, researchers found agricultural and residential pesticides present in 39 homes. With that level of chemical exposure, it comes as no surprise that the Bureau of Labor Statistics reported in 2000 that skin diseases and disorders account for almost half of all reported agriculture-related illnesses. Many of the chemicals and pesticides used in tobacco are known carcinogens, and although the transitory lifestyle of many tobacco workers has limited the ability to do research, higher rates of cancer among tobacco workers are suspected.

Substandard living and working conditions, including poor water quality for drinking and bathing, lack of proper sanitation facilities, and poor housing conditions, may lead to infectious disease propagation in the community. Lack of economic resources dictates that many tobacco farmworkers live in environments that foster the development of infectious diseases such as tuberculosis, dysentery, and parasitic diseases.

Although tobacco had been cultivated in America since 1621, cigars did not appear in the colonies until a British military officer, Israel Putnam, brought a selection of Cuban cigars and tobacco leaves back to his home in Connecticut 150 years later. By the early part of the 19th century, small-scale cigar factories featuring domestically grown tobacco were operating in several states, while an active cigar trade flourished between Cuba and the United States.

During the 1800s Cuba was a Spanish colony—the island prospered economically, but politically the residents became increasingly resentful of foreign rule. In 1868 Cubans launched an unsuccessful ten-year revolution against Spain. The continuing conflict resulted in a large-scale exodus of several thousand Cubans to the United States, with the majority heading to Key West, Florida, bringing their cigar-making skills with them. Where there had been only one cigar factory in Key West in 1831, more than 100 were in operation by the latter half of the century. Among those leaving Cuba for Key West was Vincente Martínez Ybor. Ybor had owned a cigar factory in Cuba, but the revolution, along with high tariffs and labor unrest, convinced him to move his factory and most of its workers to Key West in 1868. As Key West prospered, workers attempted to unionize, with the resulting conflicts nearly ruining the local economy. The labor problems convinced Ybor and other factory owners to relocate again. This time they chose the Tampa area. In 1885 Ybor purchased 40 acres and, along with Don Ignatio Haya, established the first factories in the area that came to be known as Ybor City.

Ybor City grew rapidly as other cigar factory owners moved their operations to the area. Eventually it had more than 200 factories, employing 12,000 workers, and producing 700 million cigars a year—the city became known as the Cigar Capital of the World. Ybor City, incorporated as part of Tampa in 1887, and the factories in the area prospered for more than 50 years, until competition from machine-rolled cigar manufacturers, cheap cigarettes, and the Great Depression of the 1930s drove many out of business. As the factories faltered, the workers were forced to find other work, often in other parts of the country. Today, few cigar factories are left, but the Latino influence in Tampa and most of south Florida remains.

RELATED ARTICLES

Agriculture; Farmworkers Movement; Florida; Health; Key West; Labor; North Carolina; Ybor City.

FURTHER READING

Billingsley, Janice. "Pesticide Exposure High in Migrant Workers." *HealthDay News* (December 12, 2002).

Buland, David. "NRCS Support of Hispanic Farmers by the Numbers." Washington, D.C.: U.S. Department of Agriculture, Natural Resources Conservation Service, 2002 [prepared for the 2002 Annual Training Conference of Professional Hispanic NRCS Employees (NOPH-NRCSE)].

Effland, Anne B., and Jack L. Runyan. "Hired Farm Labor in U.S. Agriculture." *Agricultural Outlook.* Economic Research Service/USDA (October 1998).

Larson, Alice. "Environmental/Occupational Safety and Health." *Migrant Health Issues.* Monograph 2. Buda, Tex.: National Advisory Council on Migrant Health/National Ctr. for Farmworker Health, 2001.

Quandt, Sara A., et al. "Farmworker and Farmer Perceptions of Farmworker Agricultural Chemical Exposure in North Carolina." In *Illness and the Environment: A Reader in Contested Medicine.* Ed. by Steve Kroll-Smith, et al. New York: N.Y. Univ. Press, 2000.

SELECTED WEB SITES

Economic Research Service. http://www.ers.usda.gov

Hispanicvista.com. http://www.hispanicvista.com

U.S. Census Bureau. http://www.census.gov

U.S. Department of Agriculture Census. http://www.nass.usda.gov/census

MIKE MILLER

TOPONYMY

This discipline is dedicated to the study of the names associated with places. Classification is made according to etymological, geographic, and historical information. Toponyms are used to identify a geographic referent—for example, a population center or a geographical feature of the terrain. Accordingly, toponyms are classified into two broad categories: names associated with population concentrations and names associated with geographical features.

Toponymy studies the name formation process, which includes both the origin of the name itself as well as the historical reason for choosing that particular name. A clear example would be the Caribbean island of Navidad. The word *Navidad* refers, within the Christian tradition, to the day that Jesus was born. The name was chosen, according to Christopher Columbus's *Journals,* because this island was "found" on Christmas Day 1492.

Two main forces that guide the study of toponyms are the origin of the word and the choice of the word. At times one of these two identifying factors might be obscured because of lack of information. For example, a name might have been chosen from an indigenous tongue for which there is little or no referent. In other cases, a name's origin could be easily identified, but historical or physical documentation is insufficient to substantiate a reason associated with the naming process. In the case of the Latino names in the United States, these two identifying factors might be further obscured if the information about the settlement or exploration of an area was not properly documented. The detailed and specific record keeping of the Spanish as they explored the New World and chronicled their ventures has permitted, in many instances, a particular toponym to be traced to the person who first coined it.

The toponyms related to the Latino culture in the United States are found mostly in the areas where the Spanish influence was most extensive, including the southwestern states and the southernmost states. Latino toponyms are not limited to these areas; sometimes we can even find such toponyms in unexpected locations, for example, Toledo, Ohio. When the Ohio villages of Port Lawrence and Vista incorporated in 1837, the name Toledo was suggested by a leader who liked the sound of the Spanish city's name.

Habitation Toponyms

Habitation toponyms are associated with population concentrations. Since the first stages of conquest of the North American continent, settlers had to name their places of habitation. The naming process, which was quite varied, depended on the exploration of the land and the consolidation of population on the land. The Spanish explorers were aided by indigenous peoples in their journeys of discovery, and sometimes the names that they gave to the new settlements were based on the indigenous name. Many times, however, the explorers had different criteria and gave other names. For example, Saint Augustine and Miami, Florida: the first is a name that was provided by the Spanish settlers of the town, the second is a name adopted from the indigenous people of the area. Both names however, became official under the Spanish rule.

Habitation toponyms are often classified into the following categories:

Names with Spanish Referent. These names referred to population centers that already existed in Spain and were chosen for two main reasons: to honor the city in Spain or its authorities or because of the relationship of the founders to the original city in Spain, for example, the city of Valencia, California. In some instances these names are preceded by the adjective "new," such as New Madrid, Missouri.

Names with Ecclesiastic Referent. Such names were given to population centers to honor saints within the Roman Catholic tradition. The main reason for such naming was to dedicate the population center to a patron saint who would protect the center. The assignment of a patron saint would also result in annual festivities in the town or village on that saint's day.

Other reasons include the proximity of a mission to the population center, which would adopt the name of the mission. There are many examples of these, including Los Angeles, California; Santa Barbara, California; and San Antonio, Texas.

Descriptive Names. Some of the names were descriptive, referring to a geographical feature of the area (Boca Raton, Florida, refers to a small bay, for example). Other names refer to the location itself (Perdido, Alabama, remotely located) or perhaps to a color, as is the case with Amarillo (yellow), Texas.

Other Names. These names escape a clear classification, often because of the distance from the original referents that prompted the assignment of the names, for example, Palo Alto (tall tree), California.

Another habitation toponym that is broadly used is the word *barrio*. This Spanish word did not change meaning in its voyage across the Atlantic, at least among the Latino population. This word has also been adopted by the English speakers in the United States, but it has brought with it a semantic innovation: it refers to a neighborhood populated by Latinos. It is now common to refer to the Latino neighborhood of a city as the barrio. *Barrio*, however, has also undergone a semantic change from its original meaning. The original refers to a section of a habitation area; for the Latino population, *barrio* can mean the neighborhood where they grew up or a place at times neglected by the government; for the non-Latino population of the United States, *bar-*

rio can have a negative connotation. The referent in this case eludes the original meaning and conveys the idea of an area that is poor and plagued with urban social ills, drug sale and usage, crime, and poverty.

The urban habitation toponym *plaza* is also used broadly in English. The Spanish original refers to an open square or marketplace. In the Latino culture the idea of plaza conveys a sense of a gathering of people; a place to socialize. Originally, the urban structures that were created by the Spanish always centered on a plaza, which would serve as the marketplace and the meeting place of the populace. The government buildings, the church, and many businesses were located in or around the plaza, hence the plaza became the nucleus of the town or city. Nowadays in the Latino culture within the United States, the word *plaza* has changed substantially—it refers to a shopping area, artificially created on the outskirts of a habitation area.

Geographic Toponyms

These toponyms are also derived from the first explorations and settlements of the U.S. South and Southwest. The explorers named the various geographical features of the terrain in their native tongues; these toponyms have remained and have even become part of the English toponymic system. All English speakers in the United States would understand the word *sierra* as defining a mountain range.

These types of toponyms can be further divided into the categories shown below:

Oronyms.
These toponyms refer to relief features. The most commonly used oronym is the word *sierra,* or saw, which is used in both Spanish and English to refer to a mountain range. Other oronyms such as *mesa, llano,* and so on, are also extensively used through the geography of the regions of Spanish influence. Sometimes these oronyms have even become the names for habitation-area toponyms; a clear example would be Loma Linda, California. *Loma* refers to a hill and *Linda* refers to beauty.

Hydronyms.
These toponyms refer to water features. The generic name associated with the hydronym can be used in either Spanish or in English. For example, Rio Grande and Colorado rivers—if the generic name is used in Spanish, the hydronym will be used after the noun following the syntax of Spanish. If the generic name is used in English, the hydronym will usually be placed before the noun, following the syntax of English.

Names of Geographical Areas.
These toponyms refer to areas that vary in characteristics and are used for the description of extensions such as states: Florida, Nevada, Arizona, California, Texas, and so on. They can also be used to refer to valleys or depressions—for example, San Joaquin Valley, California. Often when Spanish toponyms integrate with the generic nouns in English, they conform to the syntax of English.

The Latino toponyms that are used in the United States are extensive and cover all the areas of toponymy as discussed above. Concentration of the Latino toponyms is more dense in the areas that have a past associated with the settlement by Spain, but such toponyms are not restricted to those areas. In urban areas, a Latino toponym is usually associated with the area where much of the Latino community has settled. The word *barrio* would be an example.

RELATED ARTICLES

Explorers and Chroniclers; Missions; Onomastics; Spanish in the United States.

FURTHER READING

Ashley, Leonard R. N. "Amerindian Toponyms in the United States." In *Namenforschung/Name Studies/Les Noms Propres.* Berlin, Germany: de Gruyter, 1996.

Basso, Keith H. *Landscape and Language among the Western Apache.* Albuquerque: Univ. of N.Mex. Press, 1996.

Bright, William, ed. *International Encyclopedia of Linguistics.* New York: Oxford Univ. Press, 1992.

Bright, William. "The NAPUS (Native American Placenames of the United States) Project: Principles and Problems." In *Making Dictionaries: Preserving Indigenous Languages of the Americas.* Ed. by William Frawley, et al. Berkeley: Univ. of Calif. Press, 2002.

Feld, Steven, and Keith H. Basso, eds. *Senses of Place.* Santa Fe, N.Mex.: School of Am. Res. Press, 1996.

Gudde, Erwin G. *California Place Names: The Origin and Etymology of Current Geographical Names.* 3d ed. Berkeley: Univ. of Calif. Press, 1969.

Lamarque, P. V. "Names and Descriptions." In *Encyclopedia of Language and Linguistics.* Ed. by R. E. Asher. Oxford, England: Pergamon, 1994.

Lehrer, Adrienne. "Names and Naming: Why We Need Fields and Frames." In *Frames, Fields, and Contrasts: New Essays in Semantic and Lexical Organization.* Ed. by A. Lehrer and E. F. Kittay. Hillsdale, N.J.: Erlbaum, 1992.

Lehrer, Adrienne. "Proper Names: Linguistic Aspects." In *Encyclopedia of Language and Linguistics*. Vol. 6. Ed. by R. E. Asher. Oxford, England: Pergamon, 1994.

CÉSAR ALEGRE

TOURISM

The tourist industry in the United States underwent enormous changes in the second half of the 20th century. With culture becoming a marketable commodity, museums, historical sites (battlegrounds, churches, prisons, and so forth), parks, missions, and reservations became destinations of pilgrimage, and some even acquired an aura of sanctity. The marketing of tourist guides, the manufacturing of tourist goods, and the mass publication of history books were by-products of these changes. From Mount Rushmore to the Grand Canyon, from the U.S. Holocaust Museum in Washington, D.C., to the Liberty Bell in Philadelphia, Americans have an insatiable appetite for visiting the places that have defined their identity.

Ethnicity is a major component in the expansion of the tourist industry. Sites with relevance to African Americans and Native Americans are essential stops on the national pilgrimage. The Latino past, on the other hand, has not been a source of tourist interest. Only in the past couple of decades has an attempt to build monuments that relate to Hispanic life in the United States begun to take shape.

As a community Latinos themselves are only now beginning to travel within the United States and abroad. To a large extent this is a result of the growing Hispanic middle-class in the United States, with increased numbers, purchasing power, and leisure time. Consequently, the travel industry and related businesses have focused increasingly on the needs and habits of these ethnic groups. Simultaneously, sites and events in the United States relevant to Latino history and culture—such as the Alamo in San Antonio, Texas; Calle Ocho in Miami, Florida; Santa Fe, New Mexico; and the Puerto Rican Day Parade in New York City—have become important destinations for both Latino and non-Latino tourists.

According to *The Minority Traveler,* a report published in early 2004 by the Travel Industry Association of America (TIAA), Latino travel volume increased from 64.1 million in 2000 to 77.1 million person-trips in 2002, or up 20 percent. This increase is significantly higher than the 2 percent growth in travel within the United States overall in the same period. Sixty-four percent of Latino travel originates in six states: California, Texas, Florida, New Mexico, New York, and Arizona. Almost 50 percent of Latinos who travel do so within their state of residence. The report points to a significant fact for those businesses targeting Latino travelers: Latinos spend more than the average American when they travel. On average, Latinos spend $480 per household trip, more than the U.S. average ($457); on 15 percent of trips, Latino households spent more than $1,000, not including transportation to the destination. The report includes other important observations:

- One in seven (15 percent) Latino person-trips includes air transportation. Rental cars are used as the primary mode of transportation by seven percent of Latino travelers—more than twice as much as overall travel (3 percent).
- 77 percent of Latino travel is for leisure; 10 percent is for business; and another 10 percent combines business and pleasure.
- Spending time with family is important to Latino travelers, with 33 percent of Latino trips including three or more people from the same household, compared with the average U.S. trip (25 percent). One-third (33 percent) of trips by Latino households include children under 18 years old.
- Of 11 common trip activities, shopping is the favorite activity for Latinos (34 percent of person-trips), followed by outdoor recreation (16 percent), visiting theme or amusement parks (14 percent), visiting historical places or museums (13 percent), and going to beaches (13 percent).
- 53 percent of Latino households book accommodations in hotels, motels, or bed-and-breakfast establishments, while 42 percent will opt to stay with friends or relatives.
- 46 percent of Latino traveling households are headed by someone with a college degree; the median annual income of Latino traveling households is $45,400.
- Latino travelers tend to be between ages 18 and 44, while the average age for U.S. travelers overall is 47.

The rise in travel among Latinos is seen in the business, nonprofit, and individual segments. Latino-owned companies are growing at nearly double the national average. Most of those businesses are in significant metropolitan areas. Improving revenues mean that they have disposable income for business and personal travel. In addition, the rise in Latino professional and nonprofit organizations has contributed significantly to travel within the United States and the amount of money that these organizations contribute to the local economy.

According to the TIAA data, Las Vegas is the top U.S. destination for Latinos. Also, Latinos travel a lot in states where there are large Latino populations, particularly Arizona, California, Florida, and Texas. Yet Latinos do not limit their travel only to areas with a predominantly Latino population. Atlanta, for example, appears as the sixth most popular destination. Marketing played a big role; the city and travel-related businesses have focused marketing campaigns to attract minorities to visit Atlanta since the late 1990s. The top ten destinations for Latino travelers in the United States are Las Vegas; Los Angeles; San Antonio; San Diego; Houston; Orlando; Orange County, California; Riverside and San Bernardino, California; Phoenix and Mesa, Arizona; and San Francisco.

Los Angeles is an appealing destination because of its Mexican American identity. One out of every twelve Mexicans in the United States lives in this metropolis. Its museums, restaurants, parks, and neighborhoods, such as East Los Angeles, serve as magnets to Latino tourists. Similarly, San Diego, Riverside, San Bernardino, San Francisco, and Orange County, California, and Houston, Texas, all have alluring Spanish histories. Plus, Spanish is frequently spoken in these areas as the second tourist language.

San Antonio is a third favorite destination for Latino travelers. In general, the Alamo receives approximately 2.5 million visitors a year from the United States and all over the world. Although the site has meaning as a 17th-century mission, visitors are attracted to it because of its significance as the site of the military loss by Texans and *Tejanos* that led indirectly to the Texas victory over the Mexican government at San Jacinto in 1836.

Other important tourist sites for Latinos are Santa Fe and the California missions. The Spanish mission movement in general offers mixed historical interpretations. For 100 years after their 1833 secularization, many missions fell into decline. However, as cultural tourism has increased in the United States and around the world, some missions have been restored—especially those in affluent areas in which non-Latinos have taken the lead—and are major tourist attractions, especially the missions at Santa Barbara, San Luis Obispo, and San Juan Capistrano, all in California. There has also been an attempt to reconsider the missions' roles during the colonial period, which often results in a demonization of many Spanish clerics of that period.

Other historic sites, such as the landing places of Spanish explorers, have been appropriated by small communities as cultural tourism has increased. Several towns near Tampa, Florida, publish tourist pamphlets claiming that they were the 1528 landing place for Alvar Núñez Cabeza de Vaca in his failed conquest of North America. Various locations along the Mississippi River have claimed visits from Hernando de Soto in the 1530s. As local museums and historical societies have grown in response to the attraction of cultural tourism, particularly in the Southwest, interest in southwestern cuisine has increased, and a recognition of the long history of intercultural relations between Latinos and southwestern Indians has

© JIMMY DORANTES/LATIN FOCUS

A family gathers around the Disney character Goofy at Disneyland in Anaheim, California.

attracted additional visitation to those states from both Latinos and non-Latinos. Latinos also travel to indigenous towns in Arizona and New Mexico, which were conquered by the Spanish in the 16th and 17th centuries.

Although Miami, Florida, does not rank in the top ten destinations for Latinos, it has come to be known as "the capital of Latin America." Its Cuban, Brazilian, and Central American (Nicaraguan, Salvadoran, Guatemalan) populations are a distinctive component in its urban mix. For its longevity, the Cuban presence is the most significant. Along with its Jewish population, Miami's Cuban community is one of the most culturally active, putting its imprint on events such as the Latin Emmy Awards and the Miami Book Fair. Miami has hosted a Latino event—Calle Ocho—for 26 years, which is the largest celebration of Latino culture in the United States. It comprises entertainment and booths selling food and other goods, and has been known to attract more than 1 million visitors a day. Finally, the Puerto Rican Day Parade in New York City is also important. Promoted as an occasion of ethnic pride, it attracts a slightly higher number of visitors.

Emphasizing linguistic and cultural ties, countries such as Spain, Mexico, the Dominican Republic, and Costa Rica have also been increasing their focus on Latino travelers. Puerto Rico is also a popular destination, particularly for those of Puerto Rican background on the East Coast of the United States.

Not only have Latino-owned businesses and overall purchasing power increased, leading to more travel, but travel marketing has focused increasingly on Latinos and other ethnic groups. During the 1990s all travel sectors, including hotels, airlines, and transportation, focused more specifically on the Latino market. At the same time, the proper training of Spanish-speaking hotel, airline, and travel reservation agents, along with tour operators, had a positive effect on expanding Latino travel. There has also been a rise in Latino-owned travel agencies, whose management caters particularly to Latinos.

Another factor influencing Latino travel is the availability of travel Web sites. The number of Latinos using travel sites overall grew by 7 percent in the first six months of 2003, compared with the same period a year earlier. This rate is higher than the growth rate of 4 percent among the total Internet-using population in the United States during the same period. In fact, every one of the top ten travel sites experienced double-digit growth in Latino visits.

RELATED ARTICLES

Alamo, Battle of the; Arizona; California; Calle Ocho; Cuisine; Culture, Popular; Florida; Little Havana; Missions; New Mexico; New York City; Puerto Rican Day Parade; Texas.

FURTHER READING

Kirshenblatt-Gimblett, Barbara. *Destination Culture: Tourism, Museums, and Heritage.* Berkeley, Calif.: Univ. of Calif. Press, 1998.

Meethan, Kevin. *Tourism in Global Society: Place, Culture, Consumption.* New York: Palgrave, 2001.

The Minority Traveler. The Travel Industry Association of America (January 2004).

Sears, John. *Sacred Places: American Tourist Attractions in the Nineteenth Century.* Amherst, Mass.: Univ. of Mass. Press, 1998.

Wilson, Chris. *The Myth of Santa Fe: Creating a Modern Regional Tradition.* Albuquerque: Univ. of N.Mex. Press, 1997.

SELECTED WEB SITES

The Alamo. http://www.thealamo.org/main.html

California Missions.
   http://www.notfrisco.com/almanac/missions/

Calle Ocho. http://www.calle8.com/

Multicultural Travel News.
   http://www.multicultural.com/products/travel.html

MAYRA RODRÍGUEZ VALLADARES

TRANSLATION

Translation is at the heart and soul of the Latino experience in the United States. As an immigrant-based culture, Latinos are defined by the encounter—or perhaps the clash—of two languages, Spanish and English, and of two civilizations, Hispanic Catholic and Anglo-Protestant. Translation is an inevitable daily strategy for life that results from this encounter; Latinos live within and between the two languages and civilizations.

Translation as a way of life goes far and deep in Hispanic Catholic culture. From the so-called discovery of the Americas by Christopher Columbus in 1492, the Castilian language (*el castellano*), described by grammarian Antonio de Nebrija of the Universidad de Salamanca as "*la compañera del imperio*" (the empire's companion), became the colonizing tool in the Americas. Portuguese, English, French, and Dutch served a similar purpose in Brazil, parts of the Caribbean, and the Guyanas, but Spanish in the end was the one language acquired by the majority of the population in the Western Hemisphere. By the middle of the 16th century, it was already the political and business vehicle of communication in the former Aztec and Inca empires. How did it become such an integral part of society in such a short period of time? To this day several dozen pre-Columbian languages and dialects are still in use in the hemisphere, but they exist in marginalized form. Spanish is the lingua franca of Latin America, the only way for an Argentine and a Colombian, for instance, to engage in dialogue.

Given the vastness of the region, it is clear that the colonizing enterprise was monumental and that language played a fundamental role in the indoctrination of the population. So too did translation. Miguel León-Portilla, a leading scholar devoted to the understanding of translation as linked to national identity, studies the chronicles left behind by explorers and missionaries such as Alvar Núñez Cabeza de Vaca, Bernal Díaz del Castillo, Guamán Poma de Ayala, Fray Bernardino de Sahagún, "El Inca" Garcisalo de la Vega, Fray Bartolomé de Las Casas, and Motolinía. Their works, among numerous others, offer a record of the translation exercises, the borrowing of words, and the coining of fresh terms to cope with the challenging new reality that resulted from the encounter of the two languages and civilizations.

There are several mythical and folkloric characters in Latin America who are connected to translation. Probably the most famous one is Mexican: Malinalli Tenepal, known in Spanish as Marina and nicknamed "La Malinche" (circa 1505–1530). An Indian woman known as Hernán Cortés's mistress, she is infamous for having connected sex and interpretation. Apparently her translations of what the Aztec rulers said in their communication to Cortés, and vice versa, were inaccurate. That inaccuracy was motivated by a self-serving need to consolidate her position among the Spanish conquerors. Thus today a *malinchista* in Mexico is an individual who puts his own objectives ahead of those of his country. La Malinche is ubiquitous in literature: aside from incomplete biographies (the historical sources available on her are quite limited), she appears in novels, stories, and plays.

It is not surprising, then, that Latin America has generated a long tradition of literary works written in languages other than Spanish (Náhuatl, Maya, Mixtec, Mazatec, Zapotec, Otomí, Purepecha, and Tlapanec). Sacred and dramatic books such as the *Popol Vuh, Chilam Balam of Chumayel,* and *Rabinal Achí* are essential to the pre-Columbian mentality; and contemporary authors such as Natalio Hernández Xocoyotzin, Librado Silva Galeana, Humberto Ak'abal, Feliciano Sánchez Chan, Briceida Cuevas Cob, Juan Gregorio Regino, Gabriel López Chiñas, and Mario Molina Cruz have kept that tradition alive.

Significant works written in Spanish south of the Rio Grande have attempted to reflect the fertile linguistic environment. An early and famous example is the work of Mexican colonial nun Sor Juana Inés de la Cruz, who died in 1695. Among 20th-century authors following the same path are José María Argüeda (*The Fox from Up Above and the Fox from Down Below*) from Peru, and Augusto Roa Bastos (*I, the Supreme*) from Paraguay.

Hispanic literature has been translated into English since the Renaissance. Part one of *Don Quixote of La Mancha* by Miguel de Cervantes, for instance, was rendered into English only decades after it appeared in 1605. The literature produced in Central and South America as well as the Caribbean basin has also been present in English since the 17th century. Bartolomé de Las Casas's *An Account of the First Voyages and Discoveries Made by the Spaniards in America* appeared in London in 1699, although it was translated from the French (and the author is showcased as Don Bartholomew de las Casas, bishop of Chiapa). In the 19th century the efforts to render Spanish-language texts from south of the Rio Grande began to be more systematic. The job was mainly left to the spouses of well-known scholars and educators. Among the early practitioners were Mary Tyler Peabody Mann (wife of Horace Mann) and Fanny Bandelier (wife of Adolph Francis Alphonse Bandelier).

It was not until the 1920s and 1930s that the works of writers such as Mexicans Jorge Isaacs (*María*), Mariano Azuela (*The Underdogs*), and others made it to the United States. A number of prominent midcentury translators consolidated admirable careers, including Angel Flores and Harriet de Onís. Then, in reaction to the narrative boom of the 1960s, there appeared a plethora of new, talented translators into English. The most famous is Gregory Rabassa, a distinguished professor at Queens College and the person responsible for the translations of Gabriel García Márquez's *One Hundred Years of Solitude,* Julio Cortázar's *Hopscotch,* and Luis Rafael

Sánchez's *Macho Camacho's Beat*. Rabassa, who also translated from Portuguese, led a cadre that included Gregory Kolovakos (after whom a PEN award devoted to the promotion of Hispanic culture in the United States is named), Edith Grossman, Helen Lane, Suzanne Jill Levine, Alfred MacAdam, and Margaret Sayers Peden. Grossman then took the mantle, continuing the translations of García Márquez's oeuvre and embarking on renditions of works by Mayra Montero, Augusto Monterroso, Alvaro Mutis, and Mario Vargas Llosa. In 2003 Grossman published a critically acclaimed translation of *Don Quixote of La Mancha*.

Seeking a larger audience, a number of Latin American authors have actually translated their own work into English or rewritten their work in it. These include María Luisa Bastos, Guillermo Cabrera Infante, Ariel Dorfman, Rosario Ferré, Carlos Fuentes, and Manuel Puig.

Translation has also been a feature in Latin American films and television programs distributed in the United States. Questioning the accuracy of the translations of American films dubbed for a Spanish-speaking audience has been a practice in the Hispanic world since the 1950s. Since the 1970s, subtitles have become more attractive. (In 1931 a Spanish version of the film *Dracula* was produced in Hollywood under the direction of George Melford. The cast included Pablo Alvarez Rubio, Barry Norton, Lupita Tovar, and Carlos Villarías Villar. This experiment—shooting the same movie in different language versions of the same script with actors fluent in that language was not uncommon.) In the English-speaking world, the use of subtitles in foreign films to reach a national audience always has been preferred. It is the case of movies by canonical directors such as Luis Buñuel and of contemporary commercial successes such as Alfonso Arau's *Like Water for Chocolate* and Alfonso Cuarón's *Y Tú Mamá También*.

Latino authors in the United States, including Gloria Anzaldúa, Juan Felipe Herrera, and Demetria Martínez, regularly address translation in their oeuvre. Word play is a feature of this literature. Some writers have produced memoirs that have translation as their leitmotif.

The use of translation in Latino life goes far beyond the arts. It is part of diplomacy, the judicial system (especially the court houses), sports (particularly baseball), education, gastronomy, and, in general, romance. Hallmark Cards, Inc., has lines of greeting cards for sale from coast to coast in Spanish and Spanglish (aside from English). This might be taken as strong evidence of the extent to which the two languages and two civilizations have coexisted on the continent since the 15th century.

RELATED ARTICLES

Bible in Spanish; Bilingualism; Literature; Publishing; Spanish in the United States.

FURTHER READING

Argüedas, José María. *The Fox from Up Above and the Fox from Down Below.* Tr. by Frances Horning Barraclough. Pittsburgh: Univ. of Pittsburgh Press, 2000.

Cabrera Infante, Guillermo. *Holy Smoke.* 1985. Reprint. Woodstock, N.Y.: Overlook Press, 1997.

Cervantes, Miguel de. *Don Quixote.* Tr. by Edith Grossman, intro. by Harold Bloom. New York: Ecco, 2003.

Cortázar, Julio. *Hopscotch.* Tr. by Gregory Rabassa. 1966. Reprint. New York: Pantheon Bks., 1987.

Dorfman, Ariel. *Heading South, Looking North: A Bilingual Journey.* New York: Farrar, Straus, 1998.

García Márquez, Gabriel. *One Hundred Years of Solitude.* Tr. by Gregory Rabassa. 1970. Reprint. New York: Perennial Classics 1998.

Juana Inés de la Cruz, Sor. *Poems, Protest and a Dream: Selected Writings.* Tr. by Margaret Sayers Peden, intro. by Ilan Stavans. New York: Penguin, 1997.

León-Portilla, Miguel. *Endangered Cultures.* Tr. by Julie Goodson-Lawes. Dallas, Tex.: Southern Methodist Univ. Press, 1990.

León-Portilla, Miguel, and Earl Shorris, et al. eds. *In the Language of Kings: An Anthology of Mesoamerican Literature—Pre-Columbian to the Present.* New York: Norton, 2001.

Messinger Cypess, Sandra. *La Malinche in Mexican Literature from History to Myth.* Austin: Univ. of Tex. Press, 1991.

Roa Bastos, Augusto. *I, the Supreme.* Tr. by Helen Lane. 1986. Reprint. New York: Vintage, 1987.

Sokol, Neal. "Translation and Its Discontents." In *Ilan Stavans: Eight Conversations.* Madison: Univ. of Wis. Press, 2004.

Stavans, Ilan. *On Borrowed Words: A Memoir of Language.* New York: Viking, 2001.

ILAN STAVANS

TREATIES OF VELASCO. See VELASCO, TREATIES OF.

TREATY OF ADAMS-DE ONIS. See ADAMS-DE ONIS, TREATY OF.

TREATY OF GUADALUPE HIDALGO. See GUADALUPE HIDALGO, TREATY OF.

© MARK LENNIHAN/AP/WIDE WORLD PHOTOS

Students from New York City's Public School 38 watch the Tres Reyes Magos Parade in Spanish Harlem.

TRES REYES MAGOS

A religious and popular tradition celebrated on January 6 in Latin American countries and Latino communities throughout the United States, the Christian feast of the Epiphany, or *el Día de Los Reyes Magos,* commemorates the journey of the three kings or magi, who, according to biblical accounts, traveled from the East to pay homage to the newborn Jesus in Bethlehem. New Testament narratives describe the kings being guided by a star. The magi first arrived in Jerusalem and informed King Herod of their intentions to honor the newborn king. Herod, threatened by the birth of a possible rival, asked them to return and advise him about the child's whereabouts "so that I may also pay him homage." Warned in a dream not to return to Herod, the magi returned to their homelands by a different route. In the Christian faith, the Epiphany represents the manifestation of the Christ to the Gentile world, an indication that Jesus came for all people.

Traditionally, the kings—Melchor (Melchior), Gaspar (Kaspar), and Baltasar (Balthasar)—bore gifts of gold, frankincense, and myrrh for the child and are the subjects of popular devotions including *promesas* (promises) and rosaries in exchange for miracles. In Cuba and Puerto Rico, particular attention is given to Melchor, who is traditionally portrayed as African and standing between the two lighter-skinned magi, symbolizing the importance of African and mestizo heritage in those cultures. In other countries, Baltasar is considered to be *el Rey Negro* (the Black King).

On the eve of *el Día de los Reyes,* children place boxes filled with hay or grass and water beneath their beds for the kings' camels. In the morning, the grass and water are gone and the "kings" have left toys in their place. Latinos place special emphasis on the *Tres Reyes* feast rather than Christmas. In many U.S. Latino areas, community-based organizations and other institutions (such as El Museo del Barrio and

El Puente in New York City, and Sociedad Latina in Boston) celebrate Three Kings' Day with theatrical reenactments of the Epiphany narrative culminating in the arrival of three adults dressed as the kings who then distribute toys and other gifts to all children present.

In Latin America, while traditions vary from country to country, the feast marks the culmination of the 12 days of Christmas. In Mexico and parts of Central America, children celebrate the season by participating in *posadas*—processions from house to house carrying figures of Joseph and Mary, reenacting the couple's journey prior to the birth of Jesus, and singing hymns at each home. Children are then given refreshments and toy-filled piñatas by their neighbors.

In Puerto Rico groups of musicians and singers will spontaneously gather and form a *parranda,* also going from house to house and offering a lively and surprising late-night serenade of *aguinaldos* (traditional carols) until they are invited in for a party and feast that often lasts until dawn.

RELATED ARTICLES

Catholicism; Holidays; Navidad; Posadas.

FURTHER READING

Blanco, T. *Los Aguinaldos del Infante: Glosa de Epifanía* (A Child's Gifts: A Twelfth Night Tale). Philadelphia: Westminster, 1976.

Figueroa, J. L. M. *Melchor, Gaspar y Baltasar: Los Tres Reyes Magos en la religiosidad popular puertorriqueña* (Melchior, Kaspar and Baltasar: The Three Kings in Puerto Rican Popular Religion). San German, P.R.: Instituto de Cultura Puertorriqueña, 2001.

McConnie Zapater, B. *Three Kings' Day*. Cleveland, Ohio: Modern Curriculum Press, 1992.

ANTHONY DE JESÚS

TREVIÑO, JESÚS SALVADOR

Born: March 26, 1946; El Paso, Texas

Jesús Salvador Treviño, filmmaker and documentarian, is recognized for being one of the founders of Chicano cinema. His interest in and involvement with recording the Chicano experience on film

© MARK J. TERRILL/AP/WIDE WORLD PHOTOS

The stars of *Resurrection Boulevard* Nicholas Gonzalez (*left*) and Elizabeth Peña, with director Jesús Salvador Treviño.

began in the 1960s when civil rights agitation reached its height. Surrounded by the events of *el movimiento,* including the farmworkers' strikes, school walkouts, and the formation of the La Raza Unida Party, Treviño seized the opportunity to document the conflicts with his super-8 camera.

Treviño graduated from Occidental College in 1968. He joined a tide of activist Chicanos who were finding an outlet in film. After a stint at the public television station KCET in Los Angeles, Treviño went on to produce and direct several documentaries that were heralded for giving voice to the Chicano experience in the United States, including one of his earliest, *Yo Soy Chicano* (1972). Early in his filmmaking career, Treviño wrote and produced *Raíces de Sangre* (Roots of Blood, 1975), a bold work that is one of the hallmarks of Chicano cinema and was recognized by the Spain International Film Festival in 1991 as one of the outstanding 25 Latin American films of all time. In 1975 he worked with the first national Chicano Film Festival in San Antonio to form his own production company, New Vista Productions. Several years later, in 1978, the filmmaker formed the Chicano Cinema Coalition, a Los Angeles–based professional organization that met in Treviño's living room to screen and analyze classic Hollywood films. As historian Chon Noriega asserts, "the coalition would serve as a resource for filmmakers and as a platform for protests against exploitation films and industry hiring practices." The following year, Treviño cofounded the First New Latin American Cinema Festival in Havana, Cuba.

Treviño then began producing for television. He was executive producer for the first documentary on the Chicano civil rights struggle to air on PBS, *Chi-cano: The History of the Mexican American Civil Rights Movement* (1996). Turning next to historical subjects, Treviño explored the infamous battle of the Alamo from a Tejano (Mexican Texan) perspective with the American Playhouse television drama, *Seguin* (1982).

In addition to his work with Chicano and Mexican American subjects, Treviño has had a prolific career in prime-time television. He has produced episodes of major miniseries such as *Star Trek: Deep Space Nine, NYPD Blue, Chicago Hope, ER, Resurrection Boulevard,* and *Crossing Jordan.* He has twice won the Directors Guild of America Award for his prime-time work; he also won an Alma Award for *Resurrection Boulevard.*

Treviño has published several books of short stories and a memoir. The first of these, *The Fabulous Sinkhole and Other Stories,* was published in 1995; in 2001 he published *Eyewitness: A Filmmaker's Memoir of the Chicano Movement,* a personal chronicle of the Chicano struggle.

RELATED ARTICLES

Film; Literature, Latin American; Television.

FURTHER READING

Noriega, Chon. *Between a Weapon and a Formula: Chicano Cinema and Its Contexts.* Donostia-San Sebastián: Festival Internacional de Cine de Donostia-San Sebastián, 1993.

Noriega, Chon ed. *Chicanos and Film: Representation and Resistance.* Minneapolis: Univ. of Minn. Press, 1992.

Treviño, Jesús Salvador. *Eyewitness: A Filmmaker's Memoir of the Chicano Movement.* Houston, Tex.: Arte Público Press, 2001.

SELECTED WEB SITE

Chuy Treviño, Jesus Salvador Treviño. www.chuytrevino.com

JOSEPH TOVARES

UNITED CANNERY, AGRICULTURAL, PACKING, AND ALLIED WORKERS OF AMERICA

Founded in 1937, the United Cannery, Agricultural, Packing, and Allied Workers of America (UCA-PAWA) would become the seventh-largest union affiliated with the Congress of Industrial Organizations (CIO). From the outset, union leaders actively recruited workers of color, and the *San Francisco News* noted the union's popularity among farmworkers in California, especially Mexican migrants. Mobilizing a multi-ethnic rank and file (including Mexicans, African Americans, Filipinos, and European Americans), the union staged several strikes in the state's San Joaquin Valley. However, UCA-PAWA would achieve its greatest stability and success in the canneries and packinghouses of southern California.

In August 1939, led by union and Communist Party activist Dorothy Healey, over 400 workers, predominately Mexican and Russian Jewish women, staged a successful strike at the California Sanitary Canning Company (Cal San), one of the largest Los Angeles canneries. Carmen Bernal Escobar emerged as a dynamic local leader and the workers extended their militancy beyond the picket line at the factory gates. When local grocers refused to take Cal San products off their shelves, strikers picketed their stores. The Shapiro brothers, owners of Cal San, came to the bargaining table after children marched on their front lawns, carrying signs that read, "I'm underfed because my Mama is underpaid." By November the brothers met most of the workers' demands, including union recognition. In 1941 UCAPAWA vice president Luisa Moreno, a Guatemalan immigrant, expanded union organization throughout southern California and helped build Local 3, the second-largest affiliate. Moreno actively encouraged women's leadership, and in 1943 women held 12 of the 15 elected positions. They negotiated innovative benefits, such as a hospitalization plan, free legal advice, and, at one plant, management-financed day care. In 1944 UCAPAWA became the Food, Tobacco, Agricultural, and Allied Workers of America (FTA). During an era when few unions addressed the concerns of women, UCAPAWA/FTA blazed a new path. By 1946, 66 percent of its contracts nationwide contained equal-pay-for-equal-work clauses and 75 percent provided for leaves of absence without loss of seniority. The union was also known for including more Mexican workers in its ranks than any other CIO affiliate.

In 1945 Moreno led a union drive among northern California cannery workers competing directly with the Teamsters. Although the FTA won a convincing victory in an election that covered 72 plants, the National Labor Relations Board rescinded the results as the Teamsters began a campaign of sweetheart contracts, red baiting, and physical assaults. In 1946 the FTA narrowly lost the second election. In 1950 the union, battered by red baiting, was expelled from the CIO for alleged communist domination. Moreno herself would leave the United States that year under terms listed as "voluntary departure under warrant of deportation," on the grounds she had once belonged to the Communist Party. Despite its demise, UCAPAWA-FTA's legacy should not be written off as one of failure; rather it should be remembered as one of the first national unions to incorporate people of color as both members and leaders, providing a model of grassroots democracy in the U.S. labor movement.

RELATED ARTICLES

California; Labor.

FURTHER READING

Ruíz, Vicki L. *Cannery Women, Cannery Lives: Mexican Women, Unionization, and the California Food Processing Industry, 1930–1950.* Albuquerque: Univ. of N.Mex. Press, 1987.

Weber, Devra. *Dark Sweat, White Gold: California Farm Workers, Cotton, and the New Deal.* Berkeley: Univ. of Calif. Press, 1994.

VICKI L. RUÍZ

UNITED FARM WORKERS UNION.

See CHÁVEZ, CÉSAR.

UNITED STATES–CENTRAL AMERICA RELATIONS

Relations between the United States and the seven republics of Central America (Guatemala, Belize, El Salvador, Nicaragua, Honduras, Costa Rica, and Panama) have been close owing to geography, but because of divergent political and economic interests, they have not necessarily been friendly. Since the early 20th century the United States has asserted a special right to defend its strategic interests, protect its trade and investments, and maintain political stability. The United States has pursued these objectives using political, economic, and military means, and it has acquired a sphere of influence over the region in the process. While Central Americans have often suffered from American intervention, they have frequently looked to the United States for political guidance, economic assistance, and refuge.

The Central American republics occupy a critical geographical position, straddling two continents and bridging two oceans. With limited natural resources, the region has primarily served the international community as a transit route. The United States has placed a high priority on the maintenance of order and stability in a region that guards the sea lanes on which its commerce travels, but Central American interests have not often coincided with American interests. The unfortunate result is a history of violent conflicts that have marred relations between close neighbors with different cultures, perspectives, and aspirations.

While the United States was born a great power, the Central American republics came into existence in 1821 as weak countries that had been on the margins of the Spanish empire for three centuries. Their weakness invited intervention by foreign powers. The Americans and British competed for Spain's former colonies through most of the 19th century; the British navy's dominance assured Great Britain an advantage over the United States for most of that time. This rivalry shaped American policy toward the region in the 19th century. In 1823, with the prospect of a Spanish reconquest looming over all Latin America, the British had asked the Americans to join them in a joint declaration that the former Spanish colonies were off limits to further colonization. President James Monroe, however, preferred a unilateral declaration that would not tie his hands in the hemisphere. The result was a statement of policy known as the Monroe Doctrine, the foundation of American policy toward Latin America for nearly 200 years. According to this doctrine, the United States would not tolerate any further European colonization, encroachment, or intervention in any part of the Americas; the Americas were to be for the Americans, not Europeans. The European powers ridiculed Monroe's assertion of dominion over the hemisphere, but as the power of the United States increased dramatically in the 19th century, Monroe's bold statement became a geopolitical reality for Central Americans.

Initially, Latin American leaders welcomed Monroe's bold declaration of the anticolonial principles that they shared. They came to learn, however, that the United States had no intention of forging alliances with any of the new American republics. In 1826 Simón Bolívar, the liberator of South America, convened a congress of Pan-American states in Panama, hoping to forge a confederation. The United States, however, refused to encourage, let alone join, any such confederation. Despite the anticolonial tone of the Monroe Doctrine, the United States harbored expansionist aspirations of its own. After the United States acquired the Louisiana territory by purchase in 1803, many American leaders coveted territories to the west and south, including Central America. The weak Central American republics lay in the path of a growing American empire.

The completion of America's continental expansion by virtue of victory in the Mexican-American War (1846–1848) sharpened the United States's interest in control of the Central American isthmus. With gold-rich California in the union, Americans looked for the quickest, safest, and cheapest transportation from the Atlantic seaboard to the Pacific coast. Prior to the construction of a transcontinental railroad in the United States, the quickest transit route brought travelers by ship to Central America, across the isthmus by horse or rail, and thence by ship to California. The construction of a canal would reduce travel time considerably.

Great Britain, with a colony in British Honduras (Belize) and economic interests throughout the region, refused to cede control of the isthmus to the United States. The United States was determined to prevent the British from building their own canal. Rivalry between the two powers, fueled in part in the United States by a growing conviction of a special "manifest destiny," nearly resulted in war. Fortunately, cooler heads prevailed and the superpowers agreed to joint control of any transit route with the signing of the Clayton-Bulwer Treaty in 1850.

The expansionist interests of the United States soon clashed with the nationalistic ambitions of the Central Americans. In 1855 William Walker, an American-born soldier of fortune who believed himself and his country to have a special destiny, invaded Nicaragua with a small army and soon declared himself president. He reintroduced slavery, declared English the official language, and offered land grants to American settlers, hoping that the United States would annex Nicaragua as a slave state. Central American nationalists from Guatemala to Costa Rica rose against Walker in the great "National War," a bitter struggle to reclaim their sovereign rights. In 1857 the Central Americans drove Walker and his troops out of Costa Rica and onto an American warship. Walker was taken back to the United States, the only country that had officially recognized him as the president of Nicaragua. Although Walker failed in this and two subsequent attempts to conquer Central America, the Central Americans recognized in him the imminent danger posed by United States expansionists.

The American Civil War (1861–1865) delayed but did not diminish the expansionist zeal that had prompted William Walker. In the late 19th century, as liberal governments throughout Central America promoted the modernization of their economies by developing the coffee and banana industries, North American and European trade and investment in Central America grew dramatically. The United States, France, Great Britain, and Germany competed peacefully in the region, each one interested in the construction of a canal across the isthmus. A French company began digging a canal across Panama in the 1880s, while an American firm acquired the rights to build a canal across Nicaragua. Both projects failed, leaving the imperial powers still clamoring for an isthmian canal.

The quick victory of the United States over Spain in 1898 gave the United States a decided advantage in its rivalries with the European powers for domination of Central America and the Caribbean. The United States annexed Puerto Rico and the Philippines, established a protectorate over Cuba, and acquired bases in each country. At the same time, the United States acquired the Hawaiian Islands and Guam. These acquisitions reflected and promoted America's growing economic and military power. The completion of a canal across Central America now became a strategic and economic imperative for the United States.

Under the administration of President Theodore Roosevelt, the United States moved quickly to acquire the rights to build a canal. Frustrated by Nicaragua and Colombia, both of which refused to give Roosevelt the terms he demanded, Roosevelt sponsored a Panamanian rebellion that gave independence to Panama (1903) and a canal to the United States. Not surprisingly, the new Panamanian government authorized the construction of a canal across a 10-mile (16-km) strip of land on the terms that Roosevelt demanded. Within this zone the United States would hold complete sovereignty, with Panamanian "independence" guaranteed by the United States. Panama was thus born as a protectorate of the United States, its independence compromised by a permanent foreign presence within its borders. Roosevelt nevertheless boasted of his imperial behavior: "I took the canal while Congress debated."

The questionable origins of Panama and the Panama Canal, however, should not overshadow the technological achievement that the construction of the canal (1904–1914) represented. The United States spent $352 million to complete its most cherished strategic objective, more than the cost of all previous territorial acquisitions. To complete the canal, the United States had to eradicate the two diseases that had defeated the previous French effort: malaria and yellow fever. Offsetting this remarkable achievement was a tremendous loss of life: each mile came at the cost of 500 lives, most of them West Indian laborers.

The construction of the canal coincided with and encouraged a surge in American investment in Central America. The United Fruit Company of Boston led the way with the development of banana plantations, railroads, and port facilities along the Caribbean coasts of Costa Rica, Guatemala, Honduras, and Panama. The protection of these properties, and the commercial traffic that would soon ply the Panama Canal, became the primary objectives of the Latin American policy of the United States.

To safeguard U.S. interests in the Caribbean and Latin America, Roosevelt issued a corollary to the Monroe Doctrine in his 1904 State of the Union address. Roosevelt asserted: "Chronic wrongdoing, or an impotence which results in a general loosening of the ties of civilized society, may in America as elsewhere ultimately require intervention by some civilized nation, and in the Western Hemisphere the adherence of the United States to the Monroe Doctrine may force the United States, however reluctantly, in flagrant cases of such wrongdoing or impotence to the exercise of an international police power."

The Roosevelt Corollary meant, in practice, that the United States exercised a self-proclaimed right to maintain order and stability in all the Central American countries, ostensibly to protect the security and neutrality of the Panama Canal. In his controversial doctrine, Roosevelt implicitly asserted that the people of these regions were uncivilized and incompetent, unable to maintain the stable political order that Roosevelt demanded. Central Americans joined with their South American brothers in denouncing the paternalistic and racist implications of this doctrine to no avail.

The Roosevelt Corollary provided the political foundation for American policy toward Central America until 1933. During this time the United States exercised formal protectorates over Nicaragua and Panama. The other countries remained nominally in-

dependent but, with the exception of El Salvador, each country experienced some form of U.S. military intervention during the so-called Protectorate Era. Gunboats appeared frequently in Central American harbors to demonstrate American resolve, and Central American leaders ignored American policy at their own peril. Those who protected and promoted American interests, either democrats or dictators, stayed in power. Those who dared to challenge American interests soon found themselves out of office.

American investment in and trade with Central America continued to increase, while the economic interests of Europeans decreased, driven out by competition or the demands of World War I. As American political and economic domination increased, so did Central American nationalism. Some Central Americans collaborated with or profited from American hegemony, while others, primarily a younger generation of Central American idealists, challenged the right of the Americans to intervene in their internal affairs. More importantly, they began to see the United States as an obstacle to their development and independence. The United States, they concluded, was more interested in maintaining order and stability than promoting their general welfare.

A Nicaraguan general named Augusto César Sandino presented the first serious challenge to American hegemony in 1927, when he rebelled against the American occupation of his country. From 1909 to 1925 Nicaragua had been a protectorate of the United States, which attempted in vain to moderate the endemic conflict between liberals and conservatives. In 1927 the two parties fought for control of the government, bringing down yet another American military intervention. Although an American diplomat negotiated a truce between the warring parties, Sandino refused to lay down his weapons as long as a single marine remained in his country. For the next six years Sandino waged a guerrilla war against American troops. From his mountain base, Sandino defied the Americans, his tactics foreshadowing the guerrilla campaigns of revolutionaries a generation later. In the process he became a popular symbol of Nicaraguan nationalism and an internationally celebrated anti-imperialist hero. As the Nicaraguan war dragged on, the United States faced mounting criticism at home and abroad. The interventionist policies that had been justified by the Roosevelt Corollary, always lacking in legal foundation, lost political legitimacy as well. On January 1, 1933, the United States withdrew its military forces from Nicaragua.

Sandino achieved his primary objective of driving the marines out of Nicaragua, but a year later Anatasio Somoza García, commander of the Nicaraguan National Guard and a favorite of the American embassy, betrayed Sandino and had him executed. By 1936 Somoza had established a dictatorship and laid the foundations for his family's political dynasty, which governed Nicaragua until 1979. Through Somoza, the Americans eliminated the Nicaraguan challenge to American hegemony, but at a great cost—the repression of Nicaraguan hopes for a sovereign and democratic country.

Following the withdrawal of the marines from Nicaragua, the administration of Franklin D. Roosevelt inaugurated a new policy toward Latin America known as the Good Neighbor Policy. In his inaugural address of March 1933, Roosevelt pledged to form his foreign policy on the basis of mutual respect and nonintervention. Nine months later, at the seventh Pan-American Conference in Montevideo (December 1933), the United States formally approved a policy that "no state has the right to intervene in the internal or external affairs of another." Roosevelt's Good Neighbor Policy ended three decades of acrimonious and occasionally violent relations between Central America and the United States. Central Americans responded by establishing closer military and economic ties to the United States. During World War II, the Central American republics allied with the United States and collaborated with the war effort by opening bases and ports to the American military.

Although Central America and the United States enjoyed warm and cordial relations during the Good Neighbor era, Central Americans did not enjoy the democratic freedoms for which the Americans fought in World War II. With the exception of Costa Rica, dictators dominated the political landscape of Central America, with Jorge Ubico in Guatemala (1931–1944), Maximiliano Hernández Martínez in El Salvador (1931–1944), Tiburcio Carías Andino in Honduras (1932–1948), and Somoza in Nicaragua (1936–1956). These dictators maintained order and stability on behalf of the United States, but they repressed the democratic aspirations of their citizens.

The frustrations of Central Americans exploded in democratic and reformist movements after World War II, with Guatemala leading the way. A unique coalition of students, workers, and young military officers overthrew Ubico in 1944 and ushered in a ten-year period of reform and revolution that culminated during the administration of President Jacobo Arbenz (1951–1954). Although Arbenz did not belong to the Communist Party of Guatemala, he shared the Marxist perspectives of the communists and allied with the party to implement his revolutionary program. Arbenz intended to restructure the Guatemalan political and economic system. The centerpiece of his program was the agrarian reform law of 1952, which authorized the government to confiscate uncultivated lands and distribute them to peasant families. As a result, the United Fruit Company lost more than two-thirds of its landholdings. The company and the administration of President Dwight D. Eisenhower concluded that the agrarian reform was evidence of communist infiltration of the Arbenz government. With the Cold War turned decidedly hot in Korea, the Eisenhower administration feared that the Soviet Union was conspiring with the Guatemalan revolutionaries to convert Guatemala into the first Soviet beachhead in the Americas.

Evidence of such a communist conspiracy was lacking. Although Arbenz was a Marxist, he appointed no communists to his cabinet and only a few communists served in the legislature. More importantly, the Guatemalan military remained firmly under anticommunist control, and they had no intention of allowing Arbenz to forge an alliance with the Soviet Union. Arbenz therefore represented no military threat to the United States or even his Central American neighbors, but at the height of the Cold War, the United States identified the reformist program of Arbenz with an anti-American conspiracy. In a previous era the United States would have responded to the perceived threat by dispatching the marines; however, with the Good Neighbor Policy still in effect, the United States had to dispose of Arbenz secretly. The Central Intelligence Agency (CIA) trained and equipped a rebel army of 150 men led by Colonel Carlos Castillo Armas, which invaded Guatemala in June 1954. Arbenz and his military officers refused to fight the invading force, fearing that they would soon find themselves in a direct military confrontation with the United States. Arbenz resigned and fled in disgrace, bringing the Guatemalan revolution to an end.

The Guatemalan intervention of 1954 marked a low point in U.S. relations with Central America.

Although the United States had technically upheld its commitment to nonintervention, Central American political leaders knew that the United States had covertly organized the counterrevolution. The intervention confirmed what many reformists and radical political leaders had already concluded: the United States was an obstacle to their political and economic progress.

Ironically, the 1954 Guatemalan operation led to a substantial revision in American policy toward all of Latin America. Central Americans demanded political and economic reforms, and they expected the United States to finance their development programs. President John F. Kennedy recognized that Central Americans faced serious social and economic problems, which, if not addressed quickly, would promote revolutionary movements like the one that brought Fidel Castro to power in Cuba in 1959. Those who make peaceful evolution impossible, Kennedy argued, made violent revolution inevitable. Thus, in order to prevent revolutions, Kennedy initiated the Alliance for Progress, an ambitious ten-year development program designed to raise the standard of living in Latin America, diversify its economies, construct affordable housing, eradicate illiteracy, and provide better health care to the poor. All this was to be done under democratic regimes committed to reform with American economic assistance.

Although the Alliance for Progress fell far short of Kennedy's lofty goals, it contributed to significant political, social, and economic changes. The economies grew at measurably higher rates, spurred in part by industrial development. The urban centers of Central America grew, swelled by the working and middle classes. The democratization promised in the Alliance for Progress, however, occurred only to a limited extent in Costa Rica. The military dominated the regimes of Guatemala, El Salvador, and Honduras, while the Somoza family continued to dictate Nicaraguan affairs. Political tensions mounted as social and economic progress accelerated.

Central America exploded in revolution and civil war in the late 1970s. The revolutionary movements Kennedy had hoped to eliminate resurfaced in Guatemala, El Salvador, and Nicaragua. The first revolutionary group to seize power was the Sandinista National Liberation Front (FSLN) of Nicaragua, a coalition of leftist political forces inspired by the Cuban revolution. With substantial military assistance from Cuba, Costa Rica, and Panama, the FSLN

toppled Anastasio Somoza Debayle in July 1979, following a bloody military campaign that claimed the lives of nearly 50,000 Nicaraguans. The revolutionary government that came into power, led by Daniel Ortega, would not accept American interference in Nicaragua's internal affairs. They intended to implement revolutionary legislation, including an agrarian reform, regardless of American opposition. For military and economic assistance, the Sandinistas turned to Cuba and the Soviet Union.

Once again, the specter of Soviet penetration of an American sphere of influence alarmed Washington. President Jimmy Carter attempted to moderate the course of the revolutionary program, but the Sandinistas continued on a path that brought them into conflict with his successor, the staunch anticommunist Ronald Reagan. In December 1981, President Reagan authorized the CIA to train and equip an army to fight the Sandinista government. For the next eight years, this army of counterrevolutionary soldiers, known simply as the "Contras," waged a low-intensity insurgency against Nicaragua. With no more than 15,000 soldiers in the field, the Contras had little hope of toppling the Sandinista government. They did, however possess the inexhaustible resources of a determined American president, who funded the Contras even in defiance of U.S. congressional law. The Contras never presented a serious military threat to the Sandinistas, but the Sandinistas could not eliminate them either. The intent of the Contras, however, was not to overthrow the government, but to exhaust it. To prosecute the war against the Contras, the Sandinista governments spent as much as 50 percent of their meager budgets on the war effort.

The Contra War produced a relatively minor political scandal in the United States, but it caused devastation in Nicaragua. Over 30,000 were killed, 250,000 were displaced, and the Nicaraguan economy was in ruins. The Sandinistas had no option but a negotiated peace, followed by an agreement to respect the outcome of a free and fair election in 1990. In that campaign Daniel Ortega and the Sandinistas lost to Violeta Barrios de Chamorro, bringing a definitive end to the Contra War and hostilities between Nicaragua and the United States.

While the Contras ravaged the Nicaraguan countryside, death squads and guerrilla groups plunged El Salvador and Guatemala into bloody civil wars. The Reagan administration, convinced that the guerrillas represented a threat to the security of the United States, increased military aid and economic support to the governments of El Salvador and Guatemala, despite the notorious human rights violations committed by those regimes. While the armies slugged it out in the mountains and forests of Central America, death squads kidnapped, raped, tortured, and killed suspected subversives and sympathizers in the cities. The murder of Archbishop Oscar Romero in 1980, followed by the rape and murder of four American churchwomen in El Salvador, were only the most notorious death squad killings. Critics blasted the Reagan administration for providing military and economic assistance to governments guilty of such gross atrocities, but the war against suspected communist conspiracies wore down the guerrillas in El Salvador and Guatemala.

To escape conflict, poverty, and repression, Central Americans fled the war zones and sought refuge in the capital cities and abroad. The civil wars of the 1980s thereby resulted in a large migration of Central Americans to the United States. By 2000, over 1.6 million Central Americans lived in the United States, representing 4.8 percent of the total Latino population of the United States. With large concentrations of Central Americans in south Florida, California, and Washington, D.C., these Central Americans began to make their presence felt in Latino society and culture.

The collapse of the Soviet Union and the end of the Cold War did not bring an end to American intervention in Central America. In December 1989 the United States invaded Panama, captured General Manuel Noriega, and brought him to stand trial in the United States. The Panamanian invasion was, perhaps, the first of a new type of intervention in Central America, one not conditioned by Cold War suspicions of communist subversion. Noriega had run afoul of American law, and the administration of President George H. W. Bush was determined to bring him to justice, but outside of Panama, Latin American leaders condemned the American operation as another unacceptable intervention in the internal affairs of a sovereign country.

As the United States and Central America entered the 21st century, relations between the countries

AP/WIDE WORLD PHOTOS

Three nuns of the Maryknoll Catholic Order pray beside the bodies of their four sisters who were kidnapped and slain in El Salvador near the San Vincente volcano, 1981.

were close and cordial. Peace reigned throughout the region, and the governments shared an interest in promoting a neoliberal agenda that called for further political and economic integration. It remains to be seen whether the neoliberal reforms will address fundamental political, economic, and social problems. The Central American republics will remain firmly within the United States political and economic orbit, and the region will be even more tightly integrated into the American system. The conflicts between an elusive quest for national sovereignty and the needs and interests of a superpower will continue to present formidable challenges to the political leadership of all countries.

RELATED ARTICLES

Costa Rican Americans; Good Neighbor Policy; Guatemalan Americans; Honduran Americans; Immigration, Latino; Monroe Doctrine; Nicaraguan Americans; Panamanian Americans; United States Presidents and Latinos.

FURTHER READING

Burns, E. Bradford. *At War in Nicaragua: The Reagan Doctrine and the Politics of Nostalgia.* New York: Harper, 1987.

Conniff, Michael. *Panama and the United States: The Forced Alliance.* 1992. 2d ed. Athens: Univ. of Ga. Press, 2001.

Danner, Mark. *The Massacre at El Mozote: A Parable of the Cold War.* New York: Vintage, 1994.

Gleijeses, Piero. *Shattered Hope: The Guatemalan Revolution and the United States, 1944–1954.* Princeton, N.J.: Princeton Univ. Press, 1991.

LaFeber, Walter. *Inevitable Revolutions: The United States in Central America.* Rev. ed. New York: Norton, 1984.

Langley, Lester D. *The Banana Wars: United States Intervention in the Caribbean, 1898–1934.* 1983. Reprint. Wilmington, Del.: SR Bks., 2002.

LeoGrande, William M. *Our Own Backyard: The United States in Central America, 1977–1992.* Chapel Hill: Univ. of N.C. Press, 1998.

Leonard, Thomas M. *Central America and the United States: The Search for Stability.* Athens: Univ. of Ga. Press, 1991.

Longley, Kyle. *In the Eagle's Shadow: The United States and Latin America.* Wheeling, Ill.: Harlan Davidson, 2002.

PAUL DOSAL

UNITED STATES CONGRESS

Addressing the relationship between the United States Congress and the Latino community requires an understanding of Latino history in the United States as a complex equation of race, culture, ethnicity, discrimination, and conquest. This intricate relationship is colored by entrenched cultural prejudices, unequal distribution of resources, policies of exclusion, market inequalities, and skewed social and educational resources and services.

The U.S. Congress is central to Latino identity and position in today's society. In turn, Latino representation in Congress is critical to the fair distribution of benefits and services. In 2003 several key policy issues affected Latinos disproportionately: access to health care, bilingual education, quality education, housing and labor issues, and immigration concerns. Responsive representation at the national and state levels are essential to address these issues. This essay will highlight some of these policy issues against the backdrop of Latino representation in Congress.

Representation is a central issue in United States politics and governance, corresponding directly to political and legislative influence. At the dawn of the 21st century, there were 26 active Latino members of Congress; although the Latino electorate was emerging as a powerful presence in the American political arena, Latino representation was dismally skeletal. For example, given the percentage of the overall population Latinos represent, as a group they should have held approximately 50 congressional seats. As of 2002, 81 Latinos had served in Congress, 3 of them as U.S. senators. Following the 2004 election, there were 25 Hispanics in Congress, and two Hispanics were elected to the Senate, Republican Mel Martinez (Florida) and Democrat Ken Salazar (Colorado).

Latinos have had a presence—minimal or not—in Congress since 1822. The first Latino to serve in the U.S. Congress was Joseph Marion Hernandez, from the territory of Florida. A member of the Whig party, he served in the House of Representatives from September 30, 1822, to March 3, 1823. The first Latino senator was Octavio Larrazolo. Born in Chihuahua, Mexico, in 1859, Larrazolo moved to the United States as a boy and helped write the constitution of the state of New Mexico in 1910. He was elected to fill the unexpired term of Democratic senator Andieus A. Jones in 1928 but served only six months before falling ill and dying on April 7, 1930. Some of the earlier, most prominent Latinos in Congress were Dennis Chávez (New Mexico), the first directly elected Latino to the U.S. Senate; Edward Roybal (California), Kika de la Garza (Texas), Herman Badillo (New York), Baltasar Corrada (Puerto Rico), and Henry González (Texas). They are considered pioneers.

De la Garza, for example, had a distinguished 32-year career as a U.S. congressman, stepping down in 1996. Roybal served for 30 years. He, along with de la Garza and others, was a founding member of the Congressional Hispanic Caucus, introduced the first Bilingual Education Act, and served as a member of the powerful House Appropriations Committee. More recent prominent Latino members who have shaped policy in Congress include Ed Pastor (Arizona), Jose Serrano (New York), Solomon Ortiz (Texas), and Luis Gutiérrez (Illinois).

During the 19th and the early 20th century, Congress sporadically included one or two Latino members. Since 1905 Congress has always included at least one Latino member, and since the 88th Congress, the number of Latinos has never fallen below five. In 2003 there was no Latino senator, and there had not been one elected for over 20 years. Although Latinos have served in Congress since the 1820s, there were no Latinas elected to Congress until 1988. In 1992 Nydia Velázquez was the second Latina elected to the U.S. House of Representatives, and the first Puerto Rican woman elected to Congress. In 1996 Loretta Sánchez (California) was the first Mexican American woman elected to the House of Representatives, defeating a nine-term Republican incumbent.

Efforts from within Congress to educate Latinos and to increase their participation in the American political system began formally in 1976, when five prominent Latino congressmen organized the Congressional Hispanic Caucus (CHC). The CHC was originally created to strengthen federal commitment to Latinos, to monitor legislative and governmental activities that affect Latinos, and to ensure that official actions address the Latino population's needs. Two years later the Congressional Hispanic Caucus Institute (CHCI) was established as a nonprofit, nonpartisan subsidiary of the CHC. The CHCI creates and promotes programs that benefit the Latino community; its mission is to develop the next generation of Latino leaders.

One of the most important means of increasing Latino representation in Congress is redistricting or reapportionment. This is a powerful political vehicle used to create new electoral districts (or revamp old ones) to give local demographic majorities greater electoral power, ensuring proportional representation. In communities where Latinos make up the majority of the population, district lines have been redrawn to ensure that Latino voting power puts candidates into office who are responsive to the community's needs. Redistricting can determine national or local political office. Reapportionment, in conjunction with the continued enforcement of the provisions of the Voting Rights Act of 1965, has the potential to increase significantly the number of Latinos elected to Congress.

Immigration law and policy is of immense significance to Latinos because it mirrors American society's willingness to share resources with a significant immigrant population. According to a U.S. Census Bureau report, half of the foreign-born population—an estimated 14.5 million people—in the United States is from Latin America. Mexico accounts for more than one quarter of all immigrants and more than half of the immigrant Latin Americans in the United States. Cuba, the Dominican Republic, and El Salvador were also among the nation's top ten countries of foreign birth. Geographic distribution of Latinos often correlates to their countries of origin. Three out of four people born in the Caribbean live in New York City or Miami. Those born in Mexico are found predominantly in Los Angeles and Texas.

Throughout American history, immigration policies have played a significant role in shaping Latino politics and in creating obstacles to proportional representation. Latino politics began with a spirit of resistance toward American oppression and domination. Mexicans, as the first group to immigrate in significant numbers to the United States, were the first to engage in resistance politics. Their struggle resulted from the American occupation and conquest of Mexico's northern territory and the subsequent push to relegate Mexican immigrants to subservience. From the Gold Rush to the end of World War I, there was significant immigration of Mexican workers. Mexican laborers took on mining and farming work that Anglos were unwilling to do; the work was backbreaking and low paying. Prevailing theories about race during this time, coupled with the call for Manifest Destiny, led Americans to stereotype foreign workers and to develop discriminatory attitudes toward Latinos and other minority groups.

One of the first responses to immigration was Congress's enactment of the Bracero Program, allowing Mexican workers—but not Asians or southern or eastern Europeans—to temporarily enter the United States to work. After the admission into the Union of California and New Mexico, the Compromise of 1850 gave Mexicans in these territories legitimacy as United States political units.

In 1952 Congress—which has complete authority over immigration—enacted the Immigration and Nationality Act (INA). The INA, with a number of amendments, continues to be the basic immigration law of the United States. The 1965 amendment to the INA, which repealed the national origin quota system that had favored immigration from nations in northwestern Europe, was the most significant. Latinos have figured prominently since 1965 in the immigration patterns of both legal and undocumented aliens.

In 1986 Congress enacted the Immigration Reform and Control Act (IRCA), which sought to address growing concerns with illegal immigration. The act mandated criminal sanctions for employers of illegal aliens, denied undocumented immigrants federally funded welfare benefits, and legitimized some illegal aliens by means of an amnesty program. Edward Roybal (California), Democratic congressman and chair of the CHC, led the opposition against IRCA. Roybal introduced an alternative bill that called for creation of a National Immigration Commission to study long-term solutions to problems surrounding undocumented immigrants and employment. Although the House leadership had promised to give alternative measures serious consideration, the Roybal bill was largely ignored, and President Reagan signed IRCA into law on November 6, 1986.

Increasing foreign-born Latinos' American citizenship is crucial to improving their political representation. Despite the large proportion of Latinos within the foreign-born population, Latinos seek U.S. citizenship in dramatically lower numbers than do other immigrant groups. In 2000, 28 percent of foreign-born Latinos were American citizens. The citizenship rates for Europeans (52 percent) and Asians (47 percent) were significantly higher. A number of Latino immigrants do not wish to relinquish their citizenship or cultural identity. Because of this sense of "dual identity," Latinos' lower naturalization rates contribute to less political influence for Latinos than for other immigrant groups.

In the 1990s a wave of anti-immigrant sentiment, born of increasing economic hardship and the growing size and visibility of the Latino population, concentrated on foreign-born Latin Americans. In 1994 California voters approved Proposition 187, which prohibits illegal aliens in California from receiving government-funded health care and primary, secondary, and postsecondary education. According to Proposition 187, public schools must verify the legal status of children enrolling in or attending school, and authorities must report to the government any person suspected of being an illegal alien.

Bilingual education is a major concern in American society. This issue affects Latinos disproportionately because they represent the largest group of nonnative speakers of English; prominent Latino political organizations have supported the subject as part of the national agenda. The Bilingual Education Act (BEA) of 1968 was the first legislative acknowledgment of students with limited English proficiency (LEP). The BEA appropriated $85 million to fund 76 local school district programs through 1970. Throughout the 1960s and 1970s bilingual education was considered an essential tool for Latinos to gain a sense of ethnic pride, and the importance of bilingual instruction continued to grow along with the increasing number of immigrant children in American public classrooms. Official support for bilingual education was bolstered in 1974 when the Supreme Court ruled that LEP students who were taught exclusively in English were "foreclosed from any meaningful education" (Lau v. Nichols). The Court did not mandate a specific remedy, but the same year Congress amended BEA to show a decided preference for bilingual education.

In the 1970s and 1980s, bilingual education was a Latino policy issue associated with individuals who were—or were in the process of becoming—citizens. As an increasing percentage of Latinos remained immigrants and noncitizens in the 1990s, the government began to distance itself, and on January 8, 2002, President George W. Bush signed into law the No Child Left Behind Act of 2001 (NCLB). Title III of NCLB reflects profound shifts in educational and political attitudes toward bilingual education. Although NCLB does not withdraw all federal funding from bilingual programs, the statute mandates that LEP students demonstrate measurable yearly improvement in academic English, therefore making the transition to English immersion programs almost compulsory for schools seeking a portion of the new funds.

It is likely that the only way bilingual education will survive is if parents demand it. No Child Left Behind requires that parents be notified within 30 days of their child's placement in an English-language instruction program. If an alternative is available, parents have the right to place their children in a program other than the one chosen by the local educational agency. Faced with the possible monopoly of English-only movements, advocacy groups such as the National Association of Bilingual Education (NABE) and the Mexican American Legal Defense and Educational Fund (MALDEF) will certainly increase awareness about bilingual education's academic and cultural benefits. These groups are encouraged by the fact that under NCLB the parental waiver remains intact; they stress that bilingual education can continue to thrive in the many states where it is still mandated by state law.

Although many Americans might think that efforts to make English the official language of the United States is one of the newer political trends, John Adams lobbied to establish English as the official language in 1780. The effort was rejected as undemocratic. In 1981, 1983, and 1985, the English Language Amendment (ELA) was introduced in both houses of Congress in an effort to protect and underscore the role of English in the United States. The 1981 Senate version of ELA was introduced by Senator S. I. Hayakawa, founder and honorary chairperson of a nonprofit organization called U.S. English, which, it estimates, comprises over a million members throughout the country.

English-only proponents maintain that official language laws help governments save money by allowing publication of official documents in a single language and saving on administrative expenses for translation and printing. Groups such as U.S. English contend that English-only laws promote the learning of English by new immigrants and point out that such laws generally have exceptions for public safety and health needs.

Two versions of the English Language Amendment to the U.S. Constitution were introduced in 1985, one in the House and one in the Senate. The Senate version stated "1. The English Language shall be the official language of the United States. 2. The Congress shall have the power to enforce this article by appropriate legislation." In 1996 the Emerson English Language Empowerment Act was introduced in Congress. The Emerson Bill identifies "help[ing] immigrants better assimilate and take full advantage of economic and occupational opportunities in the United States" as its goal. Although federal English-only legislation continues to be introduced, to date

Congress appears to view this as a matter for the individual states to decide. As of the late 1990s, 27 states had existing official language laws on their books.

The relationship between Congress and the Latino community is indeed complex and richly historical. From a need to increase Latino representation in Congress to addressing legislation directly affecting the Latino community to the rising participation of Latino interest groups influencing the policy agenda, the number of issues that this topic encompasses can occupy several volumes.

RELATED ARTICLES

Bilingual Education; Bracero Program; Census, United States; Congressional Hispanic Caucus; Democratic Party; Demographics; Discrimination; English Only/First Movements; Fair Labor Standards Act; Immigration Acts; Immigration, Latino; Jones Act; Labor-Management Relations Act; Limited English Proficiency; Mexican American Legal Defense and Education Fund; Politics, Latino; Proposition 187; Republican Party; Supreme Court, United States; Voting.

FURTHER READING

Brunner, Barbara J. "Bilingual Education under the No Child Left Behind Act of 2001: se quedara atras?" *West's Education Law Reporter* (November 21, 2002).
Delgado, Richard, and Jean Stefancic, eds. *The Latino/a Condition.* New York: N.Y. Univ. Press, 1998.
Haney López, Ian F. *White By Law: The Legal Construction of Race.* New York: N.Y. Univ. Press, 1996.
Hero, Rodney E., and Caroline J. Tolbert. "Latinos and Substantive Representation in the U.S. House of Representatives: Direct, Indirect, or Nonexistent." *American Journal of Political Science* 39, no. 3 (August 1995) 640–652.
Johnson, Kevin R. "Civil Rights and Immigration: Challenges for the Latino Community in the Twenty-First Century." *La Raza Law Journal* 42 (1995).
Lawrence, Karl A. *Hispanic Americans: Issues and Bibliography.* New York: Nova Science Pubs., 2002.
Moran, Rachel F. "Demography and Distrust: The Latino Challenge to Civil Rights and Immigration Policy in the 1990s and Beyond." *La Raza Law Journal* 1 (1995).
Rodriguez, David. *Latino National Political Coalitions: Struggles and Challenges.* New York: Routledge, 2002.
Sierra, Christine Marie, et al. "Latino Immigration and Citizenship, in Latino Politics in the United States Symposium." *Political Science* (September 2000).
Stavans, Ilan. *The Hispanic Condition: Reflections on Culture and Identity in America.* New York: HarperCollins, 1995.
Suárez-Orozco, Marcelo M., and Mariela M. Páez, eds. *Latinos: Remaking America.* Berkeley: Univ. of Calif. Press, 2002.
Valente, Michael. "One Nation Divisible by Language: An Analysis of Official English Laws in the Wake of *Yniguez v. Arizonans* for Official English." *Seton Hall Constitutional Law* 205 (1997).
Vigil, Maurilio E. *Hispanics in Congress: A Historical and Political Survey.* Lanham, Md.: Univ. Press of Am., 1996.

SELECTED WEB SITES

Library of Congress, Hispanic Reading Room.
www.lcweb.loc.gov/rr/Hispanic/congress/chron.html
The Congressional Hispanic Caucus Institute.
http://www.chci.org/about/about.html

ANA MARIA MERICO-STEPHENS
AMY WALLACE-HAVENS

UNITED STATES–MEXICO RELATIONS

The relationship between the United States and Mexico is characterized by a series of paradoxical challenges and opportunities. Challenges emerge from differences in perspectives about particular enduring issues, such as trade and economic development, political stability, and immigration. For example, in the case of Mexican migration to the United States, the U.S. economy benefits from low-wage labor streams into border states such as California and Texas (whose agribusiness and service industries have long relied on migrant labor) and other states such as Georgia and Tennessee. However, the American public largely perceives this sojourner migration negatively. As a result the sojourner population and corresponding pool of immigrant labor has proved to be a politically volatile issue for U.S. presidents and legislators.

The overall dynamic of U.S.-Mexico relations is the mutual accommodation of each nation's objectives. It can be argued that because of the conditions of geopolitical proximity, especially with the U.S. as the world's largest oil importer and Mexico as the world's fifth largest oil exporter, the resulting interdependence of trade, labor, and economic markets forces the United States and Mexico to engage in a unique, reciprocal relationship. While one can cite numerous crises and disagreements regarding illegal immigration, differences in foreign intervention in Latin and Central American political systems, and public perceptions within each nation regarding the other's negative influence on its civic and political society, U.S.-Mexico relations have generally reflected a continuing attentiveness to economic and political stability by the institutional leaders of both nations, particularly after World War II.

Foundation

Starting in the 1820s both the United States and Mexico found themselves in a period of significant political instability. The United States's internal divisions over slavery and whether new states and territories would be subject to slavery sparked intense drives toward annexation of territories that would decide the nationalist policy on slavery. This internal division eventually resulted in the U.S. Civil War of 1861–1865. Prior to the Civil War, United States relations with Mexico were fueled by the United States's quest for annexation.

In Mexico this same period was rife with political instability as different leaders vied for control. Mexico won independence from Spain in 1821, although this independence did not herald stability. The country would be fraught with a series of political struggles and changing governments well into the 20th century. The confluence of political instability in the two nations resulted in war between the United States and Mexico and a radical reconstruction of territorial boundaries owing to war, secession, annexation, and conquest.

After a series of battles and long-standing conflicts with the Mexican government, the Anglo settlers (primarily from the United States) in the territorial area known as Texas, or Tejas, declared secession from the Mexican state. The newly declared republic fought a series of battles with the Mexican government as the Mexican leader General Antonio López de Santa Ana attempted to quell the secession. Santa Ana's troops were eventually defeated at the battle of San Jacinto in 1836. The Mexican government accepted the secession of Texas, and other nations, including the United States, recognized Texas's sovereignty.

Almost a decade later the United States and Mexican government relations again became acrimonious over Texas, as a result of the loss of its independence. The United States annexed Texas in 1845, which caused competing claims between the United States and Mexico regarding the western border of Texas. Mexico claimed that the border should be set at the Nueces River, while the United States and Texas claimed that the border should be the Rio Grande. United States expansion into this disputed area resulted in a declaration of war between the two countries. The Mexican-American War spanned two years and ended in 1848 with the signing of the Treaty of Guadalupe Hidalgo. The treaty provisions resulted in Mexico ceding a significant portion of its northern territory to the United States, including what is now Arizona, Utah, California, and parts of New Mexico, Colorado, and Wyoming. This territory amounted to approximately 500,000 square miles (about 1.3 million sq km).

Relations between the United States and Mexico from the late 19th century to the early 20th century were marked by U.S. concerns about the spread of political instability into the United States both from its southern neighbor and from abroad. The relationship was asymmetrical; the United States remained dominant, could only engage in intermittent coercion, and needed Mexico's cooperation. Part of the United States's concern stemmed from international political instability as evidenced by the revolution in czarist Russia as well as the Mexican Revolution of 1910. The U.S. policy of curtailing revolutions and other political activity was seen by some as a potential threat to internal U.S. political stability. United States–Mexico relations turned on U.S. direct military intervention in 1914 and military raids in 1916, when U.S. troops under General John Pershing crossed into Mexican territory. The United States intervened in Mexican civil unrest a number of times during the first years of the 20th century.

United States–Mexico relations were also shaped by a new consideration: significant shifts in international migration patterns. This change emerged in the early 1900s and became a cornerstone issue of United States-Mexico relations well into the 21st Century. The United States's political culture was becoming increasingly hostile toward immigrants, in part because of the increasing numbers of immigrants who entered the United States between 1880 and 1910. The number of all immigrants arriving in the United States jumped from 2,812,191 during the 1870s to 5,246,613 during the 1880s. Immigration flows were the highest in U.S. history during the first decade of the 20th century, with 8,795,386 entering the United States. Anti-immigrant sentiment came to a head through a coalescence of different powerful political groups throughout the nation, eventually leading to the passage of the 1921 Immigration Act and the 1924 Johnson-Reed Act. Migration flows shifted dramatically downward after the passage of the Johnson-Reed Act, from 4,107,209 immigrants in the 1920s to 528,431 immigrants in the 1930s. These acts effectively curtailed immigration from southern and eastern European countries and barred immigration from Asian countries. Immigration was not curtailed from Western Hemisphere

nations. Mexico was exempt from the race-based quota provisions of the 1921 and 1924 Immigration Acts.

The Mexican Revolution fueled Mexican migration to the United States in the 1910s as hundreds of thousands of Mexicans fled from civil strife. A second factor in Mexican migration to the United States was the result of the restrictions placed on immigration from other countries. The drop in immigration from Asian and southern European nations, a previous source of cheap labor, drove up the demand for such labor. Mexican laborers had long crossed the U.S.-Mexico border for work, and the United States now looked to Mexico for cheap sources of labor. Since the Johnson-Reed Act did not exclude migration from the Western Hemisphere, U.S. employers could avail themselves of Mexican labor, and Mexican laborers could take advantage of work opportunities offered by their northern neighbors. Thus, Mexican migration to the United States rose from 49,642 documented immigrants in the 1900s to 459,287 in the 1920s, dropping to 22,319 in 1930. The eventual increase in legal Mexican immigration in the 1940s by 60,589 migrants, and by 299,811 in the 1950s, was facilitated by a bilateral project between the United States and Mexico called the Bracero Program.

The Bracero Program ran from 1942 to 1964 and allowed both the U.S. and Mexican governments to address significant economic pressures. The U.S. government needed to address the shortage of cheap labor for its growing agribusiness in the southern and southwestern states. For Mexico, the Bracero Program allowed for much-needed remittances from Mexican workers and provided employment opportunities.

The Bracero Program offered advantages to the governments, domestic economies, and political stability in both countries. However, it also prompted anti-Mexican sentiment within the United States. The U.S. federal government periodically responded to local and national public xenophobia by conducting deportation raids against those of Mexican descent. Ostensibly, the U.S. government expressed concern regarding increases in undocumented Mexican migration during the 1940s and 1950s. In 1953 the federal government, through the Immigration and Naturalization Service, conducted Operation Wetback, deporting between 500,000 and 1,000,000 Mexican nationals and U.S. citizens of Mexican descent. Mexican immigrant labor, along with U.S. antipathy toward Mexican nationals within its borders, remained a key factor in U.S.-Mexico relations.

Another institutional development that shifted U.S.-Mexico relations was the rise of Partido Revolucionario Institucional (PRI) and its consolidation of political power across different industrial and economic classes in Mexico. This consolidation allowed PRI to bring political stability to the nation for longer periods and allowed for a shift in U.S.-Mexico relations: military intervention was less viable than economic assistance. With the consolidation of the PRI in the 1930s, U.S.-Mexico relations were less about direct intervention and more about developing bilateral trade and economic relations. This was evidenced by U.S. economic aid during the post–World War II period.

Institutions

Both the United States and the United Mexican States have republican forms of democracy. This allows for accommodation of popular will and the vision of institutional leadership. However, there are distinct differences in the way particular governing institutions operate that create challenges and opportunities for bilateral interaction. Unlike the two party system in the United States, a single party has dominated the party system in Mexico for several generations. The PRI members have held major political offices for over 70 years. Founded in 1929, the PRI has effectively constructed a party system with a single dominant party and weak opposition parties.

The Mexican Constitution provides for both direct election and proportional representation. The president is directly elected. The legislature consists of 628 members; 128 members serve as senators in the upper house and 500 members serve in the lower house, called the Chamber of Deputies. The legislature is elected by both direct and proportional representation. Half of the Senate and 300 members of the lower house are directly elected. The remaining 200 lower house seats and 64 senate seats are elected via proportional representation.

Since the adoption of the 1917 Constitution, 18 of the country's 19 presidents have been from the PRI. The election of Vicente Fox Quesada in 2000 marked the first president from outside of the PRI. Fox, a former governor of Guanajuato, is a member of the Partido Accion Nacional (PAN), one of the two major opposition political parties. He was elected with 42.5 percent of the popular vote.

Issues

Several enduring issues have shaped U.S.-Mexico relations. These include trade and economic development, immigration, and political stability.

Trade and Economic Development. Since World War I, Mexico's primary domestic issue has been economic development. Traditionally, Mexico's primary resource for economic development was its oil reserves. However, investment in oil development could not sustain Mexico's economy. Several Mexican presidential administrations generated national plans to diversify Mexico's economy and to align it with the world markets. The United States has recognized the importance of economic stability in Mexico. During the 1980s, when Mexico faced default on billions of dollars in foreign loans, the United States and other foreign lenders assisted Mexico in a loan forgiveness program. Since the 1980s Mexico has moved away from reliance on oil production as its primary opportunity for economic development. The focus has been on expanding trade with the United States and increasing foreign domestic investment in manufacturing and other trade oriented industries.

One opportunity for economic development in Mexico involves the transfer of finances from Mexican nationals. In 2003, remittances from Mexican sojourners were estimated at over $14 billion. Researchers found that from 1965 to the early 1980s, over 60 percent of Mexican migrants in the United States sent back (remitted) funds to their families in Mexico. Remittances provide the Mexican economy with a significant source of income, exceeded only by income from oil exportation. A 2003 survey conducted by the Pew Hispanic Center showed that 18 percent of Mexican respondents received remittances from abroad. The highest percentage of these remittances, 44 percent, went to residents living in five of Mexico's 31 states: Guanajuato, Jalisco, Michoacan, San Luis Potosi, and Zacatecas. These same states are the traditional immigrant-sending districts, accounting for a significant percentage of Mexican emigration to the United States.

Mexico and the United States are close trading partners. Mexico is the second largest U.S. trading partner and the United States is Mexico's largest trading partner. The trade patterns have tended to be asymmetrical. Mexican exports to the U.S. include oil, gas and other oil products, light manufactured goods, and agricultural products. American exports include heavy manufactured goods, machinery, and electrical products. The North American Free Trade Agreement (NAFTA) was devised to ease the flow of trade, services, and goods between the two nations. In the mid–1980s, U.S. president George H. W. Bush and Mexican president Carlos Salinas de Gortari spearheaded antecedents to NAFTA. NAFTA was then shepherded under the Clinton administration. Congress passed the agreement in 1992 and it was activated in 1994.

Immigration. Mexican migration to the United States is one of the most enduring issues in U.S.-Mexico relations. The issue of Mexican migration tends to spark political controversy on the local, national, and international levels. Often, immigration from Mexico is perceived in contradictory ways. It has been characterized in the United States as a much needed (and desired) labor source in service and agricultural sectors, a source of labor market competition to native workers, a fiscal burden on state and national economies, and a threat to law and order. The multidimensionality of Mexican immigration creates challenges for political leaders. However, no U.S. president has lost a bid for election or reelection because of his stance on immigration. Similarly, Mexican presidents have been able to address Mexican emigration without paying any significant electoral costs.

There has always been a significant flow of Mexican migration into the United States. Labor-hungry industries along the U.S.-Mexico border pulled Mexican migrants, particularly when Mexico experienced significant unemployment rates. For the period 1992–2002, yearly figures of Mexican legal immigration as a percentage of total number of admitted immigrants ranged from a high of 22 percent to a low of 13 percent. The average number of legal admissions from Mexico in this same period was 157,400. The decade 1991–2000 marked the highest Mexican migration to the U.S. (2,249,421 admitted). This increase was in part a result of the 1990 Immigration Act, which further liberalized immigration channels.

Historical response by the United States to Mexican migration swung from relatively open provision and collaboration with the Mexican government for guest worker programs to stringent, even draconian measures of repatriation. During the early 1940s the U.S. and Mexico agreed to provide protection to Mexican agricultural laborers working in the American Southwest (Texas and California) under the Bracero Program. World War II created labor scarcity in the United States, which concurred with Mexico on the mutual benefit of developing a stable labor supply—the migration would ease the unemployment tension in Mexico while easing the tight labor market in the United States. However, the resultant concern regarding undocumented immigrants prompted the United States to implement a border policy specifically targeting Mexican nationals. Operation Wetback operated along the Texas-Mexico border, deporting both Mexican nationals and American citizens of Mexican descent. While this policy strained U.S.-Mexico relations, Mexico was not in a strong enough position to provide a policy alternative.

While both nations were able to devise a free trade agreement under NAFTA, it proved to be much more problematic to devise a bilateral agreement addressing the movement of labor and persons across borders. During the development of NAFTA, immigration, and particularly undocumented Mexican immigration, became a central issue on the American public agenda. California voters passed an initiative (Proposition 187) that sought to deny undocumented migrants access to social and educational services. In 1996 Congress passed stringent immigration reforms through the Illegal Immigrant Reform and Immigrant Responsibility Act (IIR-IRA), which prohibited social services to specific classes of immigrants.

Political Stability

The United States and Mexico share a 2,000-mile- (3,218-km-) long border. On the U.S. side of this shared border are two of the largest American states: California and Texas, both of which have long-standing histories of relations with Mexico, as well as influence over national policy priorities regarding border control, immigration, trade, and labor. On the Mexican side of the border is the northern region of Mexico, which holds several of the nation's poorest states (Durango, Nayarit and Zacatecas) and one of its oil-producing states, Tamaulipas.

Both nations are regional powers in Latin America. Mexico's political heritage as a revolutionary state and its significant oil reserves (Mexico ranks second in North America and ninth worldwide) make it a political force in both Latin America and the world political arena. The combination of these geopolitical factors necessitates that the two nations negotiate internal, national, and international issues.

At times, the United States and Mexico have clashed over foreign policy objectives and actions, such as the political instability in El Salvador, Guatemala, and Nicaragua in the 1980s. The Reagan Administration supported intervention while Mexican president José López Portillo (1976–1982) supported a more middle-of-the road approach to the civil unrest. During the same period the two nations differed in their approach to international drug trafficking, the assignment of accountability, and appropriate policy solutions for stemming the influx of drugs into the United States from Latin America by way of Mexico.

The terrorist attacks against the United States on September 11, 2001, brought two seemingly disparate issues together on the U.S. political agenda: immigration and terrorism. While legal immigration had been an enduring issue that generated both national and international policies between Mexico and the United States, illegal immigration had been defined as an economic and social threat, rather than a national security threat to the United States. Mexican migration in particular had become a highly contested issue in the United States, both on the federal and the state levels. Public policies that involved border control operations, such as Operation Hold the Line in El Paso–Ciudad Juárez; Operation Gatekeeper in California; Operation Safeguard in Nogales, Arizona; and Operation Rio Grande in the Rio Grande Valley, were indicative of U.S. efforts to stem illegal migration. However, the policy usually amounted to a focus on apprehensions and deportations at vital entry points (for example, Tijuana–San Diego).

Prior to the attacks, border security focused on mediating the influx of economic and social migration streams. While there has been some increase of political asylum seekers attempting to enter the United States across the U.S.-Mexico border, the predominant migration was for economic and family unification reasons. A significant number of Mexican immigrants came to the United States intending to return to their home states once they had fulfilled their economic or work goals. These sojourners, as

© ROD AYDELOTTE/WACO TRIBUNE HERALD/GETTY IMAGES

President George W. Bush meets with Mexican president Vicente Fox at Bush's ranch in Crawford, Texas.

well as those who stay in the United States, are traditionally considered threats to the economic or labor market competition in the border areas.

After September 11, institutional changes and shifting priorities of the presidents converged to create new pressures on U.S.-Mexico relations. With the elections of Fox and Bush, the stage was set for the two presidents to continue the cordial relationship that had developed between them when they were both governors (Fox of Guanajuato and Bush of Texas). They had opened their respective presidencies with a shared agenda of potentially contentious policy solutions, such as illegal immigration, guest-worker programs, and trade and economic development issues. Each president made public pronouncements about the need to address immigration and labor concerns for the United States and Mexico, with immigration at the top of President Bush's agenda. September 11 changed President Bush's agenda, focusing his attention on national security and terrorism. This led to the dismantling of several existing bureaucracies and the creation of others designed to address these new issues.

The two most significant changes were the passage of the Homeland Security Act (Public Law 107-296) and the Patriot Act (Public Law 107-56). The

Homeland Security Act effectively overhauled more than 20 bureaucracies and agencies, the most sweeping bureaucratic institutional change since the Cold War. The act created a new department, and a cabinet level secretary transferred the functions of these bureaucracies to the new department. The Patriot Act effectively redefined national security to incorporate new understandings of internal and external threats to national security. The act also provided infrastructure for identification, surveillance, and apprehension of terrorists within the country, both among the citizenry and among noncitizens residing in the United States.

The Homeland Security Act dismantled the Immigration and Naturalization Service, reassigning its primary functions to two newly created bodies: the Bureau of Citizen and Immigration Services and the Bureau of Border Enforcement. These two new bureaus reflect the former functions of the INS: the implementation of immigration and naturalization policies as well as border control and deportation policies. A primary consequence of the Patriot Act vis-à-vis U.S.-Mexico relations was a change in the flow of commercial goods and services between the two countries as a result of border security policy changes.

Incidents of illegal border crossing shifted from traditional crossings in California and Texas to the southern regions of Arizona. Desert crossing in Arizona is much more dangerous. This shift in point of entry resulted in a marked increase in fatalities. Wayne Cornelius, a U.S.-Mexico relations scholar, found in his 2004 analysis "Evaluating Enhanced Border Enforcement" that deaths along the Texas-Arizona stretch have increased tenfold. However, the issue of "deaths at the border" has not become a significant sticking point between the U.S. and Mexico.

The Homeland Security Act changed original policy rationale and focus regarding these border operations. Title IV of the act specifically redefines border security in terms of threats to the nation via terrorism. Before the act, border security policy focused on reinforcing certain limited segments of the border; the 14-mile sector of San Diego–Tijuana border and the 20-mile (32-km) stretch in El Paso–Ciudad Juarez. After Homeland Security, the focus has shifted to securing much more of the border, which could have the effect of pushing the unlawful entry of economic migration streams deeper into the

dangerous regions of the country, with the potential for increased fatalities. This issue may become of greater concern in U.S.-Mexico relations in the future.

September 11 also proved to be one of Fox's primary challenges to his new administration. The terrorist attacks on the United States overshadowed U.S.-Mexico relations on the U.S. agenda, moving it away from the forefront of both presidents' immediate concerns. While the United States focused on issues of national security, Fox had to solidify his political base during the midterm election of 2003, in which PAN lost some of its power in the Chamber of Deputies.

In the United States, economic issues including both outsourcing in major U.S. industries and jobs have brought immigration and immigrant labor back to the public's attention. President Bush, recognizing the importance of U.S.-Mexico relations, visited Mexico in early 2004, where he publicly addressed the Mexican people regarding his plan to implement a temporary worker program for Mexican immigrants. He also promoted this plan in several prominent public addresses within the United States, redefining these efforts to formalize the temporary worker program as a separate issue from U.S. national security concerns about migration.

Overall, U.S.-Mexico relations have withstood both the unique challenges of institutional constraints and the challenges presented by September 11, as well as the ongoing concerns of trade and immigration. While new issues such as terrorism and the desire for stronger national security have shifted certain priorities on the U.S.-Mexico agenda, each nation's leaders have maintained a relatively accommodative approach to policy formation. The continued expansion and commitment to NAFTA, the creation of policy alternatives for ongoing immigrant labor market issues, and the investment by the presidential leaders in long-term bilateral agreements signal that U.S.-Mexico relations should improve in the 21st century.

RELATED ARTICLES

Border, United States-Mexico; Bracero Program; Civil War; Guadalupe Hidalgo, Treaty of; Immigration, Latino; Labor; Mexico; Mexican Americans; Mexican-American War; Operation Wetback; Politics, Mexican American; Velasco, Treaty of.

PLATE 1 • Grammy Award-winning guitar legend Carlos Santana performing in 2000.

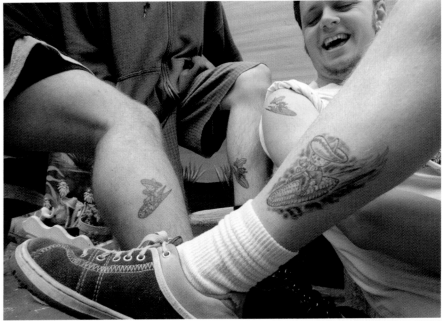

PLATE 2 • Customers display their tattoos featuring a logo of "Jimmy the Corn Man," which won them free lunches for life at the Casa Sanchez Mexican restaurant.

© RANDI LYNN BEACH / AP/WIDE WORLD PHOTOS

© ERIC RISBERG / AP/WIDE WORLD PHOTOS

PLATE 3 • Cuban trumpeter Arturo Sandoval performs during the 40th anniversary show of the Monterey Jazz Festival, 1997.

PLATE 4 • Sculptor Judith Nicolaidis in Chula Vista, California, atop her 20-foot-high statue of the Virgin of Guadalupe.

PLATE 5 • Politically charged artwork by Adal Maldonado.

PLATE 6 • Nicaraguan Contra rebel chief Siri-aco "Charro" Palacios, a most-wanted fugitive, gained popularity for protecting the poor.

PLATE 7 • Soccer fans wrapped in an American flag watch a match be-tween the United States and Germany, 2002.

PLATE 8 • Poster for the 2003 Pulitzer Prize-winning play *Anna in the Tropics* by Nilo Cruz.

PLATE 9 •
Georgia farmer holds
dried tobacco leaves.

PLATE 10 • Saint Augustine, Florida, previously known as Pagus Hispanorum; copper engraving, 1673.

PLATE 11 • Beloved Mexican singer Selena performing in concert in 1995, a month before she was fatally shot by the president of her fan club.

FURTHER READING

Baumgartner, Frank, and Bryan D. Jones, eds. *Policy Dynamics.* Chicago, Ill.: Univ. of Chicago Press, 2002.

Calavita, Kitty. *Inside the State: The Bracero Program, Immigration and the INS.* New York: Routledge, 1992.

Cornelius, Wayne. *Mexican Political System in Transition.* La Jolla, Calif.: Ctr. for U.S.-Mexican Studies, Univ. of Calif., San Diego, 1991.

Cornelius, Wayne. "Death at the Border: Efficiency and Unintended Consequences of U.S. Immigration Control Policy." *Population and Development Review.* 27, no. 4 (2001): 661–685.

Cornelius, Wayne A., et al., eds. *Mexico's Alternative Political Futures.* La Jolla, Calif.: Ctr. for U.S.-Mexican Studies, 1989.

García, Juan Ramón. *Operation Wetback: The Mass Deportation of Mexican Undocumented Workers in 1954.* Westport, Conn.: Greenwood Press, 1980.

Massey, Douglas, et al. *Beyond Smoke and Mirrors: Mexican Immigration in an Era of Economic Integration.* New York: Russell Sage, 2003.

Suro, Roberto. *Remittance Senders and Receivers: Tracking the Transnational Channels.* Washington, D.C.: Pew Hispanic Ctr., 2003.

U.S. Department of Homeland Security, Office of Immigration Statistics. *2002 Yearbook of Immigration Statistics.* Washington, D.C.: Department of Homeland Security, 2003.

VALERIE F. HUNT

UNITED STATES PRESIDENTS AND LATINOS

The relationship between American presidents and Latinos is reciprocal. Presidents can shape policies to hurt or help Latinos, and they can sincerely campaign for or pander to Latino votes at election time. However, Latinos have also used presidential politics to display their political muscle and to catapult Latino issues to a national stage.

Nineteenth-century American foreign policy reflected the imperialist aims of American presidents. Early in the 19th century, President James Monroe proclaimed the Monroe Doctrine, which said that the United States would defend Central and South America and the Caribbean against European imperialism. Some argue, though, that the Monroe Doctrine was promulgated and used for justification of American imperialism and paternalism in the region. For example, President James Polk used the concept of Manifest Destiny (the United States had the right to expand its landholdings) to justify acquiring California during the Mexican-American War (1846–1848). Polk also tried to buy Cuba from Spain; President William McKinley did win temporary control of Cuba after the Spanish-American War, when the United States also acquired Puerto Rico. These wars are significant because, in addition to acquiring more territory, the United States also had to incorporate the Latinos who lived in these newly acquired territories. In the case of California, some American legislators wanted the land but did not want the Mexican people—public discourse reflected this antipathy toward Latinos.

Theodore Roosevelt continued to justify American imperialism in Latin America with his Roosevelt Corollary. The Roosevelt Corollary said that the United States reserved the right to intervene in any Latin America country exhibiting political instability—perpetuating the paternalistic idea that Latin America and its peoples were uncivilized and needed American protection.

Franklin D. Roosevelt instituted measures to ensure that Mexican American workers benefited from New Deal relief programs during the Depression. The Federal Emergency Relief Association gave Mexican Americans temporary assistance with jobs and finances. Mexican American skilled laborers were able to participate in Works Progress Administration building projects. Unfortunately, the president's efforts were sometimes stymied by actions of local government officials, who, during the Depression, deported Mexican and Mexican American workers to reduce competition for agricultural jobs.

John F. Kennedy's 1960 presidential campaign prompted the creation of a national political agenda for Mexican Americans. Significant participation in the campaign and at the polls were important prerequisites to obtaining political access and to promoting political unity among Mexican Americans dispersed across several states in the Southwest, Midwest, and Northeast. To that end, Mexican Americans created ¡Viva Kennedy! clubs, mainly in Texas and California, to mobilize voters for Kennedy. While affiliated with the official Democratic Party campaign, the party allowed the clubs a measure of autonomy. The organizers hoped that by demonstrating their ability to independently mobilize a bloc of voters, they would be able to gain an audience with the president to discuss issues and gain access to federal appointments and employment. The strategy was successful. Mexican American voters were critical to Kennedy's winning Texas's electoral votes. Once he was inaugurated, Kennedy appointed Reynaldo Garcia to a federal judgeship in Texas.

As time went on, though, Cuban Americans lost confidence in Kennedy. In 1962 the Central Intelligence Agency recruited Cuban exiles living in the United States to return to Cuba to overthrow Fidel Castro. When Kennedy withdrew key military support for the attack, he left the Cuban exiles to invade Cuba basically on their own. Stranded in the Bay of Pigs, the exiles were defeated and captured. After the abandonment and defeat, many Cuban Americans felt that the Kennedy administration had betrayed them. Cuban Americans began to rethink their allegiance to the Democratic Party and began to vote Republican.

Subsequent presidential candidates have also attempted to reach out to Hispanic voters. For instance, in 1988, as Michael Dukakis selected a Spanish-speaking Anglo from Texas, Lloyd Bentsen, as his running mate, George H. W. Bush emphasized that his son Jeb (who became governor of Florida) was married to a Mexican American woman. Jeb and Columba Bush's son, George Prescott Bush, was a very visible member of his uncle George W. Bush's 2000 presidential campaign, addressing the Republican National Convention and actively campaigning in Latino areas.

Nevertheless, the record of presidential responsiveness is mixed. Lyndon Johnson's pro–civil rights and antipoverty initiatives benefited Latinos. Jimmy Carter directed federal grants to communities in the most need (including Latino communities) in the form of Urban Development Action Grants. Carter also accepted the 125,000 Cuban refugees in the 1980 Mariel boat lift.

While Carter's grant policies would indirectly aid Latino constituents, Ronald Reagan cut federal aid to urban centers when he consolidated numerous federal grants designated for specific purposes into broad block grants. Block grants gave states great discretion for spending in certain areas. Unlike the previous categorical grants, block grants were more likely to be issued to state rather than local governments; state governments have historically been less sensitive to minority concerns. While Reagan was able to consolidate many programs in block grants, he was unable, because of political pressure, to eliminate the grant for bilingual education by subsuming it into the larger education block grant.

Reagan and George H. W. Bush were also proponents of majority–minority districts, though for strategic reasons. After the Supreme Court allowed for the division of districts to increase the election of blacks and Latinos, both presidents encouraged these measures. This led to the increase in Latino representation in the House of Representatives after the 1990 redistricting. However, these districts also increased the probability of creating safe, white, conservative districts—likely to vote Republican—near the majority–minority districts.

During Bill Clinton's administration, the United States entered the North American Free Trade Agreement (NAFTA) with Canada and Mexico. This agreement allowed for the free flow of goods and labor throughout North America. Chicano organizations and politicians supported the agreement because it would allow people to freely cross the U.S.–Mexican border and promote neighborly relations with Mexico. Others, labor groups among them, did not support NAFTA because they believed it would jeopardize American jobs. They were joined in dissent by Puerto Rican and Cuban politicians.

Clinton also angered the Cuban American community with the forced removal of Elián Gonzalez in 2000. Five-year-old Elián was the sole survivor of a November 1999 attempted escape by boat from Cuba; his mother died in this attempt. His father, who was still in Cuba, sought to regain custody of his son, who had been rescued and taken to relatives in Miami. The relatives wanted to adopt the boy and raise him in the United States, but the Clinton administration agreed that the father's parental rights outweighed the extended family's claim. Elián was forcibly removed from his Miami family and returned to his father in Cuba, which angered many in Miami's Cuban American community.

George W. Bush has made numerous efforts to reach out to Latinos since becoming president in 2001. He has worked on establishing a strong relationship with Mexican President Vicente Fox. He also became the first president to deliver a bilingual, English–Spanish weekly radio address. His efforts paid off in 2004 when he was elected to a second term, receiving 44 percent of the Latino vote.

RELATED ARTICLES

Democratic Party; Good Neighbor Policy; Kennedy, John F.; Monroe Doctrine; Politics, Latino; Republican Party; Voting.

FURTHER READING

García, Ignacio. *Viva Kennedy: Mexican Americans in Search of a Camelot.* College Station: Tex. A&M Univ. Press, 2000.

Hero, Rodney. *Latinos and the US Political System: Two-Tiered Pluralism.* Philadelphia: Temple Univ. Press, 1992.

Montejano, David. "On the Future of Anglo-Mexican Relations in the United States." In *Chicano Politics and Society in the Late Twentieth Century.* ed. by David Montejano, 234–257. Austin: Univ. of Tex. Press, 1999.

ANDRA GILLESPIE

UNITED STATES–SOUTH AMERICA RELATIONS

The countries of South America have a peculiar geographic relation to the United States. They are neither as close to the United States as are Mexico, Central America, and the Caribbean, nor as far from it as other continents. Consequently, South America has not experienced the recurrent, profound U.S. interventionism typical of U.S. relations with its closer neighbors, nor has it been largely overlooked as many countries in Central Asia and Africa have been.

The combination of reluctant attention followed by semi-neglect is a salient feature of U.S.–South America relations. There have been exceptions, such as the heavy-handed efforts by the United States to change the foreign policy of the first Peronist administration in Argentina in 1946, to undermine the socialist administration of Salvador Allende in Chile between 1970 and 1973, and to block drug trade in the Andes since the mid-1990s. But for the most part, South America has not felt the impact of U.S. interventionism as heavily or consistently as have other regions of the world.

Episodic and inconsistent attention by the United States creates confusion as well as acrimonious polemics in the region. South Americans are often divided between those who feel that the United States is too involved in the region and those who feel that it is too distant. These positions depend on the perceived desirability of contact with the United States. Those who like U.S. involvement tend to regard the United States as too neglectful of South America; those who dislike the United States regard it as too meddlesome.

There is a much narrower range of opinions in the United States. At least at the level of policymakers, there seems to be a consensus that except during moments of exceptional security crises, South America matters little to the United States, certainly not as much as South Americans feel they ought to matter.

Interventionism until the 1930s

Early in the 19th century the United States made two declarations that implied that it would take all of the Western Hemisphere seriously. The first was the No Transfer Resolution (1811), in which the United States stipulated that it would not see "without serious inequitude" the passing of any territory in the Western Hemisphere to European hands. The second was the Monroe Doctrine (1823), in which the United States declared that any effort by Europeans to extend their political systems to this hemisphere would be seen as "dangerous to our peace and security." The few South Americans who noticed the Monroe Doctrine tended to welcome it, thinking that it foretold a close alliance between the United States and the fledgling Hispanic republics.

In South America, however, the United States ignored both principles during most of the 19th century, even when there were explicit European attempts to "extend its system" into the continent. U.S. policy toward the countries of South America during most of the 19th century remained exactly as it was during the South American wars of independence: the United States wished them well but did not wish to see them as close partners.

At the beginning of the 19th century some South American countries, such as Brazil, Argentina, Chile, and possibly Peru, might have been able to keep up with the United States, at least in terms of gross domestic product per capita, if only they had achieved rapid economic growth. Like the United States, these countries had fertile lands, links to the international economy, and republican constitutions; but by the 1870s such hopes were dashed. Most South American nations stagnated or grew less rapidly than the United States, and in less than 60 years, South America fell far behind the United States, leading to a pronounced economic asymmetry that lasted into the 21st century.

This asymmetry gave rise to resentment toward the United States from both ends of the political spectrum. For instance, conservatives such as the Brazilian Eduardo Pardo and the Uruguayan José Enrique Rodó argued that the United States had too "shallow" a culture to deserve such wealth and prestige, whereas the left worried about the imperialist appetite of the giant to the north. Like the United States, the largest South American nations pursued territorial expansion in the 19th century, often at the expense of their weaker neighbors; but because the United States was by far the hemisphere's most powerful nation, the title of the "new imperialist" was bestowed on the United States.

With the rise in the military and economic power of the United States and the expansion of commercial opportunities in South America toward the end of the 19th century, the United States could no longer afford to take the region for granted. Although the United States helped U.S. firms penetrate South American markets, the main focus of U.S. incursions was not South America but Mexico, the Caribbean, and Asia. Between 1898 and 1932 the United States deployed troops 15 times to eight Caribbean countries (including Mexico) and waged a war to subjugate the Philippines. It did not intervene militarily once in unstable South America.

Fighting Totalitarianism (1939–1989)

This complacency with South American politics came to an end with a major structural change in world politics starting in the 1930s: the rise of two great powers embracing totalitarian, antiliberal ideologies—Nazi Germany and communist Russia. These powers posed the most serious security threat to the United States since perhaps Great Britain had in the early 19th century, prompting the United States to deploy a worldwide policy to contain Germany in the early 1940s and the Soviet Union after 1948. At last the United States began to pay a bit more attention to South America.

To contain fascism, the United States made diplomatic efforts to obtain South American cooperation with the Allies during World War II. As during World War I, Brazil cooperated, but most South American nations remained neutral until 1945; in contrast, Mexico and the Caribbean nations declared war on the Axis by 1941. South American reluctance to go along with the United States was clear.

As some Realist theories of international relations would predict, the most difficult country proved to be the richest and most up-and-coming—Argentina. In 1946, unrepentant about Argentina's long delay to join the war, newly elected President Juan D. Perón entered into a high-profile political fight with the U.S. ambassador, Spruille Braden, who exaggerated the fascist threat emanating from Argentina. This conflict was an ideological dispute as well as a large South American nation's effort to assert its independence vis-à-vis the United States.

Once global fascism receded as a security threat to the United States by 1947, U.S. policy's focus shifted toward communism. The anticommunist credentials of Perón trumped his fascist proclivities, and soon relations with the United States improved.

The first U.S. policy instrument to fight communism in South America was a series of military pacts against external aggression, which most South American nations signed gladly. Then, in the early 1960s the United States experimented with another tool—the expansion of economic aid, which many South Americans had been longing for. The idea came from South American leaders themselves. They proposed that the United States offer more aid to democratic regimes in return for agrarian and social reforms. President John F. Kennedy's administration quickly signed on to the idea.

The Alliance for Progress, as this program came to be known, lasted only "1,000 days," according to Arthur Schlesinger, one of its promoters in the United States. The Alliance proved to be too controversial in South America; conservatives in South America resented the conditions, and radicals were unimpressed by the extent of social change expected. Participating governments were weakened by formidable domestic detractors from both ends of the political spectrum.

Inspired by the Cuban Revolution between 1959 and 1961 and Mao Tse-Tung's (Mao Zedong) peasant-based revolution in China in the 1940s, radicals in South America intensified their pressure against weak, U.S.-supported democracies, often turning to violence. Conservatives panicked, and a rash of coups followed, establishing so-called bureaucratic-authoritarian regimes throughout South America, with the exception of Venezuela and Colombia. The United States was shocked. The antidote to communism that worked so brilliantly in postwar Europe—cash disbursements in return for reform—turned out to be destabilizing in South America.

The Alliance for Progress was quickly replaced by the Mann doctrine, named after Thomas Mann, adviser to U.S. president Lyndon B. Johnson. Mann advocated granting U.S. aid to Latin America while remaining neutral on questions of social reform, in effect jettisoning the Alliance's principle of trading aid for social democracy.

The Mann doctrine inaugurated one of the darkest periods in U.S.–South American relations. The United States came to tolerate, sometimes prefer, authoritarian regimes. They were considered preferable to unstable democracies, which were deemed too vulnerable to communist influence.

United States policy toward the region since the Cold War has had two contradictory faces, each stemming from different branches of government. In the early 2000s based on recently declassified documents, Peter Kornbluh of the National Security Archives revealed that the Central Intelligence Agency (CIA) was more involved in destabilizing the leftist government of Salvador Allende (1970–1973) in Chile and more collaborative with Augusto Pinochet and other South American dictators than originally thought. At the same time, research in the 1990s by Robert Pastor showed that the U.S. Congress often acted as a counterweight, demanding that the executive branch pay more attention to human rights and blocking some South American counterinsurgency initiatives.

Even at the peak of the Cold War, however, actions by the U.S. executive branch were not consistent either. While the Richard Nixon administration became obsessed with destabilizing Allende, it reached an entente with the socialist military regime of Juan Velasco Alvarado in Peru. This regime committed otherwise unforgivable "sins" (including agrarian reform, nationalizations of U.S. multinationals, purchases of tanks and supersonic fighter bombers from the Soviet Union). The United States also countenanced the Brazilian military junta's close contacts with Marxist regimes and movements in lusophone Africa. After condoning military regimes in his first administration, President Ronald Reagan suddenly began to support prodemocracy opposition forces against authoritarian rulers in the 1980s, including Pinochet in Chile. Variation in U.S. interventionism against "communist threats"—or tolerance for risk—has been far greater in South America than is often recognized.

Facing these inconsistencies, South American citizens often responded in similarly divided ways. Some believed that the United States was too involved in the region; others felt the United States was not sufficiently involved. South American governments, on the other hand, were not as divided. They figured that as long as they could demonstrate commitment to fighting communism at home (something that was

not too difficult to do) the United States would grant them latitude in their policies. South American governments, both democratic and authoritarian, began to diversify their international contacts and domestic economic policies (increasing trade with the Soviet bloc, reestablishing relations with Cuba, joining the Non-Aligned Movement, supporting efforts to create a New International Economic Order, voting against the United States in international forums, nationalizing firms, tightening trade restrictions). In the words of political scientist Peter Smith, they were trying to find "a third way" between extreme pro- and anti-Americanism.

The turn to authoritarianism in South America fueled a change in society-to-society relations between the United States and South America. Progressives in the United States, shocked by human rights abuses in South America, became more attentive to the region and pressed the U.S. government to change policies. Progressive intellectuals from South America, facing repression at home, sought asylum in the previously vilified United States. Many found jobs teaching at U.S. universities.

The influx of South American intellectuals into the U.S. university system in the 1960s and 1970s had a symbiotic effect. The universities began to offer more courses on the region, and, simultaneously, South American exiles became more appreciative of the U.S. political system. A good example is the case of Fernando Henrique Cardoso, who, as a young Marxist sociologist, was forced to leave Brazil in 1964. After spending time in exile, which included teaching at U.S. universities, Cardoso underwent an intellectual evolution, softening his anti-Americanism and anticapitalism by the early 1990s. In 1994 and again in 1998 Cardoso was elected president of Brazil and became a leading promoter of market reforms and good relations with the United States.

1980s to the Present

Since the 1980s, U.S. political relations with South America have focused on promoting and consolidating democracy. The United States's only experience with the successful promotion of democracy was in postwar Europe. Compared with Europe, South America had many disadvantages, including high levels of economic underdevelopment and inequality, a tradition of military involvement in politics, a weak civil society, and a recent history of U.S. support of nondemocratic right-wing forces. In many ways, the task of promoting democracy seemed harder in South America than it ever was in Western Europe.

On the other hand, the United States had learned from its earlier attempts in South America. The U.S. government did not try to control the process by restricting efforts to state-to-state initiatives. Instead, it encouraged pluralistic and multichannel transnational contacts between the two regions. Legislators, academics, labor leaders, pollsters, party leaders, military officials, U.S. Agency for International Development (USAID) staff with training and sensitivity to social issues, state department officials, journalists, religious groups, and White House staff worked with their South American counterparts to bolster democratic institutions. They helped allay apprehensions about the United States and its political allies.

The U.S. efforts to promote democracy in South America in the 1980s were more diplomatic than economic, considering how little economic aid was earmarked for this purpose. However, this trade-off was not entirely unfortunate. One positive result of U.S. attention to diplomacy was to convince South American leaders that the defense of democracy required relaxing notions of absolute sovereignty. To prevent electoral fraud, it helps to have international observers; to deter potential coups, it helps to create a mechanism of automatic international condemnation, and even international intervention, in the event that a coup gets under way. But accepting these prescriptions meant abandoning traditional conceptions of sovereignty that ban interventions under any circumstances, a well-entrenched notion in international law widely promulgated by 19th century South American jurists (Chilean Andrés Bello and Argentine Carlos Calvo). By the late 1980s, with the help of the United States, Latin American leaders were persuaded to embrace the notion of "collective defense of democracy."

This diplomatic breakthrough paved the way for the historic 1991 Resolution 1080 of the Organization of American States (OAS), which instructs the secretary general to call for an immediate meeting of the Permanent Council in the event of any interruption of democracy among member nations. Of even more consequence, in September 2001 the OAS approved a historical Democratic Charter, which authorizes the OAS to "suspend" a member if the constitutional order is interrupted, a far departure from the traditional notion of sovereignty.

There have been coup attempts in South America in the 1990s, but no government has come to power by way of a coup since 1976. This is an unquestionable democratic victory. Methodologically, it is difficult to identify the cause of nonevents, so it is hard to establish what exactly has caused this decline, but there is reason to believe that this diplomatic, multichannel, multilateral approach to democracy may have had some impact.

Nevertheless, there have been constitutional crises in South America in the 1990s. In at least five of them, either Resolution 1080 of the OAS was invoked or South American nations played a role to diffuse tensions. Examples include the self-coup in Peru 1992, the coup attempts in Paraguay in 1996 and Ecuador in 2000, the rigged elections in Peru in 2000 (which included two coup attempts), and the coup attempt in Venezuela in 2002. Except in the Peruvian 2000 crisis, international condemnation played a role in defusing the constitutional usurpers, and except in the Venezuelan crisis of 2002, the United States was a major presence.

Preventing coups has proven easier than promoting good governance in South America. The USAID defines good governance as a "government's ability to maintain social peace, guarantee law and order, promote or create conditions necessary for economic growth, and ensure a minimum level of social security." Poor governance has been the plague of South American democracies. These regimes seem institutionally strong enough to survive coups but not strong enough to achieve the rule of law. In the 1900s many South American presidents have faced accusations of manipulating institutions, committing corruption, or looking the other way.

These institutional irregularities, which are serious enough to raise questions about the quality of democracy but do not reach the level of a constitutional crisis, have left the United States at a loss for policies. In contrast to situations where coups have been attempted, for which the United States has an official policy of condemnation, there is simply no consensus in the United States as to what to do in the event of governance crises—that is, how far to sanction the incumbents and how far to support the opposition. It is likely that U.S. reaction will continue to be erratic, inconsistent, and occasionally timid, and that the United States will repeat the pattern of semi-neglect and semi-intervention that has always characterized its policies toward South America.

After the terrorist attacks of September 11, 2001, the United States began to focus again on terrorism and the Middle East. This change of focus may undermine efforts to promote democracy and good governance in South America. By focusing on terrorism exclusively, the United States seems to have reduced the number of tests that countries in the region need to pass to qualify for good relations. In the late 1980s and 1990s, the United States had more numerous tests for South American nations, such as showing respect for democratic institutions, commitment to markets, openness to U.S. investments, alignment with U.S. foreign policy, progress in civilian controls over the military, and fulfillment of international financial obligations. But since 2001 the list of tests is shorter. As long as countries cooperate in the fight against international terrorism, they are likely to have good relations with the United States, even if they neglect issues of governance and democratization. In effect, the U.S. War on Terror has lessened international incentives for governments to worry about good governance.

The Debt Crisis and the Brady Plan

In addition to democratization, the other turning point in U.S.–South America relations was the debt crisis of the 1980s. The debt problem was a mostly South American (and Mexican) phenomenon. In 1983, five South American nations and Mexico were among the top ten debtor nations of the world (in terms of debt as a percentage of merchandise exports); they threatened to default, possibly bringing down the international financial system. South American nations and the United States realized that they could not continue to do business as usual: South Americans came to understand that they could not afford to neglect distortions in their economy, and the United States accepted that it could not afford to ignore the financial problems of the region.

After some initial hesitation, most South American nations began to reform their economies in earnest by the late 1980s, some going farther than many other nations in the world. The typical reform package included reducing state investments in unprofitable areas, raising fiscal revenues, cutting inefficient spending, and injecting stronger market forces in the domestic private sector. This set of pre-

scriptions became known as the Washington Consensus, a phrase coined by economist John Williamson. The term proved to be catchy, but infelicitous. It gave the impression that there was a consensus in Washington, when in reality there was none, and worse, that the reforms were being imposed from Washington-based actors such as the International Monetary Fund (IMF), the World Bank, and the U.S. Treasury.

The truth was more subtle. South American politicians themselves, after experiencing or coming close to experiencing hyperinflation, realized that heavy state intervention in the economy was no longer viable. After watching the relative success of Chile and Spain with market reforms, and the unquestionable disaster of Peru trying to avoid the same reforms in the 1980s, they became convinced of the need for change.

Likewise, the United States also realized that debt-relief was a crucial incentive for reform and for foreign investment. Previously, the U.S. approach had been to rely on the IMF to press countries to raise savings and generate trade surpluses so as to stay current on interest payments. Recognizing that this approach was failing, U.S. treasury secretary Nicholas Brady offered a different plan in 1989. Countries could reduce the face value of their debt, extend the time period of their obligation, and receive new infusions of cash in return for some domestic reform. One novel feature of this "Brady Plan" was to allow countries to reduce the face value of their debt through buybacks in secondary markets and to swap old loans for 30-year bonds with a 30–35 percent discount. Everyone gained. Debtor countries had the chance to reduce their debts, and lenders obtained different, realistic plans for converting bad debt into good debt that could also serve as a vehicle for investment. Mexico (1990, 1996), Venezuela (1990), Uruguay (1991), Bolivia (1992), Argentina (1993), Ecuador (1995), and Peru (1996) all signed Brady deals.

The early 1990s was thus a period of great political convergence between South America and the United States. Each was committed to market economics, democratic development, and greater trade with the other. Many South American nations became convinced that soon after the signing of the North American Free Trade Agreement (NAFTA) in 1993, the United States would extend similar agreements to South American nations; but the turn

© JUAN BARRETO/AFP/GETTY IMAGES

César Gaviria, secretary-general of the Organization of American States, inspects a point set up to collect signatures for a referendum to recall the president and several opposition representatives in Caracas, Venezuela.

toward cooperation was not as complete as first imagined. Except for Chile, South American nations did not prove to be as thorough at economic reform as originally believed, and some countries, such as Venezuela, Ecuador, and Paraguay, hardly reformed at all. Meanwhile, the United States proved less committed to closer cooperation with South America. The lack of commitment can be seen in the difference between U.S. relations with Argentina and with Mexico. While the United States gave Argentina some nontrivial rewards for its economic reforms in the 1990s (it eliminated the visa requirement for Argentine tourists), it never offered Argentina a free-trade agreement or lowered tariffs on Argentine main exports. When Argentina faced financial troubles in 2000–2001, the United States did not offer financial help (and reintroduced the visa requirement). In contrast, Mexico not only became a partner in NAFTA, but when it faced an exchange-rate crisis in 1994–1995, it received a handsome rescue package assembled by the White House.

Can Brazil Fill the Hole?

In the mid to late 1990s Brazil tried to take advantage of U.S. relative inattention to the region and become the champion of South America. During the Cold War, Brazil's foreign policy—always one of the most professional in the region—focused on two goals: maintain a friendly independence vis-à-vis the United States and engage in an economic

and arms race against Argentina. These goals changed in the 1990s. Brazil's new goals are to act as a friendly counterweight to the United States and convince its South American neighbors to accept Brazilian leadership.

Brazil has taken constructive steps toward its new goals. It curtailed its nuclear program in the 1980s; enthusiastically endorsed the creation of the South American Common Market (MERCOSUR/MERCOSUL), a trading agreement with Argentina, Uruguay, and Paraguay. It has invited other countries such as Chile (which is more interested in joining NAFTA), Venezuela (which has closer trade with Mexico and the Caribbean), and Peru (which has a small economy) to trade more with MERCOSUR. It has taken impressive steps to stabilize and modernize its economy and has begun to promote Spanish-language teaching in schools. It played a constructive role in the democratic crises of neighboring Paraguay (1996) and has tried to serve as the mediator in the Venezuelan and Colombian domestic strife. It has even created a new top position in the foreign ministry—undersecretary for South America in 2003. Brazil hopes to become the soft, benign leader in South America that the United States has failed to be.

Yet there are obstacles to Brazil's new goals. Brazil cannot easily compete with the United States because it has very few tangible resources to offer. Furthermore, the rise in Brazil's assertiveness is likely to provoke resistance, not just from the United States but from nations that feel they deserve the same stature, such as Mexico and Chile.

Brazil may be caught in a trap. The best it can offer South American nations is leadership in coordinating regional positions, thereby granting South American nations stronger bargaining power in its dealings with the United States, the European Union, and international organizations. For Brazil to have international leverage, it must show that it has the support of South American nations; yet, for South American nations to support Brazil, they want evidence that Brazil has leverage in international forums. It is a "Catch-22" situation.

The Andean Region

The most noticeable exception to the pattern of episodic and mild interventionism in South America is in the area of counternarcotics. In 1986, facing a nationwide epidemic of cocaine and crack consumption, U.S. president Ronald Reagan declared the drug trade a national security threat. This paved the way for two developments. First, efforts by the United States to fight drugs would be heavy-handed. Second, they would involve the military. Because the Andean region (Colombia, Peru, and Bolivia) is one of the world's largest suppliers of drugs, it instantly became a principal battleground of the U.S. "War on Drugs."

In Colombia the drug trade has fueled two political cancers: drug cartels and guerrillas. The guerrillas are sometimes accused of being involved in the drug trade. Most belligerents profit from drugs, either directly or indirectly, by extorting from other groups involved in the drug trade. Either way, drugs are feeding these two cancers, which now pose a grave security threat to Colombia and, increasingly, to its neighbors.

Colombian president Andrés Pastrana approached U.S. president Bill Clinton for help, and in 1998 they launched "Plan Colombia," a program of aid aimed to help Colombia defeat both the drug dealers and the guerrillas by eradicating coca production. This program leaned more toward military spending than Colombia had asked, but Colombia accepted it nonetheless. Between 2000 and mid-2003, the United States injected more the $2.4 billion into Plan Colombia, making that country the largest recipient of U.S. aid outside of the Middle East.

In the Andes U.S. counternarcotics efforts—heavy-handed and militaristic—have been criticized from all angles. One criticism focuses on the war's effects on democracy: the United States is inflating the budgets and operations of military institutions in countries where civilian control of the military is fragile, to say the least. Another criticism focuses on the futility of the effort: drug interdiction results in relocation, rather than reduction, of drug production. Yet another criticism focuses on the irrationality of the political economy of the drug war: drug production is cheap and profitable (despite U.S. efforts to make drug trafficking costly), but the War on Drugs offers weak economic incentives for actors to move away from the drug business. Yet another criticism focuses on the hypocrisy of the effort: the United States is the world's largest consumer of illicit drugs and has ineffective policies to restrain this demand.

The criticisms are numerous and devastating, but alternative solutions are scarce and flawed. This will mean that U.S. military involvement in the Andes

will continue. It is one of the few exceptions to the historical U.S. attitude of relative detachment toward South America.

The New Latinos

Traditionally, Latinos in the United States have comprised mostly those of Mexican, Caribbean, and Central American descent. The turn toward authoritarianism in South America in the 1960s began to change this, expanding the number of South American exiles coming into the United States; a massive influx of South Americans started with the debt and drug crises of the 1980s. The number of South American immigrants went from 257,940 from 1961 to 1970 to 461,847 from 1981 to 1990. The proportion of foreign-born residents of the United States from South America is still small (6.2 percent of the total foreign-born population, compared with Central Americans, who represent 36.4 percent), but the number is likely to continue to increase.

The majority of South American immigrants are not economic elites, and the proportion coming from middle- and upper-income sectors and enjoying higher levels of education is larger among South American immigrants than among immigrants from Mexico and the Caribbean. A study by the U.S. Census Bureau shows that 14.2 percent of South American–born residents live below the poverty line, compared with 22.6 percent of those from Central America. Further, 80.9 percent of South Americans have a high school education compared with only 37.3 percent of Central Americans.

There are two reasons for the higher socioeconomic profile of the South American cohort. First, many of the people-exporting countries in South America are far more economically developed, with larger middle classes, than many countries in the Caribbean. Second, the debt crisis and subsequent financial turmoil affected all income groups, generating outflows from each of them.

South Americans settling in the United States thus include a diverse profile: economic elites who lost investment opportunities back home, middle-class citizens who lost salaried jobs, and low-income workers whose lot simply turned more desperate. In terms of socioeconomic profile, the new South American cohort in the United States resembles more the Cuban cohort of the 1960s and the Puerto Rican cohort that has settled in Orlando, Florida, since the 1980s.

How this new South American cohort will shape U.S. domestic and foreign policy, if at all, remains an open question. South American Latinos are unlikely to compel the United States government to alter the tendency, discussed in this essay, to treat South America cavalierly. But because of their numbers and socioeconomic background, they stand a good chance of penetrating U.S. society easily, not just U.S. universities but also the corporate world, the entertainment industry, and the middle-class suburbs. Like the first generation of South American immigrants of the 1960s, this may mean that they stand a better chance of making U.S. society more attentive to political, cultural, and economic developments in South America, even if their impact on the U.S. government is minimal.

RELATED ARTICLES

Argentine Americans; Brazilian Americans; Chilean Americans; Ecuadorian Americans; Immigration, Latino; Monroe Doctrine; United States Presidents and Latinos; Venezuelan Americans.

FURTHER READING

Atkins, G. Pope. *Latin America in the International Political System.* 3d ed. Boulder, Colo.: Westview Press, 1995.

Baily, Samuel L. *The United States and the Development of South America.* New York: New Viewpoints, 1976.

Corrales, Javier, and Richard E. Feinberg. "Regimes of Cooperation in the Western Hemisphere: Power, Interests, and Intellectual Traditions." *International Studies Quarterly* 43 (1999): 1–36.

Farer, Tom J., ed. *Beyond Sovereignty: Collectively Defending Democracy in the Americas.* Baltimore: Johns Hopkins Univ. Press, 1996.

Kelly, Janet, and Carlos A. Romero. *The United States and Venezuela: Rethinking a Relationship.* New York: Routledge, 2002.

Kornbluh, Peter. *The Pinochet File: A Declassified Dossier on Atrocity and Accountability.* New York: New Press, 2003

Norden, Deborah L., and Roberto Russell. *The United States and Argentina.* New York: Routledge, 2002.

Pastor, Robert. *Exiting the Whirlpool: U.S. Foreign Policy Toward Latin America and the Caribbean.* 2d ed. Boulder, Colo.: Westview Press, 2001.

Pike, Frederick B. *Hispanismo, 1898–1936: Spanish Conservatives and Liberals and Their Relations with Spanish America.* Notre Dame, Ind.: Univ. of Notre Dame Press, 1971.

Roett, Riordan, ed. *Mercosur: Regional Integration, World Markets.* Boulder, Colo.: Rienners Pubs., 1999.

Schoultz, Lars. *Beneath the United States: A History of U.S. Policy toward Latin America.* Cambridge, Mass.: Harvard Univ. Press, 1998.

Smith, Peter. *Talons of the Eagle: Dynamics of U.S.–Latin American Relations.* 2d ed. New York: Oxford Univ. Press, 2000.

Tulchin, Joseph S. *Argentina and the United States: A Conflicted Relationship.* Boston: Twayne, 1990.

JAVIER CORRALES

VALDEZ, LUIS

Born: June 26, 1940; Delano, California

The founder of El Teatro Campesino, Luis Valdez is the main playwright of the Chicano movement as well as an actor, poet, essayist, director, screenplay author, and filmmaker. Valdez serves on the National Council on the Arts, holds three honorary doctorates, and has received countless awards, including an Obie (1968), an Emmy (1973), and a Peabody (1987). Jorge Huerta believes that "no other individual has made as important an impact on Chicano theater as Luis Valdez." Valdez is not without his detractors, however, who accuse him of abandoning his political activism in favor of assimilation and box office success since the 1980s. He has also been criticized for creating seemingly one-dimensional and traditional female characters: Yolanda Broyles-González, for example, has called the "deplorable representation of Mexican and Chicana women . . . a chronic weakness and signature of Luis Valdez's mainstream productions."

Valdez, the second of ten children of migrant farmworkers, entered San Jose State College in 1960 on a scholarship. While completing his bachelor's degree in English, Valdez was writing plays; one of them, *The Shrunken Head of Pancho Villa,* was produced by the school's drama department. After graduating from college in 1964, he joined the San Francisco Mime Troupe, an agitprop theater company.

The following year Valdez returned to Delano to assist César Chávez in his efforts to establish a farm-workers' union. Having worked in the fields himself since the age of six, Valdez was familiar with the plight of migrant field hands. He founded El Teatro Campesino, a theater company made up of farm laborers, which staged vignettes of Mexican American life to promote political and social activism as well as unionization. The format Valdez chose was that of the *acto,* a flexible sketch that uses the language of working-class Chicanos to convey a clear message. Numerous sketches that had started out as improvised performances were later reworked into a final form and collected as *Actos* (1971). As one of the authors of *El Plan Espiritual de Aztlán* (the manifesto passed in 1969 by a group of young Mexican Americans postulating a Chicano homeland and emphasizing the importance of a Mexican American cultural presence in the United States), Valdez saw his theater as being in the service of Chicano nationalism.

In 1967 El Teatro Campesino left the union movement, toured the United States, and widened its range of topics, while remaining focused on Mexican American identity. It shifted from *actos* to *mitos:* symbolic mythic plots in stylized poetic forms; in 1971 the company settled in San Juan Bautista, California, where it continues to operate.

Valdez has written, cowritten, and directed more than 130 plays dealing with the experience of Mexican Americans (many of them one-act plays, some unproduced, the majority unpublished). Among his

Playwright and director Luis Valdez, near a statue of Aztec chief Cuactemos at the Plaza de la Raza Cultural Center and Park in Los Angeles.

better-known works are *Bernabé* (1970), *La gran carpa de la familia Rascuachi* (1973), *El Fin del Mundo* (1976), *Tibercio Vasquez* (1980), *Bandido!* (1982), and *I Don't Have to Show You No Stinking Badges!* (1986). His best-known play, however, remains *Zoot Suit* (1978), which toured nationally and internationally and which Valdez directed as a motion picture in 1981. A docudrama on the 1942 Sleepy Lagoon murder trial in Los Angeles, *Zoot Suit* broke all previous records for the Mark Taper Forum in Los Angeles, playing to full houses for 11 months. *Zoot Suit* was also the first play by a Chicano writer to be produced on Broadway. It portrays the discrimination against young Mexican Americans by the press, the police, and the courts; using an episodic structure and the figure of a pachuco stage manger, it questions stereotypes of urban Latinos and explores the divided loyalties of Mexican Americans (to their families, ethnic group, and country) as well as efforts at overcoming ethnic boundaries.

The film version of *Zoot Suit* marked a movement of Valdez's career toward Hollywood and public television. His directing credits include *The Ballad of Gregorio Cortez* (1982), *Corridos: Tales of Passion and Revolution* (1987), *La Pastorela, or A Shepherd's Play* (1991), and a remake of the 1950s television series *The Cisco Kid* (1994). Valdez's biggest motion picture success was *La Bamba* (1987), which he wrote and directed. While his earlier work had been characterized by protest and opposition, *La Bamba,* a dramatization of the short life of the Mexican American rock-and-roll singer Ritchie Valens, advocates a syncretism of Mexican and Anglo elements into a hybrid cultural identity. Rather than stressing division (as in much of his earlier work), Valdez argues for ethnic border crossings by presenting Valens and his hit song as exemplary of an intercultural dialogue.

Despite shifting from an oppositional discourse, the focus of Luis Valdez's work—whether in film or theater or as a public figure—remains the challenge to stereotypes of U.S. Latinos. As he said in an interview, he also considers it his task to infuse new life into American culture: "Chicano art in the context of American art, I think, is like an influx of new blood which this country needs. . . . We are the future."

RELATED ARTICLES

Chicano Movement; Farmworkers Movement; Sleepy Lagoon Case; Theater; Valens, Ritchie; Zoot Suit Riots.

FURTHER READING

Broyles-González, Yolanda. *El Teatro Campesino: Theater in the Chicano Movement.* Austin: Univ. of Tex. Press, 1994.

Elam, Harry J., Jr. *Taking It to the Streets: The Social Protest Theater of Luis Valdez and Amiri Baraka.* Ann Arbor: Univ. of Mich. Press, 1997.

Flores, Arturo. *El Teatro Campesino de Luis Valdez.* Madrid: Pliegos, 1990.

Fregoso, Rosa Linda. *The Bronze Screen: Chicana and Chicano Film Culture.* Minneapolis: Univ. of Minn. Press, 1993.

Kanellos, Nicolás, ed. *An Overview of Hispanic Theatre in the United States.* Houston, Tex.: Arte Público Press, 1984.

Valdez, Luis. *Zoot Suit and Other Plays.* With an introduction by Jorge Huerta. Houston, Tex.: Arte Público Press, 1992.

SELECTED WEB SITE

El Teatro Campesino. www.elteatrocampesino.com

JOSEF RAAB

VALENS RITCHIE

Born: May 13, 1941; Pacoima, California
Died: February 3, 1959; Clear Lake, Iowa

Ritchie Valens, born Richard Steve Valenzuela to Concepción and Joseph Steve Valenzuela, had a professional recording career of less than one year, yet his influence can still be felt by garage bands, musicologists, and cultural historians. Raised among close family in California's San Fernando Valley, Valenzuela was attracted to the guitar and the potential of rock 'n' roll as performed by the likes of Elvis Presley, Little Richard, and Chuck Berry. Through the mid-1950s Valenzuela performed on the guitar at local parties and occasional dances on his own and with a group, the Silhouettes. Eventually the San Fernando performer became known as "the Little Richard of the Valley," and his talent was brought to the attention of Bob Keane, a Los Angeles record company owner and music producer.

Keane recorded Valenzuela on the Del-Fi recording label and distributed his records, first regionally, then, as their fame spread, nationally. He proposed that the teenager shorten his professional name to Valens for a broader, more mainstream acceptance, a suggestion that met little to no resistance. In the short time his 45 rpm records, such as *Come On, Let's Go* and the two-sided hit *La Bamba* and *Donna,* proved popular, Valens, who graduated from Pacoima Junior High School in 1957, performed locally (at venues such as the 1958 Los Angeles County Fair); at shows in Hawaii, New York City, and elsewhere; on national television (*American Bandstand* among other programs); in Hollywood (the movie *Go, Johnny, Go!*); and on the still nascent rock 'n' roll concert circuit. By all accounts a talented, confident, well-mannered youth, Valens learned his trade fast and well, and he showed enormous potential.

With his earnings Valens bought his mother a house in Pacoima—his parents had long-since separated and his father had died—and in January 1959 he left for a tour of the Midwest as a headliner with Dion and the Belmonts, Buddy Holly, and The Big Bopper. The tour, billed as the Winter Dance Party, traveled the upper Midwest, plagued by a bus whose heater and engine performed poorly. By the time they got to the Surf Ballroom in Clear Lake, Iowa,

Jimmy Clanton and Ritchie Valens (left) in a scene from *Go, Johnny, Go!* (1959).

on Monday, February 2, Buddy Holly decided to charter a small aircraft to ferry himself and two others to their next show in Minnesota. Following the Clear Lake show, Valens, the youngest musician of the group, persuaded one of Holly's musicians to flip a coin for space on the plane. Valens won the toss, took his seat, and minutes after takeoff the plane crashed in subfreezing temperatures. Ritchie Valens died three months shy of his 18th birthday.

Valens's best-known hit was *La Bamba,* still a staple of garage bands and oldies radio stations. The song was originally a *son jarocho*—distinctive music from Veracruz, Mexico, that fused the region's African, native, and Spanish elements—which can be traced back to the 17th century. *La Bamba* gained popularity through Mexico with traveling minstrel shows, and when recorded music and movies developed, it became known to the rest of Latin America. *La Bamba* moved north into the United States with the Bracero Program and general migration, settling in rural labor camps and urban barrios. Ritchie Valenzuela of the San Fernando Valley had grafted a joyous, electrified rock 'n' roll rhythm to a centuries-old song and had given it a new life.

Valens lived in a period when Mexican American consciousness had not yet coalesced, and his identity as an entertainer rested solely on his talent. As more southern California Mexican Americans formed bands and a pattern developed, Valens was seen as a groundbreaker whose success was both model and precedent. In 1987, attracted to the Valens story and its music, Luis Valdez, best known as cofounder of El Teatro Campesino, directed a Hollywood movie of the entertainer's life called *La Bamba,* starring Lou Diamond Phillips as Valens. The film, which has remained popular since its release, includes the band Los Lobos playing the song on-camera in its *jarocho* style and off-camera in Valens's rock version. In 1990 Valens was posthumously awarded a star on Hollywood's Walk of Fame, and the following year he was inducted into the Rock and Roll Hall of Fame. In 1993 the U.S. Postal Service issued a stamp in his memory, and the next year Pacoima's Recreation Center was named for its famous son; a fair is held there celebrating his memory every May. A generation and more since Valens's brief career, he can be seen as a pivotal character in the intersection of rock 'n' roll and Chicano pride, both just then taking shape.

RELATED ARTICLES

Music, Popular; Popular Culture; Rock-en-Espanol; Valdez, Luis.

FURTHER READING

Mendheim, Beverly. *Ritchie Valens: The First Latino Rocker.* Tempe, Ariz.: Bilingual Press, 1987.
Reyes, David, and Tom Waldman. *Land of a Thousand Dances: Chicano Rock 'n' Roll from Southern California.* Albuquerque: Univ. of N.Mex. Press, 1998.

TOM MILLER

VARELA, FÉLIX

Born: November 20, 1788; Cuba
Died: February 25, 1853; Saint Augustine, Florida

One of Cuba's most important political and literary figures of the 19th century, Félix Francisco José María de Varela y Morales—Father Félix Varela—is known particularly as a philosopher-priest and a prolific intellectual writer, who was also an ardent advocate for independence from Spain. Considered an exemplary figure, he has been hailed because of his role as an educator who taught Cubans critical thinking; as a pioneering Cuban revolutionary who advocated for independence; as a founding father of the nation; as a model of integrity, decency, and superior intelligence who served as a positive mentor for young generations; and as a great humanitarian. In the 1990s there was a movement to canonize him, and in 1997 the U.S. Postal Service issued in his honor a new 32-cent commemorative stamp.

Varela was born on November 20, 1788. In Havana he studied for the priesthood at the San Carlos Seminary. After his ordination in 1811, he stayed at this seminary, where he not only reformed its educational pedagogy but also taught physics, chemistry, philosophy, rhetoric, and constitutional law. Varela wrote profusely in Latin, Spanish, and English, and by 1820 he already had printed two books in Latin and had produced textbooks on the course content of his classes, including a four-volume text on his *Lessons on Philosophy* (1818–1820). As an educator, Varela favored teaching in Spanish rather than in Latin, and he contributed to the intellectual formation of future Cuban leaders and scholars such as José de la Luz y Caballero, Domingo del Monte, and José Antonio Saco. He excelled, furthermore, as an accomplished violinist, as a great orator, and, above all, as a political citizen critical of the colonial status of his native island.

During the first half of the 19th century, in which Spanish history was marked by the Napoleonic invasion of 1808, despotic reigns such as the one of Ferdinand VII, and the emancipation of most of the Spanish American territories from Spain, Varela advocated for independence and the abolition of slavery in Cuba. In 1822–1823 Varela was among those who represented Cuba in the meetings of the Spanish *cortes* (courts) in Spain. With the return of Ferdinand VII, however, many Spaniards and Spanish Americans were forced to seek exile. Varela escaped to Gibraltar, and from there he made his way to the United States, arriving on December 17, 1823. Philadelphia, the city where most of the intellectual exiles who had been fighting for the emancipation of Spanish America resided, welcomed Varela. Here he founded *El Habanero,* a political newspaper which openly militated for Cuban freedom, and devoted part of his time to translating into Spanish Thomas Jefferson's "A Manual of Parliamentary Practice" and Humphry Davy's "Elements of Agricultural Chemistry." Critics credit him also with the authorship of the first Spanish American historical novel, *Xicoténcatl,* a novel about the conquest of Mexico and an outcry for freedom from Spain, published anonymously in Philadelphia in 1826.

In 1825 he departed for New York City, where he was devoted to help the largely impoverished immigrant populations and to serve the poor and the sick. During most of the 19th century, New York City was smaller than the two other economic and cultural centers, Boston and Philadelphia. The Brooklyn Bridge was not finished until 1863 and the then separate boroughs of the Bronx, Queens, and Staten Island did not join Manhattan until 1898. The city mirrored the economic expansion, growth, and changes of the country and experienced during the Era of Good Feeling an unprecedented cultural, commercial, and economic growth thanks to its importance as a seaport and manufacturing center. Amid a vibrant literary and cultural city with much printing activity, the emergence of a strong middle and wealthy class, rapid industrialization, advances in transportation, and democratization of education (for example, in 1847 the Free Academy, later City College, was chartered), there were also many problems and challenges.

Millions of Germans, Irish, and other northern European immigrants flocked to work on the docks and in the mills in this strongly Protestant and Anglo-Saxon city, leading to conflicts over temperance, city government, religion, and public education and the proliferation of Nativism, an anti-Catholic movement that opposed immigration and accused Irish and German workers of undercutting the wages of American-born workers. Clashes and ethnic and racial confrontation reached a peak during the draft riots of 1863. Immigrant neighborhoods were hard hit by the lack of social and health services such as sewers and running water, and residents suffered from overcrowded living conditions, illiteracy, and high rates of illness and death. The famous cholera epidemic of 1832 was devastating to those neighborhoods.

It is within this context that Father Varela worked. He was the pastor of Christ Church of St. Peter until March 23, 1827, when the congregation moved to Christ Protestant Episcopal Church at 41 Ann Street. Eventually the congregation divided into two branches, and Varela became in 1836 the priest of one that he named the Church of Transfiguration, located on Chambers and Park streets. Father Varela financed the church with his income and money from relatives and friends, since most of the churchgoers were poor residents of Five Points. This neighborhood, visited by Charles Dickens and described in his *American Notes* (1842), was characterized by its poverty, crime rate, and physical decay. It became a symbol of the "other" New York through the text of Jacob A. Riis's *How the Other Half Lives* (1922). Varela was instrumental in establishing parochial schools and day care centers for working mothers there.

As a theologian, he attended important church reunions, such as in Baltimore in 1837, and became vicar general of New York. In 1841 Saint Mary's Seminary granted him a doctorate in theology. His stay in New York allowed him to engage in publishing books on philosophy and on the poetry of Manuel de Zequeira, and his *Letters to Elpidio on Impiety, Superstition and Fanaticism* (1835–1838). He became a noted journalist who wrote on religion, patriotism, and literature in both English and Spanish papers such as *Truth Teller, New York Weekly Register, Catholic Diary, El mensajero semanal* (all in New York), and *Revista bimestre* (in Cuba). In *El mensajero semanal,* which he coedited with José A.

Saco, he defended the Catholic faith against the Nativist and Protestant attacks made in American periodicals such as *The Protestant Abridger* and the *Annotator*. He served as editor of *Young Catholic's Magazine,* and *Catholic Expositor and Literary Magazine.*

RELATED ARTICLES

Catholicism; Cuba; Cuban Americans; Journalism; Philosophy.

FURTHER READING

Burrows, Edwin G., and Mike Wallace. *Gotham: A History of New York City to 1898.* New York: Oxford Univ. Press, 1999.

Cortina, Rodolfo. "Varela's *Jicoténcatl* and the Historical Novel." In *Recovering the U.S. Hispanic Literary Heritage.* Vol. 3. Ed. by María Herrera-Sobek and V. Sánchez-Korrol. Houston, Tex.: Arte Público, 2000.

Esquenazi-Mayo, Roberto, ed. *El Padre Varela: Pensador, sacerdote, patriota.* Washington, D.C.: Georgetown Univ. Press, 1990.

Leal, Luis. "Jicoténcatl: Primera novela histórica en castellano." *A Luis Leal Reader.* Ed. by Ilan Stavans. Madison: Univ. of Wis. Press, 2005.

McCadden, Joseph, and Helen McCadden. *Father Varela: Torch Bearer from Cuba.* New York: U.S. Catholic Hist. Soc., 1969.

Varela y Morales, Felix. *Cartas a Elpidio: Sobre la impiedad, la superstición y el fanatismo en sus relaciones con la sociedad.* Miami: Editorial Cubana, 1996.

Varela y Morales, Felix. *El Habanero, papel político, científico y literario.* Miami: Ediciones Universal, 1997.

Varela y Morales, Felix. *Xicoténcatl: An Anonymous Historical Novel about the Events Leading Up to the Conquest of the Aztec Empire.* Tr. and intro. by Guillermo I. Castillo-Feliú. Austin: Univ. of Tex. Press, 1999.

ASELA RODRÍGUEZ LAGUNA

VASCONCELOS, JOSÉ

Born: 1882; Oaxaca, Mexico
Died: June 30, 1959; Mexico City, Mexico

José Vasconcelos was one of the most complex and polemic Mexican intellectuals and writers of the 20th century. He was born in Oaxaca and spent part of his childhood on the U.S.-Mexican border, where he crossed daily to attend primary school in Eagle Pass, Texas. Vasconcelos studied law in Mexico City, where he joined the Ateneo de la Juventud (Athenaeum of Youth). This group of thinkers (Alfonso Reyes, Antonio Caso, Martín Luis Guzmán, and Pedro Henríquez Ureña), who represented a humanist reaction against positivism, shaped his early intellectual development. The Ateneo had a significant impact on Mexican cultural and intellectual history.

In 1909 Vasconcelos became one of the leaders of the Anti-Reelectionist Movement in Mexico City and was the editor of its newspaper. He was an active supporter of Fransisco Madero, an important leader of the Mexican Revolution; Vasconcelos was himself a participant in the Mexican Revolution. Later he was forced to flee to the United States for political reasons.

On his return to Mexico City, Vasconcelos headed the National University of Mexico and was named minister of education (1921–1924). During this period he worked vigorously to renovate the educational system in Mexico; he reformed rural education, built new schools, and was committed to promoting literacy for all Mexicans, including Indians. Vasconcelos enlisted the aid of prominent figures, notably the poet Gabriela Mistral, to carry out many of his educational reforms. As minister of education, Vasconcelos supported libraries and public access to the fine arts. He was responsible for the publication of inexpensive editions of the classics of world literature and promoted literacy through the distribution of more than 2 million workbooks to teach people to read. In addition, he fostered the arts, during the period when the Mexican muralists Diego Rivera, David Alfaro Siqueros, and José Clemente Orozco were gaining international recognition.

Vasconcelos is most well known for his famous and controversial *La raza cósmica* (1925; translated as *The Cosmic Race*). In this book Vasconcelos develops his theory of "the Cosmic Race," which refers to a synthesis of all of the races of Latin America. According to this theory, the Latin American mestizo is racially superior to the Anglo and should be able to resist and in the future triumph against U.S. imperialism. In *Indología* (1927; *Indigenology*) he affirms the superiority of the mestizo race, whose strength comes from the combination of different bloods.

Because of his concept of a cosmic race, which results from the mixing of different races, Vasconcelos has been important for many U.S. Latinos and, especially, Chicano intellectuals who affirm their mestizo identity, in particular the indigenous roots of their Mexican heritage. Many Mexican Americans argue that because of the experience of living between Mexican and Anglo cultures, they are able to negotiate their identity, appropriating elements from both worlds and cultures.

In 1929 Vasconcelos was defeated as a presidential candidate in a fraudulent election and was forced into exile. He lived in voluntary exile for many years, traveling and lecturing throughout Latin America, Europe, and the United States. Abandoning his liberal thinking, during the decade of the 1930s, he became quite conservative and reactionary. In 1940 Vasconcelos returned to Mexico and founded *Timón,* an openly pro-German and fascist journal. In his later years he became a devout Catholic and an apologist for conservative Spanish tradition. Although Vasconcelos is best known for his essays covering a wide range philosophical, historical, cultural, and political topics, he also cultivated other genres. *Ulises criollo* (1935; *The Creole Ulysses*) is a semiautobiographical novel about the Mexican Revolution. This was the first and most well received of his four-volume autobiography.

The reason Vasconcelos is considered so polemic, especially within the context of Mexican intellectual history, is that racism (the concept of racial superiority of the so-called cosmic race) forms the foundation of his thinking and his interest in fascism led to his support of racism during World War II.

RELATED ARTICLES

Literature, Mexican American; Mestizaje; Race.

FURTHER READING

De Beer, Gabriela. *José Vasconcelos and His World.* New York: Las Américas Publ., 1966.
Haddox, John H. *Vasconcelos of Mexico, Philosopher and Prophet.* Austin: Univ. of Tex. Press, 1969.

JUDY MALOOF

VÁSQUEZ, TIBURCIO

Born: August 11, 1835; Monterey County, California
Died: March 19, 1875; San Jose, California

Born at his parents' modest ranch in Monterey County, northern California, Tiburcio Vásquez grew up with three brothers and one sister. Vásquez's childhood in Mexican-controlled California included a formal education that gave him a command of the English language by age 16; by most accounts Vásquez's early life was that of a law-abiding person who went about his daily and weekly routines of school, work, and fandangos (Spanish dancing).

Tiburcio Vásquez's political convictions matured shortly after the United States's conquest of Mexico in 1848. Recalling this period in his life, Vásquez stated in the *Los Angeles Star* (1874), "My career grew out of the circumstances by which I was surrounded as I grew into manhood. . . . I was in the habit of attending balls and parties given by the native Californios, into which the Americans, then beginning to become numerous, would force themselves and shove the native-born men aside, monopolizing the dances and the women. . . . A spirit of hatred and revenge took possession of me. I had numerous fights in defense of what I believed to be my rights and those of my countrymen."

In spring 1851 Vásquez attended a dance along with several companions. Feeling slighted by the Anglos, Vásquez and his companions engaged in a fight with several Anglos that resulted in the death of a man by the name of Hardimount. Thus, at age 16, the young Vásquez was forced into a life on the run, beginning a career that was considered heroic to many Mexicans but criminal to many recently arrived European American immigrants.

His convictions ignited in Vásquez a passion to organize like-minded individuals to rob cattle and goods, mostly from those they considered to be invading Americans. He once commented that "Given $60,000 I would be able to recruit enough arms and men to revolutionize southern California." During winter and spring 1856–1857, Vásquez and his group took horses and rustled cattle, much of which was distributed among impoverished Mexicans in the Salinas Valley. Such distribution occurred both as a matter of generosity and in exchange for refuge.

In 1857 Vásquez was arrested in Los Angeles for horse stealing and spent time in San Quentin Prison. He returned to his parents' home in 1863 after his release and soon became a fugitive owing to accusations of confederacy. In 1873 Vásquez's notoriety as a bandit gained statewide attention and alarm. In August of that year, a plot to rob Snyder's Store in Tres Pinos resulted in the public murder of three Anglos who were chased and gunned down in the streets of the town. A series of similarly planned robberies followed.

Some of the group's monetary gain was utilized to satisfy its taste for gambling and women. One affair included Vásquez's relations with Rosaria Leiva, the wife of Adbon, one of the men in his group. Leiva turned on Vásquez and later assisted in the hunt for the band. She testified against Vásquez for the Tres Pinos murders after he was captured 10 miles (16 km) west of Los Angeles at the house of George

Allen in May 1874. Vásquez was extradited north aboard the steamer *Senator* later that month to face charges. He was convicted in January 1875 and hanged at 1:30 P.M. on the afternoon of March 19, 1875.

RELATED ARTICLES

Criminals and Bandidos.

FURTHER READING

Castillo, Pedro, and Albert Camarillo. *Furia y Muerte: Los Bandidos Chicanos.* Los Angeles: Aztlán Publications Chicano Studies Center, Univ. of California, Los Angeles, 1973.

Rambo, Ralph F. *Trailing the Bandit Tiburcio Vásquez, 1835–1875.* San Jose, Calif.: Rosicrucian Press, 1968.

Sawyer, Eugene T. *The Life and Career of Tiburcio Vásquez, The California Stage Robber.* Oakland, Calif.: Biobooks, 1944.

GABRIEL GUTIÉRREZ

VEGA, BERNARDO

Born: January 14, 1885; Cayey, Puerto Rico
Died: June 1965; Unknown

A prominent labor activist in New York City in the first half of the 20th century, Bernardo Vega was born in 1885 in the mountain town of Cayey, Puerto Rico. He was exposed at an early age to the poverty that overwhelmed the lives of the majority of the island's peasant population, and he also witnessed the end of Spanish colonial rule in Puerto Rico and the changes that came as a result of the Spanish-American War of 1898 and the U.S. occupation. As a young man, Vega was drawn into the world of the *tabaqueros* (cigarmakers), an enlightened sector of the artisan class. He was trained in cigar making and learned a great deal about the socialist ideals that were such an important component of the island's labor movement at the time. It was common practice for the *tabaqueros* to hire a *lector* (reader) at the workplace who read from daily newspapers and from some of the major works in social and political thought and creative literature. This environment familiarized Vega with workers' struggles and their exploitation by the island's creole propertied class and the U.S. corporations that controlled the Puerto Rican agricultural economy.

During the early decades of North American rule, Puerto Rico remained a neglected colony, although the island was of strategic military importance to the United States and was also a source of low-wage contract labor for mainland industries. The new colonial government promoted labor migration as a way of dealing with poverty and unemployment. Discouraging economic opportunities on the island forced Vega and many others to migrate to New York City. He left the island in 1916, a year before the U.S. Congress approved the Jones Act that made Puerto Ricans U.S. citizens. At the time, although there were only approximately 20,000 Puerto Ricans in New York City, it was the major center of Puerto Rican settlement; a Puerto Rican *colonia* (ethnic neighborhood) of a few thousand people had existed there since the mid-19th century. Tobacco-industry workers were among those drawn to New York during this period, since there were about 200 cigar-making shops and factories around the city.

In New York City Vega identified with the plight of other migrants like him who had come to the United States to improve their lives but were confronted with racial discrimination and labor exploitation. He soon became a labor activist and community organizer, participating in the establishment of several grassroots organizations aimed at promoting unity, social interaction, and advocacy around specific issues that affected the lives of Puerto Ricans and other Latino migrants. One of those worker-focused organizations was *Alianza Obrera*

DAY-TO-DAY LIFE IN NEW YORK AND OTHER DETAILS

In about 1918 entertainment for Puerto Ricans in New York was confined to the apartments they lived in. They celebrated birthdays and weddings and, of course, Christmas Eve, New Year's Day, and the Feast of the Epiphany. But always at home, with friends and neighbors.

There would be dancing, and between numbers somebody would recite poetry or hold forth about our distant homeland. At some of the parties there were *charangas,* lively groups of Puerto Rican musicians. But most of the time we played records. By that time Columbia Records was recording *danzas, aguinaldos,* and other kinds of music from back home.

Excerpt from *Memoirs de Bernardo Vega* by Bernardo Vega (1977).

(Workers' Alliance). He also wrote for Spanish-language newspapers.

Vega's interest in journalistic activities led him to purchase the newspaper *Gráfico* (Illustrated) (1926–1931), a weekly publication aimed at a working-class audience, that had been started by a group of *tabaqueros*. First edited by Afro-Cuban actor and playwright Alberto O'Farrill, the newspaper described itself as a "defensor de la raza hispana" (defender of the Hispanic race). Along with a few other newspapers, *Gráfico* promoted a pan-ethnic sense of *hispanismo* (Hispanic identity) among the various Latino nationalities living in the city. Vega's journalistic activities were not limited to *Gráfico*; however, years later he collaborated with the Spanish-exile newspaper *Liberación* (Liberation) (1946–1949). But Vega's most important legacy came in the form of his memoirs, which he began to write in the 1940s. For many years he recorded a meticulous and detailed account of his experiences as a Puerto Rican immigrant, as well as those of other migrants during the formative years of New York's Puerto Rican community. His narrative begins in 1857 with the arrival in New York City of his uncle Antonio Vega, who, along with many other Hispanic Caribbean émigrés, came to the United States to work and became involved with the Antillean separatist movement to liberate Cuba and Puerto Rico from Spanish colonial rule. Vega provides detailed information about many of the leading personalities of the expatriate separatist movement and about the organizations and publications that were created to serve the community and promote the islands' liberation from Spain.

Vega's memoirs represent a valuable historical record of the New York City Puerto Rican community, especially during the decades between the two world wars and prior to the mass migration of the late 1940s and 1950s. Vega had returned to the island in the 1950s and had shown the completed manuscript of his memoirs to his friend and socialist comrade, César Andreu Iglesias, a well known Puerto Rican writer. He asked Andreu Iglesias to edit the manuscript for publication, but the project did not come to fruition for many years. To honor his old friend's memory, Andreu Iglesias revived the project and published the edited manuscript in 1977, more than a decade after Vega's death, under the title *Memorias de Bernardo Vega*. A few years later, the historical value of the memoirs was acknowledged by Juan Flores, a U.S. Puerto Rican studies scholar.

He translated Vega's memoirs into English in a volume published in 1984. In the translator's preface, Flores comments on the significance of this publication: " . . . the English language edition of *Memoirs* is an event to celebrate, marking a new stage in the people's historical self-awareness. No book offers the millions of Puerto Ricans in the United States so many continuities and connections, so many recognizable and identifiable life experiences, so many incentives to recapture the buried past and to strike out against an unsatisfactory present." In the years since their publication, however, questions have been raised about Andreu Inglesias's editing, about the authenticity of the memoirs, and whether they were written by Vega as autobiography or as fictionalized narrative.

RELATED ARTICLES

Journalism; Labor; Newspapers and Magazines; New York City; Puerto Ricans on the Mainland.

FURTHER READING

Acosta-Belén, Edna. "The Building of a Community: Puerto Rican Writers and Activists in New York City." In *Recovering the U.S. Hispanic Literary Heritage*. Vol. 1. Ed. by Ramón Gutiérrez and Genaro Padilla. Houston, Tex.: Arte Público Press, 1993.

Andreu Iglesias, César, ed. *Memorias de Bernardo Vega: Contribución del la historia de la comunidad puertorriqueña en Nueva York*. 1977. 3d ed., rev. Río Piedras, Puerto Rico: Ediciones Huracán, 1984.

Vega, Bernardo. *Memoirs of Bernardo Vega: A Contribution to the History of the Puerto Rican Community in New York*. Ed. by César Andreu Inglesias, tr. by Juan Flores. New York: Monthly Review Press, 1984.

EDNA ACOSTA-BELÉN

VELASCO, TREATY OF

On May 14, 1836, Mexican general Antonio López de Santa Anna and representatives of the newly independent Texas government signed two peace accords collectively known as the Treaty of Velasco. Named after the port city where they were signed, these documents declared an official end to the Texas Revolution—a war for independence from Mexico—and foreshadowed the United States's acquisition of 529,189 square miles (1,370,600 sq km) of Mexican territory following the 1846–1848 Mexican-American War.

Settlement of the Texas region by U.S. citizens began in the early 1820s, when the Mexican government began selling land contracts to Anglo farmers.

Although Mexican leaders had hoped internal migration to this sparsely populated area would increase once it became more developed, by the mid-1830s the Texas population was estimated at 15,000 Anglo-Americans, 2,000 slaves, and only 4,000 Mexican Texans. Tensions rose as the Mexican Congress tried to stem the flow of Anglo immigrants and maintain control over the region. The situation came to a head in the summer of 1835. No longer willing to submit to the authority of the Mexican federal government, residents of Texas took up arms and captured several cities. On March 2, 1836, a convention of Texas representatives officially declared themselves an independent nation.

Santa Anna, Mexico's president at the time, personally accompanied a contingent of Mexican troops sent to put down the Texas rebellion. After Mexican victories at the Battle of the Alamo and the Battle of Goliad, the insurgent forces appeared destined for defeat. The tide turned, however, on April 21 when Santa Anna himself was captured at the Battle of San Jacinto and fighting was suspended.

The "public agreement" contained ten articles. Santa Anna was to cease all hostilities toward the people of Texas, evacuate his troops south of the Rio Grande, and return all property (including slaves) and prisoners taken during the fighting as quickly as possible. Mexican prisoners would also be returned, and troops from both sides were to avoid further contact while arrangements for safe travel could be made. Santa Anna was also forced to sign a "secret treaty," which was to remain sealed until it could be implemented. This second document reiterated that Mexican troops lay down their arms and withdraw from Texas. In addition, Santa Anna was to convince the Mexican government to officially recognize Texan independence and establish a commerce treaty between the two countries with the Rio Grande as the international border.

President Santa Anna later rejected the Velasco Treaty, arguing that his captors coerced his signature and in any case had voided the agreement by violating a clause requiring his "immediate embarkation" to Veracruz. The clause regarding the Texas boundary, however, proved permanent despite the fact that the Mexican government held onto the hope of recapturing its lost territory until signing the Treaty of Guadalupe Hidalgo in 1848.

Mexican citizens living in Texas felt the impact of the Treaty of Velasco almost immediately. Over-

night, what had been the native population came to be viewed as foreigners of suspect loyalty. Racial prejudice grew more apparent as U.S. migration to Texas increased and residual resentment for Santa Anna's excesses at the Alamo and Goliad lingered. Nonetheless, a significant number of Mexicans remained in Texas and many more immigrated in the years to follow.

RELATED ARTICLES

Mexican-American War; Mexico; Santa Anna, Antonio Lopez de; Southwestern United States, Anglo Immigration to; Texas.

FURTHER READING

De la Teja, Jesús F. "Texas." In *The Encyclopedia of Latin American History and Culture.* 5 vols. Ed. by Barbara A. Tenenbaum. New York: Scribner, 1996.

De León, Arnoldo. "Life for Mexicans in Texas after the 1836 Revolution." In *Major Problems in Mexican American History: Documents and Essays.* Ed. by Zaragosa Vargas. Boston: Houghton Mifflin, 1999.

Lack, Paul D. *The Texas Revolutionary Experience: A Political and Social History, 1835–1836.* College Station: Tex. A&M Univ. Press, 1992.

Winders, Richard Bruce. *Crisis in the Southwest: The United States, Mexico, and the Struggle over Texas.* Wilmington, Del.: Scholarly Resources, 2002.

SELECTED WEB SITE

Texas State Library & Archives Commission. www.tsl.state.tx.us/treasures/republic/velasco-01.html

DOUGLAS KEBERLEIN GUTIÉRREZ

VENEZUELAN AMERICANS

Before the 1980s, Venezuela was a stable country with a center-left democratic system, a functioning upper-middle-class economy, and a petroleum industry that successfully linked it to developed-nations' goals. It was also primarily an immigrant receiving, not sending, country. Historically the study of Venezuelan migration has been focused on immigrants entering Venezuela—from neighboring Colombia, Europe (primarily Spain, Italy, and Portugal), the Caribbean, other South American countries (such as Argentina and Uruguay), and Asia and the Middle East. Only recently have Venezuelan emigrants received much attention.

This shift occurred because various debt, banking, and currency crises and rising inflation and unemployment plagued Venezuela during the 1980s and 1990s, increasing incentives for emigration. During the 1980s, Venezuela witnessed economic stagnation and political discontent as its petroleum industry began going into long-term decline. In 1983 "Black Tuesday" marked the beginning of a long line of currency devaluations that would incite riots in February 1989. Then, during the 1990s, Venezuela witnessed two coups (1992), a presidential impeachment (1993), another major financial crisis (1994), and finally, the gradual collapse of its traditional party system and subsequent election of populist Hugo Chávez Frías as president (1998), much to the chagrin of Venezuelan elites and business leaders. As Javier Corrales poignantly documents, real wages in Venezuela decreased almost 70 percent over two decades, the probability of being poor increased from 2.4 to 18.5 percent over one decade, and over two-thirds of the population now lives below the poverty line. Politico-economic unrest in Venezuela has worsened in recent years, especially following an attempted coup against Chávez on April 11, 2002, continued declines in petroleum values, and labor strikes and protests.

Like elsewhere in South America, these crises have made a middle-class lifestyle much harder to attain and protect. As Venezuela painfully worked its way through not one but two "lost decades," increased emigration to the United States and elsewhere took on a powerful shape. A photo caption in a January 2003 *New York Times* article on conflict in Venezuela read, "Hundreds of people stood in line to apply for visas to go to Spain. Efforts by diplomats to resolve the stalemate between the president and his foes have been unavailing so far."

As with Argentine emigration, U.S. figures are not recent enough to document the new movement. However, between 1971 and 2001, the Immigration and Naturalization Service (INS) admitted 59,953 documented Venezuelan immigrants, and the U.S. Census counted 38,120 Venezuelan immigrants in 1980; 50,823 in 1990; and 114,677 in 2000 (149,309 by adjusted 2000 Hispanic/Latino figures). Specific to post-1989 Venezuelan emigration are rising incentives for Venezuelan elites, entrepreneurs, and upper-level bureaucrats—as well as professionals and manual laborers—to migrate abroad in order to protect their personal property and capital investments, especially since Chávez and his populist policies have begun challenging them more seriously since 1998. In this respect, early analyses have likened Venezuelan emigration under Chávez's presidency to Cuban emigration under Fidel Castro. Indeed, according to

Venezuelan immigrant and sociologist Miguel Salazar, key elements of many Venezuelan Americans' experience today are political as well as practical: settling in the United States, becoming politically active to oppose Chávez, and becoming more active in American politics.

The Venezuelan American community is based primarily in south Florida, and Venezuelans are more residentially concentrated than other South American immigrant groups, with the exception of the Guyanese and Ecuadorians. In 2000, Venezuelan immigrants settled primarily in Florida (44.2 percent), New York (9.6 percent), Texas (7.3 percent), New Jersey (6.5 percent), and California (5.3 percent). Also, Venezuelans in the United States have long been younger and more educated than most other Latin American immigrant groups; in 2000, 42.8 percent of Venezuelan immigrants boasted a bachelor's degree or higher, and 35.2 percent worked in professional or managerial occupations. However, like many other South Americans, recent Venezuelan immigrants are increasingly battling the pressures of undocumented status, ethnic concentration, and uncertainty about politico-economic stability in Venezuela and the possibility of return home.

Because the Venezuelan community in the United States is so new and young, there have been few famous Venezuelan American icons and few large-scale Venezuelan American institutions, at least until recently. Florida-based *El Venezolano* newspaper (which communicates news about Venezuela to residents in the United States) and the Venezuelan American Brotherhood Foundation (which strives to "assist Venezuelan and other Latin communities in south Florida and in their countries") are just two examples of emerging Venezuelan American institutions and associations at present. As the Venezuelan community in the United States grows and matures into the future, more associations are sure to arise in order to assist new immigrants in maintaining valuable cultural values, managing adaptation pressures, organizing politically, and promoting greater knowledge of Venezuelan history and culture in the United States.

RELATED ARTICLES

Cuisine, South American; Immigration, Latino; United States–South America Relations.

FURTHER READING

Cordova, Carlos, and Raquel Pinderhughes. "Central and South Americans in the United States." In *A Nation of Peoples: A Sourcebook on America's Multicultural Heritage*. Ed. by Elliott R. Barkan. Westport, Conn.: Greenwood Press, 1999.

Corrales, Javier. "Venezuela in the 1980s, the 1990s, and Beyond: Why Citizen-Detached Parties Imperil Economic Governance." *ReVista: Harvard Review of Latin America* (Fall 1999).

Orlov, Ann, and Reed Ueda. "Central and South Americans." In *The Harvard Encyclopedia of American Ethnic Groups*. Ed. by Stephan Thernstrom, et al. Cambridge, Mass.: Harvard Univ. Press.

Salazar, Miguel. *The Formation of a Transnational Community: The Highly-Skilled Venezuelan Diaspora in the U.S.A. and Canada*. Qualifying Paper in Sociology. Cambridge, Mass.: Harvard Univ., 2002.

HELEN B. MARROW

VIEQUES

The island of Vieques, or "Isla Nena," (Little Girl Island) is located 8 miles (13 km) off the east coast of Puerto Rico. It is merely 20 miles (30 km) long and 4.5 miles (7 km) wide at its widest point. Its name derives from the indigenous name Bieque, or "Little Island." Vieques became a municipality of Puerto Rico in 1843.

From the beginning of the relationship between Puerto Rico and the United States in 1898, military analysts foresaw the strategic importance of both Vieques and a small island to its west, Culebra. This importance became realized in 1936, when the U.S. Navy began to use Culebra for target practice. In

© LYNNE SLADKY/AP/WIDE WORLD PHOTOS

A youngster stands beside a sign reading "Vieques Yes! Navy No!" during a protest against military exercises on the Puerto Rican island of Vieques, 2003.

1941 the U.S. military expanded its operations onto Vieques, condemning many acres of land to destruction and becoming the islet's largest landowner. Thirty years later, in 1971, the navy ceased using Culebra for military practice. In turn, Vieques went on to play a central role in America's foreign policy as a training site.

This growing American influence turned Vieques into a major cultural and political symbol. In the eyes of many in both Puerto Rico and Vieques, to side with the military and its growing presence on the islet would be to side with injustice and against human rights. Consequently, those participating in the movement for Puerto Rican independence from the United States have generally been in close allegiance with efforts to terminate navy training and weaponry testing on and around Vieques. In contrast, those who aim for Puerto Rican statehood must tread a much more careful course, since they do not wish to antagonize federal officials in Washington, D.C.

With time, Puerto Rican cultural nationalism overrode most other sentiments concerning Vieques. Rather than a struggle for independence, the controversy surrounding Vieques soon became a struggle for autonomy for the people of Vieques, a struggle to which Puerto Ricans of all political persuasions could subscribe.

The intensity of the protests changed on April 19, 1999. On this day two FA-19 Hornets flew off course while conducting war games in the Vieques passage and released two bombs near an observation post. The bombs killed a security guard, David Sanes Rodriguez, and wounded four civilians. This incident galvanized the Puerto Rican communities both in Puerto Rico and the United States and called much needed attention to the plight of the people of Vieques. In Puerto Rico, polling data showed that up to 73 percent of Puerto Ricans sided with Vieques and wished to see the U.S. Navy pull out. Many activists and political figures in the United States came to Vieques to voice their disapproval. Others performed acts of civil disobedience, in Vieques as well as in the United States.

In response to this turmoil, President Bill Clinton appointed a panel in summer 1999, which ultimately recommended a reduction of navy exercises and a stop to the bombing after a term of five years. When the bombing resumed, protests once again ensued. Under mounting political pressure, the navy ended its bombing exercises on May 1, 2003, and pulled out of Vieques.

RELATED ARTICLES

Military, United States; Politics, Puerto Rican; Puerto Rico.

FURTHER READING

Barcelo, Amílcar Antonio. *Vieques, the Navy, and Puerto Rican Politics.* Gainesville: Univ. of Fla. Press, 2002.
McCaffrey, Katherine T. *Military Power and Popular Protest: The U.S. Navy in Vieques, Puerto Rico.* New Brunswick, N.J.: Rutgers Univ. Press, 2002.
Mullenneaux, Lisa. *Ni una bomba más: Vieques vs. U.S. Navy.* 2d ed. New York: Pennington Press, 2000.
Murillo, Mario. *Islands of Resistance: Vieques, Puerto Rico and U.S. Policy.* New York: Seven Stories Press, 2001.

LUIS FUENTES-ROWHER

VIETNAM WAR

From 1883 to 1945, Vietnam was divided as a French colony into Cochin China (south), Annam (central), and Tonkin (north). In 1945 the Revolutionary League for the Independence of Vietnam led by Ho Chi Minh gained independence from foreign rule and established the Democratic Republic of Vietnam (DRV). With aid from Great Britain, France regained control of South Vietnam and signed an agreement with Minh in 1946 that acknowledged Vietnam as a free state within the French union. When France attempted to regain control of the north, the French War erupted. As an attempt at peace, the Geneva Conference of 1954 created a temporary demarcation line dividing the DRV from the state of Vietnam until free elections to be held the following year would determine the government of a united Vietnam. With U.S. support, however, the southern government rejected the national elections and declared its independence as the Republic of Vietnam. As a counter-reaction the National Liberation Front of South Vietnam (NLF) was created and revolted against the southern regime in 1960.

The Vietnam War refers to direct U.S. military intervention in Vietnam in support of South Vietnam from 1961 to 1975. Although the United States provided military aid to the Republic of Vietnam prior to 1961, the impact of the Vietnam War did not hold great significance until the United States began to heighten military assistance in Vietnam through the creation of new draft policies. One of the most prominent policies that specifically affected working-class, Latino, and black communities in the country was Project 100,000, which lowered the minimum test scores required for military service.

Project 100,000

Proposals to increase the strength of the military in Vietnam were publicized as a means to socialize and improve the lives of the poor through military service. The U.S. military promised work skills, desirable benefits, and socioeconomic growth upon completion of service, specifically appealing to the working-class, Latino, and black communities in the United States with hopes of socioeconomic mobility. Proposals such as Project 100,000 provided for those who initially failed the mental proficiency section of the military exam to be retested and most likely inducted into the military under the new test score requirements. This allowed for many Latino citizens who were minimally fluent in English or monolingual in Spanish to be inducted into the military as "New Standards" men. Counter to the promises of Project 100,000, low scores channeled a majority of the Project 100,000 men into semi- or unskilled occupations and prevented them from obtaining promotions. Low scores also almost guaranteed these men combat duties. Of the 240,000 men inducted from 1966–1968, 40 percent were trained for combat while only 6 percent received educational training. The men of Project 100,000 had a death rate that was double that of the entire U.S. military.

Project 100,000 also waived the national test requirement that determined eligibility for draft deferment; grades for deferment eligibility were now locally decided. Easier access to draft deferments was only available to those enrolled as full-time college students; in specific careers such as engineering, the medical field, and teaching; or enrolled in the reserves, which maintained stringent requirements. This suggested that those who could not afford to attend college full-time and maintain "acceptable" grades were ineligible for draft deferment. It also suggested that those who were not proficient in the English language were eligible for Project 100,000 but were not eligible for the reserves.

Latinos, who were not accounted for as an inclusive group or by ethnicity, were counted by the U.S. military as Caucasian or non-Caucasian; therefore there is no record of how many Latinos served in Vietnam. However, over 90 percent of Project 100,000 inductees came from southern Texas, a pre-dominately Latino region, as well as from other southern states and Puerto Rico. Approximately 48,000 Puerto Ricans from the island served in Vietnam, many of whom did not speak English. These estimates do not include Puerto Ricans who lived on the mainland. In 1967 Chicanos were approximately 9 percent of the population in California but 21 percent of the dead in Vietnam.

Latino Communities Respond to the Vietnam War

Latino communities perceived draft and deferment laws as racially and culturally biased and believed that Latinos and blacks were more likely to be drafted and serve combat duties but less likely to gain military benefits. Through an antiwar and draft agenda, many Latino militant and civil rights groups nationwide mobilized into a united political force to raise community consciousness on specific issues that applied to Latinos locally and throughout the nation. Among those that initiated national solidarity between the various political groups was the National Chicano Moratorium Committee (NCMC), founded by Chicano students at the University of California at Los Angeles.

This united force was demonstrated by the presence of representatives from multiple Latino groups in NCMC marches throughout the late 1960s and early 1970s that consisted of members from the Brown Berets, the Young Lords Party, and the Movimiento Estudiantil Chicano de Atzlán (MEChA). These antiwar and draft demonstrations also focused on issues of education, police brutality, and national and international solidarity. At the height of their political effectiveness, these groups mobilized almost 30,000 antiwar demonstrators at Laguna Park in East Los Angeles on August 29, 1970. Although the aim was for a peaceful demonstration, it ended in a police riot with 3 civilian deaths.

Bilingual pamphlets, open letters, and oral narratives were other strategies produced to provide information and critiques on the Vietnam War. Some pamphlets were geared toward informing young Latinos on how to avoid the draft; others were more critical of U.S. imperialist intervention, urging Latinos not to participate in foreign U.S. oppression that was too similar to their own experiences as Americans. Additionally, many Latinos responded in support of the antiwar agenda through art. Poems and screenplays were produced and performed locally with similar antiwar and anti–U.S. oppression agendas. The united front for the antiwar and antidraft agenda began to dissolve between 1971 and 1972 owing to internal ideological differences between the different organizations; however, many of these political groups still exist today and continue to struggle for Latino rights locally, nationally, and internationally.

RELATED ARTICLES

Military, United States; National Chicano Moratorium of Vietnam.

FURTHER READING

Appy, Christian G. *Working-Class War: American Combat Soldiers and Vietnam.* Chapel Hill: Univ. of N.C. Press, 1993.

Garcia, Manny. *An Accidental Soldier: Memoir of a Mestizo in Vietnam.* Albuquerque: Univ. of N.Mex. Press, 2003.

Gettleman, Marvin E., et al. *Vietnam and America: A Documented History.* 2d ed., rev. and enl. New York: Grove, 1995.

Mariscal, George, ed. *Atzlán and Viet Nam: Chicano and Chicana Experiences of the War.* Berkeley: Univ. of Calif. Press, 1999.

LISA CALAVENTE

VILLA, FRANCISCO

Born: 1878; Durango, Mexico
Died: July 20, 1923; Parral, Mexico

Francisco "Pancho" Villa is one of the most controversial figures of the Mexican Revolution. To Mexicans, he is a revolutionary hero. In the United States, the Hearst newspapers of the time portrayed him as a bloodthirsty bandit, particularly after his incursion into New Mexico in 1916. Among Chicanos he is an emblematic figure who personifies both bravery and rowdiness.

Villa was born in 1878 in the state of Durango and baptized with the name of Doroteo Arango. According to the writer Martín Luis Guzmán, the young Doroteo shot the local landowner for an offense to his sister, then fled to the hills and assumed the name of Francisco or "Pancho" Villa after the real Francisco Villa, the leader of a gang of rustlers, was killed in a shootout. For several years, Villa lived as an outlaw, at the head of a gang that robbed from rich miners and landowners. In the early years of the 20th century, Mexican society was very divided, with a few rich landlords and a huge peasantry living in almost feudal conditions. As Villa robbed and killed

for gain, to the dispossessed he came to seem like a Robin Hood figure, robbing from the rich to give to the poor; to the authorities he was nothing more than a thief who tortured and killed people.

A new chapter in Villa's life began when the Mexican Revolution broke out in 1910. Groups from all over Mexico united behind the liberal leader Francisco Madero to overthrow the dictator Porfirio Díaz. In Chihuahua, the battle was seen as winning land for the poor peasants, and Villa soon joined the fray, both out of a sincere belief in Madero's political views and from a wish to see change in the provinces he knew. By 1911 Madero and his supporters had succeeded in toppling Díaz, but Madero himself was soon ousted and killed. Villa was suspicious of the new president, Victoriano Huerta, and refused to disarm. Villa's reputation as a military commander grew, and he earned himself the nickname of Centaur of the North, while his troops became the División del Norte. It was one of the most successful revolutionary armies, scoring many important victories over the regular government forces, thanks especially to daring cavalry charges. Villa and his men took the cities of Torreón and Zacatecas, but they were kept out of Mexico City, where a new provisional president, Venustiaño Carranza, had been installed.

By 1913–1914 Pancho Villa was one of the most charismatic figures of the Revolution—he was even filmed in action by D. W. Griffith. He was also a serious social reformer: he proposed sweeping land reform and other radical changes at the Aguascalientes Convention. He enjoyed the support of Emiliano Zapata, the other great popular leader from the south of Mexico, but was regarded with suspicion by Carranza and his main military leader, Alvaro Obregón. Villa soon found himself fighting the government.

In 1914 Villa's forces finally managed to enter Mexico City. But Carranza and Obregón counterattacked from the north. Villa's first defeat came at the battle for the city of Celaya—some 3,000 of his men were killed, with another 6,000 captured. Villa retreated to his northern hideouts and plotted revenge, which brought him into conflict with the United States and contributed to the change of Villa's image to that of a ruthless killer.

Villa blamed the United States for the defeat of his forces at Celaya because the United States had allowed the transport of Mexican government troops

© JIMMY DORANTES/LATIN FOCUS

Pancho Villa on his horse.

barracks in the city of Chihuahua, releasing all the prisoners from the city jail. Pershing and his "Punitive Expedition" finally had to withdraw empty-handed in February 1917. Villa's reputation as a bandit was thus born in the United States.

By now Villa had given up his ambitions for power. He made a truce with the government and went back to Chihuahua. Many of his revolutionary contemporaries, including Zapata, had met violent deaths; Villa was gunned down, apparently on the orders of a colonel in charge of the local garrison, while driving his car into the town of Parral. He died on July 20, 1923.

After his death, "Pancho Villa" quickly became a legendary figure. Rumors flew that he had not been buried, that his cadaver had been decapitated, and that his head had been stolen. He is the hero of Martín Luis Guzmán's *Memorias de Pancho Villa* and of several novels of the Revolution, including Guzmán's *The Eagle and the Serpent*. His exploits were also recounted in many *corridos,* or songs, of the Mexican Revolution. The sympathetic articles by the North American writer John Reed and the films of D. W. Griffith also added to his mythical status in the United States. In more recent years, the myth of Pancho Villa, who dared take the fight for Mexican freedom to the United States, has given him a place in the pantheon of Latino icons, although he has always been a more ambiguous figure than Emiliano Zapata, because of his undeniable cruelty and the mixed motives behind his actions.

RELATED ARTICLES

Criminals and Bandidos; Mexican Revolution; Zapata, Emiliano.

FURTHER READING

Clendenen, Clarence Clemens. *The United States and Pancho Villa: A Study in Unconventional Diplomacy.* Ithaca, N.Y.: Cornell Univ. Press, 1961.

Guzmán, Martín Luis. *The Eagle and the Serpent.* Tr. by Harriet de Onís. New York: Knopf, 1930.

Guzmán, Martín Luis. *Memoirs of Pancho Villa.* Tr. by Virginia H. Taylor. Austin: Univ. of Tex. Press, 1965.

Katz, Friedrich. *The Life and Times of Pancho Villa.* Stanford, Calif.: Stanford Univ. Press, 1998.

Krauze, Enrique. *Mexico: Biography of Power.* New York: HarperCollins, 1997.

McLynn, Frank. *Villa and Zapata—A Biography of the Mexican Revolution.* London: Jonathan Cape, 2000.

Osorio, Rubén. *The Secret Family of Pancho Villa: An Oral History.* Tr. by John Klingemann. Alpine, Tex.: Ctr. for Big Bend Studies, Sul Ross State Univ., 2000.

through its territory. In March 1916, Villa attacked the New Mexican town of Columbus, following the incineration in nearby El Paso of 20 Mexicans who were burned alive after being covered in kerosene—allegedly to get rid of their lice. Villa sent some 400 of his soldiers into Columbus, where they fired on U.S. troops in their barracks and attacked and set fire to a hotel, killing several guests. The U.S. troops chased the Villistas back across the border. The next day, President Woodrow Wilson announced that he was sending General John J. Pershing into Mexico to capture Pancho Villa dead or alive.

Historians have argued ever since whether his March attacks were a deliberate strategy by Villa to induce the United States to invade Mexico. Some historians claim that Villa wanted to unite Mexicans against the invader, hoping he would be chosen as the national resistance leader. Pershing and his 5,000 men never succeeded in capturing Villa, however; nor did Mexican government troops. Indeed, Villa was able to outflank both forces, when, in September 1916, he led about 2,000 fighters to attack the

Reed, John. *Insurgent Mexico.* New York: Greenwood Press, 1969.

NICK CAISTOR

VILLARREAL, JOSÉ ANTONIO

Born: July 30, 1924; Los Angeles, California

Novelist José Antonio Villarreal is considered one of the "pioneers" who helped to shape contemporary Chicano literature. He spent the first years of his childhood in Los Angeles and then moved with his parents (migrant farmworkers originally from Zacatecas, Mexico) to northern California. In Santa Clara, California, his parents were finally able to secure steady employment, and young Villarreal could attend school. Though Spanish was his primary tongue, he quickly picked up reading and writing in English at school and by the fifth grade had already discovered his passion for writing fiction. As a teenager with a tremendous hunger for reading, Villarreal became increasingly aware that the Chicano experience was not represented in American letters. When he entered the University of California at Berkeley in 1950, he chose to pursue his lifelong goal of becoming a fiction writer. In 1956, while studying for his Ph.D. at Berkeley, he conducted research on early-20th-century Mexican history that he would later transform into fiction in his first novel, *Pocho* (1959). To help transform into fiction those facts that inform *Pocho*—the Mexican Revolution, World War I, and the assimilationist pressures he and his family experienced in the 1930s—he turned to James Joyce's *Portrait of the Artist as a Young Man* as a model. Instead of texturing an Irish Catholic outsider who comes into his own as a writer, however, he invented the Chicano protagonist, Richard Rubio, who struggles with the tensions and contradictions of forming a new identity that is culturally neither Mexican nor American. Though Villarreal's writing style is in itself undistinguished, the development of the superconsciousness of a character who was neither Mexican nor American gave birth to the Chicano literary consciousness, and *Pocho* is widely considered to be the first Chicano novel.

Although Villarreal continued to be passionate about writing novels, he realized that he would not be able to support his family as a writer; during the 1960s he therefore worked variously as an editor and technical writer for the aerospace industry in Palo Alto, as a public-relations insurance officer, and as a delivery truck operator. After Anchor Books bought the reprint rights to *Pocho* in 1970 and the book became a best-selling Chicano novel, Villarreal secured work as a visiting professor at such schools as the University of Colorado, Boulder; the University of Texas at El Paso; and the University of Santa Clara. Teaching gave him the time he needed to continue to work on his craft, and in 1974 he published *The Fifth Horseman.* This novel follows the hard road that the protagonist, Haraclio Inés, chooses to follow after soldiering in "Pancho" Villa's army. That road leads him north, across the border into the United States, where he, too, learns to discard the heavy baggage of Mexican culture and to shrug off the assimilationist forces of America to find a sense of balance as a Chicano.

It would be ten years before Villarreal would publish the third part in this informal trilogy. In what is arguably his most accomplished novel, *Clemente Chacón,* Villarreal experiments with narrative form—and looks yet again to a Joycean model—by creating a story that unfolds over a period of one day. Here he uses flashbacks and interior monologue to give depth to his Horatio Alger–like protagonist, Ramón Alvarez (also known as Clement Chacón). He, too, comes to identify as someone who exists in-between cultures, proclaiming at one point, "I am Mexican and I am an American, and, there is no reason in the world why I can't be both."

Villarreal's place in Chicano letters has not always been secure. In the late 1960s and early 1970s many of the artists and writers active in the Chicano civil rights movement (*el movimiento*) were harshly critical of the character Richard Rubio's lack of a *raza,* or political sensibility. After a growing dissatisfaction with U.S. society and amid harsh criticism of his work, in 1973 Villarreal moved to Mexico, where he lived for about ten years, returning to teach at various universities in the American Southwest. Most critics consider Villarreal to be an early literary proponent of contemporary Chicano literary consciousness. His novels have creatively complicated the social, political, and cultural dimensions that make up Chicano identity and experience, contributing to the massive redrawing and expansion of Latino and U.S. American letters.

RELATED ARTICLES

Literature, Mexican American.

FURTHER READING

Bruce-Novoa. *RetroSpace: Collected Essays on Chicano Literature, Theory and History.* Houston, Tex.: Arte Público Press, 1990.

Lomelí, Francisco A., and Carl R. Shirley. *Chicano Writers: First Series.* Detroit, Mich.: Gale Res., 1989. [Second Series, 1992; Third Series, 1999].

Tatum, Charles M. *Chicano Literature.* Boston: Twayne, 1982.

FREDERICK LUIS ALDAMA

VIRGEN DE GUADALUPE

La Virgen de Guadalupe (English, the Virgin of Guadalupe) is the patron saint of Mexico and, since 1910, of Latin America. Her feast day, December 12, is celebrated in every Catholic diocese of the United States. She is also known in Spanish as La Virgen de Tepeyac, Santa María de Guadalupe, La Criolla, La Guadalupana, La Virgen Ranchera, La Morena, and La Pastora, and in English as translations of all these terms as well as the Madonna of the Barrios, Queen of the Americas, the North Star of Mexico, and Sovereign Woman. Her basilica in Mexico City receives more visitors than does any other Christian pilgrimage site (that is, a site of a miracle or where relics are kept) in the world. According to tradition, the Virgin appeared in a series of visions to an Indian, Juan Diego, from December 9 to 12, 1531, asking that a temple be built in her honor. In one of Diego's visits to the bishop to relate his vision, her image appeared miraculously on his *tilma* (cloak) of agave-fiber cloth, and this image became the central focus of her worship. It is housed in a hermetically sealed frame in the basilica and reproduced in countless Mexican and Mexican American households (not to mention stores, offices, schools, cemeteries, buses, and taxis). The Virgin's most basic role is as a curer of illness and disease, but she may be called on for a host of other interventions. The old basilica (the fourth church on the site) was constructed in 1709, and the present one in 1976. In 1747 the Virgin of Guadalupe was canonized as the patron saint of New Spain.

Origins and Development of the Cult

The Virgin appeared on a hill in Tepeyac, which today has become part of greater Mexico City but at the time was outside the city limits. Significantly, in 1531 Mexico had been under Spanish domination for just a decade. Tepeyac had been the site of a temple dedicated to Tonantzín, an Aztec fertility and earth goddess. It is likely that an image existed in the local Christian church of the Virgin of Guadalupe of Extremadura, Spain, who was a favorite of the conquistadores, and it is difficult otherwise to explain the name Guadalupe, which conforms neither to the place-name nor to Nahuatl phonetics (though some have suggested that the name is a corruption of the Aztec goddess Coatlalopeuh) and is not adequately explained in the earliest accounts of the visitation. Thus it is possible to interpret the appearance of the Virgin as the syncretic rebirth of a Mexican goddess into a Christian context.

The story of the appearance follows clearly European lines and indeed shows basic similarities with the Spanish Guadalupan narrative. María requests that a chapel be built in her honor and chooses a simple shepherd to carry the message to the authorities. She works several miracles, including causing roses to bloom on rocky soil in winter for Juan Diego to take to the bishop, curing the messenger's uncle of a mortal illness, and reviving a deceased Chichimec Indian on the very day of the translation of her image into the newly built church. The worshiped image also derives from European artistic traditions, though the woman's complexion is olive rather than white, and the dress and background are imbued with native symbols.

Bishop Juan de Zumárraga, who supposedly was finally convinced of the truth of Juan Diego's story by the appearance of the image on the *tilma,* left no written record of his experience or of his opinion on the Virgin. The earliest records include so-called *cantares,* or Nahuatl, hymns to the Virgin, and a narrative titled the *Nican mopuha,* after its first two words, written by a learned Aztec between 1530 and 1540. The first printed narrative, written by Father Miguel Sánchez in Spanish, was not published until 1648, though numerous sources of the 16th century make reference to the cult and to the various miraculous effects of the image. Sánchez's account seems to have given major impetus to the cult among the *criollos* (those of Spanish descent born in the New World) of Mexico. It was followed by a published Nahuatl narrative in 1649. The cathedral chapter of Mexico City conducted an investigation of the miracle from 1665 to 1666, and heard *criollo,* peninsular, and Indian witnesses, then for the first time requested that the pope name December 12 as the official feast day. The Virgin was credited with eradicating the plague of 1737, from which point her reputation increased without abatement, and she became increasingly associated with the national aspirations of Mexico.

Theological Aspects of the Virgin

Marian appearances everywhere are significant because the role of Mary receives relatively little theological elaboration in the New Testament itself. Theologians across the Americas have felt compelled to interpret the meaning of the Virgin of Guadalupe, beginning with the words she is recorded as having spoken. For example, the Virgin of Guadalupe begins by declaring herself both a virgin and a mother of God, something she never does in the Bible. She also explicitly declares her role as a merciful Mother, giving her love, her compassion, her help, and her protection to those who need it. She further offers these benefits to all those living in the land, a seeming response to the myriad ethnic, racial, and class hierarchies dividing people of the Americas from each other, then and now. In short, she defines her role as mediator between God and humans.

To comfort Juan Diego, the Virgin asks him why he should be afraid, since his mother is there at hand. Liberation theologians, in particular Virgilio Elizondo, have developed an interpretation of the Virgin as mother to the hybrid races of the new world, relieving their anxiety over being illegitimate offspring of conquest and rape. The light olive complexion (*morena* in Spanish) of the figure in the image would hint at her race as mestiza rather than Indian or white. Statements from devotees confirm this interpretation. Studies have shown that more Mexicans name the Virgin Mary as their supreme being than they do God.

Political and Social Aspects of the Virgin

Given the apparently syncretic origins of the Virgin, popular history has tended to see her as instrumental in the conversion and transculturation of the Indian peoples of Mexico. Certainly there is much to be said for her role as a common symbol allowing the spread of Mexicans across a vast and diverse land to become a nation. Her crowning as "Queen of Mexico" in 1895 testifies to this aspect, as do commonplaces such as "We Mexicans are all Guadalupans." On the other hand, the Virgin has also on occasion divided Mexicans from each other, and the

THE GRANGER COLLECTION

Banner featuring an image of the Virgen de Guadalupe used by followers of Father Hidalgo, circa 1810.

relative loyalty of various groups to her has shifted over time. Her image has been shot at and bombed as well as adored.

Through the 18th century the Virgin was overshadowed by another Mary figure, Nuestra Señora de los Remedios, also known as La Conquistadora. It would seem that the latter was favored by colonizers, while *criollos* and eventually Indians were drawn to the former. Miguel Hidalgo's insurrection of 1816 took the Virgin as its symbol of Mexican independence, while the loyalist forces emblazoned La Conquistadora on their flags, and this war of Marys continued through eventual independence. The first president of Mexico, José Fernández y Félix, assumed the name Guadalupe Victoria for his tenure in office from 1824 to 1829. In contrast, the extreme anticlerical years following the positivist and Marxist phases of the Mexican Revolution probably represent a low point in divided opinion: a bomb was detonated in 1921 in front of the *tilma* image, which (miraculously) escaped harm.

More recently, Latina feminists have tended to see the Virgin critically, as a coercive model supporting patriarchal behaviors and attitudes. A favored response has been not to reject the figure but to uncover the more powerful, ambiguous, and sexualized Aztec women goddesses, Tonantzín and Coatlicue, whom the Virgin supposedly syncretized, and to emphasize their powers and characteristics rather than those of Catholic Mary.

The Virgin in the United States

The first Spanish settlers of New Mexico brought the Virgin of Guadalupe north with them, and she has been a constant of social life in that state since the 1690s. Her chapel in Santa Fe, constructed around 1795, is the oldest continuously standing building dedicated to her in the United States. New Mexico undoubtedly maintains the greatest diversity of devotional practices, including full-dress Indian dances and a variety of pilgrimages. Localities bearing the name Guadalupe are found in every southwestern state, and it is also a popular name for persons of either gender (as it is in Mexico). Junípero Serra seems not to have been aware of the cult; there is no mention or image of Guadalupe in any California mission records or artifacts. Today, however, the celebration of her feast day at the Our Lady Queen of Angels church in downtown Los Angeles is probably the largest gathering outside Mexico.

It is routine for Mexicans immigrating to the United States to pray to the Virgin before leaving, and the additional nickname, Our Lady Crosser of Borders, has been suggested by some. Writer Guillermo Gómez-Peña has remarked on the different perspective emigration gave him vis-à-vis the Virgin. In Mexico he had perceived her with some distaste as an official, nationalistic Mexican icon. In California he discovered that his Chicano colleagues had turned the Virgin into a symbol of resistance for overcoming racism and immigration authorities, and into a visible icon in the marches of César Chávez's United Farm Workers and other demonstrations of Latino power. While there is a great deal of overlap in social attitudes toward the Virgin in Mexico and the United States, one can probably say that she is more of a national symbol in the former country, and more a protector of minorities, the oppressed, and the unconventional in the latter.

Representations of the Virgin

Since the center of Virgin worship has always been an image, reproductions of that image in almost any and every medium imaginable have helped to spread her impact across the broadest segment of societies. The most basic reproduction is called a *santo,* and the skilled artisan who produces it is known as a *santero.* Tin and cloth are favored traditional media, though almost anything can and has been used.

Dramatic pieces featuring the Virgin nearly always take on the sacred character of liturgy. They arise naturally out of the framework of the religious group, in particular out of the dramatic way in which the story is framed and the dialog among characters that occurs in the Sánchez narrative. In the colonial period the Franciscans encouraged plays on religious themes in Nahuatl, and two from the 18th century tell the story of the appearance to Juan Diego. (It is not clear what role, if any, they played in evangelization.) Such plays can be compared with, for example, the *Novena narrativa y ofrendas nuevomexicanas* (1986; written in Spanglish) by Denise Chávez, whose title identifies its liturgical nature. A vast number of folk, religious, and secular dramas come in between these examples. Numerous hymns, called *alabados,* are composed specifically on the topic of the Virgin and sung by folk minstrels. There appear to be relatively few fictional prose narratives focused mainly on the Virgin; rather, she appears as part of the cultural landscape in countless narratives of Latino life. In Rudolfo Anaya's seminal Mexican American novel, *Bless Me, Ultima,* for example, the Virgin is presented very traditionally, as an uncontestedly good maternal figure in contrast to the darker, more ambiguous *curandera,* or witch, of the title—in essence, the Mary-Tonantzín duality.

The Virgin also intersects with folkways such as lowriding, whose hobbyists she frequently accompanies as an elaborate painting on hoods of cars. Occasionally, entire "Guadalupanamobiles" may be outfitted, covered with images inside and out. Tattooing is another practice where the image of the Virgin has been a constant; gang members and prison inmates in particular favor her image as a protection against danger and pain.

Capitalism has brought with it the commodification of the Virgin's image on mass-produced souvenirs, trivia, and housewares, so that few categories remain that have not yet been Guadalupanized. T-shirts, coffee mugs, baseball caps, refrigerator magnets, night-lights, and key rings are just a few examples out of thousands. Since the eternal presence of the Virgin's image to those of all income levels has always been a feature of her worship, mass-production techniques have not encountered the opposition that creative and critical artistic representation has. For example, in 1987 the exhibition of a collage wherein the face of Marilyn Monroe was superimposed on the image of the Virgin at a prominent museum in Mexico City caused its director to be fired.

RELATED ARTICLES

Catholicism; Diego, Juan; Guadalupanismo; Religion.

FURTHER READING

Castillo, Ana, ed. *Goddess of the Americas / La Diosa de las Américas: Writings on the Virgin of Guadalupe.* New York: Riverhead Press, 1996.

Dunnington, Jacqueline Orsini. *Guadalupe: Our Lady of New Mexico.* Santa Fe: Mus. of N.Mex. Press, 1999.

Elizondo, Virgilio. *Guadalupe, Mother of the New Creation.* Maryknoll, N.Y.: Orbis Bks., 1997.

Lozano-Díaz, Nora O. "Ignored Virgin or Unaware Women: A Mexican-American Protestant Reflection on the Virgin of Guadalupe." In *A Reader in Latina Feminist Theology.* Ed. by María Pilar Aquino, et al. Austin: Univ. of Tex. Press, 2002.

Poole, Stafford. *Our Lady of Guadalupe.* Tucson: Univ. of Ariz. Press, 1996.

Rodriguez, Jeannette. *Our Lady of Guadalupe: Faith and Empowerment among Mexican-American Women.* Austin: Univ. of Tex. Press, 1994.

Sousa, Lisa, et al., eds. and trs. *The Story of Guadalupe: Luis Laso de la Vega's "Huei tlamahiçoltica" of 1649.* Stanford, Calif.: Stanford Univ. Press, 1998.

Watson, Simone. *The Cult of Our Lady of Guadalupe.* Collegeville, Minn.: Liturgical Press, 1964.

THOMAS O. BEEBEE

VIRGEN DE LA CARIDAD DEL COBRE

La Virgen de la Caridad (the Virgin of Charity), or Ochun, the goddess of love and fiscal management in the Yoruba language and the Santería pantheon, is the patron saint of Cuba. Originating as a Catholic deity in the 17th century, she was officially crowned by Pope John Paul II as the island's spiritual protector on January 24, 1998, in a Mass celebrated in Santiago de Cuba during the pontiff's historic trip to the island.

© CRISTOBAL HERRERA/AP/WIDE WORLD PHOTOS

Believers attend a pilgrimage honoring La Virgen de la Caridad del Cobre, Cuba's patron saint, in Havana.

La Virgen de la Caridad had first been declared Cuba's patron saint in 1916, after a petition from veterans of the Cuban War of Independence, also known as the Spanish-American War, to the Cuban government. September 8 was selected as her feast day, following a custom that had already been well established for centuries among her followers on the island.

According to tradition, a statue was found circa 1607 by three ten-year-old boys, commonly known as The Three Juans (Los Tres Juanes), two of them indigenous and one a black slave. The boys were en route by boat from Barajagua, a village of mostly indigenous and slave miners and ranchers, to Nipe Bay, in search of salt to cure meat.

In 1687 the last living witness, the black slave Juan Moreno, approximately 85 years old, gave this testimony to church authorities about the Virgin's first sighting. His recollections are preserved in the General Archives of the Indies in Spain (translated by Achy Obejas):

> " . . . Because the sea was calm that morning, we exited from the French Key at dawn, Juan and Rodrigo Hoyos and myself, the witness speaking. Traveling by canoe, once some distance from the French Key, we saw something white amidst the sea foam, which we could not distinguish, and as we approached it, we thought it might be a bird or dried tree branches. The Indian boys said that it looked like a little girl and during this conversation we recognized and laid eyes upon the Holy Mother, the Holy Virgin, with the Christ child in her arms, mounted on a small board, and on that board there were large letters which Rodrigo de Hoyos read, and which said: 'I am the Virgin of Charity,' and we were awed that her clothes were not wet, and we were full of joy and happiness."

The three boys—who, with their small boat, immediately became an integral part of the Virgin's iconography—returned to Barajagua, where the statue was installed in a village hermitage. Within days the Virgin disappeared overnight and reappeared in the morning. This happened several times, which the villagers interpreted as the saint's desire to be moved to a more convivial place. Consequently, she was installed in the main altar of the village church, although she continued to disappear and reappear intermittently over the years. Eventually, she was moved to a sanctuary (now a basilica) on a hilltop near the copper mines, completed in 1927; thus her longer denomination in Spanish, La Virgen de la Caridad del Cobre—the Virgin of Charity of Copper, or of the Copper Mines.

That the Virgin, who is sometimes depicted as mulatta or mestiza, would be an immediate favorite in Barajagua is not surprising given the history of that village. According to a 1980 monograph by historian Levi Marrero, the population around the copper mines was for centuries composed mostly of royal slaves who lived "as if free" because of the absence or near absence of imperial authority. Although there was a parochial presence, and the vast majority of the population formally adhered to Catholicism, there was—and continues to be—a strong current of animism and syncretism running through the religious practices of the locals.

In animist practice in Cuba—specifically the Yoruba version—the Virgin of Charity is Ochun, who is also the wife of the promiscuous Chango. Ochun is the patron saint of sweet water: creeks, lakes, rivers are all her domain. Newly consecrated priests, or *santeros,* must always go to a body of sweet water and render homage to her before starting to practice, no matter who their patron may be. Ochun cures with honey and is credited with saving humankind on several occasions.

In the United States, Cuban Americans have been formally celebrating the feast of the Virgin of Charity since 1961, when the icon from the parish of Guanabo, a village just outside Havana, was given formal asylum by the Italian ambassador to Cuba. Transported to Miami via diplomatic pouch by a Panamanian delegate to Cuba, this icon was immediately taken to Miami Stadium, where thousands awaited it for a Mass in the Virgin's honor.

In 1967 a hermitage was built in Miami to house the icon. The hermitage contained in its foundation earth from all six of Cuba's prerevolution provinces. This representation of the Virgin receives formal annual visits from each of Cuba's municipalities-in-exile, as well as from each Latin American community represented in South Florida.

Unquestionably, however, it is Ochun, the Virgin's animist aspect, that has the greater following in the United States, especially among Caribbean peoples but also among African Americans. A staple at botánicas, or Santería shops, she is consulted regularly—through intermediaries, usually *santeros* or *babalaos*—on matters of love, fidelity, coupling, fertility, and household management. As Ochun, she is always black or mulatta, voluptuous and flirtatious.

RELATED ARTICLES

Afro-Latino Influences; Catholicism; Cuba; Cuban Americans; Religion; Saints.

FURTHER READING

Matovina, Timothy, and Gerald E. Poyo, eds. *¡Presente! U.S. Latino Catholics from Colonial Origins to the Present.* Maryknoll, N.Y.: Orbis, 2000.

ACHY OBEJAS

VIRGEN DE MONSERRATE

La Virgen de Monserrate, Milagro de Hormigueros is originally from Cataluña, Spain, where a Benedictine abbey and shrine were built in her honor near Barcelona in the 12th century. The church is in the rugged (*serrat*) mountains of this region, therefore the name Montserrat in Catalan. La Virgen de Monserrate is also known as La Moreneta, or little *morena,* of dark color. She is one of many black Madonnas in the Catholic church.

Many stories explain why the Monserrate of Cataluña and the baby Jesus are black. La Virgen de Monserrate is believed to have been moved to Cataluña to hide her in the mountains to protect her from infidels—one story tells of how the statue, after being hidden for a long time, was found in a coal mine. When brought out, both the Virgin and the Christ child were black. After attempts at cleaning the statue, she still remained "miraculously black." The Virgin in the shrine in Cataluña is enthroned with the baby Jesus on her lap: she holds a globe in her right hand and the baby Jesus holds the same globe in his left hand.

La Virgen de Monserrate was brought to Puerto Rico by Catalan immigrants early in the colonial period and immediately became popular. Devotion increased after an apparition of her appeared in 1599—this event was related in a 1699 document *La Monserrate negra con el niño blanco* (The Black Montserrat with the White Child), which was found in Vidal. Another story of La Moreneta involves Gerardo González, a peasant from the town of Hormigueros, who was about to be charged by a bull when he invoked La Virgen de Monserrate. She appeared before him and the bull kneeled in front of her, sparing González's life. González then founded a church to the Monserrate in the town of Hormigueros, in which a painting hangs with the same iconography as the statue in the abbey in Cataluña.

The Puerto Rican version of this virgin is known as La Virgen de Monserrate, Milagro de Hormigueros (The Virgin of Montserrat, Miracle of Hormigueros). In Puerto Rico, as well as among the Puerto Rican community in the United States mainland, her popularity is manifested in the abundance of carvings or *santos* found in the popular religious imagery that dates to the 16th century and that covers much of the island. Devotion is also shown by the many pilgrimages to the church in Hormigueros. The Monserrate has become a repository of ideas about *puertorriqueñidad* and reflects the variety of skin colors in Puerto Rico. She is shown as white, *trigueña* (the color of wheat), black, or *achocolatá* (the color of chocolate). The image in Spain always appears as a black Madonna with a black baby. The image in Puerto Rico and among Puerto Ricans on the mainland appears in different permutations (black virgin with white baby, white virgin with white baby, black virgin with black baby, and so on)—attesting to the ways in which Puerto Rican ideas about and understanding of race became embodied in the image of this virgin.

RELATED ARTICLES

Brownness; Catholicism; Puerto Ricans on the Mainland; Puerto Rico; Race; Religion.

FURTHER READING

Nigra Sum. Iconografía de Santa María de Montserrat (We are Black: Iconography of Santa María de Montserrat). Cataluña: Publicaciones de la Abadía de Montserrat, 1995 [Catálogo, exposición en el Museo de Montserrat].

Quintero Rivera, Angel G. *Vírgenes, magos, y escapularios: Imageginería, etnicidad y religiosidad popular en Puerto Rico* (Virgins, Magi and Scapulars: Imagery, Ethnicity, and Popular Religiosity in Puerto Rico). San Juan, Puerto Rico: Centro de Investigaciones Sociales, 1998.

Vidal, Teodoro. *Los Espada. Escultores Sangermeños* (The Espada: San Germain's Sculptors). San Juan, Puerto Rico: Ediciones Alba, 1994.

Vidal, Teodoro. *La Monserrate negra con el niño blanco: una modalidad iconógrafica puertorriqueña* (The Black Montserrat with the White Child: An Iconographic Modality from Puerto Rico). San Juan, Puerto Rico: Ediciones Alba, 2003.

MARVETTE PÉREZ

VOCALISTS, POPULAR

The precursors of Latin popular vocal music emerged in the 1930s with the internationalization of the lilting Cuban ballad rhythm known as bolero. Agustín Lara, a tall, slender pianist, singer, and composer from

Mexico, became the bolero's greatest composer. His life was full of troubled relationships and his face carried a scar from where a jealous woman had slashed it with a broken bottle; but he channeled his sensitivity and pain into Latin American classics such as *Farolito, Solamente una vez,* and the highly personal *María Bonita,* written in 1946 for his third wife, Mexican screen legend María Félix. Confirming the latter song's enduring sentiment, pop crooner Mijares rerecorded the song as the title track to a smash 1992 nostalgia album.

The bolero remained a lingua franca for border-crossing trio groups in the 1940s and 1950s. The groups' three members, all of whom played guitar and sang in harmony, were almost always male. Thanks in part to their exposure in popular Mexican movies during Mexican cinema's 1940s–1950s golden age, trios such as Los Panchos and Los Tres Reyes were able to undertake international tours during a time when mass communication was far less developed and protective tariffs were in full force.

Other genres such as Argentine tango, Mexican *ranchera,* Spanish rumba, and Afro-Cuban mambo gained international fame by way of Latin American movies. Mexico in particular carried on a love affair with Cuban rhythms in its *cabaretera* films of the 1940s and 1950s. These films often portrayed pathos-inducing stories of crime and heartbreak among Mexico City's cabaret dancers, who would shake their hips to the "exotic" rhythms of Cuba in order to care for a layabout husband or send a sister to finishing school.

The mambo exploded during the 1950s as Cuban-born bandleader Perez Prado ruled the American pop charts with hits such as *Cherry Pink and Apple Blossom White* and *Patricia.* Cuba's Latin music had broken the language barrier, though its stay was short-lived, as Fidel Castro led a communist overthrow of the Cuban government in 1959, setting off a decades-long economic embargo by the United States.

In the late 1950s Mexican composer Armando Manzanero entered the scene, becoming known for sentimental boleros, such as *Contigo Aprendí, Adoro,* and *Somos Novios,* that could be convincingly sung by a street-corner trio or a tuxedo-wearing crooner. In America the latter song is better known by its English translation, *It's Impossible,* with which crooner Perry Como scored a comeback hit in 1970. Although Como was among the last of a breed in

America, the upscale crooner genre remains a strong current in Latin popular music even today.

As technology helped make the world seem smaller, the potential market for Latin superstars became bigger. The 1970s saw the advent of what came to be known as the "international ballad" period, featuring such megastars as Julio Iglesias (Spain), José José (Mexico), José Luis Rodríguez (Venezuela), Raphael (Spain), Braulio (Canary Islands), and Juan Gabriel (Mexico).

The songs that epitomized the period include such nuggets as José Luis Rodríguez's *Voy a perder la cabeza por tu amor,* Julio Iglesias's *Manuela,* José José's *Gavilan o Paloma,* and Juan Gabriel's *No tengo dinero.* Other period tunes would also include Heleno's *Anoche te vi de nuevo,* Raphael's *Toco madera* and *Yo soy aquel,* Braulio's *En bancarrota,* Camilo Sesto's *Perdóname,* and Emmanuel's *Quiero dormir cansando.* These songs were characterized by penetrating lyrics and soaring vocals and often boasted full orchestral arrangements. The focus, though, was on the power of the lyrics in songs that typically spoke of first love, heartbreak, and rediscovery. The songs, especially live, featured dynamic yet melodic arrangements with impeccable vocal delivery.

Another unique aspect that helped the international ballad stand apart from any salsa, Tejano, or regional Mexican song was its ability to be widely and readily accepted in various Latin American countries from Panama and Peru to Colombia and Chile. The artists were marketed to appeal to a wide cross-section of people; however, their success came at the expense of anyone who might have recorded anti-authoritarian lyrics or overly "aggressive" arrangements. Anything smacking of rock 'n' roll or protest was often suppressed or discouraged by the Latin American governments of the 1970s.

Musically, the crooners' universal appeal came at the expense of regional variety or musical fire. Sometimes the material lapsed into a bland, overproduced formula. Latin pop's more energetic side in the early 1980s could be found with prefab bubblegum groups such as Puerto Rico's Menudo and Mexico's Timbiriche. Akin to predecessors like the Monkees or the Partridge Family, these acts specifically targeted teens and preteens, helping the music market expand and better weather the business cycle.

Not much can be said about the musical contributions of these acts, although Menudo's hits *Dulces besos* and *Quiero ser* are still embedded in the minds of many Latinos; however, members of Menudo and Timbiriche would set the stage for the Latin pop renaissance that began in the mid-1990s. Menudo's most famous alumnus, Ricky Martin, broke through in 1995 with his international hit *María*. With thundering Afro-Latin percussion, the song proved that rootsy influences could mix beautifully with pop's slick production and instrumentation. Timing was important, too. Immigration was fueling an explosion in the U.S. Latin music market, which by 2002 would become the world's largest in sales. A new multiculturalist ethos and nostalgia for a land left behind increased the longing for Latin roots, and a song like *María*, which was irresistibly danceable and unmistakably Latino, sent the message that it was cool to be Hispanic.

Other artists mined the same vein. After having mixed results in the early 1990s with flower-child rock, former Timbiriche member Thalía turned to renowned producer Emilio Estefan, husband of Gloria Estefan, to inject some fire into her music. The Estefans had earlier had success with pop-tropical fusion in English, with Miami Sound Machine's 1980s hits *Dr. Beat, Conga,* and *1, 2, 3*. Thalía scored in 1995 with *En Extasis,* whose smash hit *Piel Morena* celebrated brown skin and fused dance music with Colombian *cumbia*. It was further proof of the increasing marketability of ethnic pride.

The influential year 1995 also saw the debut of Enrique Iglesias, son of Julio. Raised in Miami, Enrique Iglesias did things the old-fashioned way; there was still a market for lush, adult contemporary ballads with sugary lyrics, especially when performed by someone with Iglesias's good looks and romantic voice. Luis Miguel also updated the crooner template, making orchestral bolero hip again with his 1990s trilogy *Romance* (1991), *Segundo romance* (1994), and *Romances* (1997). The albums also represented a comeback for Manzanero, whose *Somos novios* and *Voy a apagar la luz* were revived by Luis Miguel. Manzanero also wrote some new songs for the sets and helped produce them. Other stars who crooned to generations X and Y in the late 1990s and early 2000s included Brazil's Alexandre Pires, Puerto Rico's Carlos Ponce, Spain's Alejandro Sanz, and the Mexican Argentine duo Sin Bandera.

The fusion template was by then standard—being proud of one's roots a given. Pires would add Brazilian percussion such as *pandeiro,* Ponce and Sanz incorporated salsa and Spanish rumba, while Sin Ban-

dera, whose name means "without flag," was influenced by American soul.

Latin pop also turned out to be the genre most suited to crossovers to the English market. Ricky Martin was first in 1999 with *Livin' la Vida Loca,* whose bilingual lyrics and Latin ska rhythm signaled Latino culture's increasing influence in the United States. Marc Anthony, a New York City–born singer of Puerto Rican descent who began a successful salsa career in 1993, followed later that year with the brassy *I Need to Know,* which featured a breakdown on the Latin percussion instrument known as *timbale*. Also helping to make 1999 the year of the Latin pop explosion, Enrique Iglesias dominated the airplay charts with *Bailamos,* a fusion of disco and Spanish flamenco that was more roots-tinged than most of his Spanish material. Still, mainstream top-40 audiences loved it. Shakira, a Colombian singer and songwriter who poured fuel on the fusion wildfire with her heartfelt, energetic combinations of rock with mariachi, *vallenato,* and even Middle Eastern rhythms—her father is of Lebanese descent—debuted in Spanish in 1996 but made the crossover in 2001 with *Laundry Service,* whose first single *Wherever, Whenever* used Andean flute and Afro-Cuban percussion. Jennifer "J-Lo" Lopez has recorded in both English and Spanish and incorporated Latin instrumentation on hits such as *Ain't It Funny* (Spanish guitar) and *Let's Get Loud* (brass).

Today, Latin pop artists enjoy much more liberty to speak out on political and social matters. Ricardo Arjona pokes fun at Catholic teachings in songs such as *Si usted la viera (El Confesor)* and *Santo Pecado*. Shakira forcefully criticized the Iraq war during her 2003 tour. Latin pop has come a long way since its quiet beginnings, incorporating traditional regional styles and continually reinventing itself by being open to new influences from rock to rap to rumba.

RELATED ARTICLES

Bolero; Corrido; Cruz, Celia; Estefan, Gloria; Lopez, Trinidad; Music, Popular; Popular Culture; Selena; Tejano; Valens, Ritchie.

FURTHER READING

Diego, Ximena. *Shakira: Woman Full of Grace*. Tr. by Francheska Farinaccio. New York: Fireside, 2001.
Marrero, Letisha. *Ricky Martin: Livin' la Vida Loca*. New York: HarperEntertainment, 1999.

Roberts, John Storm. *The Latin Tinge: The Impact of Latin American Music on the United States.* 1979. 2d ed. New York: Oxford Univ. Press, 1998.

RAMIRO BURR
DOUG SHANNON

VOTING

The act of voting is one of the most important privileges of U.S. citizenship. Through voting, Americans are able to choose their leaders and make changes in governmental policy. The 15th Amendment to the Constitution of the United States—ratified and enacted in 1870—prohibits federal or state governments from infringing on any citizen's right to vote "on account of race, color, or previous condition of servitude."

However, the federal government also gave each state broad powers to set up its own qualifications and restrictions for voters. These restrictions vary considerably from one state to another, and within decades a plethora of insidious tactics were employed in an effort to prevent African Americans and Latino Americans from exercising their voting rights. Consequently, the voting rights of Latinos from the 19th century well into the second half of the 20th century were frequently the object of arbitrary controls inflicted by state legislatures and the will of the state majority. These restrictions were most evident in two states with fairly significant Hispanic populations. In 1894 the people of California voted to approve an English literacy requirement for California's voting booth. Because of this test, many native-born Mexican American citizens who were uneducated or whose primary language was Spanish were unable to vote. In 1901 the Texas legislature passed the poll tax, which required voters to pay $1.75 at the voting booth, and in November 1902 Texas voters ratified the poll tax by a two-to-one margin. Such an expense was equally effective in keeping many poor Tejanos from exercising their right to vote. In effect, the poll tax was able to circumvent the rights that had been guaranteed to Tejano citizens by the 14th Amendment.

At the end of World War II, however, young Latino soldiers who had defended America on the battlefields of Europe and Asia returned home with new ideas about their rights as citizens and, in particular, about their rights as voters. The American GI Forum, founded in 1948, was organized by Mexican American veterans in Texas who began to campaign vigorously to increase electoral participation of Latinos in the political arena. In an effort to get Hispanics to vote, they initiated local "pay your poll tax" drives to register Tejano voters. In California a similar phenomenon took place. When World War II veteran Edward R. Roybal ran for a seat on the Los Angeles City Council, community activists established the CSO (Community Service Organization). The CSO was effective in registering 15,000 new voters in the Latino neighborhoods of Boyle Heights, Belvedere, and East Los Angeles. With this new-found support, Roybal was able to win the 1949 election race against the incumbent Anglo councilman and become the first Mexican American since 1881 to win a seat on the Los Angeles City Council.

The Mexican American Political Association (MAPA), founded in Fresno, California, came into being in 1959 and drew up a plan for direct electoral politics. MAPA soon became the primary political voice for the Mexican American community of California. Edward Roybal, elected the first president of MAPA, would become the first Chicano representative to Congress from Los Angeles in the 20th century, in large part owing to the efforts of MAPA and the CSO.

One of the primary Latino organizations contributing to increased Latino voter registration on a nationwide level was the Southwest Voter Registration Education Project (SVREP), founded in San Antonio, Texas, in 1974. Reminding Latinos that the democratic process was their right and privilege, the SVREP conducted 2,200 voter registration campaigns in 14 states and initiated "Get-the-vote-out" campaigns throughout the Southwest. Because of these extraordinary efforts, Latino voter rates increased from 2 million voters in 1974 to 7.7 million in 2001.

In 1981 the National Association of Latino Elected and Appointed Officials Educational Fund (NALEO) was established to promote the integration of Latino immigrants into American society and encourage them to become citizens so that they might participate in the electoral process. The efforts of MAPA, SVREP, NALEO, and CSO were instrumental in the dramatic increase in the Latino electorate that took place between 1960 and 2000.

On January 23, 1964, the U.S. Congress ratified the 24th Amendment to the U.S. Constitution, which stated that "the right of citizens of the United States to vote in any primary or other election . . . shall not be denied or abridged by the United States or any State by reason of failure to pay any poll tax . . . " The 24th Amendment paved the way for the Voting Rights Act of 1965, which was signed into law by President Lyndon B. Johnson on August 6, 1965. Section 2 of this act prohibited any state or political subdivision of a state from using any "standard, practice, or procedure" that would result "in denial or abridgement of the right of any citizen of the United States to vote on account of race or color." This act temporarily suspended California's literacy test, which was subsequently ruled unconstitutional in 1970 by the California Superior Court. The Voting Rights Act had not included a provision prohibiting poll taxes but had directed the attorney general to challenge its use. In *Harper* v. *Virginia State Board of Elections* (1966), the Supreme Court held Virginia's poll tax to be unconstitutional under the 14th Amendment, thus nullifying Texas's poll tax.

The Voting Rights Act of 1965 gave African Americans access to the voting booth in places where access had previously been denied to them and was beneficial in increasing the African American vote in the southern states. The Mexican American Legal Defense and Education Fund (MALDEF) and other Latino activist groups took note of this fact and began to lobby intensely for an extension of the Voting Rights Act for Latinos. On hearing extensive testimony about voting discrimination that had been suffered by Hispanic citizens, Congress responded to these lobbying efforts in 1975 by amending the Voting Rights Act to include provisions that affected Latinos and "minority-language citizens." The revised act now prohibited discriminatory election devices, including both literacy tests and poll taxes. The act also required bilingual ballots in areas where a minority group exceeded 5 percent of the vote, and it safeguarded minorities against gerrymandering schemes that would dilute the power of their vote. These legislative interventions permitted the Latino voting base to expand in the years to come.

In 1960 Hispanics represented only 3.2 percent of the national population. But it was during the 1960 presidential election that the potential influence of Latinos in very close elections was first recognized and appreciated. Early in the year, "Viva Kennedy" clubs were organized by Mexican Amer-

ican activists in nine states to support the election of John F. Kennedy to the presidency. When the general election was held in November, it was one of the closest in history, with Kennedy winning by a plurality of only 144,673 votes. With such a small margin of victory, many political analysts believe that the Hispanic vote helped Kennedy to win. Although Latinos made up a very small portion of the electorate, they voted in large numbers for Kennedy, who received about 85 percent of the national Hispanic vote. Even more significant was the fact that Kennedy received 91 percent of the Hispanic vote in Texas, a state with a significant Mexican American population. However, even with the Latino vote, Kennedy's victory in Texas was by a razor-thin margin, having carried the state by only 46,000 votes. Kennedy also carried Illinois by only 9,000 votes, another state in which the Latino vote had been mobilized by the Viva Kennedy movement.

With the significant increase in the Latino population, the voting power of Latinos gradually gained in importance over a period of three decades. The table on the following page illustrates the evolution of the Latino electorate through the presidential and midterm elections from 1972 to 2002. The Latino Voting Age Population (VAP) is the number of Latinos who were qualified by age to vote in American elections. Traditionally, only a percentage of these qualified individuals actually registered to vote (second column) and the number of Latinos who actually voted was even smaller (third column).

In 1980 the SVREP drew a profile of the average Mexican American voter in the Southwest. According to this profile, the voter was an older citizen, probably foreign born, who was unable to speak English, lived in a low-income status, and lacked a formal education. These characteristics usually typify the nonvoter. The SVREP also pointed out that 85 percent of the Hispanic voters in 1980 were concentrated in nine states, which controlled 193 electoral votes, 71 percent of the 270 votes needed to win the presidency at that time.

By the time of the 1980 presidential election, Hispanic Americans had come to represent 6.4 percent of the national population, but only 56 percent of Latino residents age 18 and over were actually American citizens, and, according to U.S. Census Bureau estimates, only 36.3 percent of qualified Hispanic citizens were actually registered to vote. When the

THE LATINO VOTING AGE POPULATION, REGISTRATION AND VOTING STATISTICS (1972–2002)

Year	Latino Voting Age Population (VAP)	Percent of Qualified Latinos Registered to Vote	Number of Latinos Who Voted	Percentage of Latino VAP that Actually Voted
1972	5,616,000	44.4	2,103,000	37.5
1974	6,095,000	34.9	1,397,000	22.9
1976	6,594,000	37.8	2,098,000	31.8
1978	6,788,000	32.9	1,593,000	23.5
1980	8,210,000	36.3	2,453,000	29.9
1982	8,765,000	35.3	2,217,000	25.3
1984	9,471,000	40.1	3,092,000	32.6
1986	11,832,000	35.9	2,866,000	24.2
1988	12,893,000	35.5	3,710,000	28.8
1990	13,756,000	32.3	2,894,000	21.0
1992	14,688,000	35.0	4,238,000	28.9
1994	17,476,000	31.3	3,522,000	20.2
1996	18,426,000	35.7	4,928,000	26.7
1998	20,321,000	33.7	4,068,000	20.0
2000	21,598,000	34.9	5,934,000	27.5
2002	25,162,000	32.6	4,747,000	18.9

Source: Federal Election Commission Web site.
http://www.fec.gov/pages/raceto.htm

election took place in November, only 2,453,000 Latinos—or 29.9 percent—actually voted for president.

According to CBS and *New York Times* exit polls, the Democratic candidate, President Jimmy Carter, received more than 60 percent of the Hispanic vote. Although his Republican challenger, Ronald Reagan, received only 35 percent of the Hispanic vote, he received 80 percent of the vote in the predominantly Cuban American precincts of southern Florida. This was the beginning of a trend that would continue through all of the presidential elections into the 21st century.

In the presidential elections held between 1972 and 2000, the vast majority of the Latino electorate usually voted for the Democratic candidate. The primary exception to this trend was the Cuban vote, which began to show a distinct preference for the Republican Party in the late 1970s and early 1980s.

Latino Voting Patterns in California

The evolution of California's Latino electorate from 1960 to 2000 is a significant event in the political arena. In 1961, after the redistricting of the Los Angeles, political boundaries took place based on the 1960 census, the Hispanic vote was essentially frag-

mented. Even the majority Chicano community of East Los Angeles was not able to send Hispanic representatives to Sacramento or Washington, D.C. Gerrymandering had split greater East Los Angeles into nine different Assembly districts, seven state Senate districts, and six different congressional districts. Most of these districts were combined with neighboring Anglo communities so that Hispanics rarely made up more than 20 percent of any one district's population. This district manipulation was effective in diminishing the Latino vote and, as a result, very few Chicano candidates were elected to state or federal positions during the next 20 years.

In the 1970 census, the Chicano population of California was tallied at 2,369,292. Although Latinos at that time made up 10.8 percent of the state's total population, their voting power was dramatically reduced by the presence of 490,892 foreign-born Hispanics, who represented 22.9 percent of the total Hispanic population. Many of these people were not citizens and were therefore ineligible for American voting privileges. This represented a significant stumbling block in electing Chicanos to public office.

In 1994 the controversial California ballot measure Proposition 187—also referred to as the "Illegal Immigration Act"—represented a challenge to all California Latinos. Proposition 187 was the first of several legislative initiatives that were directed against immigrant groups in California. Although the provisions of the proposition were specifically directed at undocumented residents of California, many Latinos saw the initiative as the hallmark of an anti-Hispanic vendetta directed at the entire Latino community. Proposition 187 aroused passions among Latino voters throughout California and led to a flurry of naturalizations and voter registrations. According to INS (Immigration and Naturalization Service) statistics, a record 879,000 immigrant adults had been naturalized in California between 1994 and 1997. These new citizens led to a dramatic increase in the number of voters who had been naturalized. In 1992 foreign-born Latino voters made up only 19 percent of Latino voters in California; by 1996 this had increased dramatically to 32.9 percent.

The 1996 Presidential Election

At the time of the 1996 presidential election, the Latino voting-age population of the United States had reached 18,426,000, but only 11,209,000 of these Hispanics were citizens qualified to vote, and of this group only 6,573,000 were registered to vote. Almost 60 percent of the Latinos registered to vote lived in four crucial states: California (2.1 million voters), Texas (1.6 million), Florida (570,000), and New York (540,000). During the 1990s, these four states held 133 electoral votes between them: California (47 votes), Texas (29), New York (36), and Florida (21). However, the number of Hispanics who actually voted in the election of 1996 was 4,928,000, representing 26.7 percent of the total Latino population. The Latino electorate voted overwhelmingly Democratic, with Bill Clinton winning 71 percent of the Hispanic votes. The Republican senator Bob Dole received only 21 percent, while 10 percent of the vote went to third-party candidates.

The Cuban vote in Florida turned out to be an important factor in Clinton's reelection. Clinton received 35 percent of the traditionally Republican Cuban American vote, a 15-percentage-point improvement over his 1992 showing. This vote helped Clinton to win the state, which no Democrat had won since 1976. In Arizona, Clinton also won 90 percent of the Latino vote, making him the first Democrat to win the state since 1948.

Many political analysts believe that the poor showing of the Republican Party in the 1996 elections was related to the anti-immigrant proposals that were sweeping the country during the mid-1990s. For Cuban, Mexican, and Central American immigrants, the passage of the so-called Welfare Law in 1996—which excluded noncitizen immigrants from many benefits—represented a personal attack on them.

The 2000 Presidential Election

In the controversial presidential election of 2000, the Democratic candidate, Vice President Albert Gore, Jr., ran against George W. Bush, the Republican candidate. Candidate Bush lost the popular vote by 539,897 votes but won the electoral vote by a razor-thin margin of 271 to 266, thus securing the presidency. Many analysts believed that the outcome of this election was influenced by events that took place in Florida's Cuban American community months earlier.

In 1999 a six-year-old Cuban boy named Elián González had been picked up off the Florida coast after his mother and other Cuban refugees died when their boat capsized after fleeing Castro's Cuba. Miami-based Cuban relatives of Elián had gained control of the young boy and campaigned vigorously to keep him from being returned to his father in Cuba. However, in April 2000, the Clinton administration enraged Miami's Cuban community when federal agents seized Elián in a dramatic predawn raid. In June 2000, after several court battles, Elián was returned to Cuba with his father. The anger directed toward Clinton and the Democratic Party caused many Cuban American citizens—both Democratic and Republican—to cast their votes for George W. Bush. Nationwide, 67 percent of Latinos cast their votes for Gore, but in Florida he received only 19 percent of the Cuban vote—and lost Florida by a mere 537 votes. Out of 802,000 Latinos registered to vote in Florida, 678,000 showed up at the polling booths. This impressive turnout was attributed to the reaction against the Clinton administration's handling of the Elián González case.

In California, the state with the largest number of electoral votes (54) and the largest number of Latino voters, the Latino population in 2000 reached almost 11 million or 32.4 percent of the total state population. However, since many in this population were under 18 or non–U.S. citizens, only 3 million of California's Hispanic residents were registered to vote, of which 1.6 million actually voted in the 2000 election, a significant increase from previous elections. Mexican Americans represented more than 77 percent of the Hispanic population in California and were largely Democratic in their party affiliation, outnumbering Latino Republicans by almost three to one (60 percent to 22 percent). Another 18 percent of the state's Latinos were either nonpartisan or registered with another party.

In 2000 New York contained the third-largest concentration of Hispanic voters, 8.2 percent of the state electorate. An estimated 603,000 Latinos were registered at the time of the 2000 presidential election and 502,000 cast ballots, representing 29.4 percent of the total Latino population. As a group, Puerto Ricans and Dominicans usually vote for Democratic candidates. In the 2000 presidential election, Puerto Ricans in New York gave Gore 80 percent of their vote, while Bush received only 18 percent. With 33 electoral votes, New York represents one of the most important states in the electoral process.

In all, 5,934,000 Hispanic voters went to the polls in the 2000 election, representing 27.5 percent of the Hispanic voting age population. Overall, ana-

English–Spanish flyer directs voters to a Web-based voter guide.

lysts still considered the Latino turnout in the 2000 election disappointing when compared with registered voter turnout in other groups: while white (non-Hispanic) registered voters participated at a rate of 86.9 percent, African Americans voted at 85.3 percent, Asians at 83.8 percent, and Latinos at 79.3

percent. Similarly, whites led Latino registration by at least 15 percentage points.

Numerous factors contributed to the low representation of Latinos at the voting booth in 2000. One factor was that the Latino population was overwhelmingly young (representing 39.4 percent of the overall

2000 vote). More importantly, in 2000, 39 percent of the Latino voting-age population were still non-citizens and therefore ineligible to vote in the presidential election. Although naturalizations of Latinos increased dramatically during the 1990s, studies indicated that naturalized citizens were less likely to register to vote (35 percent) and less likely to vote (26 percent) than native-born citizens. Another obstacle to Latino participation in the nation's electoral process was the language barrier, complicated by the availability of bilingual ballots in some states. In the early years of the 21st century, many Latino-centered interest groups began to work diligently to overcome these obstacles and to prepare for the upcoming tide of Latino political influence.

In the past few elections Latino organizations have become actively involved in efforts to mobilize Latinos to vote by urging eligible persons to register, to vote, and to become naturalized. For many elections, such as the California gubernatorial recall election of October 2003, these efforts produced a strong Latino turnout at the polls. A similar effect was felt in 2004, when a number of organizations pushed to increase Latino voter representation in states as diverse as Illinois, Wisconsin, Florida, and New York.

The 2004 presidential election posed important issues for both political parties. Senator John Kerry, the Democratic candidate, and the Democratic Party were hopeful that Latinos would vote Democratic in as high percentages as they did in the 2000 presidential election. But Republicans also courted the Latino vote, hoping to raise the percentage of Latinos voting for Republicans toward the 50 percent mark. Both candidates, President George W. Bush and Senator Kerry, spent unprecedented sums on Spanish-language advertisements in an effort to lure Spanish-speaking voters. By the time the voting booths had closed on November 2, 2004, more than 7.6 million Latinos had voted, an increase of 1.6 million from 2000. According to one exit poll by the William C. Velásquez Institute, in 11 states, 67.7 percent of Latino voters supported Kerry. Other national polls suggested that 44 percent of Latinos had voted for Bush. In addition, two Latinos were elected to the U.S. Senate, Democrat Ken Salazar of Colorado and Republican Mel Martinez of Florida, the first Latinos to serve in the U.S. Senate since 1977.

What are the party loyalties nurtured by the Latino minority? In spite of the traditional support of Hispanics for the Democratic Party, the Latino commu-nity as a whole cannot be characterized as a monolithic group. Across the nation, the Latino population differs with regard to their views on economic, social, cultural, and political issues; and their views cannot be allocated into convenient political compartments. Some studies reveal that a large proportion of Latinos tend to favor the Democratic Party—on economic and social issues, for example—while others favor more conservative values that are more consistent with the Republican Party on issues such as abortion, divorce, religion, and gay rights.

Latino Democrats tend to be more socially conservative than other Democrats, and Latino Republicans often take a more liberal stand on taxes and the size of government than non-Latino members of that party. Therefore, even within circumscribed political groups, Latinos are not easily represented. And although one could identify areas of consensus on issues that concern the majority of Latinos, such as education, health policies, bilingual education, and economic policies, the consensus breaks down considerably when one looks at age, national origin, and length of time in the United States. On cultural and social issues, Latinos' voting patterns cannot nicely be plotted on a statistical scale that would offer either party comfort. If there is one thing that can be predicted with accuracy in this context, it is that the "Latino voter" model is a myth. The potential for capitalizing on Latinos' voting power clearly exists; however, the impetus is likely to come from the voters and organizations representing Latinos rather than from the parties.

At the dawn of the 21st century, the Latino voter comes from a multitude of communities, with diverse cultural, economic, social, and educational experiences. The three major Latino groups are Mexicans—representing almost 60 percent of all Latinos—Puerto Ricans, and Cubans. The rest of the Latino population is dispersed among different nationalities, mostly from Central and South America. Experts point out that political candidates will have to learn the various regional, cultural, and political differences among Hispanics rather than treat them as a monolithic group.

Although Latinos live in all 50 states, the largest concentration is found in California and Texas. Latinos also make up significant minorities in New York, Florida, Illinois, Arizona, New Mexico, and New Jersey. The presence of a large number of eligible Latino voters in these states has tremendous potential for affecting national politics, primarily because these states control almost 70 percent of the important Electoral College votes. Politicians and analysts realize that the Latino electorate cannot be ignored and, in fact, may play a pivotal role in all future elections. Latinos are expected to number 53 million by 2020 and 97 million—roughly one-quarter of the population—by 2050. With such incredible growth rates anticipated, it is widely expected that in some areas of the country, Latinos will actually become the primary policymakers.

RELATED ARTICLES

Civil Rights; Democracy; Democratic Party; Discrimination; Mexican American Political Association; Politics, Latino; Republican Party; United States Congress; United States Presidents and Latinos.

FURTHER READING

Allsup, Carl. *The American G.I. Forum: Origins and Evolution.* Austin: Univ. of Tex. Ctr. for Mexican American Studies Monograph 6, 1982.

Barreto, Matt, and Harry Pachon. "Latino Politics Comes of Age in the Golden State." In *Latinos and the 2000 Election.* Ed. by Louis DeSipio and Rodolfo de la Garza. Boulder, Colo.: Westview Press, 2002.

Barreto, Matt, et al. *A Glimpse into Latino Policy and Voting Preferences.* The Tomas Rivera Policy Inst. Policy Brief, March 2002.

Brischetto, Robert R. *The Hispanic Electorates.* New York: Hispanic Policy Development Project, 1984.

The Field Index. *A Digest Examining California's Expanding Latino Electorate* 1 (May 2000).

Gomez-Quiñones, Juan. *Chicano Politics: Reality and Promise, 1940–1990.* Albuquerque: Univ. of N.Mex. Press, 1990.

Isla, José de la. *The Rise of Hispanic Political Power.* Santa Maria, Calif.: Archer Bks., 2003.

Menifield, Charles E. *Representation of Minority Groups in the U.S.: Implication for the Twenty-First Century.* Lanham, Md.: Austin & Winfield, 2001.

Schmal, John P. "Electing the President: The Latino Electorate (1960–2000)." *La Prensa de San Diego,* April 30, 2004. http://www.laprensa-sandiego.org/archieve/april30-04/elect.htm

SELECTED WEB SITES

SVREP—"Important Facts about SVREP." http://www.svrep.org/aboutsvrep/fact_sheet.html

U.S. Census Bureau. http://www.census.gov/population/www/socdemo/voting.html

ANA MARÍA MERICO-STEPHENS
JOHN P. SCHMAL

WASHINGTON

Latino contact with and presence in what is now the state of Washington in the Pacific Northwest dates to 1774, prior to the American Revolution. Beginning that year, Spanish ships carrying Mexican and South American adventurers traveled along the coast and into Puget Sound. Spaniards and Latinos introduced beans, corn, tomatoes, and livestock into the area, and left many place names, including the Strait of San Juan de Fuca. With the discovery of gold in the mid-19th century, Mexican vaqueros, muleteers, and miners traveled to Washington Territory from the Southwest. Immigration in large numbers, however, resulting in permanent communities, did not occur until the 20th century.

World War II brought a huge demand for agricultural products in the Pacific Northwest. In response to urgent calls from growers across the United States, the governments of the United States and Mexico agreed on the Mexican Farm Labor Program—known as the *bracero* (one who works with his arms) program, which was signed into law in 1943. By 1947, 15,000 Mexican *braceros* helped rescue agriculture in the region. *Braceros* in Washington were unanimously praised by employers, but suffered from racial discrimination, poor housing and food, and open hostility in some communities. Accidents killed or injured many of them. After World War II, new farm labor arrived from Texas and the Southwest. These Mexican American migrants, some of whom were forced out of their own farms by the

demands of 20th century competition and technology, formed the first large family communities in the Yakima Valley in eastern Washington, which is among the highest producing and most lucrative agricultural regions in the United States. The first Spanish-language radio station in the state was established in Sunnyside in the 1950s.

By 1968 the first group of Mexican American students enrolled at the University of Washington, with others enrolling at Washington State and other colleges in the following years. At this time, the Chicano movement ignited student passions and activism; students pressured university officials to institute Chicano Studies departments at universities and community colleges. In Seattle, a group occupied an abandoned building, demanding that they be allowed to use it for a community center. Granted their demands, they organized El Centro de la Raza in 1972, which today provides human services for many city residents. During this period of activism, César Chávez, head of the United Farm Workers Union, spoke to enthusiastic crowds in eastern Washington. Farmworkers continue to be politically active in the area.

The Latino population in Washington has grown for the past 20 years. The U.S. Census for 2000 listed Latinos as the state's largest minority group. In the early 21st century many immigrants with roots in the Caribbean and Central and South America are adding to the population numbers, which total 441,509 of Washington's nearly 6 million residents. Latinos also scored a political victory in May 2003,

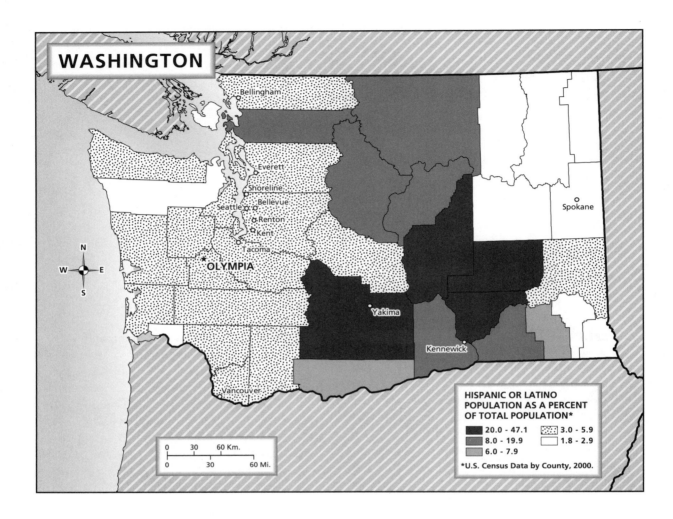

WASHINGTON

HISPANIC OR LATINO
POPULATION AS A PERCENT
OF TOTAL POPULATION*

20.0 - 47.1	3.0 - 5.9
8.0 - 19.9	1.8 - 2.9
6.0 - 7.9	

*U.S. Census Data by County, 2000.

with passage of legislation that allowed foreign-born Mexican migrant high school students to enter state universities at the same tuition as state residents.

RELATED ARTICLES

Immigration, Latino.

FURTHER READING

Gamboa, Erasmo. "Mexican Migration into Washington State: A History, 1949–1950." *Pacific Northwest Quarterly* 72 (July 1981): 121–131.

Gamboa, Erasmo. *Mexican Labor and World War II: Braceros in the Pacific Northwest, 1942–1947.* Seattle: Univ. of Wash. Press, 2000.

Johansen, Bruce E., and Roberto F. Maestas. "Washington's Latino Community: 1935–1980." *Landmarks* (Summer 1982): 10–13.

Maldonado, Carlos S., and Gilbert García, eds. *The Chicano Experience in the Northwest.* Dubuque, Iowa: Kendall/Hunt, 1995.

Schwantes, Carlos Arnaldo. *The Pacific Northwest.* Rev. ed. Lincoln: Univ. of Neb. Press, 1996.

Smyth, Willie, project director. *Gritos Del Alma: Chicano/Mexicano Music Traditions of Washington State.* Seattle: Wash. State Arts Commission, 1993.

Steiner, Stan. *La Raza: The Mexican Americans.* New York: Harper, 1970.

SELECTED WEB SITES

Association of Washington Cities. www.awcnet.org

U.S. Census Bureau, United States Department of Commerce. www.census.gov

Washington State Commission on Hispanic Affairs. www.cha.wa.gov

E. MARK MORENO

WASHINGTON, D.C.

The Greater Washington, D.C., Metropolitan Area (Washington, D.C., Maryland, and northern Virginia) is home to one of the fastest growing and most diverse Latino populations in the United States. In 2000, the U.S. Bureau of the Census estimated that more than 44,953 Latinos lived in the District of Columbia—nearly 7.9 percent of D.C.'s total population of 572,059. In 2000, Virginia's Latino population figured at 4.7 percent, while Maryland's Latino population stood at 4.3 percent. Historically, Latin American émigrés and others attached to embassies, diplomatic corps, and international organizations have settled in the region. The anthropologist David E. Pedersen links the 1980s rise in service sector jobs and immigrant laborers in the region to the expansion of the "U.S. military-industrial complex," which requires services in the areas of defense, research and development, telecommunication, transportation, international trade, finance, and legal and political work.

Terry A. Repak explains that female domestic workers and child-care providers, sponsored by diplomats, government employees, and international agencies, "pioneered the migration in the 1960s and 1970s" of Latinos to the Washington, D.C., area. The boom in regional construction, restaurant and hospitality businesses, cleaning subcontractors, and various industries opened new labor markets in the 1980s and 1990s. Throughout the 1980s, Central American immigrants, fleeing civil wars in their

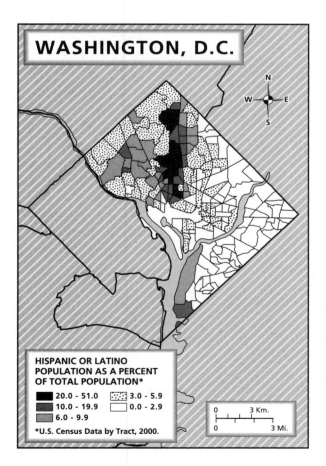

HISPANIC OR LATINO POPULATION AS A PERCENT OF TOTAL POPULATION*

- 20.0 - 51.0
- 10.0 - 19.9
- 6.0 - 9.9
- 3.0 - 5.9
- 0.0 - 2.9

*U.S. Census Data by Tract, 2000.

0   3 Km.

0   3 Mi.

countries, were attracted to the area by employment opportunities, affordable housing, and relatively easy access to jobs in the District of Columbia and its suburbs. Subsequently, the Latino population in D.C. grew, creating new tensions in an already racially stratified and economically depressed city. On May 5, 1991, race riots broke out in the Mount Pleasant Latino neighborhood, causing great damage to property and injury to people. Despite, or perhaps prompted by, the riots, businesses reopened, churches, community centers, public clinics, and service providers attended to immigrants' needs, and even a Latino festival was hosted in the ethnically diverse Adams Morgan district. In *Creating A Latino Identity in the Nation's Capital: The Latino Festival* (1998), Olivia Cadaval discusses the "multiethnic Latino community in Washington, D.C.," in the wake of race riots in the 1960s and 1990s, the civil rights movement, and the severe urban decline and renewal of Washington, D.C.

Local Latino artists such as performer and poet Quique Avilés, painter Karla Rodas (Karlísma), the bands Lilo González and los de la Mt. Pleasant, and African American and Latino youth theater troupes like LatinNegro (which was active in the 1990s) and its offshoot, Sol & Soul, document the experiences of Latino communities in Washington, D.C. In his poem, "Barrio" (1992), Avilés, a veteran of "art happenings" in the District, poignantly struggles to describe life in the Latino neighborhoods of Washington. Avilés gropes for words, "Trying to write things / without naming names / not pointing the finger / not saying what the throat wants to / say / in these arrogant times / in this arrogant place . . . " The "arrogant place" is the nation's capital, where Latinos continue to have little political representation and voice.

RELATED ARTICLES

Immigration, Latino.

FURTHER READING

Avilés, Quique. *The Immigrant Museum.* Mexico City: Pin Studio & Raíces de Papel, 2003.

Cadaval, Olivia. *Creating a Latino Identity in the Nation's Capital: The Latino Festival.* New York: Garland Publ., 1998.

Jennings, Keith, and Clarence Lusane. "The State and Future of Black/Latino Relations in Washington, D.C.: A Bridge in Need of Repair." In *Blacks, Latinos, and Asians in Urban America: Status and Prospects for Politics and Activism.* Ed. by James Jennings. Westport, Conn.: Praeger, 1994.

Pedersen, David E. "States of Memory and Desire: The Meaning of City and Nation for Transnational Migrants in Washington, D.C., and El Salvador." *Amerikastudien/American Studies* 40: n.p., n.d.

Repak, Terry A. *Waiting on Washington: Central American Workers in the Nation's Capital.* Philadelphia: Temple Univ. Press, 1995.

SELECTED WEB SITE

U.S. Census Bureau.
http://factfinder.census.gov/home/en/pldata.html

ANA PATRICIA RODRÍGUEZ

WASHINGTON HEIGHTS

Quisqueya Heights, or Washington Heights as it is otherwise known, is a neighborhood on the island of Manhattan in New York City. It is located in upper Manhattan and bordered geographically by the Harlem River and High Bridge Park on the east and Fort Washington Park and the Hudson River on the west. The population of Washington Heights is just over 200,000. The demographic makeup of the neighborhood is a mixture of racial and ethnic groups. By far the largest group in the neighborhood is recent immigrants of Hispanic origin—the vast majority from the Dominican Republic—who make up 74 percent of the population. Quisqueya Heights is the name most Dominicans use to refer to the neighborhood. The word comes from the Arawak term Quisqueya, which means "cradle of life." Quisqueya was one of the pre-Columbian names for the island of Hispaniola, the island now divided between the countries of Haiti, which in Arawak means "land of the mountains," and the Dominican Republic.

Rich in history, the neighborhood has experienced many changes since the city was established. By the late 19th century the area was primarily farmland dotted by a few estates until a subway line linked the sector with the rest of the city. Early in the 20th century, Irish, Dutch, German, and Italian immigrants moved into the area. Austrian and German Jews followed this first wave of immigrants in the 1940s. Yeshiva University, the first parochial Jewish institution of higher education in the United States, was founded in 1886 in this part of Manhattan. After World War II, African Americans from the rural South began to settle in the area, followed by increasing numbers of Puerto Rican, Cuban, and Dominican immigrants.

Washington Heights boasts a number of historic sites. The Morris-Jumel Mansion, which served as a headquarters for George Washington during the Revolutionary War, is located near High Bridge Park. The mansion is the last colonial residence left in Manhattan; nearby is Sylvan Terrace, a street lined with historic pre–World War II wooden row houses. Audubon Terrace, which was originally the estate of the famous naturalist John James Audubon, serves as home to the Hispanic Society of America, the American Numismatic Society, and the American Academy of Arts and Letters. The Church of the Intercession is located at West 155th Street and Broadway and was given landmark status in 1966 because of its neo-Gothic or Gothic Revival architecture. Fort Tryon Park, located at the highest point at the northern end of Manhattan, is the site of the Cloisters. This museum features a chapel and actual examples of cloisters from Gothic and Romanesque European monasteries, as well as a 12th-century Spanish apse. The museum also has a large collection of medieval art, and extensive gardens. Washington Heights has been home to many famous people including Duke Ellington, Thurgood Marshall, W. E. B. Du Bois, and Roy Wilkins. Malcolm X was assassinated in the Audubon Ballroom on Broadway.

The area became notorious for high crime rates and economic blight during the 1980s and 1990s. However, the Latino, mostly Dominican, community has strong cultural and ethnic pride, which contributes to a deep sense of community and creates a vibrant environment despite low income levels and problems with crime related to purported drug trade activity. The pride residents take in their community is evident in the many cultural, historic, and civic organizations active in serving the needs and interests of residents. On the third Sunday in August each year is the Dominican Day Parade, which is now held in midtown Manhattan, but which originated in 1981 in Washington Heights. The majority of immigrants coming to New York between the 1960s and the 1990s were from the Dominican Republic. Today three-quarters of Dominicans in the United States live in the New York area where they constitute approximately 10 percent of the population. Quisqueya-Washington Heights has the largest concentration of Dominicans in the city.

RELATED ARTICLES
Dominican Americans; New York City.

FURTHER READING
Aponte, Sarah. "Dominican Migration to the United States, 1970–1997: An Annotated Bibliography." *Dominican Research Monographs*. New York: CUNY Dominican Studies Inst., 1999.

Cocco de Filippis, Daisy, and F. Gutiérrez, eds. *Stories from Washington Heights and Other Corners of the World, A Bilingual Selection of Short Stories Written by Dominicans in the U.S.* New York: Latin Am. Writers Inst., 1994.

Duany, Jorge. "Reconstructing Racial Identity: Ethnicity, Color, and Class among Dominicans in the United States and Puerto Rico." *Latin American Perspectives* 25, no. 3 (1998): 147–172.

Duany, Jorge. "Quisqueya on the Hudson: The Transnational Identity of Dominicans in Washington Heights." *Dominican Research Monograph* 1. New York: CUNY Dominican Studies Inst., 1994.

JILL PINKNEY PASTRANA

WATER

No natural resource is as vital for the development of the American Hispanic community or plays as central a role in its development as water. Since the Spanish conquest of the Americas in 1521, water resources have played a key role in determining patterns of settlement, the nature of economic life, the accumulation of wealth and status, and the structures of political authority and government in the region that is today Mexico and the American Southwest. The appropriation and development of water resources was a central part of community governance in colonial times and remained so after the Treaty of Guadalupe Hidalgo (1848) incorporated the largely Hispanic population north of the Rio Grande (Rio Bravo) and Gila rivers into the young American republic.

In the 20th century, with the advent of federal reclamation policy in the United States, water policies dynamically shaped the prospects of the demographically dominant Hispanic population of the U.S.–Mexico border zone. From an earlier emphasis on agriculture and agricultural communities as the basis of regional settlement and development, water policy has shifted since the mid-20th century to support rapid urbanization and industrialization in the border region. With population growth, new concerns about water quality and the environment have been raised to challenge established practice in regional water management. That such concerns are heard reflects the growing power of Hispanic citizens in local government and their desire to secure a better quality of life for their communities. This has engendered new institutions that better incorporate the views and values of Hispanics in regional water management practice.

Colonial Period

Water and its allocation were important for the development of human settlements and agricultural production in New Spain after 1521 and very early on became a significant preoccupation of Spanish colonial municipal government. Early explorers looked for watercourses; rivers provided corridors of transit, provisions for sustenance, and bases for settlement. As Spanish explorers of the 16th and 17th centuries pushed the perimeter of New Spain northward into the more arid regions that are today's northern Mexico and the American Southwest, the conveyance and distribution of water for irrigation and domestic use were essential for both the establishment and maintenance of human settlements. Indeed, the ditching of irrigation systems usually preceded the construction of dwellings, churches, and other public facilities.

The availability of water determined patterns of settlement. The expedition of Juan de Oñate in 1598 opened the door to Spanish settlement of the upper Rio Grande–Rio Bravo river basin. Somewhat later and farther west, the exploration and mission-building of the Jesuit missionary and explorer Eusebio Francisco Kino in the later 17th century followed the Rio Sonora, Rio Magdalena, and Rio Santa Cruz. Along the California coast, spearheaded by Junípero Serra, Franciscan friars settled the river estuaries of San Diego, Carmel, San Luis, San Juan, and Dolores, among others.

While local practices varied somewhat, Spanish colonial law was highly centralized and valued uniformity in procedure and application. By 1789, general principles of water governance for the interior provinces of New Spain had been promulgated. The Plan de Pitic, developed with reference to the needs of the town of Pitic on the Rio Sonora—now Hermosillo, capital of the Mexican state of Sonora—established the following general principles of water management: a just sharing of water between Spanish settlers and Seri Indians; affirming the importance of irrigation for the well-being of the community; establishing an equal entitlement of water per family; reserving land and water for municipal functions; guaranteeing access to the main *acequia madre,* or main ditch; providing for the equitable apportionment of water resources between upstream and downstream users and stipulating responsibilities of upstream users in relation to those downstream; prohibiting waste; providing for a sharing of maintenance costs; and establishing an administrative system to ensure the proper functioning of the irrigation system, including the scheduling of water deliveries.

Colonial law also prescribed rules for settling disputes. The principle of *prior appropriation* was often employed by Spanish judges in determining a right to water, though its application was hardly uniform and decisions were modified by other established practices and principles. Prior ownership never justified squandering water resources or withholding surplus water from other community members. After 1821 and with the partition of Mexico that followed the Mexican-American War (1846–1848), as western and border region settlement intensified, this principle was adopted as a guiding legal precept for the allocation of water resources. It survives today as an important legacy of the Spanish colonial system and has been incorporated into western states' water laws.

National Period

The development and utilization of water resources heavily influenced the demographies, economy, and social development of the U.S. border region and northern Mexico. Demographically, the four states of Texas, New Mexico, Arizona, and California account for the largest concentration of Hispanic citizens in the United States. Throughout this region precipitation is scarce, from 21 inches annually along the Mexican Gulf to less than 7 inches in the parched Sonoran desert and the Imperial and Mexicali valleys along the Colorado River.

The Treaty of Guadalupe Hidalgo (1848) that partitioned Mexico is a key marker in the development of the region's water resources and a useful baseline for the most critical developments affecting Hispanic utilization of the region's scarce water supplies. The treaty failed to allocate the region's water resources, but effectively divided the region's major watershed, leaving the southern part under Mexican authority and the northern part under the authority of the U.S. states. Its failure to allocate the water of the divided territory and the ambiguity engendered by the mov-

ing boundary of rivers generated conflict that later agreements sought to resolve.

The dominant position of the United States on the major southwestern river systems gave it an upper hand in negotiating water issues with Mexico. In 1906 the waters of the upper Rio Grande were allocated, with less than 10 percent of the upper basin's water, 60,000 acre-feet, awarded to Mexico. Guided by the now-infamous Harmon Doctrine, postulated by then Secretary of State Judson Harmon, the United States as upstream riparian asserted that it had no obligation to share water with Mexico, downstream. The controversial agreement effectively limited the development of Ciudad Juárez and other Mexican communities downstream while supporting the development of El Paso, Texas, and contributing to U.S. agricultural and domestic interests upstream.

Downstream on the Rio Grande, development on both sides of the border was hindered by lack of flood control, the meandering of the river, and the uncertainty of water entitlement. On the Colorado River, the development of upstream dams added urgency to the need to resolve Mexican claims to be able to effectively allocate the river's water among U.S. basin states. Division of the water of the middle and lower Rio Grande and the Colorado was achieved in 1944. The landmark U.S.–Mexico 1944 Water Treaty abandoned the Harmon Doctrine in favor of a more equitable agreement whereby Mexico received 1.5 million acre feet of the Colorado River's estimated 15 million acre-feet average annual flow and roughly two-thirds of tributary water to the middle and lower reaches of the Rio Grande. The 1944 Water Treaty thus secured the water endowment of both countries and provided a sound foundation for needed reclamation, flood control, and hydropower projects on both the Rio Grande and the Colorado River. These projects secured the development of irrigated agriculture in the Mexicali and Imperial valleys and for Mexican and Texas cities and irrigation districts below the confluence of the Rio Conchos, both regions demographically dominated by Hispanic populations.

Policy Issues

United States–Mexico agreement on the allocation of the waters of their major international rivers by the mid-20th century provided a stable foundation for both the development of border agriculture and the growth of border cities and towns. The differential and unequal development of the U.S. and Mexican economies, however, is most evident in this region, much of which is still wracked by poverty and substandard development. On the U.S. side of the border most communities have suffered from limited investment and a preponderantly rural economy. Mexican communities, though better endowed than many of their counterparts in the interior, still lag well behind the United States in basic infrastructure, their capacity stressed by the rapid development of the assembly industries in northern Mexico. The growth and industrialization along the border have generated new pressures on water supplies and water quality in an economically challenged zone. These problems drive today's binational water policy agenda.

The problem of water supply is a matter of both allocation and distribution—both are important for the border's Hispanic communities. At one level, the supply problem is rooted in the 1944 Water Treaty's failure to adequately provide for the binational management of periodic drought. While the treaty provides some guidance for allocating Rio Grande water under short-term drought conditions, it fails to define a key concept, that of extraordinary drought, and fails to stipulate the division of water under very protracted and persistent drought conditions. In the 1990s these shortcomings surfaced as sustained drought in Mexico limited its capacity to deliver to the United States the required volume of treaty water from the Rio Conchos and other Mexican tributaries to the Rio Grande. A diplomatic conflict ensued that has yet to be adequately resolved. Both Mexican and U.S. irrigation districts and municipalities in the middle to lower Rio Grande Valley have experienced periodic water scarcity as a consequence. Diplomatic talks related to the controversy continue.

Rising water demand and drought also limit supply on the Colorado River. Despite severe drought in the Colorado River basin over the past decade, the United States continued to honor its treaty commitment to Mexico. However, upstream competition for water supplies among U.S. basin states has led to a change in river operations by the U.S. Bureau of Reclamation aimed at more efficient utilization of the river's water. Diminished flows to the Colorado River delta threaten the survival of important ecological resources and avian and marine habitat in the Gulf of California, resources that also support fishing and tourism in Mexico. Ecological concerns

are also present along the Rio Grande, particularly the river estuary, where drought and heavy demand on the river upstream have virtually eliminated outflow to the Gulf of Mexico.

Managing groundwater resources is another important challenge for border communities. Many border cities, towns, and farms rely partly or exclusively on groundwater. The U.S.–Mexico water treaties failed to address the division of important groundwater basins straddling the border, an omission that today generates considerable uncertainty concerning this source of supply. The International Boundary and Water Commission (IBWC) has recently undertaken an initiative to reliably chart and define these underground basins but the two countries remain well apart on how to manage these resources.

Distribution problems merge with water quality concerns in yet another area—the availability of water supplies to the irregular border settlements known as *colonias*. These unincorporated settlements, preponderantly Hispanic, have surged as more people are attracted to the border by the twin lures of jobs and cheap land for housing. As many as 15,000 such settlements are located on the Texas side of the Rio Grande alone. Residents often rely on shallow, contaminated wells for water, or, in some instances, on untreated river water. The provision of water infrastructure in the form of potable water and sewerage essential for public health, has proved to be a major challenge for border states and counties. It is now a focus of U.S. federal housing policy as well as concerted state and county efforts to improve water access and quality for *colonias*.

The need to improve border water infrastructure in both countries became a major public issue affecting negotiation of the North American Free Trade Agreement. In a side agreement to the main accord, the United States and Mexico agreed to establish a new set of border institutions with a mandate to support and finance needed water and environment infrastructure in both countries in a manner consistent with the modern goal of sustainable development. Since January 1994 these new institutions, the Border Environment Cooperation Commission (BECC) and the North American Development Bank (NADB), have received numerous proposals and have certified more than 80 projects for development, many eligible for financing through NADB's facility. By 2002 nearly $1 billion had been dedicated to infrastructure projects, nearly half of this in northern Mexico. These projects contribute materially to the betterment of Hispanic communities in the border region but still fall considerably short of needed overall investment, estimated by some at upwards of $20 billion. It is laudable that BECC's project certification requirements stress sustainable development and provide an avenue for the participation and empowerment of Hispanic citizens in the development of local water projects.

Policy Trends

Two recent water management trends are of particular value for Hispanic communities in developing and utilizing water resources in the border area. The first, already mentioned, is the recrafting of approaches to water management under the policy of sustainable development. This trend is evident in recent binational agreements and documents. The sustainable development principle expands and legitimizes the range of stakeholders in water development to better incorporate poor and marginalized communities. The second trend, an emphasis on watershed management, reinforces the first. While watershed management concepts have yet to be incorporated in most aspects of border water policy, they have found their way into recent binational discussions on border water management. While such approaches will not directly lead to solutions to the many water problems facing both countries, they do offer the prospect that solutions reached will better incorporate the diverse range of interests, to include Hispanic citizens on both sides of the border, in resolving problems and making provision for the well-being of the Hispanic community.

RELATED ARTICLES

Acequia System; Agriculture; Border, United States-Mexico.

FURTHER READING

Martínez, Oscar J. *Troublesome Border.* Tucson: Univ. of Ariz. Press, 1988.

Meyer, Michael C. *Water in the Hispanic Southwest.* Tucson: Univ. of Ariz. Press, 1984.

Mumme, Stephen P. *Boundary Briefing: United States-Mexico Boundary.* Durham, U.K.: University of Durham, Boundaries Research Press, 1991.

United States Environmental Protection Agency. *Border 2012: U.S.-Mexico Environmental Program.* Washington, D.C.: USEPA, 2002.

SELECTED WEB SITES

Border Environment Cooperation Commission. *Annual Report, 2002.* www.cocef.org

United States Section, International Boundary and Water Commission, United States and Mexico. *Annual Report, 2002.* www.ibwc.state.gov

STEPHEN P. MUMME

WATTS RIOTS

Less than a week after President Lyndon Johnson signed the Voting Rights Act of 1965, the nonviolent approach of the civil rights movement was disrupted by five days of rioting in the predominantly black neighborhood of Los Angles known as Watts. What had begun in the late afternoon of August 11 as a routine traffic stop of two African American brothers by the Los Angeles police turned into days of uncontrollable violence. Ultimately, peace was restored on the fifth day after Governor Pat Brown ordered in 20,000 national guard troops.

By the time the violence, arson, and looting had ended, 34 people had been killed, 1,000 wounded, 4,000 arrested, and $200 million in damages had been done. At its peak, there were as many as 35,000 people involved in the rioting. The Watts riot was a precursor for violence that would erupt during the remainder of the decade in many black neighborhoods in cities such as Detroit, Michigan; Cleveland, Ohio; Newark, New Jersey; and Chicago.

The Reverend Martin Luther King, Jr., who had advocated a nonviolent approach to the civil rights movement, would later comment that "The firebombs of Watts blasted the civil rights movement into a new phase." Until the Watts riots, black civil-rights demonstrations had been kept within the legal system; the riots ushered in a new awareness that the conditions of poverty and educational inequality were a more formidable foe than the Jim Crow laws of the South had been, because of the harsh realities of urban squalor and despair. Dr. King and his allies were now being challenged by the more militant Stokely Carmichael and Floyd McKissick, who, like Malcolm X, were advocates of "Black Power."

As a result of the violence, Governor Brown named John McCone to head a commission to study the riots. The commission concluded that the riots, even though they appeared to be the acts of common vandals, reflected more serious societal problems such as high rates of joblessness, poor housing condi-

Protesters on the burned-out streets of the Watts district of Los Angeles after the 1965 race riots.

tions, and inadequate schools in the inner cities. Chicanos were now an essential component to the picture and the media began to focus on them as well. President Johnson's Kerner Commission reached the same conclusions about most of the riots occurring in U.S. cities during that era.

The Watts riots and subsequent violence in cities such as Detroit, Michigan, and Newark, New Jersey, led many to believe that the issue was not so much a "black issue" but a condition of America's inner cities. Dr. King himself noted that "This [Watts] was not a race riot. It was a class riot." Reports had confirmed that rioters had left alone whites who were in their path, except for the police. Nearly all of the 34 people killed in the riots were black. Because attention was now focused on the conditions of America's inner cities, the Johnson administration made these areas a target of the War on Poverty legislation that was introduced in Congress. Chicanos were part of the proposed legislation.

Spontaneous violence on a large scale continued to occur in the United States on a fairly frequent basis, including Miami (1980), Los Angeles (1992), Cincinnati (2001), and Benton Harbor, Michigan (2003). In each incident the violence has been set off by a spark relating to alleged police brutality or abuse of power resulting from a history of tension between police and the black community. Most sig-

nificantly, in each case one will find the same conditions of poverty and despair—joblessness, single-parent households, substance abuse, inferior educational opportunity—that existed in South Central Los Angeles at the time of the Watts riots in 1965.

The shift to violence in the civil rights movement had an impact all over the country. In many barrios of the Southwest, Chicano students began to take a more militant view of civil-rights protest. In Los Angeles in March 1968 10,000 students walked out of five East Los Angeles high schools. These events, which lasted several weeks, were called the "blowouts." At its peak the Chicano movement involved thousands of people in Los Angeles, Santa Barbara, Sacramento, and Delano, California; San Antonio, El Paso, and Del Rio, Texas; Las Vegas, New Mexico; and other cities. In Los Angeles, at a National Moratorium Day march in August 1970, 30,000 participants from all 50 states gathered to protest the number of Chicanos that had been killed in the Vietnam War. At least 500 police and sheriff deputies attacked the marchers. Chaos and violence erupted and 30 people were killed, scores were injured, and 400 were arrested by the police; well-known *Los Angeles Times* reporter Rubén Salazar was killed by a tear-gas projectile shot into the Silver Dollar Bar by a police officer. Spontaneous violence erupted in other cities of the Southwest, ushering in more violence in the Chicano movement, much like what had occurred in the black community after the Watts Riots.

RELATED ARTICLES

African Americans, Influence and Relations; Chicano Movement; Civil Rights; Discrimination; Law Enforcement; Los Angeles; Race; Salazar, Rubén.

FURTHER READING

Bullock, Paul, ed. *Watts: The Aftermath; An Inside View of the Ghetto, by the People of Watts.* New York: Grove, 1969.

Clark, Kenneth B. *Dark Ghetto: Dilemmas of Social Power.* 1965. Reprint. Middletown, Conn.: Wesleyan Univ. Press, 1989.

Conot, Robert. *Rivers of Blood, Years of Darkness: The Unforgettable Classic Account of the Watts Riot.* New York: Morrow, 1968.

Crump, Spencer. *Black Riot in Los Angeles: The Story of the Watts Tragedy.* Los Angeles: Trans-Anglo Bks., 1966.

Governor's Commission on the Los Angeles Riots. *Violence in the City—An End or a Beginning?* Los Angeles: 1965.

Sears, David, and John B. McConahay. *The Politics of Violence: The New Urban Blacks and the Watts Riot.* 1973. Reprint. Washington, D.C.: Univ. Press of Am., 1981.

RAYMOND J. GONZALEZ

WEST SIDE STORY

West Side Story, a musical adaptation of Shakespeare's *Romeo and Juliet,* tells the story of star-crossed lovers, Tony and Maria, and is set against a backdrop of New York City streets, immigration, and gang rivalry. The musical, created by Leonard Bernstein (music), Stephen Sondheim (lyrics), and Arthur Laurents (book), opened at New York City's Winter Garden Theater on September 26, 1957.

In 1961 the film version of *West Side Story* was released; it was immediately hailed as a cinematic masterpiece, entering the canon of great American films when it won ten Academy Awards, including best picture. While film critics have often viewed the film as a cautionary tale about urban modernity, the standard interpretations have often omitted considerations of race and ethnicity. As one of the earliest and most prominent works to address the Puerto Rican presence in the United States, *West Side Story* has garnered sometimes contradictory responses from Puerto Ricans and other Latinos.

Even before production had finished, *West Side Story* was a subject of controversy. Spanish-language papers such as *La Prensa* called for the filmmakers to remove some of the more derogatory passages of the film. Of special interest to Latino activists was the song *America,* which, in its stage version, characterized the island of Puerto Rico as a dirty land of tropical disease. The concessions made by lyricist Stephen Sondheim to the demands of Latinos have been described as a move from the derogatory to the ironic by Alberto Sandoval-Sánchez.

Despite the revisions, many Puerto Rican scholars regard *America* as an argument for assimilation. Such a reading emphasizes the words sung by Anita, played by Rita Moreno, who won an Academy Award for the role. Moreno's status as the film's only Puerto Rican actor placed a special burden on her performance. While generations of Latina performers have taken inspiration from Moreno's various talents evident in her portrayal of Anita, others have viewed her as a sellout for giving voice to distasteful sentiments. To evaluate Moreno's performance on the sole basis of *America* fails to account for Anita's later disillusionment with her idealized image of American life and her affirmation of cultural difference. Considering the song as a whole, other Puerto Rican scholars have noted that *America* conveys an ambivalent picture of life in America for immigrants.

America is a term no Puerto Rican would use to refer to the United States, according to Sidney Mintz. The song is thus one more instance of fantasies about Puerto Ricans that proliferate in the film. In *West Side Story,* Puerto Ricans are criminal (if male), victims (if female), devoid of any African composition, eager to colonize urban spaces, and inherently musical (though not in ways related to island musical traditions). If the Jets represent, in their name, a proper urban subject (modern, white, male, blond), the Sharks represent a dark, animalistic threat that is as unreal as the brown makeup George Chakiris donned to portray the Sharks' leader Bernardo or the Spanish accent Natalie Wood affected to be the desirable Maria.

Indeed, Wood's Maria is one of the vehicles through which the film's racial liberalism is exposed as a fraud. Stealing a moment together away from warring gangs and their disapproving families, Tony and Maria sing *Somewhere,* evincing a utopian longing for a "place for us," a place where interethnic and interracial marriages are possible. However, to get to the point where this can even be hinted at, the ethnic subject has to be rendered in Anglo form,

The Jets confront members of the Sharks in a scene from the movie *West Side Story*.

one that loudly betrays itself with a poorly executed accent.

RELATED ARTICLES

Film; Moreno, Rita; Popular Culture; Theater.

FURTHER READING

Garebian, Keith. *The Making of* West Side Story. Toronto: ECW Press, 1995.

Mintz, Sidney. "The Island." In *Puerto Rico Mío: Four Decades of Change*. Ed. by Jack Delano. Washington, D.C.: Smithsonian Inst. Press, 1990.

Negrón-Muntaner, Frances. "Feeling Pretty: *West Side Story* and Puerto Rican Identity Discourses." *Social Text* 18, no. 2 (2000): 83–106.

Sandoval-Sánchez, Alberto. *José, Can You See? Latinos On and Off Broadway*. Madison: Univ. of Wisc. Press, 1999.

WILLIAM ORCHARD

WILLIAMS, WILLIAM CARLOS

Born: September 17, 1883; Rutherford, New Jersey
Died: March 4, 1963; Rutherford, New Jersey

William Carlos Williams is a unique figure in American Latino literature. Rejecting Europe in favor of his native United States, he saw himself in opposition to the ideals of the expatriate poets Ezra Pound and T. S. Eliot. A champion of the American way of life, he was appointed poet laureate consultant at the Library of Congress, but the offer was withdrawn because of his supposed associations with communism. The child of a Puerto Rican mother and an English father, Williams was not considered a Latino writer during his lifetime.

Much of Williams's life was spent in Rutherford, New Jersey, from his birth through 40 years of medical practice until his death. He earned a medical degree from the University of Pennsylvania, was an intern in New York City, and did postgraduate studies at the University of Leipzig. In 1910 he opened a medical practice, which he continued until 1951. He married in 1912 and was the father of two sons. Hardworking in his practice and exacting in his writing, he wrote and published continually from 1909 until his death in 1963.

Williams's poetry displays characteristics of both Romanticism and modernism. An imagist poet, he

© EVE ARNOLD/MAGNUM PHOTOS

Poet William Carlos Williams at his typewriter, 1957.

experimented with new poetic techniques and wrote about the common people with whom he had contact in his medical practice. His writings include poetry, short stories, essays, plays, an autobiography, and novels. Williams received a Dial Award in 1926, a National Book Award in 1950, and two posthumous awards: a Pulitzer Prize and a gold medal from the American Academy of Arts and Letters.

It was in the last decades of the 20th century that Williams was included in the Latino canon, perhaps because of his middle-class origins and his mixed ethnicity. Unlike the Puerto Rican writers Julia de Burgos and Jesús Colón, Williams was not born in Puerto Rico and did not write in Spanish. Critics have stated that Williams sought to hide his Latino heritage, but Julio Marzán, in *The Spanish American Roots of William Carlos Williams* (1994), concludes that Williams "remained true to and forthright about his Latin American roots." His 1917 book of poems was titled *¡Al Que Quire!* (Four Seas), and the fact that he chose to write under his full name argues

against the assumption that he wished to deny his Latino blood. In a 1939 letter Williams commented on his mixed ancestry and expressed his conviction that the United States was the best home for persons of mixed heritage.

Williams's influence continues as later generations discover his writing. By acting as a mentor, he influenced the writing of several young poets, including Denise Levertov and Allen Ginsberg. In *Something to Declare* (1999) the author Julia Alvarez writes of her immediate connection to the syntax of Williams's poem that begins, "So much depends," and how she, also the child of a Spanish-speaking mother, found in Williams's writings an antidote to self-doubt. A selection of works by Williams includes *The Autobiography of William Carlos Williams* (1951); *The Collected Poems of William Carlos Williams, Volume 1, 1909-1939*, edited by A. Walton Litz and Christopher MacGowan (1986); *The Collected Poems of William Carlos Williams, Volume II, 1939-1962*, edited by Christopher MacGowan (1988); and *Paterson* (1963).

RELATED ARTICLES

Alvarez, Julia; Literature; Literature, Puerto Rican on the Mainland.

FURTHER READING

Contemporary Authors. Ed. by James G. Lesniak. New Revision Series. Vol. 34. Detroit: Gale Research, 1991.

Marzán, Julio. *The Spanish American Roots of William Carlos Williams*. Austin: Univ. of Tex. Press, 1994.

SHERRY YORK

WORLD WAR I

Although World War I (1914–1918) involved more nations and resulted in greater destruction than any other war up to that time, its direct impact on Latinos in the United States was limited. The fact that America entered the war quite late, that no fighting took place on U.S. soil, and that relatively few Hispanic U.S. citizens participated in the fighting all lessened the war's effect on Latinos. Nonetheless, U.S. foreign policy toward Latin America in the years immediately preceding and following the conflict, along with the Mexican Revolution (1910–1920), made World War I an important turning point in the history of Latinos in the United States.

During World War I, the United States became Latin America's most important trade partner—a title it has held ever since. The early decades of the 20th century also witnessed a pattern of direct U.S. intervention in Latin American politics that was closely related to increased investments by American companies. Following the Spanish American War (1898), which resulted in Cuba and Puerto Rico becoming U.S. protectorates, but especially after the United States completed construction of the Panama Canal in 1914, successive administrations in Washington adopted a paternalistic attitude toward Latin American governments and people that reflected social Darwinist notions of racial superiority. The most obvious example was President Woodrow Wilson's famous quote, "I am going to teach the South American republics to elect good men!" This culturally pervasive attitude, combined with economic and political security concerns that were heightened during World War I, has been manifested in repeated U.S. military occupations of Caribbean nations, several of which became U.S. protectorates for varying lengths of time.

The United States's economic, diplomatic, and military expansion into the Caribbean in and around the time of the war created more opportunities than ever before for Latin Americans to interact with the United States. For example, the 1917 Jones Act, a law allowing all Puerto Ricans to be considered U.S. citizens, facilitated an increase in the number of Latinos in cities such as Miami, New Orleans, and New York. This was tempered, however, by laws also passed in 1917 that required immigrants to pay head taxes and meet a host of requirements, including passing a literacy exam if older than the age of 16. As a result, the Latino population remained almost exclusively of Mexican descent for years to come. Many had ancestors who had been living in the U.S. Southwest since at least as far back as the 1848 Treaty of Guadalupe Hidalgo, which transferred close to half of Mexico's territory at the time to U.S. control. Sadly, decades of discriminatory practices had dispossessed most Mexican American families of their landholdings and relegated them to agricultural wage labor.

When the Mexican Revolution began, the number of Mexican Americans in the United States already exceeded 500,000. Then, during the decade of fighting, an estimated 1.5 million Mexicans fled to the United States. Many simply sought temporary refuge from the dangers of war, but others were lured northward by labor agents to work on farms and in mines and railroad construction. The wartime economy also created new opportunities for Mexican Americans to obtain higher-paying employment in the war industries. Continued discrimination, however, led many Mexican Americans to join organized labor unions and establish civic groups to assist in their fight for equality. In 1929 several of these groups joined to form the League of United Latin American Citizens (LULAC).

RELATED ARTICLES

Jones Act; League of United Latin American Citizens; Mexican Americans; Military, United States; World War II.

FURTHER READING

Coerver, Don M., and Linda B. Hall. *Tangled Destinies: Latin America and the United States.* Albuquerque: Univ. of N.Mex. Press, 1999.

Holden, Robert H., and Eric Zolov, eds. *Latin America and the United States: A Documentary History.* New York: Oxford Univ. Press, 2000.

Longley, Kyle. *In the Eagle's Shadow: The United States and Latin America.* Wheeling, Ill.: Harlan Davidson, 2002.

Vargas, Zaragosa, ed. *Major Problems in Mexican American History.* Boston: Houghton Mifflin, 1999.

DOUGLAS KEBERLEIN GUTIÉRREZ

WORLD WAR II

World War II (1939–1945) was a time of contradictions for Latinos in the United States. On the one hand, the war effort created new job opportunities that prompted increased migration from south of the border. On the other hand, nativism and racial discrimination counterbalanced advances in political and social equality and underlay incidents such as the famous Zoot Suit Riots in Los Angeles.

The decade preceding World War II was difficult for Latinos in the United States. The Great Depression saw soaring unemployment rates and fostered an anti-immigrant attitude that bordered on hysteria. Residents of Mexican descent were particularly vulnerable, with an estimated 500,000 forcibly deported during the 1930s. Thousands more left voluntarily or were coerced into leaving by government agencies that threatened to withhold welfare aid to families who rejected the offer of transportation to the border.

When the United States entered the war in December 1941, new economic opportunities in fields from agriculture to the defense industry materialized and reversed the outward migratory trend of the Depression era. One of the principal contributors to this shift was the negotiation of an intergovernmental accord (the Bracero Program) between the United States and Mexico in August of 1942. *Braceros,* Mexican laborers granted temporary work permits, were to receive protection under both U.S. and Mexican labor laws regarding work-site safety, living expenses, and wages.

Unfortunately, many *braceros* entered into contracts without fully understanding their rights or realizing that they were required to return to Mexico upon completion of their contracts. As a result, *braceros* not only were frequently abused by employers, they often chose to remain in the United States as illegal immigrants rather than seek legal remedies. Although the program was terminated in 1964, it nonetheless allowed hundreds of thousands of labor-

ers to make their way across the border and incorporate themselves into American society permanently.

Latinos of Mexican descent, although accounting for the vast majority of the Spanish-speaking population in the United States, were not the only Latinos affected by the war. The Puerto Rican population had an unusual relationship with the U.S. government that extended back to the 1917 Jones Act, a law that granted citizenship to all Puerto Ricans but did not incorporate the island politically into the U.S. government. Although Puerto Ricans were free to travel to the United States, prior to the war relatively few islanders immigrated to the mainland permanently. Those that did tended to congregate in New York City. With the start of the war, however, tens of thousands began entering the country annually in search of jobs; this trend continued in

U.S. LATINO AND LATINA WWII ORAL HISTORY PROJECT

Four Latino soldiers during World War II.

the 1950s and 1960s. The result, according to María Pérez y González, was that by 1973 "40 percent of Puerto Rico's population was living in the United States."

Latinos were not only workers during World War II—many joined or were drafted by the American military. An estimated 375,000 Latinos served in the armed forces during World War II. More than 65,000 Puerto Ricans served in the United States armed forces between 1940 and 1946; 200 Puerto Rican women served as linguists in the Women's Army Corps. Other groups are more challenging to identify. Many of the National Guard units and infantry and artillery divisions, regiments, and battalions from California, Arizona, New Mexico, Texas, and Colorado were composed largely of Spanish-speaking personnel. Hispanic servicemen received many commendations and decorations, including 12 Medals of Honor.

Despite the many important contributions Latinos made to the war effort, on the home front the Spanish-speaking population faced widespread intolerance and was often stereotyped as lazy, unpatriotic, and prone to criminality. The most notable example of bigotry against Latinos during World War II is undoubtedly the Los Angeles Zoot Suit Riots. On June 3, 1943, a gang of zoot suit clad Mexican boys roughed up a small group of uniformed servicemen. After newspapers publicized the assault, the following night a group of approximately 200 revenge-seeking sailors began combing Mexican neighborhoods in taxis, jumping out to beat up anyone wearing the signature zoot suit that was so popular among young Mexican Americans at the time. On the third night, the scene repeated itself with the difference that servicemen simply marched through the Mexican sectors wrecking havoc. For the most part, the police turned a blind eye to the attackers but did arrest tens of Mexican boys caught in the fray. The rioting continued for two more days until the military temporarily forbade all servicemen from setting foot in Los Angeles. Even so, not until June 9 did the disturbances finally subside. Ultimately, the Los Angeles City Council responded by passing a law making the wearing of zoot suits a punishable offense.

The prejudice that was the root cause of the Zoot Suit Riots affected Latinos everywhere. Still, any balanced account of the World War II era needs to point out that Hispanics made important gains dur-

ing and because of the war. Latino servicemen were able to take advantage of the G.I. Bill of Rights and receive government assistance for college and the purchase of a home. Latino veterans, armed with a confidence born of their service to country, often became instigators of change and leaders in new movements. For example, in 1949, when a funeral home in Texas refused to bury war veteran Félix Longoria, fellow soldiers and Hispanic community leaders created the American GI Forum, a civil rights and advocacy group for Latino veterans of war. Finally, the visibility of incidents like the Zoot Suit Riots and others prompted government agencies such as the Fair Employment Practices Commission and the Office of the Coordinator of Inter-American Affairs to investigate job discrimination and assist local communities in improving Anglo-Latino relations. It also encouraged a new generation of Latinos to become more directly involved with politics, thus setting the stage for important gains in governmental representation as the 20th century progressed.

RELATED ARTICLES

Bracero Program; Los Angeles; Military, United States; World War I; Zoot Suit Riots.

FURTHER READING

Borgardus, Emory S. "Repatriation and Readjustment." In *The Mexican Americans: An Awakening Minority*. Ed. by Manuel P. Servín. Beverly Hills, Calif.: Glencoe Press, 1970.
González, Juan. *Harvest of Empire: A History of Latinos in America*. New York: Penguin Bks., 2000.
Longley, Kyle. *In the Eagle's Shadow: The United States and Latin America*. Wheeling, Ill.: Harlan Davidson, 2002.
Marden, Charles F., and Gladys Meyer. *Minorities in American Society*. 3d ed. New York: Am. Bk., 1968.
Pérez y González, María E. *Puerto Ricans in the United States*. Westport, Conn.: Greenwood Press, 2000.

SELECTED WEB SITES

The Bracero Program. www.farmworkers.org/bracerop.html
The Hispanic Experience.
    www.houstonculture.org/hispanic/memorial.html

DOUGLAS KEBERLEIN GUTIÉRREZ

WRESTLING

Since the mid-19th century, wrestling has been successfully marketed as a blend of sport, comedy, and theater in different parts of the world, including the United States, Latin America, Europe, and Japan. Although archeological evidence dates the origins of competitive hand-to-hand struggle to Sumerian cul-

A male Hispanic teen arm locks his female opponent during a high school wrestling match.

tures in Mesopotamia, the addition of wrestling troupes to European circuses beginning about 1840 boosted wrestling's popularity and helped bring about the establishment of the first international wrestling leagues. In the early 20th century, competing visions of wrestling's future emerged between promoters who turned profits by rigging matches and advocates of wrestling as a regulated and competitive sport. The former would later effectively control professional wrestling's international development. However, professional wrestling matches were barred from some major U.S. athletic venues into the 1940s owing to the efforts of supporters of wrestling as a sport rather than entertainment.

Although wrestling was popular among some pre-Columbian North and South American indigenous groups, professional wrestling spread to the Americas from Europe. During the early 20th century, professional wrestling pervaded popular culture in Mexico. The Mexican Wrestling Company (EMLL) was founded in 1933, and until the early 1990s it virtually monopolized the commercialization of professional wrestling in the country. Under the EMLL professional wrestling in Mexico developed unique rules and traditions, and it came to be known as Mexican Wrestling, or Lucha Libre. In Spanish *lucha libre* is a common term referring to wrestling in general and as a proper noun alludes specifically to

Mexican Wrestling. Since the 1940s, Mexican professional wrestlers have been featured in comic book and television cartoon series. *El Santo* (The Saint), perhaps the most famous Mexican wrestler of all time, starred in over one hundred movies between the 1950s and the 1970s. In contrast, U.S.-style professional wrestling ("American Wrestling") began to be marketed to a mass audience only in the 1960s. The World Wrestling Federation (WWF), which in 2002 changed its name to the World Wrestling Entertainment (WWE), began to broadcast events on national television in the early 1980s.

Participants in Lucha Libre, called *luchadores,* tend to use more acrobatic, complex, and explicitly choreographed moves than American wrestlers, who often rely more on brawn. As in American Wrestling, Lucha Libre matches are staged between two rival camps: *rudos* (villain-types, akin to American Wrestling's "heels," who attempt to use taunts to elicit animus from the audience), and *técnicos* (hero-types, equivalent to American Wrestling's "faces," who seek to provoke expressions of support from the audience). Whereas one referee presides over American Wrestling matches, two partial officials oversee Lucha Libre contests—one allied with the rudos and the other with the técnicos. Mexican wrestlers' use of masks during practices and matches also conspicuously sets them apart from their American counterparts. Luchadores' sense of honor and identity are symbolized by and partially derived from their masks. The public stripping of the luchadore's mask is considered the greatest shaming he or she can suffer, befalling only losers of the infrequently staged "mask v. mask" contests. The inseparableness of a luchadore's mask and his public image is exemplified by the fact that El Santo never appeared unmasked in any of his movies.

Ultimately, Mexican and American wrestlers alike strive to integrate story lines and displays of out-of-control violence to include their audiences in comedic, yet suspenseful, revel. Talent and charisma, rather than wins and losses, are accepted measures of wrestlers' success. In the United States, Latinos make up a crucial segment of the fan bases of both Mexican and American professional wrestling. *WWE Smackdown* and *WWE Raw Zone* are among the top rated network and cable television programs, respectively, among Hispanic viewers. Several Latino wrestlers have thrived in the WWE, including Eddie Guerrero, who held the WWE Champion title for part of 2004, and Rey Misterio (Mystery King), a successful luchadore in Mexico who has helped popularize quicker, more acrobatic techniques since his July 2002 WWE debut. The U.S. Lucha Libre fan base is also growing and diversifying, especially in southern California. Contemporary Lucha Libre superstars regularly face off in major athletic venues in Los Angeles, San Diego, and Tijuana, Mexico. Amateur leagues often stage matches in smaller, local venues, especially in predominantly Latino neighborhoods. The rising popularity among Latinos and non-Latinos alike of Lucha VaVoom, a take off on Lucha Libre that includes slapstick and burlesque influences and comedic arena announcers, is further proof that Lucha Libre is marketable to a broader American audience.

RELATED ARTICLES

Sports in Latino Life.

FURTHER READING

Mazer, Sharon. *Professional Wrestling: Sport and Spectacle.* Jackson: Univ. of Miss., 1998.

World Sports Encyclopedia. Ed. by Kevin Hagarty. St. Paul, Minn.: MBI Pubs., 2003.

SELECTED WEB SITES

Consejo Mundial de Lucha Libre (World Council of Lucha Libre). www.cmll.com

Roma Pro Wrestling. www.luchalibreusa.com

Triple A. www.triplea.com.mx

Viva La Lucha Libre. www.vivalaluchalibre.net

World Wrestling Entertainment, Inc. www.wwe.com

ADRIAN ALTHOFF

YBARRA-FRAUSTO, TOMÁS

Born: January 22, 1938; San Antonio, Texas

Ybarra-Frausto is an important arts administrator and scholar of Latino art who has lectured and published extensively. His undergraduate work was completed at the University of Texas at Austin in 1960, where he was employed as a folklore archivist. Ybarra-Frausto was awarded his doctorate in Spanish from the University of Washington, Seattle, in 1979, where he had received his master's degree in 1973. Prior to completing his doctorate, he was a public school teacher and an instructor at the University of Washington. Ybarra-Frausto received tenure in the Department of Spanish and Portuguese at Stanford University in 1985 and served as the board chair of the Mexican Museum in San Francisco in 1984–1985. In 1989 he became the associate director for Creativity and Culture at the Rockefeller Foundation, where he worked with the Fellowship Program in the Humanities, directed the Museum's program, and curated cultural projects in Latin America. Domestically, he is in charge of community cultural development programs.

In 1998 Ybarra-Frausto was awarded the Joseph Henry Medal by the Smithsonian Institution for "exemplary contributions" to the institution. The citation noted that as a professor, scholar, and foundation executive, he was devoted to "encouraging diverse communities in the United States to better understand and appreciate each other's art and culture, values, and traditions." Ybarra-Frausto donated his collections of Mexican and Chicano prints to the Smithsonian's National Museum of American Art and donated his archives pertaining to the Chicano movement to the Smithsonian's Archives of American Art. He chaired the Smithsonian Council as well as the Latino Oversight Committee. A member of the National Museum of American History's Latino Initiative Advisory Board, he also served as an adviser to the Smithsonian Institution Traveling Exhibition Service (SITES). Recently he donated his collection of Mexican folk art to the Mexican Fine Arts Center Museum in Chicago.

As a scholar Ybarra-Frausto has made wide-ranging contributions. He was a coeditor of the pioneering anthology *Literatura Chicana: Texto y contexto* (Chicano Literature: Text and Context), published in 1972. In 1977 his influential article on Chicano poetic consciousness appeared in *New Scholar,* fostering a new way of understanding Mexican American esthetics. But he is perhaps best known for *Arte Chicano* (1985), an exhaustive compendium of the literature on Chicano art, coauthored with Shifra Goldman. The frequently cited essay "Rasquachismo: A Chicano Sensibility" (1991) treats good taste within bad taste. And yet it is through his activities with the Rockefeller Foundation and the Smithsonian Institution that Ybarra-Frausto has exerted his greatest influence, benefiting numerous programs and organizations in the United States and Latin America.

RELATED ARTICLES

Art Criticism; Chicano Studies; Museums.

FURTHER READING

Castañeda, Antonia, Tomás Ybarra-Frausto, and Joseph Sommers, eds. *Literatura Chicana: Texto y Contexto.* Englewood Cliffs, N.J.: Prentice-Hall, 1972.

Goldman, Shifra, and Tomás Ybarra-Frausto. *Arte Chicano: A Comprehensive Annotated Bibliography of Chicano Art, 1965–1981.* Berkeley: Chicano Studies Lib. Pubns. Unit, Univ. of Calif., 1985.

Ybarra-Frausto, Tomás. "The Chicano Movement and the Emergence of a Chicano Poetic Consciousness." *New Scholar* 6 (1977): 81–109.

Ybarra-Frausto, Tomás. "Rasquachismo: A Chicano Sensibility." In *Chicano Art: Resistance and Affirmation.* Ed. by Richard Griswold del Castillo, et al. Los Angeles: Wight Art Gallery, Univ. of Calif. at Los Angeles, 1991.

Ybarra-Frausto, Tomás. "Santa Barraza: A Borderlands Chronicle." In *Santa Barraza, Artist of the Borderlands.* Ed. by María Herrera-Sobek. College Station: Tex. A&M Univ. Press, 2001.

RUBEN CORDOVA

YBOR CITY

Ybor City has played a fascinating dual role in both the history of U.S. Latino (mainly Cuban American) labor and in the literary imagination. As one of the first places in the U.S. eastern regions to be dominated by Spanish speakers, Ybor City was a symbol of Caribbean Hispanic culture on the mainland.

In 1884 Henry Plant brought the southern railroad to the western coast of Florida, which established the city of Tampa as the transportation hub of southwest Florida and an industrial island in the largely agrarian Deep South. The region had a long history of Hispanic presence, as far back as the 1528 disembarkation of Alvar Núñez Cabeza de Vaca. In 1885 Vicente Martínez Ybor founded Ybor City in the western sections of Tampa, signaling a new era in the history of Hispanic residence. Among early immigrants from Cuba, political refugees brought with them the dream of Cuban independence from Spain and signaled the political and social consciousness for which Ybor City would become known. The Cuban independence movement gained momentum in 1891, when the poet and politician José Martí made the first of a dozen trips to Ybor City from his exile in the Northeast. In the 1890s Ybor City was a fund-raising center on behalf of Cuban independence.

While outsiders always perceived Ybor City to be a solely Cuban enclave, other immigrant groups also populated the community, including Italians and Spaniards. Hundreds of cigar makers' cottages dotted Ybor City, a powerful manifestation of the American dream of owning one's home. By 1900 over 7,000 Cubans, Spaniards, and Italians—called "Latin" in the local vernacular—had settled in Ybor City and West Tampa and had built the city's infrastructure, including housing, roads, and monuments, and established effective mutual aid societies and modern hospitals, which offered "cradle to grave" health care. The Ybor City cigar industry buoyed Tampa's economy, making the city's name synonymous with cigars. Thousands of *tabaqueros* (cigar workers) sat at benches, rolling millions of premium cigars every year, entertained by *lecturas* (readings). *El lector* (the reader) was selected by fellow workers to read literature, always in Spanish. Workers controlled every phase of the democratic process: they elected readers, paid the readers' salaries, and even selected favorite novels.

In the early decades of the 20th century, doctrines of socialism and anarchism competed against nationalism and capitalism. Turbulent, impassioned struggles marked Tampa's labor movement, while a thriving Spanish-language press supplied residents with myriad newspapers, pamphlets, and books. Labor disturbances erupted frequently, with strikes occurring in 1899, 1901, 1910, 1920, and 1931. The last great strike of 1931 involved the role of the reader. City leaders and factory owners felt that the reader fomented discord. Workers resisted, but they lost the strike; the readers were replaced by the radio precisely at the moment that machines were replacing workers.

The 1931 affair was not only the last great strike, it symbolized the decline of the once great cigar industry devastated by the Great Depression. On the eve of World War II, Ybor City was still almost exclusively Latin, but the war marked a great watershed in its evolution. Hundreds of young Latin Americans volunteered to fight, and their military service opened new horizons of travel, courtship, and education. Finding the community's housing dilapidated, many young returning veterans moved to the new suburbs or the comfortable quarters of West Tampa.

In the 1950s Ybor City underwent a demographic change from a city with a large concentration of skilled laborers to a neighborhood-in-transition, as poor blacks replaced upwardly mobile Latinos. Then in the 1960s federal funding began to exert its influence. Interstate 4 sliced through the community and a massive urban renewal effort was begun, which resulted in the demolition of 700 homes and other structures; Ybor City became one of Tampa's poorest neighborhoods. In the late 1980s, however, the city's heritage once again began to draw new residents.

RELATED ARTICLES

Cuban Americans; Florida; Immigration, Latino; Labor.

FURTHER READING

Greenbaum, Susan. *More Than Black: Afro-Cubans in Tampa.* Gainesville: Univ. Press of Fla., 2002.

Hewitt, Nancy. *Southern Discomfort: Women's Activism in Tampa, Florida, 1880s–1920s.* Urbana: Univ. of Ill., 2001.

Mormino, Gary R., and George E. Pozzetta. "'The Reader Lights the Candle': Cuban and Florida Cigar Workers' Oral Tradition." *Labor's Heritage* 5 (Spring 1993): 4–27.

Mormino, Gary R., and George E. Pozzetta. *The Immigrant World of Ybor City: Italians and Their Latin Neighbors in Tampa, 1885–1985.* Gainesville: Univ. Press of Fla., 1988.

GARY MORMINO

YERBEROS

Yerberos (herbalists) are specialized practitioners of Latino folk medicine who treat folk illnesses and conventional ailments by prescribing and concocting traditional herbal remedies, including teas, baths, and poultices. Besides knowledge of herbal folk medicine, no uniform determinant of who qualifies as a *yerbero* exists in the United States; thus the title's meaning varies depending on the size of the Latino neighborhood and the community's cultural origin. The term *yerbero* can be applied to many individuals, ranging from a person who prescribes and creates herbal cures as an occupation, often operating out of *bótanicas* (retail shops for herbal and other curative remedies), to someone in a Latino neighborhood who has experience treating friends and family with herbal remedies.

Yerberos are part of a hierarchy of Latino folk healers, or curers, that exists, in various forms and incarnations, in all Latin American cultures. At the top of this hierarchy is a healer par excellence such as a *curandero*, shaman, *rezador de los cerros*, or *santero*; these curers are the most revered figures in folk medicine, as they use multiple modalities—many rooted in religion or superstition—to treat illnesses of mind, body, and spirit. The healing powers of these curers are sometimes perceived as gifts from the divine. *Yerberos* belong to a secondary tier of folk healers that includes healers who specialize in a specific area of

medical care, along with *sobadores* (massage therapists), *parteras* (midwives or pediatricians), *pulsadores* (healers who diagnose by reading the pulse), and *hueseros* (bone doctors and chiropractors). While rituals and practices are frequently shared among the various kinds of folk healers, especially in the use of medicinal plants, *yerberos* remain the outstanding authority on herbal remedies.

Studies have determined that 90 percent of Latino folk medicine patients do not utilize the services of preeminent healers like *curanderos*, but rather procure health remedies from specialists among the secondary tier of folk healers, especially *yerberos*. Many Latinos view herbal healers, in contrast to the more mystical and spiritual *curanderos* and other shamanistic curers, as legitimate sources of medical treatment. The use of *yerberos* in the United States is partly attributable to the lack of affordable health care available to Latinos. Even when Latinos do avail themselves of conventional medicine, believers in folk medicine commonly consult *yerberos* also.

Origins of the *Yerbero*

The use of medicinal plants and the existence of herbal healers is not unique to Latino culture—to survive, all civilizations have looked to active substances in native plants to treat and prevent illnesses and diseases. Ethnobotanists believe that primitive herbalists first began to cultivate plants for medicinal use nearly 10,000 years ago. By 2000 B.C. Chinese botanists and Indian adherents of the Ayurvedic practices had compiled encyclopedias of herbal remedies, and, by the first century of the common era, Dioscorides, a doctor traveling with the Roman army, had written *De Materia Medica*, a catalog of nearly 600 medicinal plants now considered a classic in botanical and pharmacological history. By the time of the Spanish conquest of the Americas, European society had already developed an intricate science of herbal healing.

Similarly, the civilizations of pre-Columbian Latin America possessed an expansive pharmacopeoia of about 1,500 efficacious medicinal plants. Many areas of the continent are covered by tropical regions where the absence of cold weather eliminates threats to plant life, for example, insects, herbivorous animals, fungi, and other organisms. Thus, tropical plants live in a fierce environment, causing them to produce chemicals to help them survive. These chemicals give certain plants healing properties.

Understanding and using the plants that possessed these properties became a central part of indigenous cultures; early medicine men such as *yerberos* may have been responsible for discovering and experimenting with these plants. However, few original documents from the ancient Mayan, Aztec, and Inca cultures, or the indigenous civilizations of the Amazon and the Caribbean, survive; thus we are ignorant. Ancient *yerberos* and other curers were the only repositories of indigenous medicinal knowledge, orally transmitting techniques, practices, and remedies.

Highly spiritual, indigenous herbal medicine was inseparably intertwined with religious ceremony and ritual. Disease was caused by the will of deities or the intervention of mystical entities, and therefore no regimen of somatic herbal healing lacked an accompanying psychosomatic spiritual or religious cleansing; for example, to treat skin diseases Aztecs might apply a plaster of crushed leaves from the hairy contribo vine while ceremonially wearing the skin of sacrificial victims to appease Xipe Totec, the god deemed responsible for such an affliction.

Once Europeans arrived in Latin America, a major cultural exchange took place in the area of herbal medicine as scientists and explorers rushed to incorporate the indigenous pharmacopoeia into their own, legitimating the folk practice of *yerberos* while introducing to the Americas new plants and herbs such as chamomile, aloe vera, rosemary, and garlic. The influx of African religion and culture, especially in the Caribbean, also added to the variety and breadth of medicinal plant use in the region. Pressure to acculturate suppressed the supernatural characteristics of traditional indigenous and African folk medicine, extinguishing some practices and philosophies and forcing others to exist under the guise of Catholicism.

Modern Latino *yerberos* are inheritors to the herbal pharmacopoeias and medicinal philosophies of both the indigenous and European societies that slowly meshed into the hybrid mestizo culture of postconquest Latin America, and many also incorporate traditional African elements that heavily influenced regions such as the Caribbean. Whereas many other Latino folk healers, such as *curanderos,* maintain a rigid connection between the somatic and the spiritual or mystical facets of their practices, to varying degrees *yerberos'* herbal treatments may be divorced from magical and spiritual remedies. This is less common among Latino herbalists of Caribbean origin, where the herbal and the spiritual remain more strongly intertwined.

Techniques Used by *Yerberos*

The contemporary *yerberos'* principal job as specialists in herbal medicine is to restore harmony and balance to the minds and bodies of their patients through a combination of internally ingested and externally applied herbal remedies. Modern medicine has occasionally dismissed their techniques, along with those of other folk practitioners, as providing their patients with only a psychological benefit, similar to that of the placebo. However, Latino herbalists' practices and diagnoses have successfully treated illnesses and diseases for thousands of years because of five principal benefits of *yerbero* healing:

(1) presence of alkaloids, an organic base, in some medicinal plants;

(2) factors of nourishment received from wild plants;

(3) tonic effects of plants taken over long period of time;

(4) synergistic effects of plants taken in combination; and finally,

(5) psychological effects of participating in a traditional healing procedure.

In Latino folk medicine, illness stems from an imbalance between hot and cold principles within the body. According to *yerberos,* a person can be beset by an imbalance of hot and cold literally through exposure to extreme temperature or, as with some folk illnesses such as *susto* (shock), via severe emotional stress. "Hot" illnesses include afflictions such as hypertension, diabetes, acid indigestion, *susto,* and *mal ojo* (evil eye) and are characterized by vasodilation and high metabolic rate; "cold" illnesses are menstrual cramps, pneumonia, colic, *coryza, frío de la matriz* (cold uterus), and *empacho* (locked bowels), all characterized by vasoconstriction and low metabolic rate. *Yerberos* will treat "cold" illnesses with "hot" plants, often bitter-tasting herbs that contain alkaloids, and "hot" illnesses with "cold" medicinal plants, mostly nourishing and refreshing herbs that lack alkaloids and act as natural diuretics.

While regional variations exist among the herbal remedies that *yerberos* prescribe, most operate with a core group of plants and herbs: chamomile, peppermint, eucalyptus, ginger, papaya, annatto, and aloe vera. These and other medicinal plants are commonly used as treatment for both folk illnesses and mild con-

PARK STREET / PHOTOEDIT

Panaderia and *yerberia* with a mural painted near the entrance in east Austin, Texas.

ventional ailments. *Yerberos* will relieve the stress and insomnia of *susto* with tea infused with chamomile, an herb with a sedative effect, and extract the oil of peppermint, *la yerba buena* (the good herb), to use as an antispasmodic on the muscles of the digestive tract for treating colic, diarrhea, and stomach aches. If a patient is a believer in the spiritual elements of Latino folk medicine, some *yerberos* will recommend the services of a *curandero* or other folk healer in addition to herbal treatment, especially for the more supernatural folk illnesses such as *mal ojo*.

Public health agencies have warned patients of *yerberos* to be cautious with herbal treatments. Many of the plants used in Latino folk medicine have not been examined by modern science, and the incorrect dosage of some of the *yerberos*' most commonly used remedies can be fatal, especially for children and the elderly. Health officials are also concerned that Hispanics may seek the help of *yerberos* for diseases more appropriately treated by conventional medicine. *Yerberos* in the United States will generally treat mild illnesses by prescribing herbal remedies, but will advise patients with more severe problems to utilize modern health care. Many Latinos move freely from herbal folk healing to modern medicine depending on the seriousness of their illness.

Validity of *Yerberos* in the United States

While the herbal remedies prescribed by *yerberos* are folk remedies specifically developed to address the folk illnesses of Latino American culture, pharmaceutical companies have already begun to realize that within the Latino herbalists' palette of medicinal plants and herbs lie many safe and effective treatments for a multitude of illnesses and diseases—from the common cold to the AIDS virus. Medicinal plants from the Latino folk pharmacopoeia that have been adopted by modern medicine include diosgenin, a source of cortisone for use against rheumatoid arthritis, sciatica, dermatitis, and Addison's disease, and the herb *sosa,* a natural antibiotic.

In addition, medical experts are currently considering the importance of *yerberos*' herbal remedies, including those self-administered by Hispanic families across the United States without consulting a professional *yerbero,* as one potential explanation for the so-called Latino epidemiological paradox; the paradox, a phenomenon confirmed through various studies, exists because Hispanics have been shown to experience better overall health than non-Hispanic whites, despite living with higher risk factors such as less access to health care, lower income, and less education.

The presence of *yerberos* in Latino communities also serves several functions that relate to Latino culture and acculturation. While the specific way Latino herbalists function has changed since the craft was brought to the United States, contemporary *yerberos*' work provides a continuity of traditional functions that helps maintain communities' familiarity with and faith in folk medicine, an important element of Latino culture. A *yerbero*'s success in treating a folk illness such as *susto* or *mal ojo* with herbal remedies vindicates traditional Hispanic forms of medicine and systems of belief, reinforcing ethnic and cultural identity. In addition, modern science's success in producing empirical evidence of the efficacy of many of the *yerberos*' traditional medicinal plants gives the herbalists' ancient techniques an air of modern authority that legitimizes the practice of folk medicine. Serving as a functional bridge between Latino folk culture and modern health care, *yerberos* keep their patients' minds and bodies healthy while reinforcing and spreading an important part of Latino culture and identity.

RELATED ARTICLES

Botánicas; Curanderismo; Health; Medicine.

FURTHER READING

Applewhite, Steven Lozano. "Curanderismo: Demystifying the Health Beliefs of Elderly Mexican Americans." *Health and Social Work* 20 (1995): 247–253.

Benedetti, María. *Earth and Spirit: Medicinal Plants and Healing Lore from Puerto Rico.* Orocovis, P.R.: Verde Luz, 1998.

DeStefano, Anthony M. *Latino Folk Medicine: Healing Herbal Remedies from Ancient Traditions.* New York: Ballantine, 2001.

Kidwell, Clara S. "Aztec and European Medicine in the New World, 1521–1600." In *The Anthropology of Medicine: From Culture to Method.* Ed. by Lola Romanucci-Ross, et al. New York: Praeger, 1983.

Neff, Nancy. *Folk Medicine in Hispanics in the Southwestern United States.* Baylor College of Medicine: Hispanic Health. www.rice.edu/projects/HispanicHealth/Courses/mod7/mod7.html

Press, Irwin. "Urban Folk Medicine: A Functional Overview." *American Anthropologist* 80 (1978): 71–74.

ADAM JUDE GONZALES

YOUNG LORDS. *See* PUERTO RICAN YOUNG LORDS.

YZAGUIRRE, RAÚL

Born: July 22, 1939; San Juan, Texas

Raúl Humberto Yzaguirre is among the most respected contemporary Hispanic civil rights leaders in the United States. He is the founder, president, and chief executive officer of the National Council of La Raza (NCLR), the nation's largest constituency-based national Hispanic organization (with 4 million members) and its leading Latino "think tank," located in Washington, D.C. (he stepped down in 2004). For over 25 years, Yzaguirre has fought for better economic and political opportunities for Latinos, gaining recognition as a lobbyist and mediator between corporations and Latino-service organizations. In a 2003 address to the Congressional Hispanic Caucus Institute (CHCI), he posited that "Latinos are not only about demanding our rights, but also about fully preparing to shoulder our responsibilities."

Yzaguirre began his political career at age 15. He organized the American GI Forum Juniors, an auxiliary of the American GI Forum veterans' organization, founded in 1948 by Hector P. García to promote civil rights for Latinos. After completing high school, Yzaguirre joined the U.S. Air Force Medical Corps for four years. In 1964 he established the National Organization for Mexican American Services (NOMAS). Yzaguirre graduated from George Washington University in 1968 with a bachelor of science degree and was hired by the U.S. Office of Economic Opportunity (OEO) to become a program analyst for the Migrant Division. In 1969 he founded the Interstate Research Associates (IRA), the first Hispanic consulting firm in the country, which he built into a multimillion-dollar project.

While the NCLR serves primarily Mexican Americans, Yzaguirre has sought to incorporate other Latino national groups, including Cuban Americans as well. His strategies have not always worked and he has been involved in confrontations with other Latino organizations, among them the Cuban American National Foundation. His populist style and his alliance with African American leaders also have made him a target of criticism.

From 1989 to 1990, Yzaguirre served as the first Hispanic fellow of the Institute of Politics at the John Kennedy School of Government at Harvard University and is a member of the Council on Foreign Relations. A guest lecturer at the University of Notre Dame and the University of Texas, he has received five honorary degrees from various universities. His civil rights career extends across the U.S.–Mexico border; in 1998 he met with Mexican president Ernesto Zedillo at the official residence of Los Pinos to discuss Latino immigration and health care, education, human rights, and development in Hispanic communities in the United States.

Yzaguirre served on President Bill Clinton's Advisory Commission on Educational Excellence for Hispanic Americans and was president of the Mexican-American Solidarity Foundation. He has testified in federal hearings on numerous occasions on behalf of Latinos on topics such as ethnic and racial profiling in law enforcement and immigration policy. Among the awards and honors given him are the Rockefeller Award for Outstanding Public Service from the Trustees of Princeton University (1979), the Order of the Aztec Eagle from the Mexican government (1993), the Hubert H. Humphrey Civil Rights Award from the Leadership Conference on Civil Rights (1993), and the Charles Evan Hughes Gold Medal Award for courageous leadership from the National Conference for Community Justice.

RELATED ARTICLES

Chicano Movement; Civil Rights; National Council of La Raza; Raza Unida Party, La.

FURTHER READING

Gómez–Quihnonez, Juan. *Chicano Politics: Reality and Promise, 1940–1990.* Albuquerque: Univ. of N.Mex. Press, 1990.

National Council of La Raza. *The Road to Equality: 25 Years of Commitment.* Washington, D.C.: 1993.

Villarreal, Roberto E., and Norma G. Hernández, eds. *Latinos and Political Coalitions: Political Empowerment for the 1990s.* Westport, Conn.: Greenwood Press, 1991.

Yzaguirre, Raúl. *Cinco Años Después: A Preliminary Critique of the Sixteen Point/Spanish Speaking Program Five Years.* Washington, D.C.: National Council of La Raza, 1976.

SELECTED WEB SITE

National Council of La Raza. http://www.nclr.org/

ARCELA NUÑEZ–ALVAREZ

ZAPATA, EMILIANO

Born: 1879; Anenecuilco, Morelos, Mexico
Died: April 10, 1919; Chinameca, Morelos, Mexico

Emiliano Zapata's legendary status among people in the United States, especially Mexican Americans, is a testament to his enduring power as a revolutionary figure. Known to Americans as a bandit but to Mexicans as a war hero, he was born in the southern Mexican village of Anenecuilco, Morelos, in 1879 to a relatively prosperous, landed peasant family. Zapata observed from a young age the encroachment of the region's booming sugar *hacienda* (plantation) economy on the lands of villagers and independent farmers. Although he was never poor, Zapata empathized with the plight of people deprived of their traditional livelihoods by the haciendas' expansion.

From his 1909 election as president of the Anenecuilco village council until his 1919 murder in Chinameca, Morelos, by soldiers loyal to the government of Venustiano Carranza, Zapata unwaveringly championed traditional land and water rights in the countryside. Beginning in March 1911, Zapata led a series of armed rebellions in Morelos with considerable rural popular backing, in an attempt to bring agrarian reform to the region. At first Zapata allied his forces, called "Zapatistas," with an offensive headed by Francisco Madero in northern Mexico that aimed to force President Porfirio Díaz's resignation. When Madero took power, however, he did not make agrarian reform a top priority, and in November 1911 Madero and Zapata became sworn enemies.

The Plan de Ayala, signed by Zapata and a group of advisers that same month, established the goals of their struggle against local and central government authority.

To cope with federal forces that sought to repress them, Zapata's army often engaged in guerrilla warfare. The harsh, bloody repression of civilians by federal forces stimulated popular resentment and helped to swell the Zapatistas' ranks. By the end of 1914 Zapata had overseen a sweeping agrarian reform in Morelos and solidified his control over large portions of neighboring states as well. Although Zapata was popular in the territories he controlled, Mexico City elites generally loathed him, and in many other areas indifference to Zapata's Plan de Ayala prevailed. Unable to benefit greatly from alliances with Francisco "Pancho" Villa or other groups, the Zapatista revolt remained essentially regional in scope and lost ground to federal forces between 1916 and 1919.

Meanwhile, Mexico City's conservative press labeled Zapata "The Attila of the South" and blamed him for real and imagined atrocities. Villa, the leader of an armed revolt against Carranza's government in northern Mexico, allied militarily with the Zapatistas in 1914 and was portrayed in news headlines as Zapata's accomplice in crime and terror, "The Centaur of the North." Nonetheless, Mexico's post-1920 presidents have tended to depict Zapata in a positive light to shore up rural support and legitimize official "revolutionary" policies. In the 1920s national and local officials began to organize annual celebrations

Emiliano Zapata, leader of the agrarian rebels in South Mexico, 1913.

to commemorate Zapata's death, featuring speeches and cultural productions such as music, *corridos* (narrative songs), and art displays. Beginning in the 1930s the government widely disseminated school texts depicting Zapata as a Mexican patriot and a martyr for social justice, and in 1940 Zapatista veterans founded an organization, Frente Zapatista, to build Zapata's reputation nationally.

Today, many Mexican American communities celebrate Zapata's legacy. Since at least the 1940s Mexican immigrants to the United States have viewed Zapata as an example of resistance to oppression and as an embodiment of Mexico's nationhood. The bracero program, coordinated by the Mexican and U.S. governments to replace laborers drafted into the U.S. military during World War II, was an impor-tant source of immigration from rural Mexico at a time when state-sponsored agrarian programs were being carried out in Zapata's name. The memory and myth of Zapata have been celebrated by non-Latinos as well, as evidenced by the 1952 movie *Viva Zapata* written by John Steinbeck and starring Marlon Brando. Zapata has also been the subject of numerous theatrical productions in the United States.

Tierra y Libertad (Land and Freedom) has been the battle cry of most protesters who have invoked Zapata's name since 1919, even though Zapata himself preferred the less catchy "Reform, Liberty, Justice and Law." Mexican Americans working in agriculture have identified parallels between their hardships and Zapata's drive for agrarian reform. Striking grape workers in California in the 1960s led by César Chávez and the United Farm Workers (UFW) regularly invoked Zapata's name. The memory of Zapata has also influenced urban Latinos, even though Zapata in his time exhibited a singular dislike for everything urban. Informed by African Americans' struggles for civil rights, Chicano and Chicana student activists in the 1960s emphasized language, heritage, and ethnic contributions to urge Chicanos/as to take action to demand their rightful place in U.S. society. Many such activists looked to Mexican rebels Zapata and Villa and Cuban revolutionary Ché Guevara as models for antiestablishment action.

In 1994 the peasant uprising in Chiapas, southern Mexico, brought new attention to Zapata. He was the inspiration of the EZLN, a neo-Zapatista movement led by the enigmatic Subcomandante Marcos, who always appeared in public in a ski mask. In communiqués and through iconography, Zapata became the recognized ideological forefather of the uprising, reincarnated yet again in another popular rebellion. This legacy is likely to remain in the foreseeable future as disenfranchised *campesinos* in Mexico and Central America respond to the dismal conditions in which they live. The ubiquitous presence of Zapata's image on murals and posters and tee shirts, especially in predominantly Latino neighborhoods, serves as a reminder that Zapata has evolved into more than merely an icon of political action or rebellion. In the United States, Zapata has become a symbol of a people.

RELATED ARTICLES

Mexican Americans; Mexican Revolution; Mexico; Villa, Francisco.

FURTHER READING

Hayden, Tom, ed. *The Zapatista Reader.* New York: Thunder's Mouth Press/Nation Bks., 2002.

Lynn Stephen. *Zapata Lives! Histories and Cultural Politics in Southern Mexico.* Berkeley: Univ of Calif. Press, 2002.

Stavans, Ilan. "Unmasking Marcos." In *The Essential Ilan Stavans.* New York: Routledge, 2000.

Womack, John, Jr. *Zapata and the Mexican Revolution.* New York: Knopf, 1969.

ADRIAN ALTHOFF

ZOOT SUIT RIOTS

On the night of June 3, 1943, 11 white sailors walking along Main Street in East Los Angeles, California, alleged that they were jumped and beaten by a gang of Mexican American youths dressed in zoot suits (a clothing style distinguished by broad-rimmed hats, baggy pants tapered closely at the ankle, oversized coats, and gold watch chains hanging from the pockets). The sailors suffered only a few minor injuries, but officers of the Los Angeles Police Department (LAPD) responding to the call dubbed themselves the Vengeance Squad and arrived at the scene seeking to cleanse the area of what they viewed as the loathsome influence of zoot suit gangsters. The following day, more than 200 members of the navy hired a caravan of at least 20 taxicabs and set out for East Los Angeles. When sailors in the lead car spotted a young Mexican American in a zoot suit, a signal was sent to the rest of the procession and the boy was beaten. Violence against Mexican Americans and African Americans, many wearing zoot suits but others not, continued for the next four days and nights. Anglo soldiers and marines soon joined sailors to block sections of city streets, raid places of business, and form posses searching to beat zoot suiters, strip them of their clothes, and leave them humiliated in front of gathering crowds of onlookers.

These so-called Zoot Suit Riots were partly a result of increasing xenophobia in the United States during World War II. As the country fought fascism overseas, many Americans sought to eradicate anything or anyone thought to be subversive to the war effort. Like the thousands of Japanese Americans who were forced into internment camps following the bombing of Pearl Harbor, zoot suiters were perceived as a threat to the stability of the home front, patriotism, and national unity. Moreover, because zoot suiters openly valued leisure and recreation when most Americans expected young people to work in war industries or the armed forces, they were often characterized as juvenile delinquents.

Hostility against zoot suiters, often known as pachucos, was further fueled by their challenge to popular ideas that American race identity was fundamentally white. Although there was conflict among zoot suiters of different ethnic backgrounds over style, boyfriends or girlfriends, and neighborhood turf, they also publicly confronted the racial segregation of wartime America. The Central Avenue district in Los Angeles, for example, attracted Mexican American, African American, Filipino, Japanese American, and white youths who frequented jazz performances, patronized clothing shops, or simply checked out the latest fashions. When black, brown, yellow, and white youths joined on the dance floor in the fast-paced twists and turns of the Lindy Hop or jitterbug, for example, the sexual and interracial implications of their behavior temporarily suspended Jim Crow segregation and sparked fears of miscegenation.

The zoot suit's flamboyance also contrasted sharply with ideals of wartime manhood and womanhood. American sailors, in their all-white, tight fitting, starched uniforms, were seen as heroic and patriotic, while zoot suiters were deemed lazy and unpatriotic. Young Mexican American women, many of whom were employed in war industries themselves, had their own version of zoot style, including very short dresses, long socks, and heavy make-up. Streetwise *pachucas,* or *slick chicks,* as they were commonly termed, thus challenged popular images of wartime women who exalted the image of "Rosie the Riveter" as a dedicated factory worker dressed in heavy-duty work clothes helping to produce war materials.

Combined with the infamous Sleepy Lagoon Case in 1942, several minor rumbles between zoot suiters and sailors in the spring of 1943 and months of sensational criminalization of zoot suiters as diseased drug users in the mainstream press took racial tension in Los Angeles to an all-time high. It was not long before the city exploded in violence. Although no one was killed during the Zoot Suit Riots, countless zoot suiters were injured and scores were arrested while most servicemen went unpunished. Everyone wearing the flashy zoot garb, including Mexican Americans, African Americans, Filipinos, and even some white youths, were targets of wild mobs of Anglo servicemen. Zoot suiters did fight back, however, and some even organized trips to military bases as far away as San Diego in hopes of fighting with ser-vicepeople.

Most of the violence, however, was committed by white servicemen against Mexican American youth and supported by the rest of the city. The LAPD and the navy's shore patrol did little to discourage the rioting, and some officers refused to stop the beatings, congratulated the assailants, and participated in the abuse of zoot suiters. Witnesses also noted police cars and motorcycle officers escorting taxis full of sailors looking for zoot suiters through Mexican American neighborhoods. Finally, after several days, naval and army authorities restricted enlisted men from the city to end the violence. City officials expressed support for the police and armed forces, discounted race discrimination as a factor in the uprising, and claimed the disturbances were caused by local gangs. The city council even considered a proposal making it a jailable offense to wear a zoot suit within city limits, and the U.S. Department of Justice outlawed the manufacture and sale of zoot suits on the grounds that the material used was in violation of orders to conserve fabric by the War Production Board.

Within days of the riots in Los Angeles, Mexican American and African American zoot suiters were attacked in San Diego, Detroit, Baltimore, and Philadelphia, foreshadowing race riots in New York, Detroit, and the American South later in the summer. Across the United States, violence against zoot suiters illuminated how the racial boundaries of American identity were viciously contested and how the experiences of America's many ethnic and racial groups were intertwined. Perhaps most important, the riots illustrated how seemingly powerless youths of color played a central role in debates about race and gender in World War II America. Often considered a part of Mexican American or California history, the Zoot Suit Riots were ultimately a multiracial phenomenon that holds resonance for much of U.S. history.

RELATED ARTICLES

Discrimination; Fashion; Law Enforcement; Los Angeles; Pachuco; Sleepy Lagoon Case.

FURTHER READING

Alvarez, Luis. "Zoot Violence on the Home Front: Race, Riots, and Youth Culture During World War II." In *Mexican Americans and World War II*. Ed. by Maggie Rivas-Rodriguez. Austin: Univ. of Tex. Press, 2005.

Cosgrove, Stuart. "The Zoot-Suit and Style Warfare." *History Workshop Journal* 18 (autumn 1984): 77–91.

Daniels, Douglas Henry. "Los Angeles Zoot: Race 'Riot,' The Pachuco, and Black Music Culture." *The Journal of African American History* 87, no. 1 (Winter 2002): 98–117.

Escobar, Edward J. *Race, Police, and the Making of a Political Identity: Mexican Americans and the Los Angeles Police Department, 1900–1945*. Berkeley: Univ. of Calif. Press, 1999.

Mazón, Mauricio. *The Zoot-Suit Riots: The Psychology of Symbolic Annihilation*. Austin: Univ. of Tex. Press, 1984.

SELECTED WEB SITE

PBS. "Zoot Suit Riots." *American Experience.* www.pbs.org/wgbh/amex/zoot/index.html

LUIS ALVAREZ

ZORRO

A fictitious border superhero—a Robin Hood of sorts—active in California in the 19th century, Don Diego de la Vega, better known as Zorro (in Spanish, the word means fox) is a ubiquitous mythical character in folklore, literature, and film.

Zorro's first appearance in literature dates back to August 8th, 1919. Johnston McCulley, a police reporter, born in Ottawa, Illinois, in 1883 but residing in Southern California, published a long series of pulp novels about the life and adventures of Don Diego de la Vega. The first episode, *The Curse of Capistrano,* appeared in the pulp magazine *All Story Weekly,* on August 19, 1919. The protagonist quickly became a favorite and McCulley's 65 novels, under different titles, continued to be published until March 1949.

The action in McCulley's novels takes place in a romanticized Alta California, but since there are no historical or cultural references, except mentioning the missions, it is difficult to establish the actual period when the action takes place. McCulley characterizes Don Diego as a young *criollo* of pure Spanish blood, a member of an aristocratic, well-to-do Californio family. At night Don Diego transforms himself into a daredevil who, on horseback and wearing a mask, black dress, hat, and cape; blandishing a sword or a black whip; and wearing a pistol that he seldom uses, rides throughout the town protecting and avenging the common people from the injustices of the tyrannical local authorities.

If his physical appearance is hardly changed from day to night, with the exception of dressing in black and wearing a mask, his character undergoes a com-

A young boy dressed up as Zorro, 1960.

plete change, from an idle young man into the protector of the underdogs, who are mostly Mexicans and mestizos. This formula was very successful, as Zorro is not fighting Americans, but Spanish or Mexican government tyrants. Since McCulley, it has been said, wrote for money, he could not have his hero fighting Americans.

Indeed, what John Rollin Ridge (*Yellow Bird*) did in terms of fame for an earlier popular hero with his novel *The Life and Adventures of Joaquín Murieta, the Celebrated California Bandit* (1854), McCulley was to do with Zorro. Hollywood immediately adapted McCulley's hero to the screen, producing films in which the part of Zorro was played by the famous actors Douglas Fairbanks, Sr., and Tyrone Power, while a film about Joaquín was not made until 1936 (*The Robin Hood of El Dorado*); it was based on the 1932 novel of Walter Noble and starred Warner Baxter as Joaquín.

The first film, *The Mark of Zorro*, produced in 1920 with Fairbanks in the leading role, made Zorro known throughout the world. *The Mark of Zorro* referred to the letter Z that Zorro made with his sword on the body of the tyrants he fought, always defeating them. Zorro's fame became international, and several Zorro films were made in Italy and Mexico. During the 1950s Walt Disney Studios made a very popular Zorro series for television, and made millions with Zorro merchandise, as Zorro had become America's most popular hero, with boys everywhere playing Zorro, wearing masks and carrying wooden swords.

Ridge's novel was soon plagiarized and then imitated by several pulp novelists, among them Llewellyne Williams (*Joaquín, the Claude Duval of California, or the Marauder of the Mines,* 1865), Joseph E. Badger (*Joaquín, the Saddle King,* 1881) and others, who must have inspired McCulley to create his hero.

There are differences between the two popular characters. The action in the Zorro novels takes place when the sword was still a self-defense weapon. This tradition dates back to Spain's Golden Age period, when the most famous plays were those called *de capa y espada* (cloak and sword). More important is the fact that Murieta was a mythified historical person, while Zorro is mostly fiction.

A great difference is the fact that Zorro wears a mask, a feature that has influenced more recent movie heroes, among them The Lone Ranger, Batman, and Spiderman. The mask is an important aspect of the mythical hero for other reasons as well. It is a fixture in Mexican art and mythology. Modern authors from Samuel Ramos to Alfonso Reyes, Octavio Paz, Carlos Fuentes, and Ilan Stavans have analyzed its historical and psycho-sociological role. The fact that Don Diego de la Vega uses a mask to hide his public identity suggests a superimposition of identities. Other Mexican superheroes (the majority of whom are wrestlers), such as El Santo and Super Barrio, also use the mask to bring about social justice.

Besides other novels, influences on McCullen may have come from some California historical events. Two people have been mentioned as models for Zorro: José María Ávila and Salomón Pico. In 1833, under Vice President Valentín Gómez Farías, Mexico instituted drastic radical reforms, one of which was the secularization of the California missions and the expropriation of their lands. To see that the law was enforced, the Mexican government sent Lieutenant Colonel Manuel Victoria to California with some soldiers to make Californios comply with the law and not go back to their religious traditions. Victoria was opposed by a group of Californios, among whom was the daring young José María Ávila, who faced and defeated Victoria in a single combat. He became a hero among Californios, and may have served McCulley as a model for his Zorro.

The other possible model, Salomón Pico, was the feared stagecoach robber brother of Pío Pico, the last governor of Mexican Alta California. He was known to hide in the hills near Orcutt, as the result of which they were named Solomon Hills, a misspelling of Pico's first name. Since Pico was active during the 1850s (he was born in Salinas in 1821),

defending Mexicans against Americans, in order to use him McCulley would have had to change the period of his action from the Mexican independent period to the earlier Spanish colonial one. He did not want his hero to fight Americans.

In Hollywood and beyond, actors who have portrayed the character of Zorro include, besides Fairbanks and Power, Alain Delon (*Zorro*, directed by Duccio Tessari, 1976); George Hamilton (*Zorro: The Gay Blade*, directed by Peter Medak, 1981); and, in 1998, Antonio Banderas. There has also been a television cartoon about Don Diego de la Vega, as well as pornographic movies. The Banderas vehicle is of special interest. Released in 1998, under the direction of Martin Campbell, with Anthony Hopkins and Catherine Zeta-Jones, this new incarnation had important variants. The Banderas model in *The Mask of Zorro*, Alejandro Murieta, is not an idle *criollo*, like McCulley's character, but a Mexican mestizo, brother of Joaquín, who also appears in the film.

As in Ridge's novel, Captain Love, a historical character, kills Joaquín, but under different circumstances. The old Zorro, who gives him his mask (thus the title of the movie) trains Alejandro. The villains are supported by Enrique Montero, the last Spanish governor of California. In order to bring these two Zorros together, liberties are taken with dates and history. But Banderas's film, like the early ones, is fiction, not history—and it was produced to entertain, as were the old pulp novels at the turn of the century. One might even suggest that what the old pulp serials were to the pre–World War I audience, Hollywood movies are today: sheer escapism, using the past only as their springboard.

RELATED ARTICLES

Film; Folklore, Mexican American; Literature; Stereotypes and Stereotyping; Television.

FURTHER READING

Lie, Nadia. "Free Trade in Images? *Zorro* as Cultural Signifier . . ." *Nepantla* 2, no. 3 (2001): 489–508.

Lauria, Frank. *The Mask of Zorro*. A Novelization. New York: Minstrel Bks., 1998.

McCulley, Johnston. *The Mark of Zorro*. New York: Tom Doherty Assoc., 1998.

Yenne, Bill. *The Legend of Zorro*. Greenwich, Conn.: Brompton Bks., 1991.

LUIS LEAL

ENCYCLOPEDIA LATINA

History, Culture, and Society In the United States

Appendix I
Primary Documents

THE LAWS OF BURGOS; 1512–1513

Whereas, the King, my Lord and Father, and the Queen, my Mistress and Mother (may she rest in glory!), always desired that the chiefs and Indians of the Island of Española be brought to a knowledge of our Holy Catholic Faith, and, Whereas, they commanded that certain ordinances be drawn up, which were indeed drawn up, by their Highnesses, as well as, at their command, by the Comendador Bobadilla and the Comendador Mayor de Alcántara, former governors of the said Island, and afterward by Don Diego Columbus, our Admiral, Viceroy, and Governor of it, and by our officers who reside there, and,

Whereas, it has become evident through long experience that nothing has sufficed to bring the said chiefs and Indians to a knowledge of our Faith (necessary for their salvation), since by nature they are inclined to idleness and vice, and have no manner of virtue or doctrine (by which Our Lord is disserved), and that the principal obstacle in the way of correcting their vices and having them profit by and impressing them with a doctrine is that their dwellings are remote from the settlements of the Spaniards who go hence to reside in the said Island, because, although at the time the Indians go to serve them they are indoctrinated in and taught the things of our Faith, after serving they return to their dwellings where, because of the distance and their own evil inclinations, they immediately forget what they have been taught and go back to their customary idleness and vice, and when they come to serve again they are as new in the doctrine as they were at the beginning, because although the Spaniard who accompanies them to their village, as is there ordered, reminds them of it and reprehends them, they, having no fear of him, do not profit by it and tell him to leave them in idleness, since that is their reason for returning to their said village, and that their only purpose and desire is to do with themselves what they will, without regard for any virtue, and,

Whereas, this is contrary to our Faith, and,

Whereas, it is our duty to seek a remedy for it in every way possible, it was considered by the King, my Lord and Father, and by several members of my Council and by persons of good life, letters, and conscience, and they, having informed themselves from others who had much knowledge and experience of the affairs of the said Island, and of the life and customs of the said Indians, gave it as their opinion that the most beneficial thing that could be done at present would be to remove the said chiefs and Indians to the vicinity of the villages and communities of the Spaniards—this for many considerations—and thus, by continual association with them, as well as by attendance at church on feast days to hear Mass and the divine offices, and by observing the conduct of the Spaniards, as well as the preparation and care that the Spaniards will display in demonstrating and teaching them, while they are together, the things of our Holy Catholic Faith, it is clear that they will the sooner learn them and, having learned them, will not forget them as they do now. And if some Indian should fall sick he will be quickly succored and treated, and thus the lives of many, with the help of Our Lord, will be saved who now die because no one knows they are sick; and all will be spared the hardship of coming and going, which will be a great relief to them, because their dwellings are now so remote from the Spanish communities, so that those who now die from sickness and hunger on the journey, and who do not receive the sacraments which as Christians they are obligated to receive, will not die [unshriven], because they will be given the sacraments in the said communities as soon as they fall sick; and infants will be baptized at birth; and all will serve with less hardship to themselves and with greater profit to the Spaniards, because they will be with them more continually; and the visitors who have them in charge will visit them better and more frequently and will have them provided with everything they need, and will not permit their wives and daughters to be taken from them, as now happens while they live at a distance; and many other evils and hardships will cease which the Indians now suffer because they are so remote, and which are not described here because they are notorious; and many other advantages will accrue to them for the salvation of their souls, as well as for the profit and utility of their persons and the conservation of their lives; and so,

Therefore, for these reasons and for many others that could be adduced, it was agreed that for the improvement and remedy of all the aforesaid, the said chiefs and Indians should forthwith be brought to dwell near the villages and communities of the Spaniards who inhabit that Island, so that they may be treated and taught and looked after as is right and as we have always desired; and so I command that henceforth that which is contained below be obeyed and observed, as follows:

I

First, since it is our determination to remove the said Indians and have them dwell near the Spaniards, we order and command that the persons to whom the said Indians are given, or shall be given, in encomienda, shall at once and forthwith build, for every fifty Indians, four lodges [bohíos] of thirty by fifteen feet, and have the Indians plant 5,000 hillocks (3,000 in cassava and 2,000 in yams), 250 pepper plants, and 50 cotton plants, and so on in like manner, increasing or decreasing the amount according to the number of Indians they have in encomienda, and these shall be settled next to the estates of the Spaniards who have them in encomienda, well situated and housed, and under the eyes of you, our said Admiral [Diego Columbus, son of Christopher Columbus] and judges and officers, and of our visitor who will be in charge of it, or of the person whom you, our said Admiral and judges and officers, shall send for the aforesaid purpose, and he, I charge and command you, shall be such as will be competent in this matter.

And the persons who have the said Indians in their charge [in encomienda] shall have them sow, in season, half a fanega of maize, and shall also give them a dozen hens and a cock to raise and enjoy the fruit thereof, the chickens as well as the eggs; and as soon as the Indians are brought to the estates they shall be given all the aforesaid as their own property; and the person whom you send for this purpose shall tell them it is for their own use and that it is given them in exchange for what they are leaving behind, to enjoy as their own property. And we command that the persons to whom they are given in encomienda shall keep it for them so that they may enjoy it as their own; and we command that this property shall not be sold or taken from them by any person to whom they may be given in encomienda, or by anyone else, but that it shall belong to the said Indians to whom it is assigned and to their descendants, even though this said person sell the estate in which they are, or the said Indians be removed from him; and we declare and command that the person to whom the said Indians are given in encomienda may utilize the goods that the said Indians abandon when they are brought to the estates of the Spaniards, each according to the number of Indians he has, in order to maintain them with such goods; and after the said persons have removed the said goods I command you, our said Admiral and judges and officers, to have the lodges of the said villages burned, since the Indians will have no further use for them: this is so that they will have no reason to return whence they have been brought.

II

After the aforesaid has been done, we order and command that all the chiefs and Indians dwelling on the Island of Española, now or in the future, shall be brought from their present dwelling places to the villages and communities of the Spaniards who reside, now or in the future, on the said Island; and in order that they be brought of their own volition and suffer no harm from the removal, we hereby command Don Diego Columbus, our Admiral, Viceroy, and Governor of the said Island, and our appellate judges and officers of it, to have them brought in the manner that seems best, with the least possible harm to the said chiefs and Indians, to this end encouraging them and urging them with praise; and we charge and command them most earnestly to do this with much care, fidelity, and diligence, with greater regard for the good treatment and conservation of the said Indians than for any other respect, desire, or interest, particular or general.

III

Also, we order and command that the citizen to whom the said Indians are given in encomienda shall, upon the land that is assigned to him, be obliged to erect a structure to be used for a church, on a site selected by you, the said Admiral, judges, and officers, or by the visitor appointed by you; and in this said church he shall place an image of Our Lady and a bell with which to call the Indians to prayer; and the person who has them in encomienda shall be obliged to have them called by the bell at nightfall and go with them to the said church, and have them cross themselves and bless themselves, and together recite the Ave Maria, the Pater Noster, the Credo, and the Salve Regina, in such wise that all of them shall hear the said person, and the said person hear them, so that he may know who is performing well and who ill, and correct the one who is wrong; and since the period we command to be allowed them for rest before nightfall is principally for the purpose of having them rested at the hour of evening prayer, in case any Indian should fail to come to the said church at the said time, we command that on the day following he shall not be allowed to rest during the said period; but he shall still be urged to go to prayers the next night; and we also command that each morning, before they go to work, they shall be obliged to go to the said church and pray as they do in the evening; but they shall not be obliged on that account to rise earlier than is customary, that is, at full daylight.

IV

Also, in order to discover how each one is progressing in things of the Faith, we command that every two weeks the said person who has them in charge shall examine them to see what each one knows particularly and to teach them what they do not know; and he shall also teach them the Ten Commandments and the Seven Deadly Sins and the Articles of the Faith, that is, to those he thinks have the capacity and ability to learn them; but all this shall be done with great love and gentleness; and the person who fails to obey this shall incur a penalty of six gold pesos, two of which shall be for our treasury, two for his accuser, and two for the judge who sentences him and executes the sentence; and I command that the penalty shall be executed at once upon the persons of those who incur it.

V

Also, because I have been informed that the Spaniards and Indians who live on the estates go for a long time without hearing Mass, and since it is right that they should hear it, at least on feast days and Sundays, and since it is impossible for each estate to maintain a priest to say Mass, we order and command that where four or five estates, more or less, are within distance of a league, on that estate which is nearest the others a church shall be built, and in this church an image of Our Lady and a bell shall be placed, so that every Sunday and obligatory feast day they may come there to pray and hear Mass, and also to hear the good advice that the priests who say Mass shall give them; and the priests who say Mass shall teach them the Commandments and the Articles of the Faith, and the other things of the Christian doctrine.

Therefore, in order that they be instructed in the things of the Faith and become accustomed to pray and hear Mass, we command that the Spaniards who are on the estates with the said Indians and have charge of them shall be obliged to bring them all together to the said church in the morning and remain with them until after Mass is said; and after Mass they shall bring them back to the estates and give them their pots of cooked meat, in such wise that they eat on that day better than on any other day of the week, and, although the priest who says Mass will sometimes be absent, nevertheless they shall bring them even so to the church to pray and receive good advice. If, however, the other estates are in places where the Indians can easily come to hear Mass, the said citizens shall be obliged to bring them thither, on pain that any person who has charge of the said Indians and fails to bring them [to Mass] shall incur a penalty of ten gold pesos: six pesos as prescribed in the preceding article, and of the four remaining, two shall be for the erection of the said church and two for the priest who teaches the Indians.

VI

Also, since it is our will that the best means be sought to persuade the Indians to accept the things of our Holy Catholic Faith, and since if they should have to travel more than a league to hear Mass on Sundays and feast days it would be a grave hardship for them, we order and command that, if beyond the aforesaid league where we command the said church to be built there should be other estates, even though they should be in the same district, a church shall be erected there in the aforesaid manner.

VII

Also, we order and command the prelates and priests who, now and in the future, collect the tithes from the estates where the said Indians are, to maintain priests continually in the said churches of the said estates, to say Masses on Sundays and obligatory feast days; and [we order and command] also that the said priests shall have charge of confessing those who know how to confess, and of teaching those who do not. Thus Our Lord will be served, and, if the contrary is done, He has been and will be disserved.

VIII

Also, we order and command that at the mines where there are a sufficient number of Indians churches shall be built, in convenient places approved by you, our said Admiral, judges, and officers, or by the person selected by you, so that all the Indians who are at the mines may hear Mass on the said feast days; and we command the settlers and Spaniards who bring the said Indians to extract gold, to observe with them the same procedure that is followed on the estates, as prescribed above, under the same penalties applied in the same manner.

IX

Also, we order and command that whoever has fifty Indians or more in encomienda shall be obliged to have a boy (the one he considers most able) taught to read and write, and the things of our Faith, so that he may later teach the said Indians, because the Indians will more readily accept what he says than what the Spaniards and settlers tell them; and if the said person has a hundred Indians or more he shall have two boys taught as prescribed; and if the person who has Indians does not have them taught as ordered, we command that the visitor who in our name has charge shall have them taught at the cost of such person. And because the King, my Lord and Father, and I have been informed that several persons are employing Indian boys as pages, we order and command that the person who does so shall be obliged to teach them to read and write, and all the other things that have been prescribed above; and if he fails to do so the boys shall be taken from him and given to another, because the principal aim and desire of the said King, my Lord and Father, and mine, is that in the said parts and in each one of them our Holy Catholic Faith shall be planted and deeply rooted, so that the souls of the said Indians may be saved.

X

Also, we order and command that each and every time an Indian falls sick in a place where there is a priest, the priest shall be obliged to go to him and recite the Credo and other profitable things of our Holy Catholic Faith, and, if the Indian should know how to confess, he shall confess him, without charging him any fee for it; and because there are some Indians who already understand the things of our Holy Faith, we command that the said priests shall be obliged to have them confess once a year, and also that they shall go with a Cross to the Indians who die and shall bury them, without charging any fee for it or for the confession; and if the said Indians die on the estates we command that the Christian settlers there shall bury them in the churches of the said estates; and if they die in other places where there are no churches they shall be buried where it seems best, on pain that he who has Indians in his charge and fails to bury them or have them buried, shall pay four gold pesos, which shall be applied and distributed in the following manner: one for our treasury, one for his accuser, one for the judge who sentences him, and one for the priest at the estate or village where the said Indians are buried.

XI

Also, we order and command that no person having Indians in encomienda, or any other person, shall use Indians as carriers for transporting supplies to Indians at the mines, but that when the latter are removed from one place to another they shall carry their own effects and provisions, because we have been informed that there are no beasts of burden there; and the aforesaid is to be observed and obeyed, on pain that the person who employs the said Indians as carriers against the tenor and form of this article shall pay, for each offense, two gold pesos, which shall be for the hospital of the village where the said settler lives; and if the burden which he thus puts on the Indians is of foodstuffs, he shall lose it also and it shall go to the said hospital.

XII

Also, we order and command that all the Spanish inhabitants and settlers who have Indians in encomienda shall be obliged to have all infants baptized within a week of their birth, or before, if it is necessary; and if there is no priest to do so, the person who has charge of the said estate shall be obliged to baptize them, according to the custom in such emergencies, on pain that he who fails to obey this article shall incur, for each offense, the penalty of three gold pesos, which we command shall be for the church where the said infants are baptized.

XIII

Also, we order and command that, after the Indians have been brought to the estates, all the founding [of gold] that henceforth is done on the said Island shall be done in the manner prescribed below: that is, the said persons who have Indians in encomienda shall extract gold with them for five months in the year and, at the end of these five months, the said Indians shall rest forty days, and the day they cease their labor of extracting gold shall be noted on a certificate, which shall be given to the miners who go to the mines; and upon the day thus designated all the Indians shall be released in the district where the founding is to be done, so that all the Indians of each district shall go to their houses on the same day to rest during the said forty days; and in all the said forty days no one shall employ any Indians in extracting gold, unless it is a slave, on pain that for every Indian that any person brings to the mines in the said period of forty days he shall pay half a gold peso, applied in the aforesaid manner; and we command that in the said forty days you, the said officers, shall be obliged to finish the founding. And we command that the Indians who thus leave the mines shall not, during the said forty days, be ordered to do anything whatever, save to plant the hillocks necessary for their subsistence that season; and the persons who have the said Indians in encomienda shall be obliged, during these forty days of rest, to indoctrinate them in the things of our Faith more than on the other days, because they will have the opportunity and means to do so.

XIV

Also, since we have been informed that if the Indians are not allowed to perform their customary dances [*areytos*] they will receive great harm, we order and command that they shall not be prevented from performing their dances on Sundays and feast days, and also on work days, if they do not on that account neglect their usual work stint.

XV

Also, since the most important consideration for the good treatment and increase of the Indians is their subsistence, we order and command that all persons who have Indians shall be obliged to maintain those who are on their estates and there to keep continually a sufficiency of bread and yams and peppers, and, at least on Sundays and feast days, to give them dishes of cooked meat, as is prescribed in the article that says that on feast days when they go to Mass they shall be given better pots of meat than on other days; and on the days when meat is to be given to the Indians of the said estates it shall be given them in the same manner as is prescribed for the Indians at the mines; that is, they shall be given bread and peppers and a pound of meat a day, and on feast days fish or sardines or other things for their subsistence; and those who are on the estates shall be allowed to go to their lodges to eat, on pain that the person who has the said Indians and does not fulfill all the aforesaid contained in this article shall incur for each offense the penalty of two gold pesos, which shall be distributed as prescribed above; and if he should be fined three times and still fail to correct himself, at the fourth conviction the Indians he has in encomienda shall be taken from him and given to another.

XVI

Also, we order and command that, among the other things of our Faith that shall be taught to the Indians, they shall be made to understand that they may not have more than one wife at a time, nor may they abandon her; and if the persons who have them in encomienda see that they have sufficient discretion and knowledge to undertake matrimony and govern their households, they shall procure their lawful marriage, as our Holy Mother Church commands, with the wife of their choice; and we especially command that the chiefs be made to understand that they may not take wives related to them, and we command that the visitors shall be responsible for their understanding this, repeating it to them very frequently and telling them, or having them told, all the reasons for their so doing, and how by this action they will save their souls.

XVII

Also, we order and command that now and in the future all the sons of chiefs of the said Island, of the age of thirteen or under, shall be given to the friars of the Order of St. Francis who may reside on the said Island, as the King my Lord has commanded in one of his decrees, so that the said friars may teach them to read and write, and all the other things of our Holy Catholic Faith; and they shall keep them for four years and then return them to the persons who have them in encomienda, so that these sons of chiefs may teach the said Indians, for the Indians will accept it more readily from them; and if the said chiefs should have two sons they shall give one to the said friars, and the other we command shall be the one who is to be taught by the person who has him in encomienda.

XVIII

Also, we order and command that no pregnant woman, after the fourth month, shall be sent to the mines, or made to plant hillocks, but shall be kept on the estates and utilized in household tasks, such as making bread, cooking, and weeding; and after she bears her child she shall nurse it until it is three years old, and in all this time she shall not be sent to the mines, or made to plant hillocks, or used in anything else that will harm the infant, on pain that the person who has Indians in encomienda and fails to obey this shall, for the first offense, incur the penalty of six gold pesos, distributed as prescribed above, and for the second offense the woman and her infant shall be taken from him, and for the third, the woman and her husband and six other Indians.

XIX

Also, we order and command that all those on the said Island who have Indians in encomienda, now or in the future, shall be obliged to give to each of them a hammock in which to sleep continually; and they shall not allow them to sleep on the ground, as hitherto they have been doing; and they shall give them this hammock within the twelve months immediately following their receiving the said Indians in encomienda. And we command our visitors carefully to observe whether each Indian has the said hammock, and to urge the said persons who have them in encomienda, if they have not already supplied hammocks, to do so within the said following twelve months, [on pain that the person who fails to obey the aforesaid shall incur the penalty of . . . pesos],

and this penalty we command you, our said Admiral and judges, to execute on the person who incurs it.

And since it is said that when anything is given to an Indian he immediately wishes to exchange it for something else, we command that the said Indians be admonished by the visitors that they are not to exchange the said hammocks for other things, and if they do exchange them, we command the said visitors to punish the Indians who do so and to void the exchanges they have made.

XX

Also, we order and command that, in order that henceforth the Indians may have wherewith the better to clothe and adorn themselves, the person who has them in encomienda shall give to each of them a gold peso every year, which he shall be obliged to give them in wearing apparel, in the sight of and with the consent of our visitor, and this gold peso shall be understood to be in addition to the said hammock that we commanded above to be given to each of them. And since it is just that the said chiefs and their wives should be better dressed and better treated than the other Indians, we command that one real be deducted from the gold peso to be paid to the latter, and that with this said real the said visitor shall have clothing purchased for the said chiefs and their wives; and we command you, our said Admiral, judges, and officers, to have special care to see that this article is observed, obeyed, and fulfilled.

XXI

Also, in order that each one may employ only the Indians he has in encomienda, and that no one may employ those belonging to another, we order and command that no person or persons shall employ an Indian belonging to another, or receive him in his house or estate or mine, or anywhere; but if an Indian should be traveling from one place to another, we permit him to be detained for one night on an estate, provided that immediately on the following morning he is sent forth to go and serve his master; and we command that the person who fails to obey this, and detains an Indian not given to him in encomienda, shall incur the penalty of the loss of one Indian of his own for every Indian of another he thus detains; and the said Indian shall be given to the accuser and the other returned to his master; and if the said person has no Indians he shall suffer the penalty, for the first offense, of six gold castellanos; for the second, twelve; and for the third the penalty shall be doubled again and distributed in the prescribed manner; and if he has no Indians or money the penalty shall be commuted to one hundred lashes.

XXII

Also, we order and command that, in order that the chiefs may the more easily have people to serve them in their personal needs (provided that the Indians of the said chiefs are distributed among more than one person), if a chief has forty subjects two of them shall be given to him for his service; if he has seventy he shall be given three; if a hundred, four; from a hundred to a hundred and fifty, six; and from that point onward, even though he should have more subjects, he shall not be given more; and these said Indians who are to serve him shall be chosen by the said chief, provided they are man and wife and child; and we command that the said Indians shall be chosen from among those belonging to the person who has the largest share of the subjects of the said chief in encomienda. And we command that they [the said chiefs] shall be well treated and not forced to work save at light tasks, so that they may be occupied and not idle, thus avoiding the difficulties that might arise from idleness. And we command our visitors to look carefully after the said chiefs and Indians, and to feed them well and teach them the things of our Holy Faith better than they teach the others, because [the said chiefs] will be able to indoctrinate the other Indians, who will accept it more readily from them.

XXIII

Also, we order and command that all persons who have in encomienda Indians of the said Island of Española, as well as those brought from other islands, shall be obliged to give an accounting to the visitors, within ten days, of those who die and those who are born; and we command that the said visitors shall be obliged to keep a book in which to enter every person who has Indians in encomienda, and the Indians that each one has, with their names, so that those who are born may be entered, and those who die removed, and the visitor have continually a complete record of the increase or decrease of the said Indians, on pain of two pesos gold for each offense, levied against each of the said settlers who fails to do so; and this penalty shall be divided among the trea-

sury and the accuser and the judge who sentences him; and the visitors shall be obliged to bring to each founding [i.e. smelting of gold] an account of all the aforesaid and give it to our [treasury] officers there, so that they may know how much the Indians have increased or decreased between one founding and the next, and they shall so inform us when they remit us the gold that falls to our share in the said founding.

XXIV

Also, we order and command that no person or persons shall dare to beat any Indians with sticks, or whip him, or call him dog, or address him by any name other than his proper name alone; and if an Indian should deserve to be punished for something he has done, the said person having him in charge shall bring him to the visitor for punishment, on pain that the person who violates this article shall pay, for every time he beats or whips an Indian or Indians, five pesos gold; and if he should call an Indian dog, or address him by any name other than his own, he shall pay one gold peso, to be distributed in the manner stated.

XXV

Also, since we have been informed that many persons having Indians in encomienda employ them in commerce or trade, thereby disserving us, we order and command that each person having Indians in encomienda shall be obliged to bring the third part of them to the mines to extract gold, or more than the third part if he so desires, on pain that if he fails to observe this he shall incur a penalty of three gold pesos for each Indian lacking in the said third part to be sent to the mines; but we permit the residents of La Sabana and Villanueva de Yaquimo to be excused from bringing Indians to the mines, because of their remoteness; but we command them to employ the said Indians in the manufacture of hammocks and cotton shirts, in raising pigs, and in other activities profitable to the community. And whereas I have learned that when the Indians are removed to the estates of the settlers it is necessary to employ some of them at once in the erection of lodges, and in other tasks that the settlers will indicate to them as required for their estates, and because of which they will not immediately be able to send the third part to the mines, I command you the said Admiral, judges, and officers, forthwith to fix for all this the period you think should be allowed, making it as brief as possible.

XXVI

Also, we order and command that those who have Indians [in encomienda], but whose estates are so remote from the mines that they cannot supply provisions for the said Indians [being sent thither], shall combine their Indians with those of others who have estates in the vicinity, in order to supply provisions for the said Indians, one person supplying the provisions and the other the Indians, provided that the master of the Indians [being sent to the mines] sends along with them a miner who will see to it that they do not lack necessities; and the aforesaid shall not be done through a third party, or in any way other than that prescribed, under the penalty stated above.

XXVII

Also, since many Indians have been brought, and are daily being brought, from the neighboring islands, we order and command that these said Indians be indoctrinated in and taught the things of the Faith, in the form and manner that we have commanded to be observed with the other Indians of the said Island; also, that they shall be inspected by the said visitors, unless they are slaves, for these may be treated by their owner as he pleases; but we command that they shall not be treated with that rigor and harshness with which other slaves are customarily treated, but rather with much love and gentleness, in order the better to incline them to the things of our Faith.

XXVIII

Also, we order and command that each and every time any person vacates the Indians he has in encomienda, either by death or for some other reason for which he may deserve to lose them, the person to whom we grant the said estate in encomienda shall be obliged to purchase it from the one who has vacated the said Indians, or from his heirs, and it shall be appraised under oath by two persons who are acquainted with it, to be named by you, the said Admiral, judges, and officers; and the said owner shall be obliged to sell it at their appraisal, so that the said Indians do not have to change their residence, because the persons to whom they are given [in encomienda] must be residents of the community to which the said Indians were allotted.

XXIX

Also, we order and command that in each community of the said Island there shall be two visitors in charge of inspecting the whole community, together with its mines and estates, its shepherds and swineherds, and they shall ascertain how the Indians are being taught in the things of our Faith, and how their persons are being treated, and how they are being maintained, and how they or the persons who have them in charge are obeying and fulfilling these our ordinances, and all the other things that each of them is obliged to do; and we command them to have particular care in all this, and we charge their consciences with it.

XXX

Also, we order and command that the said visitors shall be selected and named by you, the said Admiral, judges, and officers, in the form and manner you think best, provided they are selected from among the oldest inhabitants of the communities in which they are to serve; and we command that they shall be given and assigned some Indians in encomienda, in addition to those given them for their responsibility and work in the use and exercise of the said office; and these Indians shall be chosen by you, the said Admiral, judges, and officers; and it is our will that if the said visitors should become negligent in enforcing the said ordinances, or if any of them fail to carry out the aforesaid, especially in the matter of subsistence and hammocks, their own Indians that they have in encomienda shall on that account be removed from them.

XXXI

Also, we order and command that the said visitors shall be obliged twice a year to inspect all the places where there are Indians of their charge, once at the beginning of the year, and again at the middle; and we command that one of them alone shall not make the inspection both times, but each one once, so that each may know what the other is doing and so that everything may be done with the necessary care and diligence.

XXXII

Also, we order and command that no visitor shall bring to his house or estate any lost or runaway Indians he finds in the estates or elsewhere, but that immediately upon finding them he shall deposit them with a person of good conscience whom he shall select; but first he shall endeavor to discover who their master is, and when he has done so he shall deliver the Indians to him at once; otherwise, they shall be deposited as prescribed until the said master is found, on pain that the visitor who is discovered with an Indian in his possession or in his house shall lose an Indian of his own, to be given to his accuser, and the said runaway Indian taken by the visitor shall be restored to his master.

XXXIII

Also, we order and command that the said visitors shall be obliged to have and keep in their possession a copy of these our ordinances, signed by the said Admiral, judges, and officers, together with the instructions that we command you, the said Admiral, judges and officers, to give them, by which they may the better know what they must do, observe, and obey; and upon the visitor who fails to obey, the aforesaid penalties shall be executed.

XXXIV

Also, we order and command that you, the said Admiral, judges, and officers, shall inquire once every two years into the way in which the said visitors are fulfilling their duties, and you shall have their residencias [appraisals of performance in office] taken, in which it shall be ascertained how they have enforced these ordinances, each according to his obligation. And we command that the said visitors shall be obliged, at the time of their residencias, to give you, the said Admiral, judges, and officers, a very complete accounting of all the Indians and their number, each reporting for the place in his charge, and how many have been born and how many have died in those two years, so that the said Admiral, judges, and officers may send us an accounting of it all, which shall be signed by you and the visitors, to the end that I may be well informed of everything.

XXXV

Also, we order and command that no inhabitant or resident of the said communities of the said Island of Española, or of any other island, shall have in encomienda, by grant or otherwise, more than a hundred and fifty Indians, or fewer than forty.

Therefore, I command you, our said Admiral, judges, and officers, and each and every one of you, present and future, and all other persons whatsoever to whom the contents of these ordinances may apply, to consider the ordinances incorporated above and those others mentioned, and to observe and obey them, and to have them observed and obeyed and executed completely, each according to its contents; and you shall execute and cause to be executed the penalties upon such as incur them; and also, you shall observe and obey the said ordinances yourselves, according to the manner and form prescribed therein, under the penalties stated. Moreover, in case of disobedience, you shall incur the loss of the Indians you have in encomienda, and they shall be considered vacated, so that we may assign them to whomsoever we please; and you shall not act counter to their tenor and form, nor shall you permit them to be violated at any time or in any way. And if, in order to fulfill and execute the aforesaid, you should have need of favor and aid, I hereby command all town councils, justices, regidores, knights, squires, officers, and citizens of the said Island of Española to render you such favor and aid as you shall demand of them, under whatever penalties that you in our name shall impose, which by these presents I impose and consider imposed; and I hereby give you authority to execute them upon all those who fail to obey you.

Also, so that this my letter may be brought to the attention of all, and that none may plead ignorance of it, I command that it be read in the squares and markets and other customary places of the said Island of Española by the public crier, in the presence of a notary and witnesses, none of whom shall disobey it in any way, on pain of my displeasure and 50,000 maravedís for my treasury [272 maravedís = 1 peso = 1 ounce of silver], to be levied against each offender. Moreover, I command him who shows them this my letter to cite them to appear before me at my court, wherever I may be, within one hundred days of the time they are cited, under the said penalty; and, also under the same penalty, I command any notary who should be called upon to do so, to give testimony thereof signed with his rubric, so that I may know how my command is being observed.

Done in this City of Burgos, December 27, 1512.

I, the King

I, Lope Conchillos, Secretary to the Queen, our Mistress

The Bishop of Palencia, Count [of Pernia]

AMENDMENTS TO THE LAWS OF BURGOS

Doña Juana, by the Grace of God Queen of Castile, León, Granada, Toledo, Galicia, Sevilla, Córdoba, Murcia, Jaén, the Algarbes, Algeciras, Gibraltar, the Canary Islands, and the Indies, Islands, and Mainland of the Ocean Sea; Princess of Aragón, the Two Sicilies, and Jerusalem; Archduchess of Austria; Duchess of Austria, Burgundy, and Brabant; Countess of Flanders and Tyrol; Lady of Biscay, Molina, etc.

To you, the Alcalde Mayor and constables of the Island of San Juan, which is in the Indies of the Ocean Sea, and to our officers of the said Island, and to all other justices and officers of it whatsoever, present and future, and to the town councils, justices, regidores, knights, squires, officers and citizens of the said Island, its town and villages, and to any other persons whatsoever to whom what is contained in this my letter may apply in any way, and to each and every one of thee.

Know, that the King, my Lord and Father, and I, seeing how necessary it was for the service of God Our Lord, and ours, and for the salvation of souls and the increase and good treatment of the Indians of the said Island, as well as for its citizens, consulted prelates and religious and certain members of our Council, which we convened for the purpose, after which we commanded that certain ordinances be drawn up by which the said Indians were to be indoctrinated and taught and brought to the knowledge of our Holy Catholic Faith, and by which the said Indians were to be well treated and reduced to settlements, as is explained at greater length in the said ordinances.

Thereupon the King, my Lord and Father, and I were informed that, although the said ordinances were very useful, profitable, and necessary, as well as fitting, it was said that some of them had need of further elucidation and modification. Therefore, since it has always been our intent, desire, and will, to have greater regard for the salvation of souls and the indoctrination and good treatment of the said Indians than for any other consideration, we commanded several prelates and religious of the Order of St. Dominic, and several members of our Council, and preachers and learned men of good life and conscience, very prudent and zealous in the service of our Lord, to consider the said ordinances and amend them, add to them or reduce them, and modify them as might

be necessary. Therefore, having considered the said ordinances and listened to the religious who have knowledge of the affairs of the said Island and the conditions and habits of the said Indians, they, together with other prelates and members of our Council, amended and modified the said ordinances as follows.

I

First, we order and command that Indian women married to Indian men who have been given in encomienda shall not be forced to go and come and serve with their husbands, at the mines or elsewhere, unless it is by their own free will, or unless their husbands wish to take them; but the said wives shall be obliged to work on their own land or on that of their husbands, or on the lands of the Spaniards, who shall pay them the wages agreed upon with them or with the husbands; but if the said wives should be pregnant we command that the ordinances we issued covering this situation be observed, on pain that he who does the contrary shall, besides suffering the penalty prescribed in the said ordinance, lose the Indian woman whom he thus forces to work, as well as her husband and children, who shall be given in encomienda to others.

II

Also we order and command that Indian children under fourteen years of age shall not be compelled to work at [adults'] tasks until they have attained the said age or more; but they shall be compelled to work at, and serve in, tasks proper to children, such as weeding the fields and the like, on their parents' estates (if they have parents); and those above the age of fourteen shall be under the authority of their parents until they are of age and married. Those who have neither father nor mother, we command shall be given in encomienda by the person who has our authority to do so, and he shall give them in charge to persons of good conscience who shall see that they are taught and indoctrinated in the things of our Holy Faith, and employ them on their estates in tasks set by our appellate judges, in which they can work without endangering their health, provided that they [the encomenderos] feed them and pay them their proper wages at the rate fixed by our said judges, and provided that they [the encomenderos] do not prevent their attendance at Christian doctrine at the appointed time. And if any of the said boys should wish to learn a trade, they may freely do so, and they may not be compelled to serve in, or work at, anything else while they are learning the said trade.

III

Also, we order and command that unmarried Indian women who are under the authority of their parents, mothers or fathers, shall work with them on their lands, or on the lands of others by agreement with their parents; and those not under the authority of their fathers and mothers shall, to prevent their becoming vagabonds and bad women, and to keep them from vice and teach them the [Christian] doctrine, be constrained to be with the other women and work on their estates, if they have such; otherwise, they shall work on the estates of the Indians and others, who shall pay them their wages at the rate they pay the others who work for them.

IV

Also, we order and command that within two years [of publication of this ordinance] the men and women shall go about clad.

And whereas it may so happen that in the course of time, what with their indoctrination and association with Christians, the Indians will become so apt and ready to become Christians, and so civilized and educated, that they will be capable of governing themselves and leading the kind of life that the said Christians lead there, we declare and command and say that it is our will that those Indians who thus become competent to live by themselves, under the direction and control of our said judges of the said Island, present or future, shall be allowed to live by themselves and shall be obliged to serve [only] in those things in which our vassals in Spain are accustomed to serve, so that they may serve and pay the tribute which they [our vassals] are accustomed to pay to their princes.

[Then follows a long and detailed injunction to the Admiral and all lesser officials in the Indies to obey and enforce the Laws of 1512 and the amendments.]

Given in the City of Valladolid, July 28, 1513.

I, The King

I, Lope Conchillos, Secretary to our Mistress, the Queen, caused this to be inscribed, by Order of the King her Father registered:

Licentiatus Jimenez

The Bishop of Palencia—

Count [of Pernia]

CASTANEDA, Chancellor

LOUISIANA PURCHASE TREATY; APRIL 30, 1803

The President of the United States of America and the First Consul of the French Republic in the name of the French People desiring to remove all Source of misunderstanding relative to objects of discussion mentioned in the Second and Fifth articles of the Convention of the 8th Vendémiaire on 30 September 1800 relative to the rights claimed by the United States in virtue of the Treaty concluded at Madrid the 27 of October 1795, between His Catholic Majesty & the Said United States, & willing to Strengthen the union and friendship which at the time of the Said Convention was happily reestablished between the two nations have respectively named their Plenipotentiaries to wit The President of the United States, by and with the advice and consent of the Senate of the Said States; Robert R. Livingston Minister Plenipotentiary of the United States and James Monroe Minister Plenipotentiary and Envoy extraordinary of the Said States near the Government of the French Republic; And the First Consul in the name of the French people, Citizen Francis Barbé Marbois Minister of the public treasury who after having respectively exchanged their full powers have agreed to the following Articles.

Article I

Whereas by the Article the third of the Treaty concluded at St Ildefonso the 9th Vendémiaire on 1st October 1800 between the First Consul of the French Republic and his Catholic Majesty it was agreed as follows.

> "His Catholic Majesty promises and engages on his part to cede to the French Republic six months after the full and entire execution of the conditions and Stipulations herein relative to his Royal Highness the Duke of Parma, the Colony or Province of Louisiana with the Same extent that it now has in the hand of Spain, & that it had when France possessed it; and Such as it Should be after the Treaties subsequently entered into between Spain and other States."

And whereas in pursuance of the Treaty and particularly of the third article the French Republic has an incontestible title to the domain and to the possession of the said Territory—The First Consul of the French Republic desiring to give to the United States a strong proof of his friendship doth hereby cede to the United States in the name of the French Republic for ever and in full Sovereignty the said territory with all its rights and appurtenances as fully and in the Same manner as they have been acquired by the French Republic in virtue of the above mentioned Treaty concluded with his Catholic Majesty.

Article II

In the cession made by the preceeding article are included the adjacent Islands belonging to Louisiana all public lots and Squares, vacant lands and all public buildings, fortifications, barracks and other edifices which are not private property.—The Archives, papers & documents relative to the domain and Sovereignty of Louisiana and its dependances will be left in the possession of the Commissaries of the United States, and copies will be afterwards given in due form to the Magistrates and Municipal officers of such of the said papers and documents as may be necessary to them.

Article III

The inhabitants of the ceded territory shall be incorporated in the Union of the United States and admitted as soon as possible according to the principles of the federal Constitution to the enjoyment of all these rights, advantages and immunities of citizens of the United States, and in the mean time they shall be maintained and protected in the free enjoyment of their liberty, property and the Religion which they profess.

Article IV

There Shall be Sent by the Government of France a Commissary to Louisiana to the end that he do every act necessary as well to receive from the Officers of his Catholic Majesty the Said country and its dependances in the name of the French Republic if it has not been already done as to transmit it in the name of the French Republic to the Commissary or agent of the United States.

Article V

Immediately after the ratification of the present Treaty by the President of the United States and in case that of the first Consul's shall have been previously obtained, the commissary of the French Republic shall remit all military posts of New Orleans and other parts of the ceded territory to the Commissary or Commissaries named by the President to take possession--the troops whether of France or Spain who may be there shall cease to occupy any military post from the time of taking possession and shall be embarked as soon as possible in the course of three months after the ratification of this treaty.

Article VI

The United States promise to execute Such treaties and articles as may have been agreed between Spain and the tribes and nations of Indians until by mutual consent of the United States and the said tribes or nations other Suitable articles Shall have been agreed upon.

Article VII

As it is reciprocally advantageous to the commerce of France and the United States to encourage the communication of both nations for a limited time in the country ceded by the present treaty until general arrangements relative to commerce of both nations may be agreed on; it has been agreed between the contracting parties that the French Ships coming directly from France or any of her colonies loaded only with the produce and manufactures of France or her Said Colonies; and the Ships of Spain coming directly from Spain or any of her colonies loaded only with the produce or manufactures of Spain or her Colonies shall be admitted during the Space of twelve years in the Port of New-Orleans and in all other legal ports-of-entry within the ceded territory in the Same manner as the Ships of the United States coming directly from France or Spain or any of their Colonies without being Subject to any other or greater duty on merchandize or other or greater tonnage than that paid by the citizens of the United States.

During that Space of time above mentioned no other nation Shall have a right to the Same privileges in the Ports of the ceded territory--the twelve years Shall commence three months after the exchange of ratifications if it Shall take place in France or three months after it Shall have been notified at Paris to the French Government if it Shall take place in the United States; It is however well understood that the object of the above article is to favour the manufactures, Commerce, freight and navigation of France and of Spain So far as relates to the importations that the French and Spanish Shall make into

the Said Ports of the United States without in any Sort affecting the regulations that the United States may make concerning the exportation of the produce and merchandize of the United States, or any right they may have to make Such regulations.

Article VIII

In future and for ever after the expiration of the twelve years, the Ships of France shall be treated upon the footing of the most favoured nations in the ports above mentioned.

Article IX

The particular Convention Signed this day by the respective Ministers, having for its object to provide for the payment of debts due to the Citizens of the United States by the French Republic prior to the 30th Sept. 1800 (8th Vendémiaire an 9) is approved and to have its execution in the Same manner as if it had been inserted in this present treaty, and it Shall be ratified in the same form and in the Same time So that the one Shall not be ratified distinct from the other.

Another particular Convention Signed at the Same date as the present treaty relative to a definitive rule between the contracting parties is in the like manner approved and will be ratified in the Same form, and in the Same time and jointly.

Article X

The present treaty Shall be ratified in good and due form and the ratifications Shall be exchanged in the Space of Six months after the date of the Signature by the Ministers Plenipotentiary or Sooner if possible.

In faith whereof the respective Plenipotentiaries have Signed these articles in the French and English languages; declaring nevertheless that the present Treaty was originally agreed to in the French language; and have thereunto affixed their Seals.

Done at Paris the tenth day of Floreal in the eleventh year of the French Republic; and the 30th of April 1803.

Robert R. Livingston [seal]

James Monroe [seal]

Francis Barbé Marbois [seal]

LOUISIANA PURCHASE: FIRST CONVENTION

The President of the United States of America and the First Consul of the French Republic in the name of the French people, in consequence of the treaty of cession of Louisiana which has been Signed this day; wishing to regulate definitively every thing which has relation to the Said cession have authorized to this effect the Plenipotentiaries, that is to say the President of the United States has, by and with the advice and consent of the Senate of the Said States, nominated for their Plenipotentiaries, Robert R. Livingston, Minister Plenipotentiary of the United States, and James Monroe, Minister Plenipotentiary and Envoy-Extraordinary of the Said United States, near the Government of the French Republic; and the First Consul of the French Republic, in the name of the French people, has named as Plenipotentiary of the Said Republic the citizen Francis Barbé Marbois: who, in virtue of their full powers, which have been exchanged this day, have agreed to the followings articles:

Article 1

The Government of the United States engages to pay to the French government in the manner Specified in the following article the sum of Sixty millions of francs independant of the Sum which Shall be fixed by another Convention for the payment of the debts due by France to citizens of the United States.

Article 2

For the payment of the Sum of Sixty millions of francs mentioned in the preceeding article the United States shall create a Stock of eleven millions, two hundred and fifty thousand Dollars bearing an interest of Six per cent: per annum payable half yearly in London, Amsterdam or Paris amounting by the half year to three hundred and thirty-seven thousand five hundred dollars, according to the proportions which Shall be determined by the French Government to be paid at either place: The principal of the Said Stock to be reimbursed at the treasury of the United States in annual payments of not less than three millions of Dollars each; of which the first payment Shall commence fifteen years after the date of the exchange of ratifications:—this Stock Shall be transferred to the government of France or to Such person or persons as Shall be authorized to receive it in three months at most after the exchange of ratifications of this treaty and after Louisiana Shall be taken possession of the name of the Government of the United States.

It is further agreed that if the French Government Should be desirous of disposing of the Said Stock to receive the capital in Europe at Shorter terms that its measures for that purpose Shall be taken So as to favour in the greatest degree possible the credit of the United States, and to raise to the highest price the Said Stock.

Article 3

It is agreed that the Dollar of the United States Specified in the present Convention shall be fixed at five francs 3333/100000 or five livres eight Sous tournois.

The present Convention Shall be ratified in good and due form, and the ratifications Shall be exchanged in the Space of Six months to date from this day or Sooner it possible.

In faith of which the respective Plenipotentiaries have Signed the above articles both in the French and English languages, declaring nevertheless that the present treaty has been originally agreed on and written in the French language; to which they have hereunto affixed their Seals.

Done at Paris the tenth of Floreal eleventh year of the French Republic, 30th April 1803.

Robert R. Livingston [seal]

James Monroe [seal]

Francis Barbé Marbois [seal]

MONROE DOCTRINE; DECEMBER 2, 1823

. . . At the proposal of the Russian Imperial Government, made through the minister of the Emperor residing here, a full power and instructions have been transmitted to the minister of the United States at St. Petersburg to arrange by amicable negotiation the respective rights and interests of the two nations on the northwest coast of this continent. A similar proposal has been made by His Imperial Majesty to the Government of Great Britain, which has likewise been acceded to. The Government of the United States has been desirous by this friendly proceeding of manifesting the great value which they have invariably attached to the friendship of the Emperor and their solicitude to cultivate the best understanding with his Government. In the discussions to which this interest has given rise and in the arrangements by which they may terminate the occasion has been judged proper for asserting, as a principle in which the rights and interests of the United States are involved, that the American continents, by the free and independent condition which they have assumed and maintain, are henceforth not to be considered as subjects for future colonization by any European powers . . .

It was stated at the commencement of the last session that a great effort was then making in Spain and Portugal to improve the condition of the people of those countries, and that it appeared to be conducted with extraordinary moderation. It need scarcely be remarked that the results have been so far very different from what was then anticipated. Of events in that quarter of the globe, with which we have so much intercourse and from which we derive our origin, we have always been anxious and interested spectators. The citizens of the United States cherish sentiments the most friendly in favor of the liberty and happiness of their fellowmen on that side of the Atlantic. In the wars of the European powers in matters relating to themselves we have never taken any part, nor does it comport with our policy to do so. It is only when our rights are invaded or seriously menaced that we resent injuries or make preparation for our defense. With the movements in this hemisphere we are of necessity more immediately connected, and by causes which must be obvious to all enlightened and impartial observers. The political system of the allied powers is essentially different in this respect from that of America. This difference proceeds from that which exists in their respective Governments; and to the defense of our own, which has been achieved by the loss of so much blood and treasure, and matured by the wisdom of their most enlightened citizens, and under which we have enjoyed unexampled felicity, this whole nation is devoted. We owe it, therefore, to candor and to the amicable relations existing between the United States and those powers to declare that we should consider any attempt on their part to extend their system to any portion of this hemisphere as dangerous to our peace and safety. With the existing colonies or dependencies of any European power we have not interfered and shall not interfere. But with the Governments who have declared their independence and maintain it, and whose independence we have, on great consideration and on just principles, acknowledged, we could not view any interposition for the purpose of oppressing them, or controlling in any other manner their destiny, by any European power in any other light than as the manifestation of an unfriendly disposition toward the United States. In the war between those new Governments and Spain we declared our neutrality at the time of their recognition, and to this we have adhered, and shall continue to adhere, provided no change shall occur which, in the judgement of the competent authorities of this Government, shall make a corresponding change on the part of the United States indispensable to their security.

The late events in Spain and Portugal show that Europe is still unsettled. Of this important fact no stronger proof can be adduced than that the allied powers should have thought it proper, on any principle satisfactory to themselves, to have interposed by force in the internal concerns of Spain. To what extent such interposition may be carried, on the same principle, is a question in which all independent powers whose governments differ from theirs are interested, even those most remote, and surely none of them more so than the United States. Our policy in regard to Europe, which was adopted at an early stage of the wars which have so long agitated that quarter of the globe, nevertheless remains the same, which is, not to interfere in the internal concerns of any of its powers; to consider the government de facto as the legitimate government for us; to cultivate friendly relations with it, and to preserve those relations by a frank, firm, and manly policy, meeting in all instances the just claims of every power, submitting to injuries from none. But in regard to those continents circumstances are eminently and conspicuously different. It is impossible that the allied powers should extend their political system to any portion of either continent without endangering our peace and happiness; nor can anyone believe that our southern brethren, if left to themselves, would adopt it of their own accord. It is equally impossible, therefore, that we should behold such interposition in any form with indifference. If we look to the comparative strength and resources of Spain and those new Governments, and their distance from each other, it must be obvious that she can never subdue them. It is still the true policy of the United States to leave the parties to themselves, in hope that other powers will pursue the same course. . . .

TREATY OF VELASCO; MAY 14, 1836

Articles of an agreement entered into between His Excellency David G. Burnet, President of the Republic of Texas, of the one part, and His Excellency General Antonio Lopez de Santa Anna, President General in Chief of the Mexican Army, of the other part.

Article 1st

General Antonio Lopez de Santa Anna agrees that he will not take up arms, nor will he exercise his influence to cause them to be taken up against the people of Texas, during the present war of Independence.

Article 2nd

All hostilities between the Mexican and Texian troops will cease immediately both on land and water.

Article 3rd

The Mexican troops will evacuate the Territory of Texas, passing to the other side of the Rio Grande del Norte.

Article 4th

The Mexican Army in its retreat shall not take the property of any person without his consent and just indemnification, using only such articles as may be necessary for its subsistence, in cases when the owner may not be present, and remitting to the commander of the army of Texas or to the commissioner to be appointed for the adjustment of such matters, an account of the value of the property consumed— the place where taken, and the name of the owner, if it can be ascertained.

Article 5th

That all private property including cattle, horses, Negro slaves or indentured persons of whatever denomination, that may have been captured by any portion of the Mexican army or may have taken refuge in the said army since the commencement of the late invasion, shall be restored to the Commander of the Texian army, or to such other persons as may be appointed by the Government of Texas to receive them.

Article 6th

The troops of both armies will refrain from coming into contact with each other, and to this end the Commander of the army of Texas will be careful not to approach within a shorter distance of the Mexican army than five leagues.

Article 7th

The Mexican army shall not make any other delay on its march, than that which is necessary to take up their hospitals, baggage [—] and to cross the rivers— any delay not necessary to these purposes to be considered an infraction of this agreement.

Article 8th

By express to be immediately dispatched, this agreement shall be sent to General Filisola and to General T. J. Rusk, commander of the Texian Army, in order that they may be apprised of its stipulations, and to this and they will exchange engagements to comply with the same.

Article 9th

That all Texian prisoners now in possession of the Mexican Army or its authorities be forthwith released and furnished with free passports to return to their homes, in consideration of which a corresponding number of Mexican prisoners, rank and file, now in possession of the Government of Texas shall be immediately released. The remainder of the Mexican prisoners that continue in possession of the Government of Texas to be treated with due humanity — any extraordinary comforts that may be furnished them to be at the charge of the Government of Mexico.

Article 10th

General Antonio Lopez de Santa Anna will be sent to Veracruz as soon as it shall be deemed proper.

The contracting parties sign this Instrument for the above mentioned purposes, by duplicate, at the Port of Velasco this 14th day of May 1836.

David G. Burnet

Antonio Lopez de Santa Anna

James Collinsworth, Secretary of State

Bailey Hardiman, Secretary of Treasury

P. H. Grayson, Attorney General.

TREATY OF GUADALUPE HIDALGO; FEBRUARY 2, 1848

Treaty of Peace, Friendship, Limits, and Settlement between the United States of America and the United Mexican States concluded at Guadalupe Hidalgo, February 2, 1848; ratification advised by Senate, with amendments, March 10, 1848; ratified by President, March 16, 1848; ratifications exchanged at Queretaro, May 30, 1848; proclaimed, July 4, 1848.

IN THE NAME OF ALMIGHTY GOD

The United States of America and the United Mexican States animated by a sincere desire to put an end to the calamities of the war which unhappily exists between the two Republics and to establish Upon a solid basis relations of peace and friendship, which shall confer reciprocal benefits upon the citizens of both, and assure the concord, harmony, and mutual confidence wherein the two people should live, as good neighbors have for that purpose appointed their respective plenipotentiaries, that is to say: The President of the United States has appointed Nicholas P. Trist, a citizen of the United States, and the President of the Mexican Republic has appointed Don Luis Gonzaga Cuevas, Don Bernardo Couto, and Don Miguel Atristain, citizens of the said Republic; Who, after a reciprocal communication of their respective full powers, have, under the protection of Almighty God, the author of peace, arranged, agreed upon, and signed the following: Treaty of Peace, Friendship, Limits, and Settlement between the United States of America and the Mexican Republic.

ARTICLE I

There shall be firm and universal peace between the United States of America and the Mexican Republic, and between their respective countries, territories, cities, towns, and people, without exception of places or persons.

ARTICLE II

Immediately upon the signature of this treaty, a convention shall be entered into between a commissioner or commissioners appointed by the General-in-chief of the forces of the United States, and such as may be appointed by the Mexican Government, to the end that a provisional suspension of hostilities shall take place, and that, in the places occupied by the said forces, constitutional order may be reestab-lished, as regards the political, administrative, and judicial branches, so far as this shall be permitted by the circumstances of military occupation.

ARTICLE III

Immediately upon the ratification of the present treaty by the Government of the United States, orders shall be transmitted to the commanders of their land and naval forces, requiring the latter (provided this treaty shall then have been ratified by the Government of the Mexican Republic, and the ratifications exchanged) immediately to desist from blockading any Mexican ports and requiring the former (under the same condition) to commence, at the earliest moment practicable, withdrawing all troops of the United States then in the interior of the Mexican Republic, to points that shall be selected by common agreement, at a distance from the seaports not exceeding thirty leagues; and such evacuation of the interior of the Republic shall be completed with the least possible delay; the Mexican Government hereby binding itself to afford every facility in its power for rendering the same convenient to the troops, on their march and in their new positions, and for promoting a good understanding between them and the inhabitants. In like manner orders shall be despatched to the persons in charge of the custom houses at all ports occupied by the forces of the United States, requiring them (under the same condition) immediately to deliver possession of the same to the persons authorized by the Mexican Government to receive it, together with all bonds and evidences of debt for duties on importations and on exportations, not yet fallen due. Moreover, a faithful and exact account shall be made out, showing the entire amount of all duties on imports and on exports, collected at such custom-houses, or elsewhere in Mexico, by authority of the United States, from and after the day of ratification of this treaty by the Government of the Mexican Republic; and also an account of the cost of collection; and such entire amount, deducting only the cost of collection, shall be delivered to the Mexican Government, at the city of Mexico, within three months after the exchange of ratifications.

The evacuation of the capital of the Mexican Republic by the troops of the United States, in virtue of the above stipulation, shall be completed in one month after the orders there stipulated for shall have been received by the commander of said troops, or sooner if possible.

ARTICLE IV

Immediately after the exchange of ratifications of the present treaty all castles, forts, territories, places, and possessions, which have been taken or occupied by the forces of the United States during the present war, within the limits of the Mexican Republic, as about to be established by the following article, shall be definitely restored to the said Republic, together with all the artillery, arms, apparatus of war, munitions, and other public property, which were in the said castles and forts when captured, and which shall remain there at the time when this treaty shall be duly ratified by the Government of the Mexican Republic. To this end, immediately upon the signature of this treaty, orders shall be despatched to the American officers commanding such castles and forts, securing against the removal or destruction of any such artillery, arms, apparatus of war, munitions, or other public property. The city of Mexico, within the inner line of intrenchments surrounding the said city, is comprehended in the above stipulation, as regards the restoration of artillery, apparatus of war, & c.

The final evacuation of the territory of the Mexican Republic, by the forces of the United States, shall be completed in three months from the said exchange of ratifications, or sooner if possible; the Mexican Government hereby engaging, as in the foregoing article to use all means in its power for facilitating such evacuation, and rendering it convenient to the troops, and for promoting a good understanding between them and the inhabitants.

If, however, the ratification of this treaty by both parties should not take place in time to allow the embarcation of the troops of the United States to be completed before the commencement of the sickly season, at the Mexican ports on the Gulf of Mexico, in such case a friendly arrangement shall be entered into between the General-in-Chief of the said troops and the Mexican Government, whereby healthy and otherwise suitable places, at a distance from the ports not exceeding thirty leagues, shall be designated for the residence of such troops as may not yet have embarked, until the return of the healthy season. And the space of time here referred to as, comprehending the sickly season shall be understood to extend from the first day of May to the first day of November.

All prisoners of war taken on either side, on land or on sea, shall be restored as soon as practicable after the exchange of ratifications of this treaty. It is also agreed that if any Mexicans should now be held as captives by any savage tribe within the limits of the United States, as about to be established by the following article, the Government of the said United States will exact the release of such captives and cause them to be restored to their country.

ARTICLE V

The boundary line between the two Republics shall commence in the Gulf of Mexico, three leagues from land, opposite the mouth of the Rio Grande, otherwise called Rio Bravo del Norte, or Opposite the mouth of its deepest branch, if it should have more than one branch emptying directly into the sea; from thence up the middle of that river, following the deepest channel, where it has more than one, to the point where it strikes the southern boundary of New Mexico; thence, westwardly, along the whole southern boundary of New Mexico (which runs north of the town called Paso) to its western termination; thence, northward, along the western line of New Mexico, until it intersects the first branch of the river Gila; (or if it should not intersect any branch of that river, then to the point on the said line nearest to such branch, and thence in a direct line to the same); thence down the middle of the said branch and of the said river, until it empties into the Rio Colorado; thence across the Rio Colorado, following the division line between Upper and Lower California, to the Pacific Ocean.

The southern and western limits of New Mexico, mentioned in the article, are those laid down in the map entitled "Map of the United Mexican States, as organized and defined by various acts of the Congress of said republic, and constructed according to the best authorities. Revised edition. Published at New York, in 1847, by J. Disturnell," of which map a copy is added to this treaty, bearing the signatures and seals of the undersigned Plenipotentiaries. And, in order to preclude all difficulty in tracing upon the ground the limit separating Upper from Lower California, it is agreed that the said limit shall consist of a straight line drawn from the middle of the Rio Gila, where it unites with the Colorado, to a point on the coast of the Pacific Ocean, distant one marine league due south of the southernmost point of the port of San Diego, according to the plan of said port made in the year 1782 by Don Juan Pantoja, second sailing-master of the Spanish fleet, and published at Madrid in the year 1802, in the atlas to the voyage of the schooners *Sutil* and *Mexicana*; of which plan a copy is hereunto added, signed and sealed by the respective Plenipotentiaries.

In order to designate the boundary line with due precision, upon authoritative maps, and to establish upon the ground land-marks which shall show the limits of both republics, as described in the present article, the two Governments shall each appoint a commissioner and a surveyor, who, before the expiration of one year from the date of the exchange of ratifications of this treaty, shall meet at the port of San Diego, and proceed to run and mark the said boundary in its whole course to the mouth of the Rio Bravo del Norte. They shall keep journals and make out plans of their operations; and the result agreed upon by them shall be deemed a part of this treaty, and shall have the same force as if it were inserted therein. The two Governments will amicably agree regarding what may be necessary to these persons, and also as to their respective escorts, should such be necessary.

The boundary line established by this article shall be religiously respected by each of the two republics, and no change shall ever be made therein, except by the express and free consent of both nations, lawfully given by the General Government of each, in conformity with its own constitution.

ARTICLE VI

The vessels and citizens of the United States shall, in all time, have a free and uninterrupted passage by the Gulf of California, and by the river Colorado below its confluence with the Gila, to and from their possessions situated north of the boundary line defined in the preceding article; it being understood that this passage is to be by navigating the Gulf of California and the river Colorado, and not by land, without the express consent of the Mexican Government.

If, by the examinations which may be made, it should be ascertained to be practicable and advantageous to construct a road, canal, or railway, which should in whole or in part run upon the river Gila, or upon its right or its left bank, within the space of one marine league from either margin of the river, the Governments of both republics will form an agreement regarding its construction, in order that it may serve equally for the use and advantage of both countries.

ARTICLE VII

The river Gila, and the part of the Rio Bravo del Norte lying below the southern boundary of New Mexico, being, agreeably to the fifth article, divided in the middle between the two republics, the navigation of the Gila and of the Bravo below said boundary shall be free and common to the vessels and citizens of both countries; and neither shall, without the consent of the other, construct any work that may impede or interrupt, in whole or in part, the exercise of this right; not even for the purpose of favoring new methods of navigation. Nor shall any tax or contribution, under any denomination or title, be levied upon vessels or persons navigating the same or upon merchandise or effects transported thereon, except in the case of landing upon one of their shores. If, for the purpose of making the said rivers navigable, or for maintaining them in such state, it should be necessary or advantageous to establish any tax or contribution, this shall not be done without the consent of both Governments.

The stipulations contained in the present article shall not impair the territorial rights of either republic within its established limits.

ARTICLE VIII

Mexicans now established in territories previously belonging to Mexico, and which remain for the future within the limits of the United States, as defined by the present treaty, shall be free to continue where they now reside, or to remove at any time to the Mexican Republic, retaining the property which they possess in the said territories, or disposing thereof, and removing the proceeds wherever they please, without their being subjected, on this account, to any contribution, tax, or charge whatever.

Those who shall prefer to remain in the said territories may either retain the title and rights of Mexican citizens, or acquire those of citizens of the United States. But they shall be under the obligation to make their election within one year from the date of the exchange of ratifications of this treaty; and those who shall remain in the said territories after the expiration of that year, without having declared their intention to retain the character of Mexicans, shall be considered to have elected to become citizens of the United States.

In the said territories, property of every kind, now belonging to Mexicans not established there, shall be inviolably respected. The present owners, the heirs of these, and all Mexicans who may hereafter acquire said property by contract, shall enjoy with respect to it guarantes equally ample as if the same belonged to citizens of the United States.

ARTICLE IX

The Mexicans who, in the territories aforesaid, shall not preserve the character of citizens of the Mexican Republic, conformably with what is stipulated in the preceding article, shall be incorporated into the Union of the United States and be admitted at the proper time (to be judged of by the Congress of the United States) to the enjoyment of all the rights of citizens of the United States, according to the principles of the Constitution; and in the mean time, shall be maintained and protected in the free enjoyment of their liberty and property, and secured in the free exercise of their religion without restriction.

ARTICLE X

[Stricken out]

Article XI

Considering that a great part of the territories, which, by the present treaty, are to be comprehended for the future within the limits of the United States, is now occupied by savage tribes, who will hereafter be under the exclusive control of the Government of the United States, and whose incursions within the territory of Mexico would be prejudicial in the extreme, it is solemnly agreed that all such incursions shall be forcibly restrained by the Government of the United States whensoever this may be necessary; and that when they cannot be prevented, they shall be punished by the said Government, and satisfaction for the same shall be exacted all in the same way, and with equal diligence and energy, as if the same incursions were meditated or committed within its own territory, against its own citizens.

It shall not be lawful, under any pretext whatever, for any inhabitant of the United States to purchase or acquire any Mexican, or any foreigner residing in Mexico, who may have been captured by Indians inhabiting the territory of either of the two republics; nor to purchase or acquire horses, mules, cattle, or property of any kind, stolen within Mexican territory by such Indians.

And in the event of any person or persons, captured within Mexican territory by Indians, being carried into the territory of the United States, the Government of the latter engages and binds itself, in the most solemn manner, so soon as it shall know of such captives being within its territory, and shall be able so to do, through the faithful exercise of its influence and power, to rescue them and return them to their country, or deliver them to the agent or representative of the Mexican Government. The Mexican authorities will, as far as practicable, give to the Government of the United States notice of such captures; and its agents shall pay the expenses incurred in the maintenance and transmission of the rescued captives; who, in the mean time, shall be treated with the utmost hospitality by the American authorities at the place where they may be. But if the Government of the United States, before receiving such notice from Mexico, should obtain intelligence, through any other channel, of the existence of Mexican captives within its territory, it will proceed forthwith to effect their release and delivery to the Mexican agent, as above stipulated.

For the purpose of giving to these stipulations the fullest possible efficacy, thereby affording the security and redress demanded by their true spirit and intent, the Government of the United States will now and hereafter pass, without unnecessary delay, and always vigilantly enforce, such laws as the nature of the subject may require. And, finally, the sacredness of this obligation shall never be lost sight of by the said Government, when providing for the removal of the Indians from any portion of the said territories, or for its being settled by citizens of the United States; but, on the contrary, special care shall then be taken not to place its Indian occupants under the necessity of seeking new homes, by committing those invasions which the United States have solemnly obliged themselves to restrain.

ARTICLE XII

In consideration of the extension acquired by the boundaries of the United States, as defined in the fifth article of the present treaty, the Government of the United States engages to pay to that of the Mexican Republic the sum of fifteen millions of dollars.

Immediately after the treaty shall have been duly ratified by the Government of the Mexican Republic, the sum of three millions of dollars shall be paid to the said Government by that of the United States, at the city of Mexico, in the gold or silver coin of Mexico. The remaining twelve millions of dollars shall be paid at the same place, and in the same coin, in annual installments of three millions of dollars each, together with interest on the same at the rate of six per centum per annum. This interest shall begin to run upon the whole sum of twelve millions from the day of the ratification of the present treaty by— the Mexican Government, and the first of the installments shall be paid at the expiration of one year from the same day. Together with each annual installment, as it falls due, the whole interest accruing on such installment from the beginning shall also be paid.

ARTICLE XIII

The United States engage, moreover, to assume and pay to the claimants all the amounts now due them, and those hereafter to become due, by reason of the claims already liquidated and decided against the Mexican Republic, under the conventions between the two republics severally concluded on the eleventh day of April, eighteen hundred and thirty-nine, and on the thirtieth day of January, eighteen hundred and forty-three; so that the Mexican Republic shall be absolutely exempt, for the future, from all expense whatever on account of the said claims.

ARTICLE XIV

The United States do furthermore discharge the Mexican Republic from all claims of citizens of the United States, not heretofore decided against the Mexican Government, which may have arisen previously to the date of the signature of this treaty; which discharge shall be final and perpetual, whether the said claims be rejected or be allowed by the board of commissioners provided for in the following article, and whatever shall be the total amount of those allowed.

ARTICLE XV

The United States, exonerating Mexico from all demands on account of the claims of their citizens mentioned in the preceding article, and considering them entirely and forever canceled, whatever their amount may be, undertake to make satisfaction for the same, to an amount not exceeding three and one-quarter millions of dollars. To ascertain the validity and amount of those claims, a board of commissioners shall be established by the Government of the United States, whose awards shall be final and conclusive; provided that, in deciding upon the validity of each claim, the boa shall be guided and governed by the principles and rules of decision prescribed by the first

and fifth articles of the unratified convention, concluded at the city of Mexico on the twentieth day of November, one thousand eight hundred and forty-three; and in no case shall an award be made in favour of any claim not embraced by these principles and rules.

If, in the opinion of the said board of commissioners or of the claimants, any books, records, or documents, in the possession or power of the Government of the Mexican Republic, shall be deemed necessary to the just decision of any claim, the commissioners, or the claimants through them, shall, within such period as Congress may designate, make an application in writing for the same, addressed to the Mexican Minister of Foreign Affairs, to be transmitted by the Secretary of State of the United States; and the Mexican Government engages, at the earliest possible moment after the receipt of such demand, to cause any of the books, records, or documents so specified, which shall be in their possession or power (or authenticated copies or extracts of the same), to be transmitted to the said Secretary of State, who shall immediately deliver them over to the said board of commissioners; provided that no such application shall be made by or at the instance of any claimant, until the facts which it is expected to prove by such books, records, or documents, shall have been stated under oath or affirmation.

ARTICLE XVI

Each of the contracting parties reserves to itself the entire right to fortify whatever point within its territory it may judge proper so to fortify for its security.

ARTICLE XVII

The treaty of amity, commerce, and navigation, concluded at the city of Mexico, on the fifth day of April, A.D. 1831, between the United States of America and the United Mexican States, except the additional article, and except so far as the stipulations of the said treaty may be incompatible with any stipulation contained in the present treaty, is hereby revived for the period of eight years from the day of the exchange of ratifications of this treaty, with the same force and virtue as if incorporated therein; it being understood that each of the contracting parties reserves to itself the right, at any time after the said period of eight years shall have expired, to terminate the same by giving one year's notice of such intention to the other party.

ARTICLE XVIII

All supplies whatever for troops of the United States in Mexico, arriving at ports in the occupation of such troops previous to the final evacuation thereof, although subsequently to the restoration of the custom-houses at such ports, shall be entirely exempt from duties and charges of any kind; the Government of the United States hereby engaging and pledging its faith to establish and vigilantly to enforce, all possible guards for securing the revenue of Mexico, by preventing the importation, under cover of this stipulation, of any articles other than such, both in kind and in quantity, as shall really be wanted for the use and consumption of the forces of the United States during the time they may remain in Mexico. To this end it shall be the duty of all officers and agents of the United States to denounce to the Mexican authorities at the respective ports any attempts at a fraudulent abuse of this stipulation, which they may know of, or may have reason to suspect, and to give to such authorities all the aid in their power with regard thereto; and every such attempt, when duly proved and established by sentence of a competent tribunal, they shall be punished by the confiscation of the property so attempted to be fraudulently introduced.

ARTICLE XIX

With respect to all merchandise, effects, and property whatsoever, imported into ports of Mexico, whilst in the occupation of the forces of the United States, whether by citizens of either republic, or by citizens or subjects of any neutral nation, the following rules shall be observed:

(1) All such merchandise, effects, and property, if imported previously to the restoration of the custom-houses to the Mexican authorities, as stipulated for in the third article of this treaty, shall be exempt from confiscation, although the importation of the same be prohibited by the Mexican tariff.

(2) The same perfect exemption shall be enjoyed by all such merchandise, effects, and property, imported subsequently to the restoration of the custom-houses, and previously to the sixty days fixed in the following article for the coming into force of the Mexican tariff at such ports respectively; the said merchandise, effects, and property being, how-

ever, at the time of their importation, subject to the payment of duties, as provided for in the said following article.

(3) All merchandise, effects, and property described in the two rules foregoing shall, during their continuance at the place of importation, and upon their leaving such place for the interior, be exempt from all duty, tax, or imposts of every kind, under whatsoever title or denomination. Nor shall they be there subject to any charge whatsoever upon the sale thereof.

(4) All merchandise, effects, and property, described in the first and second rules, which shall have been removed to any place in the interior, whilst such place was in the occupation of the forces of the United States, shall, during their continuance therein, be exempt from all tax upon the sale or consumption thereof, and from every kind of impost or contribution, under whatsoever title or denomination.

(5) But if any merchandise, effects, or property, described in the first and second rules, shall be removed to any place not occupied at the time by the forces of the United States, they shall, upon their introduction into such place, or upon their sale or consumption there, be subject to the same duties which, under the Mexican laws, they would be required to pay in such cases if they had been imported in time of peace, through the maritime custom-houses, and had there paid the duties conformably with the Mexican tariff.

(6) The owners of all merchandise, effects, or property, described in the first and second rules, and existing in any port of Mexico, shall have the right to reship the same, exempt from all tax, impost, or contribution whatever.

With respect to the metals, or other property, exported from any Mexican port whilst in the occupation of the forces of the United States, and previously to the restoration of the custom-house at such port, no person shall be required by the Mexican authorities, whether general or state, to pay any tax, duty, or contribution upon any such exportation, or in any manner to account for the same to the said authorities.

ARTICLE XX

Through consideration for the interests of commerce generally, it is agreed, that if less than sixty days should elapse between the date of the signature of this treaty and the restoration of the custom houses, conformably with the stipulation in the third article, in such case all merchandise, effects and property whatsoever, arriving at the Mexican ports after the restoration of the said custom-houses, and previously to the expiration of sixty days after the day of signature of this treaty, shall be admitted to entry; and no other duties shall be levied thereon than the duties established by the tariff found in force at such custom-houses at the time of the restoration of the same. And to all such merchandise, effects, and property, the rules established by the preceding article shall apply.

ARTICLE XXI

If unhappily any disagreement should hereafter arise between the Governments of the two republics, whether with respect to the interpretation of any stipulation in this treaty, or with respect to any other particular concerning the political or commercial relations of the two nations, the said Governments, in the name of those nations, do promise to each other that they will endeavour, in the most sincere and earnest manner, to settle the differences so arising, and to preserve the state of peace and friendship in which the two countries are now placing themselves, using, for this end, mutual representations and pacific negotiations. And if, by these means, they should not be enabled to come to an agreement, a resort shall not, on this account, be had to reprisals, aggression, or hostility of any kind, by the one republic against the other, until the Government of that which deems itself aggrieved shall have maturely considered, in the spirit of peace and good neighbourship, whether it would not be better that such difference should be settled by the arbitration of commissioners appointed on each side, or by that of a friendly nation. And should such course be proposed by either party, it shall be acceded to by the other, unless deemed by it altogether incompatible with the nature of the difference, or the circumstances of the case.

ARTICLE XXII

If (which is not to be expected, and which God forbid) war should unhappily break out between the two republics, they do now, with a view to such calamity, solemnly pledge themselves to each other and to the world to observe the following rules; absolutely where the nature of the subject permits, and as closely as possible in all cases where such absolute observance shall be impossible:

(1) The merchants of either republic then residing in the other shall be allowed to remain twelve months (for those dwelling in the interior), and six months (for those dwelling at the seaports) to collect their debts and settle their affairs; during which periods they shall enjoy the same protection, and be on the same footing, in all respects, as the citizens or subjects of the most friendly nations; and, at the expiration thereof, or at any time before, they shall have full liberty to depart, carrying off all their effects without molestation or hindrance, conforming therein to the same laws which the citizens or subjects of the most friendly nations are required to conform to. Upon the entrance of the armies of either nation into the territories of the other, women and children, ecclesiastics, scholars of every faculty, cultivators of the earth, merchants, artisans, manufacturers, and fishermen, unarmed and inhabiting unfortified towns, villages, or places, and in general all persons whose occupations are for the common subsistence and benefit of mankind, shall be allowed to continue their respective employments, unmolested in their persons. Nor shall their houses or goods be burnt or otherwise destroyed, nor their cattle taken, nor their fields wasted, by the armed force into whose power, by the events of war, they may happen to fall; but if the necessity arise to take anything from them for the use of such armed force, the same shall be paid for at an equitable price. All churches, hospitals, schools, colleges, libraries, and other establishments for charitable and beneficent purposes, shall be respected, and all persons connected with the same protected in the discharge of their duties, and the pursuit of their vocations.

(2) In order that the fate of prisoners of war may be alleviated all such practices as those of sending them into distant, inclement or unwholesome districts, or crowding them into close and noxious places, shall be studiously avoided. They shall not be confined in dungeons, prison ships, or prisons; nor be put in irons, or bound or otherwise restrained in the use of their limbs. The officers shall enjoy liberty on their paroles, within convenient districts, and have comfortable quarters; and the common soldiers shall be disposed in cantonments, open and extensive enough for air and exercise and lodged in barracks

as roomy and good as are provided by the party in whose power they are for its own troops. But if any officer shall break his parole by leaving the district so assigned him, or any other prisoner shall escape from the limits of his cantonment after they shall have been designated to him, such individual, officer, or other prisoner, shall forfeit so much of the benefit of this article as provides for his liberty on parole or in cantonment. And if any officer so breaking his parole or any common soldier so escaping from the limits assigned him, shall afterwards be found in arms previously to his being regularly exchanged, the person so offending shall be dealt with according to the established laws of war. The officers shall be daily furnished, by the party in whose power they are, with as many rations, and of the same articles, as are allowed either in kind or by commutation, to officers of equal rank in its own army; and all others shall be daily furnished with such ration as is allowed to a common soldier in its own service; the value of all which supplies shall, at the close of the war, or at periods to be agreed upon between the respective commanders, be paid by the other party, on a mutual adjustment of accounts for the subsistence of prisoners; and such accounts shall not be mingled with or set off against any others, nor the balance due on them withheld, as a compensation or reprisal for any cause whatever, real or pretended. Each party shall be allowed to keep a commissary of prisoners, appointed by itself, with every cantonment of prisoners, in possession of the other; which commissary shall see the prisoners as often as he pleases; shall be allowed to receive, exempt from all duties and taxes, and to distribute, whatever comforts may be sent to them by their friends; and shall be free to transmit his reports in open letters to the party by whom he is employed. And it is declared that neither the pretense that war dissolves all treaties, nor any other whatever, shall be considered as annulling or suspending the solemn covenant contained in this article. On the contrary, the state of war is precisely that for which it is provided; and, during which, its stipulations are to be as sacredly observed as the most acknowledged obligations under the law of nature or nations.

ARTICLE XXIII

This treaty shall be ratified by the President of the United States of America, by and with the advice and consent of the Senate thereof; and by the President of the Mexican Republic, with the previous approbation of its general Congress; and the ratifications shall be exchanged in the City of Washington, or at the seat of Government of Mexico, in four months from the date of the signature hereof, or sooner if practicable. In faith whereof we, the respective Plenipotentiaries, have signed this treaty of peace, friendship, limits, and settlement, and have hereunto affixed our seals respectively. Done in quintuplicate, at the city of Guadalupe Hidalgo, on the second day of February, in the year of our Lord one thousand eight hundred and forty-eight.

Nicholas P. Trist
Luis Gonzaga Cuevas
Bernardo Couto
Miguel Atristain

GADSDEN PURCHASE TREATY; DECEMBER 30, 1853

By the President of the United states of America—a proclamation.

WHEREAS a treaty between the United States of America and the Mexican Republic was concluded and signed at the City of Mexico on the thirtieth day of December, one thousand eight hundred and fifty-three; which treaty, as amended by the Senate of the United States, and being in the English and Spanish languages, is word for word as follows:

IN THE NAME OF ALMIGHTY GOD:

The Republic of Mexico and the United States of America desiring to remove every cause of disagreement which might interfere in any manner with the better friendship and intercourse between the two countries, and especially in respect to the true limits which should be established, when, notwithstanding what was covenanted in the treaty of Guadalupe Hidalgo in the year 1848, opposite interpretations have been urged, which might give occasion to questions of serious moment: to avoid these, and to strengthen and more firmly maintain the peace which happily prevails between the two republics, the President of the United States has, for this purpose, appointed James Gadsden, Envoy Extraordinary and Minister Plenipotentiary of the same, near the Mexican government, and the President of Mexico has appointed as Plenipotentiary "ad hoc" his excellency Don Manuel Diez de Bonilla, cavalier grand cross of the national and distinguished order of Guadalupe, and Secretary of State, and of the office of Foreign Relations, and Don Jose Salazar Ylarregui and General Mariano Monterde as scientific commissioners, invested with full powers for this negotiation, who, having communicated their respective full powers, and finding them in due and proper form, have agreed upon the articles following:

ARTICLE I

The Mexican Republic agrees to designate the following as her true limits with the United States for the future: retaining the same dividing line between the two Californias as already defined and established, according to the 5th article of the treaty of Guadalupe Hidalgo, the limits between the two republics shall be as follows: Beginning in the Gulf of Mexico, three leagues from land, opposite the mouth of the Rio Grande, as provided in the 5th article of the treaty of Guadalupe Hidalgo; thence, as defined in the said article, up the middle of that river to the point where the parallel of 31° 47′ north latitude crosses the same; thence due west one hundred miles; thence south to the parallel of 31° 20′ north latitude; thence along the said parallel of 31° 20′ to the 111th meridian of longitude west of Greenwich; thence in a straight line to a point on the Colorado River twenty English miles below the junction of the Gila and Colorado rivers; thence up the middle of the said river Colorado until it intersects the present line between the United States and Mexico.

For the performance of this portion of the treaty, each of the two governments shall nominate one commissioner, to the end that, by common consent the two thus nominated, having met in the city of Paso del Norte, three months after the exchange of the ratifications of this treaty, may proceed to survey and mark out upon the land the dividing line stipulated by this article, where it shall not have already been surveyed and established by the mixed commission, according to the treaty of Guadalupe, keeping a journal and making proper plans of their operations. For this purpose, if they should judge it necessary, the contracting parties shall be at liberty each to unite to its respective commissioner, scientific or other assistants, such as astronomers and surveyors, whose concurrence shall not be considered necessary for the settlement and of a true line of division between the two Republics; that line shall be alone established upon which the commissioners may fix, their consent in this particular being considered decisive and an integral part of this treaty, without necessity of ulterior ratification or approval, and without room for interpretation of any kind by either of the parties contracting.

The dividing line thus established shall, in all time, be faithfully respected by the two governments, without any variation therein, unless of the express and free consent of the two, given in conformity to the principles of the law of nations, and in accordance with the constitution of each country respectively.

In consequence, the stipulation in the 5th article of the treaty of Guadalupe upon the boundary line therein described is no longer of any force, wherein it may conflict with that here established, the said line being considered annulled and abolished wherever it may not coincide with the present, and in the same manner remaining in full force where in accordance with the same.

ARTICLE II

The government of Mexico hereby releases the United States from all liability on account of the obligations contained in the eleventh article of the treaty of Guadalupe Hidalgo; and the said article and the thirty-third article of the treaty of amity, commerce, and navigation between the United States of America and the United Mexican States concluded at Mexico, on the fifth day of April, 1831, are hereby abrogated.

ARTICLE III

In consideration of the foregoing stipulations, the Government of the United States agrees to pay to the government of Mexico, in the city of New York, the sum of ten millions of dollars, of which seven millions shall be paid immediately upon the exchange of the ratifications of this treaty, and the remaining three millions as soon as the boundary line shall be surveyed, marked, and established.

ARTICLE IV

The provisions of the 6th and 7th articles of the treaty of Guadalupe Hidalgo having been rendered nugatory, for the most part, by the cession of territory granted in the first article of this treaty, the said articles are hereby abrogated and annulled, and the provisions as herein expressed substituted therefor. The vessels, and citizens of the United States shall, in all time, have free and uninterrupted passage through the Gulf of California, to and from their possessions situated north of the boundary line of the two countries. It being understood that this passage is to be by navigating the Gulf of California and the river Colorado, and not by land, without the express consent of the Mexican government; and precisely the same provisions, stipulations, and restrictions, in all respects, are hereby agreed upon and adopted, and shall be scrupulously observed and enforced by the two contracting governments in reference to the Rio Colorado, so far and for such distance as the middle of that river is made their common boundary line by the first article of this treaty.

The several provisions, stipulations, and restrictions contained in the 7th article of the treaty of Guadalupe Hidalgo shall remain in force only so far as regards the Rio Bravo del Norte, below the ini-

tial of the said boundary provided in the first article of this treaty; that is to say, below the intersection of the 31° 47′30″ parallel of latitude, with the boundary line established by the late treaty dividing said river from its mouth upwards, according to the fifth article of the treaty of Guadalupe.

ARTICLE V

All the provisions of the eighth and ninth, sixteenth and seventeenth articles of the treaty of Guadalupe Hidalgo, shall apply to the territory ceded by the Mexican Republic in the first article of the present treaty, and to all the rights of persons and property, both civil and ecclesiastical, within the same, as fully and as effectually as if the said articles were herein again recited and set forth.

ARTICLE VI

No grants of land within the territory ceded by the first article of this treaty bearing date subsequent to the day—twenty-fifth of September—when the minister and subscriber to this treaty on the part of the United States, proposed to the Government of Mexico to terminate the question of boundary, will be considered valid or be recognized by the United States, or will any grants made previously be respected or be considered as obligatory which have not been located and duly recorded in the archives of Mexico.

ARTICLE VII

Should there at any future period (which God forbid) occur any disagreement between the two nations which might lead to a rupture of their relations and reciprocal peace, they bind themselves in like manner to procure by every possible method the adjustment of every difference; and should they still in this manner not succeed, never will they proceed to a declaration of war, without having previously paid attention to what has been set forth in article twenty-one of the treaty of Guadalupe for similar cases; which article, as well as the twenty-second is here reaffirmed.

ARTICLE VIII

The Mexican Government having on the 5th of February, 1853, authorized the early construction of a plank and railroad across the Isthmus of Tehuantepec, and, to secure the stable benefits of said transit way to the persons and merchandise of the citizens of Mexico and the United States, it is stipulated that neither government will interpose any obstacle to the transit of persons and merchandise of both nations; and at no time shall higher charges be made on the transit of persons and property of citizens of the United States, than may be made on the persons and property of other foreign nations, nor shall any interest in said transit way, nor in the proceeds thereof, be transferred to any foreign government.

The United States, by its agents, shall have the right to transport across the isthmus, in closed bags, the mails of the United States not intended for distribution along the line of communication; also the effects of the United States government and its citizens, which may be intended for transit, and not for distribution on the isthmus, free of custom-house or other charges by the Mexican government. Neither passports nor letters of security will be required of persons crossing the isthmus and not remaining in the country.

When the construction of the railroad shall be completed, the Mexican government agrees to open a port of entry in addition to the port of Vera Cruz, at or near the terminus of said road on the Gulf of Mexico.

The two governments will enter into arrangements for the prompt transit of troops and munitions of the United States, which that government may have occasion to send from one part of its territory to another, lying on opposite sides of the continent.

The Mexican government having agreed to protect with its whole power the prosecution, preservation, and security of the work, the United States may extend its protection as it shall judge wise to it when it may feel sanctioned and warranted by the public or international law.

ARTICLE IX

This treaty shall be ratified, and the respective ratifications shall be exchanged at the city of Washington within the exact period of six months from the date of its signature, or sooner, if possible.

In testimony whereof, we, the plenipotentiaries of the contracting parties, have hereunto affixed our hands and seals at Mexico, the thirtieth (30th) day of December, in the year of our Lord one thousand eight hundred and fifty-three, in the thirty-third year of the independence of the Mexican republic, and the seventy-eighth of that of the United States.

JAMES GADSDEN,

MANUEL DIEZ DE BONILLA

JOSE SALAZAR YLARREGUI.

MARIANO MONTERDE,

And whereas the said treaty, as amended, has been duly ratified on both parts, and the respective ratifications of the same have this day been exchanged at Washington, by WILLIAM L. MARCY, Secretary of State of the United States, and SENOR GENERAL DON JUAN N. ALMONTE, Envoy Extraordinary and Minister Plenipotentiary of the Mexican Republic, on the part of their respective Governments:

Now, therefore, be it known that I, FRANKLIN PIERCE, President of the United States of America, have caused the said treaty to be made public, to the end that the same, and every clause and article thereof, may be observed and fulfilled with good faith by the United States and the citizens thereof.

In witness whereof I have hereunto set my hand and caused the seal of the United States to be affixed.

Done at the city of Washington, this thirtieth day of June, in the year of our Lord one thousand eight hundred and fifty-four, and of the Independence of the United States the seventy-eighth.

BY THE PRESIDENT:

FRANKLIN PIERCE,

W. L. MARCY, Secretary of State.

TREATY OF PEACE BETWEEN THE UNITED STATES AND SPAIN; DECEMBER 10, 1898

The United States of America and Her Majesty the Queen Regent of Spain, in the name of her august son Don Alfonso XIII, desiring to end the state of war now existing between the two countries, have for that purpose appointed as plenipotentiaries:

The President of the United States, William R. Day, Cushman K. Davis, William P. Frye, George Gray, and Whitelaw Reid, citizens of the United States;

And Her Majesty the Queen Regent of Spain,

Don Eugenio Montero Rios, president of the senate, Don Buenaventura de Abarzuza, senator of the Kingdom and ex-minister of the Crown; Don Jose de Garnica, deputy of the Cortes and associate justice of the supreme court; Don Wenceslao Ramirez de Villa-Urrutia, envoy extraordinary and minister plenipotentiary at Brussels, and Don Rafael Cerero, general of division;

Who, having assembled in Paris, and having exchanged their full powers, which were found to be in due and proper form, have, after discussion of the matters before them, agreed upon the following articles:

Article I

Spain relinquishes all claim of sovereignty over and title to Cuba. And as the island is, upon its evacuation by Spain, to be occupied by the United States, the United States will, so long as such occupation shall last, assume and discharge the obligations that may under international law result from the fact of its occupation, for the protection of life and property.

Article II

Spain cedes to the United States the island of Porto Rico and other islands now under Spanish sovereignty in the West Indies, and the island of Guam in the Marianas or Ladrones.

Article III

Spain cedes to the United States the archipelago known as the Philippine Islands, and comprehending the islands lying within the following line:

A line running from west to east along or near the twentieth parallel of north latitude, and through the middle of the navigable channel of Bachi, from the one hundred and eighteenth (118th) to the one hundred and twenty-seventh (127th) degree meridian of longitude east of Greenwich, thence along the one hundred and twenty seventh (127th) degree meridian of longitude east of Greenwich to the parallel of four degrees and forty five minutes (4° 45′) north latitude, thence along the parallel of four degrees and forty five minutes (4° 45′) north latitude to its intersection with the meridian of longitude one hundred and nineteen degrees and thirty five minutes (119° 35′) east of Greenwich, thence along the meridian of longitude one hundred and nineteen degrees and thirty five minutes (119° 35′) east of Greenwich to the parallel of latitude seven degrees and forty minutes (7° 40′) north, thence along the parallel of latitude of seven degrees and forty minutes (7° 40′) north to its intersection with the one hundred and sixteenth (116th) degree meridian of longitude east of Greenwich, thence by a direct line to the intersection of the tenth (10th) degree parallel of north latitude with the one hundred and eighteenth (118th) degree meridian of longitude east of Greenwich, and thence along the one hundred and eighteenth (118th) degree meridian of longitude east of Greenwich to the point of beginning. The United States will pay to Spain the sum of twenty million dollars ($20,000,000) within three months after the exchange of the ratifications of the present treaty.

Article IV

The United States will, for the term of ten years from the date of the exchange of the ratifications of the present treaty, admit Spanish ships and merchandise to the ports of the Philippine Islands on the same terms as ships and merchandise of the United States.

Article V

The United States will, upon the signature of the present treaty, send back to Spain, at its own cost, the Spanish soldiers taken as prisoners of war on the capture of Manila by the American forces. The arms of the soldiers in question shall be restored to them.

Spain will, upon the exchange of the ratifications of the present treaty, proceed to evacuate the Philippines, as well as the island of Guam, on terms similar to those agreed upon by the Commissioners appointed to arrange for the evacuation of Porto Rico and other islands in the West Indies, under the Protocol of August 12, 1898, which is to continue in force till its provisions are completely executed.

The time within which the evacuation of the Philippine Islands and Guam shall be completed shall be fixed by the two Governments. Stands of colors, uncaptured war vessels, small arms, guns of all calibres, with their carriages and accessories, powder, ammunition, livestock, and materials and supplies of all kinds, belonging to the land and naval forces of Spain in the Philippines and Guam, remain the property of Spain. Pieces of heavy ordnance, exclusive of field artillery, in the fortifications and coast defences, shall remain in their emplacements for the term of six months, to be reckoned from the exchange of ratifications of the treaty; and the United States may, in the meantime, purchase such material from Spain, if a satisfactory agreement between the two Governments on the subject shall be reached.

Article VI

Spain will, upon the signature of the present treaty, release all prisoners of war, and all persons detained or imprisoned for political offences, in connection with the insurrections in Cuba and the Philippines and the war with the United States.

Reciprocally, the United States will release all persons made prisoners of war by the American forces, and will undertake to obtain the release of all Spanish prisoners in the hands of the insurgents in Cuba and the Philippines.

The Government of the United States will at its own cost return to Spain and the Government of Spain will at its own cost return to the United States, Cuba, Porto Rico, and the Philippines, according to the situation of their respective homes, prisoners released or caused to be released by them, respectively, under this article.

Article VII

The United States and Spain mutually relinquish all claims for indemnity, national and individual, of every kind, of either Government, or of its citizens or subjects, against the other Government, that may have arisen since the beginning of the late insurrection in Cuba and prior to the exchange of ratifications of the present treaty, including all claims for indemnity for the cost of the war.

The United States will adjudicate and settle the claims of its citizens against Spain relinquished in this article.

Article VIII

In conformity with the provisions of Articles I, II, and III of this treaty, Spain relinquishes in Cuba, and cedes in Porto Rico and other islands in the West Indies, in the island of Guam, and in the Philippine Archipelago, all the buildings, wharves, barracks, forts, structures, public highways and other immovable property which, in conformity with law, belong to the public domain, and as such belong to the Crown of Spain.

And it is hereby declared that the relinquishment or cession, as the case may be, to which the preceding paragraph refers, can not in any respect impair the property or rights which by law belong to the peaceful possession of property of all kinds, of provinces, municipalities, public or private establishments, ecclesiastical or civic bodies, or any other associations having legal capacity to acquire and possess property in the aforesaid territories renounced or ceded, or of private individuals, of whatsoever nationality such individuals may be.

The aforesaid relinquishment or cession, as the case may be, includes all documents exclusively referring to the sovereignty relinquished or ceded that may exist in the archives of the Peninsula. Where any document in such archives only in part relates to said sovereignty, a copy of such part will be furnished whenever it shall be requested. Like rules shall be reciprocally observed in favor of Spain in respect of documents in the archives of the islands above referred to.

In the aforesaid relinquishment or cession, as the case may be, are also included such rights as the Crown of Spain and its authorities possess in respect of the official archives and records, executive as well as judicial, in the islands above referred to, which relate to said islands or the rights and property of their inhabitants. Such archives and records shall be carefully preserved, and private persons shall without distinction have the right to require, in accordance with law, authenticated copies of the contracts, wills and other instruments forming part of notorial protocols or files, or which may be contained in the executive or judicial archives, be the latter in Spain or in the islands aforesaid.

Article IX

Spanish subjects, natives of the Peninsula, residing in the territory over which Spain by the present treaty relinquishes or cedes her sovereignty, may remain in such territory or may remove therefrom, retaining in either event all their rights of property, including the right to sell or dispose of such property or of its proceeds; and they shall also have the right to carry on their industry, commerce and professions, being subject in respect thereof to such laws as are applicable to other foreigners. In case they remain in the territory they may preserve their allegiance to the Crown of Spain by making, before a court of record, within a year from the date of the exchange of ratifications of this treaty, a declaration of their decision to preserve such allegiance; in default of which declaration they shall be held to have renounced it and to have adopted the nationality of the territory in which they may reside.

The civil rights and political status of the native inhabitants of the territories hereby ceded to the United States shall be determined by the Congress.

Article X

The inhabitants of the territories over which Spain relinquishes or cedes her sovereignty shall be secured in the free exercise of their religion.

Article XI

The Spaniards residing in the territories over which Spain by this treaty cedes or relinquishes her sovereignty shall be subject in matters civil as well as criminal to the jurisdiction of the courts of the country wherein they reside, pursuant to the ordinary laws governing the same; and they shall have the right to appear before such courts, and to pursue the same course as citizens of the country to which the courts belong.

Article XII

Judicial proceedings pending at the time of the exchange of ratifications of this treaty in the territories over which Spain relinquishes or cedes her sovereignty shall be determined according to the following rules:

1. Judgments rendered either in civil suits between private individuals, or in criminal matters, before the date mentioned, and with respect to which there is no recourse or right of review under the Spanish law, shall be deemed to be final, and shall be executed in due form by competent authority in the territory within which such judgments should be carried out.

2. Civil suits between private individuals which may on the date mentioned be undetermined shall be prosecuted to judgment before the court in which they may then be pending or in the court that may be substituted therefor.

3. Criminal actions pending on the date mentioned before the Supreme Court of Spain against citizens of the territory which by this treaty ceases to be Spanish shall continue under its jurisdiction until final judgment; but, such judgment having been rendered, the execution thereof shall be committed to the competent authority of the place in which the case arose.

Article XIII

The rights of property secured by copyrights and patents acquired by Spaniards in the Island of Cuba and in Porto Rico, the Philippines and other ceded territories, at the time of the exchange of the ratifications of this treaty, shall continue to be respected. Spanish scientific, literary and artistic works, not subversive of public order in the territories in question, shall continue to be admitted free of duty into such territories, for the period of ten years, to be reckoned from the date of the exchange of the ratifications of this treaty.

Article XIV

Spain will have the power to establish consular officers in the ports and places of the territories, the sovereignty over which has been either relinquished or ceded by the present treaty.

Article XV

The Government of each country will, for the term of ten years, accord to the merchant vessels of the other country the same treatment in respect of all port charges, including entrance and clearance dues, light dues, and tonnage duties, as it accords to its own merchant vessels, not engaged in the coastwise trade.

Article XVI

It is understood that any obligations assumed in this treaty by the United States with respect to Cuba are limited to the time of its occupancy thereof; but it will upon termination of such occupancy, advise any Government established in the island to assume the same obligations.

Article XVII

The present treaty shall be ratified by the President of the United States, by and with the advice and consent of the Senate thereof, and by Her Majesty the Queen Regent of Spain; and the ratifications shall be exchanged at Washington within six months from the date hereof, or earlier if possible.

In faith whereof, we, the respective Plenipotentiaries, have signed this treaty and have hereunto affixed our seals.

Done in duplicate at Paris, the tenth day of December, in the year of Our Lord one thousand eight hundred and ninety-eight.

[Seal] William R. Day
[Seal] Cushman K. Davis
[Seal] William P. Frye
[Seal] Geo. Gray
[Seal] Whitelaw Reid
[Seal] Eugenio Montero Rios
[Seal] B. de Abarzuza
[Seal] J. de Garnica
[Seal] W. R. de Villa Urrutia
[Seal] Rafael Cerero

THE OFFICIAL BRACERO AGREEMENT

Agreement of August 4, 1942. For the Temporary Migration of Mexican Agricultural Workers to the United States as Revised on April 26, 1943, by an Exchange of Notes Between the American Embassy at Mexico City and the Mexican Ministry for Foreign Affairs.

General Provisions

1) It is understood that Mexicans contracting to work in the United States shall not be engaged in any military service.

2) Mexicans entering the United States as result of this understanding shall not suffer discriminatory acts of any kind in accordance with the Executive Order No. 8802 issued at the White House June 25, 1941.

3) Mexicans entering the United States under this understanding shall enjoy the guarantes of transportation, living expenses and repatriation established in Article 29 of the Mexican Federal Labor Law as follows:

Article 29. All contracts entered into by Mexican workers for lending their services outside their country shall be made in writing, legalized by the municipal authorities of the locality where entered into and vised by the Consul of the country where their services are being used. Furthermore, such contract shall contain, as a requisite of validity of same, the following stipulations, without which the contract is invalid.

I. Transportation and subsistence expenses for the worker, and his family, if such is the case, and all other expenses which originate from point of origin to border points and compliance of immigration requirements, or for any other similar concept, shall be paid exclusively by the employer or the contractual parties.

II. The worker shall be paid in full the salary agreed upon, from which no deduction shall be made in any amount for any of the concepts mentioned in the above sub-paragraph.

III. The employer or contractor shall issue a bond or constitute a deposit in cash in the Bank of Workers, or in the absence of same, in the Bank of Mexico, to the entire satisfaction of the respective labor authorities, for a sum equal to repatriation costs of the worker and his family, and those originated by transportation to point of origin.

IV. Once the employer established proof of having covered such expenses or the refusal of the worker to return to his country, and that he does not owe the worker any sum covering salary or indemnization to which he might have a right, the labor authorities shall authorize the return of the deposit or the cancellation of the bond issued.

It is specifically understood that the provisions of Section III of Article 29 above-mentioned shall not apply to the Government of the United States notwithstanding the inclusion of this section in the agreement, in view of the obligations assumed by the United States government under Transportation (a) and (c) of this agreement.

4) Mexicans entering the United States under this understanding shall not be employed to displace other workers, or for the purpose of reducing rates of pay previously established.

In order to implement the application of the general Principles mentioned above the following specific clauses are established:

(When the word "employer" is used hereinafter it shall be understood to mean the Farm Security Administration of the Department of Agriculture of the United States of America; the word "sub-employer" shall mean the owner or operator of the farm or farms in the United States on which the Mexican will be employed; the word "worker" hereinafter used shall refer to the Mexican Farm laborer entering the United States under this understanding.)

Contracts

a) Contracts will be made between the employer and the worker under the supervision of the Mexican Government. (Contracts must be written in Spanish.)

b) The employer shall enter into a contract with the sub-employer, with a view to proper observance of the principles embodied in this understanding.

Admission

a. The Mexican health authorities will, at the place whence the worker comes, see that he meets the necessary physical conditions.

Transportation

a. All transportation and living expenses from the place of origin to destination, and return, as well as expenses incurred in the fulfillment of any requirements of a migratory nature shall be met by the Employer.

b. Personal belongings of the workers up to a maximum of 35 kilos per person shall be transported at the expense of the Employer.

c. In accord with the intent of Article 29 of Mexican Federal Labor Law, quoted under General Provisions (3) above, it is expected that the employer will collect all or part of the cost accruing under (a) and (b) of Transportation from the sub-employer.

Wages and Employment

a. Wages to be paid the worker shall be the same as those paid for similar work to other agricultural laborers under the same conditions within the same area, in the respective regions of destination. Piece rates shall be so set as to enable the worker of average ability to earn the prevailing wage. In any case wages for piece work or hourly work will not be less than 30 cents per hour.

b. On the basis of prior authorization from the Mexican Government salaries lower than those established in the previous clause may be paid those emigrants admitted into the United States as members of the family of the worker under contract and who, when they are in the field, are able also to become agricultural laborers but who, by their condition of age or sex, cannot carry out the average amount of ordinary work.

c. The worker shall be exclusively employed as an agricultural laborer for which he has been engaged; any change from such type of employment or any change of locality shall be made with the express approval of the worker and with the authority of the Mexican Government.

d. There shall be considered illegal any collection by reason of commission or for any other concept demanded of the worker.

e. Work of minors under 14 years shall be strictly prohibited, and they shall have the same schooling opportunities as those enjoyed by children of other agricultural laborers.

f. Workers domiciled in the migratory labor camps or at any other place of employment under this understanding shall be free to obtain articles for their personal consumption, or that of their families, wherever it is most convenient for them.

g. *The Mexican workers will be furnished without cost to them with hygienic lodgings, adequate to the physical conditions of the region of a type used by a common laborer of the region and the medical and sanitary services enjoyed also without cost to them will be identical with those furnished to the other agricultural workers in the regions where they may lend their services.*

h. Workers admitted under this understanding shall enjoy as regards occupational diseases and accidents the same guarantees enjoyed by other agricultural workers under United States legislation.

i. Groups of workers admitted under this understanding shall elect their own representatives to deal with the Employer, but it is understood that all such representatives shall be working members of the group.

The Mexican Consuls, assisted by the Mexican Labor Inspectors, recognized as such by the Employer will take all possible measures of protection in the interest of the Mexican workers in all questions affecting them, within their corresponding jurisdiction, and will have free access to the places of work of the Mexican workers. The Employer will observe that the sub-employer grants all facilities to the Mexican Government for the compliance of all the clauses in this contract.

j. For such time as they are unemployed under a period equal to 75% of the period (exclusive of Sundays) for which the workers have been contracted they shall receive a subsistence allowance at the rate of $3.00 per day.

Should the cost of living rise this will be a matter for reconsideration.

The master contracts for workers submitted to the Mexican government shall contain definite provisions for computation of subsistence and payments under the understanding.

k. The term of the contract shall be made in accordance with the authorities of the respective countries.

l. At the expiration of the contract under this understanding, and if the same is not renewed, the authorities of the United States shall consider illegal, from an immigration point of view, the continued stay of the worker in the territory of the United States, exception made of cases of physical impossibility.

Savings Fund

a. The respective agencies of the Government of the United States shall be responsible for the safekeeping of the sums contributed by the Mexican workers toward the formation of their Rural Savings Fund, until such sums are transferred to *the Wells Fargo Bank and Union Trust Company of San Francisco for the account of the Bank of Mexico, S.A., which will transfer such amounts to the Mexican Agricultural*

Credit Bank. This last shall assume responsibility for the deposit, for the safekeeping and for the application, or in the absence of these, for the return of such amounts.

b. The Mexican Government through the Banco de Crédito Agrícola will take care of the security of the savings of the workers to be used for payment of the agricultural implements, which may be made available to the Banco de Crédito Agrícola in accordance with exportation permits for shipment to Mexico with the understanding that the Farm Security Administration will recommend priority treatment for such implements.

Numbers

As it is impossible to determine at this time the number of workers who may be needed in the United States for agricultural labor employment, the employer shall advise the Mexican Government from time to time as to the number needed. The Government of Mexico shall determine in each case the number of workers who may leave the country without detriment to its national economy.

General Considerations

It is understood that, with reference to the departure from Mexico of Mexican workers, who are not farm laborers, there shall govern in understandings reached by agencies to the respective Governments the same fundamental principles which have been applied here to the departure of farm labor.

It is understood that the employers will cooperate with such other agencies of the Government of the United States in carrying this understanding into effect whose authority under the laws of the United States are such as to contribute to the effectuation of the understandings.

Either Government shall have the right to renounce this understanding, given appropriate notification to the other Government 90 days in advance.

This understanding may be formalized by an exchange of notes between the Ministry of Foreign Affairs of the Republic of Mexico and the Embassy of the United States of America in Mexico.

CONSTITUTION OF THE COMMONWEALTH OF PUERTO RICO

We, the people of Puerto Rico, in order to organize ourselves politically on a fully democratic basis, to promote the general welfare, and to secure for ourselves and our posterity the complete enjoyment of human rights, placing our trust in Almighty God, do ordain and establish this Constitution for the commonwealth which, in the exercise of our natural rights, we now create within our union with the United States of America.

In so doing, we declare:

The democratic system is fundamental to the life of the Puerto Rican community;

We understand that the democratic system of government is one in which the will of the people is the source of public power, the political order is subordinate to the rights of man, and the free participation of the citizen in collective decisions is assured;

We consider as determining factors in our life our citizenship of the United States of America and our aspiration continually to enrich our democratic heritage in the individual and collective enjoyment of its rights and privileges; our loyalty to the principles of the Federal Constitution; the co-existence in Puerto Rico of the two great cultures of the American Hemisphere; our fervor for education; our faith in justice; our devotion to the courageous, industrious, and peaceful way of life; our fidelity to individual human values above and beyond social position, racial differences, and economic interests; and our hope for a better world based on these principles.

ARTICLE I: THE COMMONWEALTH

Section 1. The Commonwealth of Puerto Rico is hereby constituted. Its political power emanates from the people and shall be exercised in accordance with their will, within the terms of the compact agreed upon between the people of Puerto Rico and the United States of America.

Section 2. The government of the Commonwealth of Puerto Rico shall be republican in form and its legislative, judicial and executive branches as established by this Constitution shall be equally subordinate to the sovereignty of the people of Puerto Rico.

Section 3. The political authority of the Commonwealth of Puerto Rico shall extend to the Island of Puerto Rico and to the adjacent islands within its jurisdiction.

Section 4. The seat of the government shall be the city of San Juan.

ARTICLE II: BILL OF RIGHTS

Section 1. The dignity of the human being is inviolable. All men are equal before the law. No discrimination shall be made on account of race, color, sex, birth, social origin or condition, or political or religious ideas. Both the laws and the system of public education shall embody these principles of essential human equality.

Section 2. The laws shall guarantee the expression of the will of the people by means of equal, direct and secret universal suffrage and shall protect the citizen against any coercion in the exercise of the electoral franchise.

Section 3. No law shall be made respecting an establishment of religion or prohibiting the free exercise thereof. There shall be complete separation of church and state.

Section 4. No law shall be made abridging the freedom of speech or of the press, or the right of the people peaceably to assemble and to petition the government for a redress of grievances.

Section 5. Every person has the right to an education which shall be directed to the full development of the human personality and to the strengthening of respect for human rights and fundamental freedoms. There shall be a system of free and wholly non-sectarian public education. Instruction in the elementary and secondary schools shall be free and shall be compulsory in the elementary schools to the extent permitted by the facilities of the state. No public property or public funds shall be used for the support of schools or educational institutions other than those of the state. Nothing contained in this provision shall prevent the state from furnishing to any child non-educational services established by law for the protection or welfare of children.

Section 6. Persons may join with each other and organize freely for any lawful purpose, except in military or quasi-military organizations.

Section 7. The right to life, liberty and the enjoyment of property is recognized as a fundamental right of man. The death penalty shall not exist. No person shall be deprived of his liberty or property without due process of law. No person in Puerto Rico shall be denied the equal protection of the laws. No laws impairing the obligation of contracts shall be enacted. A minimum amount of property and possessions shall be exempt from attachment as provided by law.

Section 8. Every person has the right to the protection of law against abusive attacks on his honor, reputation and private or family life.

Section 9. Private property shall not be taken or damaged for public use except upon payment of just compensation and in the manner provided by law. No law shall be enacted authorizing condemnation of printing presses, machinery or material devoted to publications of any kind. The buildings in which these objects are located may be condemned only after a judicial finding of public convenience and necessity pursuant to procedure that shall be provided by law, and may be taken before such a judicial finding only when there is placed at the disposition of the publication an adequate site in which it can be installed and continue to operate for a reasonable time.

Section 10. The right of the people to be secure in their persons, houses, papers and effects against unreasonable searches and seizures shall not be violated.

Wire-tapping is prohibited.

No warrant for arrest or search and seizure shall issue except by judicial authority and only upon probable cause supported by oath or affirmation, and particularly describing the place to be searched and the persons to be arrested or the things to be seized.

Evidence obtained in violation of this section shall be inadmissible in the courts.

Section 11. In all criminal prosecutions, the accused shall enjoy the right to have a speedy and public trial, to be informed of the nature and cause of the accusation and to have a copy thereof, to be confronted with the witnesses against him, to have assistance of counsel, and to be presumed innocent.

In all prosecutions for a felony the accused shall have the right of trial by an impartial jury composed of twelve residents of the district, who may render their verdict by a majority vote which in no case may be less than nine.

No person shall be compelled in any criminal case to be a witness against himself and the failure of the accused to testify may be neither taken into consideration nor commented upon against him.

No person shall be twice put in jeopardy of punishment for the same offense.

Before conviction every accused shall be entitled to be admitted to bail.

Incarceration prior to trial shall not exceed six months nor shall bail or fines be excessive. No person shall be imprisoned for debt.

Section 12. Neither slavery nor involuntary servitude shall exist except in the latter case as a punishment for crime after the accused has been duly convicted. Cruel and unusual punishments shall not be inflicted. Suspension of civil rights including the right to vote shall cease upon service of the term of imprisonment imposed.

No *ex post facto* law or bill of attainder shall be passed.

Section 13. The writ of *habeas corpus* shall be granted without delay and free of costs. The privilege of the writ of *habeas corpus* shall not be suspended, unless the public safety requires it in case of rebellion, insurrection or invasion. Only the Legislative Assembly shall have the power to suspend the privilege of the writ of *habeas corpus* and the laws regulating its issuance. The military authority shall always be subordinate to civil authority.

Section 14. No titles of nobility or other hereditary honors shall be granted. No officer or employee of the Commonwealth shall accept gifts, donations, decorations or offices from any foreign country or officer without prior authorization by the Legislative Assembly.

Section 15. The employment of children less than fourteen years of age in any occupation which is prejudicial to their health or morals or which places them in jeopardy of life or limb is prohibited.

No child less than sixteen years of age shall be kept in custody in a jail or penitentiary.

Section 16. The right of every employee to choose his occupation freely and to resign therefrom is recognized, as is his right to equal pay for equal work, to a reasonable minimum salary, to protection against risks to his health or person in his work or employment, and to an ordinary-workday which shall not exceed eight hours. An employee may work in excess of this daily limit only if he is paid extra compensation as provided by law, at a rate never less than one and one-half times the regular rate at which he is employed.

Section 17. Persons employed by private businesses, enterprises and individual employers and by agencies or instrumentalities of the government operating as private businesses or enterprises, shall have the right to organize and to bargain collectively with their employers through representatives of their own free choosing in order to promote their welfare.

Section 18. In order to assure their right to organize and to bargain collectively, persons employed by private businesses, enterprises and individual employers and by agencies, enterprises and individual employers and by agencies or instrumentalities of the government operating as private businesses or enterprises, in their direct relations with their own employers shall have the right to strike, to picket and to engage in other legal concerted activities.

Nothing herein contained shall impair the authority of the Legislative Assembly to enact laws to deal with grave emergencies that clearly imperil the public health or safety or essential public services.

Section 19. The foregoing enumeration of rights shall not be construed restrictively nor does it contemplate the exclusion of other rights not specifically mentioned which belong to the people in a democracy. The power of the Legislative Assembly to enact laws for the protection of the life, health and general welfare of the people shall likewise not be construed restrictively.

Section 20. The Commonwealth also recognizes the existence of the following human rights:

The right of every person to receive free elementary and secondary education.

The right of every person to obtain work.

The right of every person to a standard of living adequate for the health and well-being of himself and of his family, and especially to food, clothing, housing and medical care and necessary social services.

The right of every person to social protection in the event of unemployment, sickness, old age or disability.

The right of motherhood and childhood to special care and assistance.

The rights set forth in this section are closely connected with the progressive development of the economy of the Commonwealth and require, for their full effectiveness, sufficient resources and an agricultural and industrial development not yet attained by the Puerto Rican community.

In the light of their duty to achieve the full liberty of the citizen, the people and the government of Puerto Rico shall do everything in their power to promote the greatest possible expansion of the system of production, to assure the fairest distribution of economic output, and to obtain the maximum understanding between individual initiative and collective cooperation. The executive and judicial branches shall bear in mind this duty and shall construe the laws that tend to fulfill it in the most favorable manner possible.

ARTICLE III: THE LEGISLATURE

Section 1. The legislative power shall be vested in a Legislative Assembly, which shall consist of two houses, the Senate and the House of Representatives, whose members shall be elected by direct vote at each general election.

Section 2. The Senate shall be composed of twenty-seven Senators and the House of Representatives of fifty-one Representatives, except as these numbers may be increased in accordance with the provisions of Section 7 of this Article.

Section 3. For the purpose of election of members of the Legislative Assembly, Puerto Rico shall be divided into eight senatorial districts and forty representative districts. Each senatorial district shall elect two Senators and each representative district one Representative.

There shall also be eleven Senators and eleven Representatives elected at large. No elector may vote for more than one candidate for Senator at Large or for more than one candidate for Representative at Large.

Section 4. In the first and subsequent elections under this Constitution the division of senatorial and representative districts as provided in Article VIII shall be in effect. After each decennial census beginning with the year 1960, said division shall be revised by a Board composed of the Chief Justice of the Supreme Court as Chairman and of two additional members appointed by the Governor with the advice and consent of the Senate. The two additional members shall not belong to the same political party. Any revision shall maintain the number of senatorial and representative districts here created, which shall be composed of contiguous and compact territory and shall be organized, insofar as practicable, upon the basis of population and means of communication. Each senatorial district shall always include five representative districts.

The decisions of the Board shall be made by majority vote and shall take effect in the general elections next following each revision. The Board shall cease to exist after the completion of each revision.

Section 5. No person shall be a member of the Legislative Assembly unless he is able to read and write the Spanish or English language and unless he is a citizen of the United States and of Puerto Rico and has resided in Puerto Rico at least two years immediately prior to the date of his election or appointment. No person shall be a member of the Senate who is not over thirty years of age, and no person shall be a member of the House of Representatives who is not over twenty-five years of age.

Section 6. No person shall be eligible to election or appointment as Senator or Representative for a district unless he has resided therein at least one year immediately prior to his election or appointment. When there is more than one representative district in a municipality, residence in the municipality shall satisfy this requirement.

Section 7. If in a general election more than two-thirds of the members of either house are elected from one political party or from a single ticket, as both are defined by law, the number of members shall be increased in the following cases:

(a) If the party or ticket which elected more than two-thirds of the members of either or both houses shall have obtained less than two-thirds of the total number of votes cast for the office of Governor, the number of members of the Senate or of the House of Representatives or of both bodies, whichever may be the case, shall be increased by declaring elected a sufficient number of candidates of the minority party or parties to bring the total number of members of the minority party or parties to nine in the Senate and to seventeen in the House of Representatives. When there is more than one minority party, said additional members shall be declared elected from among the candidates of each minority party in the proportion that the number of votes cast for the candidate of each of said parties for the office of Governor bears to the total number of votes cast for the candidates of all the minority parties for the office of Governor.

When one or more minority parties shall have obtained representation in a proportion equal to or greater than the proportion of votes received by their respective candidates for Governor, such party or parties shall not be entitled to additional members until the representation established for each of the other minority parties under these provisions shall have been completed.

(b) If the party or ticket which elected more than two-thirds of the members of either or both houses shall have obtained more than two-thirds of the total number of votes cast for the office of Governor, and one or more minority parties shall not have elected the number of members in the Senate or in the House of Representatives or in both houses, whichever may be the case, which corresponds to the proportion of votes cast by each of them for the office of Governor, such additional number of their candidates shall be declared elected as is necessary in order to complete said proportion as nearly as possible, but the number of Senators of all the minority parties shall never, under this provision, be more than nine or that of Representatives more than seventeen.

In order to select additional members of the Legislative Assembly from a minority party in accordance with these provisions, its candidates at large who have not been elected shall be the first to be declared elected in the order of the votes that they have obtained, and thereafter its district candidates who; not having been elected, have obtained in their respective districts the highest proportion of the total number of votes cast as compared to the proportion of votes cast in favor of other candidates of the same party not elected to an equal office in the other districts.

The additional Senators and Representatives whose election is declared under this section shall be considered for all purposes as Senators at Large or Representatives at Large.

The measures necessary to implement these guarantees, the method of adjudicating fractions that may result from the application of the rules contained in this section, and the minimum number of votes that a minority party must cast in favor of its candidate for Governor in order to have the right to the representation provided herein shall be determined by the Legislative Assembly.

Section 8. The term of office of Senators and Representatives shall begin on the second day of January immediately following the date of the general election in which they shall have been elected. If, prior to the fifteen months immediately preceding the date of the next general election, a vacancy occurs in the office of Senator or Representative for a district, the Governor shall call a special election in said district within thirty days following the date on which the vacancy occurs. This election shall be held not later than ninety days after the call, and the person elected shall hold office for the rest of the unexpired term of his predecessor. When said vacancy occurs during a legislative session, or when the Legislative Assembly or the Senate has been called for a date prior to the certification of the results of the special election, the presiding officer of the appropriate house shall fill said vacancy by appointing the person recommended by the central committee of the political party of which his predecessor in office was a member. Such person shall hold the office until certification of the election of the candidate who was elected. When the vacancy occurs within fifteen months prior to a general election, or when it occurs in the office of a Senator at Large or a Representative at Large, the presiding officer of the appropriate house shall fill it, upon the recommendation of the political party of which the previous holder of the office was a member, by appointing a person selected in the same manner as that in which his predecessor was selected. A vacancy in the office of a Senator at Large or a Representative at Large elected as an independent candidate shall be filled by an election in all districts.

Section 9. Each house shall be the sole judge of the election, returns and qualifications of its members; shall choose its own officers; shall adopt rules for its own proceedings appropriate to legislative bodies; and, with the concurrence of three-fourths of the total number of members of which it is composed, may expel any member for the causes established in Section 21 of this Article, authorizing impeachments. The Senate shall elect a President and the House of Representatives a Speaker from among their respective members.

Section 10. The Legislative Assembly shall be deemed a continuous body during the term for which its members are elected and shall meet in regular session each year commencing on the second Monday in January. The duration of regular sessions and the periods of time for introduction and consideration of bills shall be prescribed by law. When the Governor calls the Legislative Assembly into special session it may consider only those matters specified in the call or in any special message sent to it by him during the session. No special session shall continue longer than twenty calendar days.

Section 11. The sessions of each house shall be open.

Section 12. A majority of the total number of members of which each house is composed shall constitute a quorum, but a smaller number may adjourn from day to day and shall have authority to compel the attendance of absent members.

Section 13. The two houses shall meet in the capitol of Puerto Rico and neither of them may adjourn for more than three consecutive days without the consent of the other.

Section 14. No member of the Legislative Assembly shall be arrested while the house of which he is a member is in session, or during the fifteen days before or after such session, except for treason, felony or breach of the peace. The members of the Legislative Assembly shall not be questioned in any other place for any speech, debate or vote in either house or in any committee.

Section 15. No Senator or Representative may, during the term for which he was elected or chosen, be appointed to any civil office in the Government of Puerto Rico, its municipalities or instrumentalities, which shall have been created or the salary of which shall have been increased during said term. No person may hold office in the Government of Puerto Rico, its municipalities or instrumentalities and be a Senator or Representative at the same time. These provisions shall not prevent a member of the Legislative Assembly from being designated to perform functions *ad honorem*.

Section 16. The Legislative Assembly shall have the power to create, consolidate or reorganize executive departments and to define their functions.

Section 17. No bill shall become a law unless it has been printed, read, referred to a committee and returned therefrom with a written report, but either house may discharge a committee from the study and report of any bill and proceed to the consideration thereof. Each house shall keep a journal of its proceedings and of the votes cast for and against bills. The legislative proceedings shall be published in a daily record in the form determined by law. Every bill, except general appropriation bills, shall be confined to one subject, which shall be clearly expressed in its title, and any part of an act whose subject has not been expressed in the title shall be void. The general appropriation act shall contain only appropriations and rules for their disbursement. No bill shall be amended in a manner that changes its original purpose or incorporates matters extraneous to it.

In amending any article or section of a law, said article or section shall be promulgated in its entirety as amended. All bills for raising revenue shall originate in the House of Representatives, but the Senate may propose or concur with amendments as on other bills,

Section 18. The subjects which may be dealt with by means of joint resolution shall be determined by law, but every joint resolution shall follow the same legislative process as that of a bill.

Section 19. Every bill which is approved by a majority of the total number of members of which each house is composed shall be submitted to the Governor and shall become law if he signs it or if he does not return it, with his objections, to the house in which it originated within ten days (Sundays excepted) counted from the date on which he shall have received it.

When the Governor returns a bill the house that receives it shall enter his objections on its journal and both houses may reconsider it. If approved by two-thirds of the total number of members of which each house is composed, said bill shall become law.

If the Legislative Assembly adjourns sine die before the Governor has acted on a bill that has been presented to him less than ten days before, he is relieved of the obligation of returning it with his objections and the bill shall become law only if the Governor signs it within thirty days after receiving it.

Every final passage or reconsideration of a bill shall be by a roll-call vote.

Section 20. In approving any appropriation bill that contains more than one item, the Governor may eliminate one or more of such items or reduce their amounts, at the same time reducing the total amounts involved.

Section 21. The House of Representatives shall have exclusive power to initiate impeachment proceedings and, with the concurrence of two-thirds of the total number of members of which it is composed, to bring an indictment. The Senate shall have exclusive power to try and to decide impeachment cases, and in meeting for such purposes the Senators shall act in the name of the people and under oath or affirmation. No judgment of conviction in an impeachment trial shall be pronounced without the concurrence of three-fourths of the total number of members of which the Senate is composed, and the judgment shall be limited to removal from office. The person impeached, however, may be liable and subject to indictment, trial, judgment and punishment according to law. The causes of impeachment shall be treason, bribery, other felonies, and misdemeanors involving moral turpitude. The Chief Jus-

tice of the Supreme Court shall preside at the impeachment trial of the Governor.

The two houses may conduct impeachment proceedings in their regular or special sessions. The presiding officers of the two houses, upon written request of two-thirds of the total number of members of which the House of Representatives is composed, must convene them to deal with such proceedings.

Section 22. The Governor shall appoint a Controller with the advice and consent of a majority of the total number of members of which each house is composed. The Controller shall meet the requirements prescribed by law and shall hold office for a term of ten years and until his successor has been appointed and qualifies. The Controller shall audit all the revenues, accounts and expenditures of the Commonwealth, of its agencies and instrumentalities and of its municipalities, in order to determine whether they have been made in accordance with law. He shall render annual reports and any special reports that may be required of him by the Legislative Assembly or by the Governor.

In the performance of his duties the Controller shall be authorized to administer oaths, take evidence and compel under pain of contempt, the attendance of witnesses and the production of books, letters, documents, papers, records and all other articles deemed essential to a full understanding of the matter under investigation.

The Controller may be removed for the causes and pursuant to the procedure established in the preceding section.

ARTICLE IV: THE EXECUTIVE

Section 1. The executive power shall be vested in a Governor, who shall be elected by direct vote in each general election.

Section 2. The Governor shall hold office for the term of four years from the second day of January of the year following his election and until his successor has been elected and qualifies. He shall reside in Puerto Rico and maintain his office in its capital city.

Section 3. No person shall be Governor unless, on the date of the election, he is at least thirty-five years of age, and is and has been during the preceding five years a citizen of the United States and a citizen and *bona fide* resident of Puerto Rico.

Section 4. The Governor shall execute the laws and cause them to be executed.

He shall call the Legislative Assembly or the Senate into special session when in his judgment the public interest so requires.

He shall appoint, in the manner prescribed by this Constitution or by law, all officers whose appointment he is authorized to make. He shall have the power to make appointments while the Legislative Assembly is not in session. Any such appointments that require the advice and consent of the Senate or of both houses shall expire at the end of the next regular session.

He shall be the commander-in-chief of the militia.

He shall have the power to call out the militia and summon the posse comitatus in order to prevent or suppress rebellion, invasion or any serious disturbance of the public peace.

He shall have the power to proclaim martial law when the public safety requires it in case of rebellion or invasion or imminent danger thereof. The Legislative Assembly shall meet forthwith on their own initiative to ratify or revoke the proclamation.

He shall have the power to suspend the execution of sentences in criminal cases and to grant pardons, commutations of punishment, and total or partial remissions of fines and forfeitures for crimes committed in violation of the laws of Puerto Rico. This power shall not extend to cases of impeachment.

He shall approve or disapprove in accordance with this Constitution the joint resolutions and bills passed by the Legislative Assembly.

He shall present to the Legislative Assembly, at the beginning of each regular session, a message concerning the affairs of the Commonwealth and a report concerning the state of the Treasury of Puerto Rico and the proposed expenditures for the ensuing fiscal year. Said report shall contain the information necessary for the formulation of a program of legislation.

He shall exercise the other powers and functions and discharge the other duties assigned to him by this Constitution or by law.

Section 5. For the purpose of exercising executive power, the Governor shall be assisted by Secretaries whom he shall appoint with the advice and consent of the Senate. The appointment of the Secretary of State shall in addition require the advice and consent of the House of Representatives, and the person appointed shall fulfill the requirements established in Section 3 of this article. The Secretaries shall collectively constitute the Governor's advisory council, which shall be designated as the Council of Secretaries.

Section 6. Without prejudice to the power of the Legislative Assembly to create, reorganize and consolidate executive departments and to define their functions, the following departments are hereby established: State, Justice, Education, Health, Treasury, Labor, Agriculture and Commerce, and Public Works. Each of these executive departments shall be headed by a Secretary.

Section 7. When a vacancy occurs in the office of Governor, caused by death, resignation, removal, total and permanent incapacity, or any other absolute disability, said office shall devolve upon the Secretary of State, who shall hold it for the rest of the term and until a new Governor has been elected and qualifies. In the event that vacancies exist at the same time in both the office of Governor and that of Secretary of State, the law shall provide which of the Secretaries shall serve as Governor.

Section 8. When for any reason the Governor is temporarily unable to perform his functions, the Secretary of State shall substitute for him during the period he is unable to serve. If for any reason the Secretary of State is not available, the Secretary determined by law shall temporarily hold the office of Governor.

Section 9. If the Governor-elect shall not have qualified or if he has qualified and a permanent vacancy occurs in the office of Governor before he shall have appointed a Secretary of State, or before said Secretary, having been appointed, shall have qualified, the Legislative Assembly just elected, upon convening for its first regular session, shall elect, by a majority of the total number of members of which each house is composed, a Governor who shall hold office until his successor is elected in the next general election and qualifies.

Section 10. The Governor may be removed for the causes and pursuant to the procedure established in Section 21 of Article III of this Constitution.

ARTICLE V: THE JUDICIARY

Section 1. The judicial power of Puerto Rico shall be vested in a Supreme Court, and in such other courts as may be established by law.

Section 2. The courts of Puerto Rico shall constitute a unified judicial system for purposes of jurisdiction, operation and administration. The Legislative Assembly may create and abolish courts, except for the Supreme Court, in a manner not inconsistent with this Constitution, and shall determine the venue and organization of the courts.

Section 3. The Supreme Court shall be the court of last resort in Puerto Rico and shall be composed of a Chief Justice and four Associate Justices. The number of Justices may be changed only by law upon request of the Supreme Court.

Section 4. The Supreme Court shall sit, in accordance with rules adopted by it, as a full court or in divisions composed of not less than three Justices. No law shall be held unconstitutional except by a majority of the total number of Justices of which the Court is composed in accordance with this Constitution or with law. [As amended in General Election of Nov. 8, 1960.]

Section 5. The Supreme Court, any of its divisions, or any of its Justices may hear in the first instance petitions for *habeas corpus* and any other causes and proceedings as determined by law.

Section 6. The Supreme Court shall adopt for the courts rules of evidence and of civil and criminal procedure which shall not abridge, enlarge or modify the substantive rights of the parties. The rules thus adopted shall be submitted to the Legislative Assembly at the beginning of its next regular session and shall not go into effect until sixty days after the close of said session, unless disapproved by the Legislative Assembly, which shall have the power both at said session and subsequently to amend, repeal or supplement any of said rules by a specific law to that effect.

Section 7. The Supreme Court shall adopt rules for the administration of the courts. These rules shall be subject to the laws concerning procurement, personnel, audit and appropriation of funds, and other laws which apply generally to all branches of the government. The Chief Justice shall direct the administration of the courts and shall appoint an administrative director who shall hold office at the will of the Chief Justice.

Section 8. Judges shall be appointed by the Governor with the advice and consent of the Senate. Justices of the Supreme Court shall not assume office until after confirmation by the Senate and shall hold their offices during good behavior. The terms of office of the other judges shall be fixed by law and shall not be less than that fixed for the terms of office of a judge of the same or equivalent category exist-

ing when this Constitution takes effect. The other officials and employees of the courts shall be appointed in the manner provided by law.

Section 9. No person shall be appointed a Justice of the Supreme Court unless he is a citizen of the United States and of Puerto Rico, shall have been admitted to the practice of law in Puerto Rico at least ten years prior to his appointment, and shall have resided in Puerto Rico at least five years immediately prior thereto.

Section 10. The· Legislative Assembly shall establish a retirement system for judges. Retirement shall be compulsory at the age of seventy years.

Section 11. Justices of the Supreme Court may be removed for the causes and pursuant to the procedure established in Section 21 of Article III of this Constitution. Judges of the other courts may be removed by the Supreme Court for the causes and pursuant to the procedure provided by law.

Section 12. No judge shall make a direct or indirect financial contribution to any political organization or party, or hold any executive office therein, or participate in a political campaign of any kind, or be a candidate for an elective public office unless he has resigned his judicial office at least six months Prior to his nomination.

Section 13. In the event that a court or any of its divisions or sections is changed or abolished by law, the person holding a post of judge therein shall continue to hold it during the rest of the term for which he was appointed and shall perform the judicial functions assigned to him by the Chief Justice of the Supreme Court.

ARTICLE VI: GENERAL PROVISIONS

Section 1. The Legislative Assembly shall have the power to create, abolish, consolidate and reorganize municipalities; to change their territorial limits; to determine their organization and functions; and to authorize them to develop programs for the general welfare and to create any agencies necessary for that purpose.

No law abolishing or consolidating municipalities shall take effect until ratified in a referendum by a majority of the qualified electors voting in said referendum in each of the municipalities to be abolished or consolidated. The referendum shall be conducted in the manner determined by law, which shall include the applicable procedures of the election laws in effect when the referendum law is approved.

Section 2. The power of the Commonwealth of Puerto Rico to impose and collect taxes and to authorize their imposition and collection by municipalities shall be exercised as determined by the Legislative Assembly and shall never be surrendered or suspended. The power of the Commonwealth of Puerto Rico to contract and to authorize the contracting of debts shall be exercised as determined by the Legislative Assembly, but no direct obligations of the Commonwealth for money borrowed directly by the Commonwealth evidenced by bonds or notes for the payment of which the full faith credit and taxing power of the Commonwealth shall be pledged shall be issued by the Commonwealth if the total of (i) the amount of principal of and interest on such bonds and notes, together with the amount of principal of and interest on all such bonds and notes theretofore issued by the Commonwealth and then outstanding, payable in any fiscal year and (ii) any amounts paid by the Commonwealth in the fiscal year next preceding the then current fiscal year for principal or interest on account of any outstanding obligations evidenced by bonds or notes guaranteed by the Commonwealth, shall exceed 15 percent of the average of the total amount of the annual revenues raised under the provisions of Commonwealth legislation and covered into the Treasury of Puerto Rico in the two fiscal years next preceding the then current fiscal year; and no such bonds or notes issued by the Commonwealth for any purpose other than housing facilities shall mature later than 30 years from their date and no bonds or notes issued for housing facilities shall mature later than 40 years from their date; and the Commonwealth shall not guarantee any obligations evidenced by bonds or notes if the total of the amount payable in any fiscal year on account of principal of and interest on all the direct obligations referred to above theretofore issued by the Commonwealth and then outstanding and the amounts referred to in item (ii) above shall exceed 15 percent of the average of the total amount of such annual revenues.

The Legislative Assembly shall fix limitations for the issuance of direct obligations by any of the municipalities of Puerto Rico for money borrowed directly by such municipality evidenced by bonds or notes for the payment of which the full faith, credit and taxing power of such municipality shall be pledged; provided, however, that no such bonds or notes shall be issued by any municipality in an amount which, together with the amount of all such bonds and notes theretofore issued by such municipality and then outstanding, shall exceed the percentage determined by the Legislative Assembly, which shall be not less than five per centum (5%) nor more than ten per centum (10%) of the aggregate tax valuation of the property within such municipality.

The Secretary of the Treasury may be required to apply the available revenues including surplus to the payment of interest on the public debt and the amortization thereof in any case provided for by Section 8 of this Article VI at the suit of any holder of bonds or notes issued in evidence thereof. [As amended by the voters at a referendum held Dec. 10, 1961.]

Section 3. The rule of taxation in Puerto Rico shall be uniform.

Section 4. General elections shall be held every four years on the day of November determined by the Legislative Assembly. In said elections there shall be elected a Governor, the members of the Legislative Assembly, and the other officials whose election on that date is provided for by law.

Every person over eighteen years of age shall be entitled to vote if he fulfills the other conditions determined by law. No person shall be deprived of the right to vote because he does not know how to read or write or does not own property.

All matters concerning the electoral process, registration of voters, political parties and candidates shall be determined by law.

Every popularly elected official shall be elected by direct vote and any candidate who receives more votes than any other candidate for the same office shall be declared elected.

Section 5. The laws shall be promulgated in accordance with the procedure prescribed by law and shall specify the terms under which they shall take effect.

Section 6. If at the end of any fiscal year the appropriations necessary for the ordinary operating expenses of the Government and for the payment of interest on and amortization of the public debt for the ensuing fiscal year shall not have been made, the several sums appropriated in the last appropriation acts for the objects and purposes therein specified, so far as the same may be applicable, shall continue in effect item by item, and the Governor shall authorize the payments necessary for such purposes until corresponding appropriations are made.

Section 7. The appropriations made for any fiscal year shall not exceed the total revenues, including available surplus, estimated for said fiscal Year unless the imposition of taxes sufficient to cover said appropriations is provided by law.

Section 8. In case the available revenues including surplus for any fiscal year are insufficient to meet the appropriations made for that year, interest on the public debt and amortization thereof shall first be paid, and other disbursements shall thereafter be made in accordance with the order of priorities established by law.

Section 9. Public property and funds shall only be disposed of for public purposes, for the support and operation of state institutions, and pursuant to law.

Section 10. No law shall give extra compensation to any public officer, employee, agent or contractor after services shall have been rendered or contract made. No law shall extend the term of any public officer or diminish his salary or emoluments after his election or appointment. No person shall draw a salary for more than one office or position in the government of Puerto Rico.

Section 11. The salaries of the Governor, the Secretaries, the members of the Legislative Assembly, the Controller and Judges shall be fixed by a special law and, except for the salaries of the members of the Legislative Assembly, shall not be decreased during the terms for which they are elected or appointed. The salaries of the Governor and the Controller shall not be increased during said terms. No increase in the salaries of the members of the Legislative Assembly shall take effect until the expiration of the term of the Legislative Assembly during which it is enacted. Any reduction of the salaries of the members of the Legislative Assembly shall be effective only during the term of the Legislative Assembly which approves it.

Section 12. The Governor shall occupy and use, free of rent, the buildings and properties belonging to the Commonwealth which have been or shall hereafter be used and occupied by him as chief executive.

Section 13. The procedure for granting franchises, rights, privileges and concessions of a public or quasi-public nature shall be determined by law, but every concession of this kind to a person or private entity must be approved by the Governor or by the executive official whom he designates. Every franchise, right, privilege or concession of a public or quasi-public nature shall be subject to amendment, alteration or repeal as determined by law.

Section 14. No corporation shall be authorized to conduct the business of buying and selling real estate or be permitted to hold or own real estate except such as may be reasonably necessary to enable it to carry out the purposes for which it was created, and every corporation authorized to engage in agriculture shall by its charter be restricted to the ownership and control of not to exceed five hundred acres of land; and this provision shall be held to prevent any member of a corporation engaged in agriculture from being in any wise interested in any other corporation engaged in agriculture.

Corporations, however, may loan funds upon real estate security, and purchase real estate when necessary for the collection of loans, but they shall dispose of real estate so obtained within five years after receiving the title.

Corporations not organized in Puerto Rico, but doing business in Puerto Rico, shall be bound by the provisions of this section so far as they are applicable.

These provisions shall not prevent the ownership, possession or management of lands in excess of five hundred acres by the Commonwealth, its agencies or instrumentalities.

Section 15. The Legislative Assembly shall determine all matters concerning the flag, the seal and the anthem of the Commonwealth. Once determined, no law changing them shall take effect until one year after the general election next following the date of enactment of said law.

Section 16. All public officials and employees of the Commonwealth, its agencies, instrumentalities and political subdivisions, before entering upon their respective duties, shall take an oath to support the Constitution of the United States and the Constitution and laws of the Commonwealth of Puerto Rico.

Section 17. In case of invasion, rebellion, epidemic or any other event giving rise to a state of emergency, the Governor may call the Legislative Assembly to meet in a place other than the Capitol of Puerto Rico, subject to the approval or disapproval of the Legislative Assembly. Under the same conditions, the Governor may, during the period of emergency, order the government, its agencies and instrumentalities to be moved temporarily to a place other than the seat of the government.

Section 18. All criminal actions in the courts of the Commonwealth shall be conducted in the name and by the authority of "The People of Puerto Rico" until otherwise provided by law.

Section 19. It shall be the public policy of the Commonwealth to conserve, develop and use its natural resources in the most effective manner possible for the general welfare of the community; to conserve and maintain buildings and places declared by the Legislative Assembly to be of historic or artistic value; to regulate its penal institutions in a manner that effectively achieves their purposes and to provide, within the limits of available resources, for adequate treatment of delinquents in order to make possible their moral and social rehabilitation.

ARTICLE VII: AMENDMENTS TO THE CONSTITUTION

Section 1. The Legislative Assembly may propose amendments to this Constitution by a concurrent resolution approved by not less than two-thirds of the total number of members of which each house is composed. All proposed amendments shall be submitted to the qualified electors in a special referendum, but if the concurrent resolution is approved by not less than three-fourths of the total number of members of which each house is composed, the Legislative Assembly may provide that the referendum shall be held at the same time as the next general election. Each proposed amendment shall be voted on separately and not more than three proposed amendments may be submitted at the same referendum. Every proposed amendment shall specify the terms under which it shall take effect, and it shall become a part of this Constitution if it is ratified by a majority of the electors voting thereon. Once approved, a proposed amendment must be published at least three months prior to the date of the referendum.

Section 2. The Legislative Assembly, by a concurrent resolution approved by two-thirds of the total number of members of which each house is composed, may submit to the qualified electors at a referendum, held at the same time as a general election, the question of whether a constitutional convention shall be called to revise this Constitution. If a majority of the electors voting on this question vote in favor of the revision, it shall be made by a Constitutional Convention elected in the manner provided by law. Every revision of this Constitution shall be submitted to the qualified electors at a special referendum for ratification or rejection by a majority of the votes cast at the referendum.

Section 3. No amendment to this Constitution shall alter the republican form of government established by it or abolish its bill of rights.

ARTICLE VIII: SENATORIAL AND REPRESENTATIVE DISTRICTS

Section 1. The senatorial and representative districts shall be the following:

I. SENATORIAL DISTRICT OF SAN JUAN, which shall be composed of the following Representative Districts: 1. The Capital of Puerto Rico, excluding the present electoral precincts of Santurce and Río Piedras; 2. Electoral zones numbers 1 and 2 of the present precinct of Santurce; 3. Electoral zone number 3 of the present precinct of Santurce; 4. Electoral zone number 4 of the present precinct of Santurce; and 5. Wards Hato Rey, Puerto Nuevo and Caparra Heights of the Capital of Puerto Rico.

II. SENATORIAL DISTRICT OF BAYAMON, which shall be composed of the following Representative Districts: 6. The municipality of Bayamón; 7. The municipalities of Carolina and Trujillo Alto; 8. The present electoral precinct of Río Piedras, excluding wards Hate Rey, Puerto Nuevo and Caparra Heights of the Capital of Puerto Rico; 9. The municipalities of Cataño, Guaynabo and Toa Baja; and 10. The municipalities of Toa Alta, Corozal and Naranjito.

III. SENATORIAL DISTRICT OF ARECIBO, which shall be composed of the following Representative Districts: 11. The municipalities of Vega Baja, Vega Alta and Dorado; 12. The municipalities of Manatí and Barceloneta; 13. The municipalities of Ciales and Morovis; 14. The municipality of Arecibo; and 15. The municipality of Utuado.

IV. SENATORIAL DISTRICT OF AGUADILLA, which shall be composed of the following Representative Districts: 16. The municipalities of Camuy, Hatillo and Quebradillas; 17. The municipalities of Aguadilla and Isabela; 18. The municipalities of San Sebastián and Moca; 19. The municipalities of Lares, Las Marías and Maricao; and 20. The municipalities of Añasco, Aguada and Rincón.

V. SENATORIAL DISTRICT OF MAYAGUEZ, which shall be composed of the following Representative Districts: 21. The municipality of Mayaguez; 22. The municipalities of Cabo Rojo, Hormigueros and Lajas; 23. The municipalities of San Germán and Sabana Grande; 24. The municipalities of Yauco and Guanica; and 25. The municipalities of Guayanilla and Peñuelas.

VI. SENATORIAL DISTRICT OF PONCE, which shall be composed of the following Representative Districts: 26. The first, second, third, fourth, fifth and sixth wards and the City Beach of the municipality of Ponce; 27. The municipality of Ponce, except for the first, second, third, fourth, fifth and sixth wards and the City Beach; 28. The municipalities of Adjuntas and Jayuya; 29. The municipalities of Juana Díaz, Santa Isabel and Villalba; and 30. The municipalities of Coamo and Orocovis.

VII. SENATORIAL DISTRICT OF GUAYAMA, which shall be composed of the following Representative Districts: 31. The municipalities of Aibonito, Barranquitas and Comerio; 32. The municipalities of Cayey and Cidra; 33. The municipalities of Caguas and Aguas Buenas; 34. The municipalities of Guayama and Salinas; and 35. The municipalities of Patillas, Maunabo and Arroyo.

VIII. SENATORIAL DISTRICT OF HUMACAO, which shall be composed of the following Representative Districts: 36. The municipalities of Humacao and Yabucoa; 37. The municipalities of Juncos, Guarabo and San Lorenzo; 38. The municipalities of Naguabo, Ceiba and Las Piedras; 39. The municipalities of Fajardo and Vieques and the Island of Culebra; and 40. The municipalities of Río Grande, and Loíza and Luquillo.

Section 2. Electoral zones numbers 1, 2, 3 and 4 included in three representative districts within the senatorial district of San Juan are those presently existing for purposes of electoral organization in the second precinct of San Juan.

ARTICLE IX: TRANSITORY PROVISIONS

Section 1. When this Constitution goes into effect all laws not inconsistent therewith shall continue in full force until amended or repealed, or until they expire by their own terms.

Unless otherwise provided by this Constitution, civil and criminal liabilities, rights, franchises, concessions, privileges, claims, actions, causes of action, contracts, and civil criminal and administrative proceedings shall continue unaffected, notwithstanding the taking effect of this Constitution.

Section 2. All officers who are in office by election or appointment on the date this Constitution takes effect shall continue to hold their offices and to perform the functions thereof in a manner not inconsistent with this Constitution, unless the functions of their offices, are abolished or until their successors are selected and qualify in accordance with this Constitution and laws enacted pursuant thereto.

Section 3. Notwithstanding the age limit fixed by this Constitution for compulsory retirement, all the judges of the courts of Puerto Rico who are holding office on the date this Constitution takes effect shall continue to hold their judicial offices until the expiration of the terms for which they were appointed, and in the case of Justices of the Supreme Court during good behavior.

Section 4. The Commonwealth of Puerto Rico shall be the successor of the People of Puerto Rico for all purposes, including without limitation the collection and payments of debts and liabilities in accordance with their terms.

Section 5. When this Constitution goes into effect, the term "citizen of the Commonwealth of Puerto Rico" shall replace the term "citizen of Puerto Rico" as previously used.

Section 6. Political parties shall continue to enjoy all rights recognized by the election law, provided that on the effective date of this Constitution they fulfill the minimum requirements for the registration of new parties contained in said law. Five years after this Constitution shall have taken effect the Legislative Assembly may change these requirements, but any law increasing them shall not go into effect until after the general election next following its enactment.

Section 7. The Legislative Assembly may enact the laws necessary to supplement and make effective these transitory provisions in order to assure the functioning of the government until the officers provided for by this Constitution are elected or appointed and qualify, and until this Constitution takes effect in all respects.

Section 8. If the legislative Assembly creates a Department of Commerce, the Department of Agriculture and Commerce shall thereafter be called the Department of Agriculture.

Section 9. The first election under the provisions of this Constitution shall be held on the date provided by law, but not later than six months after the effective date of this Constitution. The second general election under this Constitution shall be held in the month of November 1956 on a day provided by law.

Section 10. This Constitution shall take effect when the Governor so proclaims, but not later than sixty days after its ratification by the Congress of the United States.

Done in Convention, at San Juan, Puerto Rico, on the sixth day of February, in the year of Our Lord one thousand nine hundred and fifty-two.

Appendix II: Statistical Tables

Table 1: Hispanic Population by Type: 2000

Subject	Number	%
Hispanic or Latino Origin		
Total Population	281,421,906	100.0
Hispanic or Latino (of any race)	35,305,818	12.5
Not Hispanic or Latino	246,116,088	87.5
Hispanic or Latino by Type		
Hispanic or Latino (of any race)	35,305,818	100.0
Mexican	20,640,711	58.5
Puerto Rican	3,406,178	9.6
Cuban	1,241,685	3.5
Other Hispanic or Latino	10,017,244	28.4
Dominican (Dominican Republic)	764,945	2.2
Central American (excludes Mexican)	1,686,937	4.8
Costa Rican	68,588	0.2
Guatemalan	372,487	1.1
Honduran	217,569	0.6
Nicaraguan	177,684	0.5
Panamanian	91,723	0.3
Salvadoran	655,165	1.9
Other Central American	103,721	0.3
South American	1,353,562	3.8
Argentinean	100,864	0.3
Bolivian	42,068	0.1
Chilean	68,849	0.2
Colombian	470,684	1.3
Ecuadorian	260,559	0.7
Paraguayan	8,769	0.0
Peruvian	233,926	0.7
Uruguayan	18,804	0.1
Venezuelan	91,507	0.3
Other South American	57,532	0.2
Spaniard	100,135	0.3
All other Hispanic or Latino	6,111,665	17.3
Checkbox only, other Hispanic	1,733,274	4.9
Write-in Spanish	686,004	1.9
Write-in Hispanic	2,454,529	7.0
Write-in Latino	450,769	1.3
Not elsewhere classified	787,089	2.2

Source: U.S. Census Bureau, Census 2000.

Table 2: Hispanic Population by Type for Regions, States, and Puerto Rico: 1990 and 2000

	1990			2000						
	Total population	Hispanic population		Total population	Hispanic population		Hispanic type			
Area		Number	%		Number	%	Mexican	Puerto Rican	Cuban	Other Hispanic
United States.....	248,709,873	22,354,059	9.0	281,421,906	35,305,818	12.5	20,640,711	3,406,178	1,241,685	10,017,244
Region										
Northeast............	50,809,229	3,754,389	7.4	53,594,378	5,254,087	9.8	479,169	2,074,574	168,959	2,531,385
Midwest..............	59,668,632	1,726,509	2.9	64,392,776	3,124,532	4.9	2,200,196	325,363	45,305	553,668
South..................	85,445,930	6,767,021	7.9	100,236,820	11,586,696	11.6	6,548,081	759,305	921,427	3,357,883
West...................	52,786,082	10,106,140	19.1	63,197,932	15,340,503	24.3	11,413,265	246,936	105,994	3,574,308
State										
Alabama..............	4,040,587	24,629	0.6	4,447,100	75,830	1.7	44,522	6,322	2,354	22,632
Alaska.................	550,043	17,803	3.2	626,932	25,852	4.1	13,334	2,649	553	9,316
Arizona...............	3,665,228	688,338	18.8	5,130,632	1,295,617	25.3	1,065,578	17,587	5,272	207,180
Arkansas.............	2,350,725	19,876	0.8	2,673,400	86,866	3.2	61,204	2,473	950	22,239
California............	29,760,021	7,687,938	25.8	33,871,648	10,966,556	32.4	8,455,926	140,570	72,286	2,297,774
Colorado.............	3,294,394	424,302	12.9	4,301,261	735,601	17.1	450,760	12,993	3,701	268,147
Connecticut........	3,287,116	213,116	6.5	3,405,565	320,323	9.4	23,484	194,443	7,101	95,295
Delaware.............	666,168	15,820	2.4	783,600	32,277	4.8	12,986	14,005	932	9,354
District of Columbia........	606,900	32,710	5.4	572,059	44,953	7.9	5,098	2,328	1,101	36,426
Florida................	12,937,926	1,574,143	12.2	15,982,378	2,682,715	16.8	363,925	482,027	833,120	1,003,643
Georgia	6,478,216	108,922	1.7	8,186,453	435,227	5.3	275,288	35,532	12,536	111,871
Hawaii................	1,108,229	81,390	7.3	1,211,537	87,699	7.2	19,820	30,005	711	37,163
Idaho..................	1,006,749	52,927	5.3	1,293,953	101,690	7.9	79,324	1,509	408	20,449
Illinois................	11,430,602	904,446	7.9	12,419,293	1,530,262	12.3	1,144,390	157,851	18,438	209,583
Indiana...............	5,544,159	98,788	1.8	6,080,485	214,536	3.5	153,042	19,678	2,754	39,062
Iowa	2,776,755	32,647	1.2	2,926,324	82,473	2.8	61,154	2,690	750	17,879
Kansas................	2,477,574	93,670	3.8	2,688,418	188,252	7.0	148,270	5,237	1,680	33,065
Kentucky............	3,685,296	21,984	0.6	4,041,769	59,939	1.5	31,385	6,469	3,516	18,569
Louisiana...........	4,219,973	93,044	2.2	4,468,976	107,738	2.4	32,267	7,670	8,448	59,353
Maine.................	1,227,928	6,829	0.6	1,274,923	9,360	0.7	2,756	2,275	478	3,851
Maryland............	4,781,468	125,102	2.6	5,296,486	227,916	4.3	39,900	25,570	6,754	155,692
Massachusetts....	6,016,425	287,549	4.8	6,349,097	428,729	6.8	22,288	199,207	8,867	198,367
Michigan............	9,295,297	201,596	2.2	9,938,444	323,877	3.3	220,769	26,941	7,219	68,948
Minnesota..........	4,375,099	53,884	1.2	4,919,479	143,382	2.9	95,613	6,616	2,527	38,626
Mississippi.........	2,573,216	15,931	0.6	2,844,658	39,569	1.4	21,616	2,881	1,508	13,564
Missouri.............	5,117,073	61,702	1.2	5,595,211	118,592	2.1	77,887	6,677	3,022	31,006
Montana.............	799,065	12,174	1.5	902,195	18,081	2.0	11,735	931	285	5,130
Nebraska............	1,578,385	36,969	2.3	1,711,263	94,425	5.5	71,030	1,993	859	20,543
Nevada...............	1,201,833	124,419	10.4	1,998,257	393,970	19.7	285,764	10,420	11,498	86,288
New Hampshire......	1,109,252	11,333	1.0	1,235,786	20,489	1.7	4,590	6,215	785	8,899
New Jersey..........	7,730,188	739,861	9.6	8,414,350	1,117,191	13.3	102,929	366,788	77,337	570,137
New Mexico.......	1,515,069	579,224	38.2	1,819,046	765,386	42.1	330,049	4,488	2,588	428,261
New York...........	17,990,455	2,214,026	12.3	18,976,457	2,867,583	15.1	260,889	1,050,293	62,590	1,493,811
North Carolina..........	6,628,637	76,726	1.2	8,049,313	378,963	4.7	246,545	31,117	7,389	93,912
North Dakota..............	638,800	4,665	0.7	642,200	7,786	1.2	4,295	507	250	2,734
Ohio	10,847,115	139,696	1.3	11,353,140	217,123	1.9	90,663	66,269	5,152	55,039
Oklahoma...........	3,145,585	86,160	2.7	3,450,654	179,304	5.2	132,813	8,153	1,759	36,579
Oregon...............	2,842,321	112,707	4.0	3,421,399	275,314	8.0	214,662	5,092	3,091	52,469
Pennsylvania......	11,881,643	232,262	2.0	12,281,054	394,088	3.2	55,178	228,557	10,363	99,990
Rhode Island......	1,003,464	45,752	4.6	1,048,319	90,820	8.7	5,881	25,422	1,128	58,389
South Carolina..........	3,486,703	30,551	0.9	4,012,012	95,076	2.4	52,871	12,211	2,875	27,119
South Dakota..............	696,004	5,252	0.8	754,844	10,903	1.4	6,364	637	163	3,739
Tennessee...........	4,877,185	32,741	0.7	5,689,283	123,838	2.2	77,372	10,303	3,695	32,468
Texas	16,986,510	4,339,905	25.2	20,851,820	6,669,666	32.0	5,071,963	69,504	25,705	1,502,494
Utah...................	1,722,850	84,597	4.9	2,233,169	201,559	9.0	136,416	3,977	940	60,226
Vermont.............	562,758	3,661	0.7	608,827	5,504	0.9	1,174	1,374	310	2,646
Virginia..............	6,187,358	160,288	2.6	7,078,515	329,540	4.7	73,979	41,131	8,332	206,098
Washington........	4,866,692	214,570	4.4	5,894,121	441,509	7.5	329,934	16,140	4,501	90,934
West Virginia......	1,793,477	8,489	0.5	1,808,344	12,279	0.7	4,347	1,609	453	5,870
Wisconsin...........	4,891,769	93,194	1.9	5,363,675	192,921	3.6	126,719	30,267	2,491	33,444
Wyoming............	453,588	25,751	5.7	493,782	31,669	6.4	19,963	575	160	10,971
Puerto Rico[1]........	3522,037	(NA)	(NA)	3,808,610	3,762,746	98.8	11,546	3,623,392	19,973	107,835

[1]Census 2000 was the first to ask a separate question on Hispanic origin in Puerto Rico. U.S. Census Bureau, Census 2000 and 1990.

Table 3: United States—Race and Hispanic Origin: 1970 to 2000

Census year	Total population	White/%	Black/%	American Indian, Eskimo, and Aleut/%	Asian and Pacific Islander/%	Other race(s)/%	Hispanic or Latino/%
2000	281,421,906	211,460,626/ 75%	34,658,190/ 12.3%	2,475,956/ 0.9%	10,641,833/ 3.7%	22,185,301/ 7.9%	35,305,818/ 12.5%
1990	248,709,873	199,686,070/ 80.3%	29,986,060/ 21.1%	1,959,234/ 0.8%	7,273,662/ 2.9%	9,804,847/ 3.9%	22,354,059/ 9.0%
1980	226,545,805	188,371,622/ 83.1%	26,495,025/ 11.7%	1,420,400/ 0.6%	3,500,439/ 1.5%	6,758,319/ 3.0%	14,608,673/ 6.4%
1970	203,211,926	177,748,975/ 87.5%	22,580,289/ 11.1%	827,255/ 0.4%	1,538,721/ 0.8%	516,686/ 0.3%	(NA)

Table 4: Ten Largest Places in Total Population and Hispanic Population: 2000

Place and State	Total Population Number	Total Population Rank	Hispanic Population Number	Hispanic Population Rank	% Hispanic of Total Population
New York, NY	8,088,278	1	2,160,554	1	27.0
Los Angeles, CA	3,694,820	2	1,719,073	2	46.5
Chicago, IL	2,896,016	3	753,644	3	26.0
Houston, TX	1,953,631	4	730,865	4	37.4
Philadelphia, PA	1,517,550	5	128,928	24	8.5
Phoenix, AZ	1,321,045	6	449,972	6	34.1
San Diego, CA	1,223,400	7	310,752	9	25.4
Dallas, TX	1,188,580	8	422,587	8	35.6
San Antonio, TX	1,144,646	9	671,394	5	58.7
Detroit, MI	951,270	10	47,167	72	5.0
El Paso, TX	563,662	23	431,875	7	76.6
San Jose, CA	894,943	11	269,989	10	30.2

Source: U.S. Census Bureau, Census 2000.

Table 5: Ten Places of 100,000 or More Population with the Highest Percentage Hispanic: 2002

Place and State	Total Population	Hispanic Population	% Hispanic of Total Population
East Los Angeles, CA*	124,283	120,307	96.8
Laredo, TX	176,576	166,216	94.1
Brownsville, TX	139,722	127,535	91.3
Hialeah, FL	226,419	204,543	90.3
McAllen, TX	106,414	85,427	80.3
El Paso, TX	563,662	431,875	76.6
Santa Ana, CA	337,977	257,097	76.1
El Monte, CA	115,965	83,945	72.4
Oxnard, CA	170,358	112,807	66.2
Miami, FL	362,470	238,351	65.8

*East Los Angeles, California, is a census-designated place and is not legally incorporated. U.S. Census. Bureau, Census 2000.

Table 6: Hispanic Population Projections: 2005 to 2070

Year	Total Hispanic Population	% of Total Population
2005	38,188,000	13.3
2006	39,307,000	13.5
2007	40,416,000	13.8
2008	41,515,000	14.1
2009	42,606,000	14.3
2010	43,687,000	14.6
2011	44,772,000	14.8
2012	45,872,000	15.1
2013	46,986,000	15.3
2014	48,113,000	15.5
2015	49,255,000	15.8
2016	50,410,000	16.0
2017	51,577,000	16.3
2018	52,758,000	16.5
2019	53,951,000	16.7
2020	55,156,000	17.0
2025	61,433,000	18.2
2030	68,167,000	19.4
2035	75,289,000	20.7
2040	82,691,000	21.9
2045	90,343,000	23.1
2050	98,228,000	24.3
2055	106,370,000	25.5
2060	114,796,000	26.6
2065	123,508,000	27.6
2070	132,492,000	28.6

Source: Population Projections Program, Population Division, U.S. Census Bureau, 2000.

Table 7: Detailed Occupation of the Employed Civilian Population 16 Years and Over by Sex and Hispanic Origin: 2002

Sex and detailed occupation group	Hispanic original type[1]						
	Total/ Percent	Mexican	Puerto Rican	Cuban	Central and South American	Other Hispanic	Non-Hispanic
Total	100.0	100.0	100.0	100.0	100.0	100.0	100.0
Executive, administrators, and managerial	15.2	6.8	9.4	13.2	8.3	12.4	16.2
Professional speciality	16.2	5.1	10.0	9.8	6.4	11.9	17.5
Technical and related support	3.3	1.9	2.9	3.3	2.2	4.0	3.4
Sales	11.7	8.4	12.2	12.6	8.7	11.0	12.1
Administrative support, including clerical	13.6	11.6	17.5	17.6	10.7	14.7	13.8
Precision production, craft, and repair	10.6	16.2	10.2	12.1	13.0	11.3	10.1
Machine operators, assemblers, and inspectors	4.8	8.9	5.3	3.6	8.8	4.7	4.4
Transportation and material moving	4.2	5.1	4.4	4.3	4.8	4.0	4.1
Handlers, equipment cleaners, helpers, and laborers	3.9	8.7	5.0	5.3	7.3	4.9	3.3
Service workers, private household	0.5	1.1	0.4	0.6	3.8	1.0	0.4
Service workers, except private household	13.7	20.2	21.7	17.3	23.5	18.1	12.8
Farming, forestry, and fishing	2.3	6.0	0.9	0.5	2.5	2.0	2.0
Male							
Executive, administrators, and managerial	15.6	5.5	8.0	13.2	7.0	13.9	17.0
Professional specialty	13.8	3.3	8.1	8.4	6.1	10.8	15.2
Technical and related support	2.7	1.6	1.9	3.1	2.1	4.0	2.8
Sales	11.2	5.7	9.8	13.5	6.2	9.5	11.9
Administrative support, including clerical	5.4	4.9	9.7	9.7	6.2	6.5	5.4
Precision production, craft, and repair	18.4	24.5	18.7	19.3	20.5	19.1	17.6
Machine operators, assemblers, and inspectors	5.8	8.9	6.8	2.1	9.0	5.3	5.4
Transportation and material moving	7.1	7.9	6.4	7.2	7.3	7.6	7.0
Handlers, equipment cleaners, helpers, and laborers	5.8	11.6	7.4	9.1	10.9	7.0	5.0
Service workers, private household	-	0.1	-	-	0.6	0.2	-
Service workers, except private household	10.8	17.6	21.7	13.8	20.1	12.8	9.7
Farming, forestry, and fishing	3.3	8.3	1.5	0.7	4.0	3.3	2.8
Female							
Executive, administrators, and managerial	14.8	8.9	10.9	13.3	10.1	10.9	15.4
Professional specialty	18.8	7.8	12.0	11.5	6.8	13.1	20.0
Technical and related support	3.9	2.4	3.9	3.5	2.4	4.1	4.0
Sales	12.3	12.6	14.6	11.5	12.0	12.5	12.3
Administrative support, including clerical	22.8	21.9	25.3	27.9	16.6	23.3	23.0
Precision production, craft, and repair	2.0	3.3	1.7	2.8	3.0	3.0	1.9
Machine operators, assemblers, and inspectors	3.7	8.8	3.8	5.5	8.5	4.0	3.2
Transportation and material moving	0.9	0.8	2.4	0.4	1.4	0.3	0.9
Handlers, equipment cleaners, helpers, and laborers	1.7	4.3	2.6	0.4	2.7	2.8	1.5
Service workers, private household	1.0	2.6	0.8	1.4	8.1	1.8	0.8
Service workers, except private household	17.0	24.3	21.7	21.8	28.0	23.6	16.1
Farming, forestry, and fishing	1.1	2.4	0.4	0.1	0.6	0.6	1.0

Source: U.S. Census Bureau, Current Population Survey, 2002.

[1]Hispanic refers to people whose origin is Mexican, Puerto Rican, Cuban, South or Central American, or other.

Table 8: Earnings of Full-Time, Year-Round Workers 15 Years and Over in 2001 by Sex, Hispanic Origin, and Race (numbers in thousands)

Sex and Earnings	Total		Hispanic[1]	
	Number	Percent	Number	Percent
Total (male and female) with money earnings[2]	100,351	100.0	12,012	100.0
$1 to $2,499 or less	871	0.9	84	0.7
$2,500 to $4,999	372	0.4	62	0.5
$5,000 to $9,999	2,265	2.3	500	4.2
$10,000 to $14,999	6,530	6.5	1,772	14.8
$15,000 to $19,999	9,396	9.4	2,064	17.2
$20,000 to $24,999	11,285	11.2	1,935	16.1
$25,000 to $34,999	20,932	20.9	2,431	20.2
$35,000 to $49,999	20,885	20.8	1,673	13.9
$50,000 to 74,999	16,248	16.2	1,015	8.5
$75,000 and over	11,569	11.5	476	4.0

Source: U.S. Census Bureau, Current Population Survey, March 2002.

[1]Hispanic refers to people whose origin is Mexican, Puerto Rican, Cuban, South or Central American, or other Hispanic/Latino, regardless of race.

[2]Total money earnings is the algebraic sum of money wages or salaries and net income from farm and nonfarm self-employment.

Male

Sex and Earnings	Total		Hispanic[1]	
	Number	Percent	Number	Percent
Male with money earnings[2]	58,712	100.0	7,648	100.0
$1 to $2,499 or less	501	0.9	52	0.7
$2,500 to $4,999	161	0.3	29	0.4
$5,000 to $9,999	995	1.7	230	3.0
$10,000 to $14,999	2,985	5.1	986	12.9
$15,000 to $19,999	4,242	7.2	1,285	16.8
$20,000 to $24,999	5,497	9.4	1,222	16.0
$25,000 to $34,999	11,188	19.1	1,558	20.4
$35,000 to $49,999	12,567	21.4	1,146	15.0
$50,000 to $74,999	11,292	19.2	767	10.0
$75,000 and over	9,285	15.8	373	4.9

Source: U.S. Census Bureau, Current Population Survey, March 2002.

[1]Hispanic refers to people whose origin is Mexican, Puerto Rican, Cuban, South or Central American, or other Hispanic/Latino, regardless of race.

[2]Total money earnings is the algebraic sum of money wages or salaries and net income from farm and nonfarm self-employment.

Female

Sex and earnings	Total		Hispanic[1]	
	Number	Percent	Number	Percent
Female with money earnings[2]	41,639	100.0	4,363	100.0
$1 to $2,499 or less	370	0.9	31	0.7
$2,500 to $4,999	211	0.5	33	0.8
$5,000 to $9,999	1,270	3.0	270	6.2
$10,000 to $14,999	3,545	8.5	785	18.0
$15,000 to $19,999	5,154	12.4	779	17.9
$20,000 to $24,999	5,788	13.9	713	16.3
$25,000 to $35,999	9,744	23.4	873	20.0
$35,000 to $49,999	8,318	20.0	528	12.1
$50,000 to $74,999	4,957	11.9	248	5.7
$75,000 and over	2,284	5.5	103	2.4

Source: U.S. Census Bureau, Current Population Survey, March 2002.

[1]Hispanic refers to people whose origin is Mexican, Puerto Rican, Cuban, South or Central American, or other Hispanic/Latino, regardless of race.

[2]Total money earnings is the algebraic sum of money wages or salaries and net income from farm and nonfarm self-employment.

Appendix III

Latino and Latina Members of Congress, 1822–2004,
U.S. House of Representatives

Name	State or Territory	Party	Dates
Joseph Marion Hernández	Florida	Whig	1822–1823
José Manuel Gallegos	New Mexico	Democrat	1853–1857; 1871–1873
Miguel Antonio Otero	New Mexico	Democrat	1856–1861
Francisco Perea	New Mexico	Republican	1863–1865
José Francisco Chaves	New Mexico	Republican	1865–1871
Romualdo Pacheco	California	Republican	1877–1878; 1879–1883
Trinidad Romero	New Mexico	Republican	1877–1879
Mariano Sabino Otero	New Mexico	Republican	1879–1881
Tranquilino Luna	New Mexico	Republican	1881–1884
Francisco Antonio Manzanares	New Mexico	Democrat	1884–1885
Pedro Perea	New Mexico	Republican	1899–1901
Frederico Degetau	Puerto Rico	Insular Republican	1901–1905
Tulio Larrinaga	Puerto Rico	Unionist	1905–1911
Luis Muñoz Rivera	Puerto Rico	Unionist	1911–1916
Ladislas Lazaro	Louisiana	Democrat	1913–1927
Benigo Cárdenas Hernández	New Mexico	Republican	1915–1917; 1919–1921
Félix Córdova Dávila	Puerto Rico	Unionist	1917–1932
Néstor Montoya	New Mexico	Republican	1921–1923
Dennis Chávez	New Mexico	Democrat	1931–1935
Joachim Octave Fernández	Louisiana	Democrat	1931–1941
José Lorenzo Pesquera	Puerto Rico	Nonpartisan	1932–1933
Santiago Iglesias	Puerto Rico	Coalitionist	1932–1939
Bolívar Pagán	Puerto Rico	Coalitionist	1939–1945
Antonio Manuel Fernández	New Mexico	Democrat	1943–1956
Jesús T. Piñero	Puerto Rico	Popular Democrat	1945–1946
Antonio Fernós-Isern	Puerto Rico	Popular Democrat	1945–1965
Joseph Manuel Montoya	New Mexico	Democrat	1957–1964
Henry B. González	Texas	Democrat	1961–1998
Edward R. Roybal	California	Democrat	1963–1993
Santiago Polanco-Abreu	Puerto Rico	Popular Democrat	1965–1969
Eligio "Kika" de la Garza II	Texas	Democrat	1965–1997
Jorge Luis Códova Díaz	Puerto Rico	New Progressive	1969–1973
Manuel Luján, Jr.	New Mexico	Republican	1969–1989
Herman Badillo	New York	Democrat	1971–1977
Jaime Benítez	Puerto Rico	Popular Democrat	1973–1977
Ron de Lugo	Virgin Islands	Democrat	1973–1979; 1981–1995
Baltasar Corrada del Río	Puerto Rico	New Progressive	1977–1985
Robert Garcia	New York	Democrat	1978–1990
Anthony Lee Coelho	California	Democrat	1979–1989
Matthew G. Martínez	California	Democrat	1982–2001
William B. Richardson	New Mexico	Democrat	1983–1997
Solomon P. Ortiz	Texas	Democrat	1983–present
Esteban Torres	California	Democrat	1983–1999
Jaime B. Fuster	Puerto Rico	Democrat	1985–1992
Ben Blaz Garrido	Guam	Republican	1985–1993
Albert G. Bustamante	Texas	Democrat	1985–1993
Ileana Ros-Lehtinen	Florida	Republican	1989–present
José E. Serrano	New York	Democrat	1990–present
Ed López Pastor	Arizona	Democrat	1991–present
Antonio J. Colorado	Puerto Rico	Democrat	1992–1993
Frank M. Tejeda	Texas	Democrat	1993–1997
Xavier Becerra	California	Democrat	1993–present
Henry Bonilla	Texas	Republican	1993–present
Lincoln Díaz-Balart	Florida	Republican	1993–present
Luis Gutiérrez	Illinois	Democrat	1993–present
Robert Menéndez	New Jersey	Democrat	1993–present
Carlos Antonio Romero-Barceló	Puerto Rico	New Progressive	1993–2001
Lucille Roybal-Allard	California	Democrat	1993–present
Robert A. Underwood	Guam	Democrat	1993–present
Nydia M. Velázquez	New York	Democrat	1993–present
Rúben Hinojosa	Texas	Democrat	1997–present
Silvestre Reyes	Texas	Democrat	1996–present
Ciro D. Rodriguez	Texas	Democrat	1997–present
Loretta Sanchez	California	Democrat	1997–present
Charles A. Gonzalez	Texas	Democrat	1999–present
Grace Napolitano	California	Democrat	1999–present
Joe Baca	California	Democrat	1999–present
Hilda L. Solis	California	Democrat	2001–present
Anibal Acevedo-Vilá	Puerto Rico	Democrat	2001–present
Dennis Cardoza	California	Democrat	2002–present
Mario Diaz-Balart	Florida	Democrat	2002–present
Raúl M. Grijalva	Arizona	Democrat	2002–present
Devin Nunes	California	Republican	2002–present
Linda Sanchez	California	Democrat	2002–present
Ed Pastor	Arizona	Democrat	2002–present
Xavier Becerra	California	Democrat	2002–present
Lucille Roybal-Allard	California	Democrat	2002–present
Lincoln Díaz-Balart	Florida	Democrat	2002–present

U.S. Senate

Name	State or Territory	Party	Dates
Octaviano Larrazolo	New Mexico	Republican	1928–1929
Dennis Chávez	New Mexico	Democrat	1935–1962
Joseph Manuel Montoya	New Mexico	Democrat	1964–1977
Mel Martinez	Florida	Republican	2004–
Ken Salazar	Colorado	Democrat	2004–

Source: Library of Congress "Hispanic Americans in Congress, 1822–1995."
http://lcweb.gov/rr/hispanic/congress

Synoptic Table of Contents

Directory of Contributors

MEREDITH E. ABARCA
University of Texas, El Paso
Cabeza de Baca, Fabiola; Cuisine, California;
Jaramillo, Cleofas Martínez

JORGE ABRIL-SÁNCHEZ
University of Massachusetts, Amherst
Ochoa, Ellen

REBECA ACEVEDO
Loyola Marymount University
Newspapers and Magazines

WILLIAM ACEVES
California Western School of Law
Asylum; Deportation

MARIANA ACHUGAR
Carnegie Mellon University
Internet

CHARLES W. ACKER
Independent Scholar
Peyote

JENNIFER M. ACKER
Independent Scholar
Alfaro, Luis; Comanches; HIV/AIDS

HOLLY ACKERMAN
University of Miami
Cuban American National Council; Federation for
American Immigration Reform ; League of United
Latin American Citizens; Politics, Cuban American;
Spanish-American League Against Discrimination

EDNA ACOSTA-BELÉN
State University of New York, Albany
Colón, Jesús; Jones Act; Puerto Ricans on the
Mainland; Vega, Bernardo

HELANE D. ADAMS
Miami University, Ohio
Costa Rican Americans; Cuban Studies;
Guadalupanismo; Inter-Latino Relations; Ohio;
Panamanian Americans; Proposition 187; Spiritual
Plan of Aztlán

ELENA JACKSON ALBARRÁN
University of Arizona
Alliance for Progress; Good Neighbor Policy; *I Love
Lucy*; Popular Culture

FREDERICK LUIS ALDAMA
University of Colorado, Boulder
Gamboa, Harry; Homosexuality, Male; Literature,
Gay and Lesbian; Literature, Latin American; Rap;
Villarreal, José Antonio

CÉSAR ALEGRE
Amherst College
Boscana, Gerónimo; Coronado, Francisco Vázquez
de; De Niza, Marcos; De Oñate, Juan; Menéndez de
Avilés, Pedro; Onomastics; Pérez de Villagrá,
Gaspar; Spain; Spanish Americans; Toponymy

KRISTINE M. ALPI
Weill Medical College, Cornell University
Alcohol Use and Abuse; Molina, Mario

JEANETTE ALTARRIBA
State University of New York, Albany
Mental Health

ADRIAN ALTHOFF
Independent Scholar
National Hispanic Media Coalition; Operation
Hammer; Wrestling; Zapata, Emiliano

LUIS ALVAREZ
University of Houston
Sleepy Lagoon Case; Zoot Suit Riots

SARAH APONTE
City University of New York
Moya Pons, Frank

DAVID ARBESÚ-FERNÁNDEZ
University of Massachusetts, Amherst
Arenas, Reinaldo

SARA ARMENGOT
Pennsylvania State University
Literature, Puerto Rican on the Mainland

HAROLD AUGENBRAUM
National Book Foundation
Alamo, Battle of the; Caciques; Chacón Family;
Guadalupe Hidalgo, Treaty of; Libraries and
Archives; Mexican-American War; Murrieta,
Joaquín; Núñez Cabeza de Vaca, Alvar;
Reconquista, La

HÉCTOR AVALOS
Iowa State University
Bible in Spanish; Diego, Juan; Liberation Theology; Mormonism; Protestantism; Religion

ERIC AVILA
University of California, Los Angeles
Los Angeles

MARIA ISABEL AYALA
Texas A&M University
Demographics

THOMAS O. BEEBEE
Pennsylvania State University
Jesuits; Literary Criticism; Mariachi; Popol Vuh; Virgen de Guadalupe

STEVEN W. BENDER
University of Oregon School of Law
Stereotypes and Stereotyping

ANTONIO BENÍTEZ-ROJO
Amherst College
Areíto

BERNARDO S. BERDICHEWSKY
Independent Scholar
Canada

RAVEN S. BLACKSTONE
Independent Scholar
Cuisine, Dominican American; Cuisine, Puerto Rican; Cuisine, Spanish

ISABEL ALVAREZ BORLAND
College of the Holy Cross
Literature, Cuban American

AARON BRITT
Independent Scholar
Cockfighting; Domingo, Plácido; Tennis

P. SCOTT BROWN
Independent Scholar
Corona, Juan; Galarza, Ernesto; López, Trinidad; Otero Family; Serra, Junípero

WILLIAM BURGOS
Long Island University, Brooklyn
Federación Libre de Trabajadores

MARCUS BURKE
Hispanic Society
Art, Colonial; Art, Galleries and Collections; Campeche, José; Museums; Painting; Sculpture

RAMIRO BURR
Syndicated Columnist
Norteño; Rock-en-Español; Selena; Tejano; Vocalists, Popular

NICK CAISTOR
University of Westminster, London
Black Legend; Bullfighting; Columbus, Christopher; Dorado, El; Villa, Francisco

LISA CALAVENTE
University of North Carolina, Chapel Hill
Boxing; Vietnam War

CHRISTOPHER DAVID RUÍZ CAMERON
Southwestern University School of Law
Agricultural Labor Relations Act; Farmworkers Movement; Mexican American Legal Defense and Education Fund; Mexican American Political Association; Puerto Rican Legal Defense and Education Fund

BRUCE CAMPBELL
Saint John's University
Muralism

TAÍNA B. CARAGOL
Independent Scholar
Art, Puerto Rican on the Mainland

DAVID C. CARLSON
University of North Carolina, Chapel Hill
Castro, Fidel; Cuban Revolution; Spanish-American War

MARÍA M. CARREIRA
California State University, Long Beach
Opinión, La; Radio: Spanish-Language Radio

MARTÍN CARRERA
Independent Scholar
Archeology; Exile; History; Politics, Mexican American

MARTHA CASAS
University of Texas, El Paso
Escalante, Jaime

JASON P. CASELLAS
Princeton University
Cavazos, Lauro Fred; Congressional Hispanic Caucus; Political Parties

LUZ MARÍA CASTELLANOS
Independent Scholar
Los Angeles: East Los Angeles

MAX J. CASTRO
University of Miami
English Only Movement; Miami

ARTHUR E. CHAPMAN
Independent Scholar
Kennedy, John F.; Louisiana; Seminole Wars

JESSE EDDIE CHAVARRÍA
Latino Today
El Diario/LA PRENSA; Journalism

LINDA CHAVEZ
Independent Scholar
Bilingual Education: The Case for English Immersion

FRAN CHESLEIGH
Independent Scholar
Guaracha; Jazz; Mambo; Musical Instruments; Puente, Tito; Rhumba; Son

JORGE LUIS CHINEA
Wayne State University
Michigan

TOMÁS CHRIST
University of Bielefeld
Brujería; Colonial Period; Death

JANIVA CIFUENTES-HISS
Mavin Foundation
Fast Food; Sugar

JAMES COHEN
University of Paris
Bilingual Education: The Case for Bilingual Education

JONATHAN COHEN
State University of New York, Stony Brook
Lee, Muna

M. CECILIA COLOMBI
University of California, Davis
Guatemalan Americans; Honduran Americans; Nicaraguan Americans; Parochial Schools; Salvadoran Americans

RUBÉN CORDOVA
Independent Scholar
Baca, Judith; Calaveras; Charlot, Jean; Con Safo; Goldman, Shifra; Posada, José Guadalupe; Quirarte, Jacinto; Ramírez, Martín; Rivera, Diego; Ybarra-Frausto, Tomás

WILL H. CORRAL
California State University, Sacramento
Paz, Octavio; Rodriguez, Richard

JAVIER CORRALES
Amherst College
United States-South America Relations

JOSÉ E. CRUZ
State University of New York, Albany
Operation Bootstrap; Politics, Puerto Rican; Puerto Rican Studies

INA CUMPIANO
Children's Book Press
Literature, Children's

GERMÁN R. CUTZ
University of Illinois Extension
Banking; Bodegas, Colmados, Mercados; Coffee; Corn

CAROL DAMIAN
Florida International University
Altares; Architecture, Spanish Colonial

ROXANNE DÁVILA
Brandeis University
Art, Mexican American and Chicano; Chicanismo; Mestizaje

DAISY COCCO DE FILIPPIS
Hostos Community College
Literature, Dominican American

ANTHONY DE JESÚS
Center for Puerto Rican Studies, Hunter College
Loisaida; Tres Reyes Magos

RODOLFO O. DE LA GARZA
Columbia University
Latino National Political Survey

ASELA RODRÍGUEZ DE LAGUNA
Rutgers University
1492

TATIANA DE LA TIERRA
State University of New York, Buffalo
Homosexuality, Female; Love

ARNOLDO DE LEÓN
Angelo State University
Texas

KATHARINE A. DÍAZ
Hispanic Magazine
Alonso, Alicia; Cuisine; Dancing Clubs; Limón, José; Restaurants

CRISTÓBAL DÍAZ-AYALA
Independent Scholar
Bolero; Cha-Cha; Conga; Danzón; Guajira; Rumba; Salsa

PAUL J. DOSAL
University of South Florida
Cabrera, Lydia; Cuban American National
Foundation; Cuban Missile Crisis; Guevara, Ernesto;
Key West; Mas Canosa, Jorge; United States–Central
America Relations

PAQUITO D'RIVERA
Musician
Puente, Tito

JEFFREY M. R. DUNCAN-ANDRADE
University of California, Los Angeles
Criminal Justice System; Marxism

SANDRA DUQUE
Independent Scholar
New York City

ELIZABETH R. ESCOBEDO
University of Texas, San Antonio
Pachuco

JESSE J. ESPARZA
University of Houston
Albuquerque Walkout; East Los Angeles School
Walkout

MARGARITE FERNÁNDEZ OLMOS
Brooklyn College
Alvarez, Julia; Anaya, Rudolfo; De Burgos, Julia;
Espiritismo; Ruiz de Burton, María Amparo;
Santería

ELIZABETH FERRER
Independent Scholar
Photography

JANIE FILOTEO
Independent Scholar
Demographics

GUSTAVO PÉREZ FIRMAT
Columbia University
García, Cristina; Hijuelos, Oscar

CHRISTY FLORES
University of California, Davis
Encomienda; Superstitions

RICHARD FLORES
Independent Scholar
San Antonio

YVETTE G. FLORES
Independent Scholar
Childhood and Adolescence; Family; Parenting

LUIS H. FRANCIA
New York University
Philippines

HARRY FRANQUI RIVERA
University of Massachusetts, Amherst
65th Infantry; Korean War

ILEANA FUENTES
Independent Scholar
Art Criticism

LUIS FUENTES-ROHWER
Indiana University, Bloomington
Greaser Act; Immigration Acts; Puerto Rico;
Vieques

RANDALL GANN
Independent Scholar
Radio, English-Language

ALYSSA GARCÍA
University of Illinois, Urbana-Champaign
Brothers to the Rescue; Operation Peter Pan;
Paredes, Américo; Radio Martí

DESIRÉE GARCIA
Independent Scholar
Hispanic Radio Network; Horsemanship and Horse
Racing; Immunizations; Labor-Management
Relations Act; Law Enforcement; *Miami Herald*;
Nuevo Herald, El; Olympic Games; Santa Fé
Expedition

HÉCTOR GARCÍA
University of Chicago
Illinois

KIMBERLY GARCÍA
Independent Scholar
Dance

LUPE GARCÍA
University of North Carolina, Chapel Hill
Carnaval; Mexican American Unity Council;
Mothers of East Los Angeles

MARYELLEN GARCÍA
University of Texas, San Antonio
Caló

ALEJANDRA GARCÍA QUINTANILLA
Universidad Autónoma de Yúcatan
Mayas

PAUL S. GEORGE
*Historical Association of Southern Florida, Miami-Dade
Community College*
Calle Ocho; Civil War; Little Havana; Saint
Augustine

ANDRA GILLESPIE
Yale University

Democratic Party; Discrimination; Evangelism; New Jersey; Political Association of Spanish Speaking Organizations; Republican Party; United States Presidents and Latinos

WILLARD GINGERICH
St. John's University

Huitzilopochtli; Nahuas; Quetzalcóatl

DAVID GITLITZ
University of Rhode Island

Crypto-Jews

MIMI R. GLADSTEIN
University of Texas, El Paso

Malinche, La

ADAM JUDE GONZÁLES
Amherst College

Mayas; Theater; Yerberos

ALICIA M. GONZÁLEZ
Museum of the American West

Art, Folk; Chocolate

OZZIE GONZÁLEZ
Latino Legends in Sports

Clemente, Roberto; Cordero, Angel, Jr.; De La Hoya, Oscar; Kid Chocolate; Sosa, Sammy

RAYMOND GONZÁLEZ
California State University, Monterey Bay

Hispanic Heritage Month; Lewis, Oscar; Rodeo; Watts Riots

RIGOBERTO GONZÁLEZ
The New School University

Huelga; Labor

JORGE J. E. GRACIA
State University of New York, Buffalo

Affirmative Action; Philosophy

ALEXANDRO JOSÉ GRADILLA
University of California, Irvine

Childbirth

SUSAN MARIE GREEN
California State University, Chico

Bear Flag Revolt; Católicos Por La Raza; Gadsden Purchase; Harlem Riots; Huerta, Dolores; Manifest Destiny; Mass Sterilization Campaign; Mutual Aid Societies; New Deal; Sinarquista Movement

RAÚL GUERRERO
Independent Scholar

Banana; De la Renta, Oscar; Fencing; Monroe Doctrine

DOUGLAS KEBERLEIN GUTIÉRREZ
Dominican University

Velasco, Treaty of; World War I; World War II

GABRIEL GUTIÉRREZ
Center for the Study of the Peoples of the Americas, CSU, Northridge

Californios; Criminals and Bandidos; Mexican Americans; Missions; Vasquez, Tiburcio

ANN HAGMAN-CARDINAL
Community College of Vermont

Folklore, Caribbean

EDMUND HAMANN
Brown University

Georgia

CARMEN DOLORES HERNÁNDEZ
El Nuevo Día Newspaper

Ferré, Rosario; Mohr, Nicholasa; Piñero, Miguel; Thomas, Piri

ERIKA HERNÁNDEZ
California State University, Fullerton

Feminism; Latino Studies; Lavoe, Héctor

RAMONA HERNÁNDEZ
City University of New York, Dominican Studies Institute

Dominican Americans; Dominican Studies

RAYMOND HERNÁNDEZ-DURAN
University of New Mexico, Albuquerque

Art, Popular

RUBÉN HERNÁNDEZ-LEÓN
Independent Scholar

Georgia

MARÍA HERRERA-SOBEK
University of California, Santa Barbara

Explorers and Chroniclers

VALERIE F. HUNT
Southern Methodist University

United States-Mexico Relations

KEVIN JOHNSON
University of California, Davis

Immigration, Latino; Intermarriage

TOMÁS MARIO KALMAR
Goddard College

Literacy

STEVEN KELLMAN
University of Texas, San Antonio

Literature, Latinos in Anglo-American

LUZ ANGÉLICA KIRSCHNER
Pennsylvania State University
Machismo; Navidad; Quinceañera

JOHN KRICH
Asian Wall Street Journal
Baseball

LAWRENCE LA FOUNTAIN-STOKES
University of Michigan, Ann Arbor
Stonewall Movement

ASELA R. LAGUNA
Rutgers University at Newark
Hostos, Eugenio María de; Pantoja, Antonia; Varela, Félix

LUIS LARIOS VENDRELL
Independent Scholar
Literature of Exile: Spain

LUIS LEAL
University of California, Santa Barbara
Cisneros, Sandra; Hinojosa-Smith, Rolando; Literature, Mexican American; Mexico; Rivera, Tomás; Zorro

JOSÉ E. LIMÓN
University of Texas, Austin
Chicano Studies; Cortez, Gregorio; Folklore, Mexican American

MAGALY LLORO
Independent Scholar
Botánicas; Curanderismo; Taíno

KATHRYN JEAN LÓPEZ
National Review
Abortion; Birth Control; Estefan, Gloria

PAUL LÓPEZ
California State University, Chico
Barrio Life; Civil Rights; Race

REBECCA LÓPEZ
California State University, Long Beach
Mutual Aid Societies; Protocol of Querétaro

ROBERT OSCAR LÓPEZ
Independent Scholar
Passing; Sexuality

SUSAN LUEVANO-MOLINA
California State University, Long Beach
REFORMA

WILLIAM LUIS
Vanderbilt University
Literature of Exile: Spanish Caribbean

DONNA L. LYBECKER
Pennsylvania State University, Altoona
Agriculture

JESSE H. LYTLE
University of Pennsylvania
Education, Higher

JUDY F. MALOOF
University of New Mexico
Anzaldúa, Gloria; Kahlo, Frida; Vasconcelos, José

MERCEDES MARRERO
Independent Scholar
Canseco, José; López, Nancy

HELEN B. MARROW
Independent Scholar
Argentine Americans; Brazilian Americans; Chilean Americans; Colombian Americans; Peruvian Americans; Venezuelan Americans

PHILIP MARTIN
University of California, Davis
Durst Ranch Affair; Fair Labor Standards Act

MARCOS MARTÍNEZ
Nuestra Cultura
Alianza Hispano-Americana; Anarcho-Syndicalism; Drugs; Fraternities and Sororities; Gangs

FÉLIX MASUD-PILOTO
DePaul University
Balseros; Mariel Boat Lift

EILEEN DIAZ MCCONNELL
University of Illinois, Urbana-Champaign
Indiana

PATRICIA MEARS
Fashion Institute of Technology
Fashion

VALERIE MENARD
Independent Scholar
Alvarez, Luis; American GI Forum; Austin, Texas; Auto Racing; Cinco de Mayo; Día de la Raza; Día de los Muertos; Publishing, English-Language; Santana, Carlos

MARTHA MENCHACA
University of Texas, Austin
Indigenísmo; Indigenous Heritage

RUBÉN G. MENDOZA
California State University, Monterrey Bay
Adobe; Low Riders

ANA MARÍA MERICO-STEPHENS
University of Arizona College of Law
Homestead Act; Law Professions, Latinos in; Politics, Latino; United States Congress; Voting

DORIS MEYER
University of New Mexico
Barela, Patrocinio; Golf; Taos Rebellion

NAOMI MEZEY
Georgetown University Law Center
Census, United States

ALBERTO MILIÁN
Attorney
Pau-Llosa, Ricardo Manuel

ELIZABETH MILLÁN-ZAIBERT
DePaul University
Affirmative Action

IVOR MILLER
DePaul University
Graffiti

MIKE MILLER
Independent Scholar
Tobacco

TOM MILLER
Independent Scholar
Coyotes; Diálogo, El; Journalism, Latinos in; Martí, José; *Milagro Beanfield War*; National Chicano Moratorium of Vietnam; Salt of the Earth; Three Rivers; Tijerina, Reies López; Valens, Ritchie

LUIS MOLL
University of Arizona
Bilingualism

MARIO MONTAÑO
Colorado College
Cuisine, Tex-Mex

BRIAN MONTES
University of Illinois, Urbana-Champaign
Brown Berets; Gorras Blancas, Las; National Puerto Rican Coalition; Puerto Rican Young Lords

ALFONSO MORALES
University of Texas, El Paso
Assimilation, Economic

E. MARK MORENO
Washington State University
California; Gonzales, Rodolfo; Santa Anna, Antonio López de; Washington

JOSE MORENO
California State University, Northridge
Crusade for Justice

GARY MORMINO
University of South Florida, St. Petersburg
Ybor City

STEPHEN P. MUMME
Colorado State University
Acequia System; Water

JUAN SÁNCHEZ MUÑOZ
Texas Tech University
Cortina, Juan; *Mendez* v. *Westminster School District*

ALICIA MUÑOZ SÁNCHEZ
California State University, San Marcos
Equal Education Opportunity Act; Technology

ENRIQUE G. MURILLO, JR.
California State University, San Bernardino
North Carolina

CARMEN NAVA
California State University, San Marcos
Retablos

FRANCES NEGRÓN-MUNTANER
Columbia University
Film: Films by Latinos; Muñoz Marín, Luis; Puerto Rican Day Parade

JOHN NIETO-PHILLIPS
Indiana University, Bloomington
Penitentes

ARCELA NUÑEZ-ALVAREZ
California State University, San Marcos
Acuña, Rodolfo; Alvarado, Juan Bautista; Border, United States–Mexico; Bracero Program; Corona, Humberto; Delano, Plan de; Movimiento Estudiantil Chicano de Aztlán; National Council of La Raza; Operation Wetback; San Diego, Plan de; San Diego Revolt; Santa Bárbara, Plan de; Yzaguirre, Raul Humberto

ACHY OBEJAS
University of Chicago
Virgen de la Caridad del Cobre

RAFAEL OCASIO
Independent Scholar
Saints

B. V. OLGUÍN
University of Texas, San Antonio
Brownness; Chicano Movement; Dichos

WILLIAM ORCHARD
Independent Scholar
Comics; Humor; Tattoos; *West Side Story*

GUADALUPE PACHECO
U.S. Department of Health and Human Services
Medicine

JILL PINKNEY PASTRANA
California State University, Long Beach
Holidays; School Desegregation; Washington Heights

JOHNNY PAYNE
University of Texas
Fornés, María Irene

ROBERTO PEDACE
University of Redlands
Assimilation, Economic

RICHARD PEÑA
Columbia University
Film: Latinos in Film

LORNA PÉREZ
University of Buffalo
Love, Latino Conceptions of

MARVETTE PÉREZ
National Museum of American History, Smithsonian Institute
Virgen de Monserrate

ROLANDO PÉREZ
Hunter College, Library
Cuban Americans

JEFFREY PILCHER
The Citadel
Cuisine, Mexican

REBEKAH PITE
University of Michigan
Cuisine, South American

DELIA POEY
Florida State University
Cubonics; Cuisine, Cuban American

DANNY POSTEL
Daedalus
Assimilation, Cultural; Compadrazgo

MARICEL PRESILLA
Independent Scholar
Alcohol, Culinary; Cuisine, Nuevo Latino

JASON PRIBILSKY
Whitman College
Ecuadorian Americans; Health; Infectious Diseases

TERESA PUENTE
Freelance Writer
Chicago; Colorado; Gastón Institute; Hispanic Chamber of Commerce; New York State; Orden Hijos de América

LINDA J. QUINTANILLA
North Harris College
Texas Rangers

JOSEF RAAB
University of Bielefed, Germany
Aztlán; Llorona, La; López, Yolanda; Valdez, Luis

ILIANA REYES
University of Arizona
Bilingualism

MARÍA ELENA REYES
University of Alaska, Fairbanks
Alaska

JULISSA REYNOSO
Esquire Magazine
Dominicanish; Dominican Women's Caucus

MILAGROS RICOURT
Lehman College
Dominican Women's Development Center

DIANA I. RÍOS
University of Connecticut, Storrs
Kreutzberger, Mario

ANA ROCA
Florida International University
Cruz, Celia; Spanish in the United States

JOSÉ MANUEL RODEIRO
New Jersey City University
Aesthetics; Art, Cuban American; Art, Dominican American

AMÉRICA RODRÍGUEZ
University of Texas, Austin
Class

ANA PATRICIA RODRÍGUEZ
University of Maryland, College Park
Washington, D.C.

IVELISSE RODRIGUEZ
University of Illinois, Chicago
Spanish Harlem; Spirituality

JOHN RODRÍGUEZ
City University of New York, Graduate Center
Nuyorican Poets Café

VICTOR C. ROMERO
Pennsylvania State University
Alien Contract Labor Law

VICKI L. RUIZ
University of California, Irvine
United Cannery, Agricultural, Packing, and Allied
Workers of America

ROGELIO SÁENZ
Texas A&M University
Demographics

ERNESTO SAGÁS
Southern New Hampshire University
Dominican Republic; Rubirosa, Porfirio

ANTHONY ASADULLAH SAMAD
Independent Scholar
African Americans, Influence and Relations

JORGE ABRIL SÁNCHEZ
Independent Scholar
Goizueta, Roberto Crispulo

MOISÉS SANDOVAL
Author
Catholicism

CHARLES R. VENATOR SANTIAGO
Ithaca College
Adams-Onís, Treaty of; Louisiana Purchase;
Supreme Court, United States

AZARA SANTIAGO-RIVERA
State University of New York, Albany
Marianismo; Marriage

DAVID A. SARTORIUS
Whittier College
Cuba

JOHN P. SCHMAL
Independent Scholar
Adoption; Child Labor; Crime and Latinos;
Democracy; Florida; Idaho; Indian Wars;
Massachusetts; Mississippi; Missouri; Nativism;
Nevada; Oregon; Pennsylvania; Persian Gulf Wars;
Railways; Science; South Carolina; Sports in Latino
Life; Voting

DAVID G. SCHWARTZ
Independent Scholar
Gambling

DOUG SHANNON
Independent Scholar
Norteño; Rock-en-Español; Selena; Tejano;
Vocalists, Popular

EARL SHORRIS
Independent Scholar
Gamio, Manuel; León-Portilla, Miguel;
Mesoamerica

SYLVIA SHORRIS
Independent Scholar
Hayworth, Rita; Miranda, Carmen; Quinn,
Anthony

MARIANA SOUTO MANNING
University of Georgia
Education

KATHLEEN STAUDT
University of Texas, El Paso
Activism; Maquiladoras; Raza Unida Party, La;
Sweatshops and Informal Workers

ILAN STAVANS
Amherst College
Acosta, Oscar; Alfau, Felipe; Anti-Semitism;
Castaneda, Carlos; Chávez, César;
Counter-Reformation; Dorfman, Ariel; Islam;
Jewish Life; Laws of Burgos; Leal, Luis; Marín,
Cheech; Menchú, Rigoberta; Neruda, Pablo;
Schomburg, Arthur A.; Spanglish; Translation

DITA SULLIVAN
Independent Scholar
Architecture, Modern; Bugalu; Colón, Willie

LUIS TAMARGO
Latin Beat Magazine
Barbieri, Leandro; Blades, Rubén; Bomba; Décima;
D'Rivera, Paquito; Merengue; Music, Popular;
Palmieri, Charlie; Plena; Rodríguez, Albita;
Rubalcaba, Gonzalo; Sandoval, Arturo

CARMEN HELENA TELLEZ
Indiana University
Composers; Music, Classical

ANDERSON TEPPER
Independent Scholar
Basketball; Soccer

DAVID L. TORRES
Angelo State University
Business

SILVIO TORRES-SAILLANT
Syracuse University
Dominican Americans

JOSEPH A. TOVARES
WGBH
Cantinflas; Esparza, Moctezuma; Gómez-Peña,
Guillermo; Kreutzberger, Mario; Nava, Gregory;

Olmos, Edward James; Portillo, Lourdes; Rivera,
Chita; Telenovelas; Television: Latinos in
English-Language Television; Treviño, Jesús
Salvador

RAÚL DAMACIO TOVARES
Trinity College
Arnaz, Desi; Del Rio, Dolores; Moreno, Rita;
Television: Spanish-Language Television in the
United States

SARA E. TRETTER
City University of New York, Dominican Studies Institute
Association of Progressive Women; Henríquez
Ureña Family

SERGIO TRONCOSO
Independent Scholar
Cuento; El Paso, Texas; Mexican Revolution;
Posadas

LUIS ALBERTO URREA
Independent Scholar
Salazar, Rubén

IRENE VÁSQUEZ
East Los Angeles College
Afro-Latino Influences

MAYRA RODRÍGUEZ VALLADARES
MRV Associates
Advertising; Tourism

SANTOS C. VEGA
Hispanic Research Center, Arizona State University
Arizona; Colonialism; New Mexico; Southwestern
United States, Anglo Immigration to

CARLOS G. VELEZ-IBANEZ
University of California, Riverside
Military, United States

CHARLENE VILLASEÑOR BLACK
University of California, Los Angeles
Graphic Arts

TERESA VILLEGAS
Artist
Games

ELIJAH WALD
Independent Scholar
Corrido; Narcocorrido

AMY WALLACE-HAVENS
University of Arizona
United States Congress

BRIANNA L. WATTIE
State University of New York, Albany
Mental Health

DAVID C. WAYNE
Independent Scholar
Bachata

ALAN WEST-DURÁN
Northeastern University
Bauzá, Mario; Literature; O'Farrill, Arturo

NORMA WILLIAMS
University of Texas, Arlington
Aging

SHERRY YORK
Independent Scholar
Díaz, Junot; Laviera, Jesús Abraham; Williams,
William Carlos

LEO ZAIBERT
Independent Scholar
Philosophy

ALFONSO ZEPEDA-CAPISTRÁN
Latinos United for Change and Advancement, Inc.
English as a Second Language; Limited English
Proficiency

VÍCTOR ZÚÑIGA
Independent Scholar
Georgia

Index

Page numbers in italic type indicate illustrations.

C

J

K

M

stereotypes and, **4:**145
sterilization campaigns in, **1:**311, **3:**90–91, 287
Supreme Court rulings and, **4:**159
Taíno symbolism and, **4:**162
Tres Reyes Magos observance in, **3:**231, **4:**215, 216
U.S. citizenship and, **1:**328, 333, 353, **2:**303, 407, **3:**13, 28, 85, 176, 331, 433, 434
U.S. takeover of, **1:**349, 355, **2:**363, 389, **3:**423, 424–26, **4:**121, 122, 220, 235
Vieques and, **1:**4, 329, **3:**225, 279, 351, 420, 427, 436, **4:**256–57
Puerto Rico and the American Dream (Web site), **3:**429
Puga, Amalia, **2:**450
Puig, Manuel, **3:**2, 20, **4:**214
Pujol, Ernesto, **1:**117, **3:**355
Pulido, Bobby (son), **4:**172
Pulido, Rafael, **4:**6
Pulido, Roberto (father), **4:**171, 172
Pulitzer, Joseph, **3:**364, **4:**111
Pulitzer Prizes, **3:**200, **4:**288
Hijuelos (Oscar) and, **1:**429, **2:**294, 295, **3:**410
journalism and, **2:**392, **3:**150
pulperías, **1:**205, 206, 207
pulp novels, **4:**304–5, 306
pulque, **1:**65, 66
pulquerías, **3:**188
pulsadores, **4:**296
PUMA. See Politically United Mexican Americans
Punitive Expedition, **1:**30, **4:**230, 260
punta rock movement, **2:**324, **3:**205
punto guajiro, **2:**56, **3:**201
punto guanacasteco, **2:**46
Puntos de apoyo (Medina), **2:**464
Pura Bulpré Award, **2:**461, **4:**21
purchasing power. See buying power
Pure Emotion (O'Farrill recording), **3:**275
Purépecha, **3:**104
Purim, Flora, **3:**205
Purísma, La, **2:**312
Puritans, **3:**230
Puta Vida, La—This Bitch of a Life (Povod), **3:**16
Putnam, Israel, **4:**207
Putnam/PaperStar, **3:**414
"Put the Blame on Mame" (song), **2:**288
pyramids, **3:**112

Q

Q&A (Torres), **3:**17
Qaeda, al-, **2:**380
Quakers, **3:**331
quarks, **1:**83
Quauhtlatoatzin. See Diego, Juan
Quebec, Canada, **1:**264
Quechua, **2:**454, **3:**339, 340, 440, **4:**153
Queen Bitch Goddess Success (The Madonna) (Campos), **1:**135
Queen Charlotte Islands, **1:**262
Queen Latifah (rapper), **4:**18
Queens, N.Y.
Colombian immigrants in, **1:**342
Hispanic/Latino population in, **3:**257
Queer Latina/o Artists' Coalition, **2:**318

Queer Nation, **2:**317, 320–21
queer studies, **2:**471
queer theory, **2:**317
machismo and, **3:**54–55, 57
Querétaro, Protocol of. See Protocol of Querétaro
"Qué rico el mambo" (song), **1:**375
Quero Chiesa, Luis, **1:**144, **3:**303
Queston Construction, Inc., **2:**29
Quetzalcóatl, **1:**326, **2:**432, 454, **3:**106, 107, 109, 187, **438–40**
Huitzilopochtli narratives and, **2:**332
temple of, **2:**244, 438
Quetzalpetlatl, **3:**439
Quevedo, Eduardo, **3:**119
Quiché Maya. See Mayas
quicksilver, **1:**220
Quiero dormir cansando (song), **4:**268
Quiero ser (song), **4:**268
quijada, **3:**211
Quijano, Joe, **3:**312
Quimbara (recording), **1:**410
quinceañera, **1:**125, **2:**313, **3:440–42**
Quinn, Anthony, **2:**200, 203, 213, 434, **3:**38, 326, **442–43**
Quinn, Lew, **2:**44
Quino (Joaquín Salvador Lavado), **1:**372
Quiñones, Alvin, **1:**34
Quiñones, Cristóbal de, **1:**374
Quiñones, Juan. See Gómez-Quiñones, Juan
Quiñónez, Naomi, **3:**62
Quintana, Luis, **3:**239
Quintana, Nicolás, **1:**94
Quintana, Patricia, **1:**65
Quintanilla, María L., **1:**20
Quintero, José Augustín, **1:**331
Quintero, Luis, **3:**102
Quinto Sol Generation, **3:**407
Quinto Sol Publications, **1:**169, **3:**41
Quirarte, Jacinto, **1:**128, 148–49, 152, **3:443–44**
Chicano art movement and, **1:**148–49
Quiroz, Joseph A., **1:**299
Quispe Tito, Diego, **1:**109
Quisqueya Heights. See Washington Heights
Quisqueya LaBella (Cambeira), **2:**99
Quisqueyanos, **4:**162
Quivira, **2:**75, 162
Quivira Society, **1:**363, **2:**302, 417, 438, **3:**407
Quota Law of 1921, **1:**161
quotas
affirmative action, **1:**37
immigration, **1:**157, 161, **2:**77, 345, 347, 352–53, 408, **4:**230
immigration abolishment, **2:**353, **4:**227
Quran, **2:**379

R

R&B. See rhythm and blues
Rabassa, Gregorio, **3:**1, **4:**213, 214
Rabinal Achí (sacred text), **4:**213
race, **3:445–50**
affirmative action and, **1:**36–37, 38
as Anglo stereotype, **4:**148, 150
assimilation and, **1:**153, 154, 352, **2:**349
asylum and, **1:**161

baseball and, **1:**185, **4:**136
border region and, **1:**215
Brazilian Americans and, **1:**227
Bronze Race concept and, **1:**134, 168, 231, 306, **3:**114, 115
brownness and, **1:**134, 154, 230–32, **2:**369–70
California laws and, **1:**256
carnaval and, **1:**273–74
Census categories and, **1:**51, 285–86, 288–91, **2:**429
Chicanismo and, **1:**300
Chicano movement against, **1:**301–8
citizenship and, **2:**365
civil rights and, **1:**42, 325–26, **2:**429
class and, **1:**332, 335, 359, 361, **2:**361, **3:**446–47, 448
Colombian Americans and, **1:**343
colonial period and, **1:**359, 361
comics and, **1:**370
crime and, **1:**401
Cuba and, **1:**335, 354, **4:**121
Cuban Americans and, **1:**334, 335, 425, 426–27, **2:**372, **3:**448–49
definitions of, **3:**445–46
demographic shifts in immigration and, **2:**347
derogatory terms and, **4:**146
Dominican Amerians and, **2:**100–101, 363, **3:**448
drug use and, **1:**400
English as official language proposals and, **2:**149
farmworker activism and, **2:**409, 410
gay activism and, **2:**320–21
gay and lesbian families and, **2:**172
Harlem riots and, **2:**286–87
higher-education quotas and, **2:**134–35, 138
Hispanic categorization and, **1:**290–91
Hispaniola and, **2:**106
immigration laws and, **1:**10, 160, 164, 251, 265, 403, **2:**76, 352–53, 408, **3:**226, **4:**14, 158, 223, 230
indigenismo and, **2:**361–63
indigenous heritage and, **2:**363–64, **3:**446
inter-Latino relations and, **2:**368–70
labor unions and, **4:**218, 219
Latino diversity and, **1:**231, **2:**369
Latino literature and, **2:**455–56
Latino self-identification and, **1:**333, 334, 335, **2:**373, 414, 456
Latino stereotypes and, **4:**142
Latino studies on, **2:**418
law enforcement and, **1:**401, **2:**423, **4:**145, 148
Laws of Burgos and, **2:**428
machismo and, **3:**58
Mexican American status and, **1:**288–89, 325–26, 335, **2:**364, 368, 371–76, **3:**446–47, **4:**186
Mexicans and, **3:**446–47
mixed-race nomenclature and, **1:**212
See also mestizaje
nativism and, **3:**225–28, 257, 291, 449
Nevada and, **3:**234

19th century distrust of Latinos and, **1:**29, 30
passing and, **3:**325–27
political party identification and, **4:**28
Puerto Ricans and, **1:**333, **2:**209, 363, 369, 372, **3:**447–48
Republican Party and, **4:**27
rhetoric of, **3:**119
segregation and, **1:**10–11, 42, **2:**365, **3:**99, 124, **4:**67, 81, 82–83, 158
See also school desegregation
Spanish hierarchy of, **1:**212
Spanish language and, **1:**195, 197
Spanish purity laws and, **1:**359, **2:**361
sugar symbolism and, **4:**153, 154
Supreme Court cases and, **4:**158–59
Texas and, **2:**364, **4:**185, 191, 201–2, 254
Tres Reyes Magos and, **4:**215
Vasconcelos (José) and, **1:**231, 352, **2:**455, **4:**250, 251
Virgen de Monserrate and, **4:**267
Watts and, **2:**434, **4:**284–86
See also ethnicity; intermarriage; mixed-race population
race riots. See racial conflict; Zoot Suit Riots
Racial and Ethnic Relations (Feagin and Feagin), **2:**91
Racial and Gender Report Card (2003), **1:**187
racial conflict, **2:**284–87
in Boston, **3:**86
Harlem riots and, **2:**286–87
in Los Angeles, See also Zoot Suit Riots
Los Angeles and, **3:**34, 37–38, 42
Miami riots and, **2:**219, **3:**147, **4:**285
New Jersey and, **3:**239, 240
New York City and, **3:**254
New York State and, **3:**257
Washington, D.C., and, **4:**279
Watts riots and, **2:**434, **4:**284–86
racial profiling
immigration, **2:**345
law enforcement, **1:**401, **2:**423, **4:**145, 148
Racing Hall of Fame, **2:**326
racism. See discrimination; Jim Crow laws; race; racial conflict
Racism, Sexism and the Media (Gutiérrez, et al.), **2:**391
Racketeer Influenced Corrupt Organization (RICO) laws, **2:**354
radical individualism, **1:**8
radio, **1:**105, 157, **2:**220, 395, **4:1–11**
audience for, **4:**127
bilingualism and, **4:**127
broadcasters, **4:**10–11
English-language, **4:7–11**
Hispanic Broadcasting Corporation and, **4:**2–3
Hispanic Radio Network, **2:**301, 301–2, 302
Honduran Americans and, **2:**324
information networks and, **4:**3–4
Latino journalists and, **2:**392, 393–94
as medium of choice, **4:**2
narcocorrido bans and, **3:**219, 264

T

Tigres del Norte, Los (music group), **1:**390
Title IX (1975), **4:**139
Title VII. See Elementary and Secondary Education Act of 1968
Tiwas, **2:**364
Tizol, Juan, **3:**202
Tjader, Cal, **2:**384, 385, **3:**204, 275, 312
Tlacaelel, **3:**110
tlachtli (ball game), **2:**239
Tlacopán, **3:**217
Tlacuilo (1970 Chicano art exhibition), **1:**149
Tlaloc, **3:**104, 109
Tlatelolco (Chicanocentric school), **1:**303
Tlaxcala, **3:**186, 217
Tlaxcalans, **3:**107–8, 110, 136
To a Finland Station (recording), **4:**71
tobacco, **4:204–7**
  Cuban American industry, **1:**424, **4:**119
  Florida and, **2:**216–17
  Spanish-Cuban monopoly on, **1:**416
  sugar symbolism and, **4:**154
  Ybor City and, **4:**295
  See also cigar making
Toco madera (song), **4:**268
Today's New International Version (TNIV) Bible, **1:**191
Todd, Charles, **2:**439
Todd, Mike, **1:**272
Toirac, José, **1:**119
Toledo, Francisco, **2:**188, **3:**106, 308, 310
Toledo, Isabel, **2:**180, 181–82
Toledo, Ohio, **4:**208
Tolosa, Isabel de, **2:**74
Tolsá, Manuel, **4:**88
Toltecs, **3:**106, 110, 217, 438–39
  archeology and, **1:**90, 92
  quinceañera and, **3:**440
toma todo (top game), **2:**241, 242
tomatoes, **1:**361
Tonantzín, **3:**109, **4:**34, 262, 264
Tonatiuh Quinto-Sol (TQS) Publications, **3:**407–8
Tonel (Cuban artist), **1:**119
Tongues (zine), **2:**320
Tony Awards
  Moreno (Rita) and, **3:**177, 178, 254, 435
  Olmos (Edward James) and, **3:**278
Tony G. (DJ), **4:**11
Tony Touch (rapper), **4:**18
Too Many Girls (play and film), **1:**106, 378
toponymy, **4:207–10**
  geographic, **4:**209, 277
  Guadalupe as place name, **4:**264
  habitation, **4:**208–9
  last names, **3:**282–83, 286
  saints place names, **4:**57, 111
  Spanish city names, **4:**124–25
Top Ten radio format, **4:**9
torching, **3:**28
Tordesillas, Treaty of (1494), **1:**348
Toribio, Almeida Jacqueline, **2:**100
Toribio, Antonio, **1:**120
Toro, Yomo, **3:**212
Toronto, Canada, Latino population in, **1:**262, 265–66, 268, 269
Toronto Blue Jays (baseball), **1:**187, 270
Torquemada, Juan de, **3:**136
Torrealba, J. B., **1:**33
Torres, Dara, **3:**280

Torres, David L., **1:**241
Torres, Edwin, **3:**17, **4:**201
Torres, Eloy, **3:**73, 308
Torres, Esteban, **4:**180
Torres, Felipe N., **3:**380
Torres, Gerald, **2:**456
Torres, José (boxer), **1:**223, **3:**260, 280, 435
Torres, José (mayor of Paterson, N.J.), **3:**241
Torres, Juan Pablo, **2:**118, **3:**206
Torres, Leyla, **2:**459
Torres, Luis de, **1:**411
Torres, Raffi, **4:**137
Torres, Salvador Roberto ("Queso"), **1:**133
Torres-García, Joaquín, **3:**309, 310
Torres-Llorca, Rubén, **1:**116, 118
Torresola, Griselio, **2:**424, **3:**380
Torres-Saillant, Silvio, **2:**111, 418
Torres Santiago, José Manuel, **2:**211
Torricelli, Robert, **3:**241
Torricelli Law. See Cuba Democracy Act of 1992
Torruella Leval, Susana, **1:**128, 145, 150
Tortilla Flat (Steinbeck), **3:**4
Tortilla Industry of America, **1:**384
tortillas, **1:**383, 384, **2:**16–17, 185, 347, 365, **4:**31
  packaged, **2:**26
Tortilla Soup (film), **2:**213
torture, **2:**80
Toshima, Karen, **3:**288
Totatzin, **3:**109
Touch of Evil (film), **2:**202
tourism, **4:210–12**
  bodegas, colmados, mercados and, **1:**207
  California and, **1:**251, **4:**210, 211
  Colorado and, **1:**365
  Cuba and, **1:**418, 421
  Dominican Republic and, **2:**110
  Key West and, **2:**401
  Las Vegas and, **2:**237
  Latino increased volume of, **4:**210
  Mexico and, **3:**139, 1412
  Miami and, **3:**143, 144, 247, **4:**210, 212
  Miami Latin Quarter and, **1:**257
  missions and, **1:**251, **3:**166–67, **4:**211
  New Mexico and, **3:**244, **4:**210, 212
  San Antonio and, **3:**167, **4:**68, 210, 211
  Spanish colonial art and architecture and, **1:**110
Toussaint, Frédéric Mialhe, **1:**113
Toussaint-Louverture, **2:**106
Touzet, René, **1:**209, **3:**203
Tovar, Lupita, **2:**200, **4:**214
Toward a Jewish Theology of Liberation (Ellis), **2:**437
"Towards a new mestiza consciousness" (Anzaldúa), **3:**115
Toynbee, Arnold J., **3:**137
Toypurina, **3:**33
TPS Committee for Colombia (N.Y.C.), **1:**343
TQS Publications, **3:**407–8
Traba, Marta, **1:**34
Tracks North, The: The Railroad Bracero Program of World War II (Driscoll), **4:**15
TRACY 168 (graffiti painter), **2:**269
trade
  banana, **4:**220

border region, **1:**215, **2:**411
Central America, **4:**220
chocolate, **1:**321
coffee, **1:**338–41, **4:**220
colonialism and, **1:**349, 352, 357
Cuba and, **1:**416, 418, 419
farm products, **1:**59
Mexican northern frontier, **4:**107
Native American, **1:**369–70
Philippines and, **3:**342
South American Common Market, **4:**242
sugar, **4:**151–53
U.S.-Mexican relations, **4:**231–32
See also North American Free Trade Agreement
Tradiciones (radio program), **2:**301
Traffic (film), **2:**120
traffic deaths, **1:**70
Trail of Tears (1838), **4:**92
traje, **3:**93
Transitional Bilingual Education Law (Mass.), **3:**86
translation, **4:212–14**
  of Bible, **1:**190–92, **2:**157–58
  of Neruda (Pablo), **3:**233
transnationalism, **1:**310, **2:**69
Transportation Department, U.S., **1:**365
transterrados, **3:**347
traqueros, **3:**150
Tras la tormenta la calma (Chacón), **1:**293
travel. See tourism
travel agencies, Latino-owned, **4:**212
Travel Industry Association of America, **4:**210, 211
Travels with Charley (Steinbeck), **3:**4
Travis, William Barrett, **1:**60–61
Traynor, Roger, **2:**373
Treasure of the Sangre de Cristos (Campa), **2:**226
Treasury Department, U.S., **4:**241
Treaty of Adams-Onis. See Adams-Onis, Treaty of
Treaty of Guadalupe Hidalgo. See Guadalupe Hidalgo, Treaty of
Treaty of Paris. See Paris, Treaty of
Treaty of San Ildefonso. See San Ildefonso, Treaty of
Treaty of Velasco. See Velasco, Treaty of
Trejo, Arnulfo, **4:**20
Trejo, Rubén, **1:**32, 136
Trelles, Miguel, **1:**146
TRENZA organization, **2:**420
tres (musical instrument), **3:**211
Tres cerditos, Los (Salinas), **2:**461
Tres Dedos (Three-Fingered Jack), **3:**192
Tres Juanes, Los, **4:**266
tres leches, **3:**389
Tres Marías, Los (Baca triptych), **3:**302
Tres Reyes, Los (music group), **4:**268
Tres Reyes Magos, **3:***194*, 231, 344, **4:215–16**
  Calle Ocho parade, **1:**258, **3:**25
Tres Rios Association, **3:**152
Treviño, Jesse, **1:**35, 136, **3:**306
Treviño, Jesús Salvador, **1:**304, **2:**207, **4:**180–81, **216–17**
Treviño, John, **1:**164
Treviño, Lee, **2:**260, **4:**138
Treviño, Rudy, **1:**380–81, **3:**305, 306

Treviño de Sobremonte, Tomás, **1:**412
Tri, El (music group), **4:**43
Triana, Gladys, **1:**116, 118
Triana, José, **2:**466
Tribune Company, **2:**395, **3:**293
trickster figures, **1:**397, **2:**454
Tricon Global Restaurants Incorporated, **2:**184
Trinidad, Félix, **1:**223, **2:**57, **3:**435
Trinidadian Americans, **1:**274
Trinitaria, La (secret society), **2:**107
Trío Boringuen (music group), **3:**202
trio eléctrico, **3:**201
Trio Matamoros (music group), **2:**279, 280
Trio Oriental (son group), **4:**104
tripartite hypothesis (corn), **1:**382
Triple Crown (horse racing), **2:**326
Trist, Nicholas, **3:**130
Tristezas (Sánchez), **1:**208
Troche, Rose, **2:**211
Troncoso, Sergio, **3:**12, 410
Trop F., La (music group), **4:**171
Tropical, La (film), **1:**48
Tropical America (Siquieros mural), **2:**259
Tropicalia, **1:**32
tropicalism, **1:**30, 32
Tropicalization, **3:**388
Tropicana, Carmelita, **2:**214, 319, 335, 457
Tropicana, La (Havana nightclub), **1:**31, 94, 113, 409
Trópico en Manhattan (Cotto-Thorner), **3:**15
Tropiques Magazine, **1:**32, 114
Trotsky, Leon, **2:**397, **4:**40
trova, **3:**201
Trovas del mar (Sánchez Beras), **2:**97
Troyano, Alina. See Tropicana, Carmelita
Troyano, Ela, **1:**117, **2:**214
TRPI, **2:**375–76
Trudeau, Pierre, **1:**265, 267
Trueba, Fernando, **2:**118, **3:**275
True Relation of the Vicissitudes that Attended the Governor Don Hernando de Soto and Nobles of Portugal in the Discovery of the Province of Florida now just Given by a Fidalgo of Elvas (Elvas), **2:**161
Trujillo, Carla, **2:**319, 471
Trujillo, Flor de Oro, **4:**49
Trujillo, Rafael Leónidas, **1:**81, 120, 186, **2:**96, 97, 292, 293, **3:**22, 48, 241, 254
  baseball and, **1:**185, 186
  dictatorship of, **1:**82, 119, 172, 185, **2:**108–9, **4:**49
  Dominican American literature against, **2:**468
  Henríquez Ureña family and, **2:**294
  Rubirosa (Porfirio) and, **4:**49
Trujillo, Ramfis, **1:**185
Truman, Harry S., **1:**104, 353, **2:**412, **3:**140, 380
  military desegregation and, **3:**156
  Puerto Rican assassination attempt on, **2:**424, **4:**434
  Puerto Rican government and, **3:**433
trumpet
  mariachi and, **3:**67
  Sandoval (Arturo) and, **4:**70–71
Trumpet Fantasy (O'Farrill recording), **3:**275
tuberculosis, **2:**290, 367, 368

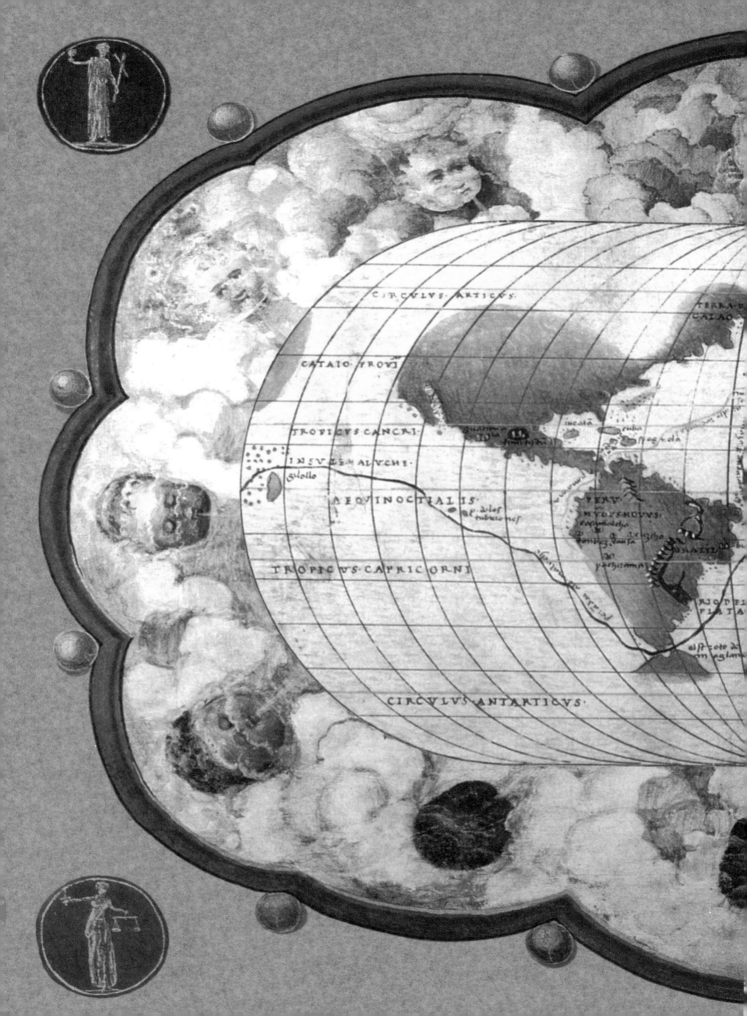

CIRCVLVS ARTICVS·

TERRA·D·
CATAO

CATAIO PROVI

TROPICVS CANCRI

INSVLE MALVCHE·

galollo

AEQVINOCTIALIS

TROPICVS CAPRICORNI

PERV
MVDVS MOVVS

BRAZIL

RIO PII
PLATA

CIRCVLVS ANTARTICVS·